ISBN 978-1-333-53562-9
PIBN 10509397

1 MONTH OF
FREE
READING

at

www.ForgottenBooks.com

By purchasing this book you are eligible for one month membership to ForgottenBooks.com, giving you unlimited access to our entire collection of over 700,000 titles via our web site and mobile apps.

To claim your free month visit:

www.forgottenbooks.com/free509397

English
Français
Deutsche
Italiano
Español
Português

www.forgottenbooks.com

Mythology Photography **Fiction**
Fishing Christianity **Art** Cooking
Essays Buddhism Freemasonry
Medicine **Biology** Music **Ancient**
Egypt Evolution Carpentry Physics
Dance Geology **Mathematics** Fitness
Shakespeare **Folklore** Yoga Marketing
Confidence Immortality Biographies
Poetry **Psychology** Witchcraft
Electronics Chemistry History **Law**
Accounting **Philosophy** Anthropology
Alchemy Drama Quantum Mechanics
Atheism Sexual Health **Ancient History**
Entrepreneurship Languages Sport
Paleontology Needlework Islam
Metaphysics Investment Archaeology
Parenting Statistics Criminology
Motivational

Genealogy

of the Descendants of

Thomas French

Who Came to America from Nether Heyford, Northamptonshire, England, and Settled in Berlinton (Burlington) in the Province and Country of West New Jersey, of which he was one of the Original Proprietors, together with William Penn, Edward Byllynge, Thomas Ollive, Gauen Laurie and Others

With some account of

Colonial Manners and Doings

Setting up of Friends' Meetings, Copies of Old Minutes and other Particular Writings of Public Interest, Curious and Rare Papers in Fac-simile, Noteworthy Happenings and Places, etc.

Together with

One Hundred and Fifty Picture Prints

Compiled and Published by

Howard Barclay French

Of the Seventh Generation

VOLUME I

PHILADELPHIA
PRIVATELY PRINTED
1909

NEW YORK PUBLIC LIBRARY

Copyright

Howard B. French

1909

IN LOVING REMEMBRANCE OF

MY HONORED AND REVERED FATHER

SAMUEL H. FRENCH

THIS WORK IS AFFECTIONATELY DEDICATED

Those who do not treasure up the memory of their ancestors, do not deserve to be remembered by posterity.—EDMUND BURKE.

LIST OF ILLUSTRATIONS

FIRE-SET BELONGING TO CHARLES FRENCH, 3RD [143].

AS A TALE THAT IS TOLD

FTER five and thirty years a work voluntarily assumed is happily and thankfully completed and placed in the hands of the members of the family who wished copies printed for their use. It is scarcely necessary to refer to the fact, always in evidence in genealogical work, that omissions constantly occur. Who among our readers can realize what the gathering of the material from countless and in many instances long hidden sources on both sides of the sea, its careful preparation, painstaking verification, laborious compilation and final passage through the press, has been? The difficulties and discouragements met with on every hand can scarcely be conceived. In some cases those who should have been the most ready and eager to help, have been strangely indifferent and seemingly hostile to honest truth seeking inquiry. Many letters have remained unanswered for unknown reasons; doubtless, in some cases, because reliable registers have not been kept, and in others are quite lost. Thus family records are left incomplete; and in some instances mistakes may have been transcribed by those sending what was in their possession. Many others have gladly and willingly cooperated to the extent of their knowledge and opportunity. Thus little by little, patiently and earnestly, the fast disappearing threads of a family history, than which there can be none more interesting and inspiring, have been gathered up and woven together day by day, month by month, year by year.

Far from complete is the story that is told. There are breaks in the narrative which cannot be covered; records have been lost, memory has failed, and half revealed facts have at times barred the way. Yet the enlarged and fascinating transcript given is one which may be reviewed with supreme satisfaction by every living descendant of the rugged and heroic pioneer who, with the scars of suffering for conscience sake upon him, stepped upon the bank of the Delaware that late summer morning, two hundred and twenty-eight years ago, with his faithful wife and nine children, the youngest only four years of age. Thomas ffrench—his quaint original way of spelling the family name—was one of the men who found empires and republics, and through the line of his descendants there runs the distinctive marks, strong and clearly defined, of a pure mind, high purpose, inflexible honesty, never flagging industry and all the essential qualities of upright and successful manhood and womanhood. The old motto of the family, MALO MORI QUAM FŒDARI (I would rather die than be debased), fully exemplifies the general characteristics of his descendants.

There has been a steadfast purpose also, widening and strengthening all the while, to make this book a living picture of the times of which it treats. It is with satisfaction that the record here submitted embraces so much of general historic interest, which in itself involved an immense amount of labor and great expense; and the photographer and engraver at their best, have been impressed to make the picture presented graphic and delightful. The publication reproduces many Friends' Meeting Houses and places of special interest to that Society, whose faithful members did so much toward laying broad and deep the foundations of the American Republic.

It is desired here to make acknowledgment of the invaluable services of many Friends some of whom have no personal interest in the book. The New Jersey State Librarian, New Jersey and Pennsylvania Historical Societies, Friends' Libraries, Philadelphia, the Philadelphia Library, Public Libraries of Woodbury, Camden, Haddonfield and Burlington, and Court Record Officials at Trenton, Mount Holly, Camden, Woodbury and Philadelphia have extended courtesies which are gratefully acknowledged. The enthusiastic work of Charles S. French and his able assistance for many years as an earnest co-laborer cannot be overestimated. This can also be said of my cousins, Sarah French Whitall and Margaret B. French; and of my secretary, Clara G. Sheppard, who has for many years devoted every spare moment to correspondence, records and data, compiling and revising with unceasing diligence and fidelity. Able assistance has been rendered by Anna M. North,* of Trenton, N. J., and also by Edwin K. Hart, the veteran journalist, whose skill and experience as writer and editor have been put to the best uses in the final revision and publication. To these and many others heartfelt appreciation is here cordially expressed.

Those who may observe statements concerning matters of historical interest somewhat different from other publications should bear in mind the fact that

* It is with feelings of deepest regret that I have to note the death of my friend and co-laborer, Anna M. North, who died 5th mo. 16th, 1908.

the information here presented was obtained from original records and accepted authorities, after most intelligent and careful research. This applies to the history of localities, meetings, and individuals, as well as to graphic reproduction of documents, wills, deeds, minutes, etc. Reliability has been the test constantly applied in all departments of inquiry, made all the more necessary by the multiplicity of current errors concerning persons and events of the past.

Let us hope that coming generations of the French family and the large number of allied families interested will make a record as worthy of remembrance and emulation as those who silently follow each other through these pages.

Howard B. French

Philadelphia, November, 1908

SPIRIT AND MISSION OF QUAKERISM

OOKING backward seven generations the thoughtful American citizen of to-day can take a calm, rational, just and philosophical review of the inspiration, rise, marvellous development, far reaching influence and beneficent effects of Quakerism. No other great movement of a reformatory and religious character ever was more timely, or more urgently needed. None ever seemed more directly the outcome of divine purpose and control over the destinies of mankind. None ever more impressively illustrated the truth contained in the burning words of Holy Writ: "Not by might, nor by power, but by my Spirit, saith the Lord of hosts."

The British realm was convulsed with a stormy revolution in which the blood of a dethroned king mingled with that of his rebellious subjects. The fierce contention of partisans thrilled the nation and fixed the wondering attention of the civilized world. The sword had been appealed to and on many fields of carnage the issue had been met. Established government had been overthrown and some advance made in human liberty and the recognition of popular rights. Yet the triumph of the Commonwealth was but fleeting. In a little while royal power was again supreme and wielded with defiant forgetfulness of the lesson taught by the headsman of Whitehall.

Meanwhile, every element of furious and relentless persecution exhausted the means of destruction aimed at the disciples and supporters of the man of peace who had found the secret of irrepressible devotion to what he believed to be the truth. It was a strange spectacle, an exhibition of human perversity, blindness, injustice and unwisdom which makes the darkest page in English history. Neither cajolery, argument, threats, shameless robbery under forms of law, imprisonment, physical torture nor edicts of banishment from home and kindred, could put out the fires that blazed within the hearts of these witnesses of the Inner Light. Within twenty years nearly ten thousand passed through prison gates, and upward of two hundred and fifty lives were directly sacrificed, yet higher and higher rose the swelling tide of testimony for righteousness.

Through it all there was no intended disrespect for legitimate authority, rightfully and justly exercised. No people the world ever knew were more intensely loyal to self-respecting rulers than the Quakers. The iron-hearted but clear-headed Cromwell had openly recognized their immovable integrity. "Here is a people," he said, "whom I cannot buy with money, gifts nor offices." And when, upon a notable occasion, a number of self-sacrificing men and women came to him to plead that they might take the places of others, worn and weary and dying in jail, he cried out to his amazed courtiers: "Who among you would do such a thing for me?" Repeated expressions of profound respect for rulers were put forth. There was no resentment, no sullen treasuring up of multiplied wrongs, with evident purpose to square the account when opportunity offered. The spirit of peace, forgiveness and blessing was ever present, ever manifest, ever active and sincere, with the self-consciousness of a happy reward that made the heavens ring with the joy that could not be confined nor suppressed.

The story of the persecution of the Quakers, at home and abroad, even in this land, whither their pursuers had fled to escape like injustice and suffering, will be pondered with amazement by future historians. Millions of the best men and women of this Republic to-day are all unconscious of the inspiring fact that they have their ancestral roots in the little companies of heroic souls who passed through the fiery furnace, seven times heated, during the last half of the seventeenth century.

And out of all this time of trial was to come a sequel little dreamed of by the drifting royal opportunist when, lazily floating in his pleasure barge on the Thames, one summer afternoon in 1677, he waved a kindly adieu and gave his kingly blessing as he saw the crowded decks of the good ship Kent, then lifting anchor and setting sail for the new world. "Are these Quakers?" indifferently asked Charles II. Aye, and more than that! They were the real advance couriers of the coming great Empire of the West. All that had gone before, all that had been done before, only comprised a fragmentary beginning. Now the serious and lasting, united and effective work of nation building was about to begin on the quiet banks of the Delaware. Only men and women of consecrated purpose, the purest lives, dauntless courage, sublime faith and never-ending endurance could have met the exacting demands, carried out faithfully and effectively the lofty aim that animated these heroic yet humble spirited pioneers.

Upon what apparently trifling things great affairs often turn. For half a century the political and commercial leaders of the old world had been learning little by little of the undeveloped continent beyond the great sea. In our own aggressive time it seems incomprehensible that more energetic and successful inquiry should not have been made, under the auspices of powerful governments with the ready coöperation of eager self-seekers. No man of that age dreamed of the commercial possibilities of America. The men of Jamestown, Plymouth, New Amsterdam, New Netherlands, Maryland and the Carolinas were regarded as fanatical zealots; suggestively and almost derisively termed in official documents and current chronicles " adventurers." And such they truly were, for every hour of their lives, on sea or land, was one of peril and uncertainty. The vast and gloomy wooded wilderness was forbidding enough; but the wild and fierce creatures of the forest comprised the least ever-present danger. Terrorizing tales of multitudes of bold and warlike savages thrilled every heart. The course pursued by many of the early colonists towards the natives had been the very essence of unwisdom and injustice. Out of it all was to come the most remarkable transformation known to mankind.

Yet it was the personal recklessness and improvidence of a few royal and semi-royal spendthrifts that directly opened the way for the industrious settlement of the new and unknown lands, contemporary with the amazing stupidity, from a national standpoint, involved in driving from their firesides and their native hillsides and hamlets tens of thousands of the best men and women of the realm. Pondering the cruel problem before them, the suffering Quakers learned that the prodigal head of the restored kingdom had flung away to his waiting brother, the Duke of York, who in a little while was to succeed him as James II, millions of acres, and that in order to have money to spend in continued luxury and extravagance, he in turn had sold this gift of fabulous richness rightly handled, for a song, to two men, neither of whom knew nor cared what it was worth, or made the least effort to find out. They likewise were ready for an easy and quick speculation, and the financial embarrassment of a third party ended in the most extraordinary land transaction in the world's history.

Not only was the greater part of colonial New Jersey sold for a little more than the money value of one hundred thousand dollars to-day, or about three cents an acre, but the short sighted King, to free himself from the burden of an annoying obligation, squared the long-standing account with the son of his deceased creditor, and thus for $400,000 William Penn became the possessor of an embryo empire. The amount paid for Pennsylvania, two hundred and twenty-five years ago, would to-day scarcely buy half a dozen corner lots in the business center of any one of its thriving cities.

It seemed as though all things were at hand for the ready carrying out of some grand scheme for the lasting benefit of humanity. Twenty-five years of trial, through which strong men and self-sacrificing women had suffered martyrdom with sublime patience and endurance, had prepared their souls and bodies for the ordeal ahead. They faced the dangers of the great deep and the unknown perils and hardships of the wilderness, with calm self-reliance and exalted faith in the guidance and care of Him whom they served with unvarying fidelity. They had sounded the depths of brotherly love and were prepared to treat with gentleness and the kindliest trustfulness the wondering natives, whose utmost confidence was thus speedily won and never lost. There is nothing more touching and beautiful in human annals than this close and happy intermingling with the untutored children of the forest. Even before these mild mannered, honest faced, open hearted strangers had stepped upon the shores of the Delaware, their wants were anticipated and a welcome extended that must have brought tears of joy to many trembling mothers holding their helpless little ones to their bosoms.

" The Indians are very loving to us," wrote one of the Burlington pioneers, and therein was revealed the whole marvellous story, the full answer to the heartfelt prayers for protection and safety which had been daily offered up during the long and weary voyage. Already conscienceless adventurers had brought evil upon the Indian and he was only too eager to make a lasting treaty of peace and sobriety and mutual protection with those of different principles and habits and purposes. " We will make a broad path," said a wise old chief, at one of the earliest councils, near Burlington. " If in passing the white man sees an Indian asleep, he will not disturb him. And if the Indian sees the white man asleep, he will pass by and not harm him." Words of child-like simplicity and goodwill that must have made the angel watchers that hovered over the camp of this new Israel drop tears of joy.

For seventy years peace reigned in Pennsylvania, until indeed, the white man's perfidy brought the destruction of war; while no conflict with the red man ever stained the history of the state founded by the peaceful and just men of Shrewsbury, Salem, and Burlington. Food was voluntarily furnished in many a crisis, when the settlers were in sore straits. Lands were released on terms that now seem incredible. Within a little more than thirty days after the arrival of the pioneer settlers in 1677, deeds were signed covering an area nearly equal to one half the acreage of the State to-day. Shelter was offered the poorest wayfarer and in the quiet little meeting houses the dark skinned hunters and trappers with their wives and children were soon found drinking eagerly from the same mysterious fountain mental and spiritual strength.

One of the earliest marriages at Burlington, number three on the recorded Friends' Meeting list, was that of a young Friend of Fenwick's colony at Salem, with an Indian maiden of winning ways and high character, as her subsequent life happily showed. This modest little daughter of a chief was treated with the same high consideration extended to her white sisters of the most influential families. Her marriage certificate was signed by the religious and social leaders of the community. The scene was one worthy to be commemorated by the most gifted artist. Often children were left in the care of Indian neighbors while their parents journeyed from home, or attended Yearly Meeting, and without a single betrayal of trust. Many of these trusty allies sought the privilege of a last resting place beside their good friends. In God's acre they sleep peacefully with those whom they welcomed when fleeing from oppression and peril in their own land. Sometime, mayhap, the darkness that has encompassed the American Indian will be penetrated and it will be revealed that these strange people, possessed of such remarkable traits and character, came from progenitors of the human race who were closely allied with the brightest type of mankind ever known.

The purpose of the Quaker colonists was, as they frankly said, to lay the foundations broad and deep, based upon the very highest principles of justice. Liberty of the individual and freedom of conscience were assured to all, not only to those of their own faith. By example and precept they sought to make Pennsylvania and New Jersey model Commonwealths, where all men should have every right guaranteed. They were constitution makers and nation builders of superior wisdom, wonderful foresight, broad minded patriotism. It was the full flower of their work which inspired the admiring tribute of the greatest English statesman of the nineteenth century. "The Constitution of the United States," said Mr. Gladstone, "is the wisest document ever conceived by the mind of man."

In the industrial arena these always zealous workers wrought mightily. The purse-proud drone and social parasite of our time was unknown amongst them. They reduced the forest, redeemed waste places, developed resources, established and fostered trade, and all the while maintained the highest standard of commercial integrity. The records of the business meetings of their religious society bear constant testimony to their determination to permit no variation from the strictest principles of honesty, while every effort was made to settle all differences quietly and peaceably, without even recourse to law. They were the original and consistent friends and exponents of arbitration, and well it would have been for those who have come after them, in all the walks of life, if this wise and just example had been followed.

Their abhorrence of every aspect of warfare forbade them bearing arms, but they were never lacking in loyalty to rightful government. During the Revolution they were often subjected to ill-founded suspicion and rash injustice. But when the conflict was over, no one bore more willing and deserved tribute to their purity of motive and upright conduct than Washington himself. Upon one occasion while he was President, he asked an esteemed Friend on what principle he had opposed the war. "On the same principle," was the reply, "that I should be opposed to a change in this government. All that ever was gained by revolutions is not an adequate compensation to the poor mangled soldier for loss of life or limb." Washington pondered deeply and then earnestly said: "I honor your sentiments; there is more in that than mankind have generally considered."

In social life the Quakers lived upon the loftiest plane. Here, again, their meeting records show how zealous they were for the preservation of the honor and safety of the home. Then as now they could not look with the least shadow of toleration upon any infraction of the moral law. Without the elaborate and pretentious hygienic knowledge of our day of scientific advancement, their homes, plain and simple in every appointment, were the abode of cleanly healthfulness, self-restraint and self-control, that rendered longevity, barring accident, the natural inheritance of almost every child of sound parentage. The blood of more than two hundred years of Quakerism, with its strain of English, Irish, Welsh and Scotch vigor and French Huguenot refinement, has produced a people of unequalled physical purity and strength. Their contribution in this respect alone, to the welfare and happiness of the American people, has been of immeasurable value. That they may not only not diminish in numbers or influence, but grow in strength everywhere, must be the earnest wish of every one having the interests of the human race at heart.

No subject was nearer the hearts of Friends than education. With earnest solicitude for the welfare of future generations—and their enlightened sympathy in this respect was not confined to their own Society circles—they founded schools of superior character in every community, in some instances before neighborhood meeting houses were built. At Burlington this matter was taken up soon after the establishment of a meeting, it being specially provided by the Assembly, in 1682, that the revenues from an adjacent island should be exclusively devoted to the cause of education. Many of these schools were the predecessors of famous institutions in the educational world. The first school in Philadelphia was established by Friends in 1683; and six years later, at the earnest suggestion of the founder of the colony, what has been known for over two hundred years as the Penn Charter School was founded, its formal charter dating from 1698. It is a significant fact that great numbers of the most discerning people having no connection with the Society of Friends have placed their children, with entire confidence and to their great benefit, in the care of Friends' teachers. The pioneer schools were generally located near meetings and were coöperative neighbors. It was an impressive union of moral, religious and intellectual forces always working for the common good.

In the higher arena of spiritual life Quakerism has fulfilled a mission as surely God-given as it has been abundantly blessed by every possible manifestation of Divine favor. It was no new thing the shepherd boy of Leicester discovered and so fervently and successfully taught. He only revealed to those sitting in darkness and others led away by empty formality and still others lost in the wilderness of sinful indulgences and neglect, the real character, possibilities, privileges and joy of the soul. Opening wide his young heart and earnestly seeking the light of truth from its true and only source, he was vouchsafed in overwhelming measure knowledge, comfort, courage, experience and strength which made him a flaming herald of righteousness.

In a single sentence George Fox summed up his conclusive faith. " I saw," said he, " that Christ died for all men and had enlightened all men and women with His divine and saving light and that no man could be a true believer but who believed in it." That he was not self-deceived, the victim of a too exalted imagination, was quickly shown by the multitude of rejoicing followers who were ready to testify to the presence within their own souls of a light and joy never before known. That there was, also, readiness for self-sacrifice was speedily demonstrated. Yawning jails and dungeons had no terrors for these devoted people. Men of refined character and delicately nurtured women bowed their necks to the yoke of oppression and endured hardships with a meekness and fortitude that must ever command the admiration of mankind.

George Bancroft, the ablest and fairest minded of American historians, beautifully sums up the lesson of that wonderful period, when he says:

" Far from rejecting Christianity, the Quaker insisted that he alone held it in its primitive simplicity. The skeptic forever vibrated, the Quaker was fixed. To him Christianity was freedom. He loved to remember that the patriarchs were graziers, that the prophets were mechanics and shepherds. To him there was joy in the thought that the brightest image of divinity on earth had been born in a manger, had been reared under the roof of a carpenter. Every avenue of truth was to be kept open. The Inner Light to the Quaker is not only the revelation of truth, but the guide of life and the oracle of duty."

The zeal of Friends for the propagation of the truth as it was revealed to them was boundless. Their feet hardly touched the ground in Burlington and elsewhere before they arranged meetings for worship, often sitting under the trees, or gathering in one another's houses or even barns, until other places could be built. There were thank offerings from full hearts and the missionary spirit was instantly manifested. Many gifted with speech and highly favored with clearness of view were eager to carry the gospel tidings to those deprived of special privileges. The story of these pioneer preachers and their journeyings to and fro through the wilderness is as fascinating as it is inspiring. Their quaint journals portray all unconsciously their own spiritual devotion and show the unity and love which pervaded the people. Wayside meetings would be held at short notice, with great comfort to all concerned. Friends never were too busy to assemble and reverently listen to the sweet story of old.

It was not stout-hearted and strong-bodied men alone who thus traveled in all directions and in all seasons to minister to those in need. Scores of devoted women left their comfortable homes, threading the bridle paths through the forests, crossing on horseback swollen streams, meeting the lone Indian by the way without fear, often stopping at his wigwam, cabin or cave, hearing the shrill cry of the panther and the wolf. They journeyed to the bleak hillsides of New England, to the far South, to the border settlements along the Susquehanna and Wyoming. They crossed again the ocean and labored with the Friends left behind in the fatherland.

The literature of memorials and journals concerning these first ambassadors of righteousness in the American wilderness will be read by coming generations with increasing interest and spiritual profit. The long roll of names tenderly recalled and talked of around the fireside by successive generations comprises a list of Christian workers worthy of everlasting remembrance. In every good word and work the Friends were and have always been zealous, self-sacrificing, unwearied. In the spirit of truth they have labored faithfully. Their mission has been to bless and help mankind, to illustrate in their own calm, pure, contented lives the teachings of the Master whom they serve in quietness and peace.

GENEALOGY

THOMAS FRENCH

THE COLONIAL DAWN

THE exact date of the first settlement of New Jersey is not fixed by accepted historical records. The earliest colonists were Dutch from Holland, about 1620, who planted a colony near the present site of Bergen. In 1623 another company, under Captain Cornelius Mey, settled on the east side of the Delaware, nearly opposite where Philadelphia was located more than half a century later. They built Fort Nassau, on what is now known as Timber creek, a stream which enters the Delaware a short distance below Camden. During the ensuing forty years, Swedes, Finns, Dutch and English struggled for supremacy, until, in 1664, Charles II, of England, disregarding all rival claims, granted all the territory between the Delaware and Connecticut rivers to his brother, the Duke of York, who later succeeded him as James II, and forcibly took possession. Pending complete subjection of the country, the Duke sold all his claims to Lord Berkley and Sir George Carteret, who named the tract New Jersey, in honor of Sir George, who as governor of the island of Jersey, had loyally sustained Charles in his contest with parliament and Cromwell. There was much difficulty in establishing permanent and satisfactory local government.

In 1673, Berkley sold his interest in the proprietorship to John Fenwick and Edward Byllynge, Quakers, who later conveyed a controlling interest to William Penn, who had become much interested in the project, and two other Quakers of financial responsibility, Gauen Laurie and Nicholas Lucas. In 1675, Fenwick brought over a colony of upwards of two hundred persons and established a settlement on the Delaware at an attractive place which he called Salem, in view of its peaceful and inviting aspect. In 1677 another company of homeseekers came from London, made up almost entirely of English and Irish Quakers, locating some sixty miles farther up the river, founding Burlington. Thus the permanent settlement of West Jersey was begun by strong men and heroic women.

For some years the province was divided into East and West Jersey. In February, 1682, the upper territory, as far north as the Hudson river, was purchased by William Penn and eleven associates, all men of means, high character and influence, and later twelve others were added. One of these, Robert Barclay, an able Scotchman and influential Friends' minister, was made Governor. Through wise and just administration the country became an asylum for the oppressed and entered upon an era of industrial development and great prosperity. Under a subdivided proprietorship and governorship, however, many difficulties arose; and in 1702 the proprietors surrendered the civil government to the British crown, retaining all personal property rights in the land, under the original agreements of purchase. Lord Cornbury became the first governor, under Queen Anne.

FIRST CONSTITUTION OF NEW JERSEY

The great charters of civil and religious liberty granted the settlers of New England were duplicated by the first Constitution of New Jersey, afterward reappearing in all essential particulars, in Pennsylvania. Formulated by Berkley and Carteret, and signed February 10, 1664, it was entitled: " The Concessions and Agreement of the Lords Proprietors of the Province of New Cæsarea, or New Jersey, to and with all and every of the Adventurers, and all such as shall settle or plant there." It was provided that government should be vested in a governor, six councillors, whom he should choose, and an Assembly, to be chosen by the people. Loyalty to the crown of England was required. The Assembly was to make all laws needful, create courts and provide for the common defense. Faithful and impartial execution of every civil trust was guaranteed. The next section was the most important of all; it declared as follows:

" That no person qualified as aforesaid, within the said province, at any time shall be any ways molested, punished, disquieted or called in question, for any difference in opinion or practice in matters of religious concernments,

SYCAMORE TREE, BURLINGTON, N. J., OVER 300 YEARS OLD
To which tradition says pioneer vessels were moored

who do not actually disturb the civil peace of the said province; but that all and every such person and persons may, from time to time, and at all times, freely and fully have and enjoy his and their judgments and consciences, in matters of religion, throughout the said province, they behaving themselves peaceably and quietly, and not using this liberty to licentiousness, nor to the civil injury or outward disturbance of others; any law, statute or clause contained, or to be contained, usage or custom of this realm of England, to the contrary thereof in any wise notwithstanding."

Seven years' occupancy and use of land secured permanency of title. As an inducement to industrious settlers it was provided that every freeman becoming a member of the colony at the beginning should be given one hundred and fifty acres of land for himself and one hundred and fifty acres for every able-bodied man servant, seventy-five acres for each minor servant above fourteen years, and seventy-five acres was to be given to each " Christian servant " at the expiration of his term of service.

FOUNDING OF THE COMMONWEALTH

Twelve years after the issuance of the Berkley-Carteret proclamation of settlement, the first organized movement towards acceptance of its liberal provisions was inaugurated in London. On the third of March, 1676, about one hundred and fifty earnest-minded men, including William Penn, Gauen Laurie, Thomas Lambert, Thomas Ollive, Thomas ffrench, Edward Byllynge and Henry Stacy, signed a paper entitled, " The Concessions and Agreements of the proprietors, freeholders and inhabitants of the province of West New Jersey in America." This now historic document, in the preparation of which William Penn played a large part, followed the main lines of the Berkley-Carteret paper, making still further provision for the successful planting of the new colony and its wise and efficient government. Commissioners were to be selected and appointed to represent the lords proprietors and the settlers and to have power to order and manage the affairs of the province. They were also to divide the land into stated provisions of ten parts each, or proprieties, these to be subdivided. Future Commissioners were to be elected by the citizens. An Assembly, or legislative body, was to succeed the Commissioners, the members being chosen by the people, by ballot.

An outline of governmental provisions and legislation was given, the purpose being to found a model Commonwealth in which the largest measure of individual liberty was to be allowed, consistent with the protection of the rights of all and the maintenance of good order. Disturbers of the peace were to be regarded as public enemies and dealt with severely, but trial by jury was provided for and impartial administration of justice assured. Imprisonment for debt was forbidden. Peace with the Indians was to be faithfully maintained. There was to be free legislative discussion and open voting before the people. The section of this immortal document which will forever command the increasing admiration of mankind, was as follows:

" That no men, nor number of men upon earth, hath power or authority to rule over men's consciences in religious matters; therefore it is consented, agreed and ordained, that no person or persons whatsoever, within the said province, at any time or times hereafter shall be any ways, upon any pretence whatsoever, called in question, or in the least punished or hurt, either in person, estate or privilege, for the sake of his opinion, judgment, faith or worship towards God, in matters of religion; but that all and every such person and persons, may from time to time, and at all times, freely and fully have and enjoy his and their judgments, and the exercise of their consciences, in matters of religious worship throughout all the said province."

Hampton L. Carson, former Attorney General of Pennsylvania, in a recent address before the Pennsylvania Historical Society, thus spoke of " William Penn as a Law Giver ":

" He severed church from State; secured the rights of conscience; wedded religious liberty to civil security; encouraged immigration; armed the citizen with the ballot; converted prisons into work-houses; abolished the infamy of jailers' fees; punished perjury and extortion; destroyed multiplicity of suits; overthrew the inequalities of primogeniture; suppressed piracy; assailed vice; stripped the criminal law of ferocious punishments; encouraged literature; rewarded science, and thus strove to secure the peace, purity and happiness of his people."

SETTLEMENT OF BURLINGTON

The rise of the Society of Friends must ever be regarded as one of the memorable events in the history of mankind. Out of the fires of persecution arose companies of consecrated men and women who crossed the sea to set up an empire of civil and religious freedom. The settlement of Burlington was one of the links in the chain of circumstances that illustrated the most

GOVERNOR SAMUEL JENNINGS' HOUSE, "GREEN HILL," NEAR BURLINGTON, N. J.

beautiful and inspiring lessons of faith, courage and heroic endurance. Following the first ship, the Kent, in 1677, within three years came upwards of fourteen hundred persons, all eager to share the trials of the pioneers. These settled along both sides of the Delaware, from Salem to the falls, near the site of the future state capital of New Jersey. Some were families of fair estate, for those times; others possessed very little with which to begin life in the wilderness. Others were modest tradesmen and useful artisans.

The first little company felt their way cautiously, leaving their ship some forty miles below Chygoe Island, where they finally determined to locate a town. Not an hour was lost, however. Within forty days negotiations were completed with the Indians whereby large tracts of land were possessed. The plan adopted resulted in the laying out of Burlington—or Bridlington, as it was first called—essentially as it is to-day. Lots were assigned and houses built as rapidly as possible, while farm lands were located and cleared for cultivation. The old chronicles present quaint pictures of this hopeful colony of busy and happy workers. Every day brought some new revelation.

"A MIGHTY FORTRESS IS OUR GOD"

The dominant note was one of reverent gratitude for divine guidance and protection. An early letter to friends in England said:

" A providential hand was very visible and remarkable in many instances, and the Indians were even rendered our benefactors and protectors. Without carnal weapons, we entered the land and inhabited therein, as safe as if there had been thousands of garrisons, for the Most High preserved us from harm, both of man and beast."

Many of the first built houses in Burlington were small wooden structures, some log huts, while a number of families for a time abode in caves along the river banks. Later substantial brick dwellings were erected and in this still old-fashioned town to-day, so quiet and restful, may be found a number of houses built in the early part of the eighteenth century and during the period prior to the Revolution. Some of these are large and imposing, showing all the distinguishing marks of the colonial era. Samuel Jennings, the first governor of West Jersey under the immigrant proprietors, had a large mansion on the river bank. He also built a fine country seat, known as " Green Hill," about two miles from Burlington, which stood with scarcely any change until a few years ago, when it was removed, but not until a picture of it was taken, which is here reproduced. Gov. Jennings was a noted Friends' minister, and at his country house meetings of ministers were often held.

BURLINGTON MEETING

That there was public worship very early is evident from the statement that open air meetings were held under sails borrowed from ships, and even marriages were thus celebrated. It was decided to organize the society in due form and the first minute, herewith given, quaintly sets forth this fact.

ince by the good Providence of god many friend ith their families have transported them selves this nto this Province of West New Iersey the said friends in hose upper parts have found it needfull according to our practice in the place wee came from to settle Monthly leetings for the well ordering the affairs of y was agreed that accordingly it should be done and accordingly it was done the 15th of y 5 Mo th 1698

First Page of "Burlington Meeting Records"

Meetings were regularly held at the houses of different members for a number of years, chiefly those of John Woolston and Thomas Gardiner. The first Yearly Meeting, taking in also Friends' societies at Salem, Shrewsbury and Crosswicks, New Jersey; Shackamaxon and Falls, Pennsylvania, was held at Thomas Gardiner's, Burlington, 6 mo. 28th 1681. Some years later the Yearly Meeting alternated with Philadelphia, until it was permanently located in the latter city in 1760.

friends
this
ds in
to our
Monthly
Church
ne and

BURLINGTON MEETING HOUSE, 1691-1785

From an old drawing

Soon after locating in Burlington, Friends took it into consideration to build a meeting house, as the society was rapidly outgrowing the capacity of private houses. Accordingly we find the following minute, under date 12 mo. 5th 1682:

> "It is ordered that a meeting house be built according to a draught of six square building of forty foot square from out to out for which he is to have 160 pounds, which ye meeting engageth to see ye Persons paid that shall disburst ye same to Francis Collings."

This important project seems to have proceeded slowly; in part, apparently, on account of the diligent attention the contractor paid to the attractive widow of Dr. Gosling, whom he finally secured as his second wife. In those days honorable courting, especially on the part of well-to-do widowers with young children, seems to have been regarded as a serious business. Finally the building was completed. The minute for 2 mo. 6 1691, says:

> "This day it is ordered that our First day Meetings at Burlington shall begin in the morning at the 9th hour, and at the 2nd hour in the afternoon; and be held both morning and evening in the meeting house."

The accompanying illustration of this historic structure is from a drawing furnished the artist, a native of Burlington. With the occupancy of the Meeting House marriages were solemnized there. Several years later a brick addition was erected, for winter use. For nearly one hundred years successive generations of Friends met in these quaint buildings for worship and counsel. The burial ground, immediately in the rear, was used meanwhile and has been since, until very little unoccupied space is left.

In 1785 the present Meeting House was built and it stands as firmly as ever, like the two great trees overshadowing it, which have stood guard for fully two hundred and fifty years. Historic relics, still in use, are the little pine table, upon which marriage certificates are signed, and the chairs, also, shown in accompanying illustrations, all more than two hundred years old and good for centuries more, though the fact is to be noted with infinite regret that the active membership of this historic Meeting is sadly reduced. In early days it was so noted for the number of ministers in attendance that it was sometimes referred to as the "School of the Prophets."

The following curious minutes are taken from early Burlington records:

At our Mens Monthly Meeting held at ye House of Tho˙ Gardiner in Bur^{ton} ye 10th of ye 7th mo: 1683

Friends saw meet to take it into their Consideration y^t It might be necefsary to have a Carriage made to Carry Such y^t are to be Laid in ye Ground who Live in remote parts from ye Burying place which is Referred to ye next meeting for further Consideration.

At our Mens Monthly Meeting held at ye House of Tho˙ Gardiner in B^{ton} ye 1st of ye 8th mo: 1683

Where the meeting ordered y^t Jno Butcher Should make a Carriage to bear Such to ye Ground y^t depart this Life who have Lived at a Distance from ye Burying Place & their Relations do now Live.

NOTABLE LAND MARKS

One of the notable land marks in the graveyard—now lying flat, as the Meeting some seventy-five years ago decreed all of like elaborate character should be placed—is the tombstone of a worthy member of one of the pioneer families of Burlington, whose descendants have ever since held positions of usefulness and influence in the Society and the religious and business world. The inscription on this memorial reads as follows:

> On the 30th day of July 1754 died
> Joseph Scattergood, Esq
> aged 40 years
> And the next day was interred here
> He was a Husband Loving & Beloved
> A Tender parent A Kind Relative
> A Sincere & faithful Friend a Good Master
> an Honest Man
> This Stone is placed over his Grave
> by his Mournful Widow as a Tribute
> Justly due to his Memory

Another impressive reminder of the early days is the great sycamore tree on the bank of the Delaware river, to which immigrant vessels were moored before a wharf was built. Accompanying picture shows this forest giant as it appears to-day, nearly three hundred years old, a wonderful specimen of long-lived trees in America. Its circumference, in 1908, was twenty-one feet eight inches.

BURLINGTON MEETING HOUSE, 1785

FOUNDING OF ST. MARY'S CHURCH

For a quarter of a century from the beginning, Friends constituted the only religious society in or about Burlington. In 1703 the Church of England established St. Mary's, first known as St. Anne's. This parish, therefore, is one of the oldest in America. The original building, erected in 1703, but not finished within for several years thereafter, has been enlarged four times and is now used chiefly for charitable purposes. The illustration given shows the front after the extension was made in 1769. A former rector, Rev. Dr. Morgan Hills, has published an elaborate history of the church. During the first seventy-three years there were but four regular ministers, namely, Revs. John Talbot, Robert Weyman, Colin Campbell and Jonathan Odell.

The first and third of these pioneer missionaries sometimes, under the spell of discouragement in consequence of many obstacles, complained to the parent society in London that the plain non-conformist people, amongst whom their lot had been cast, were too aggressive and too influential in the affairs of the province. But Dr. Odell seemed to more generously sum up the whole matter when, in 1768, he frankly declared, in a letter to his clerical superiors: "Of all Dissenters in this country, the Quakers are the most friendly to our Communion." Ten years later this zealous missionary had fresh cause to acknowledge Quaker kindness, on account of the timely aid and protection of a noted Quaker widow, Margaret Morris, whose quick wit saved him from capture and ignominious punishment by the enemies of his king.

FEATURES OF SOCIAL LIFE

Social intercourse in and around Burlington soon brightened the lives of the pioneers. Chronicles of the time relate how the members of different communities exchanged visits and in each town or hamlet a neighborly spirit prevailed. A pleasant summer time custom was out-door teas, quite informal and therefore all the more enjoyable. The quaint little porches, generally having a short bench on either side of the doorway, were almost universal. Here elderly men and women would sit in the evening, chatting with passing friends, while the young folks would occupy rustic seats upon the side lawn, or stroll to the river bank. Quarterly Meeting days, vendues and local fairs were occasions of great social interest.

Early marriage records show how busy cupid was uniting families in Pennsylvania and New Jersey. The young men did not believe in lengthy bachelorhood, and very few spinsters beyond the age of twenty-two were to be found. Early marriages and large, healthy families, domestic peace and happiness characterized those days of nation founding. It was a period of wonderful simplicity, trustfulness, honesty, purity and genuine material prosperity and spiritual development. The civic and religious records show how each community was blessed, and industrial advancement and increasing population was supplemented by the setting up of meetings throughout West Jersey. Early meetings were Burlington, Mt. Holly, Springfield, Chesterfield (Crosswicks), Rancocas (Northampton), Chester (Moorestown), Haddonfield, Newton, Evesham and Woodbury.

PENSAUKIN TRADITIONS

Definite traces of early meeting places in several instances have been quite lost; concerning others shadowy tradition points to the site of pioneer homes, as it was the custom to hold meetings in private houses until more suitable places could be provided. Old resting places for the dead have likewise been virtually obliterated. On the west bank of Pensaukin creek, near where it is crossed by the road from Camden to Moorestown, beneath a grove of trees, is an old graveyard, long since abandoned for use. A meeting house stood near by two hundred years ago. To this place the dead were sometimes brought in boats from Philadelphia. Several stones remained in position until half a century ago. Upon one was traced the faint inscription:

E. C
1713

From the same place was taken a stone, which was set up in the wall of a neighboring spring house. The following inscription was copied therefrom:

WHO ART THOU THAT

PASETH BY: LOOK ON THIS

PLACE; SEE HOW WE LIE

AND FOR THY SOLE

BE SURE CARE TAKE

FOR WHEN DETH COMS

TWILL BE TOO LATE

OLD ST. MARY'S PROTESTANT EPISCOPAL CHURCH, BURLINGTON, N. J., 1769

West front after first enlargement.   Originally built in 1703

AN INCIDENT OF THE TIME

In 1689, George Keith, an early and active Friends' minister, came from England, having been engaged as teacher of the first grammar school in Philadelphia, afterwards known as the Penn Charter School. He was regarded by contemporaries as a very learned man, and in 1691 his preaching led to a doctrinal division amongst Friends. Refusing to be admonished, the disturber was disowned by the Yearly Meeting which met at Burlington in 1692. The result was an attempt to set up separate meetings of so-called Christian Quakers, who were known as Keithians. In 1694, Keith returned to England and in a short time became identified with the Protestant Episcopal Church, receiving ordination at the hands of the Bishop of London in 1700. He again appeared in the colonies, this time as the first missionary of the Church of England to New Jersey and Pennsylvania and was known as the relentless foe of Quakerism the remainder of his days.

Friends' meeting records show some curious effects of the Keith schism. A number of cases of severe discipline are to be noted. One taken from the book of certificates of the Philadelphia Monthly Meeting, relating to a Burlington incident, is herewith given:

> "John Jones his paper of Condemnation in order to clear the truth &c
> "Whereas I did amongst many others unadvisedly sign a pernitious paper said to be given forth from ye yearly meeting at Burlington the 4th 5th 6th & 7th dayes of the seaventh month 1692 which was indeed a seperate meeting set up out of the unity of ffriends and in Opposition to Y M And the said paper Containing a severe Censure & Judgment upon ffriends Especially those ministering friends that gave forth the first Public Testimony against George Keith &c though the pretence was for peace and reconciliation and I not then percieving the mischievous design y^t was Carrying on was prevailed with to do as afores^d which as it was a great abuse to ffriends & Contributed to the Strengthening an evil spirit and wrong party: so it hath bin my sorrow and burthen Wherfore I do for satisfaction to my abused Brethren & Caution to others to beware of the Like Snare—and if it might be for the reclaiming of such as are fallen wth me all ready into it & for the removing of all Jealousies y^t might Justly raysed in ye minds of any that might hinder our unity and fellowship in the Truth Give forth this Testimony against that and all other acts done by me tending to the making or Countenancing y^t hurtfull seperation made by George Keith &c Blessing the Lord in the sence of his mercy who hath opened a way for my return and given me a place amongst his people where I desire for ever to hold the unity of the spirit in the bond of peace
> (Signed)   John Jones"

MESSAGE OF GEORGE FOX

During his visit to America, in 1672, George Fox passed through the section afterward known as West Jersey, and wrote to his friends at home commending it as a desirable place for settlement. " It is a most brave country, with good soil," he said. He always took a lively interest in the Quaker colonies, and in a letter written in March, 1676, about the time of the signing of the " Concessions and Agreements," addressed to " Friends in New Jersey and those who intend going there," he said:

> " Let your lives and words and conversations be as becomes the Gospel, that you may adorn the truth and honor the Lord in all your undertakings. Let that be your desire, and then you will have the Lord's blessing, and increase both in basket and field and storehouse; and at your lyings down you will feel him, and at your goings forth and coming in. And let temperance and patience and kindness and brotherly love be exercised among you, so that you may abound in virtue and the true humility; living in peace, showing forth the nature of Christianity; that you may all live as a family and the church of God."

COUNCIL OF PROPRIETORS

The land affairs of the province of West Jersey were at first conducted by special commissioners appointed by the proprietors, who came to America with the colony in 1677. This body was vested with authority to regulate the allotment of all lands, through surveys, make rules affecting rights of ownership, public highways, etc., in strict accord with the fundamental principles laid down in the " Concessions," signed in London, in 1676. They faithfully performed this work for ten years. The whole number of proprietors had now become so large and the members were so scattered that the transaction of business had become difficult. Therefore a general meeting of proprietors was held at Burlington, February 14, 1687, at which it was determined that there should be constituted a Council of Proprietors, to consist of eleven members, afterwards reduced to nine, to be annually chosen from among themselves.

These Councillors were fully empowered to act in all such affairs as concerned the general body. They agreed upon a system of rules relating to surveys and sales of land. In this manner the land affairs of West Jersey continued to be directed for a long period, and indeed the authority so exercised is recognized to this day in connection with unlocated and unsurveyed lands. The Council meets once a year, in May, in Burlington. The early minute books are carefully preserved in the office of the Surveyor General, at Burlington, and generally are in good condition. A few leaves have been moth-eaten, as will be seen by the photographic reproduction of part of the minute of a meeting in 1687, at which Thomas ffrench was recorded as present. Another picture shows the present Surveyor General's office, erected about one hundred years ago, in which original documents, including the " Concessions and Agreements " of 1676 are preserved.

In the Surveyor General's office is the original final deed of James, Duke of York, afterwards James II, to William Penn, Gauen Laurie and others, in trust for Edward Byllynge, bearing date August 6, 1680. It is a large parchment sheet, about 30 x 35 inches, showing but little the marks of decay. It was recently photographed, for the first time, for the compiler of this book, a copy being presented to the Historical Society of Pennsylvania. The famous " Concessions and Agreements," beautifully written on heavy vellum and bound in book form, defies the ravages of time. It is as clear as when engrossed and signed two hundred and thirty-one years ago. Three pages of this immortal document are reproduced, the title page and two others showing the signatures of Penn, Byllynge, Laurie, Ollive, Thomas ffrench and other leaders of the colonization movement.

PEN PICTURE OF COLONIAL LIFE

In many respects the quaintest story of the early settlement of Pennsylvania and New Jersey was written by Gabriel Thomas, an observant Englishman, who lived fifteen years in the colonies and wrote a truthful account of what he saw and heard. This little book was published in London, in 1698. Original copies are very rare and when found bring a fabulous price. About fifty years ago a liberal-minded antiquarian of New York, Henry Austin Brady, had the book faithfully reproduced by lithographic process. A photograph of the title page of the second part, dealing with New Jersey, is given. The author's special purpose, uniquely set forth, was to present such a favorable account of the new country that industrious persons of good character would be induced to seek homes in a land where there was wide opportunity for every one. Interesting extracts are here presented:

> " The first Inhabitants of this Countrey were the Indians, being supposed
> to be part of the Ten dispersed Tribes of Israel; for indeed they are very

like the Jews in their Persons, and something in their Practices and Worship, for they observe the New Moons with great Devotion and Reverence. And their first Fruits they offer, with their Corn and Hunting Game they get in the whole Year, to a False Deity or Sham-God, whom they must please, else, as they fancy, many Misfortunes will befall them and great Injuries will be done them. They are very loving to one another and are very kind and civil to any Christians. The Women are very ingenious in their several Imployments as well as the Men. Their young Maids are naturally very modest and their young Women when newly married are very nice and shy. As to the manner of their Language, it is high and lofty, with a short sentence.

"Burlington is become a very famous Town, having a great many stately brick houses in it. There are many fine Wharfs and large Timber Yards, Malt Houses, Bake Houses and most sorts of Tradesmen. There are many Fair and Great Brick Houses on the outside of the Town which the Gentry have built for their Countrey Houses. There are kept in this Famous Town several Fairs every year. Bread, Beer, Beef, Pork, Cheese, Butter and most sorts of Fruit here is great Plenty and very Cheap.

"There is Glocester Town, which is a very Fine and Pleasant Place, being well stored with Summer Fruits, whither Young People come from Philadelphia in the Wherries (boats) to eat Strawberries and Cream, within sight of which City it is sweetly situated. The Air is very Clear, Sweet and Wholesom; in the depth of Winter it is something colder, and as much hotter in the heighth of Summer than in England.

"They have Wheat, Rye, Peas, Oates, Barley, Rice &c in vast quantities; also Roots, Herbs and Salads in abundance. Of Fish they have many sorts in prodigious Shoals and Wild Water Fowl are numerous beyond all expectation, and Land Fowl are in extraordinary abundance and very large, with Charming and curious Birds too tedious to specify.

"I might have given a much larger Account of this Countrey, and yet without straining or deviating in the least from the Principles of my Profession, which are Truth itself. I have no Plot in my Pate, deep Design, not the least expectation of gaining anything by them that go thither, or losing by those who stay here. Reader, I wish thee all Health and Happiness in this and Everlasting Comfort in the World to come."

THE FRENCH FAMILY IN ENGLAND

NDER variously spelled surnames the French family appeared in England soon after the Norman conquest. The first of the line recorded was with William the Conqueror at the battle of Hastings, October 14, 1066, when Harold, King of the Anglo-Saxons, was defeated after an all-day struggle. Of 60,000 valiant soldiers, William lost more than 15,000. Yorkshire records of 1100 frequently show the name French. Others located in the beginning chiefly in the southeastern counties, but later appeared in the west and north as far as Scotland. They were very early in Ireland, and one branch of the family trace their descent directly from Rollo, Duke of Normandy. In England, before the close of the thirteenth century, the French family had become extensive, prosperous and influential.

Old records present curious facts. The will of Adam Frensch, of Gloucester, provided for his burial in church, beside his first wife, Maud. His clothing was to be sold for the benefit of his soul. To his widow, Alice, he left lands, but in case of her remarriage they were to be sold, one half the proceeds for her benefit, the other half for the good of the soul of Maud. In York the name was spelled Francais; in Berks, Ffrensh; in Middlesex, Frenssh; in Somerset, Frensce; in Surrey, Frensche; in Northampton, Franceis and Fraunceys; in Wiltshire, French. Two centuries later it is generally found, in Northampton, ffrench, after the manner adopted by the direct ancestors of that branch of the family whose descendants are recorded in this genealogy.

Thomas ffrench, founder of the New Jersey branch of the French family, resided, in 1680, the year of his migration to America, in Nether Heyford, a parish in the hundred of Newbottle Grove, county of Northampton, seven miles south by west from the city of Northampton, England. This parish is very ancient, the church of S. S. Peter and Paul having been erected in the early part of the thirteenth century. The first patron was Roger de Heyford, in 1216. The register that has been preserved begins in 1558, showing the French family parishioners as far back as 1560. The church

is a splendidly preserved specimen of Norman architecture.   There is a chime
of four bells; round the tenor is the inscription:

"THOMAS MORGAN GAVE ME, TO THE CHURCH OF HEY-
FORD FRANK AND FREE."

The donor was a descendant of Francis Morgan, who, about the middle
of the sixteenth century, for a time filled an honorable place upon the local
bench.   The Morgan family for more than two centuries were active and
influential in the affairs of Nether Heyford parish.   In the church a marble
tablet perpetuates the memory of Judge Morgan.   There are other notable
memorials, one to a baronet who died in 1467; another beautifully illustrates
Faith and Hope.   In this parish was born Dr. John Preston, the patriarch
of the Puritans, whom the Duke of Buckingham vainly sought to use in the
service of the king, James I.   Many members of the French family also
attended services in the ancient church of St. Michael, at Bugbrook, about
a mile and a half from Nether Heyford, and which was built early in the
thirteenth century.   Its register likewise begins in 1558.   Accompanying
illustrations, from photographs taken in 1895, show exterior view of the
church at Nether Heyford, interior view, the Village Green and the church
at Bugbrook.

The church at Heyford has been under the care of one noted family of
ministers for the past one hundred years, grandfather, father and son.   The
latter, Rev. H. H. Crawley, examined the parish register for the purposes of
this book and in a recent letter says:

> "The Heyford Register, the earliest begins in 1558, is a very interesting
> one.   I began to search from that date to 1774 and find that there are about
> 70 entries of baptisms, marriages and burials of the name and they are
> evidently members of one family.   There are at least 60 entries of the
> name between 1558 and 1680; the other entries of the name are evidently
> members of the family who did not leave the old country and I should
> say there are collateral branches of your family still living in or near
> Heyford.   Your family in old days evidently held a responsible position
> in the parish, for members of the name appear as guardians in the seven-
> teenth century.   The earliest record I can find is 1560.   A part of Hey-
> ford formerly had a right of baptism, burial, etc., in Bugbrook.   There is
> an aisle in Bugbrook church which is still called Heyford aisle, just as
> there is a Heyford aisle in the church at Stowe IX Churches."

CHURCH OF S. S. PETER AND PAUL, NETHER HEYFORD, ENGLAND, BUILT ABOUT 1200

In the earliest days of the Society of Friends a little meeting house was set up at Bugbrook.   There as at Heyford and elsewhere the members continued to outwardly conform, registering births and baptisms at the church, but it seems they often drew the line at burials and thus incurred at times severe criticism.   From the Bugbrook parish register of 1668 the following curious note is taken:

> "About this time that untoward generation of Quakers began to bury theirs distinctly by themselves in their gardens and orchards in several places of the towne, all which burialls, there being no notice given of them to the minister or parish clerke, are here omitted, nor have their names inserted in this church 'register, tho there was a considerable mortality among them, as also those of several other sort of phanaticks, who having forsaken the church, would not be buried in the church yard, but in their orchards or backside of their houses."

Thomas ffrench, father of Thomas ffrench, the progenitor of the New Jersey branch of the French family, like his ancestors of many generations, lived at Nether Heyford, where he was known as an influential and useful citizen.   He married, first, Sara ———, by whom he had the following children:

Patience, b. 1637.   Thomas, b. 1639.   Sara, b. 1643.   Elizabeth, b. 1645. Mary, b. 1648.   John, b. 1651.

By his second wife, Martha ———, he had: Robert, b. 1657.   Martha, b. 1660.

Thomas ffrench, senior, was buried May 5[th.] 1673.   Sara ffrench, his wife, was buried Feb. 9[th.] 1653.

The will of Thomas ffrench, as may be noted, is a quaint and characteristic document of the times.   It shows the thoughtful regard of a loving parent in distributing his estate carefully and making special provision for those of tender years.

WILL OF THOMAS FFRENCH, 1673

> In the Name of God Amen the Nine and twentyth day of Aprill in the five and twentyth yeare of the raigne of our Soveraigne Lord Charles the second of England Scotland Ffrance and Ireland King Defender of the faith Anno Dom 1673 I Thomas ffrench the Elder of Nether Heyford in the County of Northton being weak in body but of good and perfect Memory thanks be to Almightie God.   And Knowing the uncertaintie of this life on earth do make this my last Will and testam in manner and

In the earliest days of the Society of Friends a little meeting house was set up at Bugbrook. There as at Heyford and elsewhere the members continued to outwardly conform, registering births and baptisms at the church, but it seems they often drew the line at burials and thus incurred at times severe criticism. From the Bugbrook parish register of 1668 the following curious note is taken:

> "About this time that untoward generation of Quakers began to bury theirs distinctly by themselves in their gardens and orchards in several places of the towne, all which burialls, there being no notice given of them to the minister or parish clerke, are here omitted, nor have their names inserted in this church 'register, tho there was a considerable mortality among them, as also those of several other sort of phanaticks, who having forsaken the church, would not be buried in the church yard, but in their orchards or backside of their houses."

Thomas ffrench, father of Thomas ffrench, the progenitor of the New Jersey branch of the French family, like his ancestors of many generations, lived at Nether Heyford, where he was known as an influential and useful citizen. He married, first, Sara ———, by whom he had the following children:

Patience, b. 1637. Thomas, b. 1639. Sara, b. 1643. Elizabeth, b. 1645. Mary, b. 1648. John, b. 1651.

By his second wife, Martha ———, he had: Robert, b. 1657. Martha, b. 1660.

Thomas ffrench, senior, was buried May 5th 1673. Sara ffrench, his wife, was buried Feb. 9th 1653.

The will of Thomas ffrench, as may be noted, is a quaint and characteristic document of the times. It shows the thoughtful regard of a loving parent in distributing his estate carefully and making special provision for those of tender years.

WILL OF THOMAS FFRENCH, 1673

In the Name of God Amen the Nine and twentyth day of Aprill in the five and twentyth yeare of the raigne of our Soveraigne Lord Charles the second of England Scotland Ffrance and Ireland King Defender of the faith Anno Dom 1673 I Thomas ffrench the Elder of Nether Heyford in the County of Northton being weak in body but of good and perfect Memory thanks be to Almightie God. And Knowing the uncertaintie of this life on earth do make this my last Will and testam in manner and forme ffollowing And first being penitent and sorry for my sins past most humbly desireing forgivnesse for the same I give and Comitt my soule to Almightie God my Saviour and Redeemer in whom and by the meritts of Jesus Christ I trust and believe assuredly to be saved and to have full remission and forgivenesse of all my sins And my body to the earth from whence it was taken to be buryed in such decent and Christian manner as to my Executo^{rs} hereafter named shal be thought meet and convenient revoking and annulling by these p^rsents all and every Will and Wills testam and testaments heretofore by me made and declared and this to be taken for my last Will and testament and none other I will that all those debts and duties ^{Wch} in right or conscience I owe to any manner of person or persons whatsoever shalbe well and truely contented and paid or ordained to be paid within convenient time after my decease by my Executors hereafter named Item I give and bequeath to Thomas ffrench my eldest sone the sume of twelve pence I give and bequeath to John ffrench my second sone two shillings and six pence I give and bequeath to Patience ffrench my eldest daughter two shillings and six pence I give and bequeath to Elisabeth ffrench my second daughter two shillings and six pence I give and bequeath to Mary ffrench my third daughter two shillings and six pence all ^{Wch} said legacies I will shalbe payd by my Executors within six months after my decease All the rest of my goods cattell and chattels whatsoever I give and bequeath to Martha my loveing wife and to my sone Robert ffrench and my daughter Martha ffrench whom I make joint Executors of this my last Will and Testam I do nominate and appoint my welbeloved ffreinds Thomas Kirton and William Steffe both of Hayford aforesaid overseers of this my last Will and Testam and do give them twelvepence apeece In wittnes whereof I the said Thomas ffrench have hereunto sett my hand and seale the day and yeare first above written·

Thomas ffrench [SEAL]

Published signed and sealed
  in the presence of
    William Stif

        His
    Thomas ✕ Kirton
        Mark

        Her
    Alice ✕ Kirton
        Mark

    John Darby
Proved 16th August 1673

forme following ... being present ... for my sins past most humbly desiring ... ... I ... and Comitt my soule to Almighty God my Saviour and Redeemer ... ... and by the merites of Jesus Christ ... ... and to have full remission and forgiveness ... ... my body to the earth from whence it was taken to be buried in ... ... and Christian manner as to my Executors ... ... and and convenient revoking and ... by these ... each and every Will and Wills ... ... and this to be ... for my last Will and ... and ... ... other I will that all ... ... and debts ... ... to this manner of ... ... shall ... and ... ... and paid ... ... to be paid within ... ... by my Executors ... ... first I give and ... to Thomas ffrench my ... ... the ... of ... ... I give and bequeath to John ffrench my second sonne two shillings and six ... I give and bequeath to ... ffrench my eldest daughter two shillings and the same I give and bequeath to Elizabeth ffrench my second daughter two shillings and six pence I give and bequeath to Mary ffrench my third daughter two shillings and six pence all w'th said ... I will ... paid by my Executors within six months after my decease. All the rest of my goods cattell and chattels whatsoever I give and bequeath to Martha my loveing wife and to my sonn Robert ffrench and my daughter Martha ffrench whom I make joint Executors of this my last Will and Testam. I do nominate and appoint my welbeloved friends Thomas Kirton and William Steife both of Heyford aforesaid overseers of this my last Will and Testam and do give them twelvepence apiece. In witness whereof I the said Thomas ffrench have hereunto ...... hand and seale the day and yeare first above written

Thomas ffrench [SEAL]

Published signed and
  in the presence of
    William Stif
      His
  Thomas X Kirton
     Mark

     Her
  Alice X Kirton
    Mark

  John Darby
Proved 16th August 1653

INTERIOR, CHURCH OF S.S. PETER AND PAUL, NETHER HEYFORD, ENGLAND

THOMAS FRENCH, PROGENITOR

As will be observed, Thomas ffrench, the progenitor, was the son of Thomas and Sara ffrench. His baptism, in childhood, in 1639, in the Protestant Episcopal Church of St. Peter and St. Paul, Nether Heyford, England, is recorded, but when the religious Society of Friends arose he with other members of the family became actively identified therewith, suffering for his faith at different times. Upon one occasion he was sentenced to imprisonment for forty-two months for refusal to pay tithes to the amount of eleven shillings, he being at the time a resident of Upper Norton, Oxfordshire. Five other names of this family appear in Beese's remarkable book, namely, George, Robert, John, William and Moses. Penalty was inflicted upon the latter five times. He served altogether several years in prison.

That Thomas ffrench was a man of great force of character, intense religious conviction and earnest, consistent life, is abundantly evident. He shared with his associates trials and hardships and always resented everything bearing the slightest resemblance to injustice or oppression. A glance at the situation in England during the period of persecution will be timely. The most vigorous efforts were made to suppress the Society of Friends. Their meetings were outlawed, their property unjustly taken, through fines and the imposition of tithes, and great numbers were thrown into prison, where they were cruelly treated, hundreds suffering unto death. The sad and shameful story of this era of martyrdom would be quite incredible if the unquestioned record had not been preserved, in a book the like of which the world will never again see.

Joseph Besse, the famous English Quaker controversialist, was born about 1683 and died 1757. He was educated for the Episcopalian ministry, but becoming a convert to the teachings of Fox, refused a church living of four hundred pounds a year and became a vigorous defender of Quakerism. He wrote many religious tracts and books and edited various important works. He completed, in 1753, his great work, " The Sufferings of the People Called Quakers," from which quotations herewith given are taken. This comprises one of the most remarkable records ever compiled, being faithful transcripts, from original sources, found in the minutes of meetings, court records, petitions, personal letters, memoirs, etc. Its accuracy cannot be questioned and a testimonial to its fidelity to the truth is found in the fact that a century and a half ago the records were destroyed by the British government.

PRISONERS FOR CONSCIENCE SAKE

Following is a literal copy of references to Thomas ffrench in " Sufferings of the People Called Quakers " :

> " Thomas French, of Upper Norton, was imprisoned, in 1657, at suit of William Thomas, a lawyer and renter of Tithes, and for a demand of but eleven shillings for Tithes suffered two and forty months imprisonment." Vol. I, p. 564.

> " Thomas French was taken from meeting at Banbury, in 1662, and committed to prison." Vol. I, p. 568.

> " Thomas French, 1666, taken at meeting at house of Elizabeth White, at Coggs, near Whitney, committed to House of Correction for one month." Vol. I, p. 571.

Two pages of this extraordinary book are reproduced, one reciting instances of persecution, including imprisonment of Thomas ffrench, and the other a most impressive petition to King Charles II, 1680.

Some four score prisoners for conscience sake in Northampton jail, " who patiently suffer for worshipping the Living God in Spirit and Truth," in mid-summer, 1666, issued a warning and appeal, referring to the ravages of the plague and their view of the cause thereof. From this curious paper, headed " Truth the strongest habitation for all the People of God," we quote :

> ' There is some of thy Rulers so desperately wicked in this County of Northampton, that commit sin even with greediness at this time, as tho there were no other way to stay God's Judgments, but by provoking him more and more with their sins in persecuting, sentencing and imprisoning of the Lord's People, having lately imprisoned fifty-eight persons called Quakers, both men and women, some of the latter with little infants and shutting them all up together in the common Goal in close roomes, in the very heat of the last month, and still they continue, the number of 82 altogether. We who are sufferers in this Goal of Northampton, for the truth of the Lord, do spread these lines before the Nation, that so, if it be not too late, the Nation may see what is the cause of God's Judgments, lying so heavy upon this land and people, and may see who hath been the Troublers of England."

From a lecture on " The Baptists and Quakers in Northamptonshire, 1650–1700," by the Rev. J. Jackson Goadby, delivered in College Street Chapel, Northampton, Oct. 24, 1882, we quote the following remarkable statement :

PRISONERS FOR CONSCIENCE SAKE

Following a literal copy of references to Thomas in "Sufferings of the People Called Quakers":

CHURCH OF ST. MICHAEL, BUGBROOKE, ENGLAND, BUILT ABOUT 1200

SIXTY THOUSAND VICTIMS OF PERSECUTION

" Quakers were put in the stocks for the crime of preaching; seized by soldiers as they were quietly going to their meetings; committed for blasphemy; or when in the open fields where they had met for worship; or as vagrants; as Sabbath breakers; as men who refused to take an oath; and as seditious men. They were pounced upon suddenly when assembled for worship, and carried off to prison; crammed into crowded and reeking holes, the doors being fastened down for twelve hours every night, and refused all intercourse with their friends; and in some cases they were brutally treated both by jailors, by the jailors' wives, and by the prisoners. Men and women were seized at their meetings, carried off in carts to some ale-house, locked up in a room all night, whilst their captors indulged in ribald songs and tippling, and then hurried off the next morning to prison.

" Numbers of the imprisoned Friends, like their leaders in this county, Whitehead and Dewsbury, sent out epistles from the Northampton jail, detailing their own sufferings. Whitehead was the Quaker minister who always took his night cap with him when he went to meeting, because it was almost certain he would have to spend that night in prison. Some of the Quakers, it must be confessed, carried plain-speaking to the verge of rudeness. But this free speech is, after all, no justification of the brutal treatment received by the Friends at the hands of magistrates, and is, least of all, any palliation of the horrible fact that many hundreds of Quakers died of their harsh usage in the jails of England, and some scores in the common jail of Northampton. The Friends preserved their hold on the nation until the beginning of the eighteenth century, when they numbered 70,000.

" If the record of other religious bodies is not so full of faithful martyrs to the truth and conscience as that of the Quakers, it is not because they were any the less brutally treated, or any the less numerous. Jeremy White made a careful collection of the names of persons who suffered for their nonconformity during the reign of Charles II. Sixty thousand persons were included in this terrible list, and five thousand died of their sufferings. When James II. wished to gain possession of this dark calendar, that he might use it in his quarrel with the English State Church, and even offered 5,000 guineas for it, Jeremy White chose rather to burn the list than see it turned to such a purpose. Many of these sixty thousand brave men and women are unknown to fame, like the poor Hollanders of the days of Henry VIII.; but their deeds and their heroism have not perished. We see it to-day in the larger and more settled liberty which every Englishman possesses. They also paid part of that great sum by which our forefathers bought our freedom."

Sarah Timms, in the Grave-Yard at *Banbury,* exhorted the Prieft to fear the Lord : For which *Chriftian* Exhortation, fome of her Hearers knockt her down, and ftruck her violently. The Mayor and Magiftrates, who were prefent, inftead of reftraining them from offering fuch Illegal Abufes, fent the innocent Woman to Prifon, where fhe lay half a Year. Alfo *Jane Waugh,* for bearing her Teftimony to the Truth, and againft Deceit, in the Market-place at *Banbury,* was imprifoned five Weeks : As were *Mary Coats* and *Mary Lamprey,* for reproving the Vices of the Mayor and Magiftrates there ; the former was releafed the fame Night, but the other detained eighteen Days.

John Shackerly, for fpeaking to a Prieft, at *Oxford,* fome difpleafing Words, was by his Means fent to the City Prifon, and there detained feven Weeks. And at another Time, for the like Offence againft the Vice-Chancellor, he was imprifoned twenty eight Weeks.

ANNO 1656. *Hefter Biddle,* of *London,* was imprifoned at *Banbury* for fome zealous Reprehenfion uttered againft the Mayor and Magiftrates there.

ANNO 1657. In this Year *Alexander Harris* was imprifoned for Tithes, on two Actions ; one at the Suit of a Prieft, the other of an Impropriator : After three Years and an Half Imprifonment, he was taken fick, and his Cafe being reprefented to his Profecutors, they had Compaffion on him, and having made fufficient Proof of the Man's Sincerity, were not willing he fhould die under Confinement at their Suit, and therefore freely and generoufly difcharged him. But their Deputy afterward took the Corn off his Ground for the Tithe, Annually, in what Quantities they pleafed.

About the Middle of the Month called *February* this Year, *William Cole,* of *Charlbury,* profecuted in the *Exchequer* for Tithes, was fent to Prifon for refufing to give in his Anfwer upon Oath. Being there, he was charged alfo with an Action for Tithes, by an Impropriator ; at whofe Suit he was detained in Prifon till he died, a faithful Witnefs againft the Antichriftian Oppreffion of Tithes. The fame Impropriator took from him alfo, while in Prifon, Goods worth 20*l.* for 5*l.* demanded.

Thomas French, of *Upper-Norton,* was alfo imprifoned at the Suit of *William Thomas,* a Lawyer, and Renter of Tithes ; and for a Demand of but 11*s.* for Tithes, fuffered two and forty Months Imprifonment.

ANNO 1658. In this Year, *Richard Kite* of *Upper-Norton, Margaret Freebody* of *King's Hutton, Richard Betteris,* and *Hannah Alcock,* were at feveral Times imprifoned for their *Chriftian* and religious Exhortations and Reproofs, given to the Priefts and People on various Occafions : For which Caufe alfo, *Bathia Haflewood,* of *Borton,* was ftoned, and othewife evilly treated by the Populace at *Cropfody,* the Prieft looking on, and laughing at the Wickednefs of his Hearers.

There were, in thefe Times, fome Men advanced to the Office of Magiftrates, fo extremely fond of Perfonal Homage, as to profecute and imprifon Men for the Omiffion of that, which no Law required : Hence it was that *Simon Thompfon* and *Nathanael Knowles,* meeting *William Fines,* otherwife called Lord *Say,* and not paying him the cuftomary Ceremony of the Hat, were by him fent to *Oxford* Goal, and detained two Months. At the next Seffions, he caufed them to be fent to the Houfe of Correction, and detained there near eight Months, the faid *Nathanael Knowles* being feveral Times cruelly whipt, and otherwife ill ufed. Likewife *Ellis Hookes,* going to vifit his Mother, then refiding at the Houfe of Sir *William Waller* at *Stanton-Harcourt,* becaufe he did not pay the Knight and his Lady the Hat-honour, and cuftomary Compliments, was by them, and their Servants, beaten and abufed : And by their Influence, his own Father was fo incenfed againft him, that he turned him out of Doors.

It fo happened about this Time, that *Richard Farnfworth,* walking with one of his Friends up *Banbury-Street,* met the Mayor, and a Juftice of the Peace named *William Allen :* The Juftice looking very angrily upon *Richard,* ftruck off his Hat : W th and how

Sufferers, and of that fervent Love which the Persecuted, for the Testimony of Christ and a good Conscience, bear one towards another, praying for each others Preservation, and final Perseverance to the End of their Hope, the Salvation of their Souls.

The other Letter, or Address, was written to the King when at *Bath*, and is as follows ;

"FORASMUCH, O King! as our daily Sufferings are augmented,
" and our Number in this Place so greatly increased, as that we cannot
" any longer well hold our Peace, but do in the Fear of God, and in true
" Humility in his Sight, in all Lowliness of Mind, after long Imprisonment,
" present thee, in this thy Progress and Day of Prosperity, with our grievous
" Sufferings for our Conscience in Things relating to God ; our Souls being
" subject to the Lord that made Heaven and Earth : And against thee, O
" King! have we not done or imagined Evil, but do, according to the Truth
" and Righteousness in our Hearts, desire thy Peace and Prosperity, and that
" Mercy may establish thy Throne in Equity and Justice. And whereas we
" who are called *Quakers*, because of the Fear of God, and to keep our
" Consciences void of Offence, cannot take any Oath, many of us are by a
" severe Sentence deprived of all the Goods we have in this World, and our
" Wives and innocent Children thereby exposed to utter Ruin, unless the
" Execution thereof be prevented ; and others by Fines beyond their Abilities,
" adjudged to perpetual Imprisonment, and that for Matter of pure Conscience
" only, and not for any Design of Evil, or Wrong, intended towards thee,
" O King! or any of thy Subjects, as hath been largely testified by many
" Years Experience, through many Trials and Hardships in Bonds, wherein
" the Lord hath been with us, and preserved us innocent and upright in our
" Hearts toward thee, and for this we appeal to the Witness of God in all
" Men, whether we have not so approved our selves to this Day, in the
" Sight of God and Men. And as an Addition to our present Sufferings,
" the Goaler's Cruelty so abounds, that many of us are likely to be exposed
" to Famishment, and utter Destruction, being thrust together in such a great
" Number, and denied such necessary Accommodation, as is ordinarily given
" to the worst of Men, besides what is daily farther threatned. We therefore,
" as to our outward Man, being Objects of thy Mercy and Clemency, it
" being in thy Hands to dispose of us at thy Pleasure, do in all due Submission
" make our Appeal unto thee, as unto one who is able to relieve us : And
" the Lord open thy Heart to consider our Innocency and Distress, and to
" acquit us from our grievous Sentences, and other our Imprisonment. And
" it is the Desire of our Hearts, that in Truth and Righteousness the
" God of Peace may prosper thee to reign : And what Profit will the Death
" of the Innocent be to the King ?

From the Prisoners called Quakers,
in Ilchester, *this 4th Day of the*   Subscribed by thirty of the Prisoners.
Seventh Month 1663.

This Letter, or Address, discovers an innocent Simplicity, attended with *Christian* Courage, expressing a decent Submission void of Flattery, and professing all due Allegiance and peaceful Subjection to the King and his Government, with a noble and stedfast Resolution of keeping their Consciences undefiled and void of Offence toward God. This is the Stile of true *Christian* Confessors, whom the *Perfect Fear of God* hath exalted above an abject and servile Departure from his Commandments, in Conformity to the Laws of any Power upon Earth.

ANNO 1664. On the 7th of the Month called *May*, *Katharine Evans* and *Sarah Chevers*, Women who travelled in the Work of the Gospel, came

THE COMING OF THOMAS FRENCH

Thomas ffrench was among the first to take a practical interest in the colonization of Friends in America. With William Penn, Gauen Laurie, Thomas Ollive, Daniel Wills, Edward Byllynge and about one hundred and fifty others, he signed the famous " Concessions and Agreements," at London, in 1676, which provided for the settlement of New Jersey. It is evident from records that he made a preliminary prospecting visit to this country, to locate his land and select a home site. He has left an account of the coming of himself and family, three years after the arrival of the pioneer colonists. He sailed from London, in the ship Kent, Gregory Marlowe, master—the same vessel which brought the first company of settlers in 1677 to Burlington—about the 1st· of August, 1680, with his wife and nine children, four sons and five daughters, the oldest child being sixteen, while the youngest was not yet four years of age. He settled upon a tract of 600 acres of desirable land, located along the banks of the Rancocas, about four miles from Burlington. Throughout the remainder of his life he held an influential place in the colony and prospered in business. He was commissioner of highways 1684–5. At his death, in 1699, he was possessed of some 1,200 acres of improved land and also his proprietary share of unsurveyed lauds, approximately, 2,000 acres. During nearly twenty years residence as a leading citizen of Burlington County, Thomas ffrench trained all his children in ways of sobriety, industry, and religion, they in turn founding families in whom traits of strong character were noted. Each performed his and her share in the prosperous and happy development of colonial life.

THE PIONEER HOMESTEAD

The section of New Jersey in which Thomas ffrench located was a notable place in pioneer days. An old map, reproduced, shows the names of early settlers, two of the most conspicuous being Thomas Ollive, who served as proprietary Governor and member of the Council and who was eminent also as a Quaker preacher, and Dr. Daniel Wills, whose land joined that upon which the Friends' meeting house was built. Many fine old mansions marked the neighborhood, and some of these, over one hundred years old, remain. It is an interesting fact that part of the original plantation of Thomas ffrench is to-day owned and occupied by his descendants. Large tracts were

GOV. FRANKLIN'S HOUSE, "FRANKLIN PARK," 170

Located on original estate of Thomas French, near Rancocas, N. J.

sold early in the eighteenth century by Charles ffrench, his son, to whom the
homestead lands were willed by his father.   In 1714, Charles ffrench conveyed 250 acres to his brother-in-law, Nicholas Buzby, part of this descend-
ing to the latter's son, John Buzby, who devised the same, in 1754, to his son
John, who, in 1763, sold it to John Smith, of Burlington.   The deed stated
that the estate was thereafter to be known as " Strawberry Hill."   It is supposed the great mansion, still standing, in an excellent state of preservation,
was built by John Smith, about 1765 (see illustration).   The place was
leased soon after to Gov. William Franklin, as a summer home and purchased
by him in 1770 for two thousand pounds.   It then became known as " Franklin Park," containing a fine collection of deer and other high-class game.
A great moat was constructed, the remains of which are still visible, to keep
off poachers.

AGAIN A FAMILY POSSESSION

The Governor was removed from office, on account of his loyalty to the
King, in 1776, and taken prisoner to Connecticut.   Later he returned to
New York, where his wife had died meanwhile, being buried under the
chancel of St. Paul's historic church, Broadway.   A beautiful tablet was
erected by her husband, some years later.   Gov. Franklin retained ownership
of the Rancocas estate, without confiscation, until 1785, when he sold it to
his son, William Temple Franklin, then living in Paris and who later became
noted as the literary legatee of his grandfather, Benjamin Franklin.   He
sold the property, in 1790, to Robert Morris, the patriot financier of the
Revolution, who held it until 1794, when William Bell, a rich Philadelphia
merchant, became the purchaser, with a great amount of other land in West
Jersey owned by Morris.   Soon after Bell's death, in 1816, the property was
sold to Joseph Churchman, who in 1822, conveyed " Franklin Park " to
Mayberry McVaugh.   A two-story brick dormitory was built adjoining the
mansion, and a boarding school for boys set up, which became quite a
famous institution of its kind.   In March, 1843, Hudson Buzby [410]
bought this historic property; and in 1862, his son Richard Buzby [894]
became the owner through purchase.   In 1889, Richard Buzby's son, Thomas
T. Buzby [1689] bought the farm, about 100 acres of choice land, and the
mansion, being the present occupant.   Thus an important part of the original tract, cut out of the wilderness two hundred and twenty-eight years
ago, and having a most interesting history, is again in possession of worthy
descendants of the pioneer, Thomas ffrench.

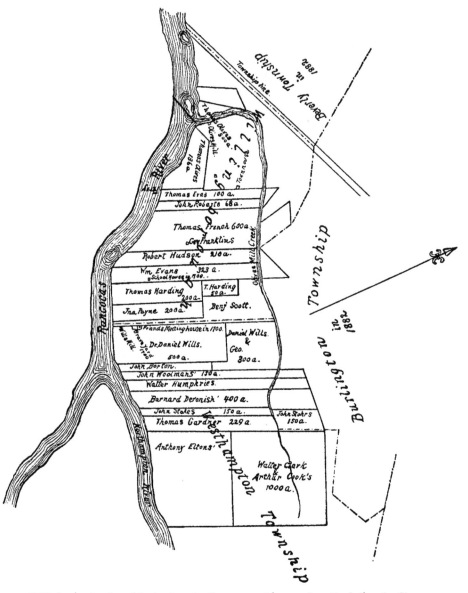

MAP showing location of lands along the Rancocas as taken up from the Indians by Thomas
ffrench and other pioneer settlers, between 1680 and 1690.

Draughted by Charles Stokes [450] from ancient surveys.

THOMAS FFRENCH'S FAMILY BIBLE

The family Bible of Thomas ffrench, printed in 1630, and brought by him to this country in 1680, is still in existence and in a fair state of preservation, although showing the effects of time.   It has always remained within the family. Accompanying illustrations are almost full size.   The record presented and transcribed is in the handwriting of the progenitor, evidently having been set down at different times, under varying circumstances and influences, throughout a period covering over thirty years, the last entry being made a little while after the death of the long-time companion who had borne him thirteen children.   Some of the lines have faded and a few words are quite illegible.   The most striking characteristic to be noted is the ever present spirit of humility, gratitude for manifold mercies and earnest desire for continued Divine guidance and protection.

52

broug

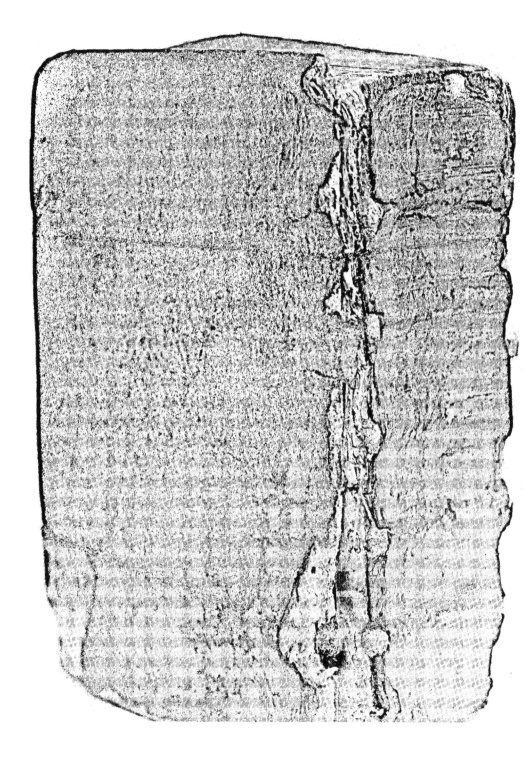

THOMAS FFRENCH'S FAMILY BIBLE

The title page of this venerable edition of the Holy Book,
" Imprinted at London by Robert Barker and John Bill,
Printers to the Kings moſt Excellent Majeſtie, 1630," was
designed after the curious manner of the time, relating to object teaching of Scriptural things.   The names on the left
refer to the twelve tribes of Israel; those on the right recite
the twelve apostles, with the writers of the four Gospels in
the centre.   The accompanying figures all have appropriate
significance in the illustration of the Biblical story.   The
New Testament title page is of the same studious and impressive character.

THE

HOLY BIBLE

CONTAINING THE OLD
TESTAMENT and the NEW:

Newly tranſlated out of the Originall Tongues:
And with the former Tranſlations diligently compared
and reuiſed, By his Maieſties ſpeciall command.

¶ Appointed to be read in Churches.

¶ IMPRINTED, AT LONDON
by Robert Barker and John Bill,
Printers to the Kings moſt
Excellent Maiestie.

M.DC.XXX.

Cum Priuilegio.

TITLE-PAGE, THOMAS FFRENCH'S FAMILY BIBLE

The title page of this venerable edition of the Holy Book, "Imprinted at London by Robert Barker and John Bill, Printers to the Kings most Excellent Majestie, 1630," was designed after the curious manner of the time, relating to object teaching of Scriptural things. The scenes on the left refer to the twelve tribes of Israel; those on the right recite the twelve apostles, with the writers of the four Gospels in the centre. The accompanying figures all have appropriate significance in the illustration of the Biblical story. The New Testament title page is of the same studious and impres-

TITLE-PAGE, THOMAS FFRENCH'S FAMILY BIBLE

THOMAS FFRENCH'S FAMILY BIBLE

Copy of writing on opposite page

Thomas ffrench and Jane his wife, and Jane and Rachel his children.
Jane was born about a fortnight before Saint James [in the Church
Calendar July 25th] in the year 1662.
Rachel was born March the 24, 1663.
Rachel was born March the 24, 1664. She alone was ris.

In the year 1673 was a very stormy year for the waters did sore
break out of their bounds and was a very wet season, such wet May
day, after which floods that flooded the meadows when they were
ready to mow and drove away in many stacks and bindings of hay,
and we had a summer like unto winter for cold and wet for the
general year.

I and my wife and nine children through the great mercy of God
came into this country and landed at Burlington, the 23 of the 7
month 1680. Thomas ffrench.

The Lord in heaven have mercy upon me.
Thomas ffrench his book. God give him grace in ————— Then
was I in great sorrow and tribulation. The Lord deliver me out
of them all.

... ____ ____ and Jane his wife and
____ his children Jane was borne about afo[re]
before Jane ____ in the year 1662
____ was borne march the 24 1663 ____
____ was borne march the 24 166[_]
in the year 1673 was a deari Steare
year for the ____ was sore prest
of ____ ____ ____ was at ____
was ____ ____ ____ may Jan[e]
with floods that flo____ the ____
where they were ____ ____
____ ____ ____ ____
____ of her ____ ____ ____
____ ____ winter for so
and ____ for the ____ ____

I and my wife and ____ child
____ the ____ many of
____ ____ this country and
at ____ the 23 of the
____ 7 month 1680 Thomas Fro[_]

The lord ____ ____ have mercy upon me

THOMAS FFRENCH'S FAMILY BIBLE

Copy of writing on opposite page

Tho. french his book. God give him grace in Jesus Lord and when the bell for me doth toll, good Lord in heaven do rest my soul.

The Lord deliver me out of all my troubles and pardon my sins. Lord bless all that [He] hath given in hand.

The Lord deliver me in time of trouble and in time of adversity, and Lord deliver me from all my enemies.

I Thomas ffrench was married to my wife Jane, June 12, 1660. December the first about ten at night my son Richard was born, 1665. The Lord give him grace that he may continually walk before Him.

I Thomas ffrench was baptized November the 3, 1639. My son Thomas was born ———— in 1667 between 8 and nine o'clock at night.
1671 my son Charles was born, the 20 day of March between 11 and 12 at night.

In the year 1673 was a very strange ————

58

Tho: ffrenk his book god gif him grat us hs
and when the bell for me douth tell god lord
In heauen to rest my sol

The lord delifer me out of all my troubles and
pardun my sines lord bles ot Thas ffar
Jnsam j i 1676

The lord delifer me in time of truble and
in time of adfarnyti and lord delifer me
form all my enimies

Memmes ffrenk was maried
to my wiff Jane June 12 1676
desamber the furst about ten at nit
my sun was borne the lord if
Richard 1661
him grat that hee may confin
walt befor him

Thomas ffrenk was baptised
march
novemember the 3 1669
my sun thomas was
before our lord j 1665 feuine ford
and was a bout at mid marke
1673 my sun wharly was borne the 20 day
of march haptima uand r at nin
for the yeare 1675 was a wed
ffra

THOMAS FFRENCH'S FAMILY BIBLE

Copy of writing on opposite page

The Lord be gracious and merciful unto me which way so ever
I go whether it be out of the land or in the land or on the sea, the
Lord be merciful unto me. This was wrote in the year 1664.

———————————

My wife Jane deceased this life the fifth day of the 8 month 1692.
My youngest child died the 12 of the same.

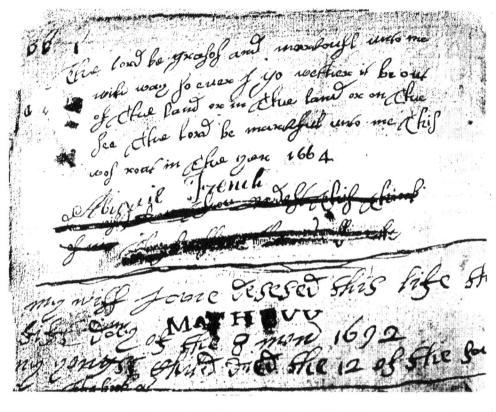

A LEAF FROM THOMAS FFRENCH'S FAMILY BIBLE

THOMAS FFRENCH'S FAMILY BIBLE

Copy of writing on opposite page

William French the son of Richard ffrench and Mary was born April the 7 in the year 1712.

———————————

Sarah French the daughter of Richard French and Mary was born the 20th day of the 7th month 1715.

———————————

All prophesies were given by inspiration and written for our learning, upon whom the ends of the world are come.

———————————

Rachel French the daughter of Richard Jun. and Rachel was born the 12th day of the 11th month 1722.

———————————

Benjamin French

1737

William French his book May 10th 17——

Thomas ffrench

62

... ...er ...

and mary was born Apri the 7...
the year 1712

Sarah French the Daughter of Richa...
and Mary was Born the 20th Day of

All scriptures weare given by in...
writen for our Learning — upon whom
ends of the world are Come

Rachal French the Dofter of Richard...
and Rachal was Born the 12th Day of
Month 1722

Benjamin French

1737

William French his Book

Thomas ffrench

A LEAF FROM THOMAS FFRENCH'S FAMILY BIBLE
Partial Family Register of Richard ffrench (5)

GENEALOGICAL RECORD

1—THOMAS FFRENCH

> b. October, 1639.
> Baptized November 3rd, 1639, at Church S. S. Peter and Paul, Nether Heyford, England.
> d. 1699, at Rancocas, N. J.
> m. First, June 12th, 1660, at " Parish Church of Whilton," England, Jane Atkins.
> She d. 8th mo. 5th, 1692, at Rancocas, N. J.
> m. Second, 7th mo. 25th, 1696, Elizabeth Stanton of Philadelphia Monthly Meeting.

2—SARA FFRENCH

Baptized March 17th, 1661, at Church S. S. Peter and Paul, Nether Heyford.
Buried April 10th, 1661.

3—JANE FFRENCH

b. about July 11th, 1662.
Baptized August 8th, 1662, at Church S. S. Peter and Paul, Nether Heyford.
Buried April 30th, 1671.

4—RACHEL FFRENCH

b. March 24th, 1664.
Baptized April 3rd, 1664, at Church S. S. Peter and Paul, Nether Heyford.
m. First, 1687, Mathew Allen.
m. Second, 12th mo. 9th, 1702, Hugh Sharp.

5—RICHARD FFRENCH

b. December 1st, 1665.
Baptized December 15th, 1666, at Church S. S. Peter and Paul, Nether Heyford.
m. First, 7th mo. 11th, 1693, Sarah Scattergood.
m. Second, 11th mo. 13th, 1701, Mary King.

6—THOMAS FFRENCH, JR.

b. 1667.
Baptized October 31st, 1667, at Church S. S. Peter and Paul, Nether Heyford.
. First, 10th mo. 3rd, 1696, Mary Allen.
m. Second, 8th mo. 9th, 1732, Mary (Pearce) Cattell.

7—HANNAH FFRENCH

Baptized September 5th, 1669, at Church S. S. Peter and Paul, Nether Heyford.
m. 8th mo. 30th, 1695, Richard Buzby.

˅ 8—CHARLES FFRENCH	b. March 20th, 1671. Baptized April 2ud, 1671, at Church S. S. Peter and Paul, Nether Heyford. . First (sup.), 1708, Elinor ————. m. Second, ———— ————.
9—JOHN FFRENCH	Baptized January 2nd, 1673, at Church S. S. Peter and Paul, Nether Heyford. m. First, 1701, Ann ————. m. Second, 6th mo. 10th, 1724, Sarah (Mason) Wickward.
ˊ 10—SARAH FFRENCH	Baptized February 23rd, 1674, at Church S. S. Peter and Paul, Nether Heyford. m. 2ud mo. 1st, 1695, Isaac Wood.
˅ 11—MARY FFRENCH	Baptized August 8th, 1675, at Church S. S. Peter and Paul, Nether Heyford. m. 8th mo. 30th, 1695, Nicholas Buzby.
12—JANE FFRENCH	Baptized November 19th, 1676, at Church S. S. Peter and Paul, Nether Heyford. m. 1st mo. 1st, 1697, Daniel Hall.
˙ 13—LYDIA FFRENCH	b. (sup.) 1682. m. (sup.) 1708, David Arnold.
14—AN INFANT	d. 8th mo. 12th, 1692.
15—REBECCA FFRENCH	b. 6th mo. 8th, 1697. m. 2nd mo. 3rd, 1729, Robert Murfin.

Thomas ffrench, in accordance with the custom of his family for generations, and that of nearly all Protestant Englishmen of his time, had his children baptized in the Church of England, notwithstanding his early sympathy and unity with the Society of Friends. The obligation thus assumed, as to religious care and training of his children, was faithfully kept, the family Bible being an impressive witness in this respect.

The following is taken from the parish records of the Church S. S. Peter and Paul, Nether Heyford, England, concerning the marriage of Thomas ffrench and Jane Atkins.

"Note. March 8 1663 The said Jane ffrench p'senting unto me John Bedford parson of Heiford A Consigned Certificate of the said Thomas ffrench jun & Jane Atkins both of Heiford pish Testifying that they the said Thomas & Jane w' marryed in the pish Church of Whilton June 12 1660 by M' Richard Morris then Minister there: Returning her Certificate of marriage backe againe into her owne custody, I thus entred the Record of y' said marriage at her request, into this my Heiford pish Register."

Thomas ffrench and Jane his wife were buried in a private burial lot, sixteen and one half feet square, on the homestead plantation, Rancocas, N. J., and this reservation was mentioned in deeds and observed for many years· Its exact location is now unknown.

MEETING RECORDS

That Thomas ffrench was a man of great force of character and independent action is evident from many things connected with his career in this country as well as in England. He early became an active and courageous member of the Society of Friends, enduring persecution with fortitude. He was not yet twenty years of age when first prosecuted. In Burlington Meeting he held a conspicuous and influential place throughout his pioneer life, covering a period of nineteen years. The meeting records concerning him, as in so many cases, are fragmentary and incomplete. Matters of a personal character often were continued indefinitely and many times no final decision was recorded. In maintaining his rights as a citizen and property holder, Thomas ffrench felt himself called upon, almost at the beginning, to take action which seems to have excited comment, but he was firm in declaring the justice of his cause, although duly regretful that his course had given occasion for criticism. Details are not given, but aside from formal acknowledgment, in deference to feelings of Friends, the sturdy progenitor calmly went his way, recording his sympathy with the " weak," and later received a certificate relating to his proposed second marriage which showed his unimpaired standing. The most striking instance of his braving public opinion was a remarkable letter to ex-Governor Ollive, in some respects the leading and most influential man in the Burlington colony. This eminent citizen was one of the original proprietors. He came with the pioneers in 1677, and at different times held the offices of land commissioner, magistrate, member of Assembly, Speaker of the same, Deputy Governor and Governor, and was one of the Council of Proprietors. In his later years, when the letter of accusation was addressed to him by Thomas ffrench, he was regarded as a sort of arbitrator in general, in the settlement of private disputes, holding informal court in his fields, on his great plantation of over 600 acres on the Rancocas, which was near that of the man who severely criticised him and stood firmly by his declaration when called to account by Burlington Meeting, in which Thomas Ollive was for many years an acceptable minister. What was the cause of this trouble can now never be known. The ex-Governor's death occurred about this time and although Thomas ffrench lived for six years thereafter no further mention of the affair is to be found in the minutes of Burlington Meeting. The following is a complete transcript of references to Thomas ffrench.

Burlington Monthly Meeting Minutes:

Friends this Know y^t I am Very Sorry & very much troubled y^t I Should give Occation of Offence in ye matter of my going to Law or Any Other matter wherein my Dear Brethern ye Lords People should be Offended Desiring you my Bretheren to forgive y^e Offence & I shall Seek all means that possibly Can be had to prevent y^e Like Occation again.

Your Friend & Brother
Thomas French

Read in y^e meeting
y^e 5th of y^e 12th mo. 1682.

At our mens monthly meeting held in Burlington in y^e House of Tho$^.$ Gardiner y^e 2nd of y^e 2nd mo. 1683.

The Meeting saw meet to desire some friend to speak with Thos$^.$ French Henry Stacy & John Borten were willing to visit him & hear his answer & return their sense wether they find him senseable y^t he sees it his place to Condemn his abrupt & Rude behavior in y^e Monthly Meeting: Elias Farr & Tho$^.$ Gardiner & Tho$^.$ Mathews are willing to assist them & give an acct. to y^e next Monthly Meeting: &c.

At y^e mens Monthly Meeting held at y^e house of Tho$^.$ Gardiner y^e 17th of y^e 3^d mo. 1683.

The Business of Tho$^.$ French yet Continued.

At y^e Mens Monthly Meeting in Burlington held at y^e House of Tho$^.$ Gardiner y^e 4th of y^e 4th mo: 1683

The meeting Still desired y^e fr$^{ds.}$ that were appoid. to Visit Tho$^.$ French (viz) Jno Bourton Henry Stacy Thomas Gardiner Elias Farr & Tho$^.$ Mathews that they would take Care to go together & hear his Answer & give this meeting an Account.

At our Mens Monthly Meeting held in Burlington in y^e House of Thos$^.$ Gardiner y^e 2nd of y$^e.$ 5th mo. 1683.

Then friends desired that Tho$^.$ French would appear at y^e next monthly meeting & in as much as Tho$^.$ Budd & Rob$^{t.}$ Powell & Willm Brightwen are desirous to Visit him the Meeting Expects their Care to Lett him know y^e meetings desire & Return this meeting an account.

At our mens monthly Meeting held in Burlington in y^e House of Tho$^.$ Gardiner y^e 6th of y^e 6th mo. 1683.

Whereas after much tenderness of Spirit & Bowels of Compaſion exercised toward Tho$^.$ French who Doth still appear in a Spirit of Opposition against y^e Truth to wit y^e Same Spirit wch he did formerly Charge y^e body of Friends wth Injustice Saying he Could have no Right done him & confidently Justifyed himself in y^e Same: We therefore for y^e Truths Sake do deny & Judge y^t Spirit in which y^e Said Tho$^.$ French doth persist in to be out of and against y^e Truth which Judgement will Stand Over his head Until he Repent.

At our Mens Monthly Meeting held in Burlington y^e 2nd of y^e 1st mo. 1684/5

Where y^e meeting gave Directions for y^e entring y^e Subscription Relating to y^e building y^e meeting Tho$^.$ French gave £2

At our Mens Monthly Meeting held at Burlington in yᵉ Houſe of Thomas Gardiner yᵉ 12ᵗʰ of yᵉ 7 mo. 1687

Whereas a Testimony is Standing upon Record in this Book against Thoˑ French for Charging yᵉ meeting with Injuſtice he hath this Day declared in yᵉ Meeting that what he had formerly Said to that Effect waſs in his haft & Paſsion for wᶜʰ he is now Sorry and In testimony whereof hath Subscribed

Your Friend   Thoˑ French

At our Mens Monthly Meeting Held at the Houſe of Thoˑ Gardiner in Bton. yᵉ 10ᵗʰ of yᵉ 7ᵗʰ Mo. 1688

Percivall Towle and Christopher Weatherill are Appointed to Speak to Thoˑ French Concerning his behaviour in Our publick Meeting at Burlingtou and if he refuſe to give them Sattisfaction to deſire his Appearance at our Next Monthly Meeting.

At our mens Monthly Meeting Held at the House of Thoˑ Gardiner in Bton yᵉ 1ˢᵗ of yᵉ 8ᵗʰ mo. 1688

Thomas Gardiner Joſeph Pope & Isaac Marriot are appointed to Speak to Jnoˑ Skeen and Thoˑ French and desire their appearance to the next Monthly Meeting.

At our Mens Monthly Meeting held at Burlington in yᵉ house of Thomas Gardiner yᵉ 12ᵗʰ of yᵉ 7ᵗʰ Month 1692

Thomas Olive made complaint to this meeting against Thomas French, for Slandering and very Grosly abusing him in a letter directed to Thomas Olive which said letter Thomas French owneth and still standeth in vendication of yᵉ same. The Meeting seeing it neceſsary to have all the Charges in the letter Examined do order Thoˑ ffrench to make proofe of his Charges by plain Evidence To Thoˑ Gardiner John Shinn John Day & Francis Devenport who are appointed to meet togather The next fourth day to here & give Account to yᵉ next meeting.

At our Mens Monthly Meeting held at yᵉ house of Thomas Gardener the 5ᵗʰ of yᵉ 4ᵗʰ Month 1693

Thomas Hackney being Minded to go for England desired a Certificate & the Meeting ordered Thoˑ Harden & Thoˑ ffrench to Enquire into his Clearness & if he be so found yᵗ James Hill is by order of this Meeting to Wright & signe a Certificate for him & his daughter Agnes.

At our Mens Monthly Meeting held at yᵉ house of Thomas Gardeners Adjorned to this Eleventh of yᵉ 7ᵗʰ month 1693 [adjourned on account of Yearly Meeting]

The Concessions and Agreements of the Proprietors Freeholders and Inhabitants of the Province of West New Jersey in America:

Chapter 1

Wee doe consent and agree as the best present expedient that w

FIRST PAGE, "CONCESSIONS AND AGREEMENTS," 1676

Thomas ffrench having laid before⋅ this Meeting his Intentions of going for England desired a Certificate & the Meeting do appoint John Paine & ffredom Lippincott to Enquire into his Clearnefs as to Marriage & also his Conversation & make report to the next Meeting.

At our Mens Monthly Meeting held at ye house of Thomas Gardners ye 2nd of ye 8th Month 1693
Peter ffretwell & James Hill appointed to enquire of ye four Friends appointed formerly to examine ye charge of Tho⋅ ffrench against Tho: Olive how it appeared to them that account may be given to next Meeting.

Att our Mens Monthly Meeting held at ye House of Tho Gardeners ye 1st of ye 11th Mo. 1693
The Meeting being informed y^t sum who frequent this Meeting hath declared sum businefs y^t hath past formerly in ye Meeting Concerning Tho ffrench being then refused a Certificate to ye abuce both to ye Meeting & also of said French ye Meeting desires all present to purge themselves by denial or else own it.

At our Mens Monthly Meeting held at ye hous of Thomas Gardeners the 6th of ye 6th Month 1694
Thomas French Intending to go for England Desired a Certificate & friends ordered y^t ffredom Lippincott & Robert Hudson Should Enquire into his Clearness upon ye Account of Marriage & by their report as also Severall other Neighbours the meeting where Satisfied to give him one from this Meting which was accordingly done.

At our Mens Monthly Meeting held at the house of Eliz⋅ Gardiner in Burlington ye 6th of the 3rd Mo. 1695
It is ordered by this meeting that ffrancis Collings Richard Love & John Day are appointed to Speak to Tho⋅ ffrench about his behaviour in Court Contrary to Truth & to make Report of his answer to the next Meeting.

At our Mens Monthly Meeting held at the House of Eliz⋅ Gardiner in Burlington ye 3rd of the 4th Mo. 1695
John Day and Richard Love giveth report to this meeting that Tho⋅ French doth Condemn the thing & is sorry that he should offend the weak.

At our Mens Monthly Meeting held at the House of Eliz: Gardiner in Bton. ye 4th of ye 9th Mo. 1695
Jno Paine & Tho⋅ French are appointed to gather ye Meetings Subscriptions for the Meeting house.

At our Mens Monthly Meeting held at the House of Eliz˙ Gardiner in
Bur'ton ye 6th mo : 1696

Tho˙ French Desired of this meeting a Certificate concerning his Clearness from Women in Relation to Marriage, fredom Lippincott & Tho˙
Eves are appointed to make Enquiry & to make report of it to the
next meeting.

Philadelphia Monthly Meeting Minutes :

At a Monthly Meeting held at the house of Robert Ewer, the twenty-
eighth of the Sixth month 1696

Milisant Hoskins & Joan Southeby presented to this Meeting Thomas
French and Elisabeth Stanton who declared their intentions of taking each
other as husband & wife, this being the first time of their appearance,
friends desire him to bring a Certificate from the Meeting where he
belongs to, against the next meeting.

At a Monthly Meeting held at the house of Robert Ewer, the twenty-
fifth day of the Seventh Month 1696

Melisant Hoskins & Joan Southeby present, Thomas French and Elisabeth Stanton to this Meeting, who declared their intentions of taking each
other in marriage he producing a Certificate of his clearnefs from others,
they were left to consummate their intended marriage in the fear of God.

DEED, THOMAS FFRENCH FROM JOHN WOOLSTON, 1680

This Indenture made & dated the Twentieth day of November in the
yeare according to the Accompt now ufed in England, one Thousand
six Hundred & Eighty Between John Woolston of Burlington in the
Province of West New Jerfey yeoman of the one pte And Thomas ffrench
of the same Towne aforesaid Cooper of the other pte witnefseth That the
said John Woolston for & in Consideracon of the sume of Twenty ffive
pounds Sterling to him in hand paid & secured to be paid by the said
Thomas ffrench the Receipt whereof hee hath hereby acknowledge and
thereof doth clearly acquitt & difcharge the said Thomas ffrench his Heires
& Afsignes forever Hath granted bargained sold releafed & Confirmed And
by thefe prefents doth grant bargaine sell Releafe & Confirme vnto the
said Thomas ffrench his Heires & Afsignes forever, one Eighth pte of a
ninetieth pte or propriety of Land Lyeing & being in the above said
Province (except one Lott of Land in Burlington Conteyning one Acre &
halfe a Rood with a dwelling houfe & fifty Acres belonging to the said
Houfe according to the said purchase within the Towne Bounds, and Except one Lott of Land more in Burlington Conteyning by eftimacon Two
Acres be the same more or lefse which the said John Woolston hath reserved
now in his owne Tenure and occupacon which said Eighth pte of a

Propriety hee the said John Woolston hath & holdeth by vertue of a deed Indented beareing date the Six and Twentieth day of ffebruary in the yeare one Thoufand Six Hundred Seaventy & Six between Thomas Ollive of Welingbrough Haberdafher of the one pte & hee the said John Woolfton of the other pte To have & to hold the said Land & prmifes (Except what before excepted) vnto the said Thomas ffrench his Heires & Afsignes forever—Togeather with all & every of the mines mineralls woods ffishings Hawkings Huntings & ffowlings, & all other priviledges profitts & Comodities whatsoever belonging to the faid prmifes.

And hee the faid John Woolston doth for himselfe his Heires Executors & Afsignes Covenant promife & grant to & with the faid Thomas ffrench his Heires Executors & Afsignes That hee the said John Woolston his Heires & Afsignes shall & will at any tyme within seaven yeares next after the date hereof at the requeft Cost & Charges of the said Thomas ffrench his Heires & Afsigns doe & Execute all & every such Lawfull conveyance & Conveyances as fhall be for the better secureing & settling all the Interest & Tytle of him y⁰ said John Woolfton of in & to the above granted prmifes in & to the faid Thomas ffrench his Heires & Afsignes. In witnefs whereof the parties ffirft above named to thefc prfent Indentures have interchangeably fett their hands & Seales 1680—

Sealed & Deliured in y⁰   The marke of
prfence of   Thomas Curtis   John Woolfton |
              Abraham Hewlings
              Tho: Enos
                        This Deed was Acknowledged y⁰ 26ᵗʰ Sept. 1681
                        before   Robert Stacye ⎫
                                        Thos: Budd   ⎬ Comrs.
                                        Benja: Scott. ⎭

SCHEDULE OR TARRY, THOMAS FFRENCH FROM JOHN WOOLSTON SENR.

This Schedule or Tarry bearing date with a Deed of bargaine & Sale Between John Woolston Senʳ of the one pte And Thomas ffrench of y⁰ other pte of one Eighth pte of a Propriety of Land in Weft Jerfey dated the Twentith day of November 1680 which y⁰ aforefᵈ Deed doth make it more at large appeare Exprefsing y⁰ Buttings & boundings of some certaine Lotts of Lott belonging to y⁰ sᵈ Eighth pte of a ppriety as they were surveyed & Lotted out to mee y⁰ sᵈ John Woolfton which sᵈ Lotts of Land Excepting thefc Lotts of Land which are Excepted in ye Deed of bargain & Sale aforefᵈ I doe hereby acknowledge that I have sold & Confirmed unto y⁰ sᵈ Thomas ffrench his beires & afsignes forever, which are as followeth That is to say Two hundred Acres of Land be it more or lefse butting upon Rancokus Creek als Northampton River y⁰ ppriety line & y⁰ Land

of William Biddle lyeing South Eaſt & John Roberts Land northwest Alſo
Two hundred Acres of Land more wᵗʰ a meadow belonging to it more or
leſse lyeing & being next to yᵉ Propriety Line below Thomas Ollives butting
upon Rancokus Creek als Northampton River aforesᵈ ye Propriety line
being on the north weſt side of it. Alſo one Lott of Land more in Burlington
in that wharfe Lott Lotted out for yᵉ ppriety of Thomas ollives ˙which
ppriety is bounded with yᵉ Highstreet Northeaſt & a Little Alley lyeing on
yᵉ southwest side of John Hollinshead houſe & fronting northweſt upon
yᵉ River Dellaware & south eaſt upon yᵉ back street which part or ſhare
of yᵉ sᵈ Lott granted in yᵉ bargaine & sale aforeſᵈ Conteyneth Twenty
five foot front upon the River aforeſᵈ be it more or leſse & goeth through to
yᵉ back street In witneſse whereof I have hereunto sett my hand & Seale

Signed Sealed & Delivʳed   The marke of
in ye pʳſence of   John ┃ Woolſton with a Seale ☉
  John Shinn   Novembʳ 11ᵗʰ 1693
  Henry Grubb   Jno. Shinn & Henry Grubb Atteſted to
        Jnᵒ Woolſtons Executing hereof before
        William Biddle & Danˡˡ Leeds Justices.

DEED, THOMAS FFRENCH FROM ANTHONY MORRIS, 1685

This Indenture made yᵉ fourteenth day of yᵉ moneth called Aprill
in yᵉ yeare according to yᵉ Accoᵗ now uſed in England One Thousand six
hundred Eighty & five—Betweene Anthony Morris of Burlington in West
Jerſey Baker of yᵉ one pt And Thomas ffrench Inhabitant neare Burlington
yeoman of yᵉ other pᵗ witneſseth that yᵉ sᵈ Anthony Morris for & in Con-
sidʳacon of yᵉ sume of fforty shillings of this Countrey Currᵗ pay. to
him paid & secured by yᵉ sᵈ Thomas ffrench at or before yᵉ ensealing &
delivery of theſe pʳsents yᵉ receipt whereof hee doth hereby acknowledge
& thereof clearly acquitt & discharge yᵉ sᵈ Thomas ffrench his heires &
aſsigns forever. Hath granted bargained sold releaſed & confirned
And by theſe prsents doth grant bargaine sell releaſe & confirm unto yᵉ
sd Thomas ffrench his beires & aſsignes forever one waterside Lott of
Land in Burlington Conteyning Eight foot front upon yᵉ great River abutting North upon yᵉ sᵈ River & South upon yᵉ Back street & East upon yᵉ
Land of yᵉ sᵈ Thomas ffrench & West upon Richard Baſnetts house it being
part of yᵉ purchaſe which hee yᵉ sᵈ Anthony Morris hath & holdeth by
vertue of a Deed Indented bearing date yᵉ Tenth of yᵉ ninth moneth
one Thouſand Six hundred Eighty & three betweene Mahlon Stacy of yᵉ
one pt & hee ye sᵈ Anthony Morris of yᵉ other pt To have & to hold yᵉ
sᵈ Lott of Land to yᵉ sᵈ Thomas ffrench his beires & aſsignes to ye
onely uſe & behoofe of him ye sᵈ Thomas ffrench his beires & aſsignes
forever with Appurtennces wayes & Eaſemᵗˢ thereunto belonging And
hee ye sᵈ Anthony Morris doth for him selfe his heires Execʳs & aſsignes

bands dated this third day of the xx
month commonly called March in
the yeare of our Lord one thousand six
hundred seaventy six

FIRST SIGNATURE PAGE, "CONCESSIONS AND AGREEMENTS," 1676

Covenant prmiſe & grant to & with yᵉ sᵈ Thomas ffrench his heires Execʳˢ & Aſsignes that hee yᵉ sᵈ Anthony Morris his heires & Aſsignes shall & will at any time within seaven yeares next after ye date hereof at yᵉ request Cost & Charges of yᵉ sᵈ Thomas ffrench doe and execute all & every such lawfull Conveyance & Conveyances as ſhall be for yᵉ better secureing & settling all yᵉ interest & tytle of him yᵉ sᵈ Anthony Morris ofin & to yᵉ above granted pʳmiſses in & to yᵉ sᵈ Thomas ffrench his heires & aſsignes forever In witneſs whereof ye ptic first above named to theſc pʳsent Indentures have interchangeably sett their hand & ſeale ye day & yeare first above written 1685.

Sealed & delivered in ye pʳsence of   Anthony Morris with a scale ⊙
  John Paine
  William Hewlings
  Tho: Eves
Novembʳ 4ᵗʰ 1685 John Paine Attested that hee did fee yᵉ sealing & Executing of this Deed according to yᵉ purport thereof
        before Tho: Revell Justice

SURVEYS OF LAND FOR THOMAS FFRENCH

Revell's Book shows following surveys for Thomas ffrench; 600 acres of upland and meadow, under date of 2ud mo. 1684; and 600 acres of upland and 21 acres of meadow, under date of 1st mo. 1689.

  Surveyed then for Thomas ffrench, Vpland & Meadowe—Begining at a Corner Tree of John Roberts by Rancokus (als) Northampton River, & runs thence by yᵉ said Land of John Roberts one hundred & Twenty chaines North North East halfe a point North to a brook called Mill Creek to another Corner tree of the said John Roberts, then up by the said Mill Creek fforty four chaines & an halfe to a white oak marked for a Corner, then South Southweſt halfe a point South to a stake for a Corner at Northampton River aforesᵈ, Then downe by the said River to the first mentioned Corner. Togeather with Twenty Acres for meadow lyeing & being the next meadow belowe Tho: ollives meadow on yᵉ same side yᵉ said Northampton River as now marked out by the vpland yᵉ northwest side of the same abutting upon the begining of that part of the River called long reach a litle Island in yᵉ River lyeing upon the South East side thereof. Surveyed for Six hundred Acres as aforesᵈ. Surveyed then for Thomas ffrench at Pensoking Creek one Tract of Land: Begining at a black oak by yᵉ said Creek next Thomas Wallis by whom it runs North East forty Chaines to a White oak & Turnes with said Thomas Wallis West North west Twenty seaven Chaines to a black oak, Corner to Jonathan ffox by whom .it runs North East & forward to the end of one Hundred and Two Chaines. Then South East Eighty Chaines to a Red oake, Corner to Thomas Rodman, by whom it runs West

South West Eighty ffive Chaines to a black oak, Corner to Sam[11] Burrows, by whom it runs west & by North Twenty Six Chaines to a white oak. Then turnes with s[d] Samuell South west Twenty nyne Chaines to a Hickory on the banck of the Creek aforesaid. Then by the said Creek to ye first station: Twenty one Acres for meadow Lyeth remote Eastwardly to the said Tract & is thus bounded: from a black oak in Thomas Hootens Lyne it runs South East & by Eaſt Twenty three Chaines to a maple for a Corner Then South South West Eleaven Chaines to a black oak; Then North west & by west Eighteene Chaines to a black oak Then North to the first station Surveyed togeather for Six hundred Twenty one Acres besides Highwayes.

DEED OF GIFT, THOMAS FFRENCH TO SON THOMAS, 1694

(See facsimile, page 116)

This Indenture made the nineteenth day of the month called February in the year according to English account one thousand six hundred ninety and four between Thomas ffrench of Wellingborough in the county of Burlington in the province of West Jersey yeoman of the one part and Thomas ffrench son of the aforesaid Thomas ffrench husbandman of the other part Witnesseth that the said Thomas ffrench Senior (for and in consideration of the natural affection good will and kindness which he hath and beareth unto his well beloved son) hath given granted and confirmed and by these presents doth give grant and confirm unto the said Thomas ffrench Junior his heirs and assigns forever three hundred acres of land lying near Pensauken Creek, begins at a hickory on the bank of the said creek near the bridge by the land of Samuel Burrows by whom it runs northeast twenty-nine chains and east by south twenty-six chains to Thomas Rodman's land, then by the same east northeast fifty-eight chains to a black oak for a corner then northwest about seventy chains to a white oak for a corner, then southwest to the land of Thomas Wallis by whom it runs east southeast about twelve chains and southeast near four chains to a white oak for a corner, then southwest to a small run of water then bounded by the same into the said creek and goes up the same about four chains to the corner first named, and also all that piece of upland and meadow containing twenty-one acres lying next to Thomas Hooton's land, together with the mines, minerals, woods, fishings, hawkings, huntings and fowlings and all and every of the appurtenances, profits and commodities whatsoever belonging to the said premises to have and to hold the said land premises and appurtenances thereof unto the said Thomas ffrench Junior his heirs and assigns unto the only use and behoof of him the said Thomas ffrench Junior his heirs and assigns forever and the said Thomas ffrench Senior for himself his heirs executors and administrators the said premises with the appurtenances unto the said Thomas ffrench Junior his heirs and assigns forever; against him the said Thomas ffrench Senior his heirs and assigns and all and every other person and persons whatsoever lawfully claiming by from or under him them or any of them shall and will warrant and forever defend by these presents. In witness whereof the parties first above named to these present indenture hath interchangably set his hand and seal the day and year first above written.

Signed Sealed and Delivered

in the presence of us,   Thomas ffrench ☉

   William Michell

   Charles ffrench

   Thomas Eves

      Feby. 20th 1694   Then acknowledged ye Deed above written before us

                              Peter Frettwell

                              Tho. Revell   Justices

      Feby. 25th 1694   Recorded ye abovewritten Deed in ye Publick Records of ye Province of West New Jersey ffol 433 Libe zz,

                        p me Tho. Revell Secy, & Regt

THOMAS FFRENCH'S CATTLE MARKS

The following is taken from the Burlington Records for 1680, filed in the office of Secretary of State, Trenton, N. J.

   The Proceedings of Co^{r}t at Burlington—

   Tho: Olive, Daniel Wills, Robt Stacy & Mahlon Stacy—

   It is further ordered That all psons within ye Jurisdiscon of ye Co^{r}t bring in to ye next Co^{r}t ye Marks & Eare Marks wherewith they have marked or intend to mark their Cattle Horſes Sheep & Swine to ye intent that— psons mark may be entered & inrolled & their Cattle Horſes Sheepe & Swine may be knowne each from other.

In accordance with the above instructions of court, Thomas ffrench adopted and registered in 1680, ear marks for his stock herewith given:

             Right   Left

WILL OF THOMAS FFRENCH, 1698

I Being intended if the Lord will to goe for Old England not knowing whether I shall ever returne againe to my ffamily doe make & ordaine this my last will & Testamt Revokeing all other Wills and promises whatsoever In manner & forme following. I give unto my wife Elizabeth after my decease if shee be the longer liver the House & Plantation where now I live with four Hundred Acres of Land belonging to it with Twenty Acres of Meadow as it is surveyed and Recorded In the place next below the Land of John Test Together with the use of all my Stock & Household goods with the Corne growing upon the ground To have & to hold the same dureing her naturall life without Impeachment of Wast. I give unto my Sonne Charles ffrench Two hundred Acres of land lyeing next John Hudsons with the ffour or ffive Acres of Clear land at Creek with ye Little Meadow lyeing by it to him and his Heirs forever allowing my wife Elizabeth Egresse & Regresse to Transport any goods or Hay: I give unto my Sonne Charles ffrench after the Decease of me & my wife to him & his Heires forever Provided that hee pay that which I shall appoint him to pay all the Plantation where now I live together with the dwelling house Barnes & other Outhouses Gardens Orchards Arrable Land & Clear land Together with four Hundred Acres of Land belonging to the Plantation aforesaid also Twenty Acres of Meadow Together with two hundred Acres of land belonging to the Meadow Also Six Hundred Acres of Land more which shall or may fall to me In my Third takeing up my Will is that my sonne Charles ffrench shall pay out of the Lands and Plantation aforesaid unto the rest of his Brothers & Sisters as followeth, I give unto my Daughter Rachell Allen to her & her Heires Twenty pounds. I give unto my Daughter Hannah Busby to her & her Heires Twenty pounds. I give unto my Daughter Sarah Wood to her & herselfe alone as she shall have need of it her Husband shall not have noe part or share in it to her & her Heires Twenty Pounds. I give unto my Daughter Mary Busby to her & her Heirs twenty pounds. I give unto my Daughter Jane Hall to her & her Heires Twenty pounds. I give unto my Daughter Lydia French Twenty pounds. I give unto my sonne Thomas ffrench Six Shillings. I give unto my sonne John French Six Shillings. I give unto my Sonne Richard French Six Shillings. I give unto my sonne Richard French all the Reversion of my Eighth part of a Propriety and that Lott at Burlington upon which Richard Bassnett hath built Houses upon to him & his Heires forever. I give unto my Sonne Charles ffrench all my Yard Land in the ppish of neather Heyford to him & his Heires forever In old England. My Will is that my Sonne Charles ffrench shall pay all my Debts and Thirty pounds to my youngest Daughter Rebecca ffrench out of

[several lines illegible due to heavy smudging]

Barnard Devenish   Albright
Thomas Vicos
Thomas French   Godfrey Hancock
Isaac Marriott   John Petty
John Butcher   Abraham Gouldnos
Geo: Hutchinson   John Newbould
Thomas Gardiner   John White
Thomas Eves   Tho: mark of Jno. Roberts
John Horton
John Paine   John Wood marke
Charles Fenton
Samuell Oldale   John Gosling
M William Bloth Burnabs   Tho Revell
Anthony Woodhouse
Daniel Leeds

LAST SIGNATURE PAGE, "CONCESSIONS AND AGREEMENTS," 1676

the Yard Land aforesaid if Rebecca shall live to the Age of Eighteen yeares and if Rebecca shall happen to die before shee come to the Age of Eighteen yeares then the Thirty pounds shall be paid unto & amongst my Five younger Daughters to Hannah Busby & Sarah Wood Mary Busby Jane Hall & Lydia ffrench my Will is that after the decease of me & my Wife that my Goods shall be divided amongst all my Daughters mentioned in my Will. And also my Will is that if I & my Wife Elizabeth shall happen to die before my youngest Daughter Rebecca is brought up that then my Sonne Charles ffrench shall bring her up or else to allow her Five pounds a year untill shee come to the Age of Ten yeares for & towards the bringing of her up. In Witness hereof I have hereunto sett my hand & Seale the Third day of the fourth month called June [1698]

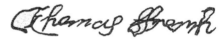

Seal

Sealed & delivered in ye p^rsence of John Paine Tho: Eves John Hollinshead jun^r

The above written is a true Coppy of the Originall will or Codecill of Thomas ffrench abovenamed, being with the same Originall Examined this Third Day of May Anno Dom 1699 As witnefse hereunto my hand & seale of Office

Tho: Revell Secry & Reg^r

THE PREROGATIVE SEAL

The Proprietors of the Province of East and West Jersey were distinctly religious, and expressed their reverence for the Almighty on every suitable occasion. The seal of the Prerogative Court under the Proprietors of East New Jersey, adopted in 1682, bears the legend, "Righteousness exalteth a Nation" and "'Tis God giveth the increase." The seal of the Prerogative Court under the Proprietors of West New Jersey, adopted in 1682, bears the inscription, "The Earth is the Lords and the Fullness Thereof," the sentence being taken from the first line of Psalm xxiv. The earliest impression of this Prerogative Seal extant is affixed to the certified copy of the will or codicil of Thomas ffrench, which bears a very fine clear impression of the seal in red wax. It is one inch and one-sixteenth in diameter. The design is not heraldic, but is evidently a conventional representation of the globe with its embracing great circles and bands.

INVENTORY OF THE ESTATE OF THOMAS FFRENCH, 1699

A true Inventory of the goods and chattels of Thomas ffrench Late of Wellingburrough in the County of Burlington Deceafed Aprifed by us whofe names are under written y⁴ 21 day of the Second Month called April 1699.

	£	s.	d.
Impᵣˢ his Books	01	00	00
one Bed and furniture	07	10	00
one Bed and furniture	05	00	00
one old Bed boulíter & blankit	02	00	00
one Lookinglaís	00	06	00
one Table Cloth	00	03	06
one old pilion	00	02	06
one old great kettle	02	10	00
one braís poridge pot	01	13	00
one braís Skimmer	00	03	00
one Iron pot and hooks	00	14	00
one Little Iron Kettle	00	07	00
one Iron dripping pan	00	05	00
one Jack and two Spitts	01	00	00
fire Shovil and tongs	00	04	00
one pare of pot hangers	00	02	00
one grind Stone	00	05	00
one old box Iron & two heaters	00	03	00
one frying pan	00	03	00
pewter	04	04	06
Iron tooles & other old Iron	03	10	01
Earthen ware	00	04	06
one old gun	00	12	00
one Cheft and two boxes	00	13	00
two milk pails	00	04	00
one table	00	10	00
two old baggs	00	02	00
3 old chears	00	03	00
one old doetrogh old barrils and other woodn Lumber	00	08	06
one grid Iron	00	02	00
one Iron barr	00	07	00
horíe gears	00	01	00
one old cart	01	10	00
plow and plow tackling	00	10	00
4 Cows	12	00	00
2 Small 3 year old Steeres	05	00	00

	£	s.	d.
2 Small 2 year olds and one yearling	04	00	00
two poore mares & 1 horſe	06	00	00
4 Sows and Some Little Shoats	04	04	00
	£ 68	05	07

A house barne & plantation with
4 hundred Acres of Land belonging to it } £200   00   00

John Paine
Thomas Harding
John Hudſon
Thomas Eves.

The within written Inventory was proved according to Law amounting to yᵉ Suᵐᵉ of Two Hundred Sixty Eight pounds five Shillings & Seaven pence this Third day of May Anno Dom 1699

Before us
Nath : Westland

Tho : Revell Secʳʸ & Regʳ   John Jewell

ADMINISTRATION BOND OF CHARLES FFRENCH, 1699

Know all men by these pʳsents That we Charles ffrench of Wellingborrow in the County of Burlington within yᵉ Province of West New Jersey yeoman Mathew Allen of yᵉ County of Burlington aforesᵈ yeoman & Henry Grubb of yᵉ Towne & County of Burlington aforesᵈ Innholder are holden & firmly bound unto yᵉ Honᵇˡᵉ ye Govʳnoʳ of the sᵈ Province in yᵉ full & just Sume of ffive hundred Thirty & Six pounds Currt. Silver money within yᵉ sᵈ Province to be paid to yᵉ said Govrnoʳ or to his Aſsignes or Succeſsors for yᵉ time being To yᵉ which paymt well & truly to be made wee binde our Selves & every of us by himselfe joyntly & severally for & in ye whole our & every of our Heires Execʳs & Admistors firmly by these prsents sealed with our Seales dated ye Third day of May Anno RRs Gulielmi tertis Angl &c vndecimo Annoq Dom 1699

The Condition of ye above written Obligacon is such that if ye above bound Charles ffrench (now admitted Admistrator of yᵉ Goods Chattells & Estate late of Thomas ffrench deceased) doe & shall truly & faithfully prforme & fullfill yᵉ mind & will of yᵉ said Thomas ffrench according as is menconed in ye Codecill annexed to yᵉ Letter of Admistracon to him yᵉ sᵈ Charles Granted bearing date abovewritten & do & shall also Render & give to ye Registrs office at Burlington abovesaid just & true accompts of & Concerning the Estate late of ye said Thomas ffrench which now is in or shall come to yᵉ poſseſsion Custody or knowledge of him ye said Admistrator when thereunto reasonably required, and also doe & shall

truly & faithfully discharge himselfe of his said Administratorshippe
according to Law. Then yᵉ Obligacon abovewritten to be voyd & of noe
effect, or elfe to be & remaine in full force & vertue.
Sealed & delivered
in ye prsence of

Nath: Westland

Charles ffrench

John Jewell

Tho: Revell

Mathorew Allou

Henry Grubb

May yᵉ 3ᵈ 1699 Charles ffrench (son of Tho: ffrench deceased) Exhibited
& proved an Instrumᵗ or Codecill of his sᵈ Tho. ffrench mind & will
& also Exhibited & proved an Inventory of his Estate according to Law,
which originall Codecil is annexed to yᵉ Letter of Administration then
granted to sᵈ Charles who then gave bond & security according to Law,
yᵉ True Coppy of which Codecil, yᵉ originall Inventory & bond being in yᵉ
office The sᵈ Codecil & Inventory being proved & administration granted
before Nath: Westland & Jno: Jewell Justices
    Tho: Revell Secry & Regʳ

We have reason to believe that Thomas ffrench did not go to England as had been
his intention when making the foregoing will. It will be noted that immediately after
his death, Charles ffrench, his son, applied for certificate from Burlington Meeting on
account of an intended visit to "Old England" (see No. 8). The estate was administered upon by the executor, and after the decease of the widow all the special provisions
of the will were faithfully carried out. The great plantation was divided into smaller
tracts, and during the ensuing two centuries many deeds of transfer were made.

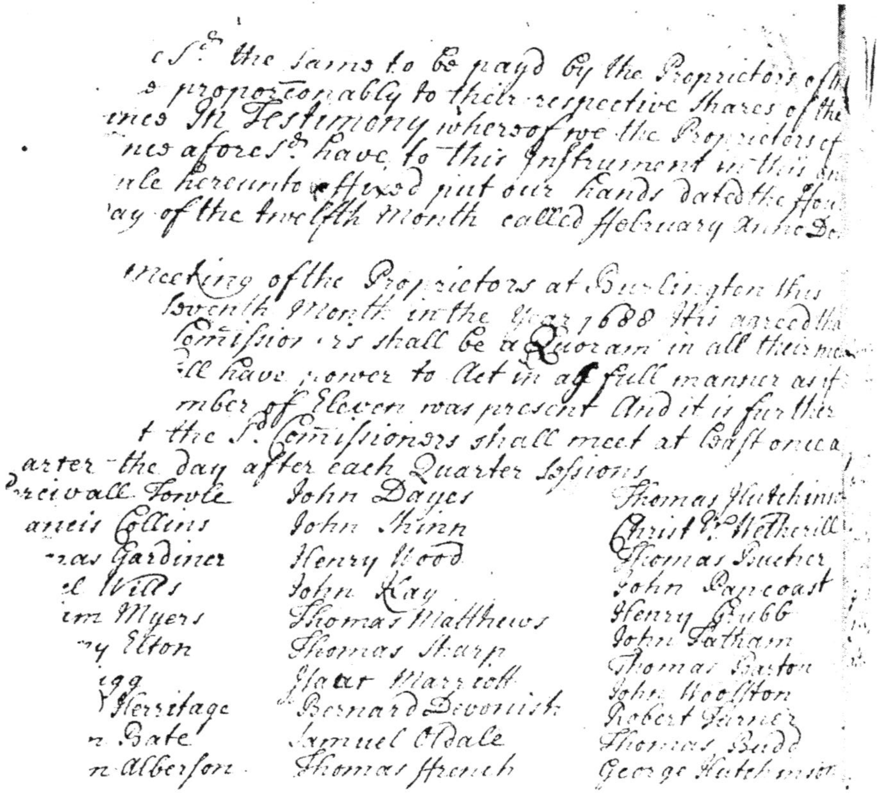

MEETING RECORDS, JANE AND LYDIA FFRENCH

At our mens monthly meeting held at the Meeting House in Burlington y^e 5th of y^e 12th mo. 1696

Dan^{ll} Hall & Jane ffrench (12) declared their Intentions of Marriage it being the first time of their coming.

At our mens monthly meeting held at our Meeting House in Bur^{ton} y^e 1st of the 1st Mo. 169$\frac{6}{7}$ Dan^{ll} Hall & Jane ffrench appeared y^e Second time & Declared their Intentions of Marriage y^e Meeting finding nothing to obstruct or hinder the Same they are Left to Consumate that weighty affair as they in a Convenient time & Place in y^e fear of y^e Lord Shall See meet.

At y^e womens meeting held in Burlington ye 3rd of ye 11th Mo. 1703 Elizabeth Gardiner & Susannah ffurniss are appointed to admonish Lidia ffrench (13) Concerning her keeping Company with one y^t is not a friend.

At ye womens meeting held in Burlington ye 7th of ye 12th mo. 1703 Elizabeth Gardiner & Susannah ffurniss being apointed last meeting to speak to Lidia ffrench had no opertunity as yet therefore they are desired to continue their care therein.

6th of ye 1st mo. 1704 Elizabeth Gardiner & Susannah ffurniss report that they have endeavoured to speak with Lidia ffrench but have had no opertunity therefore have made diligent enquiry & are informed that shee doth not now keep company with that man ye meeting was informed of.

PETITION OF JANE HALL, 1709
To be appointed administratrix to her husband's estate.

To the Honorable Richard Ingoldesby Esqr. Lieutenant Gouernor of her Majesties Provinces of New Jersey, New Yorke &c

The Petifion of Jane Hall widdow of Daniel Hall Lately Deceafed
Humbly Sheweth,

That your Petifioners husband lately died Intestate faveing that on his death-bed he verbaly declared that he left all to me and appointed me his Sole Executrix

Your petifioner therefore humbly prayes that Your Honnor would be pleafed to Committ the administration of her husbands estate to your petifioner and your petifioner as in duty bound fhall ever pray

the marke of

Jane | Hall.

Burlington the 19th Aprill 1709.

I Jane Hall doe follemnly declare in the presence of Almighty God the witnels of the truth of What I fay That Daniell Hall deceafed died without any will af farr as I know and beleive and that I will well and truely administer all and fingular the goods Chattles and Creditts of the faid deceafed and pay his Debts as farr as his goods Chattles and Creditts will thereunto extend and the Law require me and that I will make a true and perfect Inventory of all the faid goods Chattles and Creditts as alfo a Juft account when thereunto Required

the marke of

Jane ❘ Hall

Burlington the 19th Aprill 1709

Then appeared before me Richard Ingoldesby Esqr. Lieuetenant-Gouernor of her Majesty's provinces of New Jersey New Yorke &c Jane Hall widdow of Daniel Hall late of this County deceafed and praying for administration of the Goods Chattles & Creditts of the faid deceafed I doe fitt to grant the fame accordingly She haveing been duely attested faithfully to administer the faid estate & returne an Inventory thereof Accordingly.

Rich: Ingoldesby

COLONIAL OIL LAMP

4—RACHEL FFRENCH (Thomas, 1)

> b. March 24th, 1664.
> Baptized April 3rd, 1664, at Church S. S. Peter and Paul, Nether Heyford, England.
> m. First, 1687, Mathew Allen.
> He d. October, 1701.
> m. Second, 12th mo. 9th, 1702, Hugh Sharp, son of William and Hannah Sharp.
> He b. 4th mo. 3rd, 1668.
> d. 1742.

16—MATHEW ALLEN, JR.	b. 8th mo. 23rd, 1688. m. 1711, Grace Jones.
17—MERCY ALLEN	b. 1st mo. 13th, 1692. m. First, 1710, Thomas Middleton. m. Second, 10th mo. 2nd, 1730, John Hugg. m. Third, 2nd mo. 19th, 1732, Thomas Lippincott.
18—MARY ALLEN	b. 8th mo. 23rd, 1695. m. First, Jarves Stockdell. m. Second, 5th mo. 15th, 1741, John Mickle.
19—THOMAS ALLEN	b. 2nd mo. 7th, 1699.
20—HANNAH SHARP	m. 8th mo. 29th, 1724, John Brientnall.
21—REBECCA SHARP	m. First, 2nd mo. 26th, 1727, William Coate. m. Second, 1754, Joseph Lippincott.

Robert Allen, grandson of Mathew Allen, m. Mary ————. Their daughter, Margery Allen, m. Job Rogers, and their daughter, Rhoda Rogers, m. Daniel Estell. Mary Estell, daughter of Daniel and Rhoda Estell, m. Morton McMichael, Mayor of Philadelphia, 1866, 1867, 1868.

MATHEW ALLEN

A signer of the " Concessions and Agreements," Mathew Allen became one of the early English settlers of Burlington County, New Jersey. Apparently he was possessed of considerable means and had great faith in the future of the new country. In 1680, he bought of John Smith of " Christeene Creek " [Delaware] 3200 acres of land located along the Delaware near

Rancocas creek and extending eastward. Some 500 acres of the tract he conveyed to Isaac Conoroe in 1683, " out of good will and kindness which he hath and beareth unto the said Isaac Conoroe," also a further 500 acres to his brother Jacob Conoroe, under same conditions; and the descendants of these men have ever since lived in the same vicinity. Isaac and Jacob Conoroe were evidently the step-sons of Mathew Allen, as from contemporary records he appears to have been married to their widowed mother previous to his marriage to Rachel ffrench in 1687. He is frequently referred to in old deeds as the "father-in-law" of Isaac and Jacob Conoroe; a term synonymous in colonial days with step-father.

Mathew Allen became a farmer resident of Chester township; he was also a carpenter, and took an active interest in the affairs of the community. He was elected constable of Chester township in 1699 and served as tax assessor during part of 1701, the year of his death. In the month of May of that year, he was one of the signers of the address of the inhabitants of West Jersey to King William, asking his "Sacred Majesty" to assume the civil government of the Colony, many things having been suffered under proprietary control. This curious paper, so expressive of the characteristic loyalty of British subjects, concluded as follows:

> "That the great and glorious God who of his wonderfull Goodness & mercy hath sett you over his Great People will preserve your sacred Maj[ty] from the wicked contrivances, of all those who shall endeavour to oppose y[r] Maj[ty] in the great worke w[ch] lyes before You is and shall be the fervent & Constant Prayers of Us who crave leave to subscribe Our Selves your Maj[tys] most humble Suppliants."

DEED, JOHN SMITH TO MATHEW ALLEN

The following is an abstract of deed bearing date August 14th, 1680, of John Smith "of Christeene Creek in America (yeoman) to Mathew Allen of Burlington in West Jersey, in America (carpenter)."

CONSIDERATION Three score & Tenne pounds in good Country pay—grants bargains, sells &c—unto said Mathew Allen his heirs & Assigns forever (in his Actual pofsefsion now being by vertue of a bargaine & sale to him made for one whole yeare by Indenture bearing date the day before the date hereof & by vertue of y[e] statue for tranfferring vfes into pofseffion) All that his Lott or prcell of Land allready laid forth lyeing & being neare Rancokus Creek upon Dellaware River in America being comonly called the great Lott & was first laid forth conteyning by Estimacon Three Thousand Two hundred & odde Acres or thereabouts. And allfoe

all ye his Lott or Lotts of Lands lyeing or being in the Islands of
Burlington aforesaid Togeather alſoe with all such pte & pts share & shares
as ſhall belong or appertayne to the said Lott or Lotts in Burlington
Towne bounds when the said Town bounds shall be devided & laid forth
with all privileges &c to them apperteyning (except & reserved out of this
prsent deed or grant, unto the s^d John Smith his heirs & aſsigns one
Acre & an halfe of Land in Burlington Island afres^d lyeing to ye High
Street there & adjoyning to a Lott of Land belonging to the s^d Mathew Allen
and except alſoe one Lott or prcell of Land in Burlington afores^d conteyning by estimacon Eight Acres, or thereabouts be the same more leſſe
in the tenure or occupacon of William Brightwell or of his aſſignes)—all
deeds, writings coppies &c to be made at the charge of s^d Mathew Allen
his heirs & Assignes, (The Sume of one shillinge & Six pence comonly
called three Guilders yearely to be paid by said Mathew Allen his heires
& aſsignes unto the said John Smith his heires & aſsignes at the ffeast dayes
of St. John the Baptist, if lawfully demanded as a Cheiſe Rent or Quitt
Rent onlly excepted or foreprized) &c

                                                                    John Smith
Sealed & deli'rded in p^rſence of John White
                              Tho : Revell
Alſoe Sealed & Deli'rded in the p^rſence of Willm Emľey
        Thomas Lambert, Tho : ffairman & Tho : Revell.

WILL OF MATHEW ALLEN, 1701

In the Name of God Amen
This being my last will and testament: by which I make void any other
wills whatsoeuer: this ſeuententh of the ſeuenth month and in ye thirteenth
year of his maiesties Reign: and in ye year of our Lord one thousand feueu
hundred and one: I Matthew Allin of ye Prouinc of New West jerſy and
townſhip of Chester being wake of body yet of a perfect memory and
mind: I doe Conſtitute and ordeign my beloued wife Rachel Alin and
my ſon Mathew Alin to be ſole Executorſ: to performe my will as fol-
oweth: I giue to my ſon Mathew my plantation & all the land belonging
to it except two hundred Ackers where Iſaac Conorow now liveth (it
ſhall begin at the Run and ſo to John Adamſeſ path ſo along the
path half a mile ſo to the Run again) I giuc it to him when at age: to
him and his heirſ for euer also thirty pounds in Catle: I giue to my ſon
thomas Allin: the before mentioned two hundred Ackers and goshon ling
one Northhampton Ri̇uer: with thirty pounds in Catle: when at Age to
him his heirs and assigns foreuer: I doe order that my wife or her Assigns
pay to my two dafters Marſy and Mary Allin thre hundred pounds: and
my ſon Mathew or his heirs or Assigns ſhall pay one hundred pounds when
they ſhall arive at the Age of twenty years to them and their heirs or
Assigns for euer and if either Child, dye, its portion ſhall be deuided

equally between the Rest: the interest of the four hundred ſhall be for the
bringing up of the Children—

Also I giue my wife the lot of land in burlington to her or her Assigns
for euer and the remamding part of the ſtock I doe order my wif to
pay Alinor Conorow yᵉ daughter of Isaac Conorow fiue pounds when, at
Age: Also that Negro dick be ſold for yᵉ vse of the plantation allso I giue
Isaac Conorow three ſhilings. Also to Jacob Conorow three ſhilings Also
to Anthony frier three ſhillings

Sealed and delivered
in the presents of
Abraham heulings
Iſaac Conarroe

Octobʳ 17, 1701

Abraham Heulings and Isaac Conarroe appearing before us, two of yᵉ
Juſtices in the County of Burlington upon their Solemn atteſtacon did
declare that they were pʳſent and saw and heard yᵉ above Teſtator Matthew
Allen signe Seal deliver Publish and declare yᵉ above Inſtrument as his laſt
will & Teſtamᵗ & sett their hands thereto as Witneſses & further depoſeth
that to yᵉ beſt of their Underſtanding, the Teſtator was of sound and
diſpoſeing mind & memory at yᵉ Executeing thereof

Tho: Gardiner
Samˡˡ ffurnis

INVENTORY OF THE ESTATE OF MATHEW ALLEN, 1701

October yᵉ 9ᵗʰ 1701

A True Inventory of the goods and Chattels of Mathew Allen Late of
Chester in the County of Burlington in Weſt Jerſey deceaſsed, as followeth
Preiſed by us whoſe names are under written

	lb	ſ	D
Impʳⁱˢ his Ready money and Aparel	15	10	00
6 pare of ſheets	09	00	00
5 pillow beeres	00	09	00
3 table Cloths and two napkins	00	12	00
other pieces of Linin	00	07	00
bed and furniture	05	00	00
bed and furniture	05	10	00
bed and furniture	02	10	00
New Linin	02	06	06
A pcice of new woolin Cloth	05	19	00
A Remnant of new druget	00	11	00
2 great braſs kettles and one ſkillit	08	00	00

1 warming pan	00	18	00
2 braſs candleſticks	00	05	00
3 Iron potts and one Iron kettle	02	00	00
pewter	05	06	00
milk veſſils	02	00	00
Lanthorne	00	05	00
Cheſt of drawers	04	00	00
Cheſts	01	05	00
15 cows	60	00	00
1 bull	03	10	00
pare of oxen	11	10	00
pare of young ſtears	04	15	00
[— (torn)] two years old heyfors	12	00	00
5 yearlings	09	10	00
8 Calves	08	00	00
2 borſes one mare & 1 yearling Colt	14	00	00
21 Sheep	12	00	00
30 head of ſwine	20	00	00
500 pound waite of Cheeſe	12	10	00
5 barrills of boyled ſider	05	00	00
2 barrills of fiſh	02	08	00
corn in the barn & in the houſe	40	00	00
30 load of hay	18	00	00
1 Cart	01	10	00
plow and tackling	01	04	00
Iron tooles	02	04	00
ſpade and howes	00	12	00
other old Iron	00	03	00
fire Irons	01	02	08
box Irons and heaters	00	07	06
bible and other books	00	15	00
1 pare of ſtilliards & ſcales	00	15	00
1 pare of money ſcales	00	06	00
wool	02	05	00
ſaddle and pillion	01	00	00
ſpining wheelſ	01	00	00
1 gun	01	03	00
frying pan	00	07	00
peaſe [?]	02	10	00
grind ſtone	00	10	00
old ſiths and ſickles	00	10	00
one cunnooe	02	10	00
old baggs	00	10	00

	lb	f	D
chears ſtooles and other Lumber	01	17	00
3 negroes two men and one woman	115	00	00

	£ : 443	07	08
	lb	f	D
Debts oweing to the ſaid Mathew Allen....	300	00	00
brought from yᵉ other fide..............	443	07	08

	£ : 743	07	08

Preiſed by us
    John paine
    Tho: Eves
    Abraham heulings.

BOND, RACHEL ALLEN, RICHARD AND CHARLES FFRENCH, 1701.

Know all men by theſe prſents That We Rachel Allen of the County of Burlington, in the Province of Weſt New Jersey Widdow, Matthew Allen, Richᵈ ffrench, and Charles ffrench all of the same County yeom are holden and ſtand firmly bound unto the Honoᵇˡᵉ Coll. Andrew Hamilton Governoʳ of the sᵈ Province in the Sume of ffifteen hundred pounds of currᵗ silver money of yᵉ sᵈ Province To be paid to yᵉ sᵈ Governoʳ or to his lawfull Succeſſors for yᵉ time being To the wᶜʰ Paymt well and truely to be made We bind ourselves and every of us our and every of our heires Executors and Admʳˢ for the whole and in the whole joyntly and severally firmly by these Presents Sealed wᵗʰ our Seals dated in Burlington the 17ᵗʰ day of Octobʳ Anno Dm 1701 Annoqe R. Rˢ Gulielmi tertij Anglis &c decimo tertio

The Condicon of the above Obligacon is such That if the above bounden Rachel Allen, and Matthew Allen, (one yᵉ Wife the other the son and alſo) Executors of the laſt will and Teſtamᵗ of Matthew Allen late of Cheſter in ye sᵈ County of Burlington yeom decd, do and shall truely and juſtly fullfill and performe the laſt Will and Teſtamᵗ of the said Teſtator being the day of the date hereof proved and given into ye Regiſters Office at Burlington aforesᵈ juſt and true Accompts of and concerning the same Eſtate late of and belonging to ye sᵈ Teſtator wᶜʰ now is or hereafter shall come into their or either of their cuſtody poſſeſsion or knowledge when thereunto lawfully required, and thereof and of every part thereof discharge themselves according to Law That then the above Obligacon to be void & of none Effect or elſe to be and remaine in full force and virtue

                     her
       Rachel   Allen

        mark

Sealed and delivered
In the presence of

Tho: Gardiner
Sam[ll] ffurnis
Tho: Eves
Edward Hunloke

Richard ffrench

Charles ffrench

HUGH SHARP

Hugh Sharp was a native of Northampton, England, whence he came to Pennsylvania, a lad of fourteen years of age, with his father the year of Penn's arrival. His family settled in Pennsbury, where he remained until he married Rachel, daughter of Thomas ffrench, widow of Mathew Allen, of Burlington county, New Jersey. Evidently having had educational advantages he became a prominent, useful and influential citizen, of high standing in religious as well as business circles. He was a leading Friend, being a member of Burlington Monthly Meeting, and for some years an elder. He located in Chester township, becoming owner of several large plantations in that vicinity. In 1715 he received a grant of 3700 acres of unsurveyed lands from the Council of Proprietors, 230 acres of which were located in Hunterdon county and 400 acres in Morris county.

Hugh Sharp's special gifts as a writer and man of affairs were utilized in various ways. His signature, as a witness, is found on wills and other documents and he prepared many inventories. He drew petitions to the legislature, notably for a bridge over the Rancocas, in 1709. The same year he served in that body as a member for the western division of Burlington county, the first Assembly of Governor Lord Lovelace. He signed a memorial to Governor Burnet, "in obedience to the order of Council, appointing a time for the Proprietors for exhibiting their reasons why the bill for repealing an act for running and ascertaining the line of partition between the eastern and western divisions of New Jersey, should not pass." This was in 1721.

February 18, 1708-9, Hugh Sharp was appointed guardian of Thomas Allen, "a minor of the age of eleven years or thereabouts, son of Mathew Allen, late of the county of Burlington, deceased, and Rachel the now wife of the said Hugh Sharp." He entered bond in the sum of 500 pounds, April 11, 1709.

WILL OF HUGH SHARP, 1741

I Hugh Sharp of the Township of Wellingborrow and County of Burlington & province of West New Jersey Esquire thanks be to God being of perfect Sound disposing mind and memory do make & ordain this my last will and Testament in manner and form following that is to say Principally I give & Recomend my Spiritts into yᵉ hands of God yᵗ gave It and my Body to the Earth to be decently Buried att yᵉ difcretion of my Executors hereafter named And as Touching such worldly Eſtate wherewith itt hath pleaſed God to bleſs me in this Life I give and Bequeath yᵉ Same in maner and form as followeth— Item I give and Bequeath unto my dear and Loveing wife Rachel Sharp all that my Lott of Land in Burlington, fronting Pearl Street and Runing half way Back to Water Street to her and to her heirs and Aſsigns forever I alſo Give unto my Said wife yᵉ Sum of thirty pounds proclamation money to be paid to her annually out of my Eſtate dureing her Natural Life by my Executors in Lew of her thirds of my Eſtate which She is Therewith Contented.

Item I Give unto my daughter-in-Law Mary Micle yᵉ wife of John Micle all maner of Debts due or Owing unto me from her.

Item I give unto yᵉ Monthly Meeting of ffriends in Burlington yᵉ sum of five pounds to be paid into the hands of Caleb Raper Eſqʳ in twelve months after my Deceaſe for the uſe of the afforesaid Meeting. And wheras I have Sold to my Son in Law William Coate my plantation, whereon I now dwell for Eight Hundred pounds Item I Give unto my Said Son Wm. Coate the Sum of four Hundred pounds thereof he paying yᵉ Intereſt thereof for which he hath given me bonds and to my Son in Law John Brintnale the other four hundred pounds. And it is my will that after my Deceaſe and my wife's that my Eſtate Shall be Equally Divided Between my two Sons in Law as aforesᵈ, And I do nominate and appoint my Said two Sons in Law John Brientnall and William Coate Executors of this my Last will and Testament And I doe Hereby Revoake and Diſsanul all former and other Wills and Teſtaments by me Heretofore made making and ordaining this my Last will & Testament In wittneſs whereof I have hereunto Sett my hand and Seale This fifth day of yᵉ Eighth Month Comonly Called October and in the year of our Lord 1741

Signed Sealed published pronounced and
Declared by the Said Hugh Sharp as his
Last will and Testament in yᵉ preſence of

Peter ffearon
Abrᵐ ffarrington
Joshua Raper

Abraham Farrington and Joshua Raper Two of the witneſses to the within written will being of the People called Quakers on their Solemn affirmation which they took according to law did declare & affirm that they Saw Hugh Sharp the Testator therein named Sign & Seal the same & heard him publish pronounce & declare the within written Instrumt to be his last will and Testament and that at the doing thereof ye s^d Testator was of sound disposing mind memory and understanding so far as they know and as they Verily believe & that Peter ffearon the other witneſs was present and Signed his name as an evidence thereto together with these affirmants in presence of the s^d Testator

Abr^m Farrington
Joshua Raper

Affirmed at Burl^n ye Thirteenth Day of January A. D. 1742 before me

Joseph Rose, Surrogate

Be it Remember'd that the last will and Testament of Hugh Sharp dec'd having Been duly proved as aboves^d probate & letters Testamentary were granted by his Excellency Lewis Morris Esqr Governour &c. unto Wm Coates &Jo^n Brientnall the Ex^{rs} therein named who being duly affirmed well & Truly to perform the S^d will to Exhibit a True and perfect Inventory and render a Just accompt when thereunto lawfully required Given under y^e prerogative Seal of S^d province at Burlington the Second Day of March A. D. 1742 p Arch^d Home Regr. &c

HISTORIC TABLE, BURLINGTON MEETING HOUSE

Upon this table marriage certificates have been signed for more than two hundred years, and it is still in use, 1908.

5—RICHARD FFRENCH (Thomas, 1)

> b. December 1st, 1665.
> Baptized December 15th, 1666, at Church S. S. Peter and Paul, Nether Heyford, England.
> d. 1745.
> m. First, 7th mo. 11th, 1693, Sarah Scattergood, daughter of Thomas and Elizabeth Scattergood of Stepney Parish, London, England.
> She d. about 1700.
> m. Second, 11th mo. 13th, 1701, Mary King, daughter of Harmanus and Mary King of Nottingham Township, Burlington Co., N. J.

22—ELIZABETH FRENCH
b. 1694.
m. William Scholey.

23—RICHARD FRENCH, JR
b. 8th mo. 20th, 1696.
m. Rachel ————.

24—THOMAS FRENCH

25—MARY FRENCH
m. 8th mo. 15th, 1724, Preserve Brown, Jr.

26—REBECCA FRENCH
m. 2nd mo. 23rd, 1729, Benjamin Shreve.

27—WILLIAM FRENCH
b. April 7th, 1712.
m. Sept. 20th, 1748, Lydia Taylor.

28—SARAH FRENCH
b. 7th mo. 20th, 1715.
m. 2ud mo. 1741, William Marlin.

29—ABIGAIL FRENCH
b. 7th mo. 5th, 1717.
m. First, 1st mo. 1737, James Lewis.
m. Second, Jacob Taylor.

30—BENJAMIN FRENCH
b. 12th mo. 11th, 1719.
m. January 29th, 1742, Martha Hall.

31—JONATHAN FRENCH
b. 11th mo. 27th, 1722.
m. 1st mo. 12th, 1744, Esther Matlack.

Harmanus King died 5th day of 1st mo. (March) 1727/8 in his 76th year.
Mary King died 24th day of 11th mo. 1740, in her 88th year.

RICHARD FRENCH

A memorandum in the family Bible of Thomas ffrench, then residing at Nether Heyford, England, and in his own handwriting, says: " December the first about ten at night my son Richard was borne, 1665.   The Lord give him grace that hee may continually walk before him." A long and useful life shows how fully this characteristic prayer of a devout and loving father was answered.   Richard was a lad of fifteen when he came to America with the family, in 1680.   So far as known, his youth and early manhood were spent on the Rancocas homestead plantation.   That he was devoted to farm life is shown in the fact that upon his marriage, in 1693, he purchased an extensive tract of land, 460 acres, in Mansfield township, Burlington county, where he seems to have resided during the remainder of his life.   A deed of release of all claim to the home farm, after his father's death, to his younger brother, Charles, shows the kindly relationship that existed and his contentment with his own lot.

That Richard French was a faithful and zealous Friend is evident from meeting records of the period, wherein his name appears many times.   His nearest meeting was the one early established at Crosswicks.   In 1715 he is recorded as an overseer and in 1723 as an Elder and minister.   He was a frequent representative at Quarterly and Yearly Meeting.   He was now past middle age, but for a quarter of a century continued active in the work of preaching and visitation, journeying through the wilderness to New England and the South.   The original certificate of 1733, a facsimile of which is given, is wonderfully well preserved, showing many notable names of that pioneer period.   In the promotion of religious life in the colonies Richard French was conspicuous and influential.   In business affairs he was active and prosperous, as his many deeds and other papers show, particularly his will and the accompanying inventory of personal property.   In 1701 he served as tax collector for Mansfield township.   He raised a large family, all of his ten children reaching marriageable age.   The peculiar phraseology of his recorded papers shows a mind exceedingly careful of details, with a just and kindly spirit, a continuing answer to the fervent prayer of his father at his birth.   His monthly meeting fittingly testified, after his death, that in the exercise of his gift in the ministry, " he labored faithfully in his declining age, and travelled much in North America."

MEETING RECORDS

The following are extracts from various Meeting records showing reference to Richard French.

Burlington Monthly Meeting Minutes:
At our Mens Monthly Meeting held at the House of Thos. Gardiners ye 7th of ye 6th mo: 1693
Richard ffrench and Sarah Scattergood came before this Meeting and Declared their Intention of Marriage it being the first Time.

At our Mens Monthly Meeting held at ye house of Thomas Gardeners Adjorned to this Eleventh of ye 7th Month 1693.
Richard ffrench & Sarah Scattergood came this second time and declared their Intentions of Marriage & the Meeting upon Enquire finding them Clear they are prmitted to Solemnize y^e same as in y^e fear of God they see meete.

At our Mens Monthly Meeting held at our Meeting House in Bur^{ton} y^e 1st of the 1st Mo. 169$\frac{4}{5}$
Whereas Some Difference appeared between Christopher Wetherill & Richd French Concearning a Peice of Meadow in dispence between them Jno. Brown ordered to Speak to Rich^d to be here at the next Mo^{ly} Meeting.

At our Mens Monthly Meeting held at our Meeting house in Burlington y^e 5th of y^e 2nd Mo: 1697
Richard French in psuance to ye Order of ye Last meeting appeared at this Meeting & the Men by them Chosen to finally End ye Difference between them are these Joshua Humphreis ffreedom Lippincott Jno. Wills & Tho Raper.

At our Mens Monthly Meeting held at Our Meeting House in Burlington ye 7th of ye 4th Mo. 1697
The men before chosen by Christopher Wetherill & Richard French gives account to this Meeting y^t ye difference between them is ended.

Chesterfield Monthly Meeting Minutes:
4—10th Mo. 1701   Richard French and Mary King signifyed their intentions of taking each other in marriage and according to ye good order yoused amongst us, Wm. Wood and Thos. Scholey are appoynted to enquire concerning his clearness on y^t acco^t & make report to our next Mo. Mtg.

1st of 11 mo. 1701 Rich'd French and Mary King signified their intentions of marriage with each other ye 2nd time, and enquiry having been made on both parts concerning their clearness from others on y^t account and nothing appearing but that they are cleare they are left to proceed according to y^t good order yoused amongst us.

Our Women's Monthly Meeting was held at the Meeting house in Chesterfield where 4—10 mo. 1701—Richard French of this meeting and Mary King the daughter of Harmanus & Mary also of this meeting laid before this meeting their intentions of joining each together in marriage. Hannah Overton & Rebecca Davenport are to enquire of the young woman's clearness & give report to our next monthly meeting.

1—11 mo. 1701—Richard French and Mary King aforesaid have the Second time published their intentions of marriage before us: So Friends finding things clear leaves them to the men Friends.

MARRIAGE CERTIFICATE

Chesterfield Monthly Meeting Record, Book 1, Marriages, Births and Deaths.

Whereas Richard French of the Township of Mansfield & County of Burlington in the province of West Jersey yeoman, & Mary King daughter of Harmanus King of the Township of Nottingham & County & province afores^d having intentions of taking each other in Marriage did publish the same before Several Monthly Meetings of the people called Quakers & had the consent of the said Meetings & of parents & Relations concerned. And for the full determination of their said Intentions They the said Richard French & Mary King aforesaid appeared in a Solemn Afsembly of the aforesaid people met together for that end & purpose at the House of Harmenus King in the Township of Nottingham & County & province aforesaid upon the thirteenth day of the Eleventh month One Thousand Seven hundred & one Where he the said Richard French, taking the said Mary King by the hand did openly declare Friends in the fear of the Lord & in the presence of this Afsembly I take this my friend Mary King to be my Wife promifsing to be a loving & faithful husband till death Separate & the said Mary King in like manner did take the said Richard French to be her husband promifsing to be a faithful & loving Wife till death Separate us. And as a further confirmation thereof the said Richd French & the said Mary Afsuming her husband's name upon her did then & there Set their hands to thefe presents & we whose names are hereunto Subscribed were Witnefses to the said Solemnization & Susbscription.

Richard French

her

Mary m French

mark

| Francis Davenport | Hannah Woodward | Harmanis King |
| Josiah Gratton | Rose Fowler | Mary King |

Antho. Woodward   Mary Quicksall   John King
Saml. Overton   Katherine Thorne   Charles French
Jno. Bunting   Sarah Davenport   Joseph King
Jno. Leeson   Anne Davenport   Jno. French
Geo. Nicholson   Susanna Decow   Tho. Scattergood
Tho. Folkes Senr.   Bridget Davenport   Tho. Brian
Tho. Folkes Junr.   Sarah Bunting Junr.   Joseph Pancoaſt
Gervas Hall   Esther Overton   Wm. Pancoaſt
Francis Davenport Junr. Martha Shreeve   Thomasin Pancoaſt
                         Hanna Overton   Wm. Quicksall
                         Eliza. Folkes   Jos. Scattergood
                                                Hannah Pancoaſt
                                                Lydia French.

Chesterfield Monthly Meeting Minutes, Continued

4 mo—5ᵗʰ—1701—This meeting have under consideration Psons which
Profeſs truth and wass in Companey with those yᵗ Broke yᵉ Prison Dore
oppne After A Riotous Manner at Burlington to Deale with them acording
to the good order of truth.

friends Appoynted to Speake with all Such as above that be Long to
this meeting and to make Report to our next Monthly Meeting is Thomas
Scholey, William Wood and John Warren.

5 mo 3ᵈ—1701—Thomas Scholey and William Wood acquaints this Meeting yᵗ According to Appoyntmᵗ they have been with those pʳſons, and
yᵉ Meeting Again appoynts them to speak with the pʳsons above Sd to be
at our next Monthly Meeting.

6th mo. 7ᵗʰ 1701—Richard French Thomas Curtis David Curtis &
Abraham Browne (At yᵉ Requeſt of William Wood and Thomas Scholey
appoynted by the meeting) was at this meeting.

7th mo. 4ᵗʰ—1701 Whereas divers disorderly pʳſons did upon yᵉ 18ᵗʰ
day of yᵉ 1ˢᵗ mo Last Apeare in a body at Burlington And we not
understanding their wicked Intentions, but being unwareyly drawn into
yᵗ tumultious Companey Which in the End Broke forth in to A Riotus
and unlawfull Breakeing opne yᵉ Priſon Doreſ Now for yᵉ Cleareing of
ourſelves and oure Profeſſion from all Such unlawfull unwarrantable and
deteſtable actions as above Wee do here by Solemnly declare that Wee
are Absolutely Cleare from being in Aney wiſe directly or in directly
Intentionally Conserned in the InCorriageing Abeting or Aiding to yᵉ
Pſons above Sd and do forder declare yᵗ wee are hartaly Sory that our

MARRIAGE CERTIFICATE OF RICHARD AND MARY (KING) FRENCH, 1701

Signatures to this ancient document entirely worn away

unhappy Lott was to be at y^t unlawful Meeting. In teſtamony whereof we do here unto Subscribe our Names ye day and yeare Aboveſd.

Richard ffrench
Tho: Curtis
David Curtis

7th mo 4th 1701—Richard French Appeared at this Meeting and Signed A Paper to the Sattisfaction of friends. The meeting appoints Richard French and John Bunting to goe to Thomas Curtis & David for y^m to sign ye Papper as above.

8 mo 2^d 1701 John Bunting and Richard French gives this mtg account y^t they have been with Thos. and David Curtis and y^t they have both signed ye paper above mentioned.

At a Monthly Meeting at Chesterfield Meeting-house ye 2nd day of ye 11th Mo. 1706

friends by this Meeting Appointed to Attend and Accompaney Publike friend traveling this Way so far as is Neſſary is   John Murfin
Robert Willson
Edward Rockhill
John Abbott
Rich^d french
& Matthew Wattson

4th of 6th Mo. 1715—Two or three of the Overseers belonging to this Meeting for some reasons requested that there might be added to their assistance one Friend more which the Meeting having taken into consideration do appoint Richard French to be Overseer joyned to those before named.

At Meeting at Chesterfield Mtg-house 6th of the 8mo 1720. The Friends of Chester being the lower part of this County acquainted Friends of this Meeting sometime paſt that by an accident of Fire their Meeting House was burnt therefore requeſted some aſsistance of this Meeting that such as were free to contribute to so good a Work whereupon Several Friends Subſcribed to pay as soon as they could to Richard French & William Murfin the Sums contained therein to be applyed to the uſe aforesaid.

At a Monthly Meeting of Friends held at their Meeting House in Chesterfield the 5th of the 11mo 1720.

Richard French & William Murfin being formerly appointed to receive the Money Subſcribed to aſsist our Friends at Chester in order to rebuild their Meeting House that was burned brought in a Receipt to this Meeting from under the hands of Thomas French (6) & James Adams for the money paid to them being ten pounds, three Shillings new Currency.

1ˢᵗ of 6 mo. 1723 This Meeting hath thought fit to appoint our Friends and Elders Richard French and Benjamin Clarke and request that they will meet with our severall Meetings of Ministring Friends held at Burlington at the times agreed to by the General Meeting of the Ministring Friends.

6—6 mo. 1724—This meeting having considered the advantage that Friends and Truth may receive by putting in practice the weighty work of Love and service in visiting Friends families do for that service appoint our dear friends Richard French, Jos. Watts, John Sykes & Isaac Horner

At Chesterfield monthly meeting held the 6ᵗʰ of Sixth month, 1724. This meeting having considered the matter referred to this time concerning a Meeting House to be built near Stony Brook approves thereof and a subscription was made in order thereto. Richard French and John Tantum are appointed to receive for the meetings use the sums subscribed, as Friends are in readiness to pay same. John Tantum and Thomas Lambert are appointed to lay the matter before the next Quarterly meeting at Burlington for its approval and assistance.

At a Monthly Meeting of Friends held at their Meeting Houſe in Chesterfield the 7ᵗʰ of the 2ᵐᵒ 1726—
Friends of this Meeting having had for sometime paſt under their consideration the advantage it would be for Expediting the buſineſs that may be propoſed in this meeting a preparative Meeting where those that have any buſineſs to propoſe to this Meeting may have the advice of such Friends as may be present at said Meeting & that they are to be holden at the Meeting Houſe every fifth day next before our Monthly Meeting, immediately after the Week day Meeting is over & to consist of twenty four Men and Women Friends to be named by the respective Meeting or so many of thoſe named as can well be there & such other Solid Friends who are Members of our Monthly Meeting as can attend it which sd preparative Meeting shal report to yᵉ next moˡʸ Meeting such things considered by them as come properly before said Meeting. Friends appointed to attend it are as follows; Richard French, John Sykes, Joseph Worth, Abraham Farrington, Isaac Horner, John Tantum, John Abbott, Benjamin Clark, Samuel Large, Preserve Brown, John Wood & Thomas Lambert. Named by our Women as followeth Mary Bunting, Rebecca Waring, Hannah Overton, Hannah Woodward, Anne Abbott, Mary Brown, Joanna Sykes, Thomasin Pancoast, Elianor Horner, Alice Bunting, Elizabeth Tantum, & Sarah Murfin.

At A Monthly Meeting of Friends held at their Meeting Houſe in Chesterfield the 6ᵗʰ of the 8ᵐᵒ 1726.
Our Friends Richard French & John Sykes propoſed that if this Meeting

approved of it they thought it might be of good Service not only to their and many other Friends fameleys but give an opportunity to some who would be willing to come sometimes if near to Settle at some convenient place near them a Meeting to be every firſt day during the winter Quarter which propoſal this Meeting approves of and leaves the Settling of the Same to them and Friends that way.

5—11 mo. 1726 In answer to our friends request and the Quarterly Meeting directions, this meeting thinks fit to appoint our Friends Richard French, Abraham Farrington, Benjamin Clark and Thos. Lambert to make themselves acquainted as much as they can of the labors and service of that worthy servant of the Lord Thomas Wilson when in these parts and draw it in writing and bring it to our next Monthly Meeting.

2—of 5th mo. 1730 Friends subscribed to the raising of a half yearly collection for the use of our Yearly Mtg. and appointed our friends Richd French and Isaac Horner to receive the same. It is desired it may be paid in before next monthly meeting.

3—6 mo. 1732 A subscription was forwarded at this Meeting in order for the Yearly Meeting Stock and appoint our Friends Richard French and John Tantum to receive the same.

7th of 12th Month 1733 Our Friend Richard French requested a certificate of this meeting signifying that for some time he had some drawing in his mind to visit Friends in Virginia and Maryland and accordingly he had one signed.
[Facsimile of certificate above requested and granted appears upon accompanying page.]

4th of 5th mo. 1734 Our Friend Richard French being returned from his visit of Love to Friends in North Carolina and Virginia and brought certificates from Friends which are a good account & satisfactorie to this meeting.

4th of 9mo—1736—Friends appointed Isaac Horner, Richard French, William Morris, Joshua Wright and Marmaduke Watson to treat with Joseph Borden about Land to build a Meeting house on, and a grave-yard he having made an offer to some Friends concerning it.

2^d of 10mo 1736—The friends appointed to treat with Joseph Borden have been with him, and he hath ordered two pieces of Land one for a Meeting House and the other for a Grave Yard to Friends Satiſfaction;

and desire Samuel Satterthwaite, Benjamin Shreve, Thomas Newbold, Benjamin Clark Junr— Ananiah Gaunt and Joseph Gardiner to receive the Deed and Sign an acknowledgment of Truſt for it: This Meeting orders Joſeph Reckleſs to make the Writings as soon as he can with conveniency. The Declaration of Trust for the Land at Bordentown to be made to Joseph Reckleſs, Marmaduke Watson, Samuel Pancoast and Benjamin Field.

6th of 11 mo. 1736—Joseph Reckless reported that the writings were not done for the Land for a Meeting House and Grave Yard at Bordentown for want of the Survey. The Meeting orders him to get it done as soon as can be with conveniency.

3rd of 12mo 1736—Joseph Reckleſs to continue his care for getting the writing done for the Meeting House and graveyard at Bordentown.

7th of 5mo—1737—Joseph Reckleſs gives accot that the Deeds for the Meeting House and Grave Yard at Bordentown are done, this Meeting desires him to get the Declaration of Trust signed against Next Meeting.

1—1 mo. 1739—Richard French acquainted this Meeting that he had a concern on his mind to Visit Friends in New England Deſiring a Certificate on that account

5—2 Mo. 1739—Richard French had a Certificate Signed at this Meeting according to his request.

5—5 Mo. 1739—Richard French brought into this Meeting two Certificates one from Dover Monthly Meeting in New England dated the 19th day of the 3^d mo. 1739 The other from the Yearly Meeting at Newport on Road Island dated the 11th of the 4 mo. 1739 both giving a satisfactory account of his Service and of his orderly Conversation.

6—7 mo. 1739—Richard French brought a Certificate to this meeting from Long Island dated 25—of 5 mo. 1739 giving a satisfactory account of his Service there.

5—1 mo. 1741—William Marlin and Sarah French (28) the first time appeared at this meeting and declared their intentions of marriage with each other. Friends appoint Isaac Horner & Marmaduke Watson to enquire concerning his conversation and clearness on account of marriage and make report to next monthly meeting.

From our month:ly meting held at (Rastoryfield?) in
the County of Burlington the [5ᵗʰ] of 11ᵐᵒ 178[3/4]

To Friends in Maryland Vergenia or Elsewhere
where these may Come.

Deare Friends and Brethren in the unchangeable truth
this may Let you know that our antiant friend Richard
French the Bearer hereof Acquainted this meting that he
hath for some time past strained for his mind to visit friends
in your parts and having the Company of our Esteemed friend
John Sackett in that Religious visit.

These may therefore Certifye you that we have good unity with
him his plaine & Innocent Conversation being agreable to
his testimony

So we desire the Lord may be with and preserve him in his
Jorney, and when his Jorney is over among you he may return
to his famely againe with a reward of peace in his Bosome

Signed in and on behalf of ye said Meeting by

Isaac Horner

Joseph Dawes

John Sykes

John Fletcher

William Murfin

John Abbott

John King

John Black

John Bunting

William Sutterthwaite Junior

Samuel Mortsworth

Joshua Wright

James Pharoah

Thos Sanford

John Middleton

Giles Worth

Peter Brown

Peter Brown Junr

Benjamin Shreve

James Clark

Benji Plant

James Crisp

Aaron Kenny

2—2^d mo. 1741—Wm. Marlin and Sarah French the second time declared their intentions of marriage: Nothing appearing to obstruct, Friends leave them to their liberty to consumate the same to see that things are orderly.

Minutes of Chesterfield Monthly Meeting of Women Friends:
5th of ye 1st mo. 1741   William Marlen a frequenter of our meetings for worship and Sarah French (28) hath published theire intention of marriage, two friends are appointed to make enquire concerning her and report to next meeting.

2nd of 2nd mo. 1741   William Merlen and Sarah French ye second time signified they continued theire intentions of marriage and nothing appearing to hinder their proceeding they are left to the conclusion of men friends.

William Marlin was Overseer of Roads for Chesterfield Township, 1746.

"SERTIFICATE" OF HARMANAS KING

The following is taken from a very old Book of Chesterfield Monthly Meeting Records:

ffrom our Monthly Meeting at fflushing on Long Ifland the feventh day of ye ffirst mo 1699—

Deare ffriendf wee dearly falut you in the truth and hearby fartefie that Harmanas King Lived amongft us and belonged to our Meeting and hee remouing into your parts to Live requefted of us a fertificate of his Conuerfation which was sober and orderly walking acording to his profeffion in much fimplifetti and haue Left a good report behind him hauing made prouff of his Loue to truth acording to his capafity by an Inofent Conuerfation and as fuch wee defire hee may bee Receiued amongft you hoping that hee will Contineue in ye fam nearneff to truth and itf ffoloworf.

Signed by order and on behalf of our faid meeting

pr Sam Bown.

APPOINTMENT OF RICHARD FRENCH TAX COLLECTOR, 1701

An Act of Assembly made May 1700 entitled " An Act for raifing a Tax towards an Honorable Support of Government as also to defray Several Provincial Debts &c.

And it is Hereby Enacted by the Authority of the Same "————— Governor—advice of Council and Consent and agreement of the Representatives in this General free Assembly met and Assembled) that the Persons

herein after mentioned be appointed and are hereby appointed and authorized in the several and respective Townships Precincts or Districts in the
said Province, to be Assessors and Collectors for the Aſseſsing and gathering the ſaid Tax as follows, viz; "

In Burlington Co.,—for Mansfield Thomas Curtis and James Crafts
Senr Aſseſsors;—Richard French; Collector.

At Sessions of Gen. Assembly convened at Burlington the 12th Day of
May, 1701 and ending 21st Day of same.

Andrew Hamilton—Governor, (with advice of this Council) and by
Samuel Jennings Speaker of House of Representatives

Recorded per me

Edward Hunloke Clerk Council

DEED, RICHARD FRENCH TO THOMAS BRYAN, 1714

This Indenture made and dated the Seventh day of February in the year
according to English account one thousand seven hundred and fourteen
Between Richard French of the Township of Mansfield in the County
of Burlington and the Western Division of the Province of New Jersey
Yeoman of the one part and Thomas Bryan of the Township of Northampton and County & Province aforesaid yeoman of the other part Witneſseth that the said Richard French for and in consideration of the Sum of
Twenty five pounds at nine Shillings and two pence pr ounce to him in hand
paid by the said Thomas Bryan the Receipt whereof he the said Richard
French doth hereby acknowledge and thereof and of every part and parcel
thereof doth clearly acquit and discharge the said Thomas Bryan his Heirs
Executors Administrators and every of them by these presents have
Given Granted aliened Released and confirmed and by these Presents do
Give Grant Alien Release and Confirm unto the said Thomas Bryan and
to his Heirs and aſsigns One Eighth part of a Ninetieth part of the said
Province otherways understood an Eighth part of a propriety of Land
lying and being in the said Province together with All the Right Title
property claim and demand whatsoever except all the Town bound Land
and Except Eighteen hundred Acres being taken up and Surveyed in the
said Province being usually called the first Second and third Dividend
which Eighth part of a propriety he the said Richard French hath and
holdeth by virtue of a Deed Indented bearing date the twentieth day of
No^{ber} Anno 1680 Between John Woolston of Burlington and province
aforesaid Yeoman of the one part and Thomas French father of the said
Richard French party to these presents of the other part which eighth part
of a propriety was purchased by the aforesaid John Woolston of Thomas
Olive of the Township of Wellingborough Haberdasher and was held by
Virtue of a Deed Indented bearing date the twenty sixth day of February

Anno 1676 Between the said John Woolston and Thomas Olive together with all the Right Title claim and demand whatsoever unto the said Thomas Bryan his Heirs and Aſsigns forever To have and to hold the said Land Premiſses except what before Excepted unto the said Thomas Bryan his Heirs and aſsigns forever Together with all and every of the Reversion and Reversions Remainder and Remainders with the Mines Minerals woods Fishings Fowlings Hawkings Huntings and all other priviledges profits and Commodities whatsoever belonging to the said Premiſses And he the said Richard French doth for himself his Heirs Executors Administrators doth Covenant promise Grant to and with the said Thomas Bryan his Heirs & aſsigns by these presents that at the time of the Sealing and Delivery hereof he the said Richard French is the true and Lawful Owner & proprietor of the said Premiſses and hath in himself good Right full power and absolute Authority to Sell and Confirm the said Granted and Bargained Premiſses and every part and parcel thereof unto the said Thomas Bryan his Heirs and Aſsigns forevermore And further that the said Richard French his Heirs Executors and Administrators shall and will from time to time and at all times forever hereafter at the Request cost and Charges of the said Thomas Bryan his Heirs or aſsigns make do and Execute such further Acts matters thing or things whatsoever for the better and more fully conveying and confirming the said Premiſses hereby Granted and Sold unto the said Thomas Bryan his Heirs and aſsigns according to the true Intent and meaning of these presents In witneſs whereof he the said Richard French hath to this present Indenture set his hand and seal the day and year first above written 1714.

Richard French [SEAL]

Sealed Signed and Delivered in the presence of Michael Newbould Samuel Bustill George Willis—Endorsed

Be it Remembered that on the Seventh day of February one thousand seven hundred and thirty one personally appeared before me Peter Bard Esqʳ one of His majestys Council for the Province of New Jersey Richard French and acknowledged that he Signed Sealed and Delivered the within Instrument for the use therein mentioned

Peter Bard

DEED, RICHARD FRENCH TO HUGH HUDDY, 1714

To: all Chriſtian people to whome theſe preſents Shall Cum Know ye that I Richard ffrench of manſfield In ye County of Burlington & weſtern Deviſion of New Jerſey yeoman Eldeſt Son & heir of Thomas ffrench of yᵉ County of Burlington aforeſᵈ and Legate, To his Laſt Will & teſtamt for & In consideration of yᵉ sum of Seuenteen pounds Tenn Shillings have Remiſsed Releaſed altogeather for me my heirs Executors & Adminiſtrators Haue Quit claimed vnto Hugh Huddy of yᵉ town & County of Burlington

aforeſ^d Esqr for his full & peaceable poſseſsion & Seiſin being & to his
heirs & aſsignes all my Right Eſtate Title Claim vſe Intreſt & Demand
which I ye aforeſ^d Richard ffrench any time Had haue or In any wife
foreuer may haue or my heirs at any time hearafter may haue of or In
two Lotts of Land Leying In Burlington aforeſ^d Bounded as ffolloweth
vizt. the firſt being A Water Lott Containing Eight foot ffront vpon y^e
River Dellaware Abutting North vpon ye Said River & South vpon ye
Back Street & Eaſt upon ye Land of ye said Thomas ffrench and Weſt
upon Richard Baſnett

The other: A Wharff Lott Lotted out for ye propriety of thomas olives
which propriety Lott is bounded with the High Street North Eaſt & a
Littell alle Leying on ye South Weſt side of John Hollinſhead Houſe &
ffrunting North Weſt upon ye River Dellaware & South Eaſt upon ye
back ſtreet Containing Twenty ffive ffoot frunt vpon ye River aforeſ^d; So:
yt Neither I ye aforeſd Richard ffrench my heirs or any other by vs or In
our Names any Right, Estate title Claim vſe Intreſt or Demand of and In
the said Lotts of Land bounded as Aboue and premiſses Nor In any parcell
thereof may or ought to Require Claime or Challenge But from Every
Action Right title claim vſe Intreſt or Demand to the aforeſaid premiſses
or to Any parcell thereof wee are altogeather Excluded & for euer Debarred
by theſe preſents.

In. Witneſs. whereof I ye said Richard ffrench haue Heirvnto Sett my
hand & Seale this twenty Second day of May one Thouſand seven Hundred
And ffourteen Sealed & Deliuered In ye preſence of vs

Richard Allison : ⎫
W S: Martinaux ⎬   Richard ffrench [SEAL]
Joseph Reckleſs ⎭

DEED, RICHARD FRENCH TO HIS SON THOMAS, 1729/30

This Indenture made the Sixth day of ye Eleventh Month Commonly
called January in ye year of our Lord one thousand S·ven hundred and
twenty nine Thirty & in the third year of ye Reign of King George y^e
Second over England &c.

Betweene Richard French of the township of Mancefeild & County of
Burlington in ye Weſt diviſion of new Jerſey yeoman of the one part and
Thomas french Son of ye afore named Richard French of ye same Townſhip County & division afores^d Sadler of ye other Part Witneſseth that ye
said Richard French for & in conſideration of ye Sum of tenn pounds of
Good Current money of Weſt Jerſey to him in hand by his said ſon but
more Eſpecially for and in Conſideration of ye Love good Will and affection that he hath & bareth towards his sd ſon hath Given Granted Bargained
& sold Alined Enfeoffed Conveyed and Confirmed & by theſe preſents

Doth fully freely Clearly & abfolutely Give grant Bargain & sell Alien
Enfeoffe Convey & Confirme unto his said son Thomas French and to his
heirs & Afsignes for ever one Certaine peice parcel or Tract of Land situated Lying & being in yᵉ Township of Mancefield & County of Burlington
aforesaid Containing ninty six acres & by yᵉ survey thereof it lyeth thus
bounded. Begineth at a small Black oak for a Corner in yᵉ line of
Preserve Brown's Land & runs from thence a long by yᵉ line of yᵉ Land
of Jacob Decows & Joseph Pancoast Southwestwardly fifty two degrees
fifty Eight Chains to a post by a Hickery tree marked for a corner & from
thence it Runs south Eastly seventy Degrees thirty four Chains by ye
Land of Caleb Shreve to a White oake Corner Thence Nort Eaftwardly
thirty two Degrees fourteen Chains & a half to a Maple tree for Corner
& from thence Nort Eaftwardly Seven degrees thirty five Chain & three
rod to the Corner first named Containing ninety six acres as a foresᵈ it
being part of the Land adjoyning to yᵉ farm & plantation Whereon ye
sᵈ Richard French now Inhabiteth & is a part of that four Hundred &
sixty acres of Land that he the sd Richard French purchafed of William
Biddle by Deed baring date yᵉ Eighteenth day of November Anno Domini
1693 & is Recorded in ye publick Records of Weft Jersey in book B
page 355 & 356) Relation being thereunto had it doth & will more fully
and more at Large appear Togather with all & every yᵉ Mines Minerals
Woods Ways Waters fowlings fifhings Huntings Hawkings & all other
Royalties franchifes powers profits Comodities Hereditaments & appurtenances whatsoever unto ye said Ninty six Acres of Land belonging
or in any wife appertaining alfo all yᵉ Estate Right Title Intreft ufe
pofsefsion property Claim and Demand whatfoever of him yᵉ said Richard
French Either in Law or Equity of in to or out of yᵉ said Granted land &
premifes or any part or parcell thereof and yᵉ Reverfion Reverfions
Remainder & Remainders thereof & of every part thereof To have & to
hold the said pcice parcell or tract of Land situated limited & bounded as
in maner above Exprefsed and Containing Ninty Six Acres as aforesaid &
all & singular other yᵉ before mentioned and Intended to be Granted &
bargained premifes & every part & parcel thereof with their and every
of their appurtenances unto ye said Thomas French his heirs and Afsignes
for Ever to ye onely Proper Ufe benefit & behoofe of him yᵉ sd Thomas
French his Heirs and Afsignes for Ever more and yᵉ said Richard French
yᵉ father Doth Covenant for himfelf his heirs Executˢ & Administˢ that
at the time of yᵉ sealling and Delivery of thefe prefents is Lawfully &
Rightfully seazed in the above mentioned & defcribed tract of Land &
Granted & Bargained premifses of a good sure perfect & Indefeazable
Estate of Inheritance in fee simple And hath in himself good Rightfull
power lawfull & abfolute Authority to Give Grant Bargain & Sell yᵉ Same
unto yᵉ said Thomas French his heirs & Afsignes for ever So that now
yᵉ said Thomas French his Heirs & Afsignes shall & may from time to time

& at all times for Ever hereafter peaceably & Quiatly have hold Ufe
ocqupie pofsefs and Injoy all yᵉ above mentioned & defcribed ninty six
Acres of Land & Granted premifes with all & every of their appurtenances
without yᵉ Lawfull let suit Trouble Deniall Eviction Ejection Molleftation
or other Interruption of him yᵉ sᵈ Richard French his Heirs Execut⁵ Adminiſt⁵ or any other person or persons whatfoever But against himfelfe
yᵉ said Richard French his heirs Executors or Adminiſt⁵ & against all &
every other person or perfons whatsoever having or Claiming or that shall
or may at any time hereafter have or Claim any lawfull Estate Right Title
or Intreſt of into or of the said Granted Land & premifses or any part or
percel thereof shall & will warrant & for ever defend by thefe prefents In
Witnefs whereof the sd Richard French hath sot to his Hand & seal yᵉ
Day & year first above Written 1729/30.

Richard French with a [SEAL]

Signed Sealed and Delivered In the prefents of Edmond Jones, Joseph
Stockton Job Stockton Tho Scattergood

Be it Remembered that on the Twenty Sixth Day of March In the
Year of our Lord one Thousand Seven Hundred & Thirty Three Perfonally
Appeared before me Peter Bard Esqʳ one of his Majestys Councell for
the Province of New Jerfey Edmond Jones who being sworn on yᵉ holy
Evangelist of Almighty God Did Declare he was Prefent & saw Richard
French sign seale & Deliver the Within Inftrument for ye ufe Within
mentioned

Peter Bard

Recorded June 21ᵗʰ 1733 p P. B—S.

WILL OF RICHARD FRENCH, 1745

Whereas I Richard French of Mansfield Township in County of Burlington in the western Division of the province of New Jersey this Twenty
fourth day of the Seventh Month in the year of our Lord One Thousand
Seven Hundred and fforty ffive being very weak and Sick in Body but of
perfect mind and Memory thanks be Given unto Almighty God therefore
And for all Mercies Daily received and knowing it's Appointed for all
men once to die do make and ordain this my last Will and Testament in
the following manner and form that is to Say Principally and first of all
I give and Recommend my soul into the hands of God that gave it and as
for my Body I Recommend it to the Earth to be Buried in a Christian
like And Decent Manner at the Discresion of my Executor hereafter
Named, and as touching such Worldly estate wherewith it hath pleased
God To Blefs me with all in this life I give Devise and Beftow of ye
same in the following Manner—Imprimus it is my mind and will that all
my Just Debts and funeral Expences and also the Annuity and all Legacies

hereafter Exprefsed be by my Executor well and Truly paid and performed in Convenient Time After my Decease ITEM I give and Bequeath unto my well beloved and Espoused Wife Mary French Ten pounds of good Current Money of West Jersey to be paid to her Yearly and Every year so long as she Continues to be my widow but no Longer to be paid by my said Executor I also give unto my said Wife all the Beding and Furniture belonging to ye Back Room of my house wherein we now lodge and allso to have the priviledge of ye Said Room to Dwell in so long as She Continues to be my Widow as aforesaid also I order that my Said Executor shall keep a Good Horfe and a Good Cow for my said Wife at all Seasons during her Widowhood as aforesaid And also to procure Firewood for her Sufficient for her own ufe during her Widowhood as aforesaid ITEM I give unto my son Richard French the full and Just Sum of Five Shillings Current Money of West Jersey being in full of his Portion he being Advanced by me before this time ITEM I give and bequeath unto my son Thomas French the like Sum of five Shillings of Like money aforesaid he likewise having been by me heretofore advanced ITEM I give and bequeath unto my Son Benjamin French and also to my Son Jonathan French That is to Say to each of them the full and Just Sum of Twenty pounds Current Money of West Jersey aforesaid to be paid unto each of them within ye Term of two years after my Decease ITEM I give and Bequeath unto my Daughter Elizabeth Scholey the Now Wife of William Scholey the Sum of five Shillings Current Money as the aforesaid She being by me heretofore Advanced

ITEM I give and Bequeath unto my Daughter Mary Brown the now Wife of Preserve Brown the Sum of Five Shillings of Like Money aforesaid She having likewise been by me heretofore Advanced

ITEM I give and Bequeath unto my Daughter Rebekah Shreve the Now Wife of Benjamin Shreve the like Sum of five Shillings of Like Money aforesaid She also having been by me heretofore advanced

ITEM I give and bequeath unto my Daughter Sarah Marling the now Wife of William Marling the like Sum of five Shillings of Like Money aforesaid She also having been by me heretofore Advanced

ITEM I give and Bequeath unto my Daughter Abigail Taylor the Now Wife of Jacob Taylor ye like sum of five Shillings of Like Money aforesaid She also having been by me heretofore Advanced

ITEM All and singular other the Remainder of my Estate both real and Perfonall I give bequeath and Devise unto my Son William French and to his heirs and afsigns forever to Enable him to pay my Just Debts and Legacies And I do also make and Ordain him my said Son William French to be my only whole and Sole Executor of this my Last Will and testament Revoking making Null and Utterly Void all other Wills or Will Testament and Executors by me at any time heretofore

made and Bequeathed Ratifying and Confirming this 'and no other to be
my Last Will and Testament　In Witneſs whereof I have hereunto Set
my hand and Seal the day and year being first above written.

Sign'd Sealed published pronounced
& declared by the said—Richard
French as his Last Will & Testament
in the presence of Us the Subscribers, Vizt

Richard French

William Sunderland Benjamin Shreeve & Samuel Harris the witneſses
to the within Written Will being duly affirmed according to Law did
Declare that they Saw Richard ffrench the Testator within Named Sign
& Seal the Same and heard him publish Pronounce and Declare the
within Instrument to be his Last Will and Testament and that att the
Doing thereof the Said Testator was of Sound & Disposing Mind &
Memory as far as these affirmants Know and as they verily Believe and
that they Severally Subscribed their names as witneſs thereto in the
presence of the Testator

Affirmed at Burlington the Ninth Day
of November Anno Dom; 1745　Before me

William French Sole Executor in the within Testament Named being duly affirmed according to Law did declare that the within Instrument contains the True Last Will & Testament of Richard French the Testator therein Named So far as he knows and as he verily beleives and that he will well and truly perform the Same by paying first the Debts of the Said Deceased & then the Legacies in the Said Testament Specified So far as the Goods Chattels and Credits can thereunto Extend and that he will make & Exhibit into the Prerogative Office in Burlington a True and Perfect Inventory of all and Singlar the Goods Chattels & Credits of the Said Deceased that Shall come to his Knowledge or Pofsefsion or to the Pofsefsion of any other Person or Persons for his use and render a Just and True account when thereunto Lawfully required.

Affirmed at Burlington
November y⁰ 9ᵗʰ; 1745 before me

Joˢ Scattergood Surrogate

INVENTORY OF THE ESTATE OF RICHARD FRENCH, 1745

A True and perfect Inventory of all the Goods and Chattells Rights & Credits of Richard French Late of the Township of Mansfield in County of Burlington in the Western Division of New Jersey (Deceased) Taken the Twenty fifth Day of the Eighth Month in the year of Our Lord 1745.

	£	s.	d.
To his Purſe & Apparrel & Debts Standing Out...	47	08	
To Two Indentures on Two Servants	19	00	
To Fourteen Horſes Mares & Colts	79	10	
To Thirty Three Neat Cattle	76	10	
To Twenty Two Sheep	7	10	
To Fifty fat Swine & Fifty Young Steres	73	00	
To Twelve Acres of Indian Corn	18	00	
To Seven Acres of Winter Grain in the Ground...	4	04	
To Wheat Rye Oats & Hay in the Barn	24	10	
To Hay sold & in ye Barrack & Stacks	23	00	
To Buck Wheat in Stack	2	10	
To An Apple-Mill, Cyder & Casks	12	00	
To Waggon, Cart, Sled, Gears & Ox Chains.......	16	16	
To Ploughs, Harrow, & Harrow Teeth &c...... ⎫ & a Cheeſe Preſs......................... ⎭	ᴄ	ᴄ	
To Tar in a Barrel		5	
To Sundrys in the Cellar	4	15	
In the Hall, To Sundry Goods & Furniture.......	22	12	8
In the Kitchen, To Sundry Goods & Furniture....	11	15	6
To Sythes, Axes Cycles & Hoes & Sundrys........	5	00	0
In the New Room To y⁰ Furniture thereof........	20	15	0

	£	s.	d.
In the Hall Chamber To Goods & Furniture......	19	10	—
In the New Room Loft To Sundrys	2	18	—
In the Milk House Loft to Furniture	12	00	—
In the Buttery To Sundrys	4	06	6
Carry'd Over	513	00	8
To Brought Over ....£	513	00	8
To Flax, Baggs, a Grindle Stone & Sundrys......	3	00	0
In the Back Room, vizt.			
To One Large Pewter Dish & 1/2 Doz Plates & Four Spoons & a Warming pan }...	3	00	0
To 1/2 Doz pewter porringers a Box Iron 2 Heaters Mortar and pestel }...		10	
To One Feather Bed & Furniture & 3 Sheets......	12	00	
To One Walnut Case of Drawers	4	10	
To a Tea Table and Furniture	1	5	
To Five Chairs & a Small Box		18	
To Two Table Cloths & Five Napkins		10	
To One Looking Glaſs		5	
To One Oak Chest		6	
To One Side Saddle	2	10	
Total	542	14	8

Samuel Wright
Michael Newbold
Barzillai Newbold

Samuel Wright Michael Newbould & Barzillai Newbould the appraisors of the annexed Inventory being Duly affirmed did Declare that the Goods Chattels & Credits in the Said Inventory Set down and Specifyed were by them appraised according to their Just and True respective rates and vallues after the best of their Judgment & understanding & that they appraised all things that were brought to their view for appraisement
Affirmed at Burlington the ninth
day of November A D, 1745
Before me   Joˢ Scattergood Surrogate

William French Sole Executor of the Last Will & Testamᵗ of Richard ffrench Decᵈ being duly affirmed according to Law did Declare that the annexed Writing contains a True and Perfect Inventory of all and Singular the Goods Chattels & Credits of the Said Deceased so far as hath come to his Poſseſsion or Knowledge or to the Poſseſsion of any other Person or Persons for his use
Affirmed at Burlington the 9ᵗʰ
day of November A. D. 1745
Before me   Joˢ Scattergood Surrogate

THOMAS SCATTERGOOD

Thomas Scattergood, progenitor of the family in this country, with his wife Elizabeth, came from Stepney Parish, London, England, with the Burlington pioneers, in 1677. He settled on a tract of 160 acres near the present site of Columbus, New Jersey, on Craft's creek, living for many years in a cave dwelling, where he raised a family of nine children. His only neighbors in the beginning were Indians, with whom he held kindly relationship, ever after maintained. He was an earnest minded Friend and so trained his children that they became useful members of the Society. He signed the testimony issued by Friends against George Keith in 1692.

The will of Thomas Scattergood, dated November 3rd, 1697, proved November 27th, mentioned his sons Thomas, Joseph and Benjamin; son-in-law Thomas Brian, husband of Elizabeth Scattergood, then deceased; daughters Sarah French, Hannah Pancoast, Tomsin Pancoast; servant Mary Records; son Benjamin, Executor, with Richard French (son-in-law), William Pancoast and Nathaniel Records as overseers. The inventory of personal estate, dated November 11th, 1697, showed a valuation of £125 5s. 6p.

Thomas Scattergood, Junior, was born in England, in 1668. On "ye 17th day of ye 11th mo. called January, 1694" he was married to Phoebe, daughter of Christopher Wetherill, and she became an active member of Burlington Meeting. He was clerk of Burlington Meeting from 1714 to 1738, and was very frequently appointed representative to Yearly Meeting. In 1730 he first appeared as a representative in the Yearly Meeting of Ministers. He was evidently regarded in the community as a man of superior clerical attainments and a wise counsellor concerning material things. He seems to have drawn many wills and other important papers, and his name as a witness appears in many places in the records of the time. His son Joseph, for a time mariner with Thomas Chalkley, in the West Indian trade, afterwards studied law and became Surrogate of Burlington county. His signature appears in connection with the probating of the will of Richard French. He was a citizen of estimable character, and his memory is perpetuated by a notable tombstone in the Friends' Burying Ground at Burlington, the inscription upon which is given elsewhere. His son Thomas (3rd) became an eminent Friends' minister, and from 1783 to 1814 his influence in that capacity was widely felt. He travelled considerably in England and the colonies, and left a voluminous journal which holds a high place in Friends' literature.

It will be noted that two of the daughters (Hannah and Tomsin) of Thomas Scattergood the elder, married Pancoasts. An old document in the possession of Henry Pancoast of Mesopotamia, Ohio, shows the origin of the Pancoasts in America. The following is an exact copy:

"Joseph Pancoast, son of John and Elizabeth Pancoast of Ashen, fieve miles from Northampton Town, in Northampton Shire (Eng.) born 1672, the 27th of eighth month, called October; and in the year, 1680. Oct. 4th came into America in the ship "Paradise," William Evelyn, Master; and I settled in West New Jersey, Burlington County, and on the 14th of the eighth month, October, 1696, I took to wife Thomasine Scattergood, daughter of Thomas and Elizabeth Scattergood, of Stepney Parish, London, who also transported themselves into Burlington County, in America,"

William Pancoast and Hannah Scattergood were married ye fifth day of ye 3rd month 1695.

CHESTERFIELD MEETING (Crosswicks)

The first religious organization perfected within the limits of Chesterfield township, Burlington county, N. J., was Friends' Meeting at Crosswicks in 1677, and held at the house of Thomas Lambert. In 1684 a monthly meeting was established, and held at Francis Davenport's This was called Chesterfield Monthly Meeting of Friends, by which name it is still known.

First Month 5th, 1691, it was "proposed to build a Meeting house at ye burying ground at Chesterfield." This ground had been given to the Friends by Thomas Foulke, and a deed of trust made to Francis Davenport, Samuel Bunting, John Bunting, Thomas Gilberthorpe, Roger Parke and Robert Wilson. On the 7th of ye 11 mo. 1691 "Francis Davenport, Samuel Andrews, William Wood, Samuel Bunting and Thomas Gilberthorpe were appointed to treat with the carpenters." On 10 mo. 4th 1691, this committee reported they had let the work to John Green, and the Meeting house was to be placed on a portion of the six acres of land which Samuel Bunting and John Bunting on 3 mo. 3d 1693, deeded to Robert Murfin, John Abbott, Edward Rockhill and John Willsford for ten shillings, as Trustees for Chesterfield Monthly Meeting. These six acres adjoined the burial ground. The first meeting was held in this building "ye 6th of ye 8 mo. 1693," and

CHESTERFIELD MEETING HOUSE, CROSSWICKS, N. J., 1776

in 11th mo. 1693 the Committee reported, "that they had paid John Green £40, and for buy work £1, also had given him 2 shillings over and above." The building was of frame.

On 1st mo. 7th 1706 Francis Davenport and William Wood were appointed to see after the building of a new brick Meeting house, which was located near the top of the hill, on the ground since used as a burial place. It was finished about the autumn of 1707, and used for nearly half a century.

4th mo. 5th 1753 " This Meeting thinking it needful that this house should be Repared and some Adition made thereto for the Servife of ye Women's Meetings, do appoint John Sykes, John Thorne, Joseph Thorne, Preserve Brown, William Morris, Thomas Middleton and George Middleton to confider what Repares will be wanted, and how the Adition propofed can beft be done and Repoart to the next Monthly Meeting."

5th mo. 3d 1753 " The friends appointed Concerning the Repairs and Inlargement of the Meeting House Repoart that it is there opinion that a Linto added to the North Side of the house sixteen foot wide will be the Moft Convenient.   The Meeting Concurs therewith and orders it to be Reported to the Quarterly Meeting for theire approbation Likewife."

6th mo. 7th 1753 " The Inlargement of this Meeting house having ben Confidered And Gained the Approbation of the Quarterly Meeting Therefore the Meeting Concludes to proceed And Apoints John Sykes, Preserve Brown and George Middleton to Manage the Same according to the plan Concluded on with all possible Speed."   No mention is made of the date of the completion of these repairs and enlargement.

1st mo. 7th 1773 " The Treasurer of the Monthly Meeting produced the account of the cost of a stove for the Meeting house 8– 4s. 10d."   This stove was cast from New Jersey iron ore at Atsion Furnace, Burlington Co., N. J.   It was placed in this second Meeting-house; and when the present house was finished, it was removed to it, and is still there (1907).

2d mo. 4th 1773 The subject of again enlarging the Meeting-house was introduced, but it was finally concluded to build a new one, which is the present structure, and is near the site of the first one.   It was completed in 1776.   When the British troops marched from Philadelphia on their way to Monmouth, in 6th mo. 1778, a detachment attempted to cross the bridge at Crosswicks.   The American stationed on the north side under General Dickinson in endeavoring to prevent them from crossing, shot three cannon

s

balls into the Meeting-house; two through the roof and one into the brick wall. The imprint of this latter ball is still visible, as shown in the accompanying picture. The ball measures three inches in diameter and weighs three and a half pounds. It is in possession of a resident of Crosswicks. The Meeting-house, soon after the battle of Trenton, was occupied by the American soldiers for a barracks. On First days the benches were arranged and meetings held there as usual. Many descendants of the pioneer Friends reside in and about Crosswicks and keep up the society as during the reign of their ancestors.

ANCIENT MEETING RECORDS

The following is a preface taken from the original book of minutes of Chesterfield Monthly Meeting, commencing 2nd of 8th Mo. 1684:

It hath Pleased the Mighty God And Great Jehova in this Last Age After the Greate night of Darkenefs and Appostacy Which hath Spred over Nations Kinereds tongues And People Since thofe Glorious Dayes in Which the Appoftles Lived by his outftretched Gathering Arme and by ye Word of his Etternal Power, To Gatherd People Who was Weary of All dead formes, And outfide Profefsions into A Waiting frame of fpirit Wheare Wee dorst Not thinke our owne thoughts nor fpeake our owne words in things Relating to his kingdom And Way of Worfhipe and being thus Brought down By ye Mighty Power of God Wee was ye more Cappable to Receve Councell and inftructions from him, Who through And by his fon Christ Jefus the tru Light y^t Lighteth Every one y^t Cometh in to ye World Appeared in us And tought us his way and Worfhipe whitch is in fpirit and truth this hee tought us While Wee Was in old England our native Land whitch Wee may fay through the Great mercy of ye Lord wass in this Latter Age the firft of Nattions Wheare the Lord Appeard in foe Mighty A Power And Bright fhining Glory to ye Gathering of thoufands into his fould Wheareby his People Became A Body Whereof Christ is ye head And then the Lord our God As hee Did unto Paul And ye Elders of ye Churches in ye Appostels Dayes begot A Godly Care in ye harts of fum of his People Whome hee had Gathered and brought in to a Living fense of his Worke in this day and Also of the Misteryous Working of the Enemy of All Good, who in All Ages as ye fcriptures, of truth fully teftifyes Laboured by his fubtilty and transforming to draw ye Lords People in to Loosenefs and Disorder that fo the Pretious truth and the puer Way of the Lord might be dishonoured and his Worthy name Blafphemed. Wee fay the Lord hath fet fum as Watchmen Uppon y^e Walls of Jerufalem and hath Laid A Godly Care and A Nefsefity upon fum of his People that All things in this Churches of Christ may be kept

CHESTERFIELD MEETING HOUSE, REAR VIEW

O shows mark of Revolutionary cannon ball, 1778

ſweet and Clean and yᵗ Mariages and All other things Relateing to yᵉ Church affaires may be Performed in yᵉ Good order of the Goſpell of Peace therefore in the Wiſedome And Councill of God it was ſeene mete that first daies And Weekely Meettings might be Appointed And Diligently kept unto for Eddification and yᵉ Worshiping of god And yᵗ Monthly Quarterly And yearly meetings might be Appointed and dilligently kept unto by all ſutch, who are of An honest Converſation as becomes truth and have the Weights of the Lords Worke in this our day and the Care of the Churches upon them for the ſettling and ordering affairs thereof, and to Admonish and Give Advice unto ſuch As ſtand in neede of it and yᵉ Lord by his Providence And mighty Power hath brought ſum of his People out of their Native Countery over the Great Deepe into this Wilderneſs and Remote Part of the World As Weſt Jersey And Places Ajacent Whear as hee hath Laid the ſame Weight and Care upon ſum of us as hee Did in ouer Native Land that All things may be Well Amongst us to yᵉ honouer of his Great And Worthy name Which is the Ground And End of this following Booke   John Wilsford
                                                                              ffrancis Davenport
                                                                              William Watſon

The following minute is from the same book and more particularly relates to Women's Meetings.

All Deare friends Both Men and Women When you Com to Meete About buſnis As Well As to other Meetings wait to ſeele ye power of god yᵗ ſo what you doe in things Relating to Church affairs May be Doone, in yᵉ Power which is over All decept and Disorder And then if Aney ſhould be ſo ſtuborn or Wilfull As to Appose What you Doe or to Reject your Councils or Advice the will Appose and Reject yᵉ Power of God wᶜʰ is the higher Power to Which All ſhould be ſubject both in them ſelves And in others in whome it Appeares which Power will ſtand over All yᵗ is Unruly and Rebellious And As to yᵉ Womens Meetings I Certainly know they have A Cervis for God in his Church and yᵉ Lords Power doth often Attend theire Aſſemblyes in A wonderfull manner And he hath made yᵐ And Will Make ſuch Who keepe in yᵉ Power of God to Anſwer yᵉ End for wᶜʰ they was Created (viz) to be helpe meete As yᵉ Wooman was in yᵉ begining while ſhee ſtood in Godſ Councill but when ſhee Left yᵗ And tooke Council of ye Serpent ſbee be Came hurtful to ye Man ſoe All ſhold keepe in ye Power of God that ſoe they may Receive Councils from him ſoe Will they be Coeworkerſ And fellow Labourʳˢ And helpe on in the Worke of the Lord the Elder inſtruckting the younger as yᵉ holy Woomen did in the Dayes of old

Dear friends in the Love of God are theſe few Lines written And in ye ſame I Deſire they May be Receved.

yᵉ 1: of yᵉ 12ᵗʰ mᵒ: John Wilſford
    168⅞

6—THOMAS FFRENCH, JR. (Thomas, 1).

> b. 1667.
>> Baptized October 31st, 1667, at Church S. S. Peter and Paul, Nether Heyford, England.
>
> d. 1745, buried in Friends' Burying Ground, Chester Meeting, Moorestown, N. j.
>
> m. First, 10th mo. 3rd, 1696, "5th day of week at Friends' Meeting House," Mary Allen, daughter of Judah and Mary Allen of Shrewsbury, N. j.
>> She d. about 1730.
>
> m. Second, 8th mo. 9th, 1732, Mary (Pearce) Cattell, widow of Jonas Cattell, whom she had married 2nd mo. 8th 1714, at the house of James Shinn.

32—JOSEPH FRENCH	b. 7th mo. 23rd, 1698.
33—THOMAS FRENCH, 3RD	b. 8th mo. 27th, 1702. m. May 8th, 1746, Jemima Elkinton.
34—JUDITH FRENCH	d. young.
35—ROBERT FRENCH	b. 6th mo. 1707. m. 10th mo. 1737, Hannah Cattell.
36—EDWARD FRENCH	d. 1740, unmarried.
37—MARY FRENCH	m. First, April 15th, 1736, Nathan Middleton. m. Second, 9th mo. 17th, 1761, George Matlack.

THOMAS FRENCH, JR.

Thomas French, Jr., second son of Thomas ffrench, progenitor, inherited the vigorous qualities of his father in a marked degree, and received, as a special token of parental favor, a deed of gift, conveying to him 300 acres of desirable land. A facsimile of this ancient document, dated 1694, is herewith given. The estate was located in Chester township, Burlington county, between the north branch of Pensaukin creek and what is now West Moorestown. It adjoined that of notable families of the pioneer

This Indenture Do the nineteenth day of this month called February

On the year according to English Accompt one thousand eight hundred ninety and four ——

Between Thomas ffrench of Wollingaccomp... in the County of Burlington in the Province of West
Jersey yeoman of the one part And Thomas ffrench Senor of the offoresaid Thomas ffrench
the younger of the other part Witnesseth that the said Thomas ffrench Senor (for and in Consideration
of the naturall affection goodwill and ffeelings which he hath and beareth unto his well Beloved
Sonn Hath given granted and Confirmed and by these presents Doth give grant and Confirme
unto the said Thomas ffrench the younger ... and off ... for and all that ... land & Meesuages &c

... more perticular... Cort begun and ... in the market of the said ... and over the bridge
by the said Buriall burss of Burs Northeast twenty one ... having & Sept by the
twenty five ... unto Thomas Redman ... then by the Same Eastnor East ffifty five ... thence
to the Black oak for ... to the northwest Nett garrity thence to a nett oak for the Come ...
southwest ... to the Land of Thomas Wiatt's Garden north East Southwest about ... then
Southwest more (and leaving to the west and for the ... the Southwest by the well Run) ...
Land by the ... into the said Creek and ...

... And allso all that acres of upland and meadow containing twenty acres ...
... ffrench hath Land together with the ... many meeuall ... ffishing landings ...
and ffeelings And ... every of the ... profitts and Comodities and ...
to the said premises ... to have & to hold the said premises ...

Thomas Brooks

Wm Michell
his

Thomas Cobb

Peter

February 23 1697

period, and its energetic owner soon became prominent and influential in the business, political, social and religious life of the community. He was the first tax collector of the township, being appointed in 1693, and again, by the Governor, in 1701. He also held the same office in 1723. In 1699 he was overseer of highways. In 1705 he was chosen constable, in 1707 overseer of the poor, and served as freeholder 1713–14, 1720 and 1725 to 1728.

In many ways, official and unofficial, Thomas French, junior, as he was known long after his father's death, aided in the development of the resources of the section where he resided for half a century. He was always active in the affairs of the Society of Friends, and was one of the trustees, with Mathew Allen, his brother-in-law; John Hollinshead, Joseph Heritage, Sarah Roberts, Timothy Hancock and seven other prominent Friends, to whom James Adams and Esther his wife conveyed by deed dated 2nd mo. (April) 9, 1700, the ground upon which the first meeting house at Moorestown was built the same year. His first wife, Mary Allen, belonged to a family active in the affairs of the early settlement at Shrewsbury, N. J., and with her he became a useful member of the Newton and later Haddonfield Monthly Meetings of Friends. His second wife, Mary Cattell, was likewise very active in the affairs of Haddonfield Monthly Meeting of Women Friends, being an overseer for ten years. Their names appear in many places in the remarkable record kept by Elizabeth (Haddon) Estaugh for over fifty years. Thomas was frequently appointed as representative to quarterly meetings, then held alternately at Newton, Haddonfield and Salem, and also to Yearly Meeting, at Burlington and Philadelphia; and served on various important meeting committees. Part of the original estate of Thomas French, junior, comprised the homestead property on the north side of the Camden turnpike, near West Moorestown, which remained in the family for nearly two hundred years.

RECORD OF MARRIAGE

The following is taken from an ancient Shrewsbury record.

1696, 3d of 10th mo., (in margin 9th of 4 mo., 1697), Thomas French, Jr., living in West Jersey, near Burlington, md. Mary Allen, of Shrews., 5th day of week at Friends' Meeting House:

Wits:	Thomas French, Jr.,
Thomas French	Her
Caleb Allen	Mary × French
George Allen	mark

Remembrance Lippincott	Mary Forman
John Woolley	Her
John Hance	Hannah X Allen
ffranses Borden	mark
Elizabeth Lippincott	Margrett Lippincott
Hanna Allen	Lidya Woolly
Margrett Leeds	Marcy Woolly
Elizabeth Hance	Elizabeth Allen
Elizabeth Hooton	Elizabeth Allen
Ann Lippincott	Mary Tillton
Jane Borden	John Lippincott
Nathaniell Slocom	Jedidiah Allen

MEETING RECORDS

Newton Monthly Meeting Minutes. Haddonfield Quarter:

8th of 11th mo. 1710. Att ye Afores^d meeting John Hollingshead Complaynes y^t the ffriends undernamed have Joyned with ye Inhabitants of Chester township in A legall process for the forcing of s^d John to maintaine a caseway at Ancokus ferry the meeting appoynts George Smith and Thomas Shackle to Desyer John Copperthwaite, Joseph Herritge, Thomas French, Thomas Adams and John Roberts to Appeare at the next monthly meeting to answare the Afores^d Objections.

At a monthly meeting held at the house of Thomas Shackle ye 8th of 6th mo. 1715. At s^d meeting Thomas French is appointed to be one of the overseers for the upper meeting in the Room & Stead of John Hollingshead.

10–12 mo. 1721. At said meeting ye Overseer being Enquired of Signify viz ye friends of ye upper meeting that y^e are uneasy with ye Conduct of Thomas French as an Overseer therefore Joseph Heritage is Desiered to Acquaint him that he make his appearance at our next monthly meeting.

12–1 mo. 1722. At s^d meeting whereas at our last monthly meeting it was signified that there was an uneasiness with some friend Concerning Thomas French being an Overseer, upon which he was Desiered to appear at this meeting; he accordingly hath appeared and Signified that what omissions hath happened by him in the Execution of his Office was because he thought it not to belong to his present Service at that time, therefore this meeting hath thought fitt and doth Appoint Samuel Atkinson to Act in ye room of Thos. French as overseer of that mtg.

Haddonfield Monthly Meeting Minutes:

11–7–mo. 1732 At said meeting Thomas French and Mary Cattle ye first time signifyed their intentions of taking each other in marriage, therefore Thos. Hackney & Thos. Lippincott are appointed to make inquiry as is usual & are desired to make their answer to our next monthly meeting.

9-8-mo. 1732 At said meeting Thomas French and Mary Cattle y⁰ second time signified their intentions of taking each other in marriage, therefore after this meeting rec'd satisfaction concerning his clearness with others on y⁰ account of marriage & of his conversation consents that they may take each other according to y⁰ good order used amongst us and appoint Abraham Chattin & Constantine Wood to be present at said marriage to see it orderly accomplished.

13-9-mo. 1732. At said meeting y⁰ friends appointed report that they were present at y⁰ marriage of Thos. French & Mary Cattle & that it was orderly accomplished.

Haddonfield Minutes of y⁰ Mo: Meeting of Women Friends:
Att a m°ly m⁰g of wo^m fr^ds held at Haddonfield y⁰ 11th of 7^m 1732 At s^d m⁰g Tho. French & Mary Cattle signified y^r intentions of m⁰g y⁰ m⁰g a^Pts Hannah Hains & Mary Wood to make y⁰ uſual inquiry & report to next m° m⁰g.

Att a m°ly m⁰g of wo^m fr^ds held at Haddonfield y⁰ 9th of 8^m 1732 Tho French & Mary Cattle signified y⁰ continuation of y^r intentions of m^r g return of inquirs being clear y⁰ m⁰g conſents to y⁰ accompliſhm⁰ of y^r s^d m^r g & ap^ts Eliz. Gibson & Grace Chattin to see good orders kept & report to next m° m⁰g.

Att a m°ly m⁰g of wo^m fr^ds held at Haddonfield y⁰ 13th of 9^m 1732 reported y^t y⁰ afors^d m^r g was o^rdly accompliſhd.

PROCEEDINGS OF "TOWN-MEETINGS"

Following curious minutes are taken from an old "Town Book" of Chester Township, Burlington County, N. J.:

May 26-1692
Whereas several of the inhabitants have suffered several losses & damages through the Ill Con— of the Constable being not Ready at hand when Goods or cattle be stolen. Therefore to prevent & frustrate such ill minded persons in their evil d°signs we the Inhabitants of this Township of Chester Do mutually By all consents that if any person or persons do suffer any damage in his goods or Cattle by any such Ill Minded person shall forthwith if the Constable be not ready at that Instant present time take two or three of his Neighbors with him to the dwelling house of such person that is suspected & demand the person to Search and if suspected do denie &

Refuse to do the same they may take him upon suspicion before a Magistrate forthwith & there compalain against him.

We have hereunto Set our Hands.

mathew Allen
John Cowperthwaite
mount his MK Cox
      marke
Thomas his wallis
George his R Glave
    mark
William his W Matlack
    mark

Thomas ffrench
Robert Stiles
william Clark
Thrifta Siff
Richard Pillman
Charles his mark Steelman
Thomas his marke Clenerly
Samuell Burough
John Welker
John Raddepons

NOTE May 26–1692 The Inhabitants of Chester Township Mutually agreed that if any householder & Residenter in s^d Township doth neglect his service at mending of Bridges & highways within our Township having a lawful summons shall pay 3^s/0 pr day for default.

March 18- 1693

Whereas the Inhabitants of the Townshipp of Chester have had town meetting held this 18th day of March 1693. Sessors Chosen for the County Taxe also the same for the Provincial Taxe and also Colecttors for the collecting of the s^d Taxe.

Imprimiss

> John Ruderow
> James Sherwynn, Sessorss
> Thomas French, Collector

October ye 17th day 1698.

By virtue of A town [meeting] this day held att ye dwelling house of Thomas Wallis Acording to Order thereuppon Agreed the mageer part of ye free houlders of the Town Shipp of Chester Alias ponsoking in the county of Burlington to chosse Justa ffish for A Constable in the place of ffrederick King drafted to serve out the s^d ffr Kings twelve months, Imprimis secondid. To order five pounds Lawful money of the province to Any on[e] that will discover Hoggs stollen then make sufficient prooff to be payd by John Ruderow town Clarck as soon as it evidently appears.

Tersius—If Counstable Be not to be had neer & Redey when Goods lost or Cattell lost he that loosseth have any sussbishtion of Any on[e] in the townshippe he may take two or three sufficient neighbors & demand of the suspected the previlledge to sarch & if the suspected deny & Refuseth for to do su him foorth with upon susspisstion.

Those three Articles concluded upon By uss hear under written

Mathew Allen	Richard Pittman
George Greave	W^m: Clarke
Tho: Cleverly	Robert Stilles
Tho: Walles	John Walker
W^m: Matlacke	Justa ffish
John Cowperthwaite	mount Coxe
Tho: ffrench	Charles Stoolman
Samuall Buroughs	John Rudderow, Clk.

January 25, 1698

By virtue of a Town Meeting held here the day and year mentioned and the major part of the freeholders of this Township of Chester (alias Penshawken) met together and unanimously agreed with one consent to choose Constable and overseer of the High Ways, viz Mount Cox; Constable & Thomas French over-seer of the Highways.

Allso farther concluded And Condescended to have two Highways layd
out within the town viz. one and first from the Highway leading from
Burlington to Salem Actually layd out & markt By twelve men & the overseer to the Bridge now Remaining on the westerly Branch of ponsoakin
now called Cropwell near Richard Bromley. And the other leding from
the township of Evesham to A landing By William Matlack formerly called
ponsoaking now Chester River.

The names of the twelve men & the overseer y^t layd out ye Road

William Matlack	William Clarke
James Sherwyn	John Hollinshead
George Gleave	William Hollinshead
John Cowperthwaite	Anthony ffryer
Richard Pittman	James Adams
Robert Stiles	Joseph Heritage

Thomas ffrench Overseer of ye Hwys.

March 18–1698

Whereas the constable of our Town have Recd two Warrants VIZ one
for A provincial Taxe as followeth Every hundred acres of land surveyede
not Improved 3 pence & Every Acre of land fencid and Improved half
pence & every wagon Is 3d & Every neat cattell 3 pence & every hors 6
pence & every sheep halfe peny & every hog sould or disbosed 3 pence.

And in other for A county tax which is the two thirds of the provincial
Taxe that 3 four pence of Every part of the provincial Taxe.

These two warrants was excepted by the Township the 18 day of March
1698 and Sessors choosen VIZ James Sherwyn Jo Rudderow Also collector chosen for the gathering & paying In VIZ Thomas ffrench.

March 18–1698

" Whereas Several of the Inhabitants of this Township have been Bur—
and sufferers —— great loss & damage of several of the Inhabitants By
ill qualified persons of Hogg Hunters going out contrary to Law with
Dogs & Guns to kill their Neighbors Hoggs, therefore it is concluded upon
By the Major part, and the most well minded Men of this Township of
Chester—that if any person or persons do discover and make proof of the
same—he is to have for the discovery & make sufficient proof of, the sum

of 5£ to be paid him by John Rudderow or of the Inhabitants of the Township   Signed

Mathew Allen
William Clark
Robert Stilos
George (J) gleaue
Thomas ffrench
William his W marke Matlack
Hount his MK marke Coxe

Thomas walls
John Weffron
Gustasss
John Cowporthwaite
Samuell Burrough his S mark
Tho X his mark Clenerly
Charles his marke Leelman
Rikard Pittman
John Rudderow

And further it is concluded that if any suspected Person be found alone in the woods hunting of hogs with Gun & Dog without any of his neighbors along with him, he may be taken forth with before a Magistrate & thereto be ——— and Bound over to the next Court of Quarter Sessions. Concluded March 18–1698

A CURIOUS NEW JERSEY DOCUMENT OF 1707

Illustrating the charitable spirit of colonial days and the manner in which worthy unfortunates were looked after, a quaint paper appears among the old records in the office of the Secretary of State, Trenton, N. J., of which the following is a copy.

"Richard Ingoldesby, esquire, Lieutenant Governor of her Majesty's Province of New Jersey, New York, etc.

"To all Christian people by whom these presents shall come or may concern. Greeting: Whereas, to certificate made under the oaths and attestations of Thomas French and John Hollingshead, overseers of the poor, for the township of Chester in the County of Burlington, and other sufficient inhabitants of the said County taken before Theo. Revell, J. Bass, Robert Wheeler, John Ruderroe, and Wm. Heulings, justices of the peace for the County of Burlington that Francis Lee a lame and infirme man hath lately mett with a very great loss by fire having his house burnt down and all his clothes, tooles, provisions and household goods burnt and destroyed to the value of £90 and upwards, and it likewise appearing that the said Francis Lee without the charitable contributions of pious and well disposed Christians must of necessity fall to intolerable poverty and ruin. These therefore out of a tender compassion of his sufferings and loss. We consent and doe by these presents grant unto the said Francis Lee, leave lycense and authority to ask, collect and receive for his own use all such sum or sums of money or other things as shall be by any charitable Christians given him toward the repairing of his loss, and I doe likewise ernestly recommend to them the commiseration of the said Francis Lee as an offering highly acceptable to Almighty God hereby requiring and commanding all orthodox ministers or teachers in the several Churches or other religious societies in this province that they assist the said Francis Lee by exhorting and stirring up these and those to soe good and pious a work, and all church wardens are hereby required and commanded to make collections for him the said Francis Lee.

Given unto my hand and seale at Burlington this fifth day of October in the fifth year of the reign of our Sovereign Lady Anne by the grace of God, of England, Holland, France and Ireland, defender of the faith. Anno Dom. 1707"

It would seem that such a case as here noted must excite the general pity and sympathy of a well ordered community, but in this instance great feeling was created among certain classes, particularly on account of the extraordinary order of the Governor, requiring public collections in the churches, this being authoritatively addressed to "all orthodox ministers and teachers," and evidently was intended to include Friends as well as other non-conformist bodies, although the latter were as yet few in numbers and scarcely organized.

In the Township of Chester and County of Burlington Aprill ye 12th 1732

Surveyed off from that part of Clark Rodmans lands which he the said Rodman sould to Judah Allen Twenty two Acres and one Rood unto and for Thomas ffrench which is bounded as followeth viz.t Begining at a white Oak in the line of Joseph Heritages lands and Corner to part of the same tract sould To John Adams and Runs from Thence North Sixty Eight Degr Thirty Minutes East Thirteen Chains and Thirty links By the lands of the said Adams and Thirty Six Chains and Thirty nine links by the same Course to a Stone Corner to fords lands which together makes fortynine Chains an Sixty nine links to the Second Corner Thence by said fords lands North Twenty Seven Degr West five Chains an fifty links To a post in the D ffrenches line for a Third Corner Thence by the Same South Sixty five Degr west fortynine Chains and forty links to a Spanish Oak for a forth Corner Thence South Twenty five Degr East Three Chains an fifty Links to the Corner first above named surveyed pr me

Jacob Heulings

SURVEY OF LAND FOR THOMAS FRENCH, 1732

DEED, THOMAS FRENCH FROM HASKER NEWBERRY, 1737

This Indenture—made the twenty Seventh day of May in the year of our Lord one thousand Seven hundred and thirty Seven and in the tenth year of the Raign of King George the Second of Great Brittain &c Between Hasker Newberry, Hufbandman and Mary his Wife and Naomi Heritage Daughters and Heirises to John Heritage late of Waterford in the County of Gloucefter and Weftern Divifsion of New Jerfey Deceafed of the one part—And Thomas ffrench of the Township of Chefter in the County of Burlington within the Divifsion aforesaid Yoeman of the other part Whereas Edward Bylling and trustees by their Indentures of leafe & Releafe bearing date the twenty Sixth and twenty Seventh days of March Ano.: 1682 for the Confideration therein mentioned did Grant Bargain and Sell unto Isaac Martin Six full Equal and undivided five and twenty parts of a Propriaty within the Weftern Divifion aforesaid And the said Isaac Martin by his laft will and teftament made in Writing dated the twenty fourth day of November Ano 1682 among other things by him given did Will and Devise the same to Katherine his then Wife and afterward John Sibley did Intermarry with the Said Katherine Widdow Relict of the Said Isaac Martin, whereby the Said John Sibley became pofsefsed of and Legally vefted in the above mentioned land devifed and bequeathed by her former Hufband Isaac Martin as aforesaid And Whereas the Said John Sibley and Katharine his wife by their Indentures of Leafe and Releafe under their hands and Seals Duly Executed bearing date the thirty firft day of May and firft day of June Ano. 1696 for the Confideration therein mentioned did Grant Bargain and Sell unto Richard Heritage the above mentioned land which laft recited Indenture is Recorded in the Publick Records of the Divifion aforesaid in book C folio 179 & 180 Relation unto the feveral recited Indentures laft Will and testament and records being had may more at length appear. And the—Said Richard Heritage being So thereof Seized as aforesaid Died Inteftate whereby John Heritage Son and right heir at Law to his father Richard Heritage became pofsefsed and Legally vefted in the revertion of the aforesaid lands And afterwards the Said John Heritage died Inteftate Seized as aforesaid and left two Daughters Viz Mary and Naomi to whom the Said revertion of the above mentioned lands Defended by right of Inheritance and afterwards the Said Mary Heritage Did Intermarry with the Said Hasker Newberry one of the parties to thefe prefents Now this Indenture witnesseth that the Said Hasker Newberry and Mary his Wife and the Said Naomi Heritage for and in Consideration of the Sum of Thirty Eight Shillings Current Money of the Divifsion aforesaid to them or one of them in hand paid by the said Thomas ffrench the receipt whereof they the Said Hasker Newberry and Mary his wife and the Said Naomi Heritage doth hereby own and acknowledge thereof and every part and parcel thereof do hereby acquit Exonerate and Difcharge the Said Thomas ffrench his heirs Execut's and Adminift's and every of them fforever by these prefents hath granted Bargained and Sold Aliened Enfeofed Conveyed and Confirmed and by thefe prefents doth grant Bargain and Sell Alien Enfeof Convey and Confirm unto the Said Thomas ffrench and to his heirs and afsigns fforever THIRTY EIGHT ACRES of unlocated land to be taken up laid forth and Surveyed in any part of the Divifion aforesaid where the Same hath not been Surveyed and legally purchased of the Indians and to observe the laws rules Cuftoms and Methods of the Council of Propriators in that cafe made and PROVIDED TOGETHER with all the Mines Minerals quarries ffishings ffowlings Hawkings Huntings woods Swamps Ways Waters Water Courses and allso all and Singular other the rights royalties proffits Comodities Hereditaments and Appurtenances unto the Same belonging or in any wife appertaining of them the Said Hafker Newberry or Mary his Wife or Naomi Heritage both in Law and Equity and every part and parcel thereof To have and to hold the above granted and Bargained undivided Thirty Eight acres of land as the same is above Mentioned or Intended to be here in granted Bargained and Sold unto the Said Thomas ffrench his heirs and Afsigns unto the only proper ufe and behoof of the Said Thomas ffrench his heirs and assigns fforever And the Said Hasker Newberry and Mary his Wife and the Said Naomi Heritage for themselves and for all and every of their heirs Executors and Adminiftrators doth hereby Covenant Grant and Agree to and with the Said Thomas ffrench his heirs and afsigns and by thefe prefents that they the said Hafker Newberry and Mary his Wife and the Said Naomi Heritage at the time of the Enfealing and Delivery of thefe prefents are and Standeth lawfully and Sufficiently seized in their tract or parcel of unlocated land and in every part and parcel thereof and hath good right full power lawful and abfolute authority in themfelves to grant Bargain and Sell the Same unto the Said Thomas ffrench his heirs and afsigns fforever And the Said Hafker Newberry and Mary his Wife and the Said Naomi Heritage for themselves and for their Heirs the Said Thirty Eight Acres of unlocated land within the Weftern Divifion of New Jersey aforesaid and all and singular others the herein granted and Bargained premifes and every part and parcel of the Same unto him the Said Thomas ffrench his heirs and afsigns against them the Said Hasker Newberry and Mary his Wife and againft the Said Naomi Heritage and every of their Heirs and againft all and every other perfon and Perfons any thing having or lawfully Claiming or that may or Shall at any time hereafter have or lawfully claim any Estate right title or Interest of in or unto the above mentioned premises or any part or parcel thereof Shall and Warrant and Defend the same unto the Said Thomas ffrench his heirs and afsigns fforever (The quitrents there out Ifsuing to the King his heirs and Successors and the arrears thereof if any be only Excepted) And ffurther

they the Said Hasker Newberry and Mary his Wife and the Said Naomi
Heritage shall and will from time to time and at any time or times hereafter at the reaſonable requeſt Cost and Charges in the law of the said
Thomas ffrench his heirs or aſsigns make do Execute and perform all and
every other matters or things Conveyances and aſsurances in the law whatsoever for the ffurther better and more perfect aſsuring Sure making
Conveying and Confirming the Same to the uses above mentioned in Such
manner and Sort as he the said Thomas ffrench his heirs or aſsigns or
his or their Council learned in the Law Shall lawfully deviſe adviſe or
require and So as tho.—perſon or perſons unto whom Such requeſt be made
be not compelled nor hereby Compellable to travil or go from the place
of their uſual abode further than the City of Burlington within the
Diviſion aforesaid for the doing or executing thereof and so as Such
ffurther Aſsurance contain no larger Covenants or Warranty then herein
is above Compriſed In Witness Whereof the parties first above named
in these presents hath hereunto Interchangably Sett their hands and Seals
the day and year first above written 1737

The above mentioned Indenture   Haſker Newberry   [SEAL]
was by the said Haſker Newberry   her
and Mary his wife Sealed and De-   Mary (Newberry   [SEAL]
livered in the preſence of us. Viz^t·   mark
                                          her
          John Harvy   Naomi ᴎ Heritage   [SEAL]
            his   mark
          James ◯ Maſon
            mark
          John Newberry

LEASE OF "CANOE SWAMP" BY THOMAS FRENCH ET AL TO EDWARD FRENCH, 1737

The following document recites the lease of rights in a notable woodland property by
Thomas French (6) and other owners, to Edward French (36).

This Indenture made the Seventh day of Novem'r in the year of Our
Lord one thousand Seven hundred and thirty [seven] and in the Eleventh
year of the Reign of King George the Second of Great Brittain &c Between
Thomas Evens Ann Wallis Alias Heulings Relict of Thomas Wallis late
of Burlington County in the Weſtern Diviſion of New Jersey Deceaſed
and Thomas ffrench Thomas Ballinger John Roberts all of the county of
Burlington aforesaid yeomen And Timothy Matlack and William Clark
of the County of Gloucester within the Diviſion aforesaid yeomen of the
one part And Edward ffrench of the County of Burlington aforesaid, Hus-

bandman of the other part Whereas Mount Cox, William Clark William
Evens William Matlack Thomas Wallis Thomas ffrench Henry Ballinger
Sarah Roberts John Sharp and George Smith by one Indenture of Bargain and Sale bearing date the tenth day of April Ano 1697 for the Consideration therein Mentioned did purchase of Stephen Day one hundred
acres of Land and Swamp scittuate lying and being in the county of Burlington aforesaid Commonly Called or known by the name of the CONEW
SWAMP and the Said Stephen Day did referve one Eleventh part thereof
to his own ufe and that the Said Partners Did unanimoufly agree that
if any of them did fell cut down sell or take away any tree or trees without
the confent of the Major part of the Said Partners should be Subject to
the penalties as in the Said Deed and Schedule thereunto anexed relation
unto the Said Deed and Schedule being had may more at length Appear
Now this Indenture Witnesseth that the Said Thomas Evens Ann Wallis
Alias Heuling Thomas ffrench Thomas Ballinger John Roberts Timothy
Matlack and William Clark being the Major part of the Said Partners
are Inclin'd to make the beft of the timber on the aforesaid premifes for
the ufe of every one of the Said Partners for and in confideration of the
rents and Covenants hereafter Mentioned hath Demifed Granted to farm
and letten and by thefe prefents for themfelves and for every one of the
Said partners fully Clearly and abfolutely doth Demife Grant to farm and
lett unto the Said Edward ffrench and unto his heirs and afsigns all that
their one hundred acres of Swamp Scittuate as aforesaid to git Coopers
Stuff or Staves to and for the ufe of the Said Edward ffrench his heirs
and afsigns for and during and untill the full end and term of two years
to Commence from the day of the date of thefe prefents fully to be compleat and ended Yielding and paying in each refpective year the Sum of
Ten Shillings P thoufand for every thoufand he the Said Edward ffrench
his heirs or Afsigns do git of Staves To Hold the Said Swamp and all
the herein Demifed premifes unto the Said Edward ffrench his heirs and
afsigns until the full Expiration of the above Mentioned term without
the lawful lett suit denial hindrance moleftation Eviction Ejection or any
other Interruption of them the said Thomas Evans Ann Wallis Alias
Heulings Thomas ffrench Thomas Ballinger John Roberts Timothy Matlack
or William Clark their heirs Execut's or Adminift's or any other perfon
or perfons lawfully Claiming any part or parcel thereof Shall and will
warrant and Defend the same During all the said term And Notwithftand-
ing what is here above mentioned the parties above Said the parties hereunto do hereby Covenant and agree that the said Edward ffrench his heirs
or afsigns Shall give for Barrell Staves eight shillings P thoufand and
for hogfett Staves Tenn Shillings P thoufand and for Pipe Staves and
Heading fifteen Shillings P thousand And the Said Edward ffrench his heirs
and afsigns do hereby Covenant and agree to and with the Said parties

9

that the Said Edward ffrench his heirs and aſsigns shall make no waste
or as little as possible   In witness whereof the parties aforesaid hath hereunto Interchangably sett their hands and Seals the day and year first above
written (1737)

Sealed and delivered
in the presence of us
Robert Davis
John Cowperthwaite

Edward ffrench

DEED, THOMAS FRENCH TO EDWARD FRENCH, 1738

The following Deed of Gift shows transfer by Thomas ffrench (6) of his entire
interest in the " Canoe Swamp " to his son Edward (36).

THIS INDENTURE made the twenty-fifth day of September (So
Called) in the Year of our Lord one thouſand Seven hundred and Thirty
eight and in the twelfth year of the Reign of King George the Second
of Great Brittain &c. Between Thomas ffrench of the Townſhip of Cheſter
in the County of Burlington within the Western Division of New Jersey
Yeoman of the one part And Edward ffrench his Son of the other part
Witneſseth that the Said Thomas ffrench for and in conſideration of the
Natural love and affection he hath and beareth unto his said Son Edward
ffrench and for his better Support Maintainance and livelyhood as allso
for and in Conſideration of the Sum of ffive Shillings Currt money of the
Same place to him in hand paid by his Said Son Edwd ffrench the receipt
whereof he the Said Thomas ffrench doth hereby own and acknowledge
thereof and every part and parcel thereof do hereby requit & diſcharge
the Said Edwd ffrench his heirs execut's & adminiſt's and every of them
fforever by theſe p'ſents hath given granted Bargained Sold aliened Enfeofed Conveyed & Confirmed and by theſe p'ſents fully clearly and abſolutely doth give grant Bargain Sell alien Enfeof Convey and Confirm
unto the Said Edwd ffrench and unto his heirs & aſsigns all that his one
Eleventh part of all that hundred acres of Swamp scittuate in the County
of Burlington aforesaid Purchs^d in partnership with Mounce Cock William
Clark William Evens William Matlack and others as may appear by one
indenture of Bargain and Sale made Between Stephen Day of the one
part and Mounce Cock, William Clark, William Evens, William Matlack,
Thos Wallis, & the aforeſd Thos ffrench, Henry Ballinger, Sarah Roberts,
George Smith & John Sharp bearing date the tenth day of 2^d month Ano.
1697 relation unto the Said Indenture being had may and will more fully
and at length appear Together with all and every the Timber trees woods
under woods ffishings, fflowlings and Huntings and all other the proffits
Comodities Heraditaments & Appurtenances whatsoever unto the Said one

Eleventh part of the Said one hundred acres of land belonging or appertaining and allso all the Eſtate right title Interest poſseſsion property
Claim and Demand whatsoever of him the Said Thomas ffrench as well in
law as in Equity of in or unto the said given granted & Bargained premiſes
and every part & parcel thereof To have And to hold the above given
granted and Bargained undivided Eleventh part of the Said one hundred acres
mentioned or Intended to be herein given granted and Bargained premiſes
and every part & parcel thereof unto the Said Edwᵈ ffrench his heirs and
aſsigns unto the only proper uſe and behoof of the Said Edward ffrench his
heirs and aſsigns Forever And the Said Thomas ffrench for himself his
heirs Execut's and Adminiſt's doth hereby covenant grant and agree to and
with the said Edward ffrench his heirs and aſsigns by theſe preſents that
he the said Thomas ffrench is and Standeth Lawfully and Sufficiently Seized
in his Demeaſne as of ffee of and in the above mentioned premiſes and in
every part and parcel of the Same and in their and every of their Appurtenances and at the time of the Enſealing and Delivery of theſe p'ſents hath
good right full power Lawful and abſolute authority in himself to give grant
Bargain and Sell the above mentioned one Eleventh part of the Said one
Hundred Acres of land and every part and parcel thereof with their and
every of their appurtenances unto the Said Edward ffrench his heirs and
aſsigns fforever, as is above in theſe preſents Mentioned Declared and Ex-
preſsed So that now and hence forth and forever hereafter it shall and may be
lawful to and for the Said Edward ffrench his heirs and aſsigns to have hold
uſe occupy poſsess and enjoy all and Singular the above given granted and
Bargained premiſes and every part and parcel of the Same, without the
Lawfull lett suit denial hindrance moleſtation Eviction Ejection or any
other Interuption of the said Thomas ffrench his heirs Executors or Administrators or any other perſon or perſons whatsoever Lawfully Claiming or
pretending to claim any part or parcel thereof by from or under him them
or any of them or by his or their or any of their Conſent aſsent privity
or procurement Shall and will from time to time and at all times hereafter
Warrant and Defend the Same and every part and parcel thereof unto the
Said Edward ffrench his heirs and aſsigns fforever (The quit rents thereout Iſsuing unto the King his heirs and Succeſsors and the arrears thereof
if any be only excepted) And the Said Thomas ffrench and all claiming
under him Shall and will from time to time or at any time or times hereafter at the request Costs and Charges in the law of the Said Edward
ffrench his heirs or aſsigns make do acknowledge and execute or cause or
procure to be made done suffered acknowledged and executed all and every
such ffurther and other lawfull & Reasonable acts matters & things Conveyances & Aſsurances in the law whatsoever for the further better more
perfect assuring sure making conveying and Confirming the Same to the
uſes above Said So as such other assurance contain no larger covenants or
warrants than herein is above comprised In witness whereof the party firſt

above named in these presents hath hereunto Sett his hand and seal the
day and year first above written—

And further the said Thomas ffrench for himself
his heirs Exect's and Adminiſt's do hereby Covanant
grant & agree to & with his Said Son Edward that
he yᵉ said Edward ffrench his heirs & aſsigns Shall
have all and Singular yᵉ over pluſs revertion &
Revertions remainder and remainders of him if Said
Thos ffrench which he now hath or which may at
any time appear to be due within the above said
Swamp and this was entered before yᵉ Executing
hereof

Thomas ffrench

Sealed and delivered in the presence of us Vizᵗ.

Jacob Lippincott

Edward Clendries

Samᵉ Atkinson

WILL OF THOMAS FRENCH, 1745

Let it be Recorded that I Thomas ffrench of Chefter in the County of Burlington in the Province of New Jersey Yeoman being perfect & Sound in mind and memory Thanks be given to Almighty God therefore, and having in my Mind the uncertainty of this life, & the certainty of death when it Shall pleafe God to Call and being will that Such temporals as the Lord in his Great Goodnefs hath lent me in this life [far beyond my defarts] Should Come unto Such perfon & Perfons as I Shall herein Nominate & appoint hereby revoking & making void all former & other Wills & Teftaments heretofore by me made & this only to be taken for the Same

IMPRIMIS I Give and Bequeath unto my Son Jofeph five pounds to be paid him by my Son Thomas out of the Proffits of the Plantation I do herein give & devife to him

ITEM I Give and bequeath unto my Son Robert thirty pounds to be paid by my Said Son Thomas at the time

ITEM I Give & Bequeath unto my Daughter Mary tenn Pounds

ITEM I Give & Bequeath unto my Daughter Mary's four Sons each of them five pounds when they attain their full ages

ITEM I Give & bequeath unto my Wife five Shillings all which above mentioned legacies I do hereby order my Said Son Thomas to pay them out of the proffits of the Said Plantation Current money of the Same place (ie) Jofephs Roberts Marys & my Wifes Legacies in twelve months after my Deceafe

ITEM I Give Devife & bequeath unto my Son Thomas & unto his heirs & afsigns fforever all that one hundred and fifty three acres of land whereon I Now Dwell together with all the appurtenances unto the Same belonging (be the number of acres more or less) Item I Give & devife all that my Ceder Swamp Containing twenty five acres unto my Son Robert & unto my Son Thomas their heirs and afsigns fforever to be Equally divided between them Share & Share alike

ITEM I Give & bequeath unto my Said Son Robert my Riding horfe Bridle & Saddle & my Wearing Apparrell

ITEM I do her°by give and bequeath all that my perfonal Eftate after my Juft debts are paid & difcharged unto my Son Robert & unto my Son Thomas to be Equally divided between them Share & Share alike who I do hereby ordain and appoint my Execut^rs of this my laft Will & Teftament

In Witnefs Whereof I have hereunto Set my hand and Seal this twenty Sixth day of the Sixth Month Anoque Dom one thoufand Seven hundred and forty five 1745.

Signed Sealed pronounced and declared to be his laft will and Teftament in the presence of us viz

    Joshua Bispham
    Nathan Middleton
    Sam^1. Atkinson

his

Thomas ,ffrench

mark

Joshua Bispham and Samuel Atkinson two of the Witnefses to the above Written Will being of the People called Quakers on their Solemn Affirmations which they took according to Law did Declare That they Saw Thomas French the Testator above Named Sign & Seal the Same and heard him publish pronounce & Declare the above Instrument to be his Last Will & Testament And that at the Doing thereof the Said Testator was of Sound & Disposing Mind & Memory as far as these Affirmants Know and as they verily beleive and that Nathan Middleton the Other Subscribing Evidence was Present & Signed his Name as a Witnefs to the Said Will Together with these Affirmants in the presence of the Said Testator.

Affirmed at Burlington the first Day of November Anno Domini 1745

Before me   Jo⁵ Scattergood Surrogate

Thomas French one of the Executors in the Within Testament Named (Robert French the Other Executor having disclaimed the Execution thereof) being duly affirmed according to Law Did Declare that the Within Instrument contains the True Last Will & Testament of Thomas French the Testator therein Named So far as he knows and as he verily beleives and that he will well & truly perform the Same by paying first the Debts and then the Legacies in the Said Testament Specified So far as the Goods Chattels and Credits of the Said Deceased can thereunto Extend and that he will make and Exhibite into the Prerogative Office in Burlington a True and Perfect Inventory of all & Singular the Goods Chattels & Credits of the Said Deceased that Shall come to his knowledge or Pofsefsion or to the Pofsefsion of any other person or Persons for his Use And render a Just and True Account when thereunto Lawfully required

Affirmed at Burlington this firft Day of November 1745

Before me   Jo⁵ Scattergood Surrogate

ROBERT FRENCH'S RENUNCIATION OF EXECUTORSHIP

Whereas Thomas French Late of Chester in the County of Burlington Yeoman Deceased Lately Made & published his Last Will & Testament bearing date the Sixth day of the Sixth Month one thousand Seven hundred & forty five and thereof appointed Robert French & Thomas French Executors. Now I the Said Robert French being unwilling to take upon me the Burthen of the Said Executorship have Renounced & Disclaimed and by these presence do Renounce & Disclaim the Said Executorship or any Medling or acting in the Same In Testimony whereof I have hereunto Set my Hand & Seal this first Day of November Anno Domini one thousand Seven hundred & forty five

Sealed & Delivered in the presence of

Sam¹. Atkinfon

Joseph Heritage   *Robert French*

INVENTORY OF THE ESTATE OF THOMAS FRENCH, 1745

A true and perfect Inventory of all & Singular the Goods & Chattels rights and Credits of Thomas ffrench late of Chefter in the County of Burlington &c dec^d. taken the 17th of October Ano 1745 being all the Came to our view appraifed by us under Written.

	£	S	d
Imprimis to in ye parlor to purse & Apparrell	11	14	6
in Ditto to bed furniture & Sundry other things............	08	06	0
in ye Leanto to Sundry Sorts of Beding & other things.....	08	18	0
in another Leanto to a bed & divers other things...........	02	09	0
in ye great Room to tables Chairs & divers other Lumber....	07	11	6
in ye Chamber to two bed & divers other things............	06	17	0
in ye Kitc"h to Kettles pots and divers other things.........	07	10	6
in ye Cellar to Cyder with apples & Lumber...............	09	10	0
in ye Yard to plows Cart and Hufbandry Utenfills.........	07	10	6
in the field to Winter Corn growing......................	07	10	0
in Ditto to Indian Corn & potatoes......................	15	12	0
in the Barn and Stack Yard to Wheat rye & oats...........	21	10	0
in Ditto to hay..	05	15	0
to Sheep	07	00	0
to Cattell	38	10	0
to a horfe bridle & Saddle	11	15	0
to Swine	20	00	0
to Book Debts	02	00	0
to Worfted at the Weavers	05	08	0
	215	7	0

Appraised by us { Joseph Heritage
                 { Saml. Atkinfon

Affirmed at Burlington the ffirst day of November Anno Domini 1745
Before me   Jo^s. Scattergood Surrogate

RECEIPT, MARY FRENCH TO THOMAS FRENCH (33), 1745

I Mary French of Chester in the County of (Burlington) &c. Widow have received of Thomas French of the Same place Executor to the last will and testament of my late deceased Husband Thomas French one obligation bearing even date with these presents Conditioned for the payment of twenty two pounds currt. money payable in twelve months And I do hereby acquit and Discharge the said Thomas French his heirs, executors and Administes of and from all and all mannor of actions, cause and causes of actions suits debts bills Bonds Writings obligatorys sum and sums of money quarrels and controversies of what kind soever (touching) his said late deceased Fathers Estate or any thing concerning him the above said executor had made moved or depending from the beginning of our first acquaintance to the date of these presents— In witness whereof I have hereunto set my hand seal—

Dated the twenty-first day of October in the year of our Lord One thousand Seven Hundred and forty five (1745)

Seal'd and deliver'd (first Burlington in the top line, and touching in the Margent was entered before the executing hereof) in the presence of

        his

William X Prickit
     mark
Joseph Heritage

Mary french

JOSEPH FRENCH [32]

Minutes of Newton Mo. Mtg., Haddonfield Quarter:

8th-8 mo. 1722 At said meeting, application was made for a Certificate for Joseph French, therefore the mtg. appoints Samuel Atkinson and Joseph Stokes to make Enquiery concerning his Clearness and are desiered to make their answer to our next monthly meeting.

12th-9 mo. 1722 At said meeting the Persons appointed to make Enquiery concerning Joseph French's Clearness from Women on the Account of Marriage and of his Conversation report they find that he is clear from all women amongst us to the Best of their knowledge, as to his conversation they do not find it so well as could be Desiered, therefore the meeting orders that he have a Certificate accordingly.

Joseph French, like his father, sought a wife in East Jersey, and it appears early located in or near Shrewsbury, Monmouth County, where, so far as can be learned, he continued to reside until his death in 1752. He died intestate and the estate was administered by James Farrell, who had married Joseph's daughter Mary in 1751.

NEWTON MEETING

Early Friends who came from England with the first West Jersey colonists set up a meeting at Newton, in 1682. They met at each other's houses for five years and in 1687 built a log meeting house, the first in Gloucester county. This primitive building was used for its original and other purposes for more than a century. Within this period it was a notable landmark, town meetings and elections being held there as well as stated religious services. Being located on the bank of Newton creek, people came in boats in great numbers, this being one of the customs of the time, when roads through the forest were scarcely more than bridle paths. Sometimes burials were made at night, the light of flaring pine torches making weird and picturesque scenes. Many of the old families lie in the ancient and long neglected graveyard. The old meeting house fell into decay and was abandoned some years before its accidental destruction by fire, December 22, 1817. The territory nearer the Delaware river becoming more thickly populated, the present substantial brick meeting house was erected in 1801, being located on the Mt. Ephraim road, about two miles from the original site, now in the suburbs of Camden, and known thereafter as Camden Meeting.

Thomas Sharp, an energetic young Irish Friend, afterward a noted surveyor of West Jersey, who came with the pioneers in 1681, left an account of the settlement of Newton from which we quote as follows:

" Immediately amongst us a meeting was set up and it grew and increased. Zeal and fervency of spirit was in some good degree at that time abounding among Friends; in commemoration of our prosperous success and eminent preservation, both in our crossing the great deep, as also, whereas we were but few at that time and the Indians many, whereby it put a dread upon our spirits, considering they were a savage people. But the Lord, who hath the hearts of all in his hands, turned them so as to be serviceable unto us and very loving and kind. Which cannot be otherwise accounted but to be the Lord's doings in our favor, which we had cause to praise him for. And that the rising generation may consider that the settlement of this country was directed by an impulse upon the spirits of God's people, not so much for their ease and tranquility, but rather for the posterity that should be after, and that the wilderness being planted with a good seed might grow and increase to the satisfaction of the good husbandman."

HADDONFIELD MEETING

Friends amongst the settlers in the vicinity of what is now Haddonfield first worshipped at Newton and in private houses. A Monthly Meeting was established as early as 1695. In 1721 the first meeting house, a log structure, was erected on land given by John Haddon, of England, at the instance of his daughter Elizabeth, who had married John Estaugh. She was clerk of the Women's Meeting for over half a century and performed her duties with painstaking care. These minutes are still in the custody of descendants of the Haddon family. In 1760 a substantial brick meeting house was built adjoining the old one, a picture of which, taken from an old publication, is given. In 1851 this was removed and each branch of the Society erected the houses since in use. From the separation, in 1828, until 1851, both used the old building. In 1787 a brick school house was built and this is still in use, being in an excellent state of preservation. The ancient "Indian field," cleared land, cultivated by the natives, was close to the site of the first meeting house and was an historic spot until revolutionary times. The main highway, running east and west, was called the "King's Highway" and that running north and south, facing the meeting houses, "Ferry Road." The present peaceful and beautiful surroundings are in keeping with the history of this notable place.

Friends Meeting-house, Haddonfield.

BUILT 1760. REMOVED 1851.

7—HANNAH FFRENCH (Thomas, 1).

> Baptized September 5th, 1669, at Church S. S.
> Peter and Paul, Nether Heyford, England.
>
> m. 8th mo. 30th, 1695, Richard Buzby "of yᵉ
> Province of Pensilvania," son of John and
> Mary Buzby, formerly of Milton, England.
>
> He b. 1670.
>   d. 7th mo. 1747.

38—JOHN BUZBY	b. 10th mo. 5th, 169[6].
39—THOMAS BUZBY	m. 8th mo. 1723, Mary Mason.
40—JANE BUZBY	m. 7th mo. 1731, Jonathan Fincher.
41—REBECCA BUZBY	m. 10th mo. 1724, Daniel Roberts.

RICHARD BUZBY

The Buzby family were among the earliest settlers of Pennsylvania, consisting of John Buzby, who came from Milton, England, to Philadelphia, in 1682, with his wife Mary, his sons John, William, Edward, Richard and Nicholas, and daughters Mary, Elizabeth and Sarah. He was a weaver and his sons, all sturdy young men, were for a time engaged in the same line of work. The following is a copy of certificate brought by John Buzby from England, taken from the records of the Philadelphia Monthly Meeting:

> "The 4ᵗʰ day of yᵉ 2ⁿᵈ Mo. 1682. Whereas, John Buzbey, weaver, of Milton, in the parish of Shipton and belonging to the meeting at Milton is disposed to transport himself beyond sea into pensilvania this is our testimony to whom it may Concerne he ownes the living and everlasting truth of god and hath walked amongst us blameless in his life and Conversation and wee doe beleeve he is nott Indebted unto none as wee Can understand therefore we doe sett our testimony thereof."

In 1696, William and Richard Buzby purchased large adjoining tracts of land, soon after increased to over 600 acres, located in Oxford township, Philadelphia, and now between Frankford and Olney. The greater part of this fine estate, constantly increasing in value, remained in the possession of the family for nearly two hundred years, being handed down to different direct heirs by eight wills and a number of deeds. In 1742, Richard Buzby conveyed to his son Thomas, in consideration of eighty pounds—a nominal sum, as the real value even then was much greater—"and natural love and affection," his homestead and 157 acres of land. His wife, Hannah, joined in this affectionate transaction, being dutifully cared for when she became a widow, five years later, and still further provided for through the will of her son Thomas, whom she survived, made in 1757, a few months before his death. The will of Richard Buzby, as will be observed, was confined to the distribution of personal property to his children, he having disposed of practically all his real estate. Some sixty-five years after his death part of the family estate was devoted to notable uses.

In 1813, Isaac Buzby, a descendant of William and Richard, and members of his family, for $6,754, conveyed fifty-two acres of land to the Board of Trustees of Friends' Asylum for the Insane, Frankford. Some years later a part of the original Richard Buzby farm was added to this property. Friends' Asylum was the first distinctive separate institution for the humane treatment and restoration of the insane in this country, although the Pennsylvania Hospital has always had a department for the " care and cure of Lunaticks," as declared in its charter, 1751. Now in its ninety-first year, Friends' Asylum has a record unexcelled. It has cared for nearly 4,000 patients, more than one third of whom were restored.

For thirty years Richard Buzby was a very active member of Abington Monthly Meeting, Oxford Preparative Meeting being his local home Meeting. He was a frequent representative at Quarterly and Yearly Meetings, and was zealous in the performance of special duties. He was for a long time an acknowledged minister among Friends. We quote a few interesting minutes from the Meeting Records. A manuscript found among old papers of the Yearly Meeting of the year 1750, entitled, " An account of the time of the decease of such ministers and elders belonging to the Monthly Meeting of Abington as departed this life since the year 1720, with some short memorials concerning them," contains the following:

> " In the 7th mo. of the year 1747 died Richard Buzby belonging to Oxford particular meeting. He was a Friend in the ministry whose testimony was well received and travelled with the approbation of his friends to some distant parts of this continent in Truth's service. He was inoffensive and examplary in life and conversation. Aged 77 years, was buried at Friends burying ground at Oxford aforesaid."

In 1857 the following appreciative sketch of the life and work of Richard Buzby appeared in " The Friend ":

> Richard Busby was born in England, in the year 1670. At what time he came to America, we have not been able to learn; but we find him in the year 1700, a useful member of Dublin [afterwards Abington] Monthly Meeting, and probably already in the ministry. After the year 1704, we find many marks of his dedication, and of the estimation in which he was held by his friends. In tracing him through the records of the various meetings of ministers some striking and interesting minutes were found. In the Twelfth month, 1707, after recording that " Richard Busby and John Cadwallader " reported that things were well among them at Dublin, these remarks follow: " In consideration of which, that the Lord is pleased still to continue his goodness and care over us, and to lengthen out our day and time of peace, love and brotherly kindness,—pressing more and more after perfect and fervent charity, the meeting was thankful to the Lord."
>
> In the early part of the year 1721, Richard Busby and William Walton performed a religious visit to the meetings of Maryland, Virginia and North Carolina, which, from " divers certificates " produced by them on their return, appears to have been to the comfort and edification of those among whom they had laboured. In the Quarterly Meeting of Ministers and Elders, held Twelfth mo. 3d, 1721, " The ancient love and power of God was felt, to the comforting the meeting. Tender exhortation was given to the due exercise of the heavenly gift. Whereas of late several serviceable labourers in the vineyard of Christ have been removed, we should pray to the Lord that he would raise up and send forth more faithful servants; that his work of righteousness and Truth may increase and prosper, to the church's edification and his glory."
>
> In 1722, Richard, with some other ministering Friends from Pennsylvania, attended Shrewsbury Yearly Meeting. We find but little record of his services, yet it is evident that he was considered a diligent and faithful labourer in the church. Richard Busby and the other representatives from the Quarterly Meeting of Ministers and Elders, held in the Twelfth mo., 1723, to the General Meeting of Ministers, in the following month, were directed to report, that " Friends in the ministry are careful in their conversation, diligent in attending meetings, both on First and week days; that their labour and services are well received; that they are in love and unity, and that the assistance of worthy elders is found very serviceable in these meetings."

Meeting records show that other children of John and Mary Buzby married as follows: John, Mary Taylor, of Tinicum Island, 2nd mo. 1st, 1690; William, Sarah Seary, 6th mo. 11th, 1685; Edward, Susannah Adams, 3rd mo. 7th, 1696; Sarah, Richard Tomlinson.

MEETING RECORDS

Burlington Monthly Meeting Minutes:

At our mens monthly meeting held at the house of Eliz: Gardiner in Burlington ye 2nd of ye 7th mo. 1695—Richard Busby & Hannah French declared their intentions of marriage it being ye First time of their coming they Desired ye Unity of Friends.

At our Monthly Meeting held at the house of Eliz. Gardiner in Burlington ye 7th of ye 8th Mo: 1695—Richard Busby & Hannah ffrench declared their intentions of Marriage it being the Second time & upon enquiry made the meeting find all Clear and nothing to impede or hinder the Same they are Left to Consumate ye weighty affair as they in a Convenient time & Place in the fear of the Lord Shall See meet.

MARRIAGE CERTIFICATE

Whereas an Intention of Marriage hath been duely Published according to ye Laws of this Province of West New Jersey in America and alsoe att severall of the meetings of ye people of God Called Quakers And noe obstruction appearing to obstruct or hinder them—Now These are to Certifie whom it may Concerne that the said Richard Busbey of ye Province of Pensilvania and Hannah ffrench of ye County of Burlington did on the 30th day of ye Eighth mo. in ye year 1695 in A solem Assembly of ye people Aforesd; Take & declare themselves to be Husband and wife and in Testimony they subscribe theire names & we alsoe as wittnesses—

Richard Busbey
Hannah Busbey

John Adams (Justice)	John Busbey ⎫ fathers
George Deacon	Thomas ffrench ⎭
Daniell Hall	Richard ffrench
John ffletcher	Tho. ffrench, Junr.
Richard Tomlinson	Isaac Wood
Benj. Wheate	Ed. Busbey
Will. Pancoast	John Busbey
John Woolman	Nicholas Busbey
Tho. Scatergood	John ffrench
Joseph Pancoast	Charles ffrench
Sarah Busbey	Mary Wheate
Mary Busbey	Sarah Roberts
Eliz. Adams	

Abington Monthly Meeting Minutes:

At our Mo-Meeting ye 31: 11 m^o, 1714

Whereas there hath been a complaint made by Richd Tomlinſon againſt his three Brother's by Law, viz, William, Richard & Edward Buzby, ffriends being willing to put an end to ye Said defference, have adviſed them to chooſe 4 friends to hear & determine ye Matter with all Expedition: which accordingly they did make choice of four friends, who heard ye matter debated, & put an end to ye difference.

At our Mo: Meeting ye 28: 11 m^o 1716

As to the proceding minits in relation to ye viſiting of families, it is concluded that every perticular Meeting make choice of Such weighty friends as may be of moſt Service in Such a weighty Concern, & preſent them to ye next Mo-Meeting.

At our Mo-Meeting ye 25: 12 m^o 1716

As to ye former Minits Relating to ye visiting of families, friends of Abington haue Choſen John Cadwallader, Morris Morris & Thomas Canby. Oxford Meeting have choſen Edmond orphood & Richard Buzby; Germantown Meeting have Choſon Rich— Lewis & Dennis Cunnard.

Bybury Meeting have Choſon none as yet for that Service, it is left to their further Conſideration, against next Meeting.

At our Mo-Meeting ye 24: 12 m^o 1717

In pursuance of ye Minit last month; concerning ye Viſiting of families: Oxford meeting have choſen Edmond Orphood Richard Buzby & John Shallcroſs.

At our Mo-Meeting held ye 23^d of ye 12th mo 1718

Friends from Each particular preparative Meeting have Nominated perſons to Viſit families, viz. Oxford fr^{ds} Chofe Rich^d Buſby Jno Shallcroſs & Edm^d: Orpwood.

At our Mo-Meeting held ye 27th of ye 12th mo 1720

A Certificate was Granted to Willm Walton & Richard Busby in Order to Viſsit in Maryland on ye Service of Truth.

At our Mo: Meeting held ye 31st: of ye 5th mo 1721

Whereas our friends William Walton & Richard Buſby haveing Perform'd their Viſsit in ye Service of Truth in Virginia & Maryland & Carolina & Withall have Produced Several Certificates Signifying their Great Satisfaction & Unity in their Viſsit of Love.

At our Mo: Meeting held ye 26th of ye 6th mo 1723

Whereas friends are to Appear at Philad^a: by ye Appointm^t: of ye Quarterly Meeting Relating to Danl: Potts Friends Do appoint Morris Morris John Cadwallader Robt: Fletcher Danl: Thomas Edward Bolton Griffith Jones John Duncan and Thos: Wood & Richd Busby to attend ye Service.

At our Mo-Meeting held ye 22^d of ye 12th mo 1730/1

Whereas Bybery fr^{ds} of Late have been Very much at Difference among themselves which has proved an Exercise to this Meeting therefore fr^{ds}: of this Meeting Do appoint John Cadwalader Morris Morris Nicholus Austin Rich^d. Busby & Griffith Jones to Endeavour in ye Spirit of Love to bring them to a Reconciliation.

At a M^o Mg held the 26th: 4th: m^o. 1732

Rich^d: Buzby & Thos Roberts are app^d: to Speak with James Dilworth Ju^r: & endeavour to bring him to a Sense of his outgoings in taking a wife contrary to the Discipline.

WILL OF RICHARD BUZBY, 1743

I Richard Buzbey of Oxford Township In the County of Philadelphia & Province of Pensilvania Yeoman Being Sickly & weak of Body but of Sound Memory & Judgment Thanks be unto God, Calling to mind the Uncertainty of the Time of my Continuance in this Life haue thought fitt & do hereby make this my Last will & Testament in manner & Form Following, That is to say First I Recommend my Soul & Spirit to the Merciful Protection of God that Gaue it, & my Body to the Earth to be Decently Inter'd by my Son Thomas Buzbey, when it Shall pleas the Lord so to Dispose of it, & as Touching my outward Estate I will that the Same be Disposed of as herein after Declared, Imprimis I will that all my Just Debts & Funeral Charges be paid as Soon as Possible by my Son Thomas Buzbey, ITem I Give Devise & Bequeath vnto my Son Thomas Buzbey (after mine & my wife's Decease) A Long Black Wallnut Table, & a Little Desk or Cabinet with Draws, & all my weavours Loomes & Tackling Belonging to them, ITem I Give to my Two Daughters, Jane Fincher & Rebecca Roberts & to their Children for Ever (after mine & my wifes Decease) all my Household Goods & Moveables wheresoever Lying or being (Except as before mentioned Given to my Son Thomas Buzby) & I allso Give unto my Said Two Daughters all my Cows Chattels or Living Creatures, to them & their Children for Ever (after mine & my wife's Decease) all which as before mentioned I Give Devise & Bequeath to my aforesaid Two Daughters & their Children for Ever, (after mine & my wife's Decease as aforesaid) And Lastly I hereby Constitute & nominate

& appoint my Son In Law Daniel Roberts Executor of this my Last will
& Testament, Hereby Revokeing all Former & other wills heretofore by
me made & Declareing this & no other to be my Last will & Testament
In wittnefs whereof I have hereunto Set my hand & Seal This First day
of the Sixth month August. In the Sixteenth year of the Reign of King
George the Second of Great Brittain &c anno que Dins one Thousand
Seven Hundred Forty & Three

Signed Sealed Published
& Declared by the Said
Richard Buzbey to be his
Last will & Testament In
the Presence of us
    William Sutton
    Mary Sutton
    Joseph Jones

It is my will & I do hereby allso appoint & order that my Son Thomas
Busbey shall pay my wife's Funeral Charges as well as my own & all my
Just Debts as aforefaid In wittnefs whereof I haue here vnto put my hand
& Seal the day & year mentioned on the other Side,

Signed Sealed Published
& Declared before us
    William Sutton
    Mary Sutton
    Joseph Jones

Philad[a] Dec 11th: 1747. Then psonally appeared W[m]. Sutton one of
the witnefses to the foreging Will and to the Supplemt. thereto annexed and
On his Solemn affirmacon according to Law did declare & affirm he Saw
& heard Richard Busbey the Teftator therein named Sign Seal publish &
declare the Same Will for & as his Laft will & Teftam[t]. and the s[d]. Sup-
plem[t]. for & as a part of the Same and that at the doing thereof he was
of Sound mind Memory & Understanding to the best of his knowledge and
that Jofeph Jones since Deced and Mary Sutton now absent did also Subscribe their Names as witnefs[s]. thereto in the presence of & at the request
of the Testator

                Coram
                W[m] Plumsted Reg. Genl.

10

ABINGTON MEETING

During the period immediately preceding William Penn's arrival in Pennsylvania, in 1682, settlers began to locate in the desirable territory to the north of the site of the " Green Countrey Towne " laid out by the proprietor. Amongst these Friends were numerous and influential. The setting up of meetings was a matter of very early consideration. Worship was held, after the custom of the time, in private houses. Among the earliest records we find the following historical note:

> " At a monthly meeting yᵉ 8th 9 mᵒ 1682
> " At this time Governour William Penn and a multitude of ffriends arrived here, and Errected a City Called Philadelphia about half a mile from Shackamaxon where meetings were Eſtablished."

In 1684 a log meeting house was built in Oxford township and Oxford Meeting established. Meetings were also set up about this time at Byberry and Cheltenham and primitive meeting houses erected. In 1697, John Barnes gave Friends 120 acres of land in Cheltenham for educational purposes and a burial ground. It was at once decided to build a stone meeting house, with help of Friends in Philadelphia, as the early minutes note; the building being completed in 1700. For some years theretofore the society at Cheltenham had been known as Dublin Meeting, the name of the nearby township wherein many of the members lived. It was now changed to Abington. About this time Oxford Meeting lapsed, owing to the Keith schism, a majority of its members falling away, many uniting with Trinity Protestant Episcopal Church, which secured possession of the property, erecting the first part of the present venerable building about 1711.

Some years thereafter—the first Abington minute referring thereto appearing in the record for 1723—Oxford Friends reorganized their meeting, being subject to Abington Monthly Meeting. A century later this Oxford Meeting became known as Frankford Meeting, thus continuing until the present time, though since 1827 it has been subject to Green Street Monthly Meeting, Philadelphia. There have been some changes in the meeting house and grounds at Abington, but the present solidly built edifice, a portion of which is more than two hundred years old, in no way shows the effects of passing years. The grove of great trees, many of them past the century mark, forms a beautiful view from the highway. Directly opposite has been erected one of the finest school buildings in the State, this institution having always been under the care and supervision of Friends.

Abington Meeting has always been prosperous and influential.   Quarterly Meetings held there are still occasions of great interest.   Some extracts from early minutes are here given:

> On the 24th of 11 mo. 1695, this meeting having taken into consideration ye good advice of Friends from the last yearly meeting, to put in practice their council to admonish those that profess God's truth and do not walk answerable thereto. This meeting have chosen Richard Whitefield and Edward Orphood to inspect into Oxford meeting, also two for Germantown, two for Cheltenham and the same for Byberry meeting.

> At the meeting of 31st of 11 mo. 1697, William Jenkins gave Friends a relation of Friends' proceedings at Philadelphia, concerning their assistance towards building a new meeting house at Abington. William Jenkins and Joseph Phipps are appointed to attend the next monthly meeting to acquaint y^t Friends do approve of their method of subscription and accept their love. This meeting on the 28th following do desire for ye future y^t Edward Orphord and Timothy Hanson take due inspection into the youths behavior belonging to Oxford meeting.

> 1 mo. 25, 1700. Friends appoint Joseph Phipps, Thomas Canby & Wm. Jenkins to inspect into ye accts. of Everard Bolton and Samuel Cart concerning y^e building of y^e Meeting house at Abington.

> 4th mo. 24, 1700. Friends appointed to inspect accts. of Everard Bolton & Sam'l Cart reported due Everard Bolton 18 s 6d, which Friends do order to be paid.

ABINGTON MEETING HOUSE, 1700 AND 1756

8—CHARLES FFRENCH (Thomas, 1).

> b. March 20th, 1671.
> Baptized April 2nd, 1671, at Church S. S.
> Peter and Paul, Nether Heyford, England.
> m. First (sup.), 1708, Elinor ————.
> m. Second, ———— ————.

42—CHARLES FRENCH, JR.   b. 8th mo. 12th, 1714.
                                      m. 10th mo. 6th, 1739, Ann Clement.

43—URIAH FRENCH   m. Mary McCullock.

CHARLES FRENCH

The third son of Thomas ffrench, progenitor, appears to have held a responsible relationship towards his father and other members of the family. It became his duty to administer the estate, and in this connection he visited England in 1699 and several times thereafter. A number of deeds of conveyance show his disposition of the property. In one of these special reservation is made of the family burial lot, on the homestead farm, in which Thomas ffrench and his wife were buried, this provision being continued for nearly half a century, when it seems to have been lost sight of by later owners after the tract was subdivided. The plantation was bequeathed to Charles, subject to certain legacies, his father conveying to him 200 acres of land by deed of gift dated June 3rd, 1698, and afterwards bestowing the whole 600 acres upon him by will, proved 1699. In this connection a notable incident occurred. In 1713, Richard French, in order that the will of his father might be performed, " as far as in him lyeth," and fearing that " some right might appertain to him " in said plantation, as heir apparent of Thomas ffrench, being the eldest son, that should cause hindrance of the sale and permanent transfer of the property, or lead to future complications in connection therewith, as the original will of the testator had been left in England, by deed of release (herewith given) conveyed to his brother Charles any possible right he might have in the plantation.

Charles French evidently was a man of great activity and influence during his life. He resided chiefly in the upper part of Burlington county, but had interests elsewhere and lived for a time in Gloucester county, where he is supposed to have been a neighbor of the Kay, Ellis, Coles, Fortiner, Lippincott, Inskeep and other pioneer families in Waterford township.   Many real estate and administration papers, wills, deeds, etc., of that early period have been lost and the records at the first county seat, Gloucester, were destroyed through the burning of the old court house, in 1786.   Only two curious court minute books of the time, chiefly reciting quarter sessions business, were saved and many of the leaves of one of these are charred and torn and almost illegible.   The records copied at Trenton are far from complete. Those preserved in the Surveyor General's office, at Burlington, relate to surveys and to a limited degree deal with transfers of property.

Unhappily, meeting records concerning Charles French are almost equally vague and fragmentary.   He seems to have been twice married, his first wife apparently being a member of Shrewsbury Meeting, and his second wife not being a member of the Society of Friends, although there is no record of final discipline.   It is believed he had three daughters by the second marriage, and that these were they whose marriages are recorded in the book of licenses at Trenton; viz., Jemima, who married Francis Kay in 1743; Hope, who married Isaac Kay in 1748 (both grandsons of the pioneer John Kay) ; and Bathsheba, who married Daniel Fortiner in 1748.   Francis and Jemima Kay had three children, John, Samuel and Mary.   The former, in 1807, left a large family, ten children, by two wives, Keziah Thorn, daughter of Capt. Joseph and Isabella (Cheeseman) Thorn, and Elizabeth Brown; and an estate in Waterford township of over 600 acres.   Isaac and Hope Kay were living in 1772, but no family record has been discovered.   John Kay, the progenitor, was one of the most noted citizens of his locality, he being a large land owner in Waterford township and active and influential in public life.   His homestead was near the present hamlet of Ellisburg, now Delaware township, Camden county.   In 1685 he was elected to the Assembly and he also served as one of the judges of the original Gloucester county.   He was a noted arbitrator in the community and served as chairman of the committee on the settlement of the boundary between New Jersey and New York.   He was much interested in the Indians and their proper treatment.   He was a prominent Friend and at his house early meetings were held and marriages celebrated.   He died in 1741.

Daniel Fortiner, who married Bathsheba French, was an English artisan pioneer, a worker in wood, skilful and much esteemed for good qualities. His descendants have been industrious and useful citizens, one of the most widely known being the late Elwood K. Fortiner, merchant, of Camden.

MEETING RECORDS

Burlington Monthly Meeting Minutes:

At our Mens Monthly Meeting held at our Meeting house in Burlington y[e] 8th of y[e] 3[d] mo. 1699 Charles ffrench desired of this Meeting a Certificate in order for his going for England. Tho. Eves and Henry Grubb are appointed to Inquire into his Clearness & Conversation & to give acc[t] to y[e] next Meeting.

At our Mens Monthly Meeting held att our Meeting house in Burlington y[e] 5th of y[e] 4th mo[th] 1699 The men appointed to Enquire into y[e] Clearness of Charles ffrench give report y[t] they finde him Cleare Except in his publication according to law therefore have ordered after y[e] publication y[t] y[e] Cleark draw a Certificate & it be perused by Tho Gardener Christopher Wetherill Jno. Hollenshead Tho. Raper Ben Wheat Isaac Meriott and Peter ffretwell & if liked to Signe it.

Att our Mens Monthly Meeting held att our Meeting house in Burlington y[e] 6th of y[e] 7th mo. 1703 Charls French came before this meeting & acquanted the meeting y[t] he Intended God Willing to go for ould England & desired a Certificate therefore this meeting appoint John Wills & Tho: Eves to enquire into his clearnefs & to draw up a Certificate accordingly as they find things & bring it to y[e] next meeting.

From our Monthly Meeting held at Burlington y[e] 1st of y[e] 11 mo. 1704, and continued by adjournment til y[e] 25 of y[e] same.

To all captains and other military officers concerned—wereas: Peter Fretwell, Tho. Gardiner, Thos. Scattergood, Tho. Wetherill and some 34 others for Burlington; John Fenimore, Tho. Lippincott, Charles French and some 11 others for Wellingborrou; and some 70 others for Northampton, Mancefield, Chester and Eversham—

Did att our last Monthly Meeting appear declaring that they were of y[e] Society of y[e] people called Quakers & that for conscience sake they could not bear nor use arms to y[e] destruction of y[e] lives of men, and being willing to receive y[e] benefit of y[e] favor expressed to y[e] said People in an Act of Assembly lately made & published att Burlington entituled an Act for setling the Militia of this Province; pursuant to the requirings of y[e] said Act, they do request of us that we would certifie that they were of the People called Quakers: and though most of them were well known to us, yet that we might act with more care and caution therein, we did appoint certain persons to make particular enquiry into their Behaviour & uppon such Enquiry made, we do not find any Reason to Deny them their request as aforesaid.

These are therefore to certifye that the persons above named are of y⁰
Society of People called Quakers, & were so at yᵉ time of yᵉ making of y⁰
said act.

Signed in, & by order of, yᵉ said meeting. (Signed by six representatives of each of the Meetings mentioned)

This action had reference to current excitement over the French and
Indian border wars.

Att our monthly meeting att Burlington yᵉ 2ᵈ of yᵉ 12ᵗʰ moᵗʰ 1707 Charles
French Requested of this meeting a Certificate to Srowſbury [Shrewsbury]
month meeting on the account of taking a wife thereto belonging upon
which this meeting appoints Tho. Eves & John Wills to Enquire in Relation thereto.

Att our monthly meeting att Burlington yᵉ 1ˢᵗ of yᵉ 1ˢᵗ moᵗʰ 1707/8
The friends appointed to Enquire into yᵉ Clearness of Charles French
bring report yᵗ they find nothing but that he is clear on yᵉ account of
marriage & as to his conversation nothing appears Scandolous or Roproch-
ful therefore this meeting ordereth yᵉ Cleark to draw a Certificate ready
in order to be signed at yᵉ next meeting.

Att our monthly Meeting att Burlington the 3ʳᵈ of yᵉ 6ᵗʰ moᵗʰ 1719
There was an account given that Charles ffrench hath gon Contrary to
y⁰ good order of friends in his marriage and he hath been spoken to for
itt and he seems to be sory for his so doing and is willing so far as he
can to make satisfaction for his disorders & yᵉ meeting appoints Hugh
Sharp to Speak to him to be att yᵉ next meeting in order to make satisfaction under his hand.

Att our monthly meeting att Burlington yᵉ 7ᵗʰ of 7ᵗʰ Mo. 1719 Hugh
Sharp that was appointed to Speak to Charles french and to acquaint him
that the meeting Expects that he should appear at the next meeting to give
yᵉ meeting satisfaction and according he hath spoken to him and gave him
sum Expection that he would be at yᵉ Meeting but doth not onely sen in
a paper but the meeting Expects that he should be at yᵉ next meeting and
Hugh Sharp is ordered againe to acquaint him with yᵉ order of the
Meeting.

DEED, CHARLES FRENCH AND MATHEW ALLEN TO JOHN HUDSON, 1699

This Indenture made the ffifth day of the month Called June in the year of our Lord according to English Accompt One Thousand six Hundred Ninety and nine Between Charles ffrench of Wellingbourrough in the County of Burlington in the province of West Jersey son of Thomas ffrench and Executo^r to the Last Will and Testament of his father and Mathew Allen of the Towne of Chester in the County aforesaid Yeoman of the one part And John Hudson of the said Towne of Wellingburrough in the County aforesaid Carpinder of the other part Witnefseth that whereas Thomas ffrench father of the faid of the said Charles ffrench was Lawfully pofsefsed of Six Hundred Acres of Land fronting on Northampton River and lying next to the Land of John Hudson which faid six Hundred Acres of Land fronting on Northampton River and lying next to the land of John Hudson which said Six Hundred Acres belongeth to a Sixteenth part of a Propriety which he the said Thomas ffrench purchafed of John Woolstone as by one Indenture bearing date the twentieth day of November 1680 doth and may appear And the said Thomas ffrench did give unto the said Charles ffrench two hundred Acres of the said Land by a Deed of Gift bearing date the third day of June 1698 And Afterward did confirm the whole six Hundred Acres unto the said Charles ffrench by his last will and Testament And the said Charles ffrench fince the Decease of his said father hath figned and fealed one Indenture of Mortgage to the aforesaid Mathew Allen bearing date before the date of these presents to be voyd on Payment of sundry Debts as by the said Indenture it doth now at Large apear Now these presence Witnefs that the said Charles ffrench and Mathew Allen for and in Consideration of the Sum of of five and Twenty pounds Currant fillver Money in this province to him the said Charles ffrench in hand paid and fecured by the faid John Hudson at or before the fealing and Delivery of these presents the Receipt whereof they the said Charles ffrench and Mathew doe hereby Acknowledge and thereof Clearly Acquitt and Discharge the said John Hudson his heirs Executo^{rs} and Administrato^{rs} And Every of them forever by these presents Have Granted Bargined fold Enfeoffed and Confirmed and by these presents doth Grant bargain fell Enfeoffe and confirm unto the said John Hudson his heirs and afsigns forever One Hundred Acres of Land Beginning at a ftone by the faid Northampton River Then by the said John Hudsons Land to the Milcrick to a popler being Corner to the said Land Then downe the same to a fmall White Oake feven Chaine and a halfe then south westerly twenty Eight degrees One Hundred and fourty Chaine to a white Oake by the said River then up the fame to the ftone first mintioned Together allsoe with the mines mineralls woods fishings hawkings huntings and fowlings and all and Every the Appurtences profits

SURVEYOR-GENERAL'S OFFICE, BURLINGTON, N. J., 1825

and Commodities whatsoever belonging to the said Premises And the Reversion and Reversions Remainders and Remainders thereof And all the Estate Right title Interest Use possession property Claim and Demand whatsoever of them the said Charles ffrench and Mathew Allen in or to the same—To have and to hold the said one Hundred acres of Land unto the said John Hudson his heirs and Assigns to the only proper use and behoofe of him the said John Hudson his heirs and Assigns forever And the said Charles ffrench and Mathew Allen for themselves severally and Respectively and for their Several and Respective heirs Executors Administrato^rs. and Assigns doe Covenant promise and Grant to and with the said John Hudson his heirs and Assigns by these presence that they have not wittingly or Willingly Committed or done any Act matter or thing whereby or by reason whereof the said premises hereby Granted is Shall or may be Charged Burthened or Incumbered in any title Charge Estate or otherwise Howsoever & then the rents thereout Issueing to the King and his successors and the Arrears thereof if any be And Allsoe that the said Charles ffrench and Mathew Allen Their heirs and Assigns shall and will at all times hereafter during the space of seven Years Next Ensueing the date hereof at the request Cost and Charges of the said John Hudson his heirs or Assigns make doe and Execute or Cause to be made done and Executed all and every such Lawfull Conveyance or Conveyances for the further better and more perfect Assureing and sure making the abovesaid premises unto the said John Hudson his heirs and Assigns forever as by the said John Hudson his heirs or Assigns shall be Lawfully required, soe as the partie or parties to whome such request be not Compelled nor hereby Compellable to travill from the place of his or their aboade further then to the towne of Burlington for the doing and Executing thereof And soe as such Conveyance Containe Noe further warranty then as aforesaid In Witness whereof the parties first above named to these Present Indenture have Interchangably set their Hands and feals the day and year first above written 1699

Charles French with a [seale]
Mathew Allen with a [seale]

Signed sealed & Delivered in ye presence of John Test, Sam^ll: ffurnis Thomas Eves The 9th: day of the month called August 1728 Then the within Named Thomas Eves one of the Evidences to the within Deed Came before me Underwritten being one of the Kings Council for the province of New Jersey and upon his solemn Affirmation did declare that he was present and saw the within Named Charles French and Mathew Allen sign seal and Execute the within Deed unto the within Named John Hudson and that he saw John Test and Samuel ffurnis sign as Witnesses to the same. Witness my hand the day and year abovesaid.

John Wills.

DEED, CHARLES AND RICHARD FRENCH TO HENRY
PEEPS, 1704

This Indenture made the ffirst Day of November in the year of our Lord according to English acc^t. One thousand Seven hundred and ffour Between Charles French of the Township of Wellingbourrough in the County of Burlington Within the province of New Jersey yeoman And Richard French of the Township of Mansfield in the said County of Burlington Province aforesaid yeoman of the One part And Henry Peeps of the Township of Chesterfield and County of Burlington aforesaid Husbandman of the other part Witnefseth that the said Charles French & Richard French for and in Consideration of the Sum of thirty pounds of Current Silver money within the Westerly Division of the province aforesaid to the said Charles French and of ffive Shillings like current Silver money aforesaid to the said Richard French by the said Henry Peeps to them respectively in hand paid at and before the Ensealing and Delivery hereof the receipt of which said Sum of thirty pounds the said Charles French doth hereby acknowledge & the receipt of the said ffive Shillings the said Richard French hereby acknowledgeth and thereof and of every part Pcell thereof doe and Each and Either of them—Respectively Doth acquit Exonerate and Discharge the said Henry Peeps his heirs Executors and Administrators and every of them forever by these presents Have Granted bargained and sold aliened Enfeoffed & Confirmed and by these Psents Doe ffully Clearly and absolutely Grant bargain & Sell alcyne Enfeoffe and Confirm unto the said Henry Peeps his heirs and Afsigns forever The ffull Quantity of Six hundred Acres of Land to be Taken up Laid fforth and Surveyed to and for the said Henry Peeps his heirs and Afsigns in any place within the said Westerly Division of said Province where purchased from the Native Indians and not before taken up and Surveyed which said Six hundred Acres of Land is to be taken up in right of the Share or Shares of Land for the third Dividend belonging to an Eighth part of a propriety of Land within the said Westerly Division of the said Province & by the Last Will and Testament of Thomas French Deccd: ffather of said Charles and Richard French given and Bequeathed to said Charles French as by the same will relation being thereunto had more at Large Appears. Together with all and every the Mines Minerals Woods ffishings foulings Hawkings Huntings and ffowlings and all Other profits Comodities Hereditaments and Improvements Whatsoever to said Six hundred acres of Land belonging or in any wise Appertaining and Also all the Estate right Title Interest pofsefsion Property Claim and Demand whatsoever of them the said Charles French and Richard French or Either of them as well in Law as in Equity of in Or unto the said granted and bargained Six hundred acres of Land or any part or parcell thereof with the appurtenances and the Reversion and Reversions Remainder and Remainders of the Same and of Eevery part thereof To Have and To Hold the said Six hundred acres of Land and granted and Bargained Premiſses and every part and parcell thereof with the Appurtenances unto the said Henry Peeps his heirs and Aſsigns forever.

And the said Charles French Richard French for themselves Jointly and Severally and for them and Either of their heirs Executors and Administrators Doe Covenant promise and Grant to and with the said Henry Peeps his heirs and Aſsigns by these presents that at the time of the Sealing and Delivery hereof they the said Charles French & Richard French or yᵉ one of them have Or hath good right full power and Lawfull and absolute authority to Grant bargain Sell and Confirme the said Six hundred acres of Land Granted or Mentioned to be granted pmiſses with the Appurtenances unto the said Henry Peeps his heirs and Aſsigns forever in Manner and fform as in these presents is mentioned and Exprefsed And that they the said Charles French and Richard French or either of them have not nor hath not wittingly or willingly Committed Sufferred or Done any act matter or thing whatsoever whereby or by reason whereof the said granted and Bargained premiſses or any part or pcel thereof is are shall or may be Charged Burthend or Incumbred in any Tytle Charge Estate or Otherwise howsoever Other than the Quittrents thereout Iſsuing unto Our Sovereign Lady the Queen her heirs and Succeſsors and the Arrears thereof if any be and Lastly the said Charles French for himself his heirs Executors and administrators Doth hereby Covenant promise and Grant to and with the said Henry Peeps his heirs and Aſsigns That he the said Charles French and his heirs Shall and will at all and every time and Times hereafter During the Time and Space of Seven Years Next Ensuing the Date hereof at the request Costs and Charges of the said Henry Peeps his heirs and Aſsigns make do Execute or Cause to be made done or Executed Such ffurther and Other lawful Act and Acts thing and things Conveyance & Aſsurance Whatsoever for the further better more full and perfect Conveying Confirming and Aſsuring the said Six hundred Acres of Land and granted and bargained premiſses and every or any part or parcell thereof with the appurtenances unto the said Henry Peeps his heirs and Aſsigns for ever According to the purport true Intent and meaning of these presents as by him the said Henry Peeps his heirs and Aſsigns Shall be reasonably required Soe as the person or persons to whom Such request Shall be made be not Compelled or Compellable to Travell or goe ffurther then to the Town of Burlington aforesaid for the making Doing or Executing hereof and So as Such ffurther Aſsurance Contain noe ffurther Covenants or Warranty then According to the Tenor of these presents In Witneſs whereof the said Parties first above named to these present Indenture have Set their hands and Seals the Day and Year first above written 1704

> Richard French & [Seal]
> Charles French & [Seal]

Sealed and Delivered in the presence of Daniel Leeds T Wright William Bull Tho Revell November 2ᵈ: 1704.

Then received yᵉ Sum of money respectively mentioned for the consideration of the within granted Lands by us Charles French Richard French Witnefses by us Tho: Revell Daniel Leeds.

Endorsed County of Burlington July 28ᵗʰ: 1762—Then personally Came and appeared before me Charles Read Esqʳ: one of his Majesties Council for the province of New Jersey Revell Elton Esqʳ: a person to me well known and worthy of good Credit being duly Sworn did Depose that he was acquainted with the handwriting of Daniel Leeds and Thomas Revell Esqʳ (deceaᵈ long since) had Seen them respectively write their names and verily believes that the names Daniel Leeds and Thomas Revell Signed as Witnefses to the within Deed are of the proper hand writing of the said Daniel Leeds and Thomas Revell

Jurat Coram Cha Reed

Recorded this —— Septemʳ 1762.

DEED, RICHARD FRENCH TO CHARLES FRENCH, 1713

The following is the deed of release made by Richard French [5] to his brother Charles [8], of all claims in the home plantation.

To all Perfons to whom these prefents Shall come or may Concern—Greeting Know yee, that Richard French Son & Heir apparant of Thomas French Late of Wellinborrow in the County of Burlington & Province of Weft Jerfey Deceafed, for divers good & Valuable Considerations me thereunto moving & more particularly that I may as much as in me Lyeth Endeavour that the Laft Will and Teftament of my said father should be performed, and whereas my said father by his Laft Will & Teftament bareing Date the third day of June, Anno Domini, One thoufand six hundred ninety Eight, Did Nominate & Appoint my Brother Charles French to be his Sole Executor of his said Will and did by the same Give & bequeath unto my said brother all that farm plantation or tract of Land, Scituate Lying & being in the Townfhip of Wellenborrow aforesaid Containing by the survey thereof Six hundred acres of Land In Upland & Meadow, with all & every the premifses & appurtenances belonging or in any Wife appertaining & Whereas my sd Brother being Lately In Old England there Leaving the sd Originall Will which may Caufe the hindrance to my brother of yᵉ Sale of yᵉ sd Plantation as If some right might appertain to me for want of the said Will If it should any Wife Mifcarry or be Loft I being the Eldeft Son & heir of my sd Father, Therefore to prevent & Avoid all Controverfy for touching or Concerning the same I the said

Richard French have Remiſed releaſ^d and forever Quit Claimed and I do by theſe preſents, for me my Heirs Executors and adminiſtrators & Aſsigns Remiſe Releaſe & for ever Quitt Claim, unto the sd Charles French his Heirs & Aſsigns, Remiſe Releaſe & forever Quitt Claim unto the sd—all and all manner of Right Title Intereſt property Claim & Demand whatſoever—which I the sd Richard French now have my heirs Executors shall or may have Challenge or demand of in or to the sd Mentioned Tract of Land lying & being in the Townſhip of Wellenborrow as aforesaid Containing Six hundred acres of Upland & Meadow So that I the s^d Richard French my Heirs Executors Adminiſtrators or Aſsigns shall not, nor will not at any time hereafter make any claim Challenge or Demand of in or to the said Tract of Land as aforesaid or to any part or parcel of the Same—but that both myself my Heirs Executors Adminiſtrators or Aſsigns or any or every of them shall from henceforth be thereof & of every part & parcel thereof & therein be utterly & forever Excluded & Debarred by these preſents.

In Witneſs whereof I the said Richard ffrench have hereunto Set my hand & Seal this twenty Ninth day of January, In the Twelfth year of the Reign of our Sovereign Lady Anne Queen over Great Brittain, &c. Anno Domini, One thouſand seven hundred and Thirteen.

Richard French wth a Seal   [SEAL].

Seal'd & Delivered In the preſence of,

Daniel Smith, Tho: Middleton, Tho: Scattergood.

A COLONIAL ADVERTISEMENT, 1722

In December, 1719, Andrew Bradford, the pioneer printer of Pennsylvania, son of William Bradford, began the publication in Philadelphia of the first newspaper issued in the state. "The American Weekly Mercury," as the paper was called, was "Printed and Sold by Andrew Bradford, at the BIBLE in the Second Street; and alſo by William Bradford in New-York, where Advertiſements are taken in." It was a small two-column four-page sheet of the most primitive style and often contained curious advertisements, the result of the efforts of immigrants to find each other in the new country. In several numbers of the " Mercury," beginning April 19, 1722, appeared the following notice, revealing the approximate date of one of the visits of Charles French to " Old England ":

N. B. *They have a Paſs along with them from* Col. ⸺. of Maryland *all in one Paper.*

WHereas about Twenty Years ſince, there came into theſe Parts of *America,* with one Mr. *Charles French,* who lives at *Ancocus-Creek* in *Burlington* County, in *Weſt-Jerſey,* one *Samuel Lacy* born in *Northamptonſhire,* Theſe are to give Notice, That if the ſaid Samuel Lacy be living, and will come to Henry Flower, Poſtmaſter of Philadelphia, he may be informed of ſomething very conſiderable for his Advantage; And further, If any Perſon can give any true and ſatisfactory Account or Proof of the ſaid Samuel Lacy's being now living, ſhall have a Reward of Five Pounds current Money of this Province paid them

9—JOHN FFRENCH (Thomas, 1).

> Baptized January 2nd, 1673, at Church S. S.
> Peter and Paul, Nether Heyford, England.
> d. 1729.
> m. First, 1701, Ann ———.
> m. Second, 6th mo. 10th, 1724, Sarah (Mason)
> Wickward, widow of William Wickward, and
> daughter of John Mason of Evesham Town-
> ship, Burlington Co., N. J.

44—JOHN FRENCH, JR.   b. 1702.
                             d. 1729.

45—THOMAS FRENCH   b. 1703.

46—CHARLES FRENCH   b. 1704.

47—RACHEL FRENCH   b. 1705.
                           m. First, Enoch Fenton.
                           m. Second, Dec. 1, 1735, Nathaniel Wilkinson.

48—ANN FRENCH   b. 1707.
                           m. Joshua Woolston.

William Wickward and Sarah Mason were married in 1717, and had children, Samuel,
Hannah and Rachel.

JOHN FRENCH

The youngest son of Thomas ffrench, progenitor, appears to have inherited
in good degree the qualities of success which characterized his father and
brothers. He no doubt was advanced patrimony sufficient to enable him to
make a good start in life, although his share of the paternal estate under
the will was nominal. Records show that he early acquired considerable
land in Northampton township, where he resided for a number of years
and prospered as a farmer, adding to his plantation, from time to time, and
finally possessed upwards of 500 acres. The curious and painstaking account of his executors shows extended business relationship, and the performance of this trust in accordance with the letter and spirit of the will
of the testator. In life he set a consistent example and his last formal
expressions comprised impressive admonition. His son Charles seems to
have remained in Northampton township and official records established the

fact that the latter's daughter Margaret married William Hooper, a resident of Northampton township, the license bearing date Dec. 24, 1744, and accompanying which is the following quaint endorsement:

> Dec. 24, 1744, Joshua Bishop affirmed before Joseph Scattergood, one of his Majesty's Justices for the city of Burlington, that he heard Charles French, father of Margaret French, give his consent that William Hooper should marry his said Daughter.
>
> his
Joshua × Bishop
mark
>
> Affirmed before
> Joſ Scattergood

From sundry records it would appear that William Hooper and Margaret, his wife, had two sons; Isaac who, in 1775, married Martha Tice, and Jacob who, in 1772, married Hannah Platt.

William Hooper died intestate in 1759 and his wife Margaret, renouncing her right to administer the estate, at her suggestion Thomas Budd was appointed to act in that capacity.

MEETING RECORDS

Burlington Monthly Meeting Minutes:

Att our Monthly Meeting held at Burlington yᵉ 1ˢᵗ of 4ᵗʰ Mo. 1724. John ffrench made application to this Meeting on yᵉ account of marriage with one within the Vearg of Newtown moᵗʰ meeting for which yᵉ meeting appoints Joshu Smith & James Lippincott to make Enquiry Concerning his clearness & conversation and make report to yᵉ next meeting.

Att our Monthly Meeting att Burlington yᵉ 6ᵗʰ day of yᵉ 5ᵗʰ month 1724 – – The two friends Joshua Smith and James Lippincott that was appointed to make enquire in to yᵉ Clearness of John ffrench both on yᵉ account of Marriage and also his life and conversation report to this meeting yᵗ they do not find anything to object but he is clear on yᵉ account of marriage and his conversation pretty orderly of late for which yᵉ meeting orders yᵉ Cleark to draw a Certificat accordingly.

Haddonfield Monthly Meeting Minutes:

13—5 mo. 1724 At said meeting John French and Sarah Wickwart signify their intentions of taking each other in marriage, the said John Living within the Verge of Burlington Monthly Meeting therefore he is given to understand a certificate will be expected at his next presentation from them.

10—6 mo. 1724 At said monthly meeting John French and Sarah Wickwart the second time presented their Intentions of taking each other in marriage. This meeting after receiving a Certificate from Burlington Mo. Meeting consents that they may take each other in Truth's way, and appoints John Haines and W^m. Borton to be present at sd marriage, to see it be orderly accomplished.

14th 7 mo. 1724 At said meeting John Haines reports to this meeting that he was present at ye marriage of John French and Sarah Wickwart & that it was orderly accomplished.

Haddonfield Minutes of ye Mo: Meeting of Women Friends:

Att a m^oly m^tg of w^om fr^ds held at Haddonfield ye 13th of 5th m^o 1724 At s^d m^tg Jno French & Sarah Wickware signified y^r intentions of m^rg, ye m^tg a^ppts Eliz. Evins & Mary Evees to make ye ufual inquirie & report accordingly to next m^o m^tg.

Att a m^oly m^tg of w^om fr^ds held at Haddonfield ye 10th of 6^m 1724 At s^d m^tg Jno French & Sarah Wickward signified ye continuation of y^r intentions of m^rg ye return of inquirers is they find nothing so mattierall as to obstruct y^r proceedings so ye m^tg confents to ye accomplifhm^t of ye s^d m^rg according to ye good ord^r among fr^ds &c & appoints Hannah Hains & Hannah Borton to see good o^rd^r kept.

DEED, SARAH MORREY TO JOHN FRENCH, 1717

To All to whome thefe prefents Shall Come Sarah Morrey of ye City of philadelphia in ye prouince of penfilvania widow Distiller Sends greeting—

Whereas by a Certain Draught of Certificate bearing Date in October 1693 under ye hand of Daniell Leeds there was Surveyed unto Lady Martha Roads Saml Barker and Tho: Wright two tracts of Land on ye Branches of Ancocus Creek in ye County of Burlington in west new Jerfey ye one s^d to Contain three thoufand one hundred and twenty acres and ye other twelve hundred acres as by s^d Certifycate &c and ye Record thereof in ye Secretaries office may appear And Whereas by uirtue of Seuerall mefne Conveyances and Afsurences in law She ye said Sarah Morrey now is and Stands Lawfully Seized of a good right and Estate in all that part & parts of ye before mentioned Lands with ye appurtences Whereof he s^d Tho: Wright was Seized & pofsesed in common wth s^d Roads & Barker by uirtue of ye above survey &c or otherwise howsoeuer and for as much as many Disputes in law and other wise have arifen in Relation to ye Right and title of ye s^d Rhoads Barker and Wright to ye s^d land by and between them and their Afsigns and ye present Settlers thereon who alfo by uirtue of Surueys Indian purchases and Seating Claime a right to Seuerall parts & parcells thereof in order thereof to

accomedate in a Christian and peaceable name all disputes Law Suits Con-
treuerſis Claims of Right or title by from or under yᵉ sᵈ Tho: Wright
to yᵉ part of yᵉ Lands in poſsesion of John french of yᵉ County of Burlington aforsᵈ & townſhip of Northampton yeoman which is Bounded as
followeth Vizᵗ in two tracts of yᵉ first Begins at a white oak near yᵉ
mouth of Run or Creek Stop yᵉ Jades Run thence Sᵗ. Easterly 8ᵈ: twenty
one Chains to another white oak thence Nᵒ: Easterly 73 degrees Sixty
three Chains to a gum by sᵈ Creek then down yᵉ Same by yᵉ Seuerall
Cources thereof and bounding therewᵗʰ to yᵉ Corner wᵗ oak first mentioned Surveyed for one hundred acres and yᵉ other tract Begins at a
hickery tree Corner to Jacob Lambs Land thence by his Land East by
South twenty two Chains to a black oak Corner then South East twenty
fiue Chaine to a white oak Corner then weſt South west four Chains to
a black oak then near South to a brook Called Stop yᵉ Jades Run then
Bounding down by yᵉ Same and yᵉ above last mentioned tract of Land
to a white oak Corner at yᵉ mouth thereof then north Seuenteen Chains
then East north East twenty two Chains then East by north three Chains
to yᵉ first mentioned Corner Surveyed for one Hundred and twenty acres
now theſe preſents wittneſseth yᵗ She yᵉ sᵈ Sarah Morey not only for yᵉ
Conſiderations and Cauſes aforsᵈ But alſo for yᵉ further Conſideration
of yᵉ Sum of Seuen pounds Currᵗ money of America to her in hand
paid by John french aforˢᵈ yᵉ recept whereof She doth hereby acknowledge hath Remised Released and quitt Claimed and by theſe preſents
She yᵉ sᵈ Sarah Morrey for her Selfe her heirs & aſsigns do freely Clearly
and abſolutely Remise Releaſe and for Ever Quit Claime unto him yᵉ
sᵈ John french and to his heirs and aſsigns all that her Right title Intreſt
property Clayme and Demᵈ of in to or out of yᵉ sᵈ two tracts of land
Joyned in one being in yᵉ whole two hundred and twenty acres and all
yᵉ ways waters water Cources woods Houſes Buldings fields fences im-
prouemᵗˢ marſhes Swamps meadows mines mineralls fiſhings fowlings
Hawkings huntings Rights Liberties preuilidges Hereditamᵗˢ And appurtences to Each pᵗ and parcell thereof belonging or in any wiſe appertaining
togeather with yᵉ Reuerſon and reuerſons Remainder and remainders
rents iſsues and profits thereof and pᵗ and parcell thereof to have and
to hold all yᵉ sᵈ two hundred twenty acres of Land and premises with
Euery yᵉ appurtences unto him yᵉ sᵈ John french to yᵉ only use and behoofe
of him yᵉ sᵈ John french his heirs and aſsigns for euer So yᵗ neither
he yᵉ sᵈ Tho: Wright nor his heirs nor aſsigns nor yᵉ heirs nor Aſsigns
nor Legates of George Hutchinson Decᵈ nor She yᵉ sᵈ Sarah Morrey nor
her heirs nor aſsigns nor any other perſon or perſons by from or under
them Either or any of them Shall Com will or may at any time hereafter have Clayme challenge or Demand any Estate Right title property
poſesion or other thing of in or to any part share or portion of yᵉ sᵈ
Lands & premises by theſe preſents Released or Intended to be hereby

Releaſed But from all actions and Suits cauſe and Cauſes of actions & Suits Rights titles or Clayms Either in Law or Equity Shall and will from thence forth for Euer be utterly Bared and Excluded by theſe preſents in wittneſs whereof She yᵉ sᵈ Sarah Morey hath hereunto Sett her hand & Seale this fourth day of Novembʳ in yᵉ fourth year of yᵉ Reign of King george ouer great Brittain &c Anno Domini 1717

                                        Sarah Morrey   [SEAL]

   Signed Sealed & Deliuered in presents of us
      Philo: Leeds Isaac Decou Jn° Budd

County of Burlington in yᵉ prouince of New Jersey yᵉ 20ᵗʰ of March 1720 then came before me under written one of his maieſtys Councill for yᵉ prouince of New Jerſey Isaac Decou and uppon his Solemn Afirmation declares yᵗ he saw Sarah Morrey Sign Seall and deliuer yᵉ above inſtrumᵗ as hier uolentary act and Deed for yᵉ uſe aboue mentioned taken before me yᵉ day and year aboue written.

                                        Peter Bard.

WILL OF JOHN FRENCH, 1729

   I John French of Northampton In yᵉ County of Burlington & Western Division of yᵉ Province of New Jersey, yeoman, Being very sick & weak In Body But of sound & Perfect mind & memory Thanks be given to Almighty God therefore Calling to mind yᵉ mortallity of my Body & Knowing That it is appointed for all men once to Dye Do make & Ordain This my Last will & Testament & Do hereby utterly Revoke Disanul & make void all other former wills or Testaments by me heretofore made.

   And princepally & first of all I Give & Recommend my Soul Into yᵉ hands of God that Gave It and my Body I Recommend to yᵉ Earth to be buried In a Christianlike Decent manner at yᵉ Descretion of my Executors hereafter Named. And as Touching Such worldly Estate wherewith it hath pleased God to Bless me with In This Life I Give Devise & Dispose of yᵉ Same In manner & form following—

   Imprimus—And first of all I order my funeral Charges & Just Debts to be Raised out of my moveable Estate & paid by my Executors hereafter named And as for yᵉ Remaining part of my Estate both Real & personal after my Just Debts & funerall charges is paid I Give & Dispose of yᵉ same as followeth—

   ITEM I Give Devise & Bequeath unto my oldest son Thomas French & to his heirs & Assigns forever yᵉ sum of five Pounds Current Lawfull money of America to be paid by my Executors & all my waring Cloaths to be Delivered by my Executors

ITEM I Give Devise & Bequeath unto my Second Son Charles French
& to his heirs & assigns forever all That Part & parcel of my Land Lying
adjoyning on ye East side of a line or Lines of marked Trees to be Run
Beginning at a Hickory Corner next to Jacob Lambs Land & Runing
from thence a Cross my said Land upon a streight line southerly to a
Chestnut tree marked for a Corner standing by a pond In ye Division
Between ye long field and ye Rye piece & from thence extending still across
my said Land southerly upon a streight line unto another Chestnut tree
for a Corner standing in ye south line of my said Land being by Estima-
tion one hundred & three acres he my said second son Charles French
Paying unto my Daughter Ann French ye sum of fifteen pounds current
Lawfull money of america.

ITEM I Give Devise & Bequeath unto my oldest Daughter Rachel
Fenton & to her heirs & assignes for Ever all That my mantion house
plantation & Land Lying adjoyning ye West side of ye above Described
Lines Limited & Bounded & to be Run as above mentioned scituate &
being In ye abovesaid Township of Northampton In ye County & Division
of ye province aforesaid Shee my said oldest Daughter Rachel Fenton
yeilding & Paying unto my youngest Daughter Ann French ye sum of
fifty Pounds Current Lawfull money of America.

ITEM I Give Devise & Bequeath unto my Daughter In Law Sarah
French my side saddle to be Delivered by my Executors.

ITEM I Give Devise & Bequeath unto my Son In Law Samuel Wickward when he shall arrive or Live to ye age of Twenty one years old
ye sum of six pounds Current Lawfull money of america to be paid by
my Executors.

ITEM I Give Devise & Bequeath unto my Daughter In Law Hannah
Wickward when she shall arrive or Live to ye age of Twenty one years
old ye sum of six pounds current Lawfull money of america to be paid
by my Executors.

ITEM I Give Devise & Bequeath unto my Daughter In Law Rechael
Wickward when she shall arrive or Live to ye age of Twenty one years
old ye sum of six pounds Current Lawfull money of america to be paid
by my Executors.

ITEM Also That If any one or more of my said Son In Law or
Daughters In Law ye above named Wickwards should happen to Dye
before they comes to age as abovesaid That then ye Legacie belonging
or Given to ye said Deceased person or persons shall be Given or paid
by my Executors to my son Charles French & my Daughters Rechael
Fenton & Ann French to be equally Divided to each of them their Equal
Division.

ITEM I Give Devise & Bequeath unto my well Beloved & Trusty
friends my Brother Thomas French & my neighbour James Wills whom
I Likewise Nominate Constitute & ordain my whole & sole Executors to

this my Last will & Testament to Each of them ye sum of five shillings, Giving & Granting unto my said Executers or either of them Lawfull & absolute power & authority to Take Receive sell & Dispose of all my personal Estate where & whatsoever which is not before Given Devised or Bequeathed to ye Intent That my said Executers shall be Enabled to Pay my funeral charges & Just Debts & ye Legacies herein before Bequeathed.

Item And also whatsoever part of my Estate In Goods Chattles or Credits that shall Remain In my said Executers hands or ye Survivours of them I Give Devise & Bequeath unto my son Charles , French & my Daughters Rechael Frenton & Ann French to be equally Divided to Each of them their Equal Dividen and I do hereby Ratifie & Confirm This & no other to be my Last will & Testament In witness whereof I have hereunto set my hand and seal this Thirteenth Day of Aprill Anno qe Dominey one Thousand Seven Hundred & twenty nine 1729

Signed, sealed and Delivered Pub-   his
lished pronounced & Declared by y^e
said John French to be his Last will
& Testament In ye presence of us   John French
    William Allcott
    Jacob Lamb
    Joseph Meneer   mark
    John Budd

Co— Burlington SS Be it Rememberd that on this Ninth day of May An° Don 1729 personally came and appeared before me Samuel Bustill D. Surrogate & Register of ye western Division of ye Province of New Jersey duly commissioned &c William Allcott one of the wittnesses to ye above & within will subscribed who being sworn on ye holy Evangelists of Almighty God do depose that he was present & saw John French Sign & Seal & heard him publish pronounce & declare ye Instrum^t. on this sheet of paper contained to be his last will & Testament and that at the doing thereof s^d Testator was of sound mind memory & understanding to ye best of his knowledge & belief & that at ye sametime Joseph Meneer & John Budd the other subscribed evidences were present & signed their names as Evidences to ye same in ye presence of ye Testator

                                        William Allcott

    Jurat Coram Me
        Sam^1 Bustill

INVENTORY OF THE ESTATE OF JOHN FRENCH, 1729

May the 9 Day 1729.

A Trew a praisement of yᵉ Estate of John French Sener Late Deceased Begining as followeth

	£	S	d
Purs and a parrell	12	5	9
Bed & furneture	4	0	0
to side Sadel	3	0	0
to tow Chest and Linning	1	4	0
to a table & box and other things	1	12	9
to a dow trouf	0	10	0
to a Bibles & other things	1	12	6
to potts & a pann	0	18	0
to husbandtree tooles & old iorn	3	12	0
to puter & other things	3	8	0
to 2 horsses & a mair & 2 saddels	31	10	0
to a feather Bedd and furniture & other things	6	5	0
to 2 Beds and Rey & other Lomber	5	0	0
to Bacon	10	10	0
to milk vessel & other things	1	10	0
to Rey indian Corn & oates	7	0	0
to Cart & ploues & other Lumber	4	10	0
to Hogs	4	0	0
to all the Cattell	34	0	0
to Sheep	6	0	0
to yᵉ womens a parrell and other things	12	16	
to a peace of Cassey	0	13	0
to a Chest & other things	5	8	0
to Book Debts Deu	4	6	7
to Bonds Deue	12	10	0

By a trew a praisement by   Thomas Biſhop

Test—   Michal Woolſton

    William Alcott   Totall   £167 1 7

Affirmed to May 9—1729—by Thomas Bishop

    Michal Woolſton

    Thomas french

ACCOUNT OF EXECUTORS OF

The Accompt of Thomas French and James Wills Executors of the laſt Will and deceased As well of and for such and so much of the Goods, Chattels and Credits of and disbursements out of the Same &c.

Theſe Accomptants charge themselves—   Debtors

Theſe Accomptants charge themselves with all and singular the Goods and Chattels Rights and Credits of the
said Deceased mentioned and specified in an Inventory and
Appraisement thereof made and Exhibited into the Registry   £   S   d
of the Prerogative Court in the Secretary's Office at Burling- 167   1   7
ton Amounting as by the said Inventory and appraisement
appears to the Sum of One hundred and sixty seven pounds
One Shilling and seven pence

To moneys advanced upon sale of Testators Effects above   14   18   6½
the Inventory the sum of

Theſe Accomptants pray allowance of their payments and
Disbursements out of the Estate of the said Deceased as
appears on the Contra Credit side of this accoᵗ:

WILL OF JOHN FRENCH, 1732

Teſtament of John French late of Northampton in the County of Burlington yeoman the said Dece^d. as came to their hands to be administered as of and for their payments

Pr. Contra Theſe Accomptants pray allowance

		£	S	d
Imp^e.	By moneys paid at the Registers office for the Lett^e Teſtamentary	2	5	7
Item.	By moneys paid to William Collum as appears pr. recet No (2)	0	13	6
Itt.	By Womans Apparel to Jn° Briggs as appears pr. receipt N° (3)	12	16	—
It.	By moneys paid to Ann Lamb as appears pr. receipt N° (4)...	7	6	4
It.	By moneys paid to Daniel Wills as appears pr. receipt N° (5)...	4	12	11
Itt.	By moneys paid to W^m: Murrell as appears pr. receipt N° (6)...	4	18	—
Itt.	By moneys paid to Rich^d: Smith as appears pr. Recet N° (7)....	2	15	.3
It.	By moneys paid to Dorothy Large as appears pr. Rece^t N° (8)..	24	6	0½
Itt.	By moneys paid to Wm Allcott as appears pr. Rece^t N° (9).....	2	0	0
Itt.	By moneys paid to Wm Cramer as appears pr. Rece^t N° (10)....	1	5	0
Itt.	By moneys paid to Joseph Hilliard as appears pr. Rece^t N° (11)	1	2	0
Itt.	By moneys paid to Thomas Bishop as appears pr. Rece^t N° (12)	1	6	6
Itt.	By moneys paid to Edward Shippin as appears pr. Rece^t N° (13)	1	13	2
Itt.	By moneys paid to Richard Jones as appears pr. Rece^t N° (14)	0	17	6
Itt.	By moneys paid to Jonathan Wright as appears pr. Rece^t N° (15)	0	13	3
Itt.	By moneys paid to John Briggs as appears pr. Rece^t N° (16)...	0	12	3
Itt.	By moneys paid to Thos: Griffiths as appears pr. Rece^t N° (17)..	0	12	0
Itt.	By moneys paid to William Biſhop as appears pr. Rece^t N° (18)	0	7	0
Itt.	By moneys paid to John Anderson as appears pr .Rece^t N° (19)	0	6	9
	Summa	£48	9	0½

Carryed to page (4)

Thefe Accomptants continue themselves		Debtors	
	£	S	d
To the Amount of the Inventory brought from page (1)....	167	1	7
To moneys advanced upon the sale of the Teftators Effects above the Inventory.................................	14	18	6½

Pr. Contra Thefe Accomtants pray allowance

		£	S	d
	By Sundrys brought from page (2) amounting to the sum of....	48	9	0½
It.	By moneys paid Samuel Woolfton as appears pr. rece^t N° 20/.....	0	10	6
Itt.	By moneys paid John Budd as appears pr. rece^t N° (21)..........	0	6	0
Itt.	By moneys paid to Titan Leeds as appears pr. rece^t N° (22).......	0	10	0
Itt.	By moneys paid to John Brown as appears pr. rece^t N° (23)......	0	9	4
Itt.	By moneys paid to Michael Woolfton as appears pr. rece^t N° (24)..	0	5	0
Itt.	By moneys paid to Joseph Stephens as appears pr. rece^t N° (25)...	0	3	0
Itt.	By moneys paid to Jacob Lamb as appears pr. rece^t N° (26)......	0	3	0
Itt.	By moneys paid to Isaac DeCow as appears pr. rece^t N° (27)......	0	4	4
Itt.	By moneys paid to Mary Wood as appears pr. rece^t N° (28).......	0	2	9
Itt.	By moneys paid to Thomas Bryan as appears pr. rece^t N° (29)....	0	2	0
Itt.	By moneys paid to Charles ffrench Junr a Debt Due from y^e. Dece^d.	4	2	2
Itt.	By moneys paid to James Wills Due from the Dece^d and for Disbursements for and towards the funeral of the Dece^d..........	2	0	9
Itt.	By moneys paid to Thomas ffrench one of the sons of the dec^d in full of a Legacy, as appears pr. his Rece^t N° (30).............	ɔ	0	0
Itt.	By the Wearing apparell of the Dece^d delivered to the said Thos. ffrench pursuant to the Deceased's bequeft thereof to him, which s^d. apparell was appraised in the Inv^{ry}: of the dece^{ds}. Eftate at..	10	2	9
Itt.	By a Side Saddle delivered to Sarah ffrench, pursuant to the Deceased's bequest thereof to her, appraised in the Inventory of the Deceased's Estate at the sum of......................	ɔ	—	—
Itt.	By Sundrys out of the Estate of the Deceased to Samuel Wickward, amounting to the sum of.................................	1	6	6
	Summa	£76	17	1½

Carryed to page (6)

Thefe Accomptants continue themselves

		Debtors	
	£	S.	d.
To the Amount of the Inventory brought from page (3)....	167	1	7
To Moneys advanced upon the sale of the Teftator's Effects above the Inventory the Sum of........................	14	18	6½
Summa	£182	—	1½,

Pr. Contra Thefe Accomptants pray allowance—

	£	S	d
Item. By Sundrys brought from page (4) amounting to...............	76	17	1½
By moneys allowed to these accomptants by the Residuary Lega- ates for their time trouble and Expences in the Carrying on and managing the administracon of the Testator's Estate selling receiving and paying Z^t: the Sum of.........................	4	—	—
Itt. By moneys paid to Charles ffrench in full of his Legacy out of the Teftators Estate as appears pr. his Discharge for the same and is Voucher N°: (32) the Sum of.........................	30	—	—
Itt. By moneys paid to Enoch ffenton in full of his Wive's Legacy out of the Testator's Estate, as appears pr. his Discharge for the same and is Voucher N°: (33) the sum of....................	30	—	—
Itt. By moneys paid to Joshua Woolfton in full of his Wive's Legacy out of the Teftator's Estate as appears pr. his discharge for the same and is Voucher N°: (34) the sum of....................	27	18	—
Itt. By moneys paid to the Register on the Drawing and Stating of this account crediting and pafsing the Same and Quietus Est. Z^t: the sum of	1	ɔ	—
Summa	£170	—	5½
Ballance in thefe accomptant's hands for Samuel Wickward and Rachel Wickward two of the Legattees of the said Dece^d: Six pounds Each to be paid them at the age of twenty one years without Int..	12	00	00
	£182	—	1½

A true Acco^t. Pr. us

Be it Remembered that on the twenty ninth day of August in the year of our Lord one thousand seven hundred and thirty two Thomas ffrench and James Wills Executors of the laft Will & Teftament of John ffrench late of Northampton in the County of Burlington yeoman Dece[d]: Exhibited before me Samuel Buftill Deputy Register of and for the Western Divifion of the province of New Jersey the within account of their Administration of the goods and Chattels Rights and Credits of the said Deceased, together with the proper Vouchers, which acco[ts] on Due confideration I have allowed of and approved and Caused to be filed in the office. In Teftimony—whereof I have hereunto sett my hand and seal the twenty ninth Day of August af[d]: Anno Domini One thoufand seven hundred and thirty two

Sam[l]. Bustill D Reg[r]:

WILL OF JOHN FRENCH, JR., 1729

I John French Jun[r] of Northampton In y[e] County of Burlington & Western Division of y[e] Province of New Jerfey being very sick & weak In body but of sound & Perfect mind & memory Thanks be given to almighty God Therefore calling to mind y[e] mortallity of my Body & Knowing that it is appointed for all men once to Dy Do make & ordain this my Last Will & Testiment utterly Revoking & annulling all other wills & Testaments by me heretofore made.

And principally & first of all I Give & Recommend my soul Into the hands of God that Give & for my Body I Recommend to y[e] Earth to be Buried In a Christian like Decent manner at y[e] Discretion of my Executor hereafter Named & as Touching such worldly Estate wherewith It hath pleased God to Blefs me with In This Life I Give Devise & Difpofe of y[e] same In y[e] following manner—

Imprimis and first of all I order my funerall Charges & Just Debts to be paid by my Executer and as for y[e] Remaining Part of my Estate after my funeral Charges & Just Debts is paid I Give Devise & Dispose of them as followeth viz—

Item I Give Devife & bequeath unto my oldest Brother Thomas French y[e] sum of five Shillings current Lawfull money of y[e] abovesaid province to be Paid by my Executer hereafter named

Item I Give Devise & Bequeath unto my oldest Sister Rechall Fenton y[e] sum of five Shillings Current Lawfull money of y[e] above said province to be paid by my Executer hereafter named.

Item I Give Devife & Bequeath unto my youngest Sister Ann French y[e] sum of five Pounds current Lawfull money of y[e] above said province to be paid by my Executer hereafter named

Item I Give Devise & Bequeath unto my wellbeloved & Trusty friend and Brother Charles French whom I Likewise Nominate Constitute &

ordain my whole & Sole Executer to this my Last will & Testament all
my Estate In Goods Chattles & Credits what & wheresoever he my said
Executer yeilding & Paying my funerall Charges & Just Debts & y^e
Legecies above bequeathed and I do hereby Rattifie & confirm this & no
other to be my Last will & Testament as witnefs my hand & seal this
Twenty fourth Day of March anno qe Dominey one Thousand seven hundred & Twenty eight nine & In ye second year of his majestie King George
his Reign over Great Britton &c 1728/9

Signed sealed Deliv-
ered & Published pro-
nounced & Declared
by ye said John french
as his Last will &
Testament In the pres-
ence of us

 Abraham Marriott
 Jacob Lamb
 Thomas Dawson
 John Budd

Con. Burlington ſs Be it Remembered that on ye Tenth day of May
Ano 1729 personally came & appeared before me Samuel Bustill D. Surrogate & Register of ye Western Division of ye Province of New Jersey
duly Commissioned &c Jacob Lamb one of the Witnesses In ye within
Will subscribed who on his solemn affirmacon according to Law doth
declare & affirm that He was present & Saw John ffrench ye Testator
within named Sign & Seal & heard him Publish Pronounce & Declare
ye within Instrument to be his Last Will & Testament & that at ye doing
thereof the Testator was of Sound mind memory & understanding to y^e
best of his Knowledge & belief & that at y^e Same time also Abraham
Marriott, Thomas Dawson, & John Budd y^e other Subscribing Evidences
were present & Signed their Name as Wittnefses to y^e same in y^e presence
of y^e Testator

 Jurat Coram me   Jacob Lamb
 Sam^1 Bustill, D. Rg.

FIREPLACE BELLOWS, 1730

10—SARAH FFRENCH (Thomas, 1).

Baptized February 23rd, 1674, at Church S. S.
Peter and Paul, Nether Heyford, England.

m. 2nd mo. 1st, 1695, Isaac Wood, son of Jonathan
Wood, of Woodbury Creek, N. J.

49—Mary Wood   m. 9th mo. 8th, 1738, Hugh Clifton of Salem,
                              N. J., at the house of Wm. Coate, Phila-
                              delphia.

MEETING RECORDS

Burlington Monthly Meeting Minutes:
At our Mens Monthly Meeting held at ye house of Elizabeth Gardeners
the fourth of ye 12th Mo^th 1694
Isaac Wood & Sarah ffrench declared their Intentions of marrige it
being the first time of their Comeing to this meeting.

At our mens monthly meeting held at the House of Eliz. Gardiner in
Burlington ye 1st of the Second mo. 1695
Isaac Wood & Sarah ffrench came before this meeting to Declare their
Intentions of marriage it being the Second time & the meeting find nothing
to obstruct Enquiry being made they being found clear the Meeting thought
fitt that they should Consumate the Same according to the Good order of
Truth.

11—MARY FFRENCH (Thomas, 1).

Baptized August 8th, 1675, at Church S. S.
Peter and Paul, Nether Heyford, England.

d. 1728.

m. 8th mo. 30th, 1695, Nicholas Buzby of Bur-
lingtou County, N. J., son of John and Mary
Buzby of Pennsylvania, formerly of Milton,
England.

He d. 6th mo. 28th, 1727, buried on the 29th.

50—THOMAS BUZBY   m. 1727, Margaret Haines.

51—JOHN BUZBY   m. 1731, Hannah Adams.
                       d. 1754.

52—ISAAC BUZBY   m. Martha ————.

VILLAGE GREEN, NETHER HEYFORD, ENGLAND

53—WILLIAM BUZBY	b. 5th mo. 10th, 1714.
	m. 8th mo. 25th, 1739, Mary Wills.
54—BENJAMIN BUZBY	
55—LYDIA BUZBY	m. 1718, James Marson.
56—MARY BUZBY	m. 8th mo. 13th, 1729, John Swain.
57—JANE BUZBY	m. 1727, Jacob Burtsal.
58—ELIZABETH BUZBY	
59—SARAH BUZBY	m. 1741, Samuel Wickward.

As in so many other instances of early days, no record of the births of the children of Nicholas and Mary (French) Buzby appear in Meeting minutes. The marriage record is also incomplete. The order here followed is that given in the wills of both parents.

NICHOLAS BUZBY

Of the sons of John Buzby, English immigrant, who located in Philadelphia about the time of Penn's arrival, none was more industrious, energetic and successful than Nicholas, who, some time before his marriage to Mary French, in 1695, settled in Burlington county, as a farmer. He raised a family of ten children, becoming the progenitor of a great number of worthy and useful citizens. Many of his descendants reside in New Jersey today, while others are to be found throughout a wide territory. In 1714 he became possessed, through purchase from Charles French, his brother-in-law, of 250 acres of the original Thomas ffrench estate, near Rancocas. Half a century later this tract was included in the 300 acres sold to Gov. William Franklin, a part of which, as elsewhere noted, is now owned by Thomas T. Buzby [1689], a direct descendant of Nicholas. The Burlington county pioneer Buzby was a consistent Friend, a long-time member of Burlington Monthly Meeting, with his wife Mary, who survived him only a little more than one year. Many of his descendants likewise have been active and zealous Friends, one of these, Richard [894] of Willingborough, having been noted for his upright life and worthy example.

MEETING RECORDS

Burlington Monthly Meeting Minutes:

At our mens monthly meeting held at the house of Eliz. Gardiner in Burlington ye 2nd of ye 7th mo. 1695—Nicholas Busby & Mary French declared their intentions of Marriage it being ye first time of their Coming they desire ye Consent of ffriends in it.

At our Monthly Meeting held at the house of Eliz. Gardiner in Burlington ye 7th of ye 8th Mo: 1695—Nicholas Busby and Mary ffrench declared their Intentions of marriage the Second time & upon Enquiry made find all Clear & Nothing to hinder or Impede the same they are Left to Consummate that weighty affair in a Convenient time & Place as they in the fear of the Lord Shall think fit.

MARRIAGE CERTIFICATE

Whereas An Intention of marriage hath Been dewly published according to ye Lawes of This Province of West New Jersey in America And alsoe att severall of The meetings of ye people of God called quakers And nothing appearing to obstruct or hinder them. Now these are to Certifie whome it may concerne that the sd. Nicholas Busbey and Mary ffrench of ye County Burlington did on ye 30th of ye Eighth Month in ye Yeare 1695 in a Solem Assembly of ye aforesd. People Take and declare themselves to be husband and Wife and in Testimony they subscribe there names and we allsoe as wittnesses being present.

Nicholas Busbey
Mary Busbey

John Adams (Justice)	Thomas ffrench ⎫ fathers
Benj. Wheate	John Busbey ⎭
John Siddon	John Busbey, Junr.
Thomas Stokes	Edward Busbey
John ffletcher	Richard ffrench,
Daniel Hall	Thomas ffrench
Thomas Scattergood	Richard Busbey
George Deacon	Charles French
William Pancoast	Isaac Woods
John Paine	John ffrench
Tho. P———	Sarah Busbey
Tho. Scatergood	Mary Busbey
Joseph Pancoast	Hanah Busbey
Richard Tomlinson	Eliz. Adams
Richard Mason	Sarah Roberts
John Woolman	Mary Wheats

WILL OF NICHOLAS BUZBY, 1727

I Nicolas Buzby of Wellingborough in the County of Burlington and Province of New Jersey being fick and weak of body but of found and difpofing mind and memory do make this my laft Will and Teftament and do hereby difpofe of that outward eftate which it hath pleafed God to Intruft me withall in manner and form following Viz: Imprimis My Will is that all my juft debts and funerall Charges be duly paid and discharged as foon as may be after my deceafe.

2dly I give and bequeath unto my Son Thomas Buzby forty fhillings lawfull money of America.

3dly I give unto my Son John Buzby forty fhillings like money aforefaid.

4^thly I give unto my Son Ifaac Buzby forty fhillings like money aforefaid.

5^thly I give unto my Son William Buzby forty fhillings like money aforefaid.

6^thly I give unto my Son Benjamin Buzby forty fhillings like money aforefaid.

7^thly I give unto my daughter Lydiah the wife of James Marfon forty fhillings like money aforefaid.

8^thly I give unto my daughter Mary Buzby forty fhillings like money aforefaid.

9^thly I give unto my daughter Jane Buzby forty fhillings like money aforefaid.

10^thly I give unto my daughter Elizabeth Buzby forty fhillings like money aforefaid.

11^thly I give unto my daughter Sarah Buzby forty fhillings like money aforefaid.

Lastly all the refidue and remainder of my eftate both reall and perfonall I give devife and bequeath unto my well beloved wife Mary Buzby and to her heirs and Afsignes for ever Alfo I do hereby appoint Conftitute and Ordain My faid Wife to be the fole Executrix of this my laft will and Teftament ordering her to pay all my debts and Legacies aforefaid and Impowering her to recieve all fuch debts that are juftly due and owing unto me In Witnefs whereof I have hereunto fet my hand and feal this twenty fecond day of the fixth Month 1727.

Witnesses

Jacob Burdsall
    his
John X Marfon
    mark
John Wills

Probat William Burnet Esqr Capt. General & Governour in Chief of y^e Provinces of New York New Jersey & y^e Territories Thereon depending in America & Vice Admiral of y^e Same &c. To all To whom These Presents shall Come or may Concern Greeting Know yee That at Burlington in ye province of New Jersey ye first Day of October Anno Dom: one Thousand Seven hundred & Twenty Seven —— ye last Will & Testament of Nicholas Buzby Late of ye Township of Wellinborough yeoman Dece^d was proved before Samuel Bustill who is Thereto by me Authorized & appointed for That Purpose & now Approved & Allowed of by me having while he Lived & at ye Time of his Death Goods Chattels & Credits in divers places Within this Province by means whereof ye full Disposition of all & Singular of The Goods Chattels & Credits of ye Said Dece^d & ye Granting Administration of Them also ye hearing of Account Calculation or Reckoning & ye final Discharge & Dismifsion from ye Same unto me Solely & not unto any other Inferiour Judge are Manifestly known To belong & ye Administracon of all & Singular ye Goods Chattels & Credits of ye said Dece^d & his Last Will & Testament in any manner of ways Concerning was Granted unto Mary Busby ye Executrix in ye Said Last Will & Testament named chiefly of well & Truly Administring ye Same & of making a True & perfect Inventory of all & Singular ye Goods Chattels & Credits of ye Said Dece^d & Exhibiting ye Same into ye Registry of ye Prerogative Court in ye Secretarys Office at or before ye Thirtyeth Day of March next ensuing & of Rendring a just & True Account when thereunto Required.

In Testimony whereof I have Caused ye Prerogative Seal of ye Said Province of New Jersey To be hereunto Affixed at Burlington in ye province of New Jersey Aforesaid The first Day of October in ye first Year of his Majestys Reign Anno Dom: 1727.

                                                    Ia. Smith Secry—

WILL OF MARY BUZBY, 1728

I Mary Bufby of the Townfhip of Wellingborow in the County of Burlington in the prouince of Weft New Jerfy being sick of body but of sound and difpofing mind and memory doe make this my Laft will and Teftament and doe hereby Difpofe of that outward Eftate which it hath pleafed God to Intruft me withall in maner and form folling: vizt Imprimis my will is that all my Juft Debts and funarall Charges be duly pay^d and difcharged as soon as may be after my defceas 2dly. I give unto my son John Bufby six pounds Lawfull money of America.

3dly. I give unto my son Isack Bufby Six pounds lick money as aforefaid. 4dly I give unto my son William Busby six pounds alfo like money as aforefaid 5dly I give unto my son Bengman Bufby six pounds money as aforefaid. 6dly. I give unto my Dafter Lydia Marfon wife of James Marfon six pounds Like money as aforefaid.

7dly. I give unto my Dafter Mary Bufby six pounds money as aforefaid. 8dly. I give unto my Dafter Jane Burfhall now wife of Jacob Burfhall six pounds lick money as aforefaid.

9dly. I give unto my Dafter Elezabeth Bufby six pounds lick money as abouefaid.

10dly. I give unto my Dafter Sary Bufby six pounds Lick money as aforefaid, and if any of my fones fhould dye before they arive at ye age of twenty years then their money fhall be Equaly devided among ye Reft and alfo if any of my Dafters fhould dye before they arive at ye adge of Eighteen years then their money fhall be Equaly Devided amongst ye Reft. and Laftly all ye Refidue of Remainder of my Eftate both Reaill and Parfonall I give Deuife and Bequeath unto my Son Thomas Bufby to hime and to his heirs and afsigns for euer.

Alfo I doe hereby appoint Conftitute and ordain my said son Thomas Bufby to be my fole Executor of this my Laft Will and Teftament ordring him to pay all my Juft Debts, and Legafefs aforefaid giuen by me and impowering him to Receiue all fuch Debts that are Juftly due to me. In Witnefs whereof I have hereunto fett my hand and feal this fift day of the tenth month called December 1728.

Sealed figned and Declared in y^e
sight and prefents of

Thomas Reues

    mark

Nathan n Crofby

    his

Hugh Sharp

               mark

Mary   Buzby

            hir

Pro: New Jersey fs

Be it Remembered that on the twenty first day of January Anno: Dom: One thousand Seven hundred and twenty Eight Pfonally came and appeared before me Samuel Bustill D. Surrogate and Register of the Weftern Divifion of the province of New Jersey duly Commifsioned and appointed Hugh Sharp Esqr. One of the Witnefses Subscribed to the within Will who being one of the people called Quakers on his Solemn affirmation according to law did declare and affirm that he was present and saw Mary Busby the Teftatrix in the within Will named sign and seal the same, and that he heard her publish pronounce and declare the within writing to be her laft Will and Teftament, and that at the doing thereof she the said Teftatrix was of sound mind, memory and understanding to the beft of his knowledge and belief, and that at the same time alfo Thomas Reves and Nathan Crosby the other two Subscribed Evidences were prefent and that they together with this affirmant did sign as Witnefses to the within Will in the prefence of the Testatrix—

Affirmed before me   Saml. Bustill D: Reg^r:

Pro: New Jersey ſs:

Be it Remembered that on the day of the date above written personally came and appeared before me Samuel Bustill D. Register of the Weſtern Division of the province of New Jersey duly Commiſsioned and appointed Thomas Busby the Executor within named who being one of the people called Quakers On his Solemn Affirmation according to Law doth declare and Affirm, that the within writing contains the laſt Will & Teſtament of Mary Busby the Teſtatrix within named as far as he knows and believes and that he will well and truly pform the same by paying first the Debts of the deceased and then the Legacys contained in the within Will so far forth as the goods Chattels and Credits of the said deceased will thereunto Extend or the Law will charge, and that he will make a true and perfect Inventory and alſo render a Juſt account when thereunto required—

Affirmed before me

Samˡ: Bustill D. Regʳ.

A true and perfect Inventory of the Goods and Chattels of Mary Buſby Late Widow of Nickles Buſby Deſec'd of the Townſhip of Wellingborow in the County of Burlington in Weſt New Jerſy as followeth

Appraiſed by us whoſe names are under written.

Total   £97   7   6

Hugh Sharp
John Milborn

ANCIENT CHAIR IN BURLINGTON MEETING HOUSE, 1700

15—REBECCA FFRENCH (Thomas, 1), daughter of Thomas and Elizabeth (Stanton) ffrench.

> b. 6th mo. 8th, 1697.
>
> m. 2nd mo. 3rd, 1729, Robert Murfin, son of William and Sarah (Bunting) Murfin.
>
> He b. 3rd mo. 12th, 1705.
>
> d. 1753.

60—THOMAS MURFIN

61—WILLIAM MURFIN

62—JOHN MURFIN

William Murfin was the son of Robert and Ann Murfin of the town of Eaton, Nottinghamshire, England, who came to America in the ship "Shield," which arrived at Burlington, N. J., 10th mo., 1678, O. S. William was born 1st mo. 16th, 1681; died 3rd mo. 3rd, 1742; married June 8-1704, in Chesterfield Meeting House, Sarah Bunting, daughter of John and Sarah Bunting. Sarah Bunting was born 8th mo. 3rd, 1686, and died 7th mo. 26th, 1762.

SUMMARY OF INV. OF EST. OF ROBT. MURFIN, 1753

Inventory of Goods & Chattels of Robart Murfin Deceſed Appreaſed by yᵉ vnder ſubſcribers this 13ᵗʰ Day of yᵉ 9ᵗʰ Mo 1753

		Total	£18	17	4

> Pre. Brown
> William Bunting.

William Murfin the Admr— charges himself with..............£18 17 4

To what Came to hand afterwards........................... 1   7 2

£20   4   6

WILL OF SARAH MURFIN, 1754

I Sarah Murfin of Notingham in the County of Burlington and Western Devision of New Jersey widow being in helth of body and of Sound mind and memory do make This my Last Will and Testament in form following

First My Will is That all my Just Depts and funeral charges be paid and Discharged by my Executors hereafter named.

Itam I give first in perticuler To my granson John Murfin Williams son my great Red Chist that was my son Josephs—

I give to my grandaughter Ann Murfin my Black Trunk in perticuler.

I give to my grandaughter Sarah Large my Best Bed and furniture belonging to it and a pear of sheets and pillow cases besids and my warming pan and my wool wheel With all those things that are in the high chist of Drawers Which her father Left in perticuler for their use which Things their is a perticuler account Taken of to be kept. Also a Redish Trunk with child Lining in it to be devided betwixt her and her Sister Mary Large: also my plush Side Saddle to be for the use of her and her Sister Mary Also my black walnut ouel Table I give to Sarah and big black chear.

I give to my grandaughter Mary Large my Second Best Bed bolster an pillows and 2 pear of Sheets and pillow caises 2 Blankits and a coverlid and my Black wallnut low chist of Drawers and a Red Chist that was her Mothers with all the things that are in that chist There being an account taken of the perticulers To be kept Also 6 black chears and my Lining wheel and if in case one of them die before she arrive to the age of eighteen years that then the Surviver to have what was hers and if in case boath of them should die before they be eighteen years old then what they were to have had (if they have no child or children) then to be eqqualy devided amongst the rest of my gran children

Also I give my wearing cloaths to my 3 grandaughters to be equely deuided amongst them

The Rest of my Small Estate the one half I give to my son William and his son John and his daughter Ann Murfins and the other half to my other gran children Thomas William and John Murfins the children of my son Robert Murfin decesed

Lastly I do constitute and appoint my Loving son William Murfin To be my Executor of This my Last will and Testament in Witness whereof I have hereunto Set my hand and Seal the first day of October one thousand Seven hundred and fifty fouer 1754

Signed Sealed and acknowledged to be her Last will in
the presence of us

A Teſtimony from Cheſterfield Monthly-Meeting in New-Jerſey, concerning Sarah Murfin.

" This worthy woman was one whom it pleaſed the Lord, to call out of the broad way and vanities of the world, and make acquainted with his bleſſed truth; and as She abode under the croſs, it pleaſed the almighty to manifeſt unto her, that She was a choſen veſſel or inſtrument for his Service, to preach the goſpel. She was fervent in prayer, Serviceable in viſiting families, and her godly example in life and converſation, great humility and Self-denial, much adorned her miniſtry; careful to bring up her family in the fear of the Lord, and in plainneſs of Speech and apparel; being indeed a mother in Iſrael.

" We fervently deſire that the great Lord of the harveſt, may be pleaſed to continue to his church and people, a living miniſtry; and that many may be made willing to run his errands and be Serviceable in his hand, as was this our worthy friend, who departed this life, the 26th of the Seventh month 1762, aged about Seventy-Six years."

AN EARLY ACCOUNT OF COLONIAL LIFE

The following notice of the early settlement of Burlington by the English, communicated to the Historical Society of Pennsylvania by John F. Watson, was copied from the original autograph of Mrs. Mary Smith, a Friend, who arrived with the primitive colonists, when she was only four years of age:

Robert Murfin and Ann his wife, living in Nottingshamshire, England, had one daughter born there in the year 1674, the 24th of the 2d month, named Mary, (the writer of this account, who married the first Daniel Smith of Burlington). After that they had a son called Robert. [Born 3rd mo. 24th, 1676.]

Some time after it came in their minds to move themselves and family into West Jersey in America; and in order thereto, they went to Hull and provided provisions suitable for their necessary occasion,—such as fine flour, butter, cheese, with other suitable commodities in good store; then took their passage in the good ship, the Shield of Stockton, with Mahlon Stacy, Thomas Lambert, and many more families of good repute and worth; and in the voyage there were two died and two born; so that they landed as many as they took on board. And after about sixteen weeks sailing or on board, they arrived at Burlington in the year 1678; this being the first ship that ever was known to come so high up the Delaware River. Then they landed and made some such dwellings as they could for the present time;—some in caves, and others in palisade-houses secured. With that, the Indians, very numerous, but very civil, for the most part, brought corn and venison, and sold the English for such things as they needed; so that the said English had some new supply to help their old stock, which may well be attributed to the good hand of Providence, so to preserve and provide in such a wildnerness.

I may not omit some English that came the year before, which landed lower down the river, and were gotten to Burlington, who came in some small vessels To Burlington before us,—and was consented to by the Indians.

The first comers, with the others that came near that time, made an agreement with the Indians for their land,—being after this manner :—From the river to such and such creeks; and was to be paid in goods, after this manner, say—so many match coats, guns, hatchets, hoes, kettles; two full boxes, with other materials, all in number as agreed upon of both Indians and English. When these goods were gotten from England and the Indians paid, then the above-mentioned people surrendered some part of the land to settle themselves near the river—for they did not dare to go far from it at first.

I must not forget, that these valiant subjects, both to God and their king, did buy their land in old England before they entered (upon this engagement,) and after all this, did submit themselves to mean living, taking it with thankfulness, mean and coarse; as pounding Indian corn one day for the next day; for there was no mill, except some few steed-mills, and (we) thought so well of this kind of hard living, that I never heard them say, ' I would I had never come ! ' which is worth observing, considering how plentifully they lived in England. It seems no other than the hand of God, so to send them to prepare a place for the future generations. I wish they that come after may consider these things, and not be like the children of Israel after they were settled in the land of Canaan, forgetting the God of their fathers and following their own vanities; and so bring displeasure, instead of the blessings of God, upon themselves; which fall and loss will be very great on all such.

Now to return to Robert Murfin and his wife: after they came into this land, they had one son called John [born 1679]; and in the year 1681, they had another son called William; and in the year 1684, they had a daughter called Johannah. Robert and John died young [1686].

It may be observed how God's providence made room for us in a wonderful manner in taking away the Indians. There came a distemper among them so mortal that they could not bury all the dead. Others went away, leaving their town. It was said that an old Indian king spoke prophetically before his death and said, " the English should increase and the Indians decrease."

Mary Murfin and Daniel Smith were married 5th mo. 2nd, 1695, at the house of Francis Davenport.

WARMING PAN, SEVENTEENTH CENTURY

16—MATHEW ALLEN, JR. (Thomas, 1 ; Rachel, 4).

b. 8th mo. 23rd, 1688.

m. 1711, Grace Jones, daughter of John and Rebecca Jones of Pennsylvania.

She b. 7th mo. 12th, 1693.

63—MATHEW ALLEN, 3RD	m. 1737, Martha Stokes, daughter of Joseph and Judith Stokes (Haddonfield Meeting record). d. about 1760.
64—JOHN ALLEN	m. March 26th, 1744, Mary Butcher (Christ Church record). d. about 1753.
64a—WILLIAM ALLEN	m. 1st mo. 1745/6, Judith Stokes, daughter of Joseph Stokes (Haddonfield Meeting record).

MEETING RECORDS

Haddonfield Monthly Meeting Minutes:

14th of 3 Mo. 1711 Matthew Allin signified his intention of taking a young woman to wife which is a liver in Pensilvania and desired a certificate.

13th of 6 Mo. 1711 Certificate granted to Matthew Allin in order for marriage.

Abington Monthly Meeting Minutes:

Mo-Meeting yᵉ 27: 6 mᵒ 1711

Whereas Mathew Allen of West Jerſie & Grace Jones having declared their Intentions of Marriage with each other before two Mo-Meetings Enquiry being made by perſons appointed found Clear from all others on yᵉ account of Marriage Did accomplish their Marriage in yᵉ Unity of Friends as is Signified by their Marriage Certificate.

——"TO BE SOLD"——

" A plantation, lying on Rancokus Creek, in Burlington Co, West Jersey, betwixt the New Ferry and the Mouth of the said creek, containing 400 acres, 80 Acres whereof being banked Meadow, Part improved, and Part to clear.

The said Plantation hath on it a good Dwelling-house, Kitchen and Draw well, Orchard, and cleared Upland for a Settlement, about 50 acres, Any Person inclining to purchas the same, may see the land, and Conveniences, and know the Terms and Title, by applying to Matthew Allen, living on the Premises."

From " Pennsylvania Gazette," Feb. 1st, 1759.

Mathew Allen, 3rd [63] had daughter, Grace, born 10th mo. 6th, 1741; married, first, 3rd mo. 17th, 1763, Ner. Eayre, son of Richard Eayre; married, second, 1767, William Rogers, Jr., son of William Rogers. Also son, Enoch, who married 12th mo. 1st, 1774, Hannah Collins of Waterford Township, Gloucester Co., N. J., daughter of Samuel Collins (Haddonfield Meeting records). There is reason to believe that he also had sons Mathew, Anthony and Joseph, concerning whom detailed records are not available.

17—MERCY ALLEN (Thomas, 1; Rachel, 4).

> b. 1st mo. 13th, 1692.
>
> d. 2nd mo. 17th, 1754.
>
> m. First, 1710, Thomas Middleton, Jr., son of Thomas Middleton of Springfield Township, Burlington Co., N. J.

He d. 1724.

> m. Second, 10th mo. 2nd, 1730, John Hugg, Jr., son of John Hugg of Gloucester Co., N. J.

He d. 1730.

> m. Third, 2nd mo. 19th, 1732. Thomas Lippincott, son of Freedom Lippincott of Willingborough Township, Burlington Co., N. J.

He b. 10th mo. 28th, 1686.

> d. 9th mo. 5th, 1757.

65—THOMAS MIDDLETON, 3RD

66—MATHEW MIDDLETON

67—HUGH MIDDLETON

68—HANNAH MIDDLETON   m. 1727, at Chesterfield Meeting, James Clark son of Benjamin Clark of Stony Brook, N. J.

69—REBECCA MIDDLETON

70—RACHEL MIDDLETON

THOMAS MIDDLETON, JR.

Thomas Middleton, Jr., who married Mercy Allen, was the eldest son of Thomas Middleton, who came from England about 1700 and settled upon a farm in Springfield Township, Burlington County, N. J., where he died in 1704, leaving five children, Thomas, John, Nathan, Naomi and Elizabeth. The first named bought a house and lot in Burlington, on High Street, where he conducted business for himself during the next ten years after his marriage and until his health failed. During this time he bought additional property. Under his will his estate was left to the care of his widow and brother John, with special regard for the proper education and training of his six children. His brother John, through industry and economy, became possessed of considerable property. The descendants of both have been numbered among the most respectable and useful citizens of Burlington County.

MEETING RECORDS

Haddonfield Monthly Meeting Minutes:

Att A m°ly m^{t}g of women friends held at Newton ye 13th of 1st mo. 1709/10

At s^d m^{t}g Tho. Midleton & Marcy Allin declard ye intentions of mg ye first time Esther Adams & Mary Hooten are o^{r}d^{r}d to make ye ufual inquiry to return y^r acc^t to next m^{t}g.

Att A m°ly m^{t}g of women friends held at Newton ye 8th of 3 mo 1710 Tho Midleton & Mercy Allin signified ye continuation of y^r intentions of m^{r}g, consent of parents apearing & return of inquiers clear ye m^{t}g confents to ye accomplifhm^t of y^r s^d m^{r}g according to ye good o^{r}d^r amongst friends Est^{b}l^d so.

SUMMARY OF WILL OF THOMAS MIDDLETON, JR., 1724

Thomas Middleton, Burlington Town & Co., N. J., Taylor, "weak". Date, 2 mo (Aperill) 23rd, 1724 Proved, August 10– 1724

Wife Mercy Rest of my estate to bring up children

Children, eldest son, Thomas	£25	to be put to "traides" at suitable age.
second son, Mathew	£20	
youngest son, Hugh	£20	
eldest daughter, Hannah	£15	these legacies to be paid to my sons when 21, to my daughters when 18.
second daughter, Rebeckah	£15	
youngest daughter, Rachall	£15	

Executors—Wife Mercy

Brother John Middleton

"I give my Executors full authority to sell my lott and dwelling-house in yᵉ Town of Burlington and my 20 acres of Town Bound Land purchased of Sam¹¹ Meriott" &c.

Witnesses
    John Smith
V Wᵐ Collum
    Tho: Scattergood

A True and Parfect Inventory of all and Singular the Goods and Chattils of Rights and Creaditts of Thomas Middleton of the Town of Burlington in the Prouence of Weft New Jarfey Taylor, Late Deceaſed Taken at his houſe In Burlington aboue Said by Jonathan Louitt and Isaac Pearſon of the Same place, as far forth as Came to our Ands and Knowledge, Which is as ffolloweth;

                                    Total £82—14   5

The above Inventory taken by us the 22 Day of July 1724
    Iſaac Pearſon
    Jonathan Lovett

JOHN HUGG, JR.

In the early settlement of New Jersey the Hugg family had large landed possessions in Gloucester County, owning plantations along Timber Creek, where the Irish immigrant, John Hugg, who had suffered imprisonment as a Friend, located in 1683. He died in 1706, leaving two sons, John and Elias, both of whom became prominent and influential citizens of the same neighborhood. John, Jr., in 1688, married Priscilla, daughter of Francis Collins, by whom he had nine children, four daughters and five sons. His wife having died, he married Elizabeth Newbie, daughter of Mark Newbie, the Irish pioneer, in 1714. He was active in public life. For six years, from 1695, he was one of the judges of Gloucester County. For twelve years, from 1718 to 1730, he was a member of the Executive Council, serving acceptably under Governors Hunter, Burnet and Montgomerie. From 1726 to 1730 he was sheriff of Gloucester County. He served as one of the commissioners to remove and locate the Indians, and performed this delicate duty with tact and success. He sold the Swedish settlement near the mouth of Raccoon Creek the ground for a church, the successor of which is the present Trinity Episcopal Church, at Swedesboro, erected in 1785. Late in the winter of 1730–1, shortly after his marriage to Mercy Middleton, he met with an almost tragic death.   Riding from home in the morning, he was apparently taken ill about a mile from his house.   Alighting from his horse, he spread his cloak on the ground to lie down on, and having put his gloves under the saddle girth and his whip through one of the rings, he turned the animal loose, which going home, put the family upon search, when he was found, speechless.   They carried him to his house and he died that evening.

Attempts to do violence to rulers always were severely condemned by the Quaker settlers in America.   Upon one occasion, in 1697, the Quaker members of the Assembly of West Jersey and other leading citizens set forth their renewed loyalty to King William.   Among the signers whose names were attached to this quaint paper were Francis Davenport, Thos. Gardiner, John Hugg, John Hugg, Jr., John Woolston, Mahlon Stacy and nearly two score others.   This extraordinary " agreement to uphold the interests of the King " reads as follows:

> Wee the Subscribers to this present Instrument (being vnder y⁰ Denomination of Quakers) haveing vnderstood, that a Horrid Plott, and Conspiracy, hath been contrived against ye person and Government of King William y⁰ third, over England &c : which it hath pleased God, graciously to prevent; by a timely Discovery thereof: as appears at large, by an Act of Parliament presented to vs at this time by our Governor, Andrew Hamilton : Recommending it as propper, for us after y⁰ example of England &c : to Subscribe, to ye form an association in that Act Contained.   Or at least; that such of us whose Religiouse Principles will not suffer us to Subscribe in manner and form therein Expressed; Should Answer y⁰ Intent of it, by Subscribeing to a Declaration, of our fidelity, and Loyalty, to y⁰ King and Government as now Established, which we willingly, and Chearfully doe in manner following viz :
>
> Wee doe Sollemnly Promise and Declare, in y⁰ presence of God, ye witness of y⁰ truth of what we say That we will alwayes be ffaithfull to King William and vse all such Endeavors, as we can for y⁰ preservation and Safety of his person and Government, and doe Utterly Abhorr, and Detest, all Traiterouse and Dissloyall practices, against our King and Government, and are thankfull to God, for his preservations Continued over his person; and y⁰ Realmes he Rules which we pray God long to Continue in peace and Safety.

MEETING RECORDS

Burlington Monthly Meeting Minutes:

Att our Monthly Meeting at Burlington the 5th of 8th month 1730

John Hugg & Marcy Middleton appeared at this meeting and declared their intentions of marriage it being the first time.

Att our Monthly Meeting at Burlington y[e] first of y[e] 9 Mo[th] 1730.

John Hugg and Marcy Middleton appeared att this meeting and declared they were of the same mind as att the last meeting on y[e] account of marriage for which they were left to their liberty to solemnize their intentions when they shall see meete so it be orderly performed Sam[ell] Woolman and Jonathan Wright are appointed to attend, and y[e] said John Hugg having first produced a certificate of his conversation and clearness to marriage first had which Jonathan Wright and Samuel Woolman are desired to make enquiry wether the said Marcy have performed her former Husbands will in relation to his children.

Att our Monthly Meeting att Burlington y[e] 7th of y[e] 10th Month 1730.

An account was given in to this meeting that the marriage of John Hugg & Marcy Middleton was orderly performed. The friends appointed to enquire wether the said Marcy had taken care to perform her former Husbands will report that the necessary care was taken.

MARRIAGE CERTIFICATE

Whereas John Hugg of y[e] Township and County of Glosester in the west division of New Jersey and Marcy Middleton of y[e] Town & County of Burlington and division aforesaid, widdow, Having declared their Intentions of marriage with each other before several Monthly Meetings of the People called Quakers at Burlington, in said West division of New Jersey, aforesaid, according to y[e] good order used amongst them, and haveing concent of Parents and Relations concearned their proposal of Marriage was allowed of by the said Meetings.

Now these are to Certifie whome it may concearne that for the full accomplishing of their said intentions this second day of the tenth month in , y[e] year of our lord according to English Account one thousand seven hundred and thirty. They y[e] said John Hugg and Marcy Middleton appeared at a publick Meeting of y[e] aforesaid People and others Met togather at their publick Meeting House in the Township of Northamton and County of Burlington Aforesaid near Rancokas, alias Northamton River, And the said John Hugg taking the said Marcy Middleton by the hand did in a solemn manner openly declare that he took her the said Marcy Middleton to be his wife promising by divine assistance to be unto her a loving & faithful Husband until death shall seperate them and then & there in the said assembly the said Marcy Middleton did in like manner declare that she took ye said John Hugg to be her Husband promising by divine assistance to be unto him a faithful and loving wife until death shall seperate them. And moreover they the said John Hugg and Marcy Middleton she according to ye custom of marriage assuming the name of her Husband as a farther confirmation did then and there to these presents set their hands.

And wee whose names are hereunto subscribed being present amongst others att the solemnization of said Marriage and subscription have as witnesses thereunto set their hands the day & year above written 1730.

John Hugg
Mercy Hugg.

John Wills	Elizabeth Wills	Rachel Sharp
John Stoaks	Susanna ffearon·	Mary Stockton
Isaac Connaro	Elizabeth Wills, Jun	William Ellis
Thos. Scattergood	Rebeckah Wills	Lawrence Houghton
	Jane Greene	Josiah Kay
	Ellen Connarro	Hannah Albertson
		John Hugg, Junr
		Ann Harrison
		Kathrian Ellis
		Thomas Allen
		Thomas Busby
		Rebecca Middleton
		Margret Busby

Minutes of Burlington Monthly Meeting of Women Friends:

Att our womens Monthly Meeting held att our Meeting House in Burlingtou the 4th day of the 11th Mo. 1730

Mercy Hugg made application for a certificate on account of her removal to Haddonfield Monthly Meeting.

Att our Women's Monthly Meeting held att our Meeting House in Burlingtou the first day of ye 12 Mo. 1730.

A certificate for Mercy Hugg was signed in this Meeting.

Att our Women's Monthly Meeting held at our Meeting House in Burlington the 3^d day of ye 3 Mo. 1731.

The certificate which was given to Mercy Hugg was returned and made no use of by reason of the demise of her husband and her sudden returning back.

SUMMARY OF WILL OF JOHN HUGG, JR., 1722

John Hugg, Gloucester Township and County, West New Jersey, " sick and weak ".

Date, 2nd mo. 7th 1722   Proved, March 23ᵈ 1730

Wife Elizabeth { My mulatto girl Dina (born of Negro Sue yᵗ will belong to Daughter Mary when shee is 21, by virtue of my ffather's Last will) her life and to be disposed of to my Daughter Hannah or Sarah Hugg as she shall think propper.

Children

Joseph
Gabriel { The tract of land where I now live. Joseph yᵉ lower part whereon improvements are made, 140 acres with yᵉ Island I bought of John Ladd to be bounded north by my brother Elias, &c., and yᵗ 60 acres Lying in Town bounds of Gloucester I bought of Edward Smout. 200 acres to son Gabriel.

John
Elias { Equal share of tract of land I bought of Joseph Pigeon also the neck of land where Joseph Edwards now liveth, &c.

Jacob { My tract adjoyning John Richards below Great Mantoe Creek together with yᵉ Reversions off my Proprietary Rites Excepting any overplus in any of yᵉ tracts all ready taken up provided there is no want in regard to what is assigned to yᵉ Paying off my just Debts

My wife Elizabeth to spare what she can to my two Daughters Prifsilla Ayres and Hannah Hugg.

My Executrix has power to sell that tract of Land on which Patrick Flamingham fformerly lived, which I purchased of Wᵐ White, she to make conveyances in order to pay my just debts.

Executrix, my wife Elizabeth

Witnesses, Wᵐ Eddinfield W his mark

                    his
          Wᵐ ⨯ Grow
                    mark
          Thoˢ Sharp

John Hugg

Inventory taken March 24, 1731   £339—18—0

Jnº Hinchman } Appraisors
Isaac Jennings }

RENUNCIATION OF MARCY HUGG, 1730/1

of right to administer the estate of her late husband, John Hugg, Jr.

Know all men by these p^rsents That I Marcy Hugg widow & Relict of John Hugg Late of the County of Gloucester in the province of New Jersey Esqr deced for divers good Causes and Consideracons me thereunto moveing Have Renounced and disclaimed and by these presents Do Renounce and Disclaim all the Right Title & Interest ^{Wch} I have or may have or Claim of in & to the Administracon of the Estate of the s^d Deced^t John Hugg my Late husband, Saveing unto me my Right of Dower, or thirds out of the s^d Deced^{ts} Estate, willing that the Admⁿ of the s^d Deced^{ts} Estate be Granted to such pson or psons as the Judge or proper officer thereunto appointed & authorized in the s^d province shall think fitt. In Witness whereof I have hereunto Sett my hand and Seal ye nineteenth day of March A° Dno 1730/1

Signed and Sealed	her
In presence of us	Marcy m Hugg
Saml Sharp	mark
Saml Bustill.	

ADMINISTRATION BOND OF GABRIEL HUGG, 1731

Know all men by these presents That we Gabriel Hugg, and William Harrison both of the County of Gloucester, in the province of New Jersey Gen^t are held and firmly bound unto his Excellency John Montgomerie Esquire Governour of the provinces of New York and New Jersey &c. in the Just and full sum of Six hundred pounds of good and Lawfull money of America to be paid unto the said Governour or to his Succefsours or afsigns To the which payment well and truly to be made and performed we bind our Selves our heirs Executors and Administrators, Joyntly and Severaly firmly by thefe presents. Sealed with our Seals and dated this Seveenth day of April Anno Dom One thousand Seven hundred and thirty one.

The Condition of this above Obligation is Such That WHEREAS John Hugg late of the County of Gloucefter af^d Esqr Dece^d left behind him his laft Will and Teftament in writing bearing date the Seventh day of the Second Month in the year of our Lord one thousand Seven hundred and twenty two and thereby appointed Elizabeth Hugg Sole Executrix of the said laft Will and Teftament, who Died before the said Teftator and the above bounden Gabriel Hugg being one of the Sons of the said Teftator in order to take care of the said Testator's Estate hath prayed that Letters of Administration of the said Teftators Estate with the said Will annexed may be granted to him for the ufes in the said Will mentioned AND

WHEREAS the said Will hath been lately proved in due form of Law by the Witnefses to the said Will, And the said Gabriel Hugg in Order to take care of the said Testators Estate having obtained Letters of Administration of the s^d Testator's Estate. Now if the above bounden Gabriel Hugg Administrator af^d do make or Caufe to be made a true and perfect Inventory of all and Singular the goods Chattels and Credits of the said Dece^d which have or Shall come to the hands pofsefsion or knowledge of him the said Gabriel Hugg or into the hands of any other person or persons for his ufe, and the same so made, Shall Exhibit or cause to be Exhibited into the Registery of the prerogative Court in the Secretary's office at Burlington at or before the seventeenth day of June now next Ensuing And the Same Goods Chattels and Credits of the said Deceased at the time of his Death or which at any time after shall come to the hands or Pofsefsion of the Said Gabriel Hugg, or unto the hands or Pofsefsion of any other person or persons for his ufe do well and truly administer according to Law and to the uses and intents in the said Will mentioned and declared and shall alfo make or caufe to be made a Just and true acco^t of the Said Administration at or before the Seventeenth day of June which will be in the year of our Lord one thousand Seven hundred and thirty two, Then this obligation to be void and of none Effect or Elfe to be and remain in full force and virtue.

Sealed and Delivered	Gabriel Hugg	[SEAL]
In the presence of us	Wm Harrifon	[SEAL]
Jn° Hinchman		
Saml Bustill		

THOMAS LIPPINCOTT

Thomas Lippincott, the son of Freedom and Mary Lippincott, of Rancocas, N. J., married, 9 mo. 1711, Mary, daughter of John and Esther Haines, of Evesham Township, and settled upon a tract of about 1,000 acres in Chester Township, purchased of the executors of Gov. Samuel Jennings, in 1711, for one hundred and seventy-six pounds. This estate extended from Pensaukin Creek to Swedes run and covered the site of the present village of Westfield. Thomas Lippincott was an industrious and useful citizen, frequently holding a place in the township government. In 1715 he was overseer of highways; 1717 and 1722, overseer of the poor; 1720, constable; 1725–26, county collector; 1738, surveyor of highways. Town meetings were held at his house from 1743 until 1754. His second wife, Mercy (Allen) Middleton Hugg, was very active in Haddonfield

Meeting for a number of years. After her death, in 1754, he married Rachel Smith, widow, of Mt. Holly, a noted minister in the Society of Friends. Concerning her the Mt. Holly Monthly Meeting gave the following testimony:

> She was an exemplary, sympathizing friend. Her testimony in public meetings was short, yet savory and seasonable. In her last painful illness she expressed herself in this wise: "Oh! if it be Thy will, dear Father, grant me patience to bear all that Thou in Thy wisdom may see meet to afflict me with." To a friend present she said: "Oh! that love may increase and abound in this day of outward trials, and faithfulness be kept to, is my sincere desire. My trials through life have been many; but blessed be the Lord's holy name; when He has appeared all darkness has vanished." She departed this life 9th M. 29th, 1779, aged 80 years.

MARRIAGE CERTIFICATE

WHEREAS THOMAS LIPPINCOTT of ye Township of Chester in ye County of Burlington in the West Division of New Jersey in America and Marcy Hugg late of ye County of Gloísester but now of ye County of Burlington & Division aforesaid Widdow Having declared their Intentions of Marriage with each other before several Monthly Meetings of ye People called Quakers at Burling^{ton} in said West Division of New Jersey Aforesaid according to the good order Uíed amongst them and having Consent of Parents and friends and Relations Concearned their proposal of Marriage was Allowed by the said Meetings

NOW THESE ARE TO CERTIFIE whome it may Concearne y^t for ye full accomplishing of their said Intentions this nineteenth day of ye Second Month in ye year of our Lord according to English account one thousand Seven hundred and thirty two they the said Thomas Lippincott and Marcy Hugg appeared at a publick Meeting of ye aforesaid people and others Met togather at their publick Meeting houíe in ye township of Northamton & County of Burlington afore said near rancoker alias Northamton River AND the said Thos Lippincott taking ye said Marcy Hugg by ye hand did in a Solemn Manner Openly Declare that he took her the said Marcy Hugg to be his Wife promiísing by Divine Afsistance to be unto her a loving and faithfull Huíband until death shall separate them AND then and there in the said Afsembly the said Marcy Hugg did in like manner declare that she took ye said Thomas Lippincott to be her Husband promiísing by Divine Afsistance to be unto him a faithfull and Loving Wife until death shall separate them AND MOREOVER they the said Thomas Lippincott and Marcy Hugg shee according to the Custom of Marriage aísuming the name of her present Husband as a farther Confirmation thereof did then and there to these presents set their hands AND WEE whoſe names are here under alſo subscribed being present at the solemnization of said Marriage and subſcription have as Witneſses thereunto set our hands the day and year above Written 1732:

Thomas Lippincott
Marcy m Lippincott
her mark

Nathaniel Lippincott	Mary Hooton	Hugh Sharp
Thomas Middleton	Joseph Stoaks	Rachel Sharp
Jarriott ————	Thomas ffrench	Sam Lippincott
Peter Fearon	Thomas Buzby	Freedom Lippincott
Samuel Woolman	John Wills	William Coate
Joⁿ Hollinſhead	Joseph Hollinshead	Caleb Haines
Tho Scattergood	Eliz: Wills	John Wills
John Watson	Elizabeth Woolman	Richard ffrench
John Stoaks	Jane Green	Elizabeth Lippincott
John Green .	Rebeckah Middleton	Sarah Haines
Edward Mellon	Sarah Hollinſhead	Thomas Hooton

SUMMARY OF WILL OF THOMAS LIPPINCOTT, 1755

Thomas Lippincott, Chester, Burlington Co., Colony of West N. Jersey, yeoman.

Date, 5 mo. 23ᵈ 1755   Proved at Burlington, Oct. 7 1757

To Son Isaac All my land Scittuate on Swead run, Beginning on S. side thereof in Joseph Stokes' Line; thence from the said run by said Stokes' Line to his first corner, thence to the nearest Corner of Clifton's Land; thence by the head Line thereof to the head line of Samuel Davis' Land; thence by same to the head Line of the Other Lotts till it Comes to the Lower Corner of my Land thence of a Line of marked trees to the aforesaid Sweeds run thence up the same to the place of beginning unto my sᵈ Son Isaac During his natural Life and after his Decease unto my said son Isaac's son being Grandson Thomas Lippincott and to his male heirs & in default of such issue to the use & behoof of the second, third, fourth, fifth, sixth, seventh, eighth, ninth and tenth son and sons of said Thos. Lippincott Junr Succeſsively one after the other. Also to son Isaac 150 acres Scittuate on pensaukin Creek, Beginning by sᵈ Creek in Henry Warrinton's Line, thence by same 80 chains; thence at Right Angle 10 chains; thence the Course down the said Creeke to make

the full quantity of 150 acres—to son Isaac his life then
to his son my grandson Isaac Lippincott and to his male
heirs in manner from age to age as described in first mentioned tract. Also £10 in twelve months after my decease.

To Son Nathaniel Rest of my land where I now dwell during his life, then
to his son my Grandson John Lippincott and to his male
heirs, as above described. Also to son Nathaniel £10 in
twelve months after my decease.

To three daughters Abigail £30 ⎫
 .   Esther £30 ⎬ in twelve months after my decease
            Mary   £75 ⎭

Grandchildren Mary Wills   £25 ⎫
              Hope Wills   £25 ⎬ in twelve months after my decease
              Meribah Ruddero £10 ⎭
              Daniel Wills £20 when of age
              Phebe Lippincott, daughter of deceased son Thomas £100
              when sixteen

              Hannah Andrews ⎫ daughters of my deceased daughter Pa-
              Pheby Andrews ⎬ tience Andrews, each £25 when eighteen
                             ⎭ or married.

Daughter-in-law Rebecca Middleton £15 for services done for me.

Executors—Sons Nathaniel Lippincott
               Isaac Lippincott

Thomas Lippincott —

Witnesses—Arthur Borradail
          John Matlack
          Samuel Atkinson

Inventory taken September 24, 1757   £568—0—6

          Josa. Humphris ⎫ Appraisers
          John Cox   ⎭

18—MARY ALLEN (Thomas, 1 ; Rachel, 4).

> b. 8th mo. 23rd, 1695.
>
> m. First, Jarves Stockdell.
>
> He d. October, 1726.
>
> m. Second, 5th mo. 15th, 1741, John Mickle of "Glosester Co."; at house of Hugh Sharp in Willingborough Township, Burlington Co., N. J.
>
> He d. 1744.

71—RUTH STOCKDELL   m. December 31st, 1735, John Small.

72—HANNAH STOCKDELL   b. 1718.
              m. 1743, John Stokes, Jr.

73—DARKES STOCKDELL

74—RACHEL STOCKDELL   m. 1739, William Wood.

75—PRUDENCE STOCKDELL

JARVES STOCKDELL

Among the younger men active in Friends' Society of his time, Jarves Stockdell held a leading place. He is supposed to have been the son of William Stockdale, a. noted citizen of Pennsylvania, who was for a time a member of the Assembly, and also a minister in the Society of Friends. Jarves Stockdell resided in Evesham Township and frequently represented at superior meetings the meeting early established in that township. In Haddonfield Quarterly minutes he is referred to as "a lively minister and exemplary in his deportment." His marriage with the step-daughter of Hugh Sharp brought him into relationship with an influential family. By his will proved October 27th, 1726, he bequeathed "unto my Dear and Loueing Wife Mary Stocdell all my Land and Plantation I now live upon with all my Impruments and alfo to my Trusty & Well beloued ffather-in-Law Hugh Sharp alfo all that my Land and plantation with the Improvments to them and their heirs for Ever and to Sell all or part of the same for the ufefs hereafter meneced." His movable estate was given to his wife, she to pay his just debts, and the rest for bringing up the children and paying legacies, each daughter to receive twenty pounds. The personal inventory included "a prentes boy and two bound servant boys." He departed this life at a comparatively early age, highly regarded throughout a large circle. In Thomas Chalkley's "Journal" we find the following:

> "First day morning (7 mo. 1726) I went to Evesham, New Jersey, to the burial of our serviceable friend Jervice Stockdale; he being in good esteem there was much people. The meeting was in a good tender frame and continued several hours in which divers testimonies were delivered, in order to stir up people to truth and righteousness and godly living that they might die well."

Jarves Stockdell

SIGNATURE TO WILL, 1726

This name is variously spelled in different records; herein the clearly defined autograph of Jarves Stockdell is followed.

INVENTORY OF THE ESTATE OF JARVES STOCKDELL, 1726

October 14th 1726

A true Inventory of the Goods and Chattells of Garues Stockdel late of Euesham in ye County of Burlington in Weft Jerfy decd as followeth

	£	S	d
to Purfs & Apparel	15—	6—	5
to Cow kine one pare of oxen one Bull in all 16	34—	0—	0
to Horfs 3 & one mare	16—	0—	0
to 15 Sheep	04—	0—	0
to 35 hogs and Shoots	11—	15—	0
to Corn in ye Stack wheat & Ryy	03—	00—	00
to Corn in ye ground	02—	10—	00
to 2 Loomes and Taklen with warping Bars and 2 Weels	11—	03—	06
to Ingen Corn	05—	00—	00
to ye Beft Bed and furniture	10—	00—	00
to two Beds more and furniture	06—	00—	00
to two Iorn pots one brace Cettel some puter fire shouel	01—	18—	00
to one Cheft one Box Six chairs a Remnant of new Cloth	02—	00—	00
to one mans Sadel one wooman fadel woofted & wooll & bridels	04—	10—	00
to milk vefells and Chees	04—	00—	00
to A Cart & plow & other working Tools	06—	00—	00
to one Tabel one Dow trouff & other Lumber	01—	10—	00
to one Bibel one Littel wheel and other things	01—	10—	00
to one prentes Boy and two bound Saruants Boys	15—	00—	00
to ftacks of hay in ye Meddow	10—	00—	00
	165—	02—	11

Pro: New Jersey ſs

This Twenty first day of October Anno: Dom: one thousand Seven hundred and Twenty Six pſonally came and appeared before me Samuel Bustill D. Surrogate and Register of the Weſtern Division of the province of New Jersey, Mary Stockdell and Hugh Sharp the Executrix & Executor of the laſt Will and Testament of Jarves Stockdell deceᵈ they being of the people called Quakers, On their Solemn affirmation according to Law do declare Testifie and affirm that the above written containſ a True and perfect Inventory of all and Singular the Goods Chattels and Credits of the said Deceased, So far forth as hath come to their knowledge poſſeſsion or view or to the view, poſſeſsion or knowledge of any other pſon for their uſe and that they brough every thing to the view of the appraisers.

Affirmed	her
Coram me	Mary m Stockdell
Sam¹ Bustill	mark
	Hugh Sharp

JOHN MICKLE

John Mickle, who married Mary (Allen) Stockdell, in 1741, was a grandson of the progenitor of his family in America, Archibald Mickle, an Irish Quaker, who arrived in Philadelphia in 1682, and later located in Newton Township, Gloucester County, West Jersey, and who had ten children. John Mickle became a prosperous pioneer farmer and large land owner and his will, proved December 13, 1744, shows an estate of considerable size for those days, including several houses, over 600 acres of land, half a dozen negroes, who were to be freed at forty years of age; and other personal property. His wife Mary was given " One hundred pounds and all that was hers before marriage, in lieu of dower." His landed estate was divided among his children by a former marriage, sons William, John and Samuel, daughter Hannah Ladd and grandson John, with ten pounds each to two other grand children. His inventory showed personal property to the amount of six hundred and twenty-three pounds.

SIGNATURE TO WILL, 1744

ty Six pſonally came and appeared before me Samuel
e and Register of the Weſtern Division of the province
ry Stockdell and Hugh Sharp the Executrix & Executor
l Testament of Jarves Stockdell deced they being of the
ers, On their Solemn affirmation according to Law do
d affirm that the above written containſ a True and
ſf all and Singular the Goods Chattels and Credits of
So far forth as hath come to their knowledge poſseſsion
iew, poſseſsion or knowledge of any other pſon for their
rough every thing to the view of the appraisers.

		her
		Mary **m** Stockdell
›still		mark
		Hugh Sharp

JOHN MICKLE

iarried Mary (Allen) Stockdell, in 1741, was a grand-
of his family in America, Archibald Mickle, an Irish
in Philadelphia in 1682, and later located in Newton
County, West Jersey, and who had ten children.
prosperous pioneer farmer and large land owner and
nber 13, 1744, shows an estate of considerable size for
several houses, over 600 acres of land, half a dozen
be freed at forty years of age; and other personal
Mary was given "One hundred pounds and all that
age, in lieu of dower." His landed estate was divided
a former marriage, sons William, John and Samuel,
dd and grandson John, with ten pounds each to two
His inventory showed personal property to the
d and twenty-three pounds.

SYCAMORE AND WALNUT TREES, GLOUCESTER, N. J., OVER 250 YEARS OLD

Under these trees members of the Council of Proprietors for Gloucester County have met annually since organization in 1687. Owing to decay, the sycamore tree was removed in 1906.

20—HANNAH SHARP (Thomas, 1; Rachel, 4).

> b. about 1707.
> d. 1770.
> m. 8th mo. 29th, 1724, John Breintnall, son of David and Jane (Blanchard) Breintnall of Philadelphia.
> He d. 1747.

76—RACHEL BREINTNALL	m. 9th mo. 26th, 1747, Jonathan Lewis.
77—REBECCA BREINTNALL	m. July 5th, 1751, Edward Weyman.
78—ELIZABETH BREINTNALL	m. ———— Ackley.
79—MARTHA BREINTNALL	m. May 11th, 1752, James Lowther.
80—LETITIA BREINTNALL	m. ———— Tillyer.
81—HANNAH BREINTNALL	m. ———— Milner.

Jane Blanchard, born in England in 1656, came to Philadelphia in 1682, and m. 10th mo. 6th, 1683, David Breintnall. She became a member of Philadelphia Monthly Meeting of Friends, being particularly active in the affairs of discipline. She was spoken of in the records of the time as an "improving woman." About 1700 she began a ministry which was continued until a short time before her death, 6th mo. 25th, 1725. David Breintnall d. about 1730. Their son, John Breintnall, m. first, 1717, Susannah Shoemaker, daughter of Jacob and Margaret Shoemaker. Susannah d. 1719 and left two children, David and Mary. Mary Breintnall m. 1742, Thomas Kite; they had children: Susannah, m. John Burden; Deborah, m. Stephen Phipps; Joseph, m. 1784, Susannah Letchworth; John; Benjamin, m. Rebecca Walton; Elizabeth, m. John Letchworth. John Breintnall m., second, Hannah Sharp [20].

WILL OF JOHN BREINTNALL, 1747

I John Breintnall of the City of Philadelphia being weak of Body but through the Goodness of God of sound mind and memory do make Publish and declare this my Last Will and Testament in manner following That is to say First I give devise and bequeath to my six youngest Daughters viz Rachel, Rebekah, Elizabeth, Martha, Letitia and Hannah Forty Foot apiece ffronting the alley lying—Between me and Joseph Howell and to Extend from the said alley the utmost extent of my Ground Westward To hold to them my said Daughters severally and respectively their Heirs and afsigns forever and my mind is that the youngest of my Daughters allotment shall be the remotest from Chestnut Street and the next youngest allotment next the youngest and So in that Order according to Each Daughters age the minor Daughters being remotest from the street As

concerning my Eldest Son David Brintnall towards whom I have heretofore acted the Part of a Tender ffather I do hereby give unto him the
sum of one Shilling and no more in full of his part of my Estate And
as for and concerning all the rest and residue of my Meſsuage Lot Tenements & Hereditamts with Appurtenances Goods Chattels Effects and Estate
Real and Personal whatsoever or wheresoever I do give devise and bequeath
the same unto my Dear and Loving Wife Hannah Breintnall in ffee simple
she paying my just Debts and ffuneral Expenses—I do think my meſsuage
with the Ground & appurtenances in the poſseſsion of Joseph Styles my
under tenant the most saleable and fittest for my Wife to part with. Therefore I recommend it as most proper to be sold (if need be) before any
other part of my Estate and I do Nominate her my said Dear wife Hannah
Breintnall to be the sole Executrix of this my Last Will and Testament
and I do request my Loving ffriend Joseph Scattergood of Burlington in
West New Jersey to aſsiſt my said Executrix with his Council as she shall
have occasion—And I do declare this my Last Will and Testament hereby
revoking all others in Witneſs whereof I the said John Breintnall have
set my Hand and seal hereunto the fifth Day of June in the yeare One
Thousand seven hundred and forty seven.

Signed sealed Published & Declared by the above named John Breintnall
for his Last Will and Testament in the presence of us who have hereunto
subscribed our names in his presence and at his request—Plunkit Fleeſon
Anthony Benezet & William Savery
    Approved July 1, 1747

SUMMARY OF INVENTORY OF THE ESTATE OF JOHN BREINTNALL.

Wearing Apparrell & Watch	22 " 0 " 0
Shop Goods	181 " 8 " 0
Cash	14 " 0 " 0
Household Goods	198 " 15 " 0
In the Store	13 " 0 " 0
In the Yard	23 " 0 " 0
the lease of the Pasture Ground	30 " 0 " 0
the 2 Houses & Lotts	800 " 0 " 0
	£1282 " 3 " 0

Plunket Freeſon ⎫
Joseph Howell ⎬ Appraisers, Aug. 6ᵗʰ 1747
Benjᵃ Peters   ⎭

The will of Hannah Breintnall, dated June 24th, 1769, and proved August 27th, 1770, provided for the sale of her "messuage lands &c. in Pennsylvania" and the distribution of the money arising therefrom in six equal parts to her daughters, Rachel Lewis, Rebecca Weymer, Elizabeth Ackley, Martha Lowther, "Laetitia Tillier," and "Anne Milnor." In the case of Elizabeth Ackley it was specially directed that her share of the estate should be held in trust for her during her husband's life, and at her death to go to her children, sons when 21, daughters when 18. "Friend Thomas Say of Philadelphia," Executor.

21—REBECCA SHARP (Thomas, 1; Rachel, 4).

> m. First, 2nd mo. 26th, 1727, William Coate, son of Marmaduke and Ann (Pole) Coate.
> He d. 1749.
> m. Second, 1754, Joseph Lippincott.
> He d. 1779.
> She d. 1781.

82—ANNA COATE   m. Samuel Atkinson.

83—MARMADUKE COATE   m. 1747, Sarah Matthis

84—WILLIAM COATE, JR.

85—ISRAEL COATE

86—BARZILLAI COATE   m. 4th mo. 13th, 1768, Elizabeth Stokes.

87—HANNAH COATE   m. 10th mo. 24th, 1751, William West of Mount Holly, N. J.

88—RACHEL COATE
    b. 3rd mo. 12th, 1737.
    d. 6th mo. 11th, 1797
    m. 1770, Joseph Burr of Hanover Township, Burlington Co., N. J.

89—MARY COATE
    b. 3rd mo. 16th, 1739
    m. 1761, Joseph Ridgway.

90—BEULAH COATE   m. 3rd mo. 30th, 1763, John Ridgway.

91—EDITH COATE

22—ELIZABETH FRENCH (Thomas, 1; Richard, 5).

b. 1694.

m. William Scholey, son of Robert and Sarah Scholey.

92—ROBERT SCHOLEY	b. 6th mo. 9th, 1718.
93—SARAH SCHOLEY	b. 10th mo. 4th, 1720.
94—RICHARD SCHOLEY	b. 1st mo. 22nd, 1723/4.
95—THOMAS SCHOLEY	b. 3rd mo. 10th, 1725.

The Scholey family, from Yorkshire, England, were among the earliest settlers of Pennsylvania and New Jersey. They were noted as prosperous and influential citizens, large land owners, active in business and religious affairs. Thomas and Robert were among the company of home seekers who settled in the vicinity of Burlington, 1677 and 1678; Thomas coming in the flie-boat "Martha," and Robert in the "Shield." About 1679, a large tract of land was taken up on the west side of the Delaware, near the falls (later the township of Falls, Bucks Co., Pa.), and the settlement named Crewcorne, after a town in Somersetshire, Eng. Thomas and Robert Scholey held several hundred acres. Pioneer troubles came quickly, and on April 12, 1680, an earnest petition was addressed to Governor Andros, Thomas and Robert being among the signers, asking that the inhabitants of the little colony be protected from the peril and suffering resulting from the sale of liquor to the Indians. Apparently more favorably impressed with the opportunities of West Jersey, Thomas and Robert Scholey located between 1680 and 1685 in Burlington County, where they bought several large tracts in Mansfield, Springfield and Chesterfield townships. A minute of Chesterfield Mo. Meeting, 7th mo. 2nd, 1686, shows the kindly sentiment of the community: "Whereas this Meeting is made Aquainted that Robert Scholey hath Sustained A Great Loss By the fire Burning of his Corne and Hay, hath thought fitt to make Enquierry how it is With him, and hath ordered Thomas Lambert and Mahlon Stacey to Goe And Speake With him and Give their Reports to the Next monthly Meeting."

That Robert, Thomas and John Scholey—the latter coming from England about 1680—were valued citizens is shown by the court records of the time, wherein they appear as co-executors, appraisers of estates, witnesses of property transfers, etc. Robert served as constable of Yorkshire tenth, 1682. Thomas Scholey, as a contemporary of Richard French [5] in Chesterfield Meeting, was a frequent representative to quarterly meeting and served on important committees. Robert Scholey was buried "at the ffalls the 25th day of the 1 mo. 1689." His widow, Sarah Wheatly, having married Caleb Wheatly in 1696, died 14th day of 1st month, 1714/15, "and was buried at ffriends burying ground at the ffalls."

23—RICHARD FRENCH, JR. (Thomas, 1; Richard, 5).

b. 8th mo. 20th, 1696.

m. Rachel ———.

| 96—RACHEL FRENCH | b. 11th mo. 12th, 1722. |

25—MARY FRENCH (Thomas, 1; Richard, 5).

> m. 8th mo. 15th, 1724, Preserve Brown, Jr., son of Preserve and Mary Brown of Mansfield, Burlington Co., N. J.
>
> buried 6th mo. 18th, 1746, in Friends' Burying Ground, Fourth and Arch Sts., Philadelphia.
>
> He m. Second, 8th mo. 21st, 1747, Mary Sykes, daughter of John and Joanna Sykes of Chesterfield Township, Burlington Co., N. J.
>
> She b. 9th mo. 3rd, 1707.
>
> d. 1783.
>
> He d. 5th mo. 23rd, 1760.

Children of Preserve and Mary (French) Brown.

97—PRESERVE BROWN, 3RD b. 6th mo. 26th, 1729.
 d. 9th mo. 1st, 1758.
 m. October 2ud, 1748, Elizabeth Till (Christ Church record, Philada.).

98—RICHARD BROWN b. 11th mo. 10th, 1732.
 m. 5th mo. 15th, 1755, Sarah Taylor of Chesterfield Township, Burlington Co., N. J.

99—MARY BROWN b. 3rd mo. 10th, 1735.
 m. 8th mo. 12th, 1756, John Jones, Jr., son of John and Mary (Doughty) Jones of Philadelphia.

100—SARAH BROWN b. 10th mo. 2nd, 1737.
 m. 11th mo. 11th, 1756, Joseph Scholey.

101—WILLIAM BROWN b. 1st mo. 3rd, 1740/1.
 m. 1762, Rebecca Jones, daughter of John and Mary (Doughty) Jones of Philadelphia.

102—ABIAH BROWN b. 9th mo. 28th, 1743.
 m. March 12th, 1765, Margaret Sharp.

John Jones, son of Edward Jones, "of Merion, Philadelphia County, province of Pennsylvania, Chyrurgion," and Mary Doughty, daughter of Jacob Doughty, of Crosswicks, Burlington Co., N. J., were married 12th day of 9th mo., 1717.

PRESERVE BROWN, JR.

In the year 1710, Preserve Brown, Sr., removed from Chesterfield Monthly Meeting to Burlington Monthly Meeting, residing at Mansfield, a few miles from Bordentown, N. J. About this time there lived in that vicinity four persons bearing the quaint names, Preserve Brown, Safety Borden, Safety Magee and Hananiah Gaunt. Preserve Brown and his wife were highly esteemed and regarded as "valuable Friends." At his death he was buried in Friends' Burying Ground, located on what is now Prince Street, near Church Street, Bordentown. As a mark of special honor and respect the Friends erected to his memory a tombstone bearing the inscription:

> "In Memory of
> Preserve Brown
> who died the 26 day of
> the 4 month 1744
> Aged 65 years"

This solitary tombstone, in the northwest corner of the grounds, is at the present time (1907) in a good state of preservation. It is of blue marble, about two feet high, with top scrolled in the usual style of that day, and is one of the oldest tombstones to be found in any Friends' burying ground in New Jersey. Tombstones were rarely erected by Friends at so early a date.

When John Montgomerie was appointed Governor of New Jersey, 1728, the Grand Jury addressed the King a congratulatory message of a somewhat fervid character, rejoicing in the "daily accessions to Your Glory," promising faithful adherence, etc. Preserve Brown was one of the signers, with a number of other Quakers, who added a line, saying: "We agree to the matter and Substance of this Address but make some exceptions to the Stile." From this unique paper we quote:

> "We cant without a rapture of thankfulness, recount our obligation to Your Majestie, for Your Parental care of Your People in this Distant Collonie.
> ". . . We Shall not Tresspass farther upon Your Royal Patience, but shall offer up our fervent prayers to the King of Kings, that he will please to direct Your Majesty by his unerring wisdom, & always encline Your heart to his Glory & Encompass Your Sacred Person with his Favour as with a Shield, & make your Government an universal blessing to all Your Dominions."

TOMBSTONE OF PRESERVE BROWN, FRIENDS' BURYING GROUND, BORDENTOWN, N. J., 1744

From a photograph taken in 1905

Preserve Brown and his wife Mary gave careful attention to the rearing of their son, Preserve Brown, Jr. We are told: " He was trained in the nurture and admonition of the Lord and the good effect thereof seems to have been very apparent. He was diligent in attendance upon all religious duties, was exemplary in plainness, both of speech and apparel, and of a kind and hospitable disposition." He took an active part in the building of the Friends' meeting house at Bordentown, in 1738–1741, serving on several committees in connection therewith. With Colin Campbell, Thomas Scattergood, Abraham Hewlings, Daniel Smith, Sr., Joshua Raper, Thomas Wetherill, Sr., Joseph Hollinshead, William Buckley, Thomas Mariott, William Black, William Hewlings, Samuel Black, and a number of other prominent and public-spirited citizens, he became a charter member of an organization which had for its object the purchasing and " Collection of useful Books, in order to erect a Library, for the advancement of knowledge and Literature in the City of Burlington." This library, thus founded in 1758, has continued to this day one of the notable institutions of its kind in New Jersey.

In 1741, Preserve Brown, Jr., was appointed overseer of the poor in Chesterfield Township, a position his charitable disposition well fitted him to fill. In 1743 he was elected surveyor of highways. He was a large landholder, owning many hundred acres in the vicinity of Sand Hills. He built and operated Laurie's grist mill, on Doctor's Creek, and was a very active and successful business man. In the fall of 1745 he removed with his family to Philadelphia, where he engaged in the brewing business, near Second and Vine Streets. In the summer of 1746 his wife, Mary French, died and was buried in Friends' Burying Ground, Fourth and Arch Streets. In the latter part of 1749 (11 mo. 9th) a great fire destroyed his brew house. This was a misfortune he could ill bear at that time. A subscription in his behalf was started by Israel Pemberton and his son Israel, they subscribing fifty-five pounds. John Smith, who married Hannah Logan, carried the paper around and secured altogether about two hundred pounds. In his diary he says: " I met with some very free to give and others very skillful in distinctions to excuse themselves."

In 1751, Preserve Brown, Jr., again took up his residence in Burlington County, New Jersey, continuing until his death, in 1760, an active and relia-ble member of Chesterfield Meeting. He was elder and clerk of the meet-ing for many years and a frequent representative at Quarterly Meeting. An

entry in the Chesterfield minutes, 6 mo. 1st, 1758, refers to his desiring to
be "Excused from being Clark of this Meeting on account of his Hardnefs
of hearing." On the inside of front cover of 2nd book of Chesterfield
Monthly Meeting Minutes is written: "Preferve Brown recorded 111 pages."
That this worthy Friend was successful in business is shown by his will and
inventory of his personal estate, reciting property upwards of $15,000 in
value and about the same amount due on book and bond accounts. In the
issue of June 26th, 1760, of the "Pennsylvania Gazette," appeared the following advertisement:

> All Persons indebted to the Estate of Preserve Brown, late of Nottingham,
> in West-New-Jersey, deceased, are desired to pay, and those who have any
> Demands, against said Estate, are desired to bring in their Accounts, that
> they may be adjusted and paid by Richard Brown, at the late Dwelling-
> House of said Preserve Brown, and John Jones, of Phila, Executors.
>
> To be sold, a convenient Malt and Brew-house, situate in the Northern
> Liberties, between Second and Third-Streets, just above Vine-Street; for
> Title and Terms of Sale enquire of said Executors.

Three of Preserve Brown's sons became men of note in their time. Richard Brown, like his father, was a miller, and at one time owned Waln's mills,
Crosswicks, N. J. During the Revolution he embarked extensively in the
production of salt, but the venture proved a losing one. William Brown
became a leading shipping merchant of Philadelphia, but lost all during the
Revolution by the capture of his ships. Later he established a large biscuit
bakery and his product became very popular with ship captains. Upon his
death his brand sold for five hundred dollars. For refusing to take off his
hat to the crown he was the victim of a sword blow upon the head by a
reckless British soldier, from which he never recovered. He was known as
the "honest Quaker" and was highly esteemed throughout the community.
He gave freely to charitable objects and was a zealous member of Friends'
Meeting.

Abia Brown became possessed, through inheritance from his father, of an
extensive mill property in Nottingham Township, Burlington County, which
he sold, in 1768, to Robert Lewis, of Philadelphia, for about 1,000 pounds.
In this deed of transfer he is referred to as "Ironmaster." After removing
to Sussex County, he became quite prominent in public affairs and sat in
the Provincial Congress of New Jersey during the session at Trenton, 1775,
and at New Brunswick, 1776. The "Pennsylvania Gazette," March 19,
1767, contained the following advertisement:

"TO BE SOLD BY THE SUBSCRIBER"

A VALUABLE grist mill, with two pair of stones and three boulting cloths, and turning lathe, hoisting all by water, with a good two story dwelling house, four rooms on a floor, a cellar under the whole, with two Kitchens, and a well of good water at the door; a good barn, stables, store-house, and smoak-house, with a good landing, and store house at the same, sufficient to contain 300 barrels of flour, where a shallop may load at the door, that can carry 200 barrels of flour; also a small dwelling-house for the miller, and spring-house, and cooper's shop, with about 100 acres of land, one half of the same meadow, and the remainder fit for the plough, and in fence. It is pleasantly situated on the great road that leads from Trenton to Crosswicks and Allentown, and on the road that leads from Princetown to the above landing, on a constant stream of water, the whole in good repair, and in a public place for the business of Keeping Store, where there may be plenty of wheat had, it being two miles from Crosswicks, 6 from Trenton, 12 from Princetown, 6 from Allentown, and 3 from Bordentown. Any person inclining to purchase the same, may apply to Joseph Scholey, living near the said premises, or to the subscriber, living at Sharp's iron works, in Sussex County, N. J.   ABIA BROWN

MEETING RECORDS

Chesterfield Monthly Meeting Minutes:

At a Monthly Meeting of Friends held at their Meeting Houſe in Chesterfield the 3ᵈ of the 7 mo. 1724

Preserve Brown Junʳ & Mary French daughter of Richard French both belonging to this Meeting declared their intentions of taking each other in Marriage whereupon this meeting appoints our Friends John Warren & John Sykes to make enquiry of his clearneſs from all others on account of Marriage & of his conversation & make report to our next Monthly Meeting.

At a Monthly Meeting of Friends held at their Meeting Houſe in Chesterfield the 1ˢᵗ of the 8 mo. 1724

Preserve Brown Junʳ & Mary French Junʳ the second time declared their intentions of taking each other in Marriage & nothing appearing upon enquiry but that they are clear on that account & consent of parents being had This Meeting leaves them to their liberty to accomplish their said Marriage according to the good order uſed among Friends and appoint John Warren & John Sykes to make report to our next Meeting.

At A Monthly Meeting of Friends held at their Meeting Houſe in Chesterfield the 5ᵗʰ of the 9 mo. 1724

Our Friends appointed at our laſt Monthly Meeting to have the oversight at the two Marriages paſt at our laſt Monthly Meeting Give account that they saw nothing but all things were decently mannaged.

MARRIAGE CERTIFICATE

Whereas Preserve Brown Jun[r] of Mansfield in the County of Burlington & Western division of New Jersey & Mary French daughter of Richard French of the same place having declared their Intentions of Marriage with eath other before Several Monthly Meetings of the people called Quakers at Chesterfield in the County of Burlington aforesaid According to the good order used among them whofe proceedings therein after a deliberate Consideration thereof & having consent of parents & relations concerned nothing appearing to obstruct were approved of by the said Meetings.

Now thefe are to Certifie all whom it may concern that for the full accomplishing of their said Intentions this fifteenth day of the Eighth month in the Year of our Lord One Thousand Seven hundred & twenty four. They the said Preserve Brown Jun[r] & Mary French appeared in a public Meeting of the said people & others at their public Meeting houfe in Chesterfield aforesaid. And the said Preserve Brown Jun[r] taking the said Mary French by the hand did in a solemn manner openly declare that he took her to be his Wife promifsing through the Lords Afsistance to be unto her a loving & Faithful Husband until the Lord Should by death Separate them. And then & there in the said Afsembly the said Mary French did in like manner declare that She took the said Preserve Brown to be her husband, promifsing to be to him a faithful & loving Wife till it Should pleafe the Lord by death to Separate them. And Moreover the said Preferve Jun[r] & Mary French (She according to the Custom of Marriage Afsuming the name of her husband) as a further Confirmation thereof did then & there to thefe prefents set their Hands. And we whose names are here-under Subscribed being among others present at the Solemnization of the said Marriage & Subscription in manner aforesaid as Witnefses thereunto have also to thefe prefents set our names the day & year above written 1724

Preserve Brown Jun[r]
Mary Brown

W[m] Scholey	Abra: Brown Jun[r]	Richard French
Joshua Shreeve	Rich[d] Lawrence	Preserve Brown
Tho: French Jun[r]	Tho: Newbould	Harmenius King
Benj[n] Shreeve	Tho: Johnson	Tho: French
Jn[o] Abbott	Eliz[a] Scholey	Rich[d] French Jun[r]
Jn[o] Sykes	Mercy King	Jn[o] King
Jn[o] Black	Sarah Murfin	Jos: King
Ro: Stork	Mary Ellis	Tho: King
W[m] Murfin	Phebe Bunting	Fra: King
Jos: Recklefs	Eliz[a] Tantum Jun[r]	Abra Brown

At a Meeting of Friends held at their Meeting Houſe at Chesterfield Seventh of the 10^m 1738

Isaac Horner on behalf of Friends at Bordentown requeſted Liberty to build a Meeting Houſe there which this Meeting agrees to & it is referred to the next Quarterly Meeting

At a Meeting of Friends held at their Meeting Houſe at Chesterfield the 3rd of 2mo 1740

Thomas Potts Junr & Preserve Brown Junr to get a Deed for Joseph Borden for a piece of ground on the other side of the Street for a Meeting Houſe & to deliver up the old Deed for the other piece of ground.

At a Meeting of Friends held at their Meeting Houſe at Chesterfield 6th of 9mo 1740

Preserve Brown Junr & Thomas Potts Junr have discharged their trust on account of the Land for a Meeting Houſe and Grave Yard at Bordentown.

At a Meeting of Friends held at their Meeting Houſe at Chesterfield 9th 10mo 1742

Friends allow the inhabitants at and near Bordentown to have a Meeting every First day for this winter quarter according to their request.

Philadelphia Monthly Meeting Minutes:

At a Monthly Meeting held in our Meeting House in Philadelphia the 29th of the Ninth Month, 1745

Preserve Brown produced to this Meeting a Certificate for himself and Wife and son Preserve from Chesterfield Monthly Meeting in New Jersey, dated the 5th Seventh Month last which was read and well received and sent to the Women Friends.

From Monthly Meeting held at Chesterfield 7th mo. 5th, 1745

To our Friends at their Monthly Meeting to be held at Philadelphia sendeth Greeting

Dear friends these may acquaint you that our friend Preserve Brown being removed within the Compass of your Meeting hath requested a few lines by way of Certificate for himself his wife and son Preserve, enquiry having been made according to good order it appears they have been sober and orderly in their Conversation and Just in their dealings so recommending them to Divine protection and your Christian care desireing their growth and perseverance in ye blessed Truth

Signed in and by order of the said Meeting by

Isaac Hornor
W. Morris
Providence Hewes
Thos Wright
and others

At A Monthly Meeting of ffriends held in our Meeting House in Philadelphia the 28th day of Sixth Month 1747—

Preserve Brown applied for a Certificate on Account of marriage to
Chesterfield Monthly Meeting, which Israel Pemberton and John Smith are
appointed after inquiry to prepare.

At a Monthly Meeting held in our Meeting House in Philadelphia, the
25th of 7 Month 1747

Certificate prepared for Preserve Brown to Chesterfield Monthly Meeting.

From our monthly meeting held at Philadelphia the 25th of the 7mo:
1747

To the monthly meeting of friends at Chesterfield in the County of Burlington

Dear Friends

The bearer hereof our Esteemed Friend Preserve Brown acquainted our
last monthly meeting with his Intentions of Marriage with a friend belonging to your meeting and Requested a few lines from us on his behalf—

This is therefore to Certify you that he is a person in unity with us,
being of an Orderly Life and Conversation, and as far as we can find
Clear from any person in relation to marriage Excepting with the person
with whom he intends to appear at your meeting—We Recommended him
to your Christian Care in the accomplishment of his said marriage and
with the Salutation of Dear Love Remain Your Friends and Brethren

> Signed in and on behalf }
> of our said meeting By } Israel Pemberton C[lk.]

MARRIAGE CERTIFICATE

Chesterfield Monthly Meeting Marriages, Book I.

Whereas Preserve Brown of the City of Philad[a] in the province of
Pensilvania, And Mary Sykes daughter of John Sykes of y[e] Township of
Chesterfield in the County of Burlington & Western divifion of New Jersey,
& Joanna Sykes his Wife Having declared their Intentions of Marriage
with each other before Several Monthly Meetings of y[e] people called
Quakers at their Meeting houfe in Chesterfield aforef[d] according to y[e] good
order used among them whofe proceedings therein after a deliberate consideration thereof, And having confent of Parents & Relations concerned
nothing appearing to obftruct, were approved of by y[e] said Meetings.

Now Thefe are to Certifie all whom it may concern that for the full accomplifhing of their s^d Intentions this twenty firft day ye eighth Month, in ye year of our Lord One Thoufand Seven hundred & forty Seven They ye said Preserve Brown & Mary Sykes appeared at a public Meeting of the said people & others at thier Meeting Houfe at Upper Springfield in ye County of Burlington & Western division of New Jersey afores^d And ye said Preserve Brown taking the said Mary Sykes by the hand did in a Solemn manner openly declare that he took her to be his Wife promifsing through the Lords afsiftance to be to her a loving & faithful Hufband until it Should pleafe the Lord by death to Separate them. And then & there in the s^d afsembly the said Mary Sykes did in like manner declare that She took ye s^d Preserve Brown to be her hufband promifsing through the Lords afsistance to be to him a faithful & loving Wife until it Should pleafe ye Lord by death to Separate Them. And Moreover the s^d Preserve Brown & Mary Sykes (She according to ye Custom of Marriage afsuming the name of her husband) as a further confirmation thereof did then & there to thefe p^efents set their hands And we whofe names are hereunto Subfcribed being among others prefent at ye Solemnization of ye s^d Marriage & Subfription in manner afores^d as Witnefses thereunto have also to thefc prefents set our hands ye day & year above written

Preserve Brown
Mary Brown

Edith Newbold	Michael Newbold	John Sykes
Francis Scholey	Barzillai Newbold	Joanna Sykes
Mary Wright	Benj^a Shreve	Jacob Andrews
Hannah Newbold	Tho: Boud	Saml Sykes
Efther White	W^m: French	Jn° Kirkbride
Hannah Zane	Tho: Black	Jn° Brown
Sarah Newbold	Jn° Newbold	Anne Andrews
Anne Newbold	Js: Decow Medius	Richd Brown
Mary Black	Jn° Scholey	Joanna Sykes
Rachel Scholey	Saml Black	Kezia Shreve
Rebecca Smith	Saml Pleafant	Rebecca Wright
	Edwd Black	Rebecca Wright
	Antho: Sykes	Sarah Brown
	Jn° Kirkbride J^r	Rachel Bowne
	Anne Carlile	Isabel Scholey
	Anne Brooks	Edwd Brooks
	Sarah Dilwin	Benj^a Sykes
		Tho: Brown

From Monthly Meeting at Chesterfield in the County of Burlington and Western Division of New Jersey 11th mo. 7th 1747

To the Monthly Meeting of Friends at Philadelphia in the Province Pensilvania with the Kind salutation of Love

Dear friends Application hath been made to us for a Certificate on behalf of Our frd Mary (Sykes) Brown who is removed to live within the verge of your meeting These are to Certifie that from the report of the Enquirers appointed according to good order, her Conversation appears to be sober & orderly Diligent in attending our Meetings for Worship & is owned to be a member in unity with us so leaving her to the manifestation of Truth & to her and your Godly & Christian care desireing her further Growth and perseverance in the blessed truth, We take leave and Subscribe ourselves your friends Brethren & Sisters

Signed in and on behalf of our said Meeting by	Isaac Deacon Clk
	Alice Bunting
	Eleanor Hornor
	Joanna Sykes
	Elizabeth Walton
	and many others

ANCESTRY OF MARY (SYKES) BROWN

John Sykes and Joanna Murfin, daughter of Robert and Ann Murfin, were married "in a Meeting at their publick Meeting place in Chesterfield 8th Mo. (October) 19th, 1704." She was born 5th mo., 1684. John and Joanna Sykes were both acknowledged ministers among Friends. Their married life continued for a period of upwards of sixty-seven years. They had twelve children, ten of whom grew to maturity. John Sykes was the son of Samuel Sykes who with his wife and children and aged father, John Sykes, emigrated from Ashford-in-the-water, Derbyshire, England, and arrived at Burlington in 1683. Samuel Sykes and his brother Anthony were both early and prominent adherents of Quakerism in England, the latter becoming a minister. Anthony met an untimely death about 1678. John Sykes was born in 1682 and died 1771. He was survived by his wife Joanna, four daughters and three sons. His will, proved November 18th, 1771, showed him to be possessed of considerable property in Burlington and Hunterdon counties, N. J., which was divided among his wife and children. One of the bequests mentioned in the will was, "£5 towards inclosing the Lott of ground whereon Friends Meeting House stands in Bordentown." Joanna Sykes died at about ninety years of age.

MEETING RECORDS—CONTINUED

Philadelphia Monthly Meeting Minutes:

At A Monthly Meeting of Friends of Philadelphia held in our Meeting house in Philadelphia the 26th day of Second Month 1751

Preserve Brown being about to return to reside within the Compaſs of Chesterfield Monthly Meeting by a Friend requesting a Certificate for himself and Wife.

At A Monthly Meeting of Friends of Philadelphia held in our Meeting house in Philadelphia the 31st day of Third Month 1751

Certificate prepared and read for Preserve Brown and Wife to Chesterfield Monthly Meeting.

Chesterfield Monthly Meeting Minutes:

At a Monthly Meeting of Friends at theire Meeting houſe in Chesterfield held at ye 4th of 5 mo 1751

Preſerve Brown Brought Into this Meeting a Certificate from Philadelphia Monthly Meeting for himself and Wife Which was Read and Received

At a Monthly Meeting of friends at theire Meeting houſe In Cheſterfield ye 3d of 7m 1755. Isaac Decow Declining to act as Clark any Longer Preſerve brown is apointed to that Service.

Att a monthly Meeting of Friends at theire Meeting houſe in Cheſterfield the 1 of 6 mo. 1758

Preſerve Brown deſires to be Excuſed from being Clark of this Meeting on account of his Hardneſs of hearing which the Meeting Concents to, And appoints Able Midleton Clark of the Meeting in his Sted.

At Chesterfield Monthly Meeting 11 mo 2d 1758

Preserve Brown brought one Hundred & Fifty Books to this Meeting to be Distributed in ye particular Meetings belonging to this Meeting Intitled a Mite into the Treasury by David Hall.

At Chesterfield Monthly Meeting 8 mo. 4th 1763

The Friends appointed to prepare Memorials of such Ministers and Elders within the verge of this Meeting that had not been heretofore done, laid before this Meeting three, viz: one concerning our friend Isaac Horner, one for Sarah Murfin, one for Preserve Brown which was read and approved of.

Philadelphia Monthly Meeting Minutes:

At A Monthly Meeting of Friends of Philadelphia held in our Meeting house in Philadelphia the 31st day of 1st month 1749

Preserve Brown Junr [97] produced paper acknowledging his breach of Discipline in Marriage desir'd to be continued under the Care of Friends which was read and remain for further Consideration.

Chesterfield Monthly Meeting Minutes:

At a Monthly Meeting of Friends at theire Meeting houſe in Chester-field held yᵉ 6th of 6 mo 1754

Richard Brown [98] brought in a certificate from Philadelphia Monthly Meeting, which was Read and Accepted.

11 Mo 5th 1761 William [101] and Bia Brown [102] by Amos Middleton Request Certificate of Removal to Philadelphia Monthly Meeting Timothy Abbot and the Clerk to inquire.

3rd of 12 Mo. 1761 Certificate granted to William and Abia Brown to Philadelphia Monthly Meeting.

WILL OF PRESERVE BROWN, JR., 1759

It is to be Remembered that I Preserve Brown of Notingham in the County of Burlington & Province of New Jersey Shopkeeper Being in a declining state of helth, But of sound and Disposing Mind and Memory, and knowing the uncertainty of this Life, am Minded to Dispose of such Estate Reil & Personall whereof I may dye Possesed & sized; do make this my last will & Testament in maner & forme following: That is to say first I Give & bequeth unto My Beloved Wife Mary and unto her heirs & asignes forever all that I had with her from her father or otherwise, or the valew thereof if any of the things should worne out, and the best horse I shall die Possesed of & the Riding Chear; Also I Give & Bequeth to my said Wife the use of one half of the house, Mills, Stores Land & medow hereafter devised to my Son Abia to be Possesed & Injoyed by her so long as she continues my widow, which is intended and I hope she accepts Instead of her dower or thirds out of my Estate.

Also I Give & Bequeth unto my Son Richard Brown one third Part of all the Personall Estate I shall Die Possessed of after my Debts are paid & household goods are divided as above & hereafter Expressed to be possesed by him his Heirs & asigns forever.

Also I Give & Devise unto my Son William Brown that Part of the Land I Purchased of William Morris In the Township of Nottingham aforesaid that Lyes on the Southeast Side of the Mill pond & Doctors Creek (Except one half Acre at the End of the tumbling dam which is Reserved for the use of the Mills).

Also I Give & Devise unto my said son William a Iott of Land in Notingham aforesaid Bounded Southerly by a Road & South westerly by the Road that Leads from Crosswicks to Trenton & North westerly and North-easterly by William Murfins Land, also my three houses and loots In Vine Street In Philadelphia that Stand next to Second Street he paying the

Ground rent that arises thereon, To have & to hold the said Lands and Loots of Land with the buildings thereon Errected & the apurtenancies theirto belonging unto my said Son William Brown & to his Heirs & assigns forever, Also I give & Bequeth unto my said Son William Brown and to his Heirs One third part of the Personall Estate I shall Die possessed of after my Debts are paid & household goods are divided.

Also I give & devise to my Son Abiah Brown and to his heirs Heirs and Assignes forever all the Land I Purchased of William Morris in Notingham aforesaid that lies between the Road that Leads to Trentton aforesaid and Crosswicks Creek on the North side of Doctors Creek & also one half acre of Land at the South east end of the Tumbling Dam above reserved with the Mill pond, Mills & Mill houses, Dwelling house Barnes Shops Stables Stores and Wharves thereon and all the appurtenences thereto belonging he Letting my abovesaid wife have one half of the use thereof as long as she Continues my widow, Also I give and Bequeth unto my said Son Abia & his heirs one third part of the Personall Estate I shall die possessed of aftor my Debts are paid & household goods are divided.

Also I Give and Devise unto my Daughter Mary Jones and to the Heirs of her body & to theire Heirs & assignes forever My house In Vine Street in Philadelphia adjoyning to the East End of the abovesaid three Houses, divised to my Son William with the Lott thereto belonging,

Also I Give and Bequeth unto my said Daughtor Mary one half of the household goods I shall die Possessed of after my wife hath got the goods that came by her as aforesaid.

Also I Give and Divise unto my Daughter Sarah Scholy and to the Heirs of her body & to theire Heirs & assignes forever the Land I Purchased of William Morris In Notingham Lying on the North Side of the Mill pond & bounded by the said pond, and on the West by the Road that Leads from Crosswicks to Trentton, and Northerly by a road that Leads out of that to John Taylors Land & Estorly by the said Taylors Land, Also twenty five Acres of Land I Purchased of ye said Wm. Morris bounded by Samuell Stevensons Land & Abraham Tiltons & Gisbort Hendersons & Francis Bordons Land with all the Buildings & apurtanances thereunto belonging, And like wise all my Houses & Lotts in Chestorfield in the County of Burlington with the Groundrents & all the apurtenancies thereunto belonging.

Also I Give & bequeth unto my Said Daughtor Sarah one half of the household goods that I shall Die Possesed of after my wife hath got the goods above Bequeathed to her.

Provided Also and my will farther is that if any of my Children should Die under twenty one Years of age & without issue that the part or Portion of such Child or Children shall be Equally divided among the survivors of them and Likewise If either of my daughtors should Die without

Issue that the Lands & houses Divised to her shall be Sold and the money they fech be divided Equally among the rest of my Children that shall survive or theire Heirs, And for the bettor Inabling my Executors to dischare my debts & Legasyes herein before Given.

My Will farther is that all the Residue of the Reile Estate that I shall Die Possessed of that is not hearein specifacally Divised shall be sold in fee Simple by my Executors, or the Survivor or Survivors of them, or the Executors or Administrators of such Survivor, for the best price or prices that can be had for the Same and the Moneys arrising from such Sails to be added to my Personall Estate for the Purposes aforesaid.

Lastly I nominate My Sons Richard & William Brown and Soninlaw John Jones Executors of this my Last Will and Testament, hereby revoking all former Wills by me heretofore made & Declaring this only this to be my Last will & Testament.

In Witness whereof I have hearunto afixed my hand & Seale this thirtenth day of the Sixth Month Called June In the yere of our Lord one thousand seven hundred & fifty nine.

Signed Sealled Pubblished and Declared to be the Last Will and Testament of the abovesaid Preserve Brown in our Presence who at his request and in his Presence have subscribed our Naims as witnesses thereunto.

The word Bequeth in the sixtenth Line & the word Divise in the forty Ninth Line & the word her between ye 74th & 75th Line being first made what they are.

And Lotts, being likewise Interlined between the 28th & 29th Line, & his Heirs, being Intorlined between the 46th & 47th Line.

Preserve Brown

Samuel Redford
James White
John Brown
Peter Suslmann.

James White & Peter Sousman two of the Witnesses to the Within Will the said James White being duly affirmed according to law and the said Peter Sousman did Depose that they were present & saw Preserve Brown the Testator within Named Sign and Seal the Same and heard him publish pronounce & declare the within Instrument of Writing to be his last Will & Testament, and that at the Doing thereof the said Testator was of Sound & Disposing mind Memory and Understanding as far as they know and as they verily believe and that John Brown and Samuel Redford the other subscribing Evidences were present at the same time & signed their Names as Witnesses to the same Together with this Affirmant Deponent in the presence of the said Testator.

James White
Peter Suslmann

Sworn & Affirmed at Burlington
December 11th 1760, before   S. Blackwood, Surrogate.

Richard Brown one of the Executors within named being of the people called Quakers and duly affirmed according to law did declare and Affirm that the within Instrument of writing contained the true Last Will & Testament of Preserve Brown the Testator therein Named deceased as far as he knows and as he verily believes and that he will well & truly perform the same by paying first the Debts of the said deceased and then the legacies in the said Testament Specified so farr for the as the Goods Chattels & Credits of the said decd can thereunto extend & that he will make and Exhibit a true and perfect Inventory of all the Goods & Chattels of the said deceased which have or shall come to his knowledge & possession or to the possession of any other person for his use & render a just and true account of his Administrations when thereunto lawfully required.

Richard Brown

Affirmd the day & year
above, before   S. Blackwood, Surrogate.

SUMMARY OF INV. OF EST. OF PRESERVE BROWN, JR.

Inventory of Preserve Brown late of Nottingham in the County Burlington, in West New Jersey, Merchant Deceased, Dated 6 mo 2^d 1760

	£	S	d
Goods in and about House, in the Mill, down at the Landing..	2364	18	9
5 Calves missing at time of appraising sence found at 30 S....	7	10	
Shop Goods	667	8	11
Book debts	2795	12	5

Appraisers { William Murfin
{ Samuel Stevenson

Executors { Richard Brown
{ William Brown

Affirmed at Burlington this 15th
day of April Anno Dom 1762
     before Sam¹ Allinson Surrogate

LIST OF DEBTORS BY BONDS OR BILLS

Sam¹ Depews 14 Bonds
Andrew Davises Bill
Thomas Schooley Bond
———— King   "
Wᵐ Parker Bill
Daniel Caſsels—Bond
Steven Carter's—Bill
David Kaighls—Bond
John Davis—Bond
Andrew Davison—Bill
Henry Browns—Bond & Bill
Abraham Browns—Bond
Sam¹ Bonvills   "
Wᵐ Lawrences   "
Daniel Greens—Note
James Senes's—Bill
Joˢ Gay's—Bond
  Benj Englishes—Note

Geo: Hopkins—Bond
Benj: Page's—Bill
Geo. Palmer—Bond
James Prices's—Note
John Pitmans—Bill
James McClealans—Bond
Thoˢ Stevenson—Bond
Richᵈ and John Reeds—Bond(2)
Mathew Wilson—Bill
James Shaw   "
Matthew Wright—2 Bills
Nathaniel Warner's—Bill
Archibald Silvers   "
Thoˢ. Lawries—Bond
Joˢ and Abraham Skirm—B.
Charles Vankides Bond
Robert Quigleys   "

PHILADELPHIA IN 1720

LIST OF DEBTORS BY BONDS OR BILLS

s 14 Bonds
ises Bill
ooley Bond
"
Bill
ls—Bond
r's—Bill
ls—Bond
Bond
ison—Bill
ns—Bond & Bill
owns—Bond
ls "
ces "
ns—Note
's—Bill
Bond
lishes—Note

Geo: Hopkins—Bond
Benj: Page's—Bill
Geo. Palmer—Bond
James Prices's—Note
John Pitmans—Bill
James McClealans—Bond
Thoˢ Stevenson—Bond
Richᵈ and John Reeds—Bond(2)
Mathew Wilson—Bill
James Shaw "
Matthew Wright—2 Bills
Nathaniel Warner's—Bill
Archibald Silvers "
Thoˢ. Lawries—Bond
Joˢ and Abraham Skirm—B.
Charles Vankides Bond
Robert Quigleys "

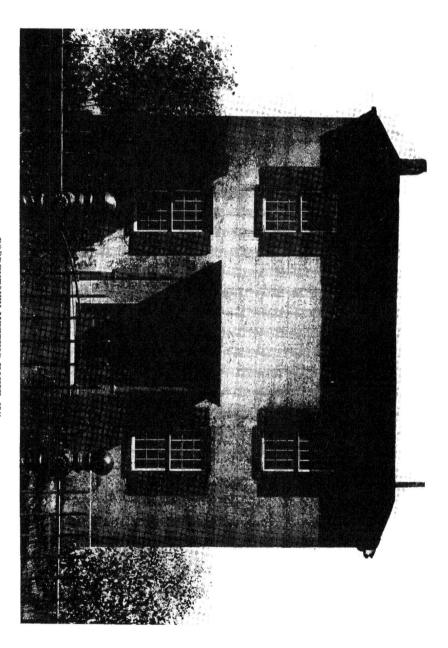

BORDENTOWN MEETING HOUSE, 1741

BORDENTOWN MEETING

Friends among the early settlers in the vicinity of Bordentown, N. J., sought and obtained privilege from Chesterfield Monthly Meeting to hold meetings for worship in their immediate neighborhood for three months in each year. No mention is made of the place of holding these meetings, and it is very probable that they were held, as in many other instances, at the house of some Friend living in or near Bordentown. About 1736, Joseph Borden made an offer to some Friends of land upon which to build a meeting house, and for a graveyard; and in the ninth month of that year a committee from Chesterfield Monthly Meeting was appointed to treat with him concerning it. In fifth month, 1737, the deeds for the meeting house and graveyard were reported finished and the Meeting directed that the " Declaration of Trust be signed against Next Meeting." For some reason the matter seems to have rested for about a year and a half. No further record of it appears upon the Meeting minutes until tenth month, 1738, when Isaac Horner, on behalf of Bordentown friends, made a request that they might have liberty to build a meeting house there, and Chesterfield Monthly Meeting agreeing, the matter was referred to the next Quarterly Meeting. On the 3rd of second month, 1740, " Thomas Potts Junr. and Preserve Brown Junr. were appointed to procure a Deed from Joseph Borden for a piece of ground on the other side of the Street for a Meeting house and to deliver up the old Deed for the other piece of ground." This trust was duly performed, and another committee, of which Preserve Brown, Jr., was an active member, was appointed to superintend the erection of the building, which was completed in 1741. This meeting house is still standing in excellent condition, as accompanying picture shows. It is located on what is now Farnsworth Avenue, opposite Crosswicks Street. In 1905 this Meeting was " laid down " as a place of worship on First and Fifth days, no Friends living there, but Chesterfield Monthly Meeting was held there in the Third, Sixth, Ninth and Twelfth Months alternately with Crosswicks and Trenton until the spring of 1907, when for various reasons it was decided to discontinue holding any meetings there.

26—REBECCA FRENCH (Thomas, 1; Richard, 5).

> m. 2nd mo. 23rd, 1729, Benjamin Shreve, son of
> Caleb and Sarah (Areson) Shreve of Mans-
> field Township, Burlington Co., N. J.
>
> He b. 6th mo. 9th, 1706.
>
> d. 1751.

103—KEZIAH SHREVE
> b. March 8th, 1730.
> m. about 1752, Moses Ivins.

104—RICHARD SHREVE
> b. 6th mo. 10th, 1732.
> d. unmarried.

105—CALEB SHREVE
> b. 8th mo. 25th, 1734.
> m. 11th mo. 19th, 1755, Grace Pancoast.

106—WILLIAM SHREVE
> b. 8th mo. 4th, 1737.
> m. First, May 8th, 1756, Anna Ivins.
> m. Second, 12th mo. 15th, 1768, Rhoda Ivins.
> m. Third, February 21st, 1779, Anne (Wood-
> ward) Reckless.

107—ISRAEL SHREVE
> b. 12th mo. 24th, 1739.
> m. First, 2ud mo., 1760, Grace Curtis.
> m. Second, 5th mo. 10th, 1773, Mary Cokley.

108—SARAH SHREVE
> b. 10th mo. 18th, 1744.
> m. First, May 4th, 1768, David Scattergood.
> m. Second, April 24th, 1779, Joseph Beck.
> m. Third, John Nixon.

109—BENJAMIN SHREVE, JR.
> b. 10th mo. 7th, 1747.
> m. First, 7th mo. 10th, 1770, Hannah Marll.
> m. Second, 1786, Susan Wood.

110—SAMUEL SHREVE
> b. 1st mo. 25th, 1750.
> m. First, ——— ———. *Mira Trout* 1/s
> m. Second, ——— ———.

BENJAMIN SHREVE

The Shreve family were among the earliest settlers of New England, \Caleb, the progenitor, being recorded as a resident of Plymouth, Mass., in 1641. Two of his sons, Caleb and John, located in Rhode Island, the former, in 1680, marrying Sarah, daughter of Dirick Areson, of Flushing, L. I. Soon after he removed to Shrewsbury, East Jersey, in the vicinity of which he remained from 1685 until 1699, when he purchased a large tract of over 300 acres from Richard French [5], Mt. Pleasant, Mansfield Township, Burlington County, West Jersey. This notable homestead has remained in the possession of successive generations of the family until this day.

Caleb Shreve had seven sons and three daughters. At his death, in 1740, sixty years after his marriage, his wife was still living. His will bequeathed to her one third of his personal property and a life interest in his real estate. In a note "inferted before signing of ye same," he requested that his wife, at her death, leave her personal property to Benjamin, the youngest son, to whom was left the entire estate, after his mother's death, except certain small legacies to his brothers, Thomas, Joshua, Joseph, Caleb, Jonathan and David, five shillings each; the same to his daughters, Mary (Shreve) Gibbs and Sarah (Shreve) Ogburn; five shillings to his son-in-law, Benj. Scattergood, and some personal property to Sarah Shreve, daughter of his son Joshua. It is supposed that the older sons were provided for in his life time. The daughter who was the wife of Benj. Scattergood evidently was deceased.

Benjamin Shreve added to his valuable patrimony by various land purchases some 450 acres. Tradition says that he died prematurely in consequence of a fall from his horse. He was not yet fifty years of age. His will shows his solicitude for his minor children and their careful bringing up. Several of his sons and one grandson distinguished themselves in the war for national independence. Although the Shreve family were honored and esteemed Friends, meeting and government records show that the various branches of the family were possessed of a martial spirit to an eminent degree. A portion of the old house, shown in accompanying picture, was built by Caleb Shreve in 1725, and another part by Benjamin in 1742, these figures being conspicuous on the eastern end. It stands upon high ground, commanding a fine view, and within has many colonial features, in old Dutch tiling, fireplaces, cupboards, etc. From Caleb [105] the property passed to his son, Benjamin, who died in 1844. In 1902 it descended to the present owner, B. F. Haywood Shreve, of Philadelphia.

DEED, RICHARD FRENCH TO CALEB SHREVE, 1699

This Indenture made ye Twynty Second day of Aprill in ye yeare of o^r Lord according to English Acc^t one Thousand Six hundred ninety & nine Betweene Richard ffrench of ye Township of Mansfield in ye County of Burlington in ye Province of West New Jersey yeoman of ye one p^t And Caleb Shreeve of ffreehold in ye Province of East Jersey yeoman of ye other p^t Witnefseth that ye sd Richard ffrench for & in Considracon of one hundred Seaventy Seaven pounds & ten shillings currant silver money within ye s^d Province to him by ye sd Caleb Shreeve at & before ye sealing & deliv^{r}y hereof in hand paid ye receit whereof he ye s^d Richard ffrench doth hereby acknowledg– & thereof & every part & pcell thereof doth acquit exon^{r}ate release & discharge ye s^d Caleb Shreeve his heires Exe^{r}s adm^{r}s & every of them forever by these p^{r}sents Hath granted bargained sold alyened enfeoffed & confirmed & by these p^{r}sents doth fully clearly & abso- lutely grant bargain sell alyen enfeoffe & confirm unto ye s^d Caleb Shreeve his heires & Afsignes forever Three hundred twenty & five acres of land Situate lieing & being at Mount Pleasant in ye Township of Mansfield & County of Burlington afores^d Begins at a Stake in John Butchers line in ye great meadow E. by N 29 chaines to a stake in same meadow thence E. 3° ; S 49 chaines, to black oak by Michael Newbolds land thence along by same 14 chaines to a white oak, thence W.N.W 20 chaines to a stake in a meadow, thence N.N.E. 26 chaines to a maple; thence E. by S 4 chaines to a white oak thence N.E. 2 chaines to a stake thence WNW 51 chaines to a stake by Joseph Pancoafts land, thence along by ye same S.W. 5 chaines to a black oak thence E. 9 chaines to a black oak thence along by ye s^d Joseph Pancoafts land SSW 71 chaines to place of beginning,—Said Three hundred twenty & five acres of land is part of that four hundred & Sixty acres of land which formerly did belong unto William Ellis & which The s^d Richard ffrench by one Indenture bearing date ye Eighteenth day of November Anno Dom 1693 did purchase of William Biddle of Mount Hope Execut^r of ye last will & testamt of ye s^d William Ellis recorded in Liber B, folio 355 & 3.56 and all dwellings &c. appertaining thereto—with liberty for s^d Caleb Shreeve to pass throu ye land of s^d. Richard ffrench to a certaine well or spring in ye same below Abraham Brown's Meadow & ifsuing out of ye South Side of a certaine Hill there & there out to take water for his and their use & that their cattle shall have free access to same.

Signed   Richard ffrench with a seale

Apr^{11} 22^q 1699 acknowledged by Richard ffrench:

before Tho: Revell Juftice.

May 11th—1699 Sarah wife of Richard ffrench declared her free & full consent to ye sale of ye p^{r}mifses in this Deed whereto shee sett her marke—A—Sarah ffrench In presence of Tho: Revell Justice

MEETING RECORDS

Chesterfield Monthly Meeting Minutes:

6—1 mo. 1729. Benjamin Shreeve son of Caleb and Sarah Shreeve and Rebbecca French daughter of Rich'd and Mary French declared their intentions of taking each other in marriage, their parents being present gave their consent. The friends appointed to enquire concerning his conversation and clearness on account of marriage are Joseph Pancoast and John Black and make report to our next monthly meeting.

3—2 mo. 1729. Benj. Shreeve and Rebecca French the second time appeared at this meeting and he signified they continued in the same mind expressed to the last meeting and the friends appointed by our last meeting report that they find nothing to obstruct their proceedings Therefore this meeting gives them liberty to accomplish their said marriage according to the good order used among friends. Friends appointed to oversee at said marriage are Preserve Brown and Joseph Pancoast and make report to our next mo. meeting.

MARRIAGE CERTIFICATE

Whereas Benjamin Shreeve son of Caleb Shreeve and Rebecca ffrench daughter of Richard ffrench both of ye Township of Mancefeild and County of Burlington in the West division of New Jersey in America having declared their Intentions of Marriage with Each other before severall Monthly Meetings of ye people Called Quakers in ye Township of Chesterfield and County of Burlington aforesaid according to the good order used and Established amongst them and having Consent of parents and relations Concerned their proposal of Marriage was allowed of by the said Meetings.

Now these are to Certifie whom it may concearn that for the full accomplishing of their said Intention this twenty third day of ye second month in the year of our lord one thousand and seven hundred & twenty nine they ye said Benjamin Shreeve and Rebecca French appeared at a publick meeting of the aforesaid People and others met to gather at their publick Meeting house at ye upper End of Springfield and County of Burlington aforesaid. And ye said Benjamin Shreeve Taking the said Rebecca ffrench by ye hand did in a Solemn manner openly declare that he took her the said Rebecca ffrench to be his Wife promising by divine Assistance to be unto her a loving & faithfull husband until death should seperate them. And then and there in ye said Assembly the said Rebecca ffrench did in like manner declare that she took ye s^d Benjamin Shreve to be her Husband promising by divine Assistance to be unto him a faithfull & loving wife until death should seperate them And Moreover they ye said Benj. Shreve and Rebecca ffrench she according to ye Custom of Marriage assuming y^e

15

name of her Husband as a farther confirmation thereof did then & there
to these presents set their hand and wee whose names are here under also
subscribed being present att yᵉ Solomnization of yᵉ said Marriage and Subscription have as Witnesses thereunto set our hand The day & year above
Written 1729

                              Benjamin Shreeve
                              Rebecca Shreeve

Thomas Shreeve	Jane Shreeve	Hope Shreeve
Elizabeth Shreeve	Sarah Ogborn	Jonathan Shreeve
Isaac Gibbs	William ffrench	Hannah Shreeve
Mary Gibbs	Caleb Shreeve	Constance King
Tho. ffrench	Richard ffrench	Isaac Gibbs
John King	Sarah Shreeve	ffrancis King
Mary Brown	Mary ffrench	Joseph King
Joseph Shreeve	Mary King	Tho. King
Joshua Shreeve	James Shreeve	

The above names are from the relatives' column, forty-two names besides
these appear on the certificate.

The pioneer Friends who settled in the upper part of Burlington County, New
Jersey, for some years worshipped in each others' houses, but as population grew they
were permitted by the Burlington Quarter to set up a permanent meeting. Joshua Shreve
gave a piece of ground and in 1727 Upper Springfield Meeting House was built. Contrary to the usual custom at that time, this was a substantial brick structure, which has
withstood the ravages of passing years. The date still clearly appears on one end,
showing this to be one of the oldest meeting houses in the country. The descendants of
many old families reside in the vicinity.

UPPER SPRINGFIELD MEETING HOUSE, 1727

WILL OF BENJAMIN SHREVE, 1750/1

IN THE NAME OF GOD AMEN The Fourteenth Day of March in the Year of our Lord 1750.51 One Thousand Seven Hundred & Fifty, Fifty One, I Benjamin Shreve of Mansfield in the County of Burlington in the Province of West new jersey Yeoman being weak and Sick in bodey but in perfect Mind and Memory thanks be given to God for the Same, therefore calling to mind the Mortality of my Body and knowing that it is Appointed for all Men once to die, do make and ordain this my last Will and Testament. AND as touching Such Worldly Estate wherewith it hath pleased GOD to bless me in this Life, I give devise and dispose of the Same in the following manner and Form. IMPRIMIS it is my Will and I do order, That in the first place, all my just Debts and Funeral Charges be paid and Satisfied by my Executors hereafter mentioned.

ITEM I give to my well beloved Wife Rebecca Shreve One Third part of all my personal Estate, to her Heirs and Assigns forever, And also the Benefit of my Real Estate if She continue my Widow till my Children come of Age each in their Order it being to enable her to bring them up, but if She happen to Marry again She Shall have no power any longer in my Real Estate or the bringing up of my Children, Saving at the Discression of my Exrs. as they Shall Appoint or order. ITEM I give to my Two Daughters (Viz) Kezia Shreve and Sarah Shreve Share and Share alike of the remainder of my Personal Estate to be paid them as they attain to the Age of Eighteen Years. Now it is my Will that Kezia she Shall have her Portion within a Year after my Decease Seeing She is of Age and Sarah as abovesaid now if either of my Daughters Die within a Year after my decease She that Surviveth Shall have the Portion of the Deceased. ITEM I give to my Son Caleb Shreve all and Singular the Estate of Lands and Tenements I now live on to him his Heirs and Assigns forever. ITEM I give to my Son William Shreve all and Singular the Lands Farm or Plantation I lately purchased of of Preserve Brown lying and being in Mansfield and part in Chesterfield in ye Said County of Burlington to be enjoyed by him when he Attaineth to the Age of Twenty One Years, his Heirs and Assigns forever. ITEM I give to my Son Israel Shreve all that Farm or Plantation I lately Purchased of Jacob Ong of Hanover and also the One Hundred Acres of Land I had by Virtue of my Fathers last Will & Testament which Land my Father Purchased of Daniel Smith, to him his Heirs and Assigns forever. AND also a right for One Hundred Acres of Land which I Purchased of Preserve Brown all which to be enjoyed by him when he attaineth to the Age of Twenty One Years his Heirs and Assigns for ever. ITEM I give to my Three Sons (Viz) Caleb, William and Israel all & Singular my Cedar Swamp to be equally Divided amongst them by North and South Lines, Caleb to have the West Side, William the middle part and Israel the residue to be enjoyed by them their Heirs and Assigns forever. Further it is my Will that if my Son Caleb Should Die before he come of Age that William Shall have the Portion that was given to Caleb, and Israels Portion shall be that is given to William and if either of ye younger Ones die before they come of Age the Survivor to enjoy both their Portions his Heirs and Assigns forever. ITEM I give to my Two Youngest Sons Benjamin and Samuel each of them Five Hundred Pounds to be paid them as they attain to the Age of Twenty One Years, and if either of them die before they come of Age the Survivor to have the whole and to be paid as followeth Caleb to pay to Benjamin Four Hundred Pounds and William to pay to Benjamin One Hundred Pounds lawful Money of the Same Place. And William to pay unto Samuel Four Hundred Pounds & Caleb One Hundred Pounds to compleat their Portions to be paid them out of their Estates given them as abovesaid. Also it is my Will that my Nigro Man Jack be immediately Set free he paying to them that enjoyeth the Homestead forty Shillings per Year for Five Years after my Decease and the Money to be kept in order to keep him in his Old Age, and the rest they that enjoyeth the Homestead Shall make up in Maintaining him. I likewise order that no Timber be cut to waste or destroyed Saving for the necessary use of ye places, nor no more upland to be cleared neither any of ye Meadows & Swamp land to be plowed. Lastly I Constitute and appoint Daniel Doughty and Michael Newbold my trusty and well beloved Friends, my only & Executors of this my last Will and Testament. AND I do hereby utterly disallow, revoke & disanul all and every other former Testaments, Wills, Legacies, & Executors, by me in any ways before this Time Named, Willed and Bequeathed, Ratifying & Confirming this and no other to be my last Will and Testament IN WITNESS whereof I have hereunto Set my Hand and Seal the Day and Year above written.

Signed, Sealed, Published and Declared
by the Said Benjamin Shreve as his
last Will & Testament in ye Presence
of us ye Subscribers
     Barzillai Newbold
     Levi Nutt
     Robt. Bland

Daniel Doughty & Michael Newbold Executors in the within Testament named being duly affirmed according to Law did declare that the within Instrument contains the true last Will and Testament of Benjamin Shreve the Testator therein named so far as they know and as they verily believe and that they will well and truly perform the same by paying first the debts of the said deceased and then the Legacies in the said Testament specifyed so far as the Goods Chattels and Credits of the said Deceased can thereunto Extend and that they will make and Exhibit into the prerogative Office in Burlington a true and perfect Inventory of all and Singular the Goods Chattels and Credits of the said deced that have or shall come their knowledge or possession or to the possession of any other person or persons for their use & render a just accot. when lawfully Required.

Affirmed at Burlington this }   Danl. Doughty
29th of March 1751. }   Michael Newbold
Cha Read Sr.

INVENTORY OF THE ESTATE OF BENJAMIN SHREVE, 1751

An Inventery of the Goods Chattels and Credits of Benjamin Shreve Late of the Township of Mansfield and County of Burlington, Dec'd. Taken & Appraised the Eighteenth Day of the Second Month 1751

	£	S	D
Purs & Apparrel	38	1	11½
Cattel	92	13	0
Horses	112	00	0
Sheep	21	6	0
Swine	13	00	0
Green Corn	28	10	0
Grain	30	13	6
Port Gemons & bacon	58	8	6
Chair & two wagons	38	00	0
Husbandry Utentials Plows Harrows &c	34	00	6
Goods in the Common Rume Clock & Chairs &c	21	09	6
in the Rume below Stairs Bed Case of Draws &c	31	16	0
in the first Chaimber Bed Cais of Draws Glass c	32	16	0
in the Second Chaimber Bed & Sondries	09	2	6
Goods in the third Chaimber Beds & Sonderies Good	31	11	10
in the Shop Rume Bed &c	09	3	0
in the Kitchin Iron putor brass &c	15	6	4
in the Old Chaimber Beds flax fithers &c	17	17	6
Goods in the Cellor Syder Sperits Molases &c	21	4	6
Shoe Lether	16	6	0
An Old Negrow Man	05	00	0
Debts Dew on Bonds Bills & Book	1300	17	3½
	1979	4	1
a womans Side saddle	1		
	1980	4	1

Wm Cooke
Thos Black } Appraisers
Anthony Sykes

Thomas Black and Anthony Sykes two of the appraisers of the within Inventory being duly affirmed according to Law did declare that the Goods Chattels and Credits in the said Inventory set down and specifyed were by them appraised according to their Just and true respective rates and Values according to the best of their Judgment and understanding and that they appraised all things that were brought to their View for appraisement.

Affirmed at Burlington this   }   Thos. Black
Eighth day of May 1751   }   Anthony Sykes
   Cha Read Sr.

Daniel Doughty and Michael Newbould Executors of the last Will and Testament of the within named Benjamin Shreve deceased being duly affirmed according to Law did declare that the within Writing contains a true and perfect Inventory of all and singular the Goods Chattels and Credits of the said deceased so far as have come to their possession or knowledge or to the possession of any other person or persons for their Use.

Affirmed at Burlington this   }   Danl Doughty
Eighth day of May ADom: 1751 }   Michael Newbold.
   Cha Read Sr.

BUILT 1725 AND 1742

27—WILLIAM FRENCH (Thomas, 1; Richard, 5).

> b. April 7th, 1712.
>
> d. 1781.
>
> m. September 20th, 1748, Lydia Taylor of Bordentown, N. J.

111—WILLIAM FRENCH, JR. b. May 10th, 1751.

> m. 9th mo. 17th, 1777, Rachel Rickey.

112—RICHARD FRENCH   b. October 15th, 1759.

> m. Mary Davis.

113—LYDIA FRENCH   b. March 19th, 1763

> m. July 16th, 1782, Gabriel Allen of Bordentown, N. J.

ADMINISTRATION OF ESTATE OF WILLIAM FRENCH, 1781

Letters of adm: was granted by his Excellency William Livingston Esq unto William French Adm^r to the Estate of William French late of the County of Burlington Deceased being first duly affirmed to administer the fame Exhibit a true Inventory & render a Just & true account of his Administration

Given under the Prerogative feal the 8th Day of December 1781

Wm. Wood, Bondsman.   Bowes Reed Reg^r.

An Inventory of the Goods & Chattels of William French Late of the County of Burlington in the Township of Hanover—Dec'd Taken the 26th day of October 1781—

                                                    £34 16

Joseph Kirby ⎱ Apprs—   Affirmed at Burlington   ⎱
John Wood   ⎰   Dec 8—1781 before me   ⎰ John Wood
                        John Phillips Surrog^{te}

29—ABIGAIL FRENCH (Thomas, 1; Richard, 5).

> b. 7th mo. 5th, 1717.
>
> m. First, 1st mo. 1737, James Lewis of Philada.
>
> He d. March, 1741.
>
> m. Second, Jacob Taylor.

114—JAMES LEWIS, JR.

MEETING RECORDS

Chesterfield Monthly Meeting Minutes:
At a Monthly Meeting of Friends held at their Meeting House in Chefterfield the 3^d of ye 12mo 1736

James Lewis and Abigail French appeared at this Meeting & declared their Intentions of Marriage Friends appoint Isaac Horner & preserve Brown Junr to enquire into his Converfation & Clearnefs on Account of Marriage & make report to next Monthly Meeting.

At a Monthly Meeting of Friends held at their Meeting Houfe in Chesterfield y^e 3^d of y^e 1$^{m.o}$ 1736/7

James Lewis & Abigail French appeared the Second time at this Meeting & declared their continuance in the same mind relating to Marriage. He producing a Certificate from Phila. nothing appearing to hinder they are to accomplish the Same according to good Order. Friends appoint Joseph Pancoast & John Sykes to attend the Marriage.

At a Monthly Meeting of Friends held at their Meeting Houfe in Chesterfield the 7th of the 2mo 1737

Joseph Pancoast Sent account that things were orderly at the Marriage of James Lewis.

Minutes of Chesterfield Monthly Meeting of Women Friends:
3rd of 12th month 1736, James Lewis and Abigal French published their intention of marriage, her parents consenting and he producing a certificate. Two friends appointed to make enquiry concerning her and make report to next meeting.

3rd of 1 mo. 1737. James Lewis and Abigal French published their intention of marriage the second time, and nothing appearing to hinder they are left to the conclusion of men friends. Two friends appointed to attend the marriage.

SUMMARY OF WILL OF JAMES LEWIS, 1740/1

James Lewis, Bordentown, Burlington Co., N. J., by will dated February 8—1740/1, proved March 28—1741, bequeathed unto

Wife Abigail " My Personal estate,—Joseph Jay to give her a title to the land I bought of him nere Bordentown & paid him for. Charles Taylor to make her a title for lot I bought of him in Bordentown & paid him for; also I give her ½ of my tract at or near Nefhaminy pa, to bring up my child "

Son James   "The other ½ of land above mentioned—when 21. He to be put to a trade when 14 "

Executor   " My wife Abigail Lewis "

30—BENJAMIN FRENCH (Thomas, 1; Richard, 5).

> b. 12th mo. 11th, 1719.
>
> d. 1747.
>
> m. January 29th, 1742, Martha Hall, daughter of Burgiss Hall, " Marriner," of Bordentown, N. J., and Abigail Hall.

115—RICHARD FRENCH

MARRIAGE LICENSE

Licence of Marriage on the Twenty nineth Day of January AD. 1742 was granted by his Excy Lewis Morris Esqr Govr unto Benjamin French of Bordenstowne in the County of Burlington Carpenter of the one party & Martha Hall Spinster, Daughter of Captn Burgiſs Hall, of the same place of the other party.

Arch^d Home, Secry.

SUMMARY OF WILL OF BENJAMIN FRENCH, 1747

Benjamin French Borden's Town, Burlington Co. N. J. " Joyner "
Date—Sept 10, 1747.   Proved Oct 16, 1747.
Wife—Martha French " to have proceeds of sale of Estate to bring up my son Rich^d "
Child—Richard—To be put to a beneficial traid when Ex^r thinks suitable.
Executor—My brother Wm French

Witnesses—Joseph Tillton
                  Saml Farnsworth Ju^r.
                  Thos Folkes.

SIGNATURE OF EXECUTOR

Inventory taken Sept 19—1747   £278—00—00

By Us Freeholders in Bordentown
       Thos Folkes
       Jno Imlay
       Sam^{11} Shourds jun^r

31—JONATHAN FRENCH (Thomas, 1; Richard, 5).

> b. 11th mo. 27th, 1722.
> m. 1st mo. 12th, 1744, Esther Matlack, daughter
> of John and Mary (Lee) Matlack.
> She m. Second, July 21st, 1744, Vespasian Kemble.
> He d. 1778.
> She d. 1795.

116—FRANCIS FRENCH   m. Elizabeth ————.

117—MARY FRENCH

118—EUNICE FRENCH   m. Jonas Thomas.

118a—JONATHAN FRENCH

119—WILLIAM FRENCH   m. May 25th, 1783, Ruth Higby.

120—RICHARD FRENCH   b. 8th mo. 6th, 1760.
                          m. 10th mo. 11th, 1784, Sophia Bendler.

MEETING RECORDS

Chesterfield Monthly Meeting Minutes:
  2—12 mo. 1743 A certificate for Jonathan French was desired to the
Monthly Meeting at Haddonfield concerning his conversation on account
of marriage. Friends appoint Michael Newbold and Barzilla to enquire
as usual and draw a certificate accordingly.

  1—1 mo. 1744 A certificate was signed at this meeting for Jonathan
French to the monthly meeting at Haddonfield.

Haddonfield Monthly Meeting Minutes:
  13—12 mo. 1743 Jona. French and Esther Matlack daughter of John Matlack declared their intention of taking each other in marriage therefore
John Hollingshead and Jos: Stokes are desired to make the usual enquiry
and to make report thereof at our next monthly meeting, the Young People's
Fathers being present consent to sd proposals.

FRANCIS FRENCH HOUSE, NEAR ALMONESSON, N. J.

Built in the early part of the eighteenth ce^tury.

12—1 mo. 1744 Jona. French & Esther Matlack appeared and signified the continuation of their intentions of taking each other in marriage The Friends appointed to make enquiry into sd Jonathan's conversation & clearness on account of marriage not find anything to obstruct and he produced a certificate from Chesterfield to Friends satisfaction they are left to their liberty to consumate their intentions according to good order and appoints Thos. Redman & Benj. Holmes to be present to see that good orders be kept.

9—2nd mo. 1744 The committee report that they were present at the marriage of Jonathan French and Esther Matlack & that it was orderly accomplished.

Haddonfield Minutes of ye Mo: Meeting of Women Friends:
Att a m^{o}ly m^{t}g of wo^m fr^{ds} held at Had^{n}fl^d ye 13th of 12^m 1743/4 at s^d m^{t}g Jonathan French & Hester Matlack signified y^r intentions of m^{r}g fr^{ds} a^{pts} Rachel Smith & Phebee Burrough to make ye uſual inquiry & report to next m^{t}g.

Att a m^{o}ly m^{t}g of wo^m fr^{ds} held at Had^{n}f^{ld} ye 12th of 1st^m· 1743/4 Jonathan French & Heſter Matlack signified ye continuation of their intentions of marriage, Conſent of parents apearing & return of inquirs clear, friends conſents to ye accompliſhm^t of y^r said marr^{e}g according to ye good order among us, & a^{pts} Rachel Smith & Eliz^a Hillman to attend ye s^d m^{r}g & report to next m^{t}g.

Att a m^{o}ly meeting of wo^m fr^{ds} held at Had^{n}fl^d ye 9th of 2^m 1744 It was reported by ye perſons a^{ptd} to attend ye mar^{gs} y^t they was orderly accompliſh^d.

Haddonfield Monthly Meeting Minutes:
12—1 mo. 1750 The Overseers of Haddonfield reported that they had Dealt with Jonathan French for a Neglect of attending our religious Meeting for Worship and disorderly conversations and that he still persists in the same; therefore Robt. French and Robt. Stephens are appointed to acquaint him that unless he makes satisfaction Friends must proceed against him and make report thereof to our next monthly Meeting.

9—2 mo. 1750 The Friends appointed to speak to Jonathan French reported that they had not had any opportunity therefore they are desired to continue their care.

14—3 mo. 1750 The affair of Jonathan French was referred to next Monthly Meeting.

4 mo. 1750 Isaac Andrews is desired to acquaint Jonathan French that Friends desire his appearance at our next monthly meeting to answer the charge for which he hath been dealt with, otherwise they must proceed.

9th of 5th mo. 1750 Isaac Andrews reported that he had spoken to Jon^a French and he gave Expectation of appearing but did not therefore that affair is referred to the Consideration of our next monthly meeting.

13—6 mo. 1750 Jonathan French not appearing to give satisfaction for his misconduct or sending any reason why he did not, therefore Wm. Forster and Edmond Hollingshead are appointed to draw a testification against him and produce it at our next monthly meeting.

10—7 mo. 1750 Wm. Foster and Edmond Hollingshead produced a testification against Jonathan French but Wm. Forster reporting that he had spoke with him and that he gave some expectation of making satisfaction therefore it was referred to the consideration of our next monthly meeting.

8—8 mo. 1750 Jonathan French appeared and Friends were of opinion that it might be better to refer the matter to the consideration of our next mo. meeting.

7—10 mo. 1750 The affair relating to Jonathan French being now reconsidered and he not appearing the testification brought against him in ye 7th mo. last was read and approved and signed by the clerk, and Sam'l Clement & Wm. Griscom are appointed to serve him with a copy thereof and acquaint him with his privilege of appeal.

14—11 mo. 1750 Samuel Clement and Wm. Griscome reported that they had served Jonathan French with a copy of the testification against him and that he did not incline to appeal, therefore Ebenezer Hopkins is appointed to read it in a publick First day meeting at Haddonfield and make report thereof at our next Mo. Mtg.

Evesham Monthly Meeting Minutes:
    At a Monthly Meeting held at Evesham ye 7th of ye 2nd mo. 1782. Friends from ye Preparative Meeting at Chester reported that Jonathan French [118a] had been treated with for the neglect of attending Meetings outgoing in marriage and being active in Military Services therefore John Roberts and Wm. Matlack are appointed to treat further with him & report to next meeting.

At a Monthly Meeting held at Evesham ye 7th of 3rd mo. 1782.
The friends appointed reported that they have performed a visit to Jonathan French who doth not appear desirous to retain his right of membership; therefore William Matlack & John Roberts are appointed to inform him that the meeting has come to a judgment to disown him & prepare a minute accordingly & produce it to next Meeting.

At a Monthly Meeting held at Evesham ye 4th of ye 4th mo. 1782.
One of the friends appointed reported that he had informed Jonathan French of the judgment of this meeting according to appointment & produced a minute of disownment against him which was read approved and signed by the Cl'k & John Collins & Abraham Warrington are appointed to give him a copy thereof inform him of his privilege of an appeal & report to next meeting.

At a Monthly Meeting held at Evesham ye 9th of ye 5th Mo. 1782.
The friends appointed reported that they have given Jonathan French a copy of the Disownment against him according to appointment & he said he should not appeal.

At a Monthly Meeting held at Evesham the 8th of 2nd Mo. 1788.
The Committee appointed to peruse the Records of this Meeting &c. produced the following report which being several times read was with some alteration approved being as follows vizt:
To the Monthly Meeting held at Evesham
We the Committee appointed in the 12th M^o last to peruse the Records of said Meeting &c having several times met and carefully examined the same, have to Report; that all the children of Jonathan [31] and Esther French not heretofore disunited, must be considered as having a right of Membership, agreeable to the Minute of the Yearly Meeting in the Year 1762 & further explained in the Year 1782.
Submitted to the Meeting 2nd Mo. 8th Day 1788, and signed on behalf of the Committee by William Matlack.

At a Monthly Meeting held at Evesham the 10th of 10th Mo. 1788.
Friends from the Preparative Meeting at Chester reported that from a late examination of the Records of this Meeting it appears that Francis [116], William [119], and Richard French [120] have a right of Membership of which they were ignorant until of late; previous wherto they have been guilty of divers matters inconsistent with our Discipline (vizt.) outgoing in their Marriages, and neglect of attending Meetings; and the two former with other reproachful conduct: which severally claiming the attention of Friends, wherein they unite in appointing John Collins, Abrm Warrington, Humphrey Owen, Joshua Lippincott, Sam'l. Allinson and Enoch Evans, to take a solid opportunity with them, and report their sense of their dispositions of Mind to next Meeting.

At a Monthly Meeting held at Evesham the 7ᵗʰ of 11ᵗʰ Mo. 1788.
The Committee appointed on a visit to Francis, William and Richard French reported attention thereto, in the performance whereof they evidenced such satisfaction as influenced them to request time for further labour with them if consistent with the judgment of the Meeting; which was granted, and they to report thereon as occasion may require.

At a Monthly Meeting held at Evesham the 5ᵗʰ of 6ᵗʰ Mo. 1789.
The Friends under whose care the case of Francis French was referred in the 10ᵗʰ mo. last, now reported that he declines making necesſary satisfaction for his deviation; therefore Saml. Roberts Jr. and Joseph Warrington are appointed to inform him that Friends have come to a judgment to disown him, prepare a Minute accordingly for the approbation of next Meeting.

At a Monthly meeting held at Evesham the 10 of 7ᵗʰ Mᵒ 1789. One of the Friends appointed to inform Francis French of the judgment of last Meeting, and produce a Disunion agst. him, having performed the same agreeable thereto, which being read, but not being fully satisfactory, was returned for amendment, & produce it to next Meeting.

At a Monthly Meeting held at Evesham the 7ᵗʰ of 8ᵗʰ Mo. 1789.
The Disunion against Francis French, returned at last Meeting for amendment, being again produced and read, was, with some alteration approved and signed by the Clk. Thomas Lippincott & Henry Warrington are appointed to give him a Copy thereof inform him of his privilege of Appealing, and report to next Meeting.

The Friends to whose care the case of William French was committed in the 10ᵗʰ mᵒ last now reported that he doth not appear desirous of continuing his right of Membership; which after being attended to, united the Meeting in the appointment of Joseph Roberts and Joshua Hunt to prepare a Minute of Disownment for the approbation of next Meeting.

At a Monthly Meeting held at Evesham the 11ᵗʰ Day of the 9ᵗʰ Mo. 1789.
The Friends appointed to give Francis French a Copy of the Disunion against him &c. reported their compliance therewith and he signified no intention of appealing.
The Committee appointed produced a Disunion against William French which being read and approved was signed by the Clk. Joseph Roberts & Henry Warrington are appointed to give him a Copy thereof, inform him of his privilege of appealing, and report to next meeting.

OLD COLESTOWN (N. J.) PROTESTANT EPISCOPAL CHURCH, 1751.

At a Monthly meeting held at Evesham the 9th of 10th Mo 1789.
One of the Friends appointed to give William French a copy of the Disunion against him &c. reported his compliance therewith and he signified no intention of Appealing.

At a Monthly Meeting held at Evesham the 10th of 6th mo. 1791.
The case of Richard French being continued under the care of Joshua Lippincott and Sam'l Allinson in the 11th mo. 1788, the latter of whom is now dec^d. Saml. Burrough is appointed to unite with the former in giving the necessary attention thereto, and report thereon as occasion may require.

At a Monthly Meeting held at Evesham the 9th of 12th Mo. 1791.
Richard French produced an acknowledgment for consummating his marriage contrary to the order established amongst us, which being several times read and attended to, it appeared the united sense of the Meeting that the same be now accepted; and is in the following words (vizt.)

> To the Monthly Meeting of Evesham—
> I the subscriber having a Birthright amongst Frds: but not having any knowledge thereof till since I consummated my marriage contrary to the good order established amongst them; on being treated with, feel love & nearness towards my Friends, and have a sincere desire to retain my right in Society, hoping this with my future orderly walking may reconcile me to my friends again, is the desire of
>
> Richard French
> 12" mo. 9" 1791

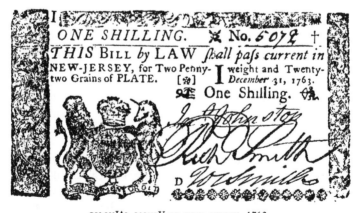

COLONIAL MONEY OF NEW JERSEY, 1763

FRANCIS FRENCH

A resident of Chester Township, Burlington County, N. J., during early manhood, Francis French [116] wrought faithfully at his trade of house carpenter until he accumulated a fund sufficient to buy a comfortable farm homestead, where he spent the remainder of a long life. May 26, 1798, he purchased of William Holmes, for 500 pounds, a "messuage, plantation and tract" of seventy-seven acres, located along Timber Creek, near the present village of Almonesson, Deptford Township, Gloucester County. This land was purchased from the original proprietaries by Thomas Matthews, in 1681, and for more than half a century subsequently was part of the great Hillman estate. The ancient house, shown in accompanying picture, evidently erected at two different times, during the eighteenth century, has all the distinguishing marks of pioneer days, rough stone, primitive clap-boarding, heavy timbers and doors, wooden latches, very low roof and immense fireplaces, long since closed in. Local tradition says it was a colonial tavern and Indian trading post. A former resident, then past four score, said the house was old in his boyhood days, about the time of Francis French's death, 1831.

After the separation of the latter from Friends' Society, he became specially interested in Old Colestown Protestant Episcopal Church, making a subscription of several pounds a year towards the maintenance of the graveyard, neglected through lack of an efficient church organization. No meeting or church record concerning his marriage or the births of his children has been found, but certain court records, at Woodbury, show his relationship to the family of Jonathan French and recite the names of his children and grandchildren and the disposition of his estate. By deed, dated March 28, 1814, "Francis French, Richard French, 'Unice' Thomas, widow of Jonas Thomas, and Mary French, single woman, of Gloucester County, heirs at law of Jonathan French, who died intestate, sold to Isaac Armstrong, of Gloucester County, for $307, nine acres of land." "Unice" made her mark and signed in the presence of George French, justice of the peace of Moorestown.

Before the Orphans' Court, Gloucester County, Dec. term, 1831, Joseph Orens, administrator of the estate of Francis French, asked for Commissioners' sale of land, mentioning as "heirs at law" the following children:

Hannah (French) Sloan, Samuel French, Jonathan French, Mary

rlington County, N. J., during early
ght faithfully at his trade of house
sufficient to buy a comfortable farm
ler of a long life. May 26, 1798, he
pounds, a " messuage, plantation and
along Timber Creek, near the present
nship, Gloucester County. This land
etaries by Thomas Matthews, in 1681,
sequently was part of the great Hill-
n in accompanying picture, evidently
he eighteenth century, has all the dis-
rough stone, primitive clap-boarding,

INTERIOR, OLD COLESTOWN (N. J.) PROTESTANT EPISCOPAL CHURCH, 1751

(French) Husk. Also the children of Sarah (French) Roberts, deceased, and children of Esther (French) White, deceased.

It is recited that "three discreet and indifferent (impartial) persons, between the parties," were appointed Commissioners, viz., John Clement, David B. Morgan and Joseph Saunders. On February 1, 1833, the farm homestead, seventy-seven acres, was sold to James Rowand, for $1,400. Two other small lots, seventeen and a half acres in all, were sold for $430. About thirty years later the Cunard family bought the farm and retained it until recently. The location of this property invests it with peculiar interest, as although only six miles from Woodbury, for more than one hundred years it was on the outskirts of civilization in Gloucester County.

ST. MARY'S EPISCOPAL CHURCH, COLESTOWN, N. J.

Next to St. Mary's, Burlington, this is, or was, the oldest Protestant Episcopal Church in West Jersey. Services were held in the vicinity, about four miles from Moorestown, as early as 1703, the year the church at Burlington was founded, but the little wooden church was not built until about 1751. It was 34 $\times$ 30 feet, with high pulpit, small chancel, high-backed benches, boxed-in seats for the choir, and a three-part cast-iron stove, for wood, brought from England, in 1760. Accompanying illustrations show this ancient and historic structure within and without. The little church had many vicissitudes and several times the society was almost abandoned. In 1796 there was serious trouble over the old graveyard, in which members of many pioneer families lie buried. Francis French [116] was one of the subscribers to a special maintenance fund. The pulpit Bible, first used, is carefully preserved; likewise a silver communion service, now cared for by Trinity Church, Moorestown. To the infinite regret of a wide circle of friends, a mysterious fire destroyed St. Mary's, November 7, 1899. In 1907 a granite monument was erected on the site to perpetuate the memory of a notable landmark in the religious and social history of West Jersey.

ST. MARY'S MON.

16

33—THOMAS FRENCH, 3RD (Thomas, 1; Thomas, 6).

> b. 8th mo. 27th, 1702.
>
> d. 4th mo. 28th, 1757, buried in Friends' Bury-
> ing Ground, Chester Meeting, Moorestown,
> N. J.
>
> m. May 8th, 1746, Jemima Elkinton of Evesham
> Township, Burlington Co., N. J.

> She b. 3rd mo. 3rd, 1725.
>
> buried 4th mo. 11th, 1782.

121—EDWARD FRENCH	b. 1st mo. 7th, 1747.
	m. Mary Wilkins.
122—URIAH FRENCH	b. 3rd mo. 14th, 1748
	m. First, June 29th, 1771, Rachel Ingersoll.
	m. Second, August 6th, 1800, Isabella Peacock.
123—GEORGE FRENCH	b. 2ud mo. 9th, 1753.
	m. 5th mo. 1775, Rachel Rakestraw.
124—MARY FRENCH	b. 6th mo. 23rd, 1755.
	m. April 4th, 1771, John Reily.
125—SARAH FRENCH	b. 9th mo. 26th, 1757.
	m. 1776, Charles Brown.

THOMAS FRENCH, 3RD

The second son of Thomas French, Jr., seems to have inherited the farming habits of his ancestors and to have remained in the same location in
which his father resided, in Chester Township. He was active in local
affairs and served as constable, overseer of highways and overseer of the
poor for Chester Township. His homestead, at the west end of Moorestown, was part of the estate conveyed to his father by Thomas ffrench,
progenitor, through the deed of gift of 1694. A special survey, made in
1752, showed that it joined other lands of his father and of his brother,
Robert French. He bequeathed this plantation to his son Edward and it
continued in family ownership until sold by one of his descendants, Sarah
(French) Ogden, about twenty-five years ago. Apparently he deferred

making his will until his strength was fast failing, but his declared intention was accepted and faithfully carried out. During his life time he added by purchase considerably to his landed patrimony.

MEETING RECORDS

Haddonfield Monthly Meeting Minutes:

14—8 mo. 1751. The Overseers of Chester meeting reported that they had dealt with Thos. French for going out in marriage & that he had given an expectation of making satisfaction which he hath not yet done. Thos. Lippincott & Jos. Stokes are appointed to acquaint him that unless he comply with Friends request & produce satisfaction, they will be obliged to proceed against him.

9—10 mo. 1751. Jos. Stokes and Thos. Lippincott reported that they had spoken to Thos. French who gave expectation of making satisfaction, but not being here he was referred to the consideration of next meeting and the clerk appointed to bring the minute or a copy of it that was made on ye returning ye above mentioned acknowledgment.

13—1 mo. 1752. Thomas French produced an acknowledgment for his outgoing in marriage which was read and received, and is as followeth:

To Friends at their Monthly Meeting at Haddonfield. I the subscriber having broke the good rules established amongst Friends by going contrary thereto in marriage am sorry for it and desire Friends to accept this as acknowledgment therefore, from your friend,

Thomas French.

Haddonfield Minutes of yᵉ Mo: Meeting of Women Friends:

Women friends of yᵉ mᵒly meeting being met at Hadⁿf¹ᵈ yᵉ 10th of 2ᵐ 1752 report by yᵉ overseers of Cheſter yᵗ Jemima French deſireˢ to come under yᵉ notice of frᵈˢ which frᵈˢ take under consideration.

Minutes of Evesham Monthly Meeting of Women Friends:

10—10 mo. 1776. The overseers being enquired of reported from Chester that Sarah Brown formerly Sarah French [125] had been treated with for outgoing in her marriage and she not appearing in a disposition of mind to be reconciled to Friends and having ye concurrence of ye mens meeting we therefore disown her according to our discipline and Hannah French is appointed to acquaint her thereof.

DEED, JOSHUA BISPHAM TO THOMAS FRENCH, 3RD, 1746

This Indenture Made the Thirteenth day of March in the year of our
Lord One Thousand Seven Hundred and Forty Six And in the twentieth
year of the Reign of our Sovereign Lord George the Second Between Joshua
Biſpham of the Township of Chester and County of Burlington and province of New Jersey Merchant of the one part, and Thomas French of the
Town County and province aforesaid Yeoman of the other part Witneſseth
that the said Joshua Biſpham for and in consideration of one Pound fifteen
Shillings Current Lawful Money of the Said Province to him in hand paid
by the Said Thomas French at and before the Sealing and delivery of theſe
presents the Receipt whereof the Said Joshua Biſpham doth hereby Acknowledge and thereof and every part and parcel thereof doth Clearly and Abſolutely acquit Exonerate and discharge the Said Thomas French His Execu^{rs}
and Admin^{rs} and every of them by these presents Hath granted Bargained
and Sold aliend Enfeoff'd and Confirm'd and by these presents for him
and his heirs doth Clearly and abſolutely grant Bargain and Sell alien
Enfeoff'd and confirm unto the aforesaid Thomas French his heirs and
aſigns all that Lot of Land Containing one Rood and Twenty perches Situated lying and being in the Township of Chester Butted and Bounded
as followeth (Viz) Beginning at a Spanish Oak Corner to Thomas French
and Runs from thence by ye Said French South Twenty Six Degd East
two Chains to a post Corner to Joseph Heritages Land thence by ye S^d
Heritages North Eighty four degd twenty Minutes West four Chains forty
three Links to a Spanish Oak Corner to the aforesaid French thence by S^d
French North Sixty Nine Degd East three Chains Seventy Six Links to
the Corner first mentioned; Containing by Survey thereof one Rood and
Twenty perches of Land which was taken up and Surveyd to Solomon
Lippincott the Nineteenth day of August 1742 And Convey'd to Joshua
Biſpham by a Instrument bearing date April the Tenth 1743 Together with
all and every ye Heridetements and appurtenances to the same one Rood
and twenty perchs of Land and premiſes belonging or in any wise apper-
taining or there with usealy Occupied or Injoy'd and the Reversion or
Reversions Remainder and Remainders Rents Iſsues and profits of the
premiſes and every part and parcel thereof and all the Estate Right title
Interest use property Claim and demand whatsoever both in Law and
Equity of him the Said Joshua Biſpham of in to and out of S^d one Rood
and twenty Perchs of Land and premiſes and every part and parcel thereof
and all writeings touching the Same premiſes only to have and to hold the
Said one Rood and twenty perchs of Land and all and Singular the premiſes hereby granted and Convey'd or meant mentioned and intended So to

be Sold with them and every of their appurtenances unto the Said Thomas French his heirs and afsigns for ever to the only proper ufe and Behoof of the Said Thomas French his heirs and afsigns forever and the Said Joshua Bifpham for himself his heirs Execu'rs and Adm'rs and for every of them doth Covenant and grant to and with the Said Thomas French his heirs and afsigns by these presents in Manner Following That is to Say that he the Said Joshua Bifpham and his heirs the aforesaid one Rood and twenty perchs of Land & premifes and every part thereof with all the appurtenances unto the Said Thomas French his heirs and afigns, against him the Said Joshua Bifpham and his heirs and against all and every other perfon or persons Claiming or to Claim by from or under him or them; or by from or under any other perfon or perfons whatsoever Shall warrant and forever defend by thefe prefents And that he the Said Joshua Bifpham and his heirs Shall and will from time to time and at all times Hereafter upon the Reasonable request and at the proper Cost and Charges in Law of him the Said Thomas French his heirs and afsigns, do acknowledge Execute and perform, or caufe to be done, all and every such further, and other Lawfull and Reafonable Acts matters and things Whatfoever Requifite and Necefsary for the further and more Sure makeing and Conveying the premifes and every part thereof with the Appurtenances unto the Said Thomas French his heirs or afigns devifed or advised or Required   In Witnefs whereof the party first above named hath to this prefent Indenture Set his hand and Seal the day and year above written.

                                        Joshua Bispham

     Signed Sealed and delivered
     in the presence of us
         Nathan Pratt
                 his
         John | Small
                mark

This Sixth day of April Ano 1752 there Came before me one of the Judges of the County Court for holding of Pleas for the County of Burlingtou Joshua Bifpham Efq' and did Acknowledge the within Deed as his act and Deed (taken and Acknowledged before me) for the ufe within Mentioned.

                                        Jos ͣ Bispham
         Revell Elton

TEN YEARS' APPRENTICESHIP INDENTURE, 1750

THIS INDENTORE Witnefseth that I Richard Jackson Son of John Jackson of The Township of Chister and County of Burlinton and Prouince of weft new Jarfey hath put him Self And by Thefe Prefents by The Confent of his Father Doth voillenta^{ry} and of his own free will and Accord put him Self Apprentice To Thomas French to Serve his Heirs or afsigns of the Township of Chifter and County of Burlington and province aforesaid—Farmor to Learn His Ocupatnt and after the Maner of an Apprentice To Serve from the Day of the Date here of for and During and unto The full End and Term of ten Years and nine Months Next Enfuing During all Which Term the Said Apprentice his Said Mafter faith fully Shall Serve his Secrets keep his Lawful Comands Every whare Readily obay he Shall Do no Damage to his Said Mafter nor See it to be Don by others with ovt Letting or Giveing Notice thare of to his Said Mafter he Shall Not wafte his Said Mafters Goods nor Lend them unlawfully to Any he Shall Not Contract Matrimony with in The Said term Att Cards Dice or any other Unlawfull Game he Shall Not play whare by his Said Mafter may have Damage with his own Good nor the goods of others with out Licence from his Said Mafter he Shall neither buy nor Sell he Shall not Abfent him Self Day nor night from His Said Mafters Service with out his Leave nor haunt ale Houfses Taverns or play hovfses but In all Things be have him Self as a faithfull Apprentice ought to Do Dureing the Said term and the Said Mafter Shall Ufe the utmost of his endavovr to teach or Cavfe to be tavght Wright and Sifer as fir as the Rule of three and the Said Mafter is to teach or Cavse to be taught the Said Apprintes The Ocap^etion which he now followeth And procure and prouide for him Sufficient Meat Drink Lodging and wafhing fiting for an apprentice During the Said term of ten Years and nine Months and at the Expiration of the Said term the said Mafter is heirs or Afsigns is to Give the Said Apprentice twenty poun^{ds} of Good Currant Money the Said Master Is to Give the Said apprentis two Suits of appirl that Is to Say one Sute for hollowdays and one Sute for working Days . . .

And for the trve Performance of all and Singular the Covenants and Agreements a fore Said the Said parties bind Them Selves Each Unto the other firmly by Thefe prefen^{es} In Witnefs whare of the Said parties have Interchangeably Set their hands and Seals here unto Dated the forth Day of April in the twenty fifth Year of Raign of our Sovenring Lord George King of Grate britain &c Annoque Domini: one Thoufand Seven Hundred and fifty —

in the prefence of
    Robert ffrench
    John Risdom

Thomas Foch

WILL OF THOMAS FRENCH, 3RD, 1757

Let it be recorded that I Thomas French of Chester in the County of Burlington Yeoman Do make this my last Will and Testament as followeth Viz.

I$_m$^{Pres}—I give and Bequeath unto my eldest son Edward French my plantation whereon I now Dwell, which was given to me by my Father to him his Heirs and assigns forever

Item—I give and bequeath unto my second Son Uriah French all that my plantation which I bought of Richard Heritage to him his Heirs and assigns forever

Item—I give and bequeath unto my youngest son George French my Two Houses and Tenements in Moors Town and also Fifty Acres of Land part of my affore Said plantation which my father gave me adjoyning the Said Houses and So to the end of the Said Land adjoyning Nathan Middletons Land

Item—I Give and bequeath unto my Daughter Mary French the Sum of Fifty pounds to be paid out of my personal Estate

Item—I Give and Devise unto my well beloved wife Jemimah all the Remainder of my personal Estate and also the use and profitts of all my Lands till my Affore-Said three Sons Attain the Age of Twenty One Years She my Said Wife paying and Discharging all my Just Debts.

The Above was declared by Thomas French to be his last Will the 28th of April 1757 but before the Same was Completed he became Senseless Died having Mentioned the above in our hearing—

John Cox
Hugh Hollinshead
Robert French

Be it remembered that on ye 29 day of April 1757 John Cox Robert French & Hugh Hollinshead appeared before me Charles Read Esqr. One of the masters of the High Court of Chancery of the province of New Jersey & being all of the people called Quakers on their respective Solemn Affirmations which Each of them took, did declare that they were present & heard Thomas French declare the contents of the within writing to be part of his Will in the ilness of which he died & about two hours before his death, but before he could finish it he was taken senseless & dyed. At the desire of the Widow of said French lett it be recorded that the son & Heir may thereby know his fathers Intentions

Chas. Read Mag Cur Con

Recorded this 20th Aug: 1761
Chas: Read, Reg^r.

INVENTORY OF ESTATE OF THOMAS FRENCH, 3RD, 1757

A True & perfect Inventory of all and Singular the Goods and Chattels rights and Credits of Thomas French Late of Chester in the County of Burlington &c. Decd. Taken the 5th Day of May Anno 1757 being all that Came to our View Appraisd By us under written—

	£	S	d
Imprs.—To Cash and wearing Apparrel in the Lodging Room.	17	15	
To a Rideing Horse Bridle & Saddle................	13	15	
To Book Debts £16: 13: 0 To and Old Watch 20S To a bedd & furniture £12........................	29	13	
To a Case of Drawrs £4: 10 To a Table and Trunk 27/6	5	17	6
To 7 Chairs 25S To Chania Delf and Glass 15S To a Chest 11/6	2	11	6
To a Small Looking Glass 3/ To warming pan 10S..		13	
Item—To a feather Bedd and Bedding in Leanto Room £7: 0: 0 To Chaf Do 40S	9		
To a Chest and Sundries therein....................	1		
Item.—To a bedd and Bedding in the Lower Room £10: To pewter 30S	11	10	
To a Settle & 2 old Tables 20S To a Small Table & Dough Trough, 15S	1	15	
To Chairs & Sundries 18/ To wooden 7/6 To a brass Kettle 20S	2	5	6
To Iron potts and Tea Kettle 28/ To pott Rax fier Shovels Tongs 25/...........................	2	13	
Item—To a Chaf Bedd in Chamber £3: To wheat & Rye flower £3: —	6		
To Spinning Wheels old Casks 2 Scythes 6 Baggs & Sundries	ɔ	9	
Item—To Hogsheads and Barrels in Celler and Hogs Lard and earthen ware	4	ɔ	
To Cyder royal 30S Tub of Soap 30S To Small Keggs &c. 4/.................................	3	4	
Item—To Bacon in Smoak House........................	4	10	
Item—To Linnin Yarn.................................	1	15	
Item—To Sundry Edge Tools and old Iron 88/ To a New plough & Irons 24/6......................	5	12	6
To 2 ploughs one Harrow 4 pair Horse Geers and an ox Chain	4		
To a pair of Steers and Yoak £8: To 6 Cows £20....	28		
To Young Cattle £9 To 20 Sheep £7: 15............	16	15	
To 21 Hoggs	18		

To an Iron Bound Waggon £8: To an Iron Bound ox Cart £4 12

To a Horse Cart £3: To a Slay 30S To a Cyder press & Mill 40S 6 10

To 15 Bushels Indien Corn 33/9 To a Stack of Rye £8: 10 .... 10 3 9

To Clean Wheat and Wheat in Sheaf £7 To Green Wheat and Rye in the Ground £10: 3........... 17 ᴣ

To 3 Horses £20: To Cutting Box & Mill to Clean Corn 27/6 .... 21 7 6

To 20 Bushel of Oates........................... 1 11 8

£262 12 11

Joshua Humphris
John Cox.

Jemima French and Robert French administrators of all and Singular the Goods Chattels & Credits of Thomas French within mentioned decd. being of the People Called Quakers on their Solemn affirmations which they Respectively took according to Law Did Declare that the within Inventory Contains a True and Perfect Inventory of all and Singular the Goods Chattels & Credits of the said Deceased which have Come to their knowledge and Possion or to the Possion of any other pson or psons for their use.

Affirmed at Burlington   Robert French
May 6th 1757 before   Jemima French
        Saml. Peart, Surrogate.

ACCT. OF ADMINISTRATRIX OF EST. OF THOMAS FRENCH, 1761

The Account of Jemima French Administratrix of all and Singular the Goods Chattels & Credits which were of Thomas French deceased, as well of and for such and so much of the Goods as of and for her payments & Disbursements out of the same.

This Accomptant Chargeth herself.............................Dr.

This Accomptant Chargeth herself with all & Singular the Goods Chattels & Credits which were of the said deceased mentioned and Specified in an Inventory & Appraisement thereof made and Exhibited into the Registry of the Prerogative Court in the Secretaries Office in Burlington, Amount: g £ s d (as by the same Inventory appears) to the Sum of.......... 262 12 11

P Contra.　This Accomptant prays Allowance Cr.

		£	s	d
No.	1. By Mony's paid Mary Stanley as p rec[t]	9	—	—
	2. By Do. paid Lucy Hurley as p Rec[t]	3	8	—
	3. By Monies paid James Cornish as p Rec[t]	2	19	—
	4. By Do paid Ezekiel Lippincott a Note	3	2	—
	5. By Do paid Samuel Shute as p Rect	1	11	—
	6. By Do paid Grace Lippincott as p Do	2	3	6
	7. By Do paid Samuel Collins- as p Do	—	8	6
	8. By Do paid John Wallis as p Do	5	14	5
	9. By Do paid Samuel Fisher as p Do	—	10	—
	10. By Do paid Daniel Toy	1	6	4
	11. By Do paid Mary Wallace as p Rect	3	12	2
	12. By Do paid Thomas Spicer as p Do	11	12	9
	13. By Do paid Thomas Morton as p Do	—	16	11
	14. By Do paid George Matlock as p Do	2	7	—
	15. By Do paid Wm. Matlock as p Do	—	17	—
	16. By Do paid Josiah White as p Do	—	6	6
	17. By Do paid Robert Hunt as p Do	—	11	5
	18. By Do paid George Weed as p Do	2	2	3
	19. By Do paid Joshua Bispham as p Do	—	17	8
	20. By Do paid for Letters of Admn as p Do	1	10	—
	21. By Do paid John Collins as p Do	5	5	1
	22. By Do paid Samuel Stokes as p Do	63	11	6
	23. By Do paid Ezekiel Lippincott as p Do	1	13	8
	24. By Cash paid Michael Linch as p Rec[t]	32	5	—
	25. By Do Paid Thomas Redman as p Rec[t]	2	3	8
	26. By Do paid Ephraim Roberts as p Do	—	7	6
	27. By Do paid Charles Ferguson as p Do	3	3	8
	28. By Do paid Jane Middleton at Bond & Intr	36	17	—
	29. By Do paid Joshua Wright. the Order of Jonath[n]. Tho[s].	1	8	5
	30. Do Do paid Mary Wallace a Bond & Intst	29	10	—
		231	0	11
	By Commissions on the Am[t] of the Inventory @ 7 £ p. Cent	18	5	8
	By Cash paid for Quietus Est. & Settlem[t] of this Acct.	1	12	—
		250	18	7
	Ballance Remaining in the Hands of this Accomptant	11	14	4
		262	12	11

WILL OF JEMIMA FRENCH, 1789

Let it be Recorded that I Jemimah French of Moores Town in the County of Burlington Widow, being weak of Body but of Sound and Disposing mind and Memory, thanks be Given unto God therefor, and being Defireous that Small Estate which it hath pleafed God to blefs me with in this Life Shall Come unto Such perfons as I shall herein Nominate and appoint do make this my Laft Will and Testament in Manner following—

Imprimis. I Will that all my funeral Charges & Just Debts be fully paid by my Executor hereafter Named . . .

Item I Give and Bequeath unto my Daughter Sarah Brown my two Bedds & furniture thereunto belonging and a Cafe of High Cherry tree Drawrs, and a Mahogany Tea Table and Looking Glafs, and a Couch and beding thereunto belonging—and a Note or Bill I have against my Son George French, and a Large Chest Standing in my Lodging Room, half a Dozen of my best Chairs & an arm Chair and a Chids high Chair, and a Large Pewter Dish that was her Father's & Six of my best Pewter plates. I also Give all my Waring Cloaths to my said Daughter Sarah and a Big wheel . . .

Item I Give and Bequeath unto my Grand Daughter Unea Keen, my little wheel . . .

Item I Give and bequeath to my said Daughter Sarah my best Dieper Table Cloaths . . .

Item I order & it is my Will that all the Refidue of my Estate be Sold as soon After my Deceafe as may be Convenient, Item and out of the money Arifing from the Sales thereof I Give and Bequeath unto my three Sons namely Edward Uriah & George French Each the Sum of Ten Shillings, they being heretofore provided for, Item I Give & bequeath unto my said Grand Daughter Unea Keen the Sum of fifteen pounds in hard Money or the Value thereof in other Currency.

Item I order and it is my Will that the Refidue of my Estate After my Just Debts funeral Charges and Legacies are paid Shall be Equally Devided between my four Childred and my said Grandaughter Unea Share and Share Alike Item & Lastly I do hereby Nominate Conftitute and appoint my said Son Edward French whole and Sole Executor of this my Laft Will and Teftament In Witnefs whereof I have hereunto Set my Hand and Seal the firft day of April in the year of our Lord one thoufand Seven Hundred and Eighty nine 1789

Signed Sealed pronounced &
Declared by the within Named
Jemimah French as and for
her Last Will & Testament
in the prefence of us—
    Joseph Newton
    John Cox

hir

Jemimah French

mark

Joseph Newton one of the witnesses of the within will being duly affirmed according to Law did affirm and say that he saw Jemimah French the Testatrix therein named make her Mark and Seal the same & heard her publish pronounce and declare the within writing to be her last will and Testament, that at the doing thereof the said Testatrix was of sound & disposing mind and memory as far as this affirmant knows and as he verily believes and that John Cox the other Subscribing Evidence was present at the same time & Signed his name as a witnefs to the said Will together with his affirmant in the presence of the S^d Testatrix—

Affirmed at Burlington the 13th ⎫
day of May 1789 before me   ⎬   Joseph Newton
    Herbert McElroy Surr ⎭

Edward French sole Executor in the within named being duly affirmed according to Law did affirm and say that the within Instrument of writing Contains the true Last Will and Testament of Jemimah French the Testatrix therein named so far as he knows and as he verily believes, that he will well and truly perform the same by paying first the Debts of the said Testatrix and then the Legacies in the said Testament Specified so far forth as the Goods Chattels and Credits of the said dec'd can thereunto Extend & that he will make and Exhibit into the Prerogative Office of New Jersey a true and perfect Inventory of all and singular the goods Chattels & Credits of the said Dec'd that have or shall come to his knowledge or pofsefsion or to the pofsefsion of any other person or persons for his use and render a Just and true Account when thereunto Lawfully required.——

Affirmed at Burlington the 13th ⎫
May 1789—before me   ⎬   Edward French
    Herbert McElroy   ⎭
Inventory dated April 15th 1789   £74—0—10

    John Cox
    Joseph Newton
    Appraisers

A FAMILY SPINNING WHEEL

35—ROBERT FRENCH (Thomas, 1; Thomas, 6).

> b. 6th mo. 1707.
> buried 9th mo. 7th, 1760, in Friends' Burying
> Ground, Chester Meeting, Moorestown, N. J.
> m. 10th mo. 1737, Hannah Cattel, daughter of
> Jonas and Mary (Pearce) Cattel.
> She b. 6th mo. 7th, 1716.
> d. 6th mo. 27th, 1801.

126—JONAS FRENCH   b. 9th mo. 17th, 1738.

127—MARY FRENCH   b. 10th mo. 4th, 1740.
                       m. First, 12th mo. 24th, 1761, William Hold-
                       craft.
                       m. Second, 3rd mo. 16th, 1797, Isaac Gibbs.

128—HANNAH FRENCH   b. 7th mo. 15th, 1743.
                       d. 11th mo. 29th, 1784, unmarried.

129—THOMAS FRENCH   b. 12th mo. 26th, 1745.
                       m. April 22nd, 1769, Mercy Cox.

130—ELIZABETH FRENCH   b. 2ud mo. 28th, 1747.
                       d. 3rd mo. 10th, 1767.
                       m. June 18th, 1766, John Ferguson (Christ
                       Church record, Philadelphia).

131—ROBERT FRENCH, JR. b. 3rd mo. 10th, 1749.
                       m. First, 2ud mo. 15th, 1785, Hannah War-
                       rington.
                       m. Second, 5th mo., 1803, Elizabeth Stokes.

132—JAMES FRENCH   b. 3rd mo. 1st, 1751.
                       m. First, July 24th, 1773, Mary Clark.
                       m. Second, October 12th, 1779, Sarah Fer-
                       guson.

133—JOSEPH FRENCH   b. 10th mo. 14th, 1753.
                       d. aged two weeks.

134—KEZIAH FRENCH   b. 5th mo. 11th, 1756.
                         m. John Thompson.

135—ANN FRENCH   b. 10th mo. 26th, 1758.
                         m. 12th mo., 1781, Samuel Carr.

ROBERT FRENCH

Robert French, third son of Thomas French, Jr., was a man of strong character, who early developed characteristic family traits. He purchased from Thomas Cowperthwaite, in 1741, thirty acres of good farm land, located on the northwest side of Moorestown, N. J.; and, three years later, his father conveyed to him by deed of gift, dated March 23, 1744, one hundred and sixty-seven acres adjoining the same. Here he resided until his death, in 1760. His will directed the sale of the property as soon after his death as his executors might think proper, and it was in part disposed of, although not immediately. In 1744 his son James [132] purchased fifty acres. The same year his son Robert [131] bought fifty-five acres; and in 1801, through the will of his mother, Robert became possessed of the remainder of the estate, subject to the care of an invalid brother.

Robert French, the elder, became a recognized minister in the Society of Friends and was much esteemed. Both he and his wife Hannah were very active in the affairs of Chester (Moorestown), Evesham and Haddonfield Meetings, being many times appointed representatives to Quarterly and Yearly Meetings. Hannah French was made overseer of Chester Meeting in 1747 and elder in 1765, serving in the latter capacity thirty-six years. In his journal, Daniel Stanton, a minister of Philadelphia Monthly Meeting, makes the following note: " I was at a large Meeting at Chester at the burial of Robert French a Friend in the ministry who was much beloved and valued as a good Example among Friends where he had lived."

" The Friend," 10 m. 1, 1859, gave the following appreciative sketch:

> Robert French was born in the township of Chester, County of Burlington, West Jersey, 1708. His parents were religious members of the Society of Friends, whose pious labors on his behalf, through the Lord's assisting grace, were blessed. He was religiously inclined from his youth and grew in favor with his heavenly Father and in the esteem of his friends. His natural abilities were not great, yet his innocent, exemplary life and faithfulness in discharging the duties laid upon him, made his way

open with all lovers of the Truth. Having received a gift of the ministry of the gospel, he was often led to exercise it, generally briefly, but in a lively manner, to the comfort of the well-minded. He was often engaged to exhort to love, and was himself a good example of that Christian virtue, watchful over his own spirit, and living in good measure agreeable to his profession therein. " His removal was a loss to the meeting he belonged to, yet we are fully satisfied it was his gain." He was a minister twenty-two years.

MEETING RECORDS

Haddonfield Monthly Meeting Minutes:

14—9—mo. 1737 Robert French and Hannah Cattle the first time signified their intentions of marriage with each other, therefore Joseph Stokes and Thos. Hackney are appointed to make enquiry as usual and make report thereof to our next Monthly Meeting, parents present give consent to said.

12—10 mo. 1737 Robt French and Hannah Cattle signified ye 2nd time they continued their intention of marriage, therefore not finding anything to obstruct this mtg. allows that they may take each other in marriage and appoints Jos. Stokes and Thos. Hackney to be present to see said intended marriage accomplished orderly.

9—11 mo. 1737 The committee report that they were present at the marriage of Robt. French and Hannah Cattle and y^t it was accomplished orderly.

Haddonfield Minutes of ye Mo: Meeting of Women Friends:

Att a m^oly m^tg of w^om fr^{ds} held at Haddonfield ye 14th of 9th m^o 1737 Robert French & Hannah Kettle signified y^r intentions of m^rg Mary Roberts & Ann Cooper are a^{ptd} to make ye usual inquirie & report to next m^tg.

Att A m^oly m^tg of w^om fr^{ds} held at Haddonfield ye 12th of 10^m 1737 Robert French & Hannah Kettle signified ye continuation of y^r intentions of. m^rg, consent of parties concernd ap^rg & return of inquiers clear, ye m^tg consents to ye accomplishm^t of y^r s^d m^rg according to ye good o^rd^r amongst fr^{ds}, & a^{pts} Eliz^a Evins & Sarah Hains to see good o^rd^{r}s kept & report to next m^tg.

Att a m^oly m^tg of w^om fr^{ds} held at Haddonfield ye 9th of 11^m 1737/8 last m^tg minuit^s being read reportd y^t persons ap^td y^t ye afors^d m^rg was orderly accomplish^d.

[Men's Meeting]

8—10 mo. 1740 Robert French, Josiah & Wm. Foster, John Hollings-head, etc. to meet at ye house of Jos. Cooper on ye first second day in next month in order to peruse the minutes of this meeting in order that they may be fairly entered in a book that is bound and that they may have power to correct said minutes

11—3 mo. 1747 Edmund Hollingshead from the Preparative Mtg of Chester requests that Robt. French might have Liberty to sit in the Meeting of Ministers and Elders which this meeting consents to and that it being signified in there report to the Quarterly Meeting of Ministers & Elders.

11—3 mo. 1747. The Overseers of each meeting are desired to meet at Haddonfield at seven in the morning before the monthly meeting with the company of Joshua Lord, Thos. Redman and Isaac Andrews, Wm. Forster, Robt. French etc. to consider what is best to be done in the case of such as walketh disorderly and has been neglected to be dealt with & discharged ourselves of them, & to make report thereof at our next monthly meeting.

12—8 mo. 1759 Chas. and Robert French are among the friends ap-pointed to meet at Haddonfield ye 28th instant at ye 10th hour in ye fore-noon to waitily consider that friends would again revive ye consideration of seperate monthly meeting for Evesham and Chester.

9—6 mo. 1760 Robt. French one of committee to inspect whether friends have wills by them and likewise to collect such births and burials as ye persons concerned neglects to do and bring them through the Preparative Mtg. to the monthly meeting to be recorded.

Evesham Monthly Meeting Minutes:

At a Monthly meeting held at Evesham ye 10th of ye 9th Mo. 1761. Isaac Evens produced an Essey of The Testimonys of this meeting, Con-cerning our Dec'd friends Robert French and Obadiah Borton which were read and with Some amendment approved and ye Clerk is Directed to Transcribe them, & sign them, & send them with ye reports to our next Quarterly meeting.

Haddonfield Minutes of ye Mo: Meeting of Women Friends:

Women friends of ye m^{o}ly m^{t}g being met at Had^{n}f^{ld} ye 11th of 3^m 1747 no other bufinefs from Chefter, but ye request of an other over-seer, to be chofen, where upon, fr^{ds} a^{Pts} Han^a French.

Evesham Monthly Meeting Minutes:
[Women's Meeting]

7" of 7" mo. 1763. The necessity of revising of the minutes of this meeting coming under consideration; therefore Hannah French, Hannah Foster, Sarah Wilkins, and Ruth Bispham are appointed to inspect all the said minutes and correct such of them as they may find needful, and set a price for transcribing the said minutes into a bound book to be purchased for that service and make report when the work is perfected.

8"—of 9"—mo. 1763 We the Committee appointed by the Mo. Mtg. at Evesham to inspect the minutes of said meeting have all met on ye occasion agreeable to direction and have performed ye service and are of the mind that it is worth one pound, five shillings to transcribe them into a bound book. Sign'd this 16th of ye 8th Mo. 1763— By Hannah Foster, Sarah Wilkins, Hannah French and Ruth Bispham.

Hannah French and Ruth Bispham are appointed to comprize the answers into one and draw the report for the Quarterly Meeting, and one of them sign it on behalf of this meeting.

[Men's Meeting]

At a monthly meeting held at Evesham ye 5th of ye first mo. 1764. Our friend Mark Reeve signified that he had Drawings in his mind to visit ye Families of Friends within ye compass of Chester Meeting, & he produced ye concurrence of Salem Monthly Meeting which was approved of Therefore Edm^d Hollinshead, John & Joshua Roberts, Hannah French, Esther & Rebukah Roberts are app^d to joyu him in that service.

[Women's Meeting]

5" of 1" mo. 1764 The meeting appoints Hannah French, Esther and Rebekah Roberts to join Mark Reeve & Joshua Thompson in visiting Families of Friends belonging to Chester.

8—of 3" mo. 1764. Hannah French requests a few lines by way of certificate to recommend her to friends of Haddonfield Monthly Meeting.

[Men's Meeting]

At a monthly meeting held at Evesham ye 8th of ye 3^d mo. 1764. The women friends requested that Certificates might be prepared to recommend Hannah French to ye monthly meeting at Haddonfield & Mary Enoch & Hannah Shinn to ye monthly meeting at Burlington therefore Enoch Roberts is appointed to prepare that for Hannah French & Mary Enoch, & Josiah Prickitt that for Hannah Shinn agreeable to ye acct. they receive from ye women & produce them to next meeting.

17

At a Monthly Meeting held at Evesham yᵉ 5ᵗʰ of yᵉ 4ᵗʰ Mo. 1764. The Friends appointed produced certificates on behalf of Hannah French, Mary Enoch, & Hannah Shinn, according to appointment which were read approved & signed by yᵉ.clerk, & sent to yᵉ women for their signing.

[Women's Meeting]
5" of 4" mo. 1764 A certificate being read approved and signed recommending our Friend Hannah French to ye care of Friends of Haddonfield Monthly Meeting.

Haddonfield Minutes of yᵉ Mo: Meeting of Women Friends:
At a Monthly Meeting of Women Friends held at Haddonfield the 9ᵗʰ 4 Mo. 1764.
A Certificate was produced from Evesham Monthly Meeting recommending Hannah French to the Notice of this Meeting as a Friend in good Unity, which was Read and Received.

Evesham Monthly Meeting Minutes:
[Men's Meeting]
At a Monthly Meeting held at Evesham yᵉ 8ᵗʰ of yᵉ 11ᵗʰ mo. 1764. Hannah French requested certificates to recommend her two.sons, Thomas and Robert to the monthly meeting at Haddonfield, Therefore Thomas Warrington & John Lippincott are appointed To make yᵉ Needful .Enquiery & prepare Them according & produce Them To Next Meeting.

At a Monthly Meeting held at Evesham yᵉ 6ᵗʰ of yᵉ 12ᵗʰ Mo. 1764. The Friends appointed, produced Certificates on behalf of Thomas & Robert French, according to appointment which were read approved and signed by yᵉ Clerk.

At a Monthly Meeting held at Evesham yᵉ 6ᵗʰ of yᵉ 6ᵗʰ mo. 1765. A Certificate was produced on behalf of Thomas French from yᵉ Monthly Meeting at Haddonfield Dated yᵉ 13ᵗʰ of yᵉ 5ᵗʰ mo. 1765 recommending him to have been orderly whilst amongst them, which was read & rec'd.

[Women's Meeting]
9ᵗʰ of 6ᵗʰ mo. 1765 Our friend Hannah French being returned from Haddonfield with a certificate which friends gladly receive.

8ᵗʰ of 8ᵗʰ mo. 1765 Hannah French, Hannah Haines, Hannah Foster, and Rebecca Roberts appointed to inspect and correct the minutes of this meeting.

5th of 9th mo. 1765   We the committee appointed by ye monthly meeting of women friends of Evesham, to inspect and correct ye minutes of ye said meeting have met agreeable to appointment and have inspected and corrected such of them as we tho't needful and agreed with Hannah Haines to transcribe them into the bound book for the sum of one pound two shillings. Signed by us, Hannah Foster, Hannah French, Rebecca Roberts, and Hannah Haines.

5th of 9th mo. 1765   There appears a necessity of another elder for Chester Preparative Meeting therefore they have nominated our Friend Hannah French to that service which was sent to ye men friends for their approbation.

[Men's Meeting]
At a Monthly Meeting held at Evesham ye 5th of ye 9th mo. 1765.
The women Friends alfo signified that they proposed Hannah French to be an appointed Elder for Chester preparative meeting which was approved of, & ye Clerk is Directed to Notifie ye Quarterly Meeting of Ministers & Elders thereof for their concurrence.

[Women's Meeting]
10th of 2^d mo. 1774   Hannah French one of a committee to visit such as are in ye neglect of attending meetings.

10—4 mo. 1783   Hannah French one of the women friends appointed to sit with the Friends of upper Evesham at some of their first Preparative Meetings.

8th 10 mo. 1784   Hannah French appointed on committee to read and revive some ancient advices of discipline.

5—1st mo. 1787   Hannah French appointed on committee to attend the meeting for parents and heads of families.

[Men's Meeting]
Extract from Record book of Sufferings of Friends of Evesham Monthly Meeting for non Compliance of Military duty. Being An Account of Friends Sufferings within the Compass of Evesham Monthly Meeting for refusing to pay a Tax for procuring Powder & other Military Stores & for refusing to be Active in Military Services. The Sums Demanded: Goods taken: the Value thereof; by whom taken, & by what Authority is as followeth.

6th mo. 1783.   Taken from Hannah French (Widdow) by Abraham Winner & John Mott a Coverlid & Blankett rated £1 : 10 : 0 Substitute Tax demanded about 10 s.

At a Monthly Meeting held at Evesham the 5th of the 3rd Mo. 1802. One Elder deceased, To wit, Our esteemed friend Hannah French, an Elder of Chester preparative, and Evesham Monthly Meetings, departed this life on the 27th day of the 6th Mo. 1801 in the 85th year of her age.

In her passage through Time, she experienced many scenes of difficulty and probation; which she was enabled to bear with Christian fortitude; through the efficacy of that Faith which worketh by love, and is the support of the Righteous through all ages. In the latter years of her life it appeared that her love towards her fellow Mortals evidently increased; she often expressing in her last illness, earnest Solicitude that her connections with others, would press after the same apprehending it a good preparative for the awful Scene to which with a becoming resignation, she appeared to be hastening.

RECEIPT, ROBERT FRENCH [35] TO THOMAS FRENCH [33], 1745

I Robert French of Chester in the County of Burlington &c., have Reseved of Thomas French of the Same place Excutor to the Last Will and Testament of my late deceased Father Thomas French one obligation bearing even date with these presents Conditioned for the payment of Thirty pounds currant money and my Fathers horse bridel and Saddel and all his wearing aperrel and I do hereby acquit and discharge The Said Thomas French his heairs Executors and Administrators from all except Thee half of the Seder Swamp that was left between us and from all other actions Cause and Causes of action Suits Debts bils Bonds writings obligations Sum and Sums of money Quarrels and conterouersies of what kind Soever touching his late Deceased Fathers Estate or anything concearning him The above Said Excutor had made moved or depending from the begining of our first acquantance To the date of these presents. In Witness whareof I have hereunto set my hand Seal Dated The Twenty forth day of October in the year of our Lord one Thousand Seven hundred and forty and five (1745)

Robert French

Sealed and delivered
in The presence of
　　Samuel Atkinson
　　Joseph Heritage

WILL OF ROBERT FRENCH, 1760

Let it be recorded that I Robert French of Chester in the County of Burlington and within the Province of West New. Jerſey Yeoman Being Sick & weak of Body, But of Sound and Dispoſing mind and memory thanks be given to Almighty God therefore; and Calling to mind the uncertainty of this life, and the Certainty of Death when it may please Almighty God to call; and being Desirous that what Temporal Estate it hath pleased God to lend me in this life Shall Come unto Such perſon and perſons, as I shall herein Nominate and appoynt. Hereby revoaking and making Void all other wills & Testaments heretofore by me made Either by word or writing; and this only to be taken for the same as followeth Viz^t.——

Imp^{rs} I Do hereby order and Direct, that all my Estate may be Sold Both Real and perſonal as Soon after my Death, as my Execu^{rs} Hereafter Named may think proper, and I Do hereby Impower my Execu^r or the Survivers of them to make as Good a Deed or Deeds of Conveyance to the purchaſer or purchaſers of my lands, as I my Self Could do were I perſonally present, and out of the firs payments ariſing from my Estate I order my Execu^{rs} to pay and discharge all my Just Debts whatsoever, and the Remainder of my Estate I Despoſe of in the following manner——

Item—I Give and Bequeth unto my Dear and well beloved Wife Hannah the Sum of One Hundred pounds Procklamation Money to her my Said Wife her heirs and aſsigns forever.

Item—I Give and Bequeth unto my Son Jonas French & to his Heirs and Aſsigns forever; the Sum of One Hundred Pounds money aforeſaid, and Also a gray Mare Bridle and Saddle which was Called his . . .

Item—I Give and Bequeth unto my Daughter Mary French and to her heirs and aſsigns for Ever a Bay Coult a Saddle and Bridle, and the Sum of fifty pounds Money Afforeſaid, to be paid to her by my Execu^{rs} as Soon after my Debts are paid as may be Convenient—

Item I Give and Bequeth unto my Daughter Hannah French the Sum of Fifty pounds money afforeſaid to be paid to her by my Execu^{rs} in Manner Afforeſaid to her my Said Daughter her heirs and Aſsigns forever—

Item I Give and Bequeth unto my other Six Children Namely Thomas French Elizabeth French, Robert French James French Kiziah French and Anne French, the Sum of Fifty pounds Each, to them and Each of them my said Children their heirs and aſsigns forever, to be paid to them as they may Severly attain their full ages or married, which may first happen, by my Execu^{rs}—

Item it is my Will and I do hereby order that all the Remainder of my Estate (after my Just debts and legacies aforeſaid are paid), shall be Equily Divided Mongst my Wife and Children Share and Share alike

Item it is my Will that my Dear and well beloved wife Should have the Interest of Each of my Children's Shares whilst they are under age the Better to Enable her to bring up and Edicate my Said Children . . .

Item My will is if any of my Said Children Should happen to Dye before they attain their full age leaving no lawfull Ishue then and in Such Case I order his her or their Share So Dying to be Equily Devided amongst my Surviving Children Share and Share alike—

Item I Give and Bequeth unto my Said Wife a Gray mare Saddle and bridle—

Item I do hereby Nominate and appoynt my Said Dear Wife Hannah Execu—and my Brother-in-law James Cattle and my Son Jonas French Executors to this my last Will and Testament in Testamoney whereof I have here unto Sett my hand and Seal the thirty first Day of the Eighth Month in the Year of our of Our Lord One thousand Seven Hundred and Sixty 1760.

Signed Sealed pronounced and declared by the within named Robert French to be his last Will and Testament in the presence of us whofe Names are hereunto Subscribed as witnefses thereto.

Robert French 🌀

Tho⁸ Morton
John Matlack
Samuel Gafkill
John Cox

Samuel Gaskill and John Coxe two of the Witnefses to the above Will being of the People called Quakers and duly affirmed according to Law did declare and Affirm that they were Present and saw Robert French the Testator above Named Sign & Seal the fame and heard him publish pronounce and declare the above Instrument to be his last Will & Testament and that at the doing thereof the said Testator was of Sound & dispofing Mind Memory and Understanding as far as they know and as they Verily believe and that Thomas Morton and John Matlacke the other Subscribing Evideuces were present and Signed their Names as Witnefses to the fame together with thefe Affirmants in the prefence of the said Testator.

Affirmed at Burlington October ⎫
1ˢᵗ Anno Dom 1760 before   ⎬   Samuel Gafkill
    S. Blackwood Surrogate. ⎭   John Cox

Hannah French and James Cattell the Exrs. within Named being of the people called Quakers on their Solemn Affirmation which they took according to Law did declare & Affirm that the within Instrument of writing contains the true last Will & Instrument of Robert French the Testator therein Named deceased as far as they know and as they Verily believe and that they will well & truly perform the same by paying first the Debts of the said deceased & then the Legacies in the said Testament Specified so farr forth as the Goods Chattles & Credits of the said deceased can thereunto extend and that they will make and Exhibit into the Registry of the Prerogative Office at Burlington a true and perfect Inventory of all & Singular the Goods Chattles & Credits of the said deceased which have or shall come to their knowledge or poſseſsion or to the poſseſsion of any other perſon or perſons for their Uſe and Render a Just & true Acct when thereunto Lawfully Required—

Affirmed October 1ˢᵗ 1760
before
    S. Blackwood Surrogate.

Hannah french
James Cattell

INVENTORY OF THE ESTATE OF ROBERT FRENCH, 1760

An Inventory of the Goods Chattels and Credits of Robert French Late of Chester in the County of Burlington Dec. Taken and Appraised by us under: written the 24ᵗʰ day of September 1760

	£	S	P
To wareing Apparrel in the Lodging Room...............	9		
To a ffether Bedd and ffurniture.......................	10		
To 2 old Chests and Sundries therein....................	1	10	
To a Case of Old Drawers 20/. To a warming pan & Bedd 15/	1	15	
To a Small Looking glass 5/ Glass Bottles &c 2/6......		7	6
To Sundries old pewter in the frunt Room...............		17	6
To pair of Stilyards Lantron old pine tables............		15	
To Sundry old chairs worsted and woollen Yarn........	2	6	6
To 2 old wheels old Sive &c 17/6 To Sundry old books &c	1	9	6
To a Bed and Bedding in the first Room upstairs........	8	10	
To an old Chest and Some Bed Cloaths therein...........	1	4	
To a ffether Bed and beding in the Second Room........	4	10	
To 2 old Chaff Beds and Beding.......................	3		
To wooll Tubs and Sundries 25/ To an old Saddle 19/...	2	4	
To an old Gun 12/ in the Kitchen.....................		12	
To a Dough Trough 5/ To Sundry Iron potts pott Rase &c 22/6	1	7	6
To End Irons and Shovel Tongs &c....................		18	

To Tubs pails &c 7/6 To Sundry old Iron Edge tools
    &c 22/6 ....   ɪ   10

To old Casks &c in the Celler...........................   1   3

To Edge tools Chains and Sundries in the Smoak house...   2   2

To Rye in the Stack Suposed to be 65 Bushel a 2/6p......   8   2   6

To wheat in the Stack Suposed to be 15 Bushel a 4/.......   3

To a Stack of Oates..................................   5

To Flax & Sundries in the Barn.......................   1   11

To Sundry Stacks of hay..............................   15

To 23 Sheep...   6   10

To 3 old ploughs and a harrow........................   2   8   6

To an Iron Bound Waggon £9—To 2 old Carts £4 : 10 :...   13   10

To 6 Cows at 70/p To 3 heffers a 40/p Yearling Dᵒ 30/...   28   10

To a Yoak of Oxen...................................   12

To a field of Indien Corn and Some punkins...........   8   10

To one thousand Shingles at home.....................   3

To Eight Thousand Shingles at the Ceader Swamp.......   16

To Scythes Grind-stone Geers old harrows &c...........   1   ɪ   6

To a piece of Buck : wheat............................   1

To a Gray Mare £10—To Dᵒ £10—To a bay coult £8......   28

To a gray Horse £7 To an old Gray Mare 10/..........   7   10

To 16 Small Hoggs & 14——Piggs.....................   14

To 16 Yards of Tomey at 4/6p.........................   3   12

John Cox
Enoch Roberts

John Coxe and Enoch Roberts the Appraisers of the above Inventory being of the People called Quakers and duly Affirmed According to Law. did declare and Affirm that the Goods Chattles and Credits in the above Inventory Set down & Specified were by them Appraised according to their Just and true Respective Rates and Values after the best of their Judgment & Understanding an that they Appraised things were brought to their View for Appraisement

Affirmed Octo 1ˢᵗ 1760 before   John Cox
     S. Blackwood Surrogate.   Enoch Roberts

Hannah French and James Cattell Executors of the last Will and Testament of Robert French deceased being duly Affirmed according to Law did declare & Affirm that the Above Writing contains a true & perfect Inventory of all & Singular the Goods Chattles & Credits of the said deceased as farr as have come to their knowledge or possion or to the possession of any other person or persons for their Use

Affirmed October 1ˢᵗ 1760.   Hannah ffrench
     before me   James Cattell
         S. Blackwood Surrogate.

SUMMARY OF WILL OF HANNAH FRENCH, 1785

Hannah French—Chester, Burlington Co., N. J. Widow.

Date—12 mo. 12th—1785   Proved, August 18—1801

Children—Robert French—After directing that her debts and funeral charges be paid—" I give all the rest, residue & remainder of my personal estate (excepting my wearing apparel) Together with all that Mefsuage, Tenement Plantation & tract of Land whereon I now dwell Situate in Chester afores^d with the Appurtenances thereunto belonging, to my Son Robert French subject to the following Incumbrance, that he maintain my Son Jonas French during his natural life."

Jonas—to be maintained during his natural life by Robert and his Heirs, Admr^s or afsigns.

Executor, Son Robert French

Witnesses:
{ Joshua Hunt
{ Esther Hunt Junr
{ William Roberts.

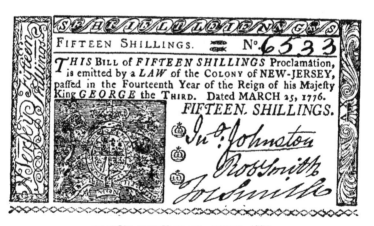

COLONIAL MONEY OF NEW JERSEY, 1776

On the reverse side is an engraving of a skeleton leaf, with the words: " Fifteen Shillings. To counterfeit is death. Burlington, New Jersey. Printed by Isaac Collins."

EVESHAM MEETING

The first account of this meeting states that Friends assembled for worship at the house of William Evans, in 1694. He was the progenitor of the Evans family in New Jersey and came with the pioneers to Burlington in 1677. The first meeting house was built about 1698, when regular meetings were established. Referring to this meeting appears the following minute in the Haddonfield records, authorizing the establishment of Preparative and Monthly meetings:

> " Request for this meeting was laid before Haddonfield Monthly Meeting 23 of ye 3ᵈ Mo. 1759 and was kept under consideration of ye Quarterly Meeting until ye 21 of 3ᵈ Mo. 1760, ye sd request was granted."

The following minute also appears:

> " It having been observed by some Friends of Evesham and Chester Meetings the great increase of a hopeful and rising generation among us, and the comfortable increase of our meetings for worship, from hence a concern arose for their further advancement in the blessed Truth; and having by experience seen the need and use of church discipline, and the necessity of waiting for Divine aid in the management thereof; and observing the increase and multiplicity of business at Haddonfield Monthly Meeting, of which we are members, by reason whereof our affairs could not be carried on with that improving calmness and deliberation which the nature of the service required; and being concerned that generations to come may ask and seek for the good old way, and may walk therein by a clear illumination of mind and simplicity of manners;—under these considerations a concern arose to request that Evesham and Chester might be constituted to hold a separate Monthly Meeting; which, after several years' deliberation, and a firm persuasion that it might be for general service, was accordingly done, as the minutes do set forth."

In 1760 the second meeting house was built. In 1798 it was enlarged and a partition put in. After 1828 both branches of the Society used the same building, a quaint specimen of old-time meeting houses. The woodwork was not painted, except around the doors and windows. On the north side of the building was a well which was filled up in 1846. The original lock on the front door was eight by eleven inches, two inches thick, fastened by heavy bolts. The key weighed nearly one half a pound. In the old house was a library filled with books as old as itself.

EVESHAM MEETING HOUSE, MOUNT LAUREL, N. J., BUILT 1760 AND 1798

37—MARY FRENCH (Thomas, 1; Thomas, 6).

> m. First, April 15th, 1736, Nathan Middleton.
> He d. 1760.
> m. Second, 9th mo. 17th, 1761, George Matlack.

136—BEULAH MIDDLETON

137—NATHAN MIDDLETON, JR.

Thomas French [6], father of Mary (French) Middleton, in his will dated 1745, bequeathed to his "daughter Mary's four sons each of them five pounds when they attain their full age." At least three of these sons appear to have been deceased at the time of the death of Nathan Middleton, in 1760, as only one son is mentioned in his will. Nathan Middleton was constable of Chester Township, Burlington Co., N. J., in 1732, and overseer of highways, 1748–49.

SUMMARY OF WILL OF NATHAN MIDDLETON, 1760

Nathan Middleton Chester, Burlington Co. N. J. Yeoman; "sick & weak in body"

Date June 6th—1760.   Proved—June 30—1760 at Burlington.

Wife   Mary remainder of my personal estate, & use of my plantation where I dwell, until son Nathan is 21, to enable her to bring up my children

Children—daughter, Bulia a lot of land to be taken off from my plantation as follows; beginning at corner of Joshua Bispham's field next adjoining the land whereon the Meeting houſe stands & to extend from sᵈ Bisphams corner a perrilal courſe with his line to my Meadow fence thence as the fence now Stands to the Road Between my plantation and the plantation late Nehemiah Haines's thence a South Courſe up the sd road to the Meeting-house Lands, thence part by the Same and part by the Said Bispham's Land to place of beginning; also give her a case of Drawers other articles of furniture, largest brass kettles and warming pan, my young Sorrel'd Mare &c &c. when 18 or married; £30 to be paid by son Nathan 3 years after he comes of age

Son Nathan rest of my lands & plantation 1 horse 2 cows when 21

Executors—Wife Mary
  friend Samˡ Stokes.   *Nathan Middleton*

Witnesses   Robt French Wᵐ Thomas John Cox

Inventory Taken June 24—1760—   £321   3   8
To Martin Hefter's a Dutch Lad's Time 4 yrs—£14.
To Phillip Acreman's a Dutch boy's time 6 yr—£18.

42—CHARLES FRENCH, JR. (Thomas, 1; Charles, 8).

b. 8th mo. 12th, 1714.
d. 1st mo. 15th, 1785.
m. 10th mo. 6th, 1739, Ann Clement, daughter of
Jacob and Ann (Harrison) Clement.
She b. 9th mo. 24th, 1720.
d. 8th mo. 9th, 1778.

138—ANN FRENCH
b. September 24th, 1740.
m. 12th mo. 12th, 1757, Jacob Wilkins.

139—ABIGAIL FRENCH
b. January 18th, 1742.
m. 9th mo. 1760, John Brick, 3rd.

140—JACOB FRENCH
b. April 28th, 1745.
m. 12th mo. 3rd, 1772, Elizabeth Stokes.

141—SAMUEL FRENCH
b. September 17th, 1748.
m. 4th mo. 7th, 1769, Sarah Heulings.

142—ELIZABETH FRENCH
b. February 18th, 1750.
m. First, 10th mo., 1768, James Wills.
m. Second, 4th mo. 11th, 1787, Moses Wills.

143—CHARLES FRENCH, 3RD. b. October 25th, 1753.
m. May 29th, 1783, Sabilla Stokes.

144—ELEANOR FRENCH
b. March 19th, 1756.
m. First, 11th mo. 23rd, 1775, Hugh Hollingshead.
m. Second, Joseph Matlack.

145—HOPE FRENCH
b. November 5th, 1763.
m. 1st mo. 1780, William Black, 3rd.

146—SARAH FRENCH
b. January 3rd, 1765.
d. 8th mo. 3rd, 1778.

(Birth dates of children are taken from Charles and Ann French family
Bible; dates of marriages are from Meeting and Church records.)

CHARLES FRENCH, JR.

Charles French, Jr. [42], learned the trade of mason, supposedly while a resident of Philadelphia, whence he removed to Moorestown, New Jersey, about 1740. He pursued his calling successfully and became a land owner in that vicinity. Yet like his forbears he was devoted to rural life and the cultivation of the soil. April 20, 1747, he purchased of James Childs a fine piece of land, 259 acres in extent, located on both sides of the south branch of Pensaukin Creek, partly in Evesham Township, Burlington County, and partly in Waterford Township, then Gloucester, now Camden County, near the present hamlet of Fellowship. This property had first been taken up by the Inskeep family, three brothers, jointly interested, James, Joseph and John, selling it to their father, November 8, 1727. He sold it, December 31, 1728, to James Childs, who, nearly twenty years later, conveyed it to Charles French, who made it his homestead throughout the remainder of his life, increasing his holding until a final survey, in 1782, showed that he owned 460 acres in that immediate neighborhood. In all lines of industrial effort he prospered greatly, exercising large influence throughout the community. In 1760 he assisted in building the second Friends' meeting house, Moorestown, one of his associate workmen being Mathew Allen, whose ancestor was a son-in-law of Thomas ffrench, the progenitor. At this time he became an overseer in Chester Meeting, Moorestown, and with his wife was active in the affairs of the Society, frequently sitting as representative in Quarterly Meetings at Haddonfield and Salem. In later life he took special interest in Evesham Meeting.

In 1771, Charles French availed himself of a special opportunity, at Sheriff's sale, at Woodbury, purchasing 1,000 acres of "land and swamp," with saw mill, farm houses, etc., located along and near Raccoon Creek, Greenwich (now Harrison) Township, about three miles from Mullica Hill. This extensive property, belonging to James Budd, was in four tracts, partly cultivated, other sections containing valuable timber. The purchase price was 505 pounds, little more than one half the amount of the judgment. Soon thereafter this property was taken charge of by the owner's son, Samuel French [141], whose inheritance it became, about ten years later. The will and inventory of Charles French [42] shows that at the time of his death, in 1784, he was a man of large possessions.

Charles French gave much intelligent attention to local affairs and to the promotion of public improvements. He became known as "straight roads"

French, on account of his vigorous advocacy of direct highways. Many amusing anecdotes were told of him in this connection. One neighbor sold out to get clear of him. Locating at some distance, he was amazed and vexed one day to find his pursuer, with a party of surveyors, prospecting across his land for a new road. After a parley he good naturedly accepted the situation. Upon another occasion the energetic roadmaker became so absorbed in his work in the woods, following the survey, he forgot his horse and buggy, going home with a neighbor at nightfall. After supper his black servant had to walk several miles to rescue the forgotten horse.

MEETING RECORDS

Haddonfield Monthly Meeting Minutes:

8—8—mo. 1739 Charles French & Ann Clement the first time Siguified their intention of taking each other in marriage, the sd. Charles is acquainted that a few lines from Frds. of Phila. will be expected at their next appearance and also appoints Joseph Stokes & John Hollingshead to make proper enquiry while sd. Charles hath had his living amongst us & make their ans. to our next Monthly Mtg.

12—9—mo. 1739. Charles French & Ann Clement y° second time Signified their intention of marriage; this meeting after receiving Satisfaction concerning Charles clearness on y° account of marriage according to y° good order used amongst us & appoints Timothy Matlack and Jos. Tomlinson to be present at sd. intended marriage to see it accomplished orderly.

11—10 mo. 1739. Joseph Tomlinson reported that he was present at the marriage of Charles French and Ann Clement and that it was accomplished orderly.

Haddonfield Minutes of y° Mo: Meeting of Women Friends:

Att a m°ly m^{t}g of wo^m fr^{ds} held at Haddonfield y° 8th of 8^m 1739 at s^d m^{t}g Charles French & Ann Clements signified y^r intentions of m^{r}g, m^{t}g a^{Pts} Marth^a Matlack & Rebecca White, to make y° ufual inquirie & report to next m^{t}g.

Att a m°ly m^{t}g of wo^m fr^{ds} held at Haddonfield y° 12th of 9^m 1739 Charles French & Ann Clement signified y° continuation of y^r intentions of m^{r}g, confent of parties concernd ap^{r}g, & retu^{r}n of inquirers clear, y° m^{t}g confents to y° accomplifhm^t y^r of, & apoints Martha Matlack, & Rebecca White, to see good o^{r}d^{r}s kept, & report to next m^{ts}

Att a m°ly m^{t}g of wo^m fr^{ds} held at Haddonf^{ld} y° 10th of 10th m° 1739 but y° fr^{ds} ap^{td} to tend C. French &c was not acquainted wth y° time.

MARRIAGE CERTIFICATE

Whereas Charles French of the County of Burlington in the province of New Jersey Brick-layer and Ann Clement Daughter of Jacob Clement Late of the County of Gloucester Deceased having Declared their Intentions of marriage with Each Other before Several Monthly Meetings of the People Called Quakers at Haddonfield within the County of Glouce^{tr} Afores^d According to the Good Order Used amongst them & Having the Consent of Relations Concerned their Said preposal of Marriage was allowed by the Said Meeting. Now These are to Certify whom it may concern that for the full accomplishing their s^d. Intentions this Sixth Day of the tenth Month in the year of our Lord one thousand Seven hundred and thirty nine they the Said Charles French takeing the said Ann Clement by the hand Did in a Sollemn Manner Openly Declare that he took her the Said Ann Clement to be his wife promising through the Lords Afsistance to be unto her a loving & faithful Husband untill Death should seperate them; & then and their in the Same Assembly the said Ann Clement did in like manner declare that she took Charles French to be her husband promising through the Lords Assistance to be unto him a faithfull & Loving wife untill Death Should Sepperate them & Moreover they the said Charles French & Ann Clement She According to the Custom of Marriage Assuming the name of her husband, as a further Confirmation thereof did then and there to these Presents Sett their hands & we whose names are here under Also Subscribed being present at the Sollemnization of the sd. Marriage & Subscription have as witnesses there unto Set our hands the Day and Year above Written.

Charles French
Ann French

Elizabeth Tyler	Samuel Clement
James Hinchman	Jacob Clement
Thomas French, Jr.	Mary Middleton
Uriah French	Hannah Hinchman
Benj. Heritage	Thomas Bate
Wm. Hinchman	Nathan Middleton
Simeon Ellis	Thomas French
Mary Ellis	Harry Bate
Sarah Ellis	Kesia Williott
Sarah Ellis, Jr.	
John Hinchman	

and 20 other names not in the relatives' column.

Haddonfield Monthly Meeting Minutes Continued:

10—1—mo. 1746 Joseph Heritage reported from the Preparative Meeting of Chester that said meeting has appointed Charles French to be one of the overseers of the Grave Yard at said Chester which was approved of by this meeting

14—4—mo. 1760 Chas. French one of the friends added to ye committee on ye affair of those whose general conduct has denied ye way of Truth.

9—6 mo. 1760 Edmond Hollingshead from ye preparative meeting at Chester reported that Robt. Hunt requested to be released from being an overseer and that he proposed Charles French in his stead which this meeting concurs with.

Evesham Monthly Meeting Minutes:

Agreeable to ye Direction of ye Quarterly Meeting held in ye 3^d & 9th months Last Friends of Evesham and Chester held their monthly meeting at Evesham on ye 9th of ye 10th m° 1760 — — Edm^d Hollinshead & Charles French are appointed overseers of Chester meetings.

At a monthly meeting held at Evesham ye 9th of ye 4th mo. 1761 Wm. Foster, Thos. Evens, Edmond Hollinshead, Thos. Wilkins, John Roberts & Charles French are appointed agreeable to ye Direction of our Last Quarterly Meeting, to confer with friends of Haddonfield monthly meeting in what manner to hold our youths meeting for ye Future & to assist in preparing a report to be Sent to ye next Quarter, but ye time for sd friends to meet is referd to f^{ds} of Haddonfield to appoint.

At a monthly meeting held at Evesham ye 8th of ye 4th Mo. 1762 Isaac Evens produced a copy of a minute importing that the monthly meeting at Haddonfield had appointed a committee to settle the Quotas for the Yearly Meeting Stock, Therefore Charles French, John Roberts, Wm. Foster, & Isaac Evens are appointed to joyn them in that Service, to meet at Haddonfield the 12th Instant at nine o'clock and report their proceeding to our next meeting.

At a monthly meeting held at Evesham ye 7th of ye 7th mo. 1763 Friends from Chester meeting reported that Charles French requested to be released from ye service of an overseer, & that they proposed Joshua Roberts to that service in his stead which was approved of. ·

Quarterly Meeting Minutes of Gloucester and Salem (Haddonfield):

1768—Joseph Gibson, William Foster, Josiah Albertson, Charles French, Solomon Lippincott, Mark Reeve, & David Cooper were "desired to prepare an Epistle of Advice and Admonition to the Several Monthly Meetings on the subject of Horse racing, fox hunting etc."

The Committee appointed at last Meeting reported in Writing as follows: We of the Committee appointed to consider the Queries from Haddonfield proposed to last Quarterly Meeting, having several times met on the Occasion & solidly deliberated thereon, in Answer to both the Queries, do give it as our Sense & Judgement, —— That, being a Party to a Horse Race and Wager is not in the Sense of our Discipline a Crime that requires to be condemned, or Testified against in a public Manner ——
That Horse-Racing is to be considered as Vain Sports, and Wagers as Lotteries:—Nevertheless, as it is of a very corrupting Nature, and many times leads into Things that are publicly Scandalous; when this is the Case, it may be necessary for Monthly Meetings to testify publicly against such Conduct, unless the Offenders will take it on themselves by a public Acknowledgment, in which Cases, the Age, & other Circumstances of the Offenders ought to be considered

Haddonfield ⎱
24th 3 mo. 1768 ⎰ All which nevertheless is submitted to ye Meeting

Joseph Gibson	William Foster
Josiah Albertson	Charles French
Solomon Lippincott	Mark Reeve
& David Cooper	

Which being twice read, after a Time of solid Consideration it was approv'd, & the Clerk is directed to deliver a Copy thereof to Haddonfield Monthly Meeting.—They also produced an Essay of a Testimony to be publicly read against Horse Racing, Fox Hunting &c. which being read was approv'd and the Clerk is directed to send Copy thereof to the several Monthly Meetings, who are to order the same to be publicly read on a First Day at each of their particular Meetings and may have the same repeated as often as they find necessary.

DEED, CHARLES FRENCH TO BARZILLIA COATES, 1769

This Indenture made the seventeenth day of January in the year of our Lord One thousand seven hundred and sixty nine Between Charles French of Waterford in the County of Gloucester and province of New Jersey Yeoman of the one part, and Barzillia Coates of Willenborough in the County of Burlington and province af^sd yeoman of the other part.

18

Witnesseth that the said Charles French for and in Consideration of the
Sum of Six pounds proclamation Money to him paid by the said Barzilla
Coates, the Receipt whereof he doth hereby Acknowledge and him the said
Barzilla Coates of and from the same doth acquit and discharge hath
granted Bargained and Sold, and by these Presents doth grant bargain &
Sell unto the said Barzilla Coates his Heirs and Assigns all that Tract of
Land Surveyed to his Grand Father Thomas French in 1684 situate in the
Township of Willenborough afs⁴ Bounded as followeth to wit, Beginning
at a Corner Tree formerly John Roberts's by Rancocas alias Northampton
River, and runs thence by the said Land of John Roberts One hundred
and twenty Chains North North East half a point North to a Brook called
Mill Creek to another Corner Tree of the said John Roberts. Then up by
the said Mill Creek forty four chains and an half to a white Oak marked
for a Corner, Then South South West half a point South to a Stake for a
Corner at Northampton River afs⁴ Then down by the said River to the first
mentioned Corner. Together with twenty Acres for Meadow lying and
being the next Meadow below Thomas Olives Meadow on the same side the
said Northampton River, as now mark'd out by the upland, the North
West side of the same, abutting upon the beginning of that part of the
River called long Reach, a little Island in the River lying upon the South
East side thereof surveyed for Six hundred Acres as by the Survey thereof
recorded in Revell's Book of Surveys fol: 83 in the Secretary's Office in
Burlington appears Excepting thereout such parts as have been already
legally granted sold and Conveyed to any Person or Persons whomsoever
Together with all and singular the Rights, Liberties Priviledges, Hereditaments and appurtenances Rents Issues & profitts thereof or any part thereof,
and all the Estate Right & Title of him the said Charles French of in and
to the same To have and to hold the said Tract or parcel of Land and
Meadow with all and singular the Rights Liberties Priviledges Hereditaments & appurtenances to the same belonging (except as above excepted)
unto the said Barzilla Coates his Heirs and Assigns To the only Use and
Behoof of the said Barzilla Coates his Heirs and Assigns for ever And
the said Charles French for himself his Heirs Executors and Administrators
doth Covenant to and with the said Barzilla Coates his Heirs & Assigns
by these presents That he the said Charles French and his Heirs, and all
and every other Person and Persons anything having or claiming in the
said Tract or parcell of Land Tenements and Premises or any part thereof
by from or under him shall and will from time to time and at all times at
the Reasonable request, and at the Costs and Charges in the Law of the
said Barzilla Coates his Heirs or Assigns make and Execute, or cause to
be made and Executed all and every such further or other lawfull & Reasonable Act or Acts thing or things Device or Devices whatsoever for the
further, better and more perfect Granting Conveying and Assuring the said
Tract or parcell of Land Tenements & Premises afs⁴ (except as before

excepted) unto the said Barzilla Coates his Heirs or assigns. To the only use & Behoof of the s^d Barzilla Coates his Heirs & Afsigns for ever as by the s^d Barzilla Coates his Heirs or Afsigns or his or their Council learned in the Law shall be reasonably devised, advised and required—provided such further Afsurance Contain no other Covenant than is Comprised in this Deed. In Witnefs whereof the parties to these presents have interchangeably set their hand and Seals dated the day & year just above written

Charles ffrench   [Seal]

Sealed & Delivered in the presence of John Lanning, John Norton.

WILL OF CHARLES FRENCH, JR., 1784

Let it be Recorded that I Charles French of the Township of Waterford in the County of Gloucester in the State of New Jersey Yeoman, being at this time of sound and disposing mind and memory, thanks be given unto Almighty God therefor. And Calling to mind the uncertainty of this Life and the Certainty of Death when it may please God to Call, and being desirous that the Temporal Estate which it pleased divine Providence to bless me with in this life, shall come unto such persons as I shall herein after nominate and appoint hereby revoking and making void all former Wills and Testaments by me made, either by word or Writing and this only to be taken for the same as followeth Viz. Imprimis I Will and order that my Executors hereafter named, do pay all my funeral Charges, and Just Debts, out of my personal Estate, as soon after my Decease as can Conveniently be done, Item I Give and Devise unto my son Jacob French a Certain piece of Land at the Eastwardly end of my Plantation whereon he now Dwells, as the same was lately ran of by David Fisher. Beginning at a stone in the old Line of my Plantation standing on the ditch Bank thence South thirty Degrees, West five Chains to a stone thence North Thirty three Degrees, West five Chains and Twenty seven links to a stone, thence South Seventy five Degrees, thirty minutes, West fourteen Chains and forty four Links to a White oak, then South Twenty Eight Degrees, West Twenty six Chains and Seventy five links to a stone, thence South Eighty Six Degrees and thirty minutes, East Eight Chains and Eighty links to a White oak, thence South Thirty nine Degrees, West nine Chains and Sixty links to a stone by the Road, thence North Eighty Eight Degrees, East thirteen Chains and Sixty links to a Black Oak in John Lippincott's line thence Along said line, North fifty nine Degrees, East Nineteen Chains and fifty links to a Black oak Corner to Thomas Hollinshead's Land, thence by the same North Twenty Six Degrees and fifteen minutes, West Ten Chains and Seventy links to a Stone, thence North Sixty six Degrees and thirty minutes, East Twelve Chains and Twenty five links, to a stone, thence North Twenty five Degrees, and thirty

minutes West Eight Chains and Ninety links to the Beginning Corner.
Containing Seventy five Acres, and one half Acre be the same more or less,
all which Seventy five Acres and half of Land, with the Buildings & Improvements thereon or thereunto belonging, I Give and Devise to my said
son Jacob French during his natural Life (Excepting only the Grist Mill
Stream of Water hereafter Devised to my son Charles French) Item in case
my said son Jacob should die before his present Wife, then and in that
case I Give and Bequeath the use and profits of the said Plantation unto
her during the time she may remain my said son Jacob French's Widow
and no longer. Item after the Decease of my said son Jacob, and the
Decease or Second Marriage of his said present Wife, I do hereby order
and it is my Will that my Executors or the Survivor of them, or any
other person or persons that he or they may Authorize or appoint, shall
sell the said Plantation to the best bidder And all the money Arising from
the sales, of the said Plantation I Give and Bequeath unto my said Son
Jacob's Children to be Equally divided amongst them share and share
alike. Item In case any or either of my said son Jacob's Children should
Die before the said money can be divided, it is my Will that if him her
or them so Deceased should leave Lawful Issue that such Issue shall have
the Parents share or devidend. Item I Give and Devise unto my son
Charles French And to his Heirs and Assigns forever, all the Remainder
of my Land and Plantation whereon I now Dwell with the Grist Mill and
other Improvements thereunto belonging, together with all my Household
Furniture and farming utensils, he my said son Charles paying out of the
same the sum of Five Hundred pounds, unto my Daughters in manner
hereafter mentioned. Item Whereas there is a Ditch that Runs through
part of the Land Devised to my son Jacob that Conveys a Stream of Water
to my Grist Mill to prevent any Dispute hereafter, I Give and Devise the
said Stream of Water unto my said son Charles his Heirs and Assigns
forever, that is to say Ten feet of Land on each side the Middle of the
Water Course, so far as the same Runs through the Land Devised to my
son Jacob as aforesaid. Item I Give and Devise unto my said son Charles,
and to his Heirs and Assigns forever, All my Cedar Swamp Reserving
so much timber out of the same as my said son Jacob may want for Rails
or Building on his own Plantation and no more. Item I Give and Devise
unto my son Samuel French and to Heirs and Assigns forever, all that my
several tracts of Land, Plantation and Saw Mill and utensils thereunto
belonging whereon he now Dwells in the County aforesaid he paying out
of the same the sum of Ten pounds Current money to each of my three
Grand Daughters namely Ann, Abigail and Sarah Brick, as they severally
arive to the Age of Eighteen years. Item if either of my said Grand
Daughters should die under Age, without Issue, I will that her Legacy so
Dying shall be paid to her Surviving sisters, or Sister, and if any Child
or Children should be left by either of them then the Legacy to be paid

to her or their Child or Children so Decd. Item I Give and Bequeath unto my Daughter Hope Black the sum of one Hundred pounds Current money of New Jersey to be paid to her by my son Charles French in one year after my Decease, she being as I think the most Necessiatie for the first payment. Item I Give and Bequeath unto my Daughter Abigail Brick the sum of one Hundred pounds money aforesaid, to be paid to her by my said son Charles French in two years after my Decease. Item I Give and Bequeath unto my Daughter Elizabeth Wills, the sum of one Hundred pounds money Aforesaid, to be paid to her by my said son Charles in three years after my Decease. Item I Give and Bequeath unto my Daughter Ann Wilkin the sum of one Hundred pounds money aforesaid, to be paid to her by my said son Charles in four Years after my Decease. Item I Give and Bequeath unto my Daughter Elenor Hollinshead, the sum of one Hundred pounds money aforesaid to be paid to her by my said son Charles in five years after my Decease. Item I Give to Chester Meeting the sum of Twenty pounds towards repairing the Meeting House, and Grave Yard, to be paid by my Executors out of the Interest Arising from the money that may be then due to me. Item I Give & Devise all the Residue and Remainder of my Personal Estate (after my Just Debts and funeral Charges are paid) unto my aforesaid five Daughters to be equally divided amongst them, share and share alike. Item it is my will and I do hereby order that in case any or either of my said Daughters should Depart this Life before their Legacy or Devidend is paid, then and in that case her or their share so dying shall be Divided amongst her or their Children. Item and Lastly I do hereby nominate Constitute and appoint, my said sons Samuel French and Charles French Executors of this my last Will and Testament.

In Witnefs whereof I have hereunto Set my Hand and Seal the thirteenth day of the Eleventh Month (November) in the year of our Lord One thoufand Seven Hundred and Eighty-four—1784

Signed Sealed published prounounced and Declared by the Said Charles French as and for his Last Will and Testament in the prefence of us the fubfcribing Witnefses who in his prefence & at his Requeft have fubfcribed our Names as Witnefses thereunto—

David Davis
Samuel Coles Davis
John Cox

David Davis and Samuel Coles Davis, two of the Witnesses to the within
Will being duly affirmed According to Law, did Severally Affirm and say,
that they saw Charles French the testator therein named Sign and Seal the
same and heard him publish pronounce and Declare the within writing to be
his last Will and Testament, and that at the doing thereof the said Testator was of sound and disposing mind and memory, as far as these affirmants
know and as they verily believe, and that John Cox the other Subscribing
Evidence was present at the same time and signed his name as a Witness
to the said Will Together with these affirmants in the presence of the said
Testator David Davis, Samuel Coles Davis.

Affirmed at Burlington March the 29th 1785 before me
                              Herbert McElroy   Surrogate

The Foregoing Will being proved Probate was Granted by His Excellency
William Livingston Esqr. unto Samuel French and Charles French, Executors in the said will named they being first duly Affirmed well and truly to
perform the same Exhibit a true and perfect Inventory & Render a Just
and true Account when thereunto Lawfully required Given under the Prerogative Seal the day and Year aforesd.

                              Bowes Reed   Regr.

INVENTORY OF ESTATE OF CHARLES FRENCH, JR., 1785

An Inventory of the Good and Chattels Rights Credits and Effects of
Charles French of Waterford In the County of Gloucefter And State of
Niew Jerfey Dec^d Taken and Appraifed this 28th Day of March 1785 by
Us the Subfcribers Which is as follows Viz :

To his Wearing apparrel and some other Small Things.£	21	7	4
To his Silver Watch	5	0	0
To A Mare Saddle & Bridle	31	10	0
To A Bond againſt William Black	52	9	6
To A Bond againſt Samuel French	56	8	4
To A Bond againſt Ephraim Hains	39	3	2
To A Bond againſt William Hinchman	346	16	2
To A Note againſt John Cox	2	3	6
To Caſh In Hard Money	24	7	1
To Sundry Book Debts	19	13	4
To a Cafe & Bottles	0	10	0
Total	599	8	5

Thomas Stokes } Appraifers
David Davis   }

David Davis one of the appraisers of the within Inventory being duly affirmed according to Law did affirm & say, that the Goods Chattels & Credits in the within Inventory Let down & Specified were by him Appraised according to their just & true respective rates & values after the best of his Judgment & Understanding & that Thomas Stokes—the other appraiser whose name is thereto subscribed was present at the same time & consented in all things to the doing thereof & that they appraised all things that were brought to their view for appraisement.   David Davis
Affirmed at Burlington March 29th 1785

Samuel French & Charles French Executors of Charles French dec^d being duly Affirmed according to Law did affirm & Say that the within Instrument of Writing Contains a true & perfect Inventory of all & Singular the Goods Chattels & Credits of the s^d deceased that have come to their Knowledge or Poſseſsion or to the Poſseſsion of any other Person or Persons for their use—

Affirm'd ut Ante Coram me   ⎱   Samuel French
    Herbert McElroy Surrogate ⎰   Chas French

ANCESTRY OF ANN (CLEMENT) FRENCH

Samuel Harrison, mariner, located in Gloucester County, N. J., sometime prior to 1688. Various genealogical investigations have discovered traditional ground for belief that this early adventurer in West Jersey was a son or grandson of General Thomas Harrison, a noted leader in the English Revolution of 1648, one of the signers of the death warrant of Charles I, and who was finally executed after the restoration of the monarchy under Charles II, in 1660.

Samuel Harrison m. Sarah, daughter of William Hunt, and had children: William, Samuel and Ann. In 1689 he bought land near Woodbury Creek from Thomas Gardiner, administrator for the estate of Thomas Matthews, original purchaser; and in 1691, an additional tract from Thomas Sharp of Newton. He was highly esteemed and respected in the community, and it is interesting to note that in 1697 he was made "heir and executor of real and personal estate," including 450 acres of land in Gloucester Co., of Thos. Penston. By will dated Aug. 5, 1700, proved March 18, 1704/5, Isaac Goodwin "left son John to the care of Samuel Harrison," who was appointed executor of "outward" estate. As the latter died in 1703, the execution of this trust became the duty of his widow, Sarah Harrison. Inventory of personal estate of Samuel Harrison, taken Feby. 9, 1703/4, amounted to £500 17s. 6d., including books £20, plate £28, four negroes £120. Letters of administration were granted to the widow, March 1, 1703/4.

Ann Harrison, daughter of Samuel and Sarah (Hunt) Harrison, m. Jacob Clement, born 1678. In 1709 and 1710 Jacob Clement served as sheriff of Gloucester County. He died prior to 1739. In 1720 a son and daughter, twins, were born to Jacob and Ann (Harrison) Clement, and named Jacob and Ann. Ann Clement, the daughter, married in 1739, Charles French [42]. Jacob Clement was a son of James and Jane Clement, who settled on Long Island. James was son of Gregory Clement, a citizen of London, England, member of the Cromwell Parliament, and one of the judges who tried and condemned Charles I, in 1648.

GREGORY CLEMENT

Gregory Clement, a member of the jury which tried and condemned Charles I., King of England, in 1648, was a London merchant. He had taken great interest in the Revolution and entered the Cromwellian parliament in 1646. He was diligent and efficient in the performance of his legislative duties, and when he was chosen to sit in judgment upon his dethroned sovereign he reluctantly obeyed the perilous summons, and at the conclusion of the trial set his hand and seal to the historic death warrant. Later he was deprived of his seat in parliament, having incurred the displeasure of some of his associates, but was restored after Cromwell's death. With most of the regicides, Gregory Clement disregarded the peril of punishment after the restoration and remained in England. He was arrested and brought to trial. At first he pleaded "not guilty," but later, upon the importunity of his relatives, who thus hoped for mercy, he acknowledged the offense charged. Instead, however, he was excepted from all clemency, both of estate and life, and barbarously executed, with several others, October 16, 1660. The terrible scenes of the hour sickened executioner and spectators, the sentence of the law calling for hanging—partial strangulation only—disemboweling and quartering of the mutilated body, after the head was cut off. Before execution he expressed extreme regret because he had pleaded guilty, which had rendered him "unworthy to die in so glorious a cause." His estates having been confiscated, one of his sons, James, came to America, in 1670, taking up a small tract of land on Long Island. From him descended the Clement family of New Jersey, one of whom was the ancestor of Ann Clement, who married Charles French, Jr., in 1739. The American descendants of the men who tried and condemned Charles I, have always encountered many difficulties in securing essential genealogical facts, on account of the fierce persecution of the regicides after the restoration and the consequent destruction of family records, to prevent discovery and possible punishment of those in any way related to them. But in some instances diligent research has been in part at least rewarded.

WARRANT TO EXECUTE KING CHARLES I, A. D. 1648

At the high Co^{r}t of Juſtice for the tryinge and judginge of Charles Steuart Kinge of England January XXIXth Anno Dm 1648.

Whereas Charles Steuart Kinge of England is and ſtandeth convicted attaynted and condemned of high Treaſon and other high crymes And ſentènce uppon Saturday laſt was pronounced againſt ·him by this Co^{r}t to be putt to death by the ſeveringe of his head from his body OF wch ſentence execution yet remayneth to be done. Theſe are therefore to will and require you to ſee the ſaid ſentence executed In the open Streete before Whitehall uppon the morrow being the Thirtieth day of this inſtante month of January betweene the hours of Tenn in the morninge and ffive in the afternoone of the ſame day wth full effect And for ſoe doing this ſhall be yor ſufficient warrant And theſe are to require All Officers and Souldiers and other the good people of this Nation of England to be aſſiſtinge unto you in this Service Given under our hands and Seales.

To Collonell ffrancis Hather Colonell Huncks
    and Lieutenant Colonell Phayre and to every of them.

Jo. Bradshawe	Ri Deane	Symon Mayne
Tho: Grey	Robert Tichborne	Tho: Horton
O Cromwell	H Edwards	J Jones
Edw. Whalley	Daniel Blagraue	John Moore
M. Livesey	Owen Rowe	Gilbt Millington
John Okey	William Pureſoy	G ffleetwood
J Dauers	Ad: Scrope	J Alured
Jo. Bourchier	James Temple	Robt Lilburne
H Ireton	A Garland	Will ſay
Tho Mauleuerer	Edm: Ludlowe	Anth: ſtapley
Har: Waller	Henry Marten	Gre Norton
John Blakiston	Vinc^t Potter	Tho. Challoner
J Hutchinson	Wm: Constable	Tho. Wogan
Willi Goff	Rich Ingoldesby	John Venn
Tho Pride	Will: Cawley	Gregory Clement
Pe Temple	Jo Barkstead	Jo: Downes
T Harrison	Iſaa Ewer	Tho Wayte
J Hewson	John Dixwell	Tho. Scot
Hen Smyth	Valentine Wauton	Jo: Carew
Per. Pelham		Miles Corbet

From original document in House of Lords.

43—URIAH FRENCH (Thomas, 1; Charles, 8).

> m. Mary McCullock.
> She m. Second, August 10th, 1759, Hugh Creighton
> of Gloucester County, N. J.

147—CHARLES FRENCH   m. 4th mo. 7th, 1773, Rebecca Taylor.

148—SAMUEL FRENCH   m. First, November 11th, 1775, Mary Wayne.
                                       m. Second, Elizabeth ———.

URIAH FRENCH

Uriah French, as was the prevailing custom among Friends in the early days, mastered a trade, becoming a bricklayer and locating in Newton Township, Gloucester County (now Camden County), N. J. In 1749 he bought of James Hinchman, a descendant of the pioneer of that name, about 100 acres of land, near Haddonfield. March 25, 1758, he sold this property to Joseph Bullock, this being a short time before his death. His estate was administered by his widow, Mary French, with her brother-in-law, Charles French [42], as bondsman, as the following memoranda, taken from Gloucester County original will files, 1754–60, will show:

Uriah French, Bricklayer Newton Township Gloucester Co. N J. Intestate. Adm^x Mary French (widow) of above place.

Bondsman Charles French, of above place
    Date of letters Aug 7—1758
    Invty taken Aug 4—1758 total....................£202   4   5
    From estate of John McCollock and other cash.....£ 47   1   11

    Jacob Clement   } Apprs
    John Gill   }
Affirmed to June 12—1759.

SIGNATURE OF ADMINISTRATRIX

Account of Hugh Creighton & Mary his wife late Mary French Relict of Uriah French late of Gloucester Co. died who charge themselves with

£208   10   5

Amount of Inventory....................£202	4	5	
Rec'd of Wm Woods Ex^r.................	2	6	0
" of Archibald Mickles' Est..........	1	17	6
Cash unappraised being paid to Nathl			
Brundage before appraisement........	2	2	6
	£208	10	5

Persons to whom payments were made

John Ladd Surrogate	Thos Champion	John Hatkinſon
Mary Hawhins	Beulah Clement	James Mulock adm^r of
Amos Archer	Chas Ferguson	Benj. Collins
Saml Hugg	John Jones	Simeon Ellis for
Elizabeth Maxwell	Jacob Clement	Sarah Norris
Isaac Kay	Wm Hinchman	Tatum Williams
Thos Edgerton	Geo. Weed	Abraham Inskeep
Elizabeth Craig	John Blackwood	John Hillman
Saml Murrell	Robt Friend Price	Jacob Albertson
Anne Sharp	John Gill	Saml Harrison for
Wm Griscom	Thos Redman	James Talman
Thos Thackra	Jacob Burroughs	and Kezia Hinchman
Richd Weeks	Henry Crawford	Nathl Brundage
Hugh Creighton	Jo^s Thomas for Exrs	John Matlack Jr
James Inskeep	of Josiah Hewey	Rich^d "
John Bailey	Job Siddons	Elizabeth Estaugh
	Isaac Andrews	Jacob Stokes adm^r
		of Joseph Ellis dec'd
		Judith Jennings—

The above account is just and True as to the Charge & Discharge thereof April 2^d—1764

Hugh Creighton
Mary Creighton

ORIGINAL SIGNATURE.

Examined this Account with the Vouchers & approved of by me this 2^d April Anno Dom. 1764

Samuel Allinson, Surrogate.

HUGH CREIGHTON—HADDONFIELD REMINISCENCES

Hugh Creighton, who married Mary (McCullock) French, was a well known citizen of Haddonfield before and during the Revolutionary War. He owned and conducted from 1777 until about 1790 the historic " Tavern House," in which the New Jersey Council of Safety and Legislature met at different times. Their daughter Mary, born 1762, married, in 1787, Dr. James Stratton, son of Benjamin and Sarah (Austin) Stratton, of Cumberland County, N. J., and resided near Swedesboro, N. J.; their son, Charles C. Stratton, born 1796, died 1859, was member of the New Jersey Assembly from Gloucester County, N. J., in 1821–23 and 1828, Representative in Congress, 1837–39 and 1841–43, and Governor of New Jersey, 1845–48.

In 1900 the State of New Jersey bought the " American House," the name by which the old hotel was known to later generations, placing it in the care of a patriotic association. On the front wall was placed a tablet bearing the following inscription:

Within this building,
then a tavern-house,
the Council of Safety
for New Jersey was
organized March 18th, 1777.
Herein also, in September
of the same year, the legislature unanimously resolved
that thereafter the word
" State " should be substituted
for " Colony " in all public
writs and commissions.
        1750   1900

[The historical accuracy of this statement has recently been questioned, by a New Jersey State official. At the time of the publication of this book the matter is a subject of further inquiry by those specially concerned.]

While the Creighton's conducted this historic inn at Haddonfield, it was the centre of political, official and social life. Here the famous Committee of Safety held many important sessions. Here were brought, by summary process, many leading citizens to answer more or less serious charges of indifference or hostility to the patriot cause. Here the gravest questions were considered and momentous decisions reached concerning the prosecution of the war and the rights of citizenship. Soldiers of distinction of both armies made the " tavern house " their headquarters. The genial proprietor and his wife, noted for her loving and unselfish disposition,

AMERICAN HOUSE, HADDONFIELD, N. J., BUILT 1750

possessed many acquaintances, friends and relatives.   Conspicuous among the young folks who participated in a round
of innocent pleasure in this ancient hostelry on the King's
Highway of Haddonfield, was a merry little Quakeress—
Dolly Payne, the bright and beautiful daughter of John
Payne, Jr., and Mary (Coles) Payne, then living in Philadelphia.   They were strict and conscientious Friends, and
before leaving the home plantation in Scotchtown, Va.,
they evidenced their devotion to high principles by freeing
their slaves.   To their bright and fun loving young
daughter, the quiet and plainness of the home life became
at times dull and monotonous, and the visits made to her
Uncle and Aunt Creighton's at Haddonfield, where she
entered so heartily into the festive occasions at the inn, were
memorable days in the life of Dolly Payne.   She greatly
enjoyed the drives taken on delightful summer days with
kind Aunt Creighton, cousins and friends, to Moorestown,
Burlington and Trenton, and the visits which they made
on these occasions to the shops.   Prominent families of
the neighborhood entertained her, and many admirers paid
court to her beauty.   Withal she remained a member of
Meeting, and at Pine Street Meeting House, Philadelphia,
1st mo. 7th, 1790, she married John Todd, a promising
young member of the bar and a Friend.   A large company
was present including Uncle and Aunt Creighton.   In the
latter part of 1793, Dolly (Payne) Todd was left a widow

1720

with a son.   She then made her home with her mother, who, owing to loss
of husband and means, was endeavoring to make her living by taking
boarders.   One of her patrons was James Madison, member of Congress
from Virginia, and future President of the United States.   He was nearly
twenty years the senior of young Mrs. Todd to whom he addressed his
attentions, and whose beauty had ripened with passing years.   There were
marked differences in their mental and physical characteristics and tempera-
ment, but in 1794 they were married and lived happily together for two
score years.   As the brilliant and popular mistress of the White House,
" Dolly " Madison remembered her happy days at Haddonfield and always
cordially welcomed visitors from that locality.

47—RACHEL FRENCH (Thomas, 1; John, 9).

> b. 1705.
>
> m. First, Enoch Fenton, son of Eleazer and Elizabeth (Stacy) Fenton.
>
> He b. 1693.
>
> d. 1732.
>
> m. Second, December 1st, 1735, Nathaniel Wilkinson.

149—ELEAZER FENTON   b. 1723.
     m. Nov. 7th, 1753, Elizabeth Atkinson.

150—VESTA FENTON   m. Jany. 21st, 1754, Obadiah Ireton.

151—RACHEL FENTON

152—ENOCH FENTON, JR.

Eleazer Fenton and Elizabeth Stacy were married February 2nd, 1690. She born 8th mo. 17th, 1673; he died 1704.

50—THOMAS BUZBY (Thomas, 1; Mary, 11).

> m. 1727, Margaret Haines, daughter of Thomas Haines.
>
> d. 1773.

152 a—DANIEL BUZBY

153—THOMAS BUZBY, JR.   b. 2nd mo. 4th, 1739.
     m. 1765, Tabitha Hugg.

154—AMOS BUZBY   b. 7th mo. 20th, 1742.
     m. First, Patience Springer.
     m. Second, Rebecca Matlack

154 a—ISAAC BUZBY

155—JOSEPH BUZBY

53—WILLIAM BUZBY (Thomas, 1; Mary 11).

> b. 5th mo. 10th, 1714.
>
> d. 9th mo. 5th, 1759.
>
> m. 8th mo. 25th, 1739, Mary Wills, daughter of Daniel and Elizabeth (Woolston) Wills of Northampton Township, Burlington Co., N. J.
>
> She b. 5th mo. 6th, 1718.
>
> d. 3rd mo. 12th, 1786.

156—WILLIAM BUZBY, JR. b. 10th mo. 23rd, 1751.
          m. 6th mo. 9th, 1773, Susannah Deacon.

157—ELIZABETH BUZBY m. 5th mo. 13th, 1767, Samuel Haines, Jr.

Daniel Wills, son of John Wills of Northampton Township, and Elizabeth Woolston, daughter of John Woolston of Mansfield Township, Burlington Co., N. J., were married at Springfield Meeting House 8th mo. 13th, 1714.

71—RUTH STOCKDELL (Thomas, 1; Rachel, 4; Mary Allen, 18).

> m. December 31st, 1735, John Small.
>
> He d. 1769.

158—ISRAEL SMALL m. October 13th, 1763, Ann Hinchman.

159—JONAS SMALL

160—WILLIAM SMALL

161—JOHN SMALL

162—ROBERT SMALL m. December 21st, 1778, Elizabeth Morris.

163—RUTH SMALL

164—MARY SMALL m. Thomas Archer.

In his will, dated August 1st, 1768, approved February 27th, 1769, John Small, yeoman, of Evesham, Burlington Co., N. J., divided his estate, real and personal, amongst his family. Unto his wife he gave the use and benefit of his houses and lands, so long as she remained his widow, in order to bring up his children. To his sons William and

John six acres of land and ten pounds each. To his son Robert six acres upon arriving at his majority and also five pounds. It was specially provided that these lands should "not to be Lett to any others but some of my sons." To his daughter Ruth Small furniture and five pounds, at 21; likewise to his daughter Mary, wife of Thomas Archer, twenty shillings. The rest of his lands to his sons Israel and Jonas Small, equally, with a dwelling house for each, they to pay to their brothers the money legacies above mentioned. Wife Ruth, son Israel and friend Edward Darnal were named Executors. Israel declined to serve. The inventory of his personal property, appraised by Samuel Garwood and Abraham Borton, showed a valuation of 93 pounds and 15 shillings.

72—HANNAH STOCKDELL (Thomas, 1; Rachel, 4; Mary Allen, 18).

> b. 1718.
> d. 6th mo. 16th, 1790.
> m. 1743, John Stokes, Jr., son of John and Elizabeth (Green) Stokes, of Willingborough Township, Burlington Co., N. J.
> He b. 5th mo. 15th, 1713.
> d. 8th mo. 24th, 1798.

165—MARY STOKES	b. 8th mo. 15th, 1745. m. Isaac Newton.
166—JOHN STOKES, 3RD	b. 6th mo. 22nd, 1747. m. Susannah Newton.
167—DAVID STOKES	b. 11th mo. 12th, 1751. m. 4th mo. 15th, 1784, Ann Lancaster.
168—JARVES STOKES	b. 11th mo. 10th, 1753. m. Nov. 27th, 1773, Elizabeth Rogers.
169—HANNAH STOKES	b. 10th mo. 12th, 1756. m. First, 4th mo. 9th, 1794, Jacob Haines. m. Second, George Browning.
170—ELIZABETH STOKES	b. 5th mo. 31st, 1759. m. 5th mo., 1803, Robert French [131].
171—RACHEL STOKES	b. 2ud mo. 2ud, 1765. m. 10th mo. 12th, 1785, Joseph Hackney, Jr.

SUMMARY OF WILL OF JOHN STOKES, JR., 1786

John Stokes, Wellingborough Burlington Co., N. J., yeoman

Date—3 Mo—7th—1786.   Proved August 30th—1798

Wife—Hannah £100 out of my personal estate

> £100 to be paid by son John one year after my decease
> £ 50 " " " David in consideration of land I shall hereinafter give to him.
> Also she is to have Use of West End of my Dwelling House, both above Stairs and Below—her widowhood Household Furniture; use of Kitchen, Oven, Pump use of Garden Place where I live, and as much Cyder as shall be necefsary for her own Family Consumtion. 600 weight of good Pork, 400 Weight of good Beef, Ten Bushels of clean Wheat and Ten Bushels of Rye; Firewood ready Cut and brought to her Door fit for her Room and Use. Also to be kept for her on the Place free of Expence a Riding Horse, two Milch Cow and Six Sheep. These to be attended to by David

Daughters Hannah ⎫ If these daughters remain unmarried at my wife's
           Elizabeth ⎭ death, they are to enjoy all privileges given to their Mother during their unmarried lives. If only one survives the Mother and is unmarried she is to enjoy all above privileges until married.

Sons—John Stokes   My lands and Improvements Lying in Haycock Township, in Bucks Co., Penna., where he now lives, he paying in One year after my Decease to his Mother £100.

> David Stokes—My Land and Plantation Lying to the Southward of a Line Beginning at a Black Oak Corner standing at the North West Corner of that Land which Aaron Wills bought of the Executors of Thomas Green and from thence to run Westward quite acrofs my Lands to a Stone standing as a Corner to my Land, and there being two Corners near together as setled by Arbitration between me and Jonathan Borden, the Westernmost Corner I fix as the Bounds of this Division; also all the Land I hold between the said Line and Ancocus Creek with the Buildings; also all my Cedar Swamp I bought of Executors of John Stockton; also one half of my Cedar Swamp which I bought of Vincent Leeds lying at Mount Skitt; also a large Brafs Kettle; he my son David to pay my wife Hannah £50. in one yr. after my death.

Gervas Stokes—that part of my plantation where he now lives lying Northerly of the above Discribed Line of Division being all my Land between the said Line and Mill Creek with the Buildings and Appurtenances; Also all that my Cedar Swamp I bought of Revel Elton; also one Equal Undivided half part of the Cedar Swamp purchased by me of Vincent Leeds.

4 Daughters—Mary Newton, Hannah Stokes, Elizabeth Stokes, Rachel Hackney — the Residue of my Perſonal Estate after Legacies & Debts are deducted, so that Hannah and Elizabeths shares be equal. Also Mary and Rachels shares be also Equal. But Mary and Rachels share to be Each of them £100. less than Hannah and Elizabeth.

Executors—
My Wife Hannah
Sons— John Stokes, David Stokes, Gervas Stokes

Witnesses, Thomas Buzby, Samuel Kille, Dan[1] Smith

Codicil—dated Aug. 17—1791. Whereas in within Will I ordered my Son John to pay to his Mother £100. in case She was left a Widow, and son David to pay her £50; but as she is deceased, in lieu thereof Son John is to pay my two Daughters Hannah and Elizabeth Stokes each £25, or £50. to the Survivor in case of the decease of Either in one year after my Death; and I order Son David Stokes to pay to said two Daughters each £25; or £50 to Survivor, in case Either dies in one year after my decease. David is to furnish them or the Survivor of them 300 Weight of pork, 300 Weight of Beef Ten Bushels of clean Wheat and Ten Bushels of Rye as long as they are unmarried; one horse—two Milch Cows and Six Sheep, all of their own choosing and kept on the place free from Expence.

John Stokeſ [Seal]

Witnesses: Jonah Woolman, Edith Peddle, Mary Stokes.

Inventory taken September 13th—1798 £2074 " 3 " 1

William Deacon, Samuel Haines — Appraisers.
Affirmed to Sept. 15—1798.

74—RACHEL STOCKDELL (Thomas, 1; Rachel, 4; Mary Allen, 18).

m. 1739, William Wood, son of Constantine Wood,
of Woodbury Creek, Gloucester Co., N. J.
He d. 1762.

172—WILLIAM WOOD, JR.   m. 1777, Hannah Ladd.

173—RACHEL WOOD

174—SARAH WOOD   m. 1773, Samuel Thompson.

175—LETITIA WOOD   m. 1772, James Mickel.

176—ANNA WOOD

William Wood was a great grandson of Henry Wood, founder of Woodbury, N. J.,
who came from Bury, England, with his son John, in 1682, and settled on the stream
which became known as Woodbury Creek. William was the eldest son of Constantine
Wood, who was the third son of John; the latter dying in 1705/6. Constantine, born
in 1683, died 1734, was the first child born of English parents in that vicinity. Henry
Wood and his son John brought with them the following certificate, recorded in Haddonfield Monthly Meeting Book of Certificates, 1681-1741:

The 20th day of ye Second Month 1682 from ye Monthly Meeting att
Clithrice [Clitheroe] in ye County of Lankeshire [Lancashire]
To ffriends in America of ye monthly meeting wheare it may fall to the
Lott of Henry Wood & John Wood his son to inhabit. These may Satisfie
you y^t ye above named Henry Wood & John Wood with their ffamilyes
goeing to those ptes is with consent of ffriends, and we farther sertifie you
y^t ye both have been faithful to the Truth and great sufferers for their
Testimony and are of good report amongst ffriends in several ptes of this
County and in several ptes of this nation, so with our Deare Loves to you,
remembered Desireing your Loving assistance to both these our Deare
ffriends wee rest your ffriends in the truth.

MEETING RECORDS

Haddonfield Minutes of ye Mo: Meeting of Women Friends:
Att a m^{o}ly m^{t}g of wo^m fr^{ds} held at Haddonf^{ld} ye 10th of 10th m^o 1739.
Wm Wood & Rachel Stockdale signified y^r intentions of m^{r}g, E. Ballinger
& M. Wilkins a^{Ptd} to make ye usual inquirie, & report to next m^{t}g.

Att a m^{o}ly m^{t}g of wo^m fr^{ds} held at Haddonfield ye 14th of 11^m 1739/40.
Wm Wood & Rachel Stockdale signified ye continuation of y^r intentions of
m^{r}g, confent of parents being had, & return of inquirers clear, ye m^{t}g
allows y^m, to accomplifh y^r s^d m^{r}g, according to ye good ord^r abovs^d, &
a^{Pts} Eliz Lord & Mary Gibfon, to see good o^{r}ders kept, & report to next m^{t}g.

SUMMARY OF WILL OF WILLIAM WOOD, 1762

The will of William Wood, dated 4 mo. 30, 1762, proved May 26, 1762, shows him to have been a man of large possessions, both real and personal. His wife Rachel and Ebenezer Miller were made exectuors. It was provided that the widow should have the choice of a personal homestead, ten acres and small house, or the use of a portion of the old homestead; this and the plantation being devised to the eldest child and only son, William. The remainder of the real estate was to be sold and proceeds equally divided between the four daughters, with 75 pounds each in money additional. Small legacies were devised to his brother Francis; Constantine Jeffries, son of his sister Leatitia; his niece, Elizabeth Smith, and cousin, Mary Small. Two hired lads were to have a suit of clothes each if they learned a trade, and one five pounds upon attaining his freedom. In case of the son's death, the widow—remaining such—was to have the care of the education of the children and she was to have the residue of income, after other provisions of the will were carried out. The following inventory of personal property makes an interesting and suggestive showing of the affairs of a prosperous farmer and business man of those days.

	£	s	d
To his horse bridle Saddle Wearing Apparel & Cash.........	107—	0—	6
To 9 Feather beds & furniture Desk bookCase & Clock & other household goods	200—	1—	6
To Carts Waggon & Other plantation Utensils with Rye Wheat Indian Corn and Oats on the Ground...................	76—16—		6
To Horses Cattle Sheep and Swine.........................	281—	6—	0
To Bonds Bills and Book Debts out Standing...............	686—	7—	3

James Whitall John Wilkins Appraisers   £1351—12—9

CHEST BROUGHT FROM ENGLAND BY HENRY WOOD, 1682

86—BARZILLAI COATE (Thomas, 1; Rachel, 4; Rebecca Sharp, 21).

    m. 4th mo. 13th, 1768, Elizabeth Stokes, daughter of Samuel and Hannah (Hinchman) Stokes.

    d. 2nd mo. 22nd, 1784.

177—EDITH COATE   m. Mahlon Budd.

178—HANNAH COATE   m. Daniel Smith.

179—WILLIAM COATE   m. Sarah Hollingshead.

89—MARY COATE (Thomas, 1; Rachel, 4; Rebecca Sharp, 21).

    b. 3rd mo. 16th, 1739.

    m. 1761, Joseph Ridgway of Springfield Township, Burlington Co., N. J.

180—ISRAEL RIDGWAY   b. 11th mo. 16th, 1762.
                            d. 1809.

181—SARAH RIDGWAY   b. 6th mo. 17th, 1764.
                            m. 12th mo. 21st, 1785, Isaac Morgan.

182—BEULAH RIDGWAY   b. 3rd mo. 5th, 1766.
                            d. 1835.

183—RACHEL RIDGWAY   b. 12th mo. 31st, 1767.
                            m. June 26th, 1796, John Butterworth.

184—MARY RIDGWAY   b. 12th mo. 11th, 1769.
                            d. 1848.

185—COATES RIDGWAY   b. 7th mo. 30th, 1771.
                            d. 4th mo. 13th, 1816.

186—CATHARINE RIDGWAY   b. 10th mo. 12th, 1773.
                            . First, Samuel Potts.
                            m. Second, Samuel Paxson.

187—ANNA RIDGWAY   b. 12th mo. 24th, 1775.
                            m. Samuel Butterworth.

188—ABIGAIL RIDGWAY   b. 6th mo. 5th, 1778.
                              m. David Bullock.

189—JOSEPH RIDGWAY   b. 6th mo. 8th, 1781.
                              d. 6th mo. 9th, 1781.

90—BEULAH COATE (Thomas, 1; Rachel, 4; Rebecca Sharp, 21).
                  m. 3rd mo. 30th, 1763, John Ridgway.
                  d. 3rd mo. 30th, 1807.

190—WILLIAM C. RIDGWAY

191—EDITH RIDGWAY

192—REBECCA RIDGWAY   m. 7th mo. 19th, 1792, Jeremiah Boone, "Jeweler of Philadelphia."

193—MIRIAM RIDGWAY

194—MARY RIDGWAY.

100—SARAH BROWN (Thomas, 1; Richard, 5; Mary, 25).
                  b. 10th mo. 2nd, 1737.
                  buried 6th mo. 2nd, 1811.
                  m. 11th mo. 11th, 1756, in Chesterfield Meeting, Joseph Scholey of Nottingham Township, Burlington Co., N. J.
            He d. 2nd mo. 10th, 1778.

195—JAMES SCHOLEY   b. 9th mo. 19th, 1757.
                              d. 2nd mo. 25th, 1826.
                              m. 9th mo. 7th, 1786, Mary Rogers, daughter of Isaac and Ann Rogers, of Windsor Township, Middlesex Co., N. J.

196—SAMUEL SCHOLEY   b. 11th mo. 18th, 1759.

197—MARTHA SCHOLEY   b. 5th mo. 18th, 1761.

198—MARY SCHOLEY   b. 7th mo. 24th, 1762.

m. 10th mo. 12th, 1780, Isaac Thorn, son of John Thorn, of Chesterfield Township, Burlington Co., N. J.

199—ANN SCHOLEY   b. 5th mo. 1st, 1766.

200—JOHN SCHOLEY   b. 4th mo. 21st, 1769.

201—RACHEL SCHOLEY   b. 9th mo. 14th, 1770.

103—KEZIAH SHREVE (Thomas, 1; Richard, 5; Rebecca, 26).

b. March 8th, 1730, in Burlington Co., N. J.

m. about 1752, Moses Ivins, son of Isaac Ivins, Sr.

He d. 1803, in Monmouth Co., N. J.

202—CALEB IVINS   b. 12th mo. 14th, 1753.

d. 8th mo. 26th, 1845, in Hornerstown, N. J.

m. Sarah Wright.

She d. 1821.

203—MOSES IVINS

204—SARAH IVINS   m. John Dixon.

205—ISRAEL IVINS   b. 2ud mo. 19th, 1760.

d. 6th mo. 11th, 1822, near Wrightstown, N. J.

m. 1780, Margaret Woodward, daughter of Anthony and Constance (Williams) Woodward.

She b. 11th mo. 12th, 1759.

d. 2ud mo. 17th, 1832.

206—REBECCA IVINS   m. March 20th, 1783, Jonathan Cleaver.

207—LYDIA IVINS   m. Adam Gibbs.

208—ANN IVINS   b. 1st mo. 12th, 1768.

d. 11th mo., 1851.

m. First, Ezra Cook.

m. Second, 1799, Aaron Ivins.

William Cleaver, son of Jonathan and Rebecca (Ivins) Cleaver [206], m. Oct. 9, 1823, Jane W. Thomas, their-daughter Mary m. Sept. 13, 1842, Hugh DeHaven, their son Holstein DeHaven, president, Real Estate Title Ins. & Trust Co., Phila., m. Nov. 12, 1891, Annah B. (Colket) Gallup, widow of Edwin C. Gallup, and daughter of Coffin and Mary Pennypacker (Walker) Colket.

105—CALEB SHREVE (Thomas, 1; Richard, 5; Rebecca, 26).

>   b. 8th mo. 25th, 1734, in Burlington Co., N. J.
>   d. 4th mo. 21st, 1792.
>   m. 11th mo. 19th, 1755, Grace Pancoast, daughter
>   of Thomas and Anne Pancoast.
>   She b. 4th mo. 7th, 1734.
>   d. 5th mo. 23rd, 1806.

209—PHEBE SHREVE

>   b. 5th mo. 12th, 1757.
>   d. 3rd mo. 26th, 1796.
>   m. 1778, Joshua Forsyth.

210—BENJAMIN SHREVE

>   b. July 7th, 1759.
>   d. April 16th, 1844.
>   m. April 13th, 1785, Rebecca Lippincott.
>   She d. 8th mo. 27th, 1821.

211—ANN SHREVE

>   b. 10th mo. 10th, 1763.
>   d. 11th mo. 3rd, 1783.
>   m. 3rd mo. 20th, 1782, Michael Rogers, Jr.,
>   son of Michael and Ann Rogers, of Not-
>   tingham Township, Burlington Co., N. J.
>   He b. 2nd mo. 9th, 1756.

212—REBECCA SHREVE

>   b. 9th mo. 30th, 1764.
>   d. 11th mo. 15th, 1821.
>   m. Isaac Perkins.

213—CALEB SHREVE, JR.

>   b. 10th mo. 30th, 1766.
>   d. 5th mo. 24th, 1836.
>   m. 6th mo. 2nd, 1802, Frances Hunt, daughter
>   of Ralph and Mary Hunt of Lawrence-
>   ville, N. J.
>   She b. 2ud mo. 27th, 1772.
>   d. 2nd mo. 15th, 1862.

214—REUBEN SHREVE

>   b. 8th mo. 16th, 1768.
>   d. 6th mo. 19th, 1841.
>   m. 11th mo. 18th, 1795, Mary Scattergood, of
>   Mansfield Township, Burlington Co., N. J.
>   She b. 3rd mo. 31st, 1773.
>   d. 2nd mo. 12th, 1821.

215—THOMAS SHREVE   b. 9th mo. 1st, 1770.
                                     d. 2nd mo. 17th, 1846, in Cincinnati, Ohio.
                                  m. 11th mo. 5th, 1801, at Indian Springs
                                        Meeting House, Maryland, Ann Hopkins,
                                        daughter of John and Elizabeth (Thomas)
                                        Hopkins, of Baltimore, Md.
                        She b. 2nd mo. 26th, 1775.
                                    d. 12th mo. 12th, 1815.

216—GRACE SHREVE   b. 10th mo. 15th, 1772.
                                     d. 6th mo. 22nd, 1843, unmarried.

217—MARY SHREVE   b. 4th mo. 10th, 1775.
                                     d. 11th mo. 30th, 1777.

CALEB SHREVE

Caleb Shreve took a conspicuous and influential part in public affairs during the critical years when the colonies were struggling for independence. As one of the representatives of Burlington County, he sat in the New Jersey Provincial Congress during its memorable session of 1776, taking an active part in the proceedings and earnestly supporting notable measures proposed by the friends of liberty, though he opposed the adoption of a test vote of allegiance for persons entitled to vote for members of the Assembly at the ensuing fall election. This was the first Assembly of New Jersey to be chosen after the adoption of the new state constitution. He favored a conciliatory policy as far as possible, evidently in accordance with his religious principles, and was fully sustained by his own electorate, through four successive elections to the Assembly. While a member of the Provincial Congress, he voted in favor of permitting paroled persons to secure the return of personal property. July 2, 1776, he voted for the adoption of the new constitution which obliterated colonial government; and on July 17 joined in the unanimous and enthusiastic endorsement of the action of the Continental Congress in declaring the colonies forever free and independent, the resolution passed pledging the members to support "the freedom and independence of the State of New Jersey with our lives and fortunes and the whole force of the State."

As noted, Caleb Shreve was elected a member of the New Jersey Assembly in 1776, 1777, 1778 and 1779. He was also elected 1783 and 1784. His course as a legislator was the same as in the Provincial Congress, independent and conservative. Some of his votes showed remarkable courage, in view of the events of the times and the excited state of the public mind. A notable instance was his recorded opposition to the confirmation of the Council of Safety. Evidently he maintained a high place in public confidence all the while. He prospered greatly in business, the inventory of his personal estate showing a valuation of nearly $12,000. He died in 1792 intestate and his estate was administered by his sons, Benjamin and Caleb.

Although a Friend, himself a non-combatant and a very conservative citizen throughout the Revolution, Caleb Shreve did not escape the consequences of war. Among the claims filed at Trenton for damages by British troops in New Jersey in December, 1776, and June, 1778, is an inventory of losses by Caleb Shreve of money, clothing, saddle, bridle, twelve large silver coat buttons, calves, sheep, geese, ducks, turkeys, fowls, shoes, pewter plates and basins, £43 3s. 0d.

MEETING RECORDS

Chesterfield Monthly Meeting Minutes:

4 mo. 5—1759 This Meeting being inform'd that Caleb [105] and Israel Shrieve [107] has been guilty of Training and William Shrieve [106] married contrary to ye good order and Discipline Established amongst Friends Jonathan Cheshire and Anthony Sykes is desired to let them know if they dont make this Meeting Satisfaction as discipline directs they will be Testify'd against.

8 mo. 5th 1759 Caleb Shrieve laid before this Meeting an Acknowledgment Condemning his being guilty of Training which was read and receiv'd.

3 mo. 6—1777 The Pre Mee of Upper Springfield reports that Caleb Shreve, John Wood, John Black, Joshua Shreve, William Newbold, Jos. Newbold, John Middleton & Wm. Wood, Junr. had been visited on account of being concern'd in Military services, and that they seemed to justify their conduct therefore Joshua Gibbs, Alex. Howard, Wm. Copperthwait & Garvas Pharo are appointed to endeavour by further Christian Labour if possible to bring them to a just sense of their Transgreſsion and report to next Meeting.

7 mo. 3^d 1777 One of the Friends appointed to that service reports that Joseph Newbold has been served with a copy of the Testification of this Meeting against him and he did not intend to appeal, Anthony Sykes and Fretwell Wright are desired to Aſsist them in performing the neceſsary labour and care of the cases of Caleb Shrieve, John Wood & John Middleton and report to next Meeting.

11 mo. 6th 1777 The Friends appointed to that service produced a Testification against Caleb Shreve Junr for acting in or promoting military measures which was read and approv'd and sign'd, and the same Friends are appointed to Read it to him give him a copy if requir'd let him know his right of appeal and report to next meeting.

12 mo 4th 1777 Joseph Forsyth reports he has read friends Testification against Caleb Shreve to let him know his right of appeal.

7 mo. 2^d 1778 Caleb Shreve's Acknowledgment condemning his repaying the money to those who had bought his goods taken for military fines was read and received.

BENJAMIN SHREVE [210]

The patriotic spirit of the Shreve family was manifested throughout the Revolutionary War, as shown by the records in the Adjutant General's office, at Trenton, N. J. In 1779, Benjamin [210], eldest son of Caleb Shreve, with his cousin, presumably Richard [220], son of William Shreve [106], enlisted at Philadelphia and served six months on board a Letter of Marque called the " Trooper," sixteen guns, commanded by Captain Samuel Howell; and afterwards served for a time under Captain Edward Thomas. In the early autumn of 1782, he joined the Company of Light Horse and Infantry, First Regiment, Burlington Co., N. J., Militia, of which William Shreve [106] was Colonel, and Richard Shreve [220] Captain; and was commissioned by Governor Livingston as First Lieutenant. This troop served in an emergency capacity, during times of special danger, until the end of the war, engaging in many skirmishes. On December 26th, 1782, it had a lively encounted with Tory refugees at Cedar Creek, Monmouth County, N. J., where several men were wounded and one killed. On January 6th, 1783, during a skirmish in the same locality, Lieutenant Benjamin Shreve was wounded in the knee, by reason of which he was compelled to retire from the service. He became a Revolutionary pensioner.

Although a mere lad, only sixteen years of age, Caleb Shreve [213], second son of Caleb, served as a private for short periods in his cousin Richard's command. He was reported with the troop on October 13th, 1782; November 5th, 1782, and December 20th, 1782; and took part in the engagement at Cedar Creek, December 26th, 1782. He also served a short time during the early part of 1783.

MEETING RECORDS

Chesterfield Monthly Meeting Minutes:

2 mo. 6th 1783 The Friends appointed report they visited Benjamin Shreve [210] in respest to his bearing Arms in a Military way, he informed them he Expected to continue therein, therefore this Meeting disowns him, the said Benjamin Shreve, from being a Member of our religious Society untill he becomes sensible of his Deviation and condemns the same as discipline directs. William Satterthwaite and Barzillai Furman are appointed to give him a Copy of this Minute, inform him of his right of appeal, and report to next Meeting.

4 mo. 3[d] 1783 The Friends appointed report Benj Shreve hath been served with a Copy of the Minute of the Meeting against him and inform'd of his right of Appeal.

SIGNATURES OF ADMINISTRATORS, ESTATE OF CALEB SHREVE [105]

106—WILLIAM SHREVE (Thomas, 1; Richard, 5; Rebecca, 26).

> b. 8th mo. 4th, 1737, in Burlington Co., N. J.
>
> d. 1812.
>
> m. First, May 8th, 1756, Anna Ivins of Spring-
> field Township, Burlington Co., N. J.
>
> m. Second, 12th mo. 15th, 1768, Rhoda Ivins.
>
> m. Third, February 21st, 1779, Anne Reckless,
> widow of Joseph Reckless, Jr., and daughter of
> Joseph and Hannah Woodward.

218—JEREMIAH WARDER SHREVE

> b. 1757.
>
> m. 1775, Sarah Beck.
>
> d. about 1783, at sea.

219—AMY SHREVE   m. ——— Ridgway.

> d. before 1810.

220—RICHARD SHREVE

> b. 9th mo. 25th, 1760.
>
> d. 9th mo. 12th, 1822, in Bloomfield Town-
> ship, Crawford Co., Penna.
>
> m. 1783, Margaret Newbold, daughter of
> Thomas Newbold.
>
> She b. 5th mo. 26th, 1766.
>
> d. 9th mo. 10th, 1852.

221—ISAAC SHREVE

222—KEZIAH SHREVE

223—SAMUEL SHREVE

224—ANNA SHREVE

> b. 9th mo. 1st, 1773.
>
> d. 12th mo. 20th, 1846, in Belfast, O.
>
> m. Nathan Shumard.

Joseph Reckless, Jr., son of Joseph and Margaret (Satterthwaite) Reckless, was born 3rd mo. 27th, 1722, died 11th mo., 1771. He was a Friend of high standing in the Meeting and in the community in which he resided. Chesterfield Meeting records show that he was frequently appointed on important committees for the consideration of "weighty affairs." From 1750 to 1768 he was clerk of Chesterfield township, N. J. He carried on the milling business at the mill formerly owned by his father, near the present site of Recklesstown, N. J. By his will, dated October 30th, 1771, and proved November 26th, 1771, he devised to his wife Anne rents and profits of his grist mill, houses and land in and about Recklesstown, to bring up and educate their children until the youngest son, Robert, was 21, when the property was to be sold and divided among their five sons, Joseph, Isaac, John, Anthony and Robert. And it was devised that these sons were to have equal share of profits arising from the sale of their father's "half of mill called Chapman's, lot containing one acre near Prince Town, 20 acres at Chees Quakes in the south ward of city of Amboy, 108 acres in Hanover township, Burlington Co., quarter part of a saw mill and Pine land." Wife Anne, Robert Field, Esq., William Wood, yeoman, appointed executors. Inventory of personal estate taken 11th mo. 21st, 1771, amounted to £533, 0s, 6d. Children of Joseph and Anne (Woodward) Reckless were Joseph, born 10th mo. 29th, 1753, died 8th mo. 10th, 1773; Isaac, born 4th mo. 19th, 1755; John, born 12th mo. 30th, 1756; Robert, born 12th mo. 8th, 1758; Anthony, born 8th mo. 13th, 1760; Robert, born 3rd mo. 1st, 1763; Mary, born 1st mo. 10th, 1765.

COLONEL WILLIAM SHREVE

Sharing the military spirit of other members of the family, William Shreve rendered himself amenable to the discipline of the Friends' Society as early as 1759, and was dealt with in that year by the Chesterfield Meeting for "Training," evidently in connection with the French and Indian wars. When the Revolution came on he resumed training. August 26, 1775, he was commissioned Second Major, First Regiment, Burlington County, N. J., Militia. September 28, 1776, he was promoted to First Major; March 15, 1777, Lieutenant Colonel, and April 18, 1778, was made Colonel, continuing to serve when occasion required for several years. In August, 1782, his son Richard [220] was elected Captain of the troop of Light Horse belonging to the same regiment.

Being active in support of the Revolutionary cause, Col. Shreve suffered with many others during the march of the British army through New Jersey in the summer of 1778. His claim for damages, submitted to the State government, showed a total loss, June 23, 1778, of nearly £1,400, including "one dwelling house 24 × 32-1/2 feet, 2 stories, high Seiled & Painted, built in the year 1765."

About the close of the Revolutionary War, Col. Shreve entered mercantile life in Burlington County, but was not successful. On November 2, 1782, he and his wife Anne made an assignment of all their "messuages, lots of ground, lands, tenements, hereditaments and real estate whatsoever and wheresoever situated, moneys, debts, credits, etc. (except Family's wearing apparel)," to three prominent Philadelphia merchants, Jeremiah Warder, Jr., Mordecai Lewis, and Samuel Coates, in trust for his creditors, "anything remaining to be for use of William Shreve and family." On December 12th, 1789, these assignees for "divers sums of money and further sum of £2537—10 shillings conveyed to Moses Ivins 304 acres of land, being the same land and premises which William Shreve and wife Ann conveyed to Jeremiah Warder, Mordecai Lewis and Samuel Coates, Nov. 2, 1782"; showing considerable of an estate for those times. It is not known how much accrued to Col. Shreve after the payment of all obligations, but in 1788 he journeyed to western Pennsylvania with his brother Israel and others. Evidently the prospect was not alluring in that locality, as he returned to Burlington County, N. J., and resumed business there with success. His will, dated May 1, 1810, proved January 1, 1813, disposed of personal estate amounting to $2,043.00. His wife Anne was given the estate that belonged to her at the time of her marriage, and also one half of the real and personal estate of the decedent, after debts and other small legacies were paid. His daughter, Keziah Shreve, received the other half of the property, and her mother's wearing apparel. His other children's share was one hundred dollars each.

VICTIMS OF BRITISH VANDALISM

The ten days' march of the British army from Philadelphia to the upper New Jersey coast was an occasion of great trial and suffering to a large number of helpless people. At Haddonfield, June 18, 1778, Sir Henry Clinton, the Commander-in-Chief, issued a stringent order against disreputable practices, declaring his intention "to execute upon the spot every man maurauding, or who shall quit his post upon the march without permission"; yet at Crosswicks, five days later, June 23, in the orders for the day the following significant statement appeared:

> The Houses of Mrs. Shreve and Mr. Tallman having been burned this morning, the Commander in Chief will (if the destruction of the Houses was intentional) give a reward of 25 Guineas to any one who will discover the person or persons who set fire to the above Houses, so that they may be brought to punishment for an act so disgraceful to the Army. The Commander in Chief gives notice that any person that may hereafter be found committing such disorders will be delivered to the Provost for immediate execution.

While near Freehold, Monmouth County, Sir Henry made his headquarters for the night at a farm house which was completely stripped of furniture and valuables, including clothing, and the inmates subjected to humiliation and suffering. The aged mistress of the plantation, 74 years old, was compelled to spend the night with her servants in the milk house. The stock was stolen and the damage sustained was very great. At Navesink two men were tried for burning a house and barn and acquitted. One woman camp follower was given 100 lashes on the bare back and drummed out of camp for plundering—the only conviction recorded. At Sandy Hook Sir Henry's order of the day (July 5) contained the following humiliating confession:

> The Commander-in-Chief is, though reluctantly, obliged to say that the irregularity of the Army during the march reflected much discredit on that discipline which ought to be the first object of an officer's attention.

Tradition says that during this memorable march the commander-in-chief, upon one occasion at least, set a deplorable example of weakness and fright. This was when he spent the night at Crosswicks, June 23, 1778. He and his staff occupied the Bunting house. Having " dined " beyond his capacity, Sir Henry Clinton was put to bed in a very much demoralized condition. A little later he was the victim of a fearful " nightmare," and rushing downstairs and out the open door, the night being very hot, he was soon floundering in the mud at the border of a little stream near the house. His cries and the excitement which followed, with his rescue, made up a most ridiculous affair. The hostess was compelled to furnish material with which to cleanse the noble Sir Henry and place him in bed again to get calmed down. This story has been preserved in an unpublished manuscript belonging to descendants of the Bunting family.

MEETING RECORDS

Chesterfield Monthly Meeting Minutes:

10 mo. 4th 1759 William Shrieve laid before this Meeting and Acknowledgment Condemning his Training and marrying contrary to good order and Discipline Established among Friends which was read and left for further proof of his conduct. Anthony Sykes is desired to read it at the close of some First Day Meeting before our next Meeting.

11 mo. 1st 1759 Anthony Sykes reports he has read William Shrieves Acknowledgment pursuant to the order of last Meeting.

5 mo. 2^d 1776 Anthony Sykes informs the Meeting that William Shreeve and Barzillai Newbold had been concerned in Military services that they have been Treated with and are not disposed to condemn the same Samuel Black and Samuel Satterthwaite are appointed to let them know that unlefs they condemn their said Transgrefsion to the satisfaction of the Meeting they will be disowned agreeable to Discipline.

6 mo. 6th 1776 The friends appointed to acquaint William Shreeve and Barzillai Newbold of the complaint against them for acting in Military Services report they have had an opportunity with them and they did not appear in a disposition of condemning their conduct therein. Therefore this Meeting disowns the said William Shreeve and Barzillai Newbold from being members of our Religious Society until they come to a sense of their misconduct and forsake it and condemn the same as our Discipline directs Richard Way Furman and Joseph Forsyth are appointed to serve them with a copy of this Minute let them know their right of appeal and report to next Meeting.

7 mo. 4th 1776 One of the friends appointed to serve William Shreeve and Barzillai Newbold with a Copy of the Minute of the Meeting against them report it has been done and they did not either of them intend to appeal.

REVOLUTIONARY DOCUMENTS

To His Excellency the Governor William Livingston Esqr Commander in Chief of the Militia of this State in New Jersey—
Agreeable to a State Law of this State for raising a Company of Light Horse to belong to the first Regiment of Burlington County Militia Commanded by Col. William Shreve to be Raised in the Several Townfhips of Chesterfield, Mansfield & Springfield & Hanover the different Inhabitants was notified to meet at the House of Solomon Rockhill in Mansfield Township the Majority then meet by plurality of voices did Ellect for Capt. Richard Shreeve [220] for Lieu^t Benjn Shreve [210] for Coronet John Brown Jr. which we beg your Honour will grant Commifsions for the fame.
Signed by order of the Company Aug 7, 1782   James Fenimore Clk.

State of New Jersey To Doct^r Aaron Swain Dr.
Dec 28 1782.
To attendance on Robt Reckless a wounded Soldier Belonging to Capt. Richd Shreves Company of Horse from the first Rigement of Burlington County Melitia at a Scurmish at Ceder Creeke in the County of Monmouth from Dec 28—1782 to Jany 10th 1783   Amount £18—10—6

I do certify that the Above named Person Robert Recklefs Was in Publick Service When Wounded Under my Command ye 27th of December 1782.
Richard Shreve Capt.

20

"PETTICOAT BRIDGE"

The section of Burlington County through which the British army passed on its march from Philadelphia to New York in the summer of 1778, was the scene of many stirring incidents. The struggling patriots destroyed bridges, obstructed roads and harassed the enemy in many ways. The English commander, Sir Henry Clinton, complained bitterly of this in his communications to his friends in New York, and officially magnified the strength of his opponents. At the crossing of Assissicunk creek, near Jacksonville, a bridge was burned. Great public inconvenience resulted and while most of the able-bodied men of the vicinity were absent, tories in hiding or following the enemy, and members of the militia on duty elsewhere, a band of sturdy women, wives and daughters of the continental soldiers, turned out and put up a temporary structure, which on account of this manifestation of patriotic energy, suggestively became known as "Petticoat Bridge." In the accompanying picture part of the old timbers may be seen under the new iron bridge. For more than a century local fire-side tales relating to this instance of the courage and energy of the women of revolutionary days, have been a feature of many family and social gatherings. Homesteads of the Shreve, Newbold, Reckless, French, Black and many other noted families were in this neighborhood and the damage done by the maurauding English troops was very great.

" PETTICOAT BRIDGE "

107—ISRAEL SHREVE (Thomas, 1; Richard, 5; Rebecca, 26).

- b. 12th mo. 24th, 1739, in Mansfield Township, Burlington Co., N. J.
- d. 12th mo. 14th, 1799, in Fayette County, Penna.
- m. First, 2nd mo. 1760, Grace Curtis of Burlington Co., N. J.
- She d. 12th mo. 12th, 1771.
- m. Second, 5th mo. 10th, 1773, Mary Cokley; Rev. Jacob Duche performing ceremony; Christ Church record, Philadelphia.
- She b. 8th mo. 17th, 1749, in Amity Township, Berks Co., Pa.

225—JOHN SHREVE

- b. 4th mo. 8th, 1762.
- d. 9th mo. 8th, 1854, in Alliance, Ohio.
- m. September 9th, 1786, Abigail Ridgway, daughter of Solomon and Mary Ridgway, of Burlington Co., N. J.
- She b. 1st mo. 4th, 1765.
- d. 6th mo. 4th, 1808.

226—ELIZABETH SHREVE

- b. 5th mo. 11th, 1765.
- d. 1769.

227—SARAH SHREVE

- b. 1769.
- d. 1769.

228—KEZIAH SHREVE

- b. 6th mo. 4th, 1771.
- d. 4th mo. 14th, 1834.
- m. 1791, Thomas Stevens.

Children of Israel and Mary (Cokley) Shreve

229—ESTHER SHREVE

- b. 8th mo. 11th, 1774.
- d. 8th mo. 8th, 1837, in Belmont Co., Ohio.
- m. 12th mo. 29th, 1790, William Briggs, son of Job and Hannah Briggs, of Fayette Co., Penna.

230—ISRAEL SHREVE, JR.

- b. 9th mo. 11th, 1778.
- d. unmarried.

231—GEORGE GREENE SHREVE
>   b. 10th mo. 14th, 1780.
>   Went to China and never heard from.

232—REBECCA SHREVE
>   b. 5th mo. 14th, 1783.
>   d. 1st mo. 23rd, 1868, in Louisville, Ky.
>   m. First, 7th mo. 24th, 1804, Fergus Moore-
>   head, of Fayette Co., Penna.
>   m. Second, James C. Blair, of Louisville, Ky.

233—HENRY MILLER SHREVE
>   b. 10th mo. 21st, 1785.
>   d. 3rd mo. 7th, 1851, in St. Louis, Mo.
>   m. First, 2ud mo. 28th, 1811, Mary Blair, of
>   Brownsville, Penna.
>   m. Second, Lydia Ann Rogers.

234—BENJAMIN SHREVE
>   b. 5th mo. 27th, 1787.
>   d. 11th mo. 11th, 1824, at sea.
>   m. Elizabeth ———.

235—MARY SHREVE
>   b. 2nd mo. 24th, 1792.
>   m. William McMillin.

236—CALEB SHREVE

COLONEL ISRAEL SHREVE

In the vigor of his young manhood Israel Shreve took an active part in the military affairs of the colony. Before the outbreak of hostilities in the war for independence he served for a time as Colonel of the First Battalion, Gloucester County Militia. When the New Jersey Continental line was first organized he was commissioned, November 8, 1775, Lieutenant Colonel of the Second Battalion Infantry. The officer in command was Colonel William Maxwell, who throughout the Revolutionary struggle commanded the famous New Jersey brigade that bore his name. These troops were enlisted for one year and rendered conspicuous service in the campaign of 1776, in northern New York and Canada, taking part in the siege of Quebec and the battle of Three Rivers. At the expiration of their term of service they were discharged and the second New Jersey Continental line recruited. In a letter, dated Point Independence, October 18, 1776, Gen. Maxwell, addressing Gov. Livingston and the New Jersey Legislature, said:

" I have the pleasure to inform you that I have as good a set of officers as any battalion in the Continental service and they will make good soldiers. I beg leave in a particular manner to recommend to your notice Col. Shreve. He has been very attentive to getting a thorough knowledge of his duty. Although I must regret his absence from any regiment I should have the honor to command, yet I cannot refrain from doing him the justice to recommend him to you as fit for first preferment in these battalions, or to command the fourth to be raised."

In accordance with this flattering testimonial from his superior officer, Colonel Shreve, November 28, 1776, was commissioned Colonel of the Second Battalion, enlisted for the war. In this capacity he participated in the campaign of the following year, taking part in engagements at Ash Swamp, near Woodbridge, New Jersey, May 31, 1777; Short Hills, N. J., June 26, 1777, and the battle of Brandywine, Pennsylvania, September 11, 1777, where he was severely wounded. Upon his recovery Col. Shreve, with his son John, a brave lad who accompanied him in several campaigns, joined the army at Valley Forge, sharing the terrible privations endured by the patriot soldiers during that memorable encampment. In the spring of 1778 his command was ordered to join the forces in West Jersey, where British troops were constantly raiding the inhabitants.

April 21, Col. Shreve was at Haddonfield. At midnight a detachment of the enemy, 1,400 strong, crossed from Philadelphia to Gloucester and stealthily marched to Haddonfield. Vigilant watch was kept, however, and the little band of American soldiers, at 3 o'clock on Sunday morning, the 22nd, escaped to Mt. Holly. Three dilatory men were overtaken and bayoneted. The enemy " gasconaded through the village," terrorizing the helpless residents, thus expressing their wrathful disappointment, and then returned at daylight to Philadelphia. This incident illustrated Col. Shreve's watchfulness and readiness in emergencies. His command was with the detachment of the American forces, under Gen. Maxwell, which harrassed the army of Gen. Clinton on its last march through New Jersey and was at the lively skirmish near Crosswicks, Burlington County, June 21, 1778. Pushing on, the battalion was at the battle of Monmouth, June 28, 1778. During the march of the British through the neighborhood of Col. Shreve's home they burned his house and destroyed the crops.

In the campaign of 1779, against the hostile Indians in Pennsylvania and New York, Col. Shreve and his battalion were active and efficient, this ser-

vice extending from May until November. In the spring of 1780 they
helped to drive the enemy from northern and eastern Jersey, taking part in
engagements at Connecticut Farms, June 7, and Springfield, June 23. In
his report of the operations around Springfield, Gen. Nathaniel Greene,
under date of June 23, 1780, said:

"Col. Shreve was stationed at the second bridge, to cover the retreat of
the first line. Here the enemy were warmly received, but as they advanced
in great force, with a large train of artillery, he had orders to join the
brigade. The troops that were engaged behaved with great coolness and
intrepidity, and the whole of them discovered an impatience to be brought
into action. The order and discipline which they exhibit do them highest
honor."

September 26, 1780, Col. Shreve was appointed to the command of the
Second Regiment of the Continental Line, and for a time commanded the
New Jersey brigade at West Point, during the critical period of Arnold's
treachery. He was placed in personal charge of the detachment which sur-
rounded the guard at Major Andre's execution. Upon the reorganization
of the army, about the 1st of January, 1781, he retired from active service,
but not until he had undergone a painful experience and given a renewed
manifestation of his loyalty and zeal. He had always set a conspicuous
example of unselfish devotion to the cause of freedom. Upon one occasion,
when a large number of the line and company officers of the New Jersey
brigade had signed and forwarded to the Legislature an earnest protest and
demand, concerning their long neglected pay, he declined to join them.
Washington was exceedingly stirred up and made a strong appeal to the
patriotism of the petitioners, promising that their wrongs should be righted,
but begging them not to leave the service at that critical hour, as they had
declared their intention of doing. The matter was adjusted. In January,
1781, several hundred private soldiers of the New Jersey line mutinied.
Their grievances were many. Col. Shreve went about amongst them and
did all he could to quell the revolt. He largely succeeded, but three ring-
leaders persisted in making trouble and two of these were tried by court
martial and shot.

Col. Shreve made large sacrifices during the war and his personal affairs
were in an unhappy condition, after six years continuous and faithful service.
Upon his retirement from the army, however, he was called upon to take up
the responsibilities of civil government, as a member of the legislature from

Burlington County, 1781–83. Some years later, in 1788, he removed with his family to southwestern Pennsylvania, locating on a tract of land in Fayette County surveyed by Washington some twenty-five years before and then owned by him, from whom it was first rented on advantageous terms and afterwards purchased. His will, made a few days before his death, and herewith published, directed final payment on this land to Gen. Washington. Further interesting papers relate incidents in the eventful life of this notable member of one of the pioneer families of New Jersey, many of whom partook of his patriotic and intrepid spirit. It was a singular coincidence that he died the same day that Washington passed away, December 14, 1799.

Col. Shreve's fourth son, Henry M., was distinguished for his improvements in steamboats in use on the western rivers and the invention of practical devices for clearing those great streams of the accumulated obstructions of centuries. Fifty years after his death, Congress granted his heirs the sum of $50,000 for this great service. Shreveport, La., was named for him.

LETTERS OF COL. ISRAEL SHREVE TO HIS SON JOHN SHREVE

Dear Son   Sorel, 12th June 1776.

You and Samuel Shute are to Go off home with Lieut Anderson, you are to take your Guns and Acutrements, your Blankets, and all your Cloathing. Git Ready as soon as possable, it is Better for you to Go than stay—John is to Go home to philadelphia—Stay there or Go up to his unkle Caleb—Go to School keep With Mr. Anderson untill you Git home Keep Samuel Shute at your mothers untill he can Git an oppertunity to Go home in some Market Waggon, be kind to your Mother and Sisters keep out of all bad Company. Go up to your Unkles when your Mother Orders you I have sent a Letter to John Stilley, one to your Unkle Caleb and one to your Mother, they are all three foalded up together and Directed to Mr. John Stilley when you Git home Deliver them to the Owners, take a Pillow Case to put your Cloathes In. Lieve my Chest in the Care of Doctor holms and Thomas Smith. Lieve the Key.—Both of you be Cheerful and set off as it is my and Capt. Shutes Commands. Anderson has money for Johns Expenses be Good Lads and I hope you will farewell Dont think hard but Go off amediately   I am your father

Israel Shreve

P. S. Keep this Letter it will Do for a pass when you Git home show it to your mother. If you are a Good Lad If I live you shall Go With Me Next Campain.

Mount Independance 25th August 1776.

Dear Son

I have the pleasure to Inform you that your Comarade Samuel Shute was yesterday appointed Ensign In Capt. Dillons Company (Write him a Letter, according to the form I here send you) My son Spend not one moment in Vain Your Mother Informs me you are at a Good School. Do all you Can to Learn, you are not to join the Regt untill we Come home which Will be some time in November. Consider now you are an officer in the Army of the United States of America. I Wrote that you Was appointed Ensign in Capt Brearley's Company a month ago to Day.— Strive to be as Good a Scholar and Soldier as Mr. Ensign Saml Shute, he is to go to School untill we Come home,—Spend not your time playing on the Streets With Mischevious Boys But Study to be the Scholar and the Soldier. Be Dutiful to your Mother, and kind to your Sisters. I have Wrote to your Unkle William to Let your Couzen Richard Shreve, Come out With me next Campaign. My Love to you hoping to here of your Welfare,—I am With Great tenderness and Respect your

Father Israel Shreve

P. S. Lt. John Higgins Died at Crown point we here nothing of Lt. Friese Read

I. S.

AN EMPHATIC ORDER FOR FORAGE

Sir,

Quarter Maſter Banks Informs me you Refuſe to Let him have forage on my order.

Col. furman told me he had placed you there to purchase forage and Deſired Me to Call on you when I wanted. An order from him is not Material. As I Command him And you, when in the Limits of My Command. I know you have grain at Several places And if you Re [parts of several lines here torn from manuscript] order I shall send for you and [————] you for Diſobedience of Order and take the grain. Your Compliance will prevent You and me trouble

I am your Moſt Hum[l]

Serv[t] I Shreve Col. Comd[r]

Newark March 25th 1779
　　to Mr. Safern.

COL. SHREVE'S JOURNEY TO WESTERN PENNSYLVANIA

The following is the journal of travel of Col. Israel Shreve and relatives and friends from New Jersey to Western Pennsylvania, 1788:

Journal of travel from Township of Mansfield, county of Burlington in the State of New Jersey, to the Township of Rostrover in the County of Westmoreland, State of Pennsylvania, of party consisting of Israel Shreve and Mary, his wife, with their children, Kezia, Hesther, Israel, George Greene, Rebecca and Henry; John Fox and James Starkey; three two horse waggons and three Cows. William Shreve and wife, with their children, Anna and Richard. Joseph Beck and Sarah, his wife, with their children, Benjamin, Rebecca, Elizabeth, Henry, Joseph and Ann; with one three horse waggon. Daniel Hervey and Sarah, his wife, and their child, Job, with a Mulatto Boy named Thomas; and Joseph and Ann Wheatly; John Shelvill; one three and one two horse Waggon and one cow. In all 29 Souls.

Monday the 7th of July, 1788—Set out and crossed the Delaware at Donkses Ferry where we parted with a Number of our Relations and friends who had accompanied us and continued on to the Sign of General Washington, 17-½ miles to-day, here staid all night, Rainy in the Night.

Tuesday the 8th of July—Set out early, halted in the City of Philadelphia several hours getting necessaries; Left the City and passed the Schuylkill over a Bridge at the Middle Ferry, halted on the Hill on the other Side. Set out again and Halted at the Sign of the Buck 21 miles to day, Stayed all Night.

Wednesday the 9th July—Set out at Sunrise, Daniel Harvey and wife being unwell halted and breakfasted at the Sign of the Spread Eagle, here for the first time in our Journey boiled the Tea Kettle, Set out again hindered by having two horse shoes put on, hard showers of Rain to-day, halted at Downington, 22 Miles to-day, Stayed all Night.

Thursday the 10th July—Set out again hindered some time getting forage at a Mill, went on over exceedingly muddy bad roads, halted and dined at Caleb Ways, here perceived the Black mare badly foundered, drenched her with salt and water and sent her to the light waggon, went on and halted at the Sign of the Marriner's Compass, kept by a Mr. Taylor, in Pequa Valley, 13-½ Miles to-day only, occasioned by Bad Roads and crossing the South Mountain and one of my waggons drove by James Starkey oversetting bottom upwards, to day the women were much fatigued by walking, Sarah Hervey walked eight and a half miles over the Hill at one heat.

Friday the 11th July—Set out and passed over Roads full of bad Mud-holes, halted and breakfasted at the Sign of the Hat kept by Andrew Coldwell, hindered this morning by getting clasps put round the felloe of a wheel, went on over muddy roads to George Prisly at the head of the Great Spring, Sign of the Bird in Hand and dined. Set out again and crossed the Canestoga Creek within two miles of Lancaster—17 miles to day, all cherry and in high spirits, stayed all night, it being the height of harvest, took particular notice of the wheat which is bad in general so far, being killed by the severity of the weather, and much mildewed.

Saturday the 12th July—Set out Early and halted some time in Lancaster, had one new horse shoe put on. Drove out of town and break-fasted late—went on, halted at Scotts Mill and dined in the woods, went on again and were obliged to halt at a Private House, paraded our beds in a barn, this did not set well. Daniel went on to Elizabethtown in the Night, 16 miles to day.

Sunday 13th July—Set out and halted at Alexander Boggs; at the Sign of the Bear in Elizabethtown, 4 miles to day; Here John Gaston and Wife overtook us on their way home to the Monongahala River.

Monday the 14th July—Set out at Sunrise, halted and breakfasted at Middletown; we are now in sight of the Susquahanna River; went on to the Chambers Ferry crossed over to Captain Simpsons,—Set out again and forded a rapid Creek called Yellow Breeches,—very mirey roads—halted at Pattersons Tavern, 8 miles to day, stayed all night—here is good level land; the wheat along the road from Lancaster to the Susquahanna, appears to have plenty of straw but is much mildewed and rusty.

Tuesday the 15th July—Set out again passed over exceedingly good level land and halted at Carlisle and dined—here lost my Dog—Set out again and passed over level roads full of bad mudholes, halted at Robert Simples Tavern, 22 miles to day—Rainy night.

Wednesday 16th July—Set out and halted at Mr. Cracken's Tavern at the head of the Great Spring and breakfasted, Road something better than yesterday, went on to Shippensburg, there halted and dined at Capt Scotts Tavern,—(when we dined at Taverns we always made use of our own provisions.) Set out again in a hard rain, by advice took the right hand road that leads over the three hills, lately opened and made by a Mr. Skinner from Jersey, halted at Joseph Fenleys Tavern at the Sign of the Ball, 19 miles to-day, a rainy night, Roads level but muddy in places to day.

Thursday 17th July—Set out and halted at Coopers Tavern at the foot of the first hill called the Blue mountain and breakfasted, all in good health and high spirits. Crops from the Susquahanna to this place exceedingly good and plenty, free from mildew and rust, then ends the good land until over all the hills except in spots, and here began sorrow. Set out and ascended the first Mountain so steep that we were obliged to double the teams to get up and very stony going down the other side, in this valley crossed a Creek called Cannogoguinop, halted at said Mr. Skinners who made the road, A hard rain coming on and our horses much worried we stopped the afternoon, 8 miles to day, stayed all night. Here Joseph Becks daughter Ann was taken sick.

Friday 18th July—Set out again and rose the second hill called the North Mountain, this as steep and stony as the first at the west fort forded a Creek in Path Valley, went on and halted at a Tavern, the Landlord drunk, a man who calls himself Noble with the Landlady on the Bed nursing the Landlord who was fast asleep;—this place affords neither forage nor water and whiskey nearly out. Coming down the last Hill Daniel Hervey left his stallion to follow the waggon, the horse took an old path and caused several hours search before he was found stripped of all his gears but the collar, consisting of a new blind bridle, a pair of leather lines, harnes, back and belly bands, and one iron trace the other having been taken to lock the waggon—about 2 o'clock in the afternoon set out and ascended the third hill called the Tuscarora Mountain which is much steeper than the other. At or near the top there are several Cabins, in one lives or stays an old woman who appears to be very sick and in distress. At the West fort of this third Hill is a good farm—Went on a mile farther to Mr. Gimmersons who keeps a Tavern and Store of Goods which he sells as cheap for hard cash as such Goods are sold in Jersey for paper money. Here had the misfortune to break one of my Waggon wheels, sent it on five miles this evening to be repaired, 8 miles only to-day: This is the place called the Burnt Cabins, where the old road that passes through Chambers Town comes into the old Road said to be twenty miles farther than the new one but much better and shuns two of the three Hills just mentioned. Our women complain heavily on account of being obliged to walk on foot over the Mountain.

Saturday 19th July—About eleven o'clock set out all but the disabled Waggon and passed over barren sideling roads, halted at Capt Birds at fort Littleton, 5 miles to day, one or two pretty good farms in this valley, here stayed for the Waggon wheel which was not finished until evening.

Sunday 20th July—Sent the repaired wheel to the Waggon, About eleven o'clock had a further hindrance by having three horse shoes put on, Set out and passed over barren roads good but much gullied, halted in the woods at a Run of Good Water at the foot of Sideling Hill, 13 miles to day, stayed all night, heavy complaints among the Women.

Monday 21st July—Set out and ascended Sideling Hill up a good new Road made by said Skinner, halted on the top and breakfasted at Henry Livingstons Tavern, went on over exceedingly stony Roads to Rays Hill, here cut saplings and chained to our Waggons, this hill steep, gullied, and very stony, Skinners men at work making a new Road down, we continued on to the crossings of the Juneatto, forded the River, halted on the Hill at a Colonel Martins Tavern, Land Lord nor Lady at home, no feed but

2 Rye sheaves cut up for which I paid 9d, the girls of the House very
uncouth and surly; went on and halted at Cabin Tavern kept by a Jersey
Dutchman; 12 miles to-day. Road from Martins barren and bad sideling
hill; one felloe of one of my Waggons gave way, Mr. Shreve put in a
new one.

Tuesday 22nd July—Set out after breakfast, went on and passed through
Bedford, halted for a horse shoe, went on four miles further and halted at
John Bonnets Tavern at the forks of the Old Pennsylvania and Glade
Roads, 15 miles today, Here is an excellent farm with more than one hun-
dred acres of the best Meadow land. Joseph Becks child very ill, stayed
here all night.

Wednesday 23rd July—Set out late in the morning, went over a poor
country and in the evening halted at a poor Dutch Hut where the Landlady was very angry with D. H. for pulling a radish. No feed at this
Tavern nor anything else but whiskey, 13 miles to day. The gnats very
bad here.

Thursday 24th July—Set out and passed on five miles to the foot of the
Allagana Mountain, having now passed twelve miles along Dry Ridge and
seen but two or three houses which are very poor,—went on and ascended
the mountain which is nothing of a Hill to what we have passed, halted
and dined a little off the road on the Hill, very rainy, we then proceeded
on from the Allagana one mile into the Glades and halted at Christian
Spikers where we stayed the remainder of the Day on account of the
illness of the child, 13 miles to day;—About eleven o'clock this evening,
Ann Beck doughter of Joseph Beck departed this life to the great grief of
her parents, more so on account of being far distant from their former
home.

Friday 25th July—Sent to Berlin for a Coffin which arrived towards
Evening when the child was decently interred in Mr. Spikers family Burying ground. Stayed here all night again. Still raining by spells.

Saturday 26th July—Hired George Pancakee and two horses to put
before my heaviest Waggon for 8—4 per day and find him and horses. Set
out, halted at a Blacksmith, had two clasps put on my Waggon wheel and
one horse shoe put on—Set out and halted at Mr. Blacks, here is a family
waiting for Judsims, [Judge John C. Symmes] went on taking a right hand
road at an empty Cabin on account of the other Road being cut so much
by heavily loaded Waggons, halted and dined at one Jacob Louts, went on
and halted at a Dunker called Perkeys, 15 miles to day. The land in the
Glades on the Roads we have passed poor.

Sunday 27th July—Set out and after going a few hundred yards missed
the most material part of Daniel Herveys property, it having gone before
and taken a wrong road, a hue and cry was raised when to his great joy
it was found unhurt. We passed on and began to rise Laurel Hill, halted
and breakfasted at a run of Water. Set out again and ascended to the top

of the Mountain over miry and stony Roads, then soon began to descend, first down a short steep hill, then a long gradual descent through Chestnut Brush, the timber appearing to have been killed by fire sometime before, huckle berries here as well as in many places before very plainly on the low green bushes,—this Road down is over logs and stones enough to dash all to pieces: At length we arrived at a house in Legenear Valley it being Sunday and rain coming on we stayed the afternoon and all night. Our women exceedingly fatigued by walking over the Mountain.

Monday 28th—Set out and after passing three miles halted and break-fasted. Set out again and found the steepest hill we had met with, in going up Chestnut Hill were obliged to put six horses to some of the heaviest waggons. Raining hard—Descend the Ridge and came into the other road which is so miry as to sink the Waggons to the hubs in many places, stopped at a Blacksmiths and had one shoe put on one of my horses. Set out again and met Joseph Wood on his way to Jersey from Little Kenhaway, he informed me that a house was ready for me in the forks of Youghaina, went on and was overtaken by John Fox with the intelligence that one of Daniel Herveys Waggons had broken down. I halted at John Bennetts junior it being the first house over all the mountain. In the evening all the waggons arrived less Daniel Herveys two. 12 miles today—D. Harvey last evening in coming from his Waggon to Mr. Bennetts, got out of the Road; it being very dark he could not find it again and was forced to take up his lodging in the Woods until day. Sarah Harvey and Sarah Beck walked six miles over very bad Roads this afternoon and arrived much wearied.

Tuesday 29th July—Sent for D. Harveys broken waggon and got a new axle-tree put in. We are now clear of the Mountains over which we have with much difficulty got so far safely except the misfortune of losing the child. The Allagania mountain, the Back Bone of America or the United States, is easy to ascend, being a long gradual ascent up Dry Ridge. Upon it, especially on the East side are very large white pines in great plenty; the Glade is a high country or piece of land 18 miles wide:—Between this and the Laurel mountain the road for many miles is through chestnut Timber, such I never before saw for size and height—In many places as many rails could be cut on an acre as could be got out of the best Cedar Swamp in Jersey. The land is of little value but for timber.

Wednesday 30th July—Set out halted and breakfasted at Mr. Robesons, went on through a settlement on good level land for this country, stopped and dined within four miles of Budds Ferry, here found a Mr. Brunt with a large family from Hunterdon in Jersey bound for Kentucky, went two miles further and found Moses Juttle waiting for Judge Symmes, went on again and forded Youghagaina River, the water being so high as to come into some of the waggons that happened to drive a little amiss—Halted and stayed all night at Budd's Ferry—14 miles to day—We are now in the forks—Here I received Colonel Bayard's letter of instructions where to find the house prepared for me.

Thursday, 31st July—Set out, and halted at Capt. Petersons, where Cawet [Carrs] formerly lived; went on, and took the Elizabethtown Road for several miles, when all the waggons left me and turned off to the right hand near the meeting house to Asher Williams. I went on with my family, and turned to the left of Mr. Walter Walls. A hard rain coming on, and the road difficult to find, I stayed the afternoon and all night. Mr. Wall is a Jerseyman, and very kind.

Friday, 1st August—Set out. Mr. Wall sent his son James as a guide with me; after going a mile or two, met Mr. Joseph Lemmon, the owner of the house I was going to, with Mr. Taylor. Walter Carr also accompanied us, with several others, to our new habitation, where we arrived about one o'clock in the afternoon—All well, after a very fatigueing journey of 25 days since leaving Jersey. The house provided for me is a new one,. 30 feet by 26, two stories high, built of hewed white oak Logs, with a very good stone chimney. The house is not finished, no family having lived in it until we came. We set to, stopped it with lime and clay, laid the upper floor with Chirety [cherry] boards, and it is now pretty comfortable for Summer.—There is a Spring of good water within about five rods of the door.

I have the privilege of pasture and fourteen acres of good land to sow this fall with wheat, and plenty of apples for house use, &c. &c.

I have ridden over some of the neighborhood, and must say that the land in general is exceedingly good, producing excellent crops of grain—Many parts are too rich for wheat, though the crops in general are good. Indian corn in some places is excellent, in other fields it has been hurt by the wet season—All that truth can say against the place is that the land in general is hilly, though even the sides of the hills are very rich, producing Walnut, Sugar Trees, Ash, with a variety of other woods, &c.—As to the inhabitants, they are mostly from Jersey, very kind to new comers, as well as to one another; they live in a plain way, not spending much in Dress and foppery, but are well provided with the real necessaries of life.

Israel Shreve

Rostrover Township, Westmoreland County, Pennsylvania,
    August 10th, 1788.

By Jacob Keelor, who faithfully discharged his duty in carefully driving a waggon.

LETTER OF COL. ISRAEL SHREVE TO HIS BROTHER CALEB SHREVE

Forks of Yough, Decr. 26th, 1789.

Dear Brother:

Having an opportunity to Philada., I embrace it, and mention my situation or intended one. Since I have been here have wished to get Washington's Bottoms, and have at last obtained the whole tract on rent for five years. I wrote to the General by his Agent in this County, Colonel Canon, who a few weeks ago returned from New York; the General was pleased to order Colonel Canon to let me have the whole of the Bottoms so called at my own offer.—The old farm contains about 80 acres of improved upland and about 40 of the best kind of meadow, a bearing orchard of 120 apple & 100 peach trees; the buildings as good as most in this Country—pretty well situated, and five other improved farms that at this time rent for £43—10—I am accountable for the whole rent, which altogether is £60—so that I shall have the old place for £16—10, to be paid either in money or wheat at 3/ per Bushel.

I considered this land at the Miami Settlement was rising fast, and that I had better pay this low rent for a well improved farm than barter away my land at a low rate for land here—Land does not rise much in this place, owing to the great emigration down the River. It seems as if people were crazy to get afloat on the Ohio· Many leave very good livings here, and set out for they know not where, but too often find their mistake. I believe this as good as any of the settlements down the River for the present. The Mississippi trade is open at this time, and all the Wheat, Whiskey, Bacon, &c., buying up by those concerned in it; the highest price for Wheat is 4/ in trade, or 3/.9. cash, whiskey, 3/. cash, and Bacon, 9d. p. lb. cash, &c.

On the farm where I am going is as good a stream for a Grist Mill as any in the whole forks, and a Mill that can be set going for, I believe, £50, and a number of years given for the repairs. I am in hopes of being able to set it going as it will produce more grain than all six farms on the tract.

I am to have possession the first of April next—and flatter myself I have as good a chance as any person in my circumstances could expect—I shall have nothing to attend to but my own private concerns—and think this way of life far preferable to any other.—Richard Shreve is to have one of the small farms; they contain of improved land as follows: one, 40 acres upland and 5 good meadow; one, 35 acres upland and 7 good meadow; one, about 35 acres upland and 6 good meadow; the other two about 25 acres upland and 5 or 6 of good meadow each; the whole in fences, they being the year before last rented for repairs only, &c. Peggy Shreve has a daughter; she and her husband have been very sickly this last fall, but have recovered. I am grandfather to another son;—John and his wife pretty well, as is our family at present, but expect the measles, as it is in

the school where our boys go. I hope you are all well also—I am, with
great respect and love,   Your Brother,

                                                    Israel Shreve

To Caleb Shreve, Esquire,
     Mansfield, Burlington County, New Jersey.

     favd. by   To be left at Charles French's, merchant,
Mr. Richard Jones   next door to Old Ferry, Philada.

WILL OF COL. ISRAEL SHREVE, 1799

     In the Name of God Amen I Israel Shreve of the Township of Franklin
County of Fayette and Commonwealth of Pennsylvania Being very weak in
body but in perfect sound mind & memory do make this my last Will and
Testament in manner following first I order all my funeral charges and
just debts fully paid by my Executor hereinafter named, Item I, Give &
bequeath to my beloved wife Mary One thousand Dollars in full for her
Dowry & share of said estate Item I give & bequeath to my sons George
Henry & Benjamin One hundred fifty Acres of Land each George to have
where Laphin lives, Henry where Spencer lives Benjamin where I live
I give and bequeath unto my daughter Rebeckah and Mary each Two hundred dollars I give and bequeath unto my son John & Israel one hundred
dollars each I give and bequeath unto my Daughters Kiziah and Esther
one hundred dollars each I do hereby nominate and appoint my trusty
friends Edward Cook John Shreve and Richard Noble to be my Executors
to this my last will and testament I do hereby order and fully Otherwise
my said Executors to sell and dispose of all the Residue of my Estate both
Real and Personal and money arising therefrom together with my out
standing debts to be apropriated to the payment of my Funeral Charges
& out standing debts and legasies and the over plus if any there be to be
divided equally amongst my wife and children I do hereby order and
request my said Executors to call upon George Washington and pay his
Demand or due with the first money that comes into their hands belonging
to said Estate and obtain a title for said land according to his Article and
when such Deed is obtained to execute Deeds to all such as I have heretofore sold to according to their Articles takeing care to obtain payments
from them as soon as it may be had I do give and bequeath unto my
beloved wife Mary my son Benjamins Part of land to her use unto he is
of age I do hereby submit this my last Will and Testament unto the judgment and management of my said Executors relying on their fidelity and
good conduct as WITNESS my hand seal this ninth day of December in
the year of our Lord one thousand seven hundred and ninety and nine

LIEUTENANT JOHN SHREVE [225]

Many youthful soldiers took part in the war for independence, none making a more commendable record than John Shreve [225]. He was a lad of thirteen, in the fall of 1775, when made an Ensign, Second Battalion, Gloucester Co., N. J., troops, of which his father, Israel Shreve, was Lieutenant Colonel. He took part in the campaign in New York and Canada the following spring and summer. In November, 1776, he was made First Ensign and in July, 1777, Lieutenant, in which capacity he served at different times until 1781. At the battle of Springfield, N. J., he received a buckshot in one of his legs, which he carried until his death, seventy-five years later. Accompanying papers give interesting personal reminiscences of his career in the army and afterward.

During the winter encampment at Valley Forge the soldierly bearing of Lieut. Shreve, then in his sixteenth year, as shown in the different scouting expeditions sent out under his command, won the admiration of a number of ladies then visiting the army. With the approbation of General Washington, they presented the young officer with a beautiful and valuable buckle, set with costly stones, for his sword belt. This precious relic was given by Lieut. Shreve to a granddaughter, when the clouds of civil war were gathering, with the patriotic warning: "Don't let it fall into disloyal hands." He enjoyed the friendship of General Washington, and while dining with the President and Lady Washington, in November, 1796, the latter called his attention to the dinner service of blue and gold of a thousand pieces, made in China, which had been presented to her husband by the Society of the Cincinnati, of which the guest was a member. At Valley Forge, General Lafayette became much interested in Lieut. Shreve. When the French patriot visited America, in 1825, and was met at Brownsville, Pa., Lafayette recognizing a tall figure in the crowd on the wharf, gave him an old familiar salute, and in a moment they were in each other's arms.

Soon after his marriage, in 1786, John Shreve moved to southwestern Pennsylvania, where he purchased a farm and lived many years. He was also engaged in the Mississippi trade, purchasing large quantities of flour, which he shipped to New Orleans, thence to the West Indies, where he exchanged it for sugar, which was brought to New York. For several terms he was a member of the Pennsylvania legislature and filled various local offices with credit to himself and advantage to the public. About the year

21

1825, his children having removed to Ohio, he went to that state and made his home with them until his death, which occurred September 8, 1854, in the ninety-third year of his age. In closing a sketch of John Shreve, the "Democratic Transcript," of Ohio, October 11, 1854, said:

"He was a man of vigorous intellect and strong memory; he was benevolent to a fault, and often contributed to relieve the wants of others beyond what his own necessities would strictly justify. He was an ardent friend of freedom, strongly devoted to the principles of liberty, for which he had fought and bled under Washington. We have noticed concisely a few of the leading incidents in the life of one who served his country, both in peace and war, with a faithfulness that won the approbation of such men as Washington and Lafayette and the community in which he resided. To his posterity he has left the inheritance of an unsullied reputation, of greater worth than the gold of California."

LIEUT. JOHN SHREVE'S REVOLUTIONARY SERVICES

The following is an abstract from the personal narrative of the services of Lieut. John Shreve, of the New Jersey Line of the Continental Army:

I, John Shreve was born April 8—1762 in Mansfield, Burlington Co. New Jersey: son of Israel Shreve, who commanded the 2^d New Jersey Regiment "Continental Line," and I was in active service during the war of the Revolution I was made Ensign in 1776, and Lieut in July 1777, in which capacity I served until I left the army in 1781. I was but 13 when I entered the army. Soon after the Battle of Bunker Hill, Congress composed of the 13 Colonies, ordered four regiments to be raised in New Jersey.

W^mMaxwell was appointed Col. of the 2^d Regiment; and my father, Israel Shreve, appointed Lieut-Col. of same. Maxwell's men were ready first & marched for Canada. My father followed the last of Feby, and took me with him. We passed through Trenton, past Sussex Court House in New Jersey, and Kingston (alias Esopus) to Albany in New York; here we stayed several weeks, waiting for ice to disappear in the lakes. As soon as possible we went up the Hudson to Old Fort Edward, then to F^t George. When the ice had gone out of Lake Champlain, we, with 25 or 30 men, cut through the ice, passed Ticonderoga, and so on down the beautiful Sorel, to the St. Laurence; then through Lake St. Peter, and next day passed & landed at Wolfe's Cove, in sight of Quebec; then up Wolfe's road to Abraham Heights & joined our other troops, I believe, on 2^d or 3^d of May 1776.

British reinforcements arriving, our army raised the siege & retired up the river on May 6—1776. We were repulsed at Three Rivers and retired to Sorel. My father was left at Sorel to collect provisions. Capt. Ephraim Anderson was sent express to Congress, and my father sent me and Samuel Shute, son of Capt. Shute, with Capt. Anderson to go home, attend school & fit ourselves better for next campaign.

Gen. Sullivan conducted our army up the Sorel, & over Lake Champlain, making a stand at Mt. Independence, where I was appointed Ensign in 2^d Regiment, a few days after the Declaration of Independence.

Capt. Anderson left me with Saml Shute at Skenesborough, contrary to promise, and took most of my money. Samuel and I went on foot by ourselves to Albany, then in a vessel to New York, and from thence on foot to Bristol (Penna). I crossed over the Delaware to Burlington, & stayed a few days with my grandmother; then on to Phil^a and to school until the Jersey troops were discharged.

New regiments were organized & mustered the first of Feby 1777. I was appointed 1st Ensign in 2^d Regiment Dec 26—1776. My father Israel Shreve was Colonel of this regiment. We had an engagement with the enemy at Short Hills & Capt. Ephraim Anderson was killed.

At the battle of Brandywine my father was wounded in the thigh. I took him to near Darby where we stayed until morning, then through Philadelphia to one of my Uncle's in New Jersey. When we stopped to dress the wound & unbuttoned his breeches at the knee, the bullet, which had been flattened on one side by striking the bone, rolled down on his boot. I believe one of my Sisters has it now.

After the British obtained possession of Philadelphia I went with my father to Reading. I joined the regiment at White Marsh, a short time after the battle at Germantown. We went into winter quarters at Valley Forge, where the whole army suffered for want of provisions and clothes. My father had now recovered sufficient to join his regiment and later was ordered to Haddonfield, New Jersey, with his command, to prevent the enemy getting supplies in that part of the country. Our patrols stopped great quantities of provisions going to the British.

I was at West Point when Gen. Arnold deserted to the enemy and saw him making his escape to the British ship. At the execution of Major Andre, though not on duty, I was with the guard and my father had command of the detachment of troops that formed a square to keep off the crowd.

I continued with the army until 1781, when my father could no longer remain, having become too fleshy to ride a horse. He desired me also to leave on account of condition of our family affairs. He had no available property left, and could obtain no pay from the Government. The surrender of Lord Cornwallis occurred the same autumn and was the only engagement the New Jersey troops were in after I left the army. I was in my minority the whole of the time, being but 21 at close of the war.

LETTER OF LIEUT. JOHN SHREVE TO HIS NIECE, 1853.

Near Salem, Ohio, April, 1853.

S. B. D.: Dear Niece—A short account of my life. I am this day ninety-one years old. I write this without spectacles. I was born on the 8th day of April, 1762, in Burlington County, New Jersey. My mother died when I was about nine years old. My father married again, in about three years after. In the year 1775 the war of the Revolution commenced. Soon after the battle of Bunker Hill the Provincial Congress ordered four regiments to be raised in New Jersey, to serve one year. My father thought it was his duty to assist in liberating his country from British tyranny, and he was appointed Lieut. Colonel of the second regiment, which was raised and equipped, and marched in February, 1776, for Canada. My father thought it was not proper to leave me with a step-mother, and took me with him in the army. I was appointed an ensign in the regiment, the 15th July, and returned to Philadelphia, and went to school to fit me better for the next campaign.

When the regiment was discharged in December, a new regiment was ordered to be raised. My father was appointed Colonel, and I, first ensign. We lost a Captain, killed in the battle at Short Hills, in New Jersey, in June. I was promoted to the rank of Lieutenant the first of July. My father was wounded in the battle of Brandywine, the 11th of September, 1777. I went with him through Philadelphia to New Jersey—then took him to the town of Reading in Pennsylvania, when the British entered Philadelphia—and I joined the Regiment at White Marsh. Shortly after, we went into winter quarters by building huts at Valley Forge, where we suffered for want of provisions and clothes. After a partial supply of the latter, my father was ordered with his regiment to cross the Delaware and take a stand at the town of Haddonfield, seven miles from Philadelphia, to watch the motions of the enemy. In March, 1778, General Washington thought they were preparing to make their escape through New Jersey to New York. When the British were moving their army over the river, General Maxwell was ordered with the other two regiments (the first and third) to join the second, and joined us at Mount Holly. When the enemy evacuated the city and crossed over the river, Washington moved the army and crossed the Delaware at Coryell's and Howell's ferries above Trenton.

I was ordered with a guard to take the baggage of the brigade to the northeast of Trenton, and stay there till the enemy passed, and our army approached the enemy, whom they met at Monmouth Court House. I followed our army, and was at Englishtown, three miles from the battle-field. The day after the battle, when the enemy had moved off in the night, and left their dead and most of their wounded, I joined the brigade with the baggage; this was in June, 1778. The enemy made their escape to Sandy Hook and New York.

Our brigade was ordered on the lines at Elizabeth Town and Newark, where we remained through the following winter. We had many skirmishes and engagements with the British and Tories that winter and spring. They came out with eight or nine thousand men and thirty waggons, in June 1779, intending to take our stores of provisions at Morris Town. We stopped them at the town of Springfield. The people said when they returned the thirty wagons were full of their dead and wounded. In September of that year, our brigade was ordered to join Gen. Sullivan, to chastise the Indians and Tories towards the Susquehanna, and their towns in the Genessee county, west of New York. On our return, we wintered near Morris Town, in New Jersey. In 1780 we were on the lines of our former station, near Newark, when the British ship brought Major John Andre (the English spy) and laid at the head of Tappan Bay, about seven miles below West Point Fort. General Greene was ordered with several brigades to lay at the little town of Orange; our brigade was one. I was ordered to take a stand with twenty-six men, near to where the ship lay, to watch her motions. While there I saw General Arnold, the traitor, go on board the ship when he made his escape; and saw Major Andre, the spy, hung.

In the year 1781, my father being very fleshy, weighing three hundred and twenty pounds, he could not get a horse that could carry his weight faster than a walk, and he retired from the army on half pay. We then had but little property, except our public securities, which could not be turned into money. He thought it best for me to leave the army also, and help to support his family. That year ended the war.

I stayed and assisted the family until the year 1786, when I was married, and remained in New Jersey until the fall of the year 1787, then removed with my wife and child to the west side of the Alleghany mountains, and purchased one hundred acres of land, with but two or three acres cleared, and a small cabin without a nail or any sawed board, on Little Red Stone Creek, a branch of the Monongahela river, about thirty-three miles south of Pittsburg, where I remained thirty-eight or forty years, and raised a family of nine children. I cleared about sixty acres of land, mostly with my own hands. I served the township a great part of the time in all the public offices. A county commissioner three years—five different times a commissioner for laying graded roads—and three times in the State Legislature. I went one trip down the river to Cincinnati—one trip to the Falls of Ohio, and returned by the wilderness, through part of Tennessee and part of Virginia. I went three times with flour down the rivers Monongahela, Ohio and Mississippi to New Orleans, and took flour from New Orleans to the West Indies, one time to Havana, in the Island of Cuba; one time to Kingston, in the Island of Jamaica. Took sugar from Cuba and rum from Jamaica to New York, and paid six thousand seven hundred dollars duty to the United States on the sugar and rum.

I was concerned with a company in a manufactory after the close of the last war with England, and lost the most of my savings from my fifty years' toil. I surveyed land occasionally for more than thirty years. I had the rheumatism in my limbs, which prevented me from following the compass, and I moved to the State of Ohio, where I have remained with my children about twenty-seven years. Congress acknowledged to be indebted to me for services rendered to the United States, and I am now receiving an annuity which enables me to provide a comfortable living in my old and declining age.   John Shreve.

108—SARAH SHREVE (Thomas, 1; Richard, 5; Rebecca, 26).

> b. 10th mo. 18th, 1744, in Burlington Co., N. J.
> d. 1821.
> m. First, May 4th, 1768, David Scattergood.
> m. Second, April 24th, 1779, Joseph Beck.
> m. Third, John Nixon.

237—BENJAMIN SCATTERGOOD

238—ELIZABETH SCATTERGOOD   m. Joseph Shumar.

239—REBECCA SCATTERGOOD   m. Aaron Horner.

Children of Sarah (Shreve) Scattergood and Joseph Beck

240—JOSEPH BECK, JR.   m. 1810, Rebecca Gibbs, of Columbus, N. J.

241—HENRY BECK   d. in Columbiana Co., Ohio.

242—ANN BECK   d. 7th mo. 24th, 1788, while family were travelling in wagons from Burlington Co., N. J., to western Pennsylvania.

109—BENJAMIN SHREVE, JR. (Thomas, 1; Richard, 5; Rebecca, 26).

> b. 10th mo. 7th, 1747.
> d. 11th mo. 18th, 1801, in Alexandria, Va.
> m. First, 7th mo. 10th, 1770, Hannah Marll, daughter of John Marll, of Philadelphia.
> She d. 12th mo. 25th, 1784.
> m. Second, 1786, Susan Wood of Alexandria, Va.

243—WILLIAM SHREVE   b. 3rd mo. 13th, 1772, in Alexandria, Va.
                        d. 10th mo. 3rd, 1773.

244—A SON
                                               b. 8th mo. 20th, 1773.
                                               d. 8th mo. 20th, 1773.

245—JOHN SHREVE
                                               b. 7th mo. 12th, 1774, in Alexandria, Va.
                                               d. 7th mo. 17th, 1774.

246—REBECCA SHREVE
                                               b. 8th mo. 7th, 1775, in Alexandria, Va.
                                               d. 7th mo. 3rd, 1793.

247—SARAH SHREVE
                                               b. 4th mo. 3rd, 1777, in Winchester, Va.
                                               d. 9th mo. 24th, 1777.

248—ISAAC SHREVE
       b. 3rd mo. 25th, 1779, in Winchester, Va.
       d. 9th mo. 24th, 1829.
       m. First, 5th mo. 2ud, 1802, Hannah Very,
              daughter of Capt. Samuel and Hannah
              Very, of Salem, Mass.
  She b. 9th mo. 10th, 1781.
       d. 1st mo. 13th, 1820.
       m. Second, 11th mo. 7th, 1820, Mary Moulton,
              daughter of Bartholomew and Elizabeth
              Moulton, of Danvers, Mass.
  She b. 1st mo. 13th, 1795.
       d. 12th mo. 20th, 1854.

249—BENJAMIN SHREVE, 3RD
       b. 12th mo. 6th, 1780, in Winchester, Va.
       d. 5th mo. 8th, 1839, in Salem, Mass.
       m. Mary Goodhue (no issue).

250—SAMUEL BUTCHER SHREVE
       b. 12th mo. 20th, 1782, in Alexandria,, Va.
       d. about 1865, in Burlington, N. J.
       m. Rachel Huffendoffer, of Alexandria, Va.

251—A SON
                                               b. 8th mo. 18th, 1784.
                                             d. 8th mo. 18th, 1784.

Child of Benjamin and Susan (Wood) Shreve

252—JOHN SHREVE
       b. 5th mo. 1st, 1787, in Alexandria, Va.
       d. 2nd mo., 1821.

BENJAMIN SHREVE, JR.

Benjamin Shreve, Jr., fifth son of Benjamin and Rebecca (French) Shreve, in early life located in Alexandria, Va., at that time a place of considerable commercial importance. He entered into partnership with James Laurason, and their business, that of shipping and commission merchants, became quite extensive. They sent large quantities of flour to New England and received shipments of leather from the same section; the town of Salem, Mass., being noted at that time for the tanning of leather with hemlock bark. Pleasant business relationship was established between Benjamin Shreve and Captain Samuel Very of Salem, Mass.; and in 1794 the former sent his son Isaac, then a lad of fifteen, to Salem, in the care of Captain Very, to learn the trade of tanner. Five of Benjamin Shreve's children had died in infancy, a daughter at the age of seventeen, and in his son Isaac was centered the hopes of a fond father. There were also two younger sons, Benjamin Shreve, 3rd, and Samuel Butcher Shreve. The mother of these boys having died while they were six, four and two years old respectively, their father married a second time and had one son, John Shreve. Isaac was attentive and diligent, and soon after the expiration of his apprenticeship married, May 2nd, 1802, Captain Very's daughter Hannah and returned with her to Alexandria, Va. His father having died a short time before, the patrimony left him was used to set up the tanning business. About ten years later Isaac Shreve and his wife left Alexandria and returned to Salem, Mass., where he conducted a profitable tanning business for the remainder of his life. He had eight children by his first wife, viz., Rebecca, Samuel, Hannah, Isaac, Jr., Benjamin, Mary, Louisa and Frances Eliza; and by his second wife (Mary Moulton) five children, viz., Elizabeth, Susan Wood, John, Mary and George. His brother, Benjamin Shreve, 3rd, married Mary Goodhue of Salem, Mass., and engaged in the East India trade quite profitably. He had no children; he died in Salem, May 8th, 1839, aged fifty-eight years.

When Isaac Shreve left home to learn his trade in Salem, Mass., his father addressed to him a remarkable letter, facsimile of which would have been herewith given, but the original was, unfortunately, lost some years ago. The following, however, is an attested copy of this thoughtful communication, so full of wisdom and tender regard:

Alexandria, 29th the 5th Month, 1794

Dear Son Isaac: Thee is now going from under the care of thy loving father, whose eyes have been ever watchful for thy good into the wide world. Thee will be now under the care of Captain Very, who will advise thee for thy good, and I would wish thee to be advised by him. I have thought it most for thy good for thee to go to Salem to learn the trade of a tanner. If Captain Very can get thee a place to suit, I would advise thee to stay; if not, come home by the first opportunity that offers. As thee will be among strangers, take good care how thee forms acquaintance. Let them be friends, if possible, and steady, sober lads, older than thyself, and the fewer the better. A young man's happiness, both in this world and that which is to come, in a great measure depends on the connections he forms when young. Keep steady to meeting and to plainness both in speech and apparel, and that God that made us will protect thee from all harm. Above all things, be true to thy trust and defraud no man, though the thing may be small. But do unto men as thee would that they should do unto thee. And by so doing thee will gain the esteem of all good men and thy master, and come up in the world a useful member of society. Thee will have peace in thy own mind, which cannot be taken away but by actions which I hope thee wilt not be guilty of. If I should be spared to live until thee comes of age, I am in hope to be able to set thee up in thy intended business, so that by care and industry thee may soon get above the frowns of this world. But if I should be taken away from works to rewards, thee may expect an equal share of what I leave behind me; provided thee conducts thyself in a sober, orderly manner. If thee agrees to stay, I shall send thee a certificate, which thee must take to the monthly meeting. As there will be many opportunities, I would have thee to write often, and let me know if thee stand in need of anything, and I will endeavor to furnish thee from time to time. I want thee to serve five years and a half. Then thee will have sometime in the winter which will give time for thee to prepare for settling thyself in the spring following. I now recommend thee to that God that has protected me from my youth until this time (my father having died when I was about four years old). And I am sure he is the same heavenly Father that ever He was, and will remain to protect and preserve all those that love and fear Him.

From thy loving father

Benj. Shreve

N. B. Take care of the little money thee has, for thee will find that to be a friend where all others have forsaken thee. I shall furnish thee with small matters of money according as I hear of thy behaviour. Often read this advice and endeavor to follow it.

110—SAMUEL SHREVE (Thomas, 1; Richard, 5; Rebecca, 26).

> b. 1st mo. 25th, 1750, in Burlington Co., N. J.
> d. about 1814.
> m. First, ——— ———.
> m. Second, ——— ———.

253—BENJAMIN SHREVE   b. near Alexandria, Va.
                           m. First, ——— Muse.
                           m. Second, Barbara Swink.

254—JOHN SHREVE   m. Anna Ball.

255—WILLIAM SHREVE   d. young, in Virginia.

256—SAMUEL SHREVE, JR.   b. 1785.
                           d. 1862, in Falls Church, Va.
                           m. First, Priscilla Payne.
                           m. Second, Mary Ann Culver.

257—MARY SHREVE   d. young.

Samuel Shreve [110] was commissioned in June, 1775, Adjutant of the First Battalion, Gloucester County, N. J., Militia, and later was promoted to Captain. In February, 1777, he was appointed Lieutenant Colonel of the same Battalion. Resigned from army in October, 1778.

111—WILLIAM FRENCH, JR. (Thomas, 1; Richard, 5; William, 27).

> b. May 10th, 1751.
> d. 10th mo. 27th, 1808.
> m. 9th mo. 17th, 1777, at Falls Meeting (Bucks Co., Pa.), Rachel Rickey, daughter of Thomas and Hannah Rickey, of Lower Makefield Township, Bucks Co., Pa.
> She d. 8th mo. 27th, 1827, in Lamberton, N. J.

258—LYDIA FRENCH   b. 8th mo. 25th, 1778.
                          d. 8th mo. 18th, 1781.

259—HANNAH FRENCH   b. 12th mo. 5th, 1779.
                          d. 5th mo. 22nd, 1782.

260—JOHN TAYLOR FRENCH b. 1st mo. 27th, 1783.
d. 11th mo. 21st, 1831.

261—WILLIAM RICKEY FRENCH
b. 11th mo. 23rd, 1785.

262—MAHLON KIRKBRIDE FRENCH
b. 6th mo. 12th, 1788.
m. May 15th, 1807, Sarah Stackhouse.

263—AMOS TAYLOR FRENCH b. 1st mo. 23rd, 1791.
m. 5th mo. 6th, 1812, Ruth Ewing.

264—RACHEL RICKEY FRENCH
b. 2ud mo. 22nd, 1794.

"Died at Lamberton, N. J., on Monday morning the 27th August, Rachel French, widow of William French, deceased, aged 80 years. The deceased was a respectable member of the Society of Friends, and has left this world with a comfortable hope of a blessed immortality beyond the grave."
From the Philadelphia "Daily Advertiser," Sept. 3, 1827.

MEETING RECORDS

Minutes of Chesterfield Monthly Meeting of Women Friends:
At a Monthly Meeting of Woman friends held at Chesterfield ye 3rd of 4th Mo. 1783—
We are informed by Men friends that Rachel French had a Certificate granted from the Falls Monthly Meeting directed to this included with her Husband William French, wich hath Neglected to Produce to this Meeting therefore Hannah Linton and Sarah Robins are to visit her in Company With men friends and Report to Next Meeting.

6th of ye 5 mo. 1783 A Certificate was brought in this meeting for Rachel French, included with her husband Wm. French from the Monthly Meeting held at the fals in buks County Pensilvany bearing date ye 3^d of ye 3^d mo. 1779 which was read and received. Likewise an acknowledgment for the Neglect of its laying so long not brought in and also the Neglecting of attending Religious meetings which was read and received.

11th of 7th mo. 1797. A Certificate was laid before this meeting for Rachel French wife of Wm. French; included in her husbands and their five minor children to wit, John, William, Malon, Amos and Rachel from the monthly meeting of Haddonfield bearing date the 8th of 5th Mo. 1797 which was read and received.

DEED OF PATENT RIGHTS, OLIVER EVANS TO WILLIAM FRENCH

Know all men by these presents, that I Oliver Evans of the City of Phil^a State of Pennsylvania, do for my self my heirs and aſsigns by these presents, for and in consideration of the sum of two hundred & fifty dollars to me in hand paid the receipt whereof I do hereby acknowledge, aſsign, Transfer & convey, and forever release to William French Millwright, of the State of New Jersey his heirs and aſsigns, all my right unto title and Interest in, my new invention, called the Screw Mill, for breaking different hard substances; in all those States of the United States situated North or east of the river Delaware, Viz The States of New Jersey, New York, Connecticut, Vermont, New Hamshire, Maſsachusetts including the Districts of Main and Rhode Island. For this invention I have received the exclusive rights of making selling and using in the United States of America by letters patent under and by the authority of the said States, & bearing date the fourteenth of February eighteen hundred and four, as by said Letters pattent will fully appear; hereby transfering & conveying to the said William French his heirs & aſsigns all my rights, power and authority in me vested by the Laws of the United States, to demand, sue for and recover any sums of money, due or that, may here after become due, for the making, selling or using of my said invention as well as all the penalties or forfeitures for the evation or infringements of my Pattent rights which may by the laws of the United States be recoverable, and all the profits and emoluments arising from my said invention in the aforesaid seven States of the United States for and during the term of time of my Pattent, yet unexpired. In Witneſs whereof I have here unto set my hand & seal the twenty sixth of July Eighteen hundred and six

Oliver Evans [SEAL]

Signed sealed and delivered
in the presence of
    Daniel French
    Samuel Satherthwaite

City of Philadelphia ſs—Be it known that on the twenty ninth day of September one thousand eight hundred and six, before me Benjamin Nones, Esquire Notary Public for the Common wealth of Pennsylvania duly commiſsioned and authorized dwelling in the City of Philadelphia personally came the above named Oliver Evans and acknowledged the foregoing to be his act and deed

In testimony whereof I have hereunto set my Hand and affixed my notarial seal the day & year last aforesaid

    Benj Nones Noty. Public 1806.

Newly Invented Plaster Works.

DRY   MILL,

Made by William French, of New-Jersey.

HE above invention and improvement confists principally, in having the Plafter ground through and
a fcrew, inftead ot clofe, heavy mill ftones by water.
he fubfcriber wifhes to call the attention of all thofe
ho are in the habit of ufing or fowing plafter, and think
proper here to obferve—That st his Plafter-Works he
ands the Plafter in fuch a manner as to meafure about
4 bufhels to the ton, which is found, by obfervation and
xperience, to be the proper proportion which the mea-
re fhould hear to the weight; whereas, at the mills
here Plafter is ground by water, it may be readily re-
uced down fo flat as to make from 30 to 32 bufhels the
on, and even as fine as duft—The refult is, thofe who
ny of my grinding, get about a ton weight in paying for
4 bufhels and in buying the fame weight, ground fo very
ne, pay for from 30 to 32 bufhels. The difference in
ubftance to purchafers is obvious and needs no explana-
ion. To roll indian corn in, or other grain, I rather may
e ground very fine; but upon no other principle fhould it
e reduced to a powder. Any perfon who will read
udge Peters' Treatife upon the ufe of Plafter and Prac-
ical Farming, (a fmall pamphlet highly worthy of the
ttention of every farmer) may thereby learn the trade of
ult and effect of Plafter, in all its various modes of ufe,
is well as upon different foils. It is undoubtedly my intreft, to promote the ufe and fale of Plafter, as I have gone
argely into the manufacturing of it—It is alfo evidemly my
nterest, that the farmers who buy of me fhould find it ans
fwer their reafonable expectations and wifhes, otherwife
t can be no object to them. The true mode of felling
Plafter which is ground, is by weight for in that mode
we, who deal in it, buy it. I hope yet to eftablifh that
mode, tho I have met with fome oppofition to it. The
caufe is evident—for when I fell 24 bufhels, which make
a ton weight, thofe who grind it dead flat, fell from 30
to 32 bufhels, which make but the fame weight, and it
has been faid by fome that they could and would fell their
Plafter under my price, be that price what it may; but
the reafon of this I fully appears from the foregoing facts.

by grinding it finer they increafe the bulk, but not the
fubftance—It is thus, by meafure, they underfel, but in
other way; yet very few farmers have confidered t
difference in purchafing this article, whether it be grou
to a proper degree of finenefs, or to a powder; there a
however, fome, who are converfant in the ufe of Plafter
and who well know the difference, as well as the nece
fity of its being properly manufactured, and all who co
tinue in the ufe of it, will, no doubt, obtain advant geo
knowledge; for experience will naturally lead to the n
ceffary information.

Since the fubfcriber publifhed his fuggeftions and ide
laft year, with refpect to Plafter being ground dow
flat, and to duft, he is happy to find, that many perfo
have paid clofe attention to it, and from real experien
they find the ftatement correct, and they alfo find,
like experience, that the Plafter ground (as it appears)
a duft or powder, has not a body or weight left in it, fu
ficient to hold it ftationary, and of courfe the body a
fubftance is blown to difperfion. It is true, that fo
omes and generally, this powdered Plafter brings fo
ward an immediate and rapid growth, or vegetation; b
obferve, it foon paffes off for want of having in or abo
it a body fufficient to fuftain, and often difcovers this wa
before the firft feafon after fowing is paft. It is likew
very difficult to get the fame placed on the ground reg
lar and even, and this. I would obferve, is a material poi
if you fow dry, it dufts and blows out of place—if wet,
clogs and will fall in lumps, and uneven.

It will be found, that when Plafter is ground to a
gular and proper fize, there will always be a fufficie
proportion of it in flour to promote and carry on an im
diate vegetation—The coarfer parts produce their eff
following:

A conftant fupply will be for fale here, warranted
the firft quality, and if it does not prove fuch, he enga
to refund the money, and the purchafer not to return t
Plafter. It will be fold on as reafonable terms as the f
fcriber can poffibly afford, and he hopes to retain, and
augment that good fhare of cuftom which he has here
fore experienced.

Now on hand and for Sale,
300 Tons in the grofs—Alfo, any qua
tity ground to a proper fize, by the bu
el, or in barrels of four bufhels each.
N. COMBES.

Lamberton, (on Delaware) Jan. 1, 1803.   201-1

ADVERTISEMENT FROM "TRENTON FEDERALIST," MARCH 21, 1803

FALLS MEETING

The early settlers of Pennsylvania in the vicinity of the Delaware river falls were mostly Friends. They met in each others' houses for worship, under the care of Burlington, N. J., Monthly Meeting, until 1683, when they set up a Monthly Meeting, the first in what was afterwards known as Bucks County, and in 1690 built a small brick meeting house, 20 × 25 feet. This was enlarged in 1700, and in 1728 a new building was erected to accommodate the increasing membership. Additions were made in 1758 and 1765, and the large and substantial stone meeting house, herewith reproduced, was built in 1789, the year the American Congress caused a survey to be made along the Delaware in Falls township, with a view to locating there the District of Columbia and the capital of the United States. Falls Meeting has always held a foremost place in the history of the Society of Friends. During the first century of its existence over five hundred marriages were recorded.

Relations between the early meetings at Burlington and Falls were very close and mutually helpful. Upon one occasion two young Friends wishing to marry disregarded the rule concerning certificates. The Burlington Meeting addressed to Friends at Falls a very earnest and characteristic letter, in vindication of their action in withholding approval, from which we quote as follows:

> To our dear friends and brethren in the monthly meeting for the County of Bucks, in Pennsylvania:
>
> Dear friends, with love unfeigned in the holy covenant of life, do we greet and tenderly salute you, blessing God for the holy communion and fellowship which he hath graciously brought his people into, and doth defend and preserve them in, where being kept, our greatest care will be for the honor of God, and the good of his people. Dear friends, we are comforted concerning many of you, being fully assured of your integrity and service in the Lord, and are glad our lot has fallen so near each other, and do desire that in this service and work of God, which he is carrying on here as well as elsewhere, and will make glorious in his time, we may be all packed together, and knit in that holy bond, which the strongest powers of darkness are not able to break.
>
> Dear friends, as to the business of ———— and his friend, we are informed that he has a certificate come, and, therefore, our exercise as to that is at an end; yet, still, we are desirous, according to our former intentions, to give you a naked serious account. Wherefore, we have laid such an injunction on all, of having certificates when their marriages were presented, that came single and marriageable into this country. We had many

FALLS MEETING

ettlers of Pennsylvania in the vicinity of the Delaware river
stly Friends. They met in each others' houses for worship,
of Burlington, N. J., Monthly Meeting, until 1683, when they
hly Meeting, the first in what was afterwards known as Bucks
1 1690 built a small brick meeting house, 20 × 25 feet. This
n 1700, and in 1728 a new building was erected to accommo-
asing membership. Additions were made in 1758 and 1765,
and substantial stone meeting house, herewith reproduced, was
the year the American Congress caused a survey to be made
ware in Falls township, with a view to locating there the Dis-
bia and the capital of the United States. Falls Meeting has
foremost place in the history of the Society of Friends. Dur-
century of its existence over five hundred marriages were

tween the early meetings at Burlington and Falls were very
ually helpful. Upon one occasion two young Friends wishing
garded the rule concerning certificates. The Burlington Meet-
to Friends at Falls a very earnest and characteristic letter, in
their action in withholding approval, from which we quote

dear friends and brethren in the monthly meeting for the County
in Pennsylvania·

FALLS MEETING HOUSE, BUCKS COUNTY, PA., 1789.

marriages that came before us where little could be certified concerning the persons, yet earnestly pressing the accomplishment of the matter, which became a great strait and exercise to honest friends on whom God had laid the care of his honor. Yet, for a time, in condescension did permit such marriages, constantly expressing ourselves not satisfied therewith, still desiring that care might be taken for the future, that things too doubtful and dangerous might not be put upon us; requesting the care and help of Friends in England to inform such as come over, that they might bring certificates with them; giving notice through our respective meetings that it was expected; also, informing all how they might be helped by the monthly meeting here in their sending. Yet, notwithstanding it was allowed, and the old practice continued and grew amongst us, and the burthen of the upright grew with it, some alleging that such and such were passed and why not we. So, finding it of that dangerous consequence, and that it strengthened the wrong, and hurt the good, we can say, in the sight of God and his people, necessity was laid upon us to do what we did, singly eyeing the glory of God, and the advancement of His truth in it. So, not doubting that we shall be felt, and credited, and strengthened by you herein, we subscribe ourselves by order, and on the behalf of our men's monthly meeting, the 2d of the fifth month, 1683, your friends and brethren in the love and travails of the truth.   Samuel Jennings, Thomas Budd

112—RICHARD FRENCH (Thomas, 1; Richard, 5; William, 27).

> b. October 15th, 1759.
> d. 2nd mo. 26th, 1823.
> m. Mary Davis.
> She b. 12th mo. 29th, 1761.
> d. 12th mo. 12th, 1829.

265—THOMAS FRENCH	b. 1st mo. 17th, 1785.
	m. Ann Headly
266—CHARLOTTE FRENCH	b. 10th mo. 17th, 1786.
	m. Jesse Van Horn.
267—LYDIA FRENCH	b. 9th mo. 19th, 1788.
	d. 9th mo. 19th, 1788.
268—LYDIA FRENCH	b. 2nd mo. 3rd, 1793.
	d. 11th mo. 11th, 1801.
269—RICHARD FRENCH, JR.	b. 11th mo. 26th, 1799.
	m. 9th mo. 12th, 1822, Sarah ·Hutchinson.

Richard French [112] served in the Continental army, and was for a time under the command of General Cadwallader of Pennsylvania. He took part in the operations against the Hessians and British in the vicinity of Trenton and Bordentown, N. J., December, 1776.

119—WILLIAM FRENCH (Thomas, 1; Richard, 5; Jonathan, 31).

m. May 25th, 1783, Ruth Higby; Gloria Dei (Old
Swedes') Church record, Philadelphia.
She d. 1801.

270—JOHN FRENCH	d. young.
271—REBECCA FRENCH	b. June 24th, 1785.
	m. Enoch Thorn.
272—RICHARD FRENCH	d. young.
273—JOSEPH FRENCH	b. February 27th, 1790.
	m. December 25th, 1815, Christiana Slim.

The Swedish colonists who settled along and near the Delaware during the seventeenth
century built four churches and maintained them for more than one hundred years.
That located near the Indian settlement of Wiccaco was for a long time the center of
religious activity and influence in the southern part of Philadelphia. Services were first
held by Rev. Jacob Fabritius, in 1677, in the block house fort, built in 1669. This was
torn down in 1698 and in 1700 the present brick church, apparently good for centuries
yet, was built by Rev. Andrew Rudman. The church came under the care of the
Protestant Episcopal Diocese of Pennsylvania in 1841. The present rector, Rev. Snyder
B. Simes, has been in charge for forty years.

GLORIA DEI (OLD SWEDES') CHURCH, PHILADELPHIA, 1700

120—RICHARD FRENCH (Thomas, 1; Richard, 5; Jonathan, 31).

b. 8th mo. 6th, 1760.

d. 12th mo. 19th, 1839.

m. 10th mo. 11th, 1784, Sophia Bendler.

She b. 8th mo. 16th, 1762.

d. 8th mo. 6th, 1845.

274—JACOB FRENCH	b. 4th mo. 22nd, 1785. d. 9th mo. 29th, 1791.
275—JONATHAN FRENCH	b. 12th mo. 25th, 1786. m. Rebecca Wilson.
276—MARY FRENCH	b. 11th mo. 25th, 1788. m. 1811, William Jones.
277—SARAH FRENCH	b. 10th mo. 4th, 1791. m. 1815, Anthony Warrick, Jr.
278—RICHARD FRENCH, JR.	b. 8th mo. 30th, 1793. d. 4th mo. 16th, 1853, unmarried.
279—SAMUEL FRENCH	b. 10th mo. 15th, 1796. m. 1820, Elizabeth Roberts.
280—ELIZABETH FRENCH	b. 10th mo. 14th, 1798. d. 2nd mo. 14th, 1800.
281—KEZIAH FRENCH	b. 6th mo. 7th, 1803. m. 1822, Samuel Hillman.

RICHARD FRENCH

Richard French [120] was a prosperous farmer and brickmaker, his homestead of over 100 acres being located on the White Horse pike, near the present village of Kirkwood, Camden County, N. J. He was a methodical business man of enviable reputation and wide influence. His home was a model of neatness and his personal habits exact. He kept all engagements with scrupulous care. An old account book, preserved by one of his grand-daughters shows profitable relations with many business men and builders of that period. During the months of September, October and November, 1801, he sold over 30,000 bricks, at an average price of £1 17s. 6d. per thousand. He died in his 80th year, leaving to his children and grand-

22

children the memory of a well spent life.   Until some time after his marriage to Sophia Bendler, in 1784, Richard French supposed he had lost his birthright in the Society of Friends, on account of the action taken in the case of his father, Jonathan French [31].   Evidently he was in full accord with Friends and when he learned that the way was open for him to renew his membership in meeting, he at once took advantage of the long desired opportunity, submitting an acknowledgment for marrying out and an appeal for recognition characteristic of the gentle spirit he always manifested.   This communication, addressed to Eveshan Monthly Meeting, appears with the entire record of proceedings taken, under Jonathan French [31], and is herewith reproduced:

> To the Monthly Meeting of Evesham
> I the Subscriber having a Birthright amongst Frds; but not having any Knowledge thereof till since I consummated my marriage contrary to the good order established amongst them; on being treated with, feel love & nearness towards my Friends, and have a sincere desire to retain my right in Society, hoping this with my future orderly walking may reconcile me to my friends again, is the desire of   Richard French
>   12" mo. 9" 1791

In 1792 Richard French was granted a certificate of removal from Evesham Monthly Meeting to Haddonfield Monthly Meeting, in which meeting he continued to take an active interest until his death in 1839.

WILL OF RICHARD FRENCH, 1839

> I Richard French of the Township and County of Gloucester and State of New Jersey being of Sound mind and Memory, do Make and Publish this For my last Will and Testament . . . First I Give and Bequeath to my dear Wife Sophah French the Income and profits of my Farm where I now leive Situate in the Township of Gloucester one Cow at her Choise one Bed Bedstid and Beding and I allso Give to her as much of my Furniture as she may think necefsary to keep house,   Second; It is my Will and I do order my Executor to sell the Balance or remainder of my Personall property after my Wife shall take what she may Think Necefsary to keep house and pay all my Just debts and Funerall Charges and the Remainder I Give and Bequeath to be Eaqually Divided Between my three daughters namely Mary Jones Sarah Warreck and Kiziah Hillman   third It is my Will and I do order my Executor at the deceas of my wife to Sell att Public or Private Sale all my Real Estate be the Same More or Lefs and where so ever Found and the Money Ariseing thereon to be Equally divided the one

half part of the neate profits to be Equeally Between My Son Samuel Frenches Four Sones namely Richard B. French Jacob French Samuel French and Jonathan French I Give and Bequeath to the above named Richard B. French Jacob French Samuel French and Jonathan the above mentioned one half part of the neate profits ariseing on the sale of my real Estate to be Eaquelly divide Between them Fourth I Give and Bequeath to my son Jonathan French and to my son Richard French and to my daughter Kiziah Hillman the other half part of the neate profits ariseing on the Sale of my real Estate to be Eaqueally divided Between them Fifth and lastly I do appoint my son in law Samuel Hillman Executor of this My Testament and Last Will I appoint Samuel Hillman Guardean to have the Care of my son Richard and his Estate and Person In Witnefs Whereof I have hereunto Set my hand and Seal this Twentininth day of August in the year of Our Lord one thousand Eight hundred and Thirty-nine 1839.

Signed sealed published and
declared by the said Richard
French to be his Testament and
last Will in the presence of us
    David Sloan
    Iazer Sickler
    Christopher Sickler

Gloucester County ſs, Samuel Hillman Executor in the within testament named, alledging himself to be confcientiously fcrupulous of taking on oath and being duly affirmed according to law upon his affirmation faith that the within inftrument contains the true last will and testament of Richard French the testator therein named so far as he knows and as he verily believes, that he will well and truly perform the fame by paying first the debts and then the legacies in the faid testament Specified so far as the goods chattels and Credits of the faid deceased can thereunto extend, and that he will make and exhibit into the Surrogates Office of the County of Gloucester a true and perfect Inventory of all and fingular the goods chattels and credits of the faid deceased that have or fhall come to his knowledge or pofsefsion or to the pofsefsion of any other person or persons for his use, and render a just and true account when thereunto lawfully required
Subfcribed and affirmed at
Woodbury this first day of
January, A. D. 1840.   Samuel Hillman
before me—   J. C. Smallwood,

121—EDWARD FRENCH (Thomas, 1; Thomas, 6; Thomas, 33).

b. 1st mo. 7th, 1747.
d. 8th mo. 21st, 1822.
m. Mary Wilkins.
She b. 5th mo. 28th, 1750.
d. 5th mo. 29th, 1827.

282—THOMAS FRENCH	b. 7th mo. 1st, 1770. d. 7th mo. 21st, 1770.
283—JEMIMA FRENCH	b. 9th mo. 27th, 1771. m. April 21st, 1790, Jacob Borton.
284—HANNAH FRENCH	b. 4th mo. 7th, 1773. m. March 7th, 1792, Nathan Evans.
285—JOSEPH FRENCH	b. 4th mo. 6th, 1774. m. (about) 1797, Elizabeth Zane.
286—JOHN FRENCH	b. 2nd mo. 16th, 1775. d. 2nd mo. 20th, 1775.
287—SARAH FRENCH	b. 4th mo. 19th, 1777. m. First, 12th mo. 19th, 1803, Gilbert Deacon. Second, ——— Currie.
288—ANNE FRENCH	b. 2nd mo. 16th, 1779.
289—EDWARD FRENCH	b. 9th mo. 7th, 1780.
290—STACY FRENCH	b. 8th mo. 5th, 1782.
291—ISAAC FRENCH	b. 10th mo. 10th, 1784. d. 10th mo. 15th, 1784.
292—SAMUEL FRENCH	b. 12th mo. 2nd, 1785. m. Sarah ———.
293—URIAH FRENCH	b. 2nd mo. 23rd, 1787. d. 3rd mo. 6th, 1788.
294—MARY FRENCH	b. 12th mo. 15th, 1789. m. Dominic Connelly.

295—SYLENIA FRENCH   b. 7th mo. 10th, 1792.
                            m. ——— Dennis.

296—CHARLES HAINES FRENCH
                    b. 11th mo. 8th, 1797.
                    m. First, 1st mo. 27th, 1820, Hannah E. Moore.
                    m. Second, 1st mo. 7th, 1826, Mary Moore.

EDWARD FRENCH

Edward French was for many years a noted and influential resident of Chester Township, N. J. He resided before, during and for many years after the Revolution, on a plantation at the west end of Moorestown, now known as " Forrest Brook Farm," some two hundred acres in extent. He was much interested in township affairs, serving as overseer of highways in 1773, and chosen freeholder in 1784 and from 1788 to 1793 inclusive. He was a member of the township committee, in many of the old records called " Representatives," in 1786 and from 1788 to 1794. He was also a long-time justice of the peace; and between 1795, when the marriage license law was passed, and 1801, he married sixty-four couples. In 1770 he sold a piece of ground on what is now the north side of West Moorestown to Samuel Lanning, upon which the latter erected a comfortable house; and in 1821, Edward French purchased this property, removing there with his wife, to whom he bequeathed at the time of his death, in 1822, a life tenancy therein. He was a man of strong character and great vigor of mind and body. Prior to 1779 he was an active member of Friends' Meeting. During the Revolutionary War an " old tippler " went to the Friends' Meeting House in Moorestown on First Day morning, while Friends were at worship, and opening the door, called out in a loud voice: " Here you are all sittin' in meetin' and the British are down at Neddie French's." It is scarcely necessary to say that the usual form of breaking meeting was not observed.

The plantation of Edward French, which he devised to his son, Charles Haines French, was formerly the property of his grandfather, Thomas French [6]. He also owned for many years an adjoining property, one hundred and fifty-three acres, on the north side of the present Camden and Moorestown turnpike, which comprised a portion of the estate conveyed by deed of gift 1694, by Thomas ffrench, progenitor, to his son Thomas, grandfather of Edward French.   Part of this property, one hundred and five acres, Edward French conveyed to his son Joseph in 1821.   The latter dying intestate, and the farm being sold, under direction of the Orphans' Court, by Commissioners, in 1838, Edward French [559], son of Joseph, bought sixty-one acres, which, with an additional tract, he bequeathed in 1871 to his daughter, Sarah A. Ogden, by whom it was sold in 1872 to Ellwood Hollinshead, after one hundred and seventy-eight years consecutive ownership by members of the French family.

Two views of the Edward French homestead, now known as " Forrest Brook Farm," are herewith given, one showing its appearance as it faced the old " King's Highway," in Revolutionary times; the other, the present front, facing the Camden and Moorestown turnpike.   On one of the small window panes, in the eastern end of the first floor sitting room, there appears the name and date, " Charles H. French 1819," scratched with a diamond. This was evidently done by Edward's youngest son, who at that time was 23 years of age, and who inherited the farm.

MEETING RECORDS

Evesham Monthly Meeting Minutes:
At a Monthly Meeting held at Evesham ^{ye} 9th of ^{ye} 8th mo. 1770. Edward French produced an acknowledgment of his out going in marriage, which was read and referred for consideration.

At a Monthly Meeting held at Evesham ^{ye} 6th of ^{ye} 9th mo. 1770. Edward Frenches acknowledgment was now accepted and is in the following words—

To Friends of Evesham Monthly Meeting, as I ^{ye} under writer having gone out in marriage which is Contrary to Friends rules, in which Conduct I allow myself in fault, & am willing to Condemn ^{ye} Same hopeing that my future Conduct may render me worthy of friends further notice.
^{ye} 9th of ^{ye} 8th mo. 1770   Edward French

At a Monthly Meeting held at Evesham ^{ye} 9th of ^{ye} 9th mo. 1779. Friends from ye preparative Meeting at Chester reported that Edward French & Enoch Allen had been treated with for paying their fines in Lieu of Military Service.   Therefore Samuel Shute & John Roberts are appointed to visit them and report to next meeting.

father of Edward French.   Part of this property, one hundred and five acres, Edward French conveyed to his son Joseph in 1821.   The latter dying intestate, and the farm being sold, under direction of the Orphans' Court, by Commissioners, in 1838, Edward French [559], son of Joseph, bought sixty-one acres, which, with an additional tract, he bequeathed in 1871 to his daughter, Sarah A. Ogden, by whom it was sold in 1872 to Ellwood Hollinshead, after one hundred and seventy-eight years consecutive ownership by members of the French family.

Two views of the Edward French homestead, now known as " Forrest Brook Farm," are herewith given, one showing its appearance as it faced the old " King's Highway," in Revolutionary times; the other, the present front, facing the Camden and Moorestown turnpike.   On one of the small window panes, in the eastern end of the first floor sitting room, there appears the name and date. "Charles H. French 1819," scratched with a diamond. This was evidently done by Edward's youngest son, who at that time was 23 years of age. and who inherited the farm.

MEETING RECORDS

Evesham Monthly Meeting Minutes:

At a Monthly Meeting held at Evesham ye 9th of ye 8th mo. 1770. Edward French produced an acknowledgment of his out going in marriage, which was read and referred for consideration.

At a Monthly Meeting held at Evesham ye 6th of ye 9th mo. 1770. Edward Frenches acknowledgment was now accepted and is in the following words—

To Friends of Evesham Monthly Meeting, as I ye under writer having gone out in marriage which is Contrary to Friends rules, in which Conduct I allow myself in fault, & am willing to Condemn ye Same hopeing that my future Conduct may render me worthy of friends further notice.
ye 9th of v^e 8th mo. 1770   Edward French

At a Monthly Meeting held at Evesham ye 9th of y^e 9th mo. 1779. Friends from y^e preparative Meeting at Chester reported that Edward French & Enoch Allen had been treated with for paying their fines in Lieu of Military Service.   Therefore Samuel Shute & John Roberts are appointed

EDWARD FRENCH HOUSE, NEAR WEST MOORESTOWN, N. J., 170

As remodeled, about 1850, to face the Camden Turnpike

At a Monthly Meeting held at Evesham ^{ye} 7th of 10th Mo. 1779. The friends appointed reported that they have visited Edw'd French & Enoch Allen but that they did not appear in a Suitable Disposition to Condemn their Misconduct therefore this meeting proceeds to Disown them ye said Edw'd French and Enoch Allen from having any Right of membership amongst us until they come to a Sight of their Misconduct & condemn ^{ye} same to friends Satisfaction, which that they may is our Sincere Desire & Jacob Hollinshead & Wm. Matlack are appointed to give them a copy of this Minute & report to Next Meeting.

At a Monthly Meeting held at Evesham ^{ye} 4th of ^{ye} 11th mo. 1779. The friends appointed reported that they have given Edw'd French a Copy of ^{ye} Minute against him; but they have not had an opportunity with Enoch Allen.

REVOLUTIONARY DAMAGES

Inventory of Damage done to Edward French by the American Troops under the Command of General Varnum and others February 15th 1777

1200 Cedar Rails @ 25/ 200 Oak d° @ 6/......................£15	12	
Hay and Grain taken by Waggoners........................... 2	5	
£17	17	

Thomas Morris being Sworn, Deposeth that he saw the Troops of the Continental take and Destroy the articles Contained in the within Inventory.

Thomas Morris

Inventory of the Goods of Edward French Plundered and Destroyed by the Troops of the British Armey in June 1778, Vizt.

1 Old Horse, 1 two year old heifer, 2 yearling D°............£12	0	0	
5 Calves, 25 Sheep, 4 large Hogs, 5 Shoats.................... 24	2	6	
80 Fowls, 9 Geese, 4 Tons Hay, 1000 Ceedar Rails............. 25	12	6	
300 Oak Rails, Harnefs for 2 Horses........................ 3	3	—	
Sundry Timber and Fruit Trees, 1 Acre Flax.................. 4	10	—	
1 Gun, Sundry Cloathing................................... 3	10	—	
£72	18	0	

Thomas Morris being Sworn, Deposeth that he lived in the Famely of the above Applicant in the time of the British Troops being at his House and Saw Said Troops Plunder and Destroy the Several Articles Contained in the Above Inventory.

Thomas Morris.

WILL OF EDWARD FRENCH, 1821

I Edward French of the Township of Chester in the County of Burlington and State of New Jersey being of Sound and disposeing Mind and Memory, Do make and publish this my last will and testament, Makeing all former and other will by me maid Void and this only to be taken for the Same in Manner & form following that is to Say

1ˢᵗ I give and bequeth to my wife Mary French the Rent and profit of the houſe and lot of Land where I now dwell which I purchased of Samuel Lanings Estate together with the Land adjoining on the North Side of the Stage Road adjoining to Joseph Frenchs land and bounding by the Same to the line of George French & the same to the Main Street or Stage Road and down the Same to the place of begining during her natural life. I also give to my Said wife two good beds and beding together with other houſehold goods such as she shall chofe to the amount of Eighty dollars to be taken at the appraised price and dispoſe of her houſehold goods to whome she may see fit. I also order my Son Charles H. French to take charge of her and to see that she shall not want for any nefsarys during her life.

2ⁿᵈ I Order my Executors here after Named, to sell and dispoſe of all my moveable Estate not otherwiſe dispoſed of, as soon after my disceaſe as can be Conveniantly Done, and pay all my Just debts and Nefseſary Expences, and to avoid disputes as much as poſsable and it is my will that all the grain and graſs standing or growing on the premises and Vigatbles of every kind I mean what I claim as mine to be dispoſed of and all my Sider works and Still and Utentials thereunto belonging & boyler in the boyler houſe, to be considered as movables and disposed of as such for the payment of debts and in cafe my movable estate Should not be Sufficient to pay my debts I order my Executors to sell and dispoſe of that houſe and lot where James Ginnet now dwells and likewiſe to sell of in Small lots Land to the Eastward of Coles Medow Road sufficient to discharge the Remainder of my Just debts and to make Deed or Deeds for the same good and sufficient as I could do in life

3ʳᵈ I give and deviſe to my Son Joseph French ten dollars, out of my movable Estate, he having Received his full Share of my estate by Deed bareing date the fifth day of June one thouſand Eight hundred and twenty one

4ᵗʰ I give & devise to my Son Charles H. French the Plantation where he now dwells with his complying with the Legecies to be paid out of the Same, beginning at a Stone in George Frenchs line below the School houſe and Corner to Joseph Frenchs land and Runing on his line to James⸱ Hinchmans land and corner to Joseph French, and from thence by Hinch⸱

WILL OF EDWARD FRENCH, 1824

I Edward French of the Township of Chester in the County of Burlington
and State of New Jersey being of Sound and disposeing Mind and Memory,
Do make and publish this my last will and testament, Makeing all former
and other will by me maid Void and this only to be taken for the Same
in Manner & form following that is to Say

1ˢᵗ I give and bequeth to my wife Mary French the Rent and profit
of the houfe and lot of Land where I now dwell which I purchased of
Samuel Lanings Estate together with the Land adjoining on the North Side
of the Stage Road adjoining to Joseph Frenchs land and bounding by the
Same to the line of George French & the same to the Main Street or Stage
Road and down the Same to the place of begining during her natural life.
I also give to my Said wife two good beds and beding together with other
houfehold goods such as she shall chofe to the amount of Eighty dollars
to be taken at the appraised price and dispofe of her houfehold goods to
whome she may see fit. I also order my Son Charles H. French to take
charge of her and to see that she shall not want for any nefsarys during
her life.

2ⁿᵈ I Order my Executors here after Named, to sell and dispofe of all
my moveable Estate not otherwife dispofed of, as soon after my discease
as can be Conveniantly Done, and pay all my Just debts and Nefsesary
Expences, and to avoid disputes as much as pofsable and it is my will that
all the grain and grafs standing or growing on the premises and Vigatbles
of every kind I mean what I claim as mine to be dispofed of and all my
Sider works and Still and Utentials thereunto belonging & boyler in the
boyler houfe, to be considered as movables and disposed of as such for the
payment of debts and in cafe my movable estate Should not be Sufficient to
pay my debts I order my Executors to sell and dispofe of that houfe and
lot where James Ginnet now dwells and likewife to sell of in Small lots
Land to the Eastward of Coles Medow Road sufficient to discharge the
Remainder of my Just debts and to make Deed or Deeds for the same good
and sufficient as I could do in life

3ʳᵈ I give and devife to my Son Joseph French ten dollars, out of my
movable Estate, he having Received his full Share of my estate by Deed
bareing date the fifth day of June one thoufand Eight hundred and twenty
one

4ᵗʰ I give & devise to my Son Charles H. French the Plantation where
he now dwells with his complying with the Legecies to be paid out of the
Same, begining at a Stone in George Frenchs line below the School houfe
and Corner to Joseph Frenchs land and Runing on his line to James
Hinchmans land and corner to Joseph French, and from thence by Hinch-

EDWARD FRENCH HOUSE, NEAR WEST MOORESTOWN, N. J., 1770

As it faced the King's Highway during Colonial and Revolutionary Days

mans Coles & Josiah Roberts land to Cowperthwaits, Chambers Hunts and
so on to a Small Run of water & down the same to a small lot quit-
claimed to Hugh Cowperthwaits to the North branch of pensaukin creek and
up the Same the Severil Courſes to a Maple Stump thence by land of
Hannah & Joseph Cowperthwaits the Severil courſes to the arch bridge in
the Haddonfield Road thence up the South side of a Large ditch And main
water courſe to a Stone in Range with Benjamin Hunts line where I and
Samuel Cowperthwait agreed it should be placed from thence along Hunts
and George French land the severil courses to the place of begining.
Likewise a lot of Seder Swamp on atco atco adjoining to a Lot given to
Joseph French containing eight or nine acres be the same more or less to
him his Heirs and aſsigns for ever providinge^d he pays the Legacies allotted
to be paid out of the Same.

5th I give and bequeth to Daughter Jemima Borton Eight hundred dollars
to be paid to her by my Son Charles H. French out of the Plantation given
to him in twelve months after my deceſe and in Case Jemima should decese,
before She Receives this Legecy the Money hereby given to her to be
divided among her Surviving Children and her husband equally share alike

6th I give and bequeth to my daughter Mary Conelly two hundred
dollars to be paid to her by my Son Charles H. French out of the plantation given to him, and Likewiſe all the houſehold goods I lent her some
years back—but in caſe my Daughter Mary should deceaſe before She
Receives this Legecy her husband is to have no part thereof, but to Remain
in the hands of my Executors to be devided equally between her Children
when they arrive to the age of twenty one or the Survivors of them. I
mean the Children of my Daughter Mary is to Receive this Legecy Not
her husband.

7th I give and bequeth to my Daughter Sarah Currie a certain Note
signed to me by my son Joseph French for one hundred dollars together
with a bed and beding Caſe of Draws looking glaſs other things I brought
from Alloways Creek yet on hand together with one hundred dollars to be paid
her by my Son Charles H. French out of the Plantation given to him but
in case she should decs$_e$ before she gits this Legecy her husband is to have
No part thereof, but to Remain in the hands of my Executors to be equally
devided between her Children she had by Gilbert Deacon when they arrive
to full age Share alike.

8th I give and bequeth to my Daughter Syllenia Dennis Eight Hundred
dollars to be paid to her by my Son Charles H. French out of the plantation given to him in one year after my deceſe, but in caſe She should die
befor She Receives this Legecy her Children she shall then have and her
husband is to share this equally between them share alike and to be paid her
in one year from my deccſe.

9th I give and bequeth to my Grand Son Samuel French the Son of my
Son Samuel French Decas^d And after the deth of his Grand Mother the

houſe and lot where I now dwell with the land adjoining as it is discribed
to his Grand Mother on the North Side of the Stage Road and bounding
on the Land of Joseph French and Rode to Coles Medow when he arrives
to the age of twenty one years and that if my Grand Son Samuel should
decíe before his Grand Mother then the land given to him after the deceſe
of his Grand Mother must be sold and the money arriſseing the sɑle thereof
must be devided between my then surviveing Children and Sarah Ann
French my Grand daughter share alike sons and Daughters I likewiſe give
to my Grand Son Samuel French the Remainder of my wood land to the
Eastward of Coles Medow Road after a ſufficency be sold for the payment
of my debts, but my Executors is to have the care of the property and see
that no wast be committed and if he should die without Lawful Iſue I
order it to be sold and dispoſed of as above but if he should survive his
grand Mother and have lawful Iſue I give it to him his heirs and aſsigns
forever.

10ᵗʰ I give and devise to my grand daughter Sarah Ann French two
hundred dollars to be paid to her by my Son Charles H. French out of the
plantation given to him and in cafe she should deceaſe before she is twenty
years of age then this Legacy to decend to all my then surviving Children
share alike.

Lastly I Nominate my Son Charles H. French and Jacob Borton my
Son-in Law to be Executors to this my last will and testament and to see
that the same be strickly complyed with. In Witneſs whereof I have hereunto Set my hand and affixed my Seal this Ninth day of June one thouſand
Eight hundred and twenty one 1821—In the preſence of the Subscribing
witneſses who at my Request have aſsigned their thereto—

Edward French

Signed Sealed pronounced and by ⎞ Hugh Hollinshead
the testator to be his Last Will & ⎬ Thomas Gill
testament in the preſence of us.   ⎠ William Hooton

Hugh Hollinshead & William Hooten two of the witneſses to the within
will being duly sworn & affirmed, to wit the said Hugh Hollinshead being
duly sworn, & the said William Hooten alleging himself to be conscientiously scrupulous of taking an oath & being duly affirmed according to law,
upon their respective oath & affirmation declare & say, that they saw
Edward French the testator therein named deceased sign & seal the fame
& heard him publish, pronounce & declare the within writing to be his last
will and testament; that at the time of the doing thereof the said testator

was of sound and disposing mind & memory so far as this deponent & affirmant know & as they verily believe; and that Thomas Gill the other Subscribing evidence was present at the ſame time & signed his name as a witneſs to the said will together with this deponent & affirmant in the preſence of the said testator

Sworn & affirmed the 7th Septʳ A. D. Hugh Hollinshead
1822 before me William Hooten
  Abrm. Brown Surrog

Charles H. French & Jacob Borton executors within named alleging themselves to be conscientiously scrupulous of taking an oath & being duly affirmed according to law declare & say that the within instrument contains the true last will & testament of Edward French the testator therein named deceased so far as they know & as they verily believe; that they will well & truly perform the ſame by paying first the debts of the said deceased and then the legacies in the said testament specified so far as the goods, chattels & credits of the said deceased can thereunto extend; & that they will make & exhibit into the Prerogative Office at Trenton a true & perfect inventory of all & singular the goods & chattels & credits of the said deceased which have or shall come to their knowledge or poſseſsion or to the poſseſsion of any other person or persons for their use & render a just & true account when thereunto lawfully required.

Charles H French
Jacob Borton

Affirmed the 7ᵗʰ day of Septʳ A. D. ⎫
1822 before me Abrm. Brown—Surrog ⎭

INVENTORY OF THE ESTATE OF EDWARD FRENCH, 1822

A True & perfect inventory of all and singular the Goods and Chattels rights & credits of Edward French Deceased Late of the township of Chester & County of Burlington Made by us whose names are hereunto subscribed The fifth day of September One thousand eight hundred & twenty two Thus 1822

	D. cts
Purse and wearing Apparel	68.02
Horse Chais & harneſs	89.00

Horned Cattle	26.00
Swine	9.00
Plate and Other household Goods	439.75
Corn Growing at the time of his Death	55.00
Hay and Grain in the barn	80.00
Potatoes & vegitables in the Ground	5.00
Cider Mill & prefses & Emty Casks	35.50
Fruit fallen	2.00
Stills & appurtenances belonging thereto	123.00
Boiler	2.00
Buckwheat standing	3.00
Implements of husbandry	27.25
Debts	945.89
	$1909.41

Appraised by us the day }   William Roberts
and year above written }   Wm Doughten

1822 Sep^t 7th 1 Sheep & 1 Cupboard since appraised............. 5.50

Affirmed the 7th day of Sept^m AD.   Wm Doughten
1822 before me—Abm. Brown Surog   Charles H. French
                                         Jacob Borton

122—URIAH FRENCH (Thomas, 1; Thomas, 6; Thomas, 33).

          b. 3rd mo. 14th, 1748.
          d. 1823.
          m. First, June 29th, 1771, Rachel Ingersoll,
             daughter of Ebenezer Ingersoll, of Great Egg
             Harbour, N. J.
          m. Second, August 6th, 1800, Isabella Peacock,
             widow.

297—MARY FRENCH   m. ——— Haines.

298—REBECCA FRENCH

299—URIAH FRENCH, JR.   b. 5th mo. 27th, 1788.
                               m. Ann Bates.

300—GEORGE FRENCH

WILL OF URIAH FRENCH, 1822

I Uriah French of the Township of Chester, County of Burlington and State of New Jersey, Senior—being of sound mind and memory, do make and publish this for my last Will and Testament.

First My Will is, that the House and Lot, or corner lot, that lies on the Burlington and Moorestown Roads, containing about one Acre of Land more or less, may be sold, and the Money arising therefrom to pay my just Debts and Funeral charges, and the residue, I give and bequeath to dear Wife Iszabella French and to Margaret Peacock, Daughter to said Iszabella—to be equally divided between them.

Second,—The House and Farm whereon I now live containing about nineteen Acres and three roods of Land, more or leſs, with all the appurtenances, And also all my Moveable effects wherever they may be found, I give and bequeath to my dear Wife Iszabella French and her said Daughter Margaret Peacock, (During the natural life of my said Wife Iszabella French) to be equally divided between them, And at my Wife's Decease, my Will is, that the same may fall to her said Daughter Margaret Peacock to her and her heirs, forever.

Third, I give and bequeath to Mary Haines, Rebecca French, Uriah French & George French, my sons and Daughters, five Dollars a piece to be paid to them, or their heirs in five years after my Decease. I appoint James Vansciver Executor, and my Wife Iszabella French Executrix, of this my Testament and last Will. In Witneſs whereof I have hereto set my hand an Seal, this twenty fouth day of September in the year of our Lord one thousand eight hundred and twenty-two.

Uriah French Senr

Signed, Sealed, published & declared   } John Ward
by the said Uriah French Senr to be his } David Ward
Testament & last Will, in presence of us } Abraham Heulings

John Ward one of the witneſses to the within will alleging himself to be conscientiously scrupulous of taking an oath and being duly affirmed according to law doth declare and say that he ſaw Uriah French Senr the testator therein named deceased sign and seal the ſame and heard him publish, pronounce and declare the within writing to be his last will and testament.

Affirmed the 30th day of May }
A. D. 1823 before me   }   John Ward
    Abrm Brown Surrog— }

Isabella French and James Vansciver executors within named being duly sworn depose and say that the within instrument contains the true last will and testament of Uriah French Sen[r] the testator therein named deceased so far as they know & as they verily believe; that they will well and truly perform the fame by paying first the debts of the said deceased and then the legacies in the said testament specified so far as the goods chattels and credits of the said deceased can thereunto extend; and that they will make and exhibit into the Prerogative Office at Trenton a true and perfect inventory of all and singular the goods chattels and credits of the said deceased which have or shall come to their knowledge or pofsefsion or to the pofsefsion of any other person or persons for their use, and render a just & true account when thereunto lawfully required.

Sworn the 30th day of May   Isabella French
A. D. 1823 before me   James Vanfciver.
     Abrm Brown Surrog

123—GEORGE FRENCH (Thomas, 1; Thomas, 6; Thomas, 33).

         b. 2nd mo. 9th, 1753.
         d. 1827.
         m. 5th mo. 1775, Rachel Rakestraw, daughter of
           Thomas Rakestraw.
     She b. 9th mo. 8th, 1755.

301—WILLIAM FRENCH   b. 3rd mo. 30th, 1776.
                           m. Abigail ———.

302—ABRAHAM FRENCH   b. 5th mo. 23rd, 1778.

303—SUSANNAH FRENCH   b. 11th mo. 16th, 1781.
                           m. 11th mo. 14th, 1811, Andrew Hollingshead.

304—BATHSHEBA FRENCH   b. 3rd mo. 15th, 1783.
                           m. 4th mo. 24th, 1806, Joseph Roberts.

305—ISAAC FRENCH   b. 9th mo. 8th, 1785.
                           d. 10th mo. 14th, 1791.

306—JACOB FRENCH   b. 5th mo. 8th, 1788.
                           d. 10th mo. 15th, 1791.

307—FIRMAN FRENCH   b. 7th mo. 29th, 1791.
                           d. 10th mo. 21st, 1791.

308—RACHEL FRENCH   b. 7th mo. 30th, 1792.
                           m. 10th mo. 13th, 1814, Enoch Roberts.

309—MATILDA FRENCH   b. 12th mo. 14th, 1795.
                           m. Thomas Quick.

GEORGE FRENCH

George French, the youngest son of Thomas [33] throughout a long and busy life was one of the most prominent and useful citizens of Moorestown. In 1774, when he was twenty-one years of age, his brother Edward conveyed to him, " for ten pounds and natural love and good will which he beareth toward his brother and for his better support," three lots, fifteen acres and a house, in the west end of Moorestown.   He at once entered into business and prospered greatly, accumulating considerable property for those days, as will be observed by his will, in which provision was made for his children and grand children.   He took an active interest in local affairs, holding various offices during a period of forty years.   In 1784 he was chosen tax collector for Chester township, assessor in 1787 and again in 1805, member of the township committee, or " representative," in 1796–99 and 1800–1.   In 1799 he served as chosen freeholder.   He was justice of the peace for many years later in life.

MEETING RECORDS

Evesham Monthly Meeting Minutes:
    At a monthly meeting held at Evesham ye 6th of ye 4th mo. 1775. George French son of Thos. French dec'd. & Rachel Rakestraw Daughter of Thos. Rakestraw Dec'd appeared and Declared their Intentions of marriage with Each other.   Therefore Wm. Matlock and John Lippincott are appointed to make ye needful Enquiery & report to next meeting his mother being present consented.

    At a monthly meeting held at Evesham ye 4th of ye 5th mo. 1775. George French & Rachel Rakestraw appeared & signified the Continuation of their Intentions of marriage with Each other ye Friends appointed to make Enquiery reporting nothing to obstruct their proceedings.   Therefore they are at Liberty to Consumate their said Intentions according to good order & Thos. Wilkins & Joseph Wilcox are appointed to be present & see that good order be kept & report to next meeting.

Minutes of Evesham Monthly Meeting of Women Friends:
6th of 4th Mo. 1775. George French and Rachel Rakestraw appeared and declared their intentions of marriage with each other. Two friends appointed to enquire intó her life & conversation & make report.

4—5 mo. 1775. George French and Rachel Rakestraw appeared and signified the continuation of their intentions of marriage.

8—6 mo. 1775. The friends appointed to attend the marriage of George French and Rachel Rakestraw report it was orderly accomplished.

[Men's Meeting]
At a Monthly Meeting held at Evesham ye 4th of ye 11th mo. 1779. Friends from the Preparative Meeting at Chester reported that Jos'n Morgan Junr & George French had been treated with for paying a fine in Lieu of their personal service in ye Militia therefore Jacob Hollinshead & John Riſdon are appointed to visit them and report to next meeting.

At a Monthly Meeting held at Evesham ye 9th of ye 12th Mo. 1779. One of ye Friends appointed reported that they had Visited Josn Morgan Junr. & George French who did not appear disposed to make Friends satisfaction, therefore this meeting Disowns them from having any right of membership with us until they are favour'd to see their Error & make ye necessary Satisfaction & Joseph Worinton & John Collins are appointed to give them a Copy of this minute and report to next meeting.

At a Monthly Meeting held at Evesham the 6th of ^{ye} 1st Mo. 1780. The friends appointed reported that they have given Joseph Morgan Junr and George French Copies of this Meeting's Minute against them.

REVOLUTIONARY DAMAGES

Inventory of Goods and Chattels of George French Plundered by the British Troops in June 1778—
1 Cow, 3 Sheep, half a Ton Clover hay......................£8 15 —

Henry Bradshaw being affirmed Declared that he Saw the British Troops Runing After the Cow above mentioned, and Soon After their Departure Saw Such Remains of her as Convinced him that the Said Cow was killed by the Said Troops, and as he lived in the Same House with the above Applicant has good Reason to Believe that the other articles Contained in the Above Inventory, was Plundered by the aforesaid British Troops.

Henry Bradshaw.

CHESTER TOWNSHIP'S AID TO PHILADELPHIA, 1793

Richard S. Smith being appointed at a Town Meeting held the 12th Day of October last to receive such monies as Should be Collected from the Inhabitants and to forward the same to the Committee appointed in Philadelphia for the Relief of the poor of that city labouring under the dreadful Malady called the Yellow Fever Reported That he had Received from the different collectors as follows:

Octr 12 1793	of	William Roberts the sum of	...........£13	1	4—1/2
20	of	do	 22	17	3
Jany 9 1794	of	do	 3	17	6
Oct 19 1793	of	Nathaniel Middleton	 7	0	7—1/2
Nov 22	of	do	 4	6	2
Jany 9 1794	of	do	 1	2	6
Oct 22 1793	of	George French	 22	10	0
Jany 9 1794	of	do	 2	19	4—1/2
Oct 22 1793	of	Samuel Shute	 5	0	0
" 29	of	do	 0	7	11
Nov 30	of	do	 4	0	0
Jany 9 1794	of	do	 0	4	0
Mch 11	of	Joseph Morgan subscribed in Pine Wood	2	9	6
		Total Sum Received	....................£89	16	2—1/2

WILL OF GEORGE FRENCH, 1825

Let is be recorded that I George French of the Township of Chester in the County of Burlington and State of New Jersey, being at this time week of body yet favour'd with Sound disposing mind and memory: I do make and ordain this to be my last will and Testament in words following—(First) I will and order that all my Just debts and funeral charges be paid by my Executor herein after named and appointed out of my personal effects, as early after my decease as convenience will admit.

(Second.) I will and bequeath to my grandson William French the Sum of Two hundred Dollars in cash to be paid to him by my Executor within one year after my decease; and also four Shares of the Stock I hold in the Camden bank.— (Third.) I will and bequeath to my grand-daughter Harriot Brown the Sum of Two hundred Dollars in cash, to be paid to her by my Executor within one year after my decease; and alsò four Shares of the Stock I hold in the Camden Bank.

(Fourth.) I will and bequeath to my grandsons George Hollinshead and Charles Roberts each of them one new Silver watch of the value of eighteen Dollars each.

23

(Fifth.) I will and bequeath to my grandson Isaac One hundred Dollars in cash, to be paid by my Executor out of my personal estate.

(Sixth.) I will and bequeath to Lydia Peacock widow of Isaac Peacock Deceased Eighteen Dollars in cash, to be paid to her by my Executor out of my Personal estate.

(Seventh.) I will and bequeath to my Daughter Susanna Hollinshead the new house and lot of Land at the corner of Bodine road So called, where She now dwells; with all the Improvements that are thereon, to have and to hold to her; her Heirs and aſsigns forever.—(Eighth.) I will and bequeath to my Daughter Bathsheba Roberts the house lot of Land and other Improvements that are thereon which I purchased of John Anderson together with a lot of land adjoining the Same marked on the draught thereof N° 3. containing three acres and three roods of Land be the Same more or leſs; to have and to hold to her, her heirs and aſsigns forever; and also one hundred Dollars in cash, to be paid to her by my Executor within one year after my Decease

(Ninth.) I will and bequeath to my Daughter Rachel Roberts the house, lot of Land and the Improvements that are thereon, where She now dwells; which I purcased of the Aſsigneese of Joshua Humpries, together with all that lot of Land I purchased of Doctor Daniel Benneville to have and to hold to her, her heirs and aſsigns forever; and also Three hundred Dollars in cash to be paid to her by my Executor within one year after my decease.—

(Tenth.) I will and bequeath to my Daughter Matilda French the house, lot of Land and the improvements that are thereon which I purchased of Uriah French together with that lot of Land adjoining the Same marked on the draught N° 2 containing Six acres two Roods and fifteen perches of Land be the Same more or leſs; to have and to hold to her; her heirs and aſsigns forever; and also the Sum of four hundred Dollars in cash to be paid to her by my Executor within one year after my decease: And I also give unto her four Shares of the Stock I hold in the Camden bank; And one good bed, bedding, and bedstead; the bureau that has been commonly called hers and the breakfast table Standing in the parlor:—It is my will that if there Should be any claim ever hereafter made on any part of the Land I have heretofore bequeathed whereby the right and interest of either of my said children should be Injured; that I do hereby subject and make liable each and every Share I have aforesaid bequeathed, in equal proportions, to make good Such injury, to the child injured if any should occour by paying to them their due proportions thereof.

(Eleventh.) All the rest, residue and remainder of my estate both real and personal whatsoever and wheresoever I will and direct my executor to Sell, hereby impowering him to make titles to the Said Lands as good and Sufficient as I myself might or could do were I personally present—and the procedes of the Sales after paying out my Just debts, funeral charges, the Legacys aforesaid and the expenses of the Settlement of my estate, I will to be divided into five equal proportions; and one fifth part thereof I will and bequeath to my Daughter Susanna Hollinshead; and one other fifth part thereof I will and bequeath to my Daughter Bathsheba Roberts and one other fifth part thereof I will and bequeath to my Daughter Rachel Roberts, and one other fifth part thereof I will and bequeath to my Daughter Matilda French; and the remaining other fifth part thereof I will to be equally divided between my grandson William French and my granddaughter Harriot Brown Share and Share alike.

And lastly I do constitute and appoint my esteemed friend Benjamin H. Lippincott Executor of this my last will and testament; herby renouncing and revokeing all other and former wills and testaments by me at any time heretofore made and this only to be taken for my last will.

In Witnefs whereof I have hereunto Set my hand and Seal this fourteenth day of the eleventh month (called November) in the year of our Lord one Thousand eight hundred and twenty five. (1825.)

Signed Sealed pronounced and declared by the above named George French to be his last will and testament in the presence of us who have Subscribed our names as witnefses thereto in the presence of the testator.

> James Todd
> Clayton Roberts
> Hugh Shotwell.

Clayton Roberts one of the witnefses to the within will alleging himself to be conscientiously scrupulous of taking an oath & being duly affirmed according to law doth declare & say that he saw George French the testator therein named deceased sign & seal the same & heard him publish, pronounce & declare the within writing to be his last will & testament that at the time of the doing thereof the said testator was of sound & disposing mind & memory so far as this affirmant knows & as he verily believes; & that James Todd & Hugh Shotwell the other subscribing evidences were present at the same time and signed their names as witnefses to the said will together with this affirmant in the presence of the said testator.

Affirmed the 25th day of September
A. D. 1827 before me
    Abm. Brown Surrog

Clayton Roberts.

Benjamin H. Lippincott sole executor within named alleging himself to be conscientiously scrupulous of taking an oath & being duly affirmed according to law doth declare & say that the within instrument contains the true last will and testament of George French the testator therein named deceased so far as he knows & as he verily believes; that he will well and truly perform the same by paying first the debts of the said deceased and then the legacies in the said testament specified so far as the goods, chattels & credits of the said deceased can thereunto extend; and that he will make and exhibit into the Prerogative Office at Trenton a true and perfect inventory of all & singular the goods, chattels & credits of the said deceased which have or shall come to his knowledge or poſseſsion or to the poſseſsion of any other person or persons for his use, and render a just and true account when thereunto lawfully required

Affirmed the 25th day of September ⎫
A. D. 1827 before me   ⎬   Benjamin H. Lippincott.
        Abrm Brown Surrog   ⎭

INVENTORY OF THE ESTATE OF GEORGE FRENCH, 1827

A True and perfect Inventory of all and Singular the goods, chattels, rights and credits of George French late of the Township of Chester in the County of Burlington deceased, made by us whose names are hereunto Subscribed the twenty first day of the ninth month in the year of our Lord 1827.

	Dol	cts.
His apparel and Silver watch	18	00
Purse	403	96
Sixteen Shares of Camden Bank Stock	640	00
Plate and other Household goods &c	233	50
Debts due on Bonds, Notes &c	2979	19
Interest on Said obligations	182	47
Rent in arrear	259	18
Due on Book accounts	310	69
Total.	$5026	99

Appraised by us the day and year above written

                                                      William Roberts
Affirmed the 25th day of September   Amos Stiles
A. D. 1827 before me
        Abrm: Brown Surrog—

127—MARY FRENCH (Thomas, 1; Thomas, 6; Robert, 35).

> b. 10th mo. 4th, 1740.
>
> m. First, 12th mo. 24th, 1761, William Hold-craft of Chester Township, Burlington Co., N. J.
>
> m. Second, 3rd mo. 16th, 1797, Isaac Gibbs.

310—ROBERT HOLDCRAFT

311—WILLIAM HOLDCRAFT

MEETING RECORDS

Evesham Monthly Meeting Minutes:

At a monthly meeting held at Evesham ye 5th of ye 11th mo. 1761 William Holdcraft, & Mary French Daughter of Robert French Dec^d appeared and Declared their Intentions of marriage with each other, therefore Edmd Hollinshead & John Lippincott are appointed to make Enquiery Concerning the young mans clearness & Conversation & make report thereof to our next meeting, her mother being present consented.

At a Monthly Meeting held at Evesham ye 10th of ye 12th mo. 1761 William Holdcraft & Mary French appeared and signified the continuation of their Intention of marriage with Each other, the friends appointed to make Enquiry reporting nothing to obstruct their proceeding, therefore they are at Liberty to proceed therein according to good order and Thos. Warrington & John Lippincott are appointed to be present and see that good order be kept and make report thereof to our next meeting.

At a monthly meeting held at Evesham ye 7th of ye 1st Mo. 1762. The friends appointed to attend the marriage of William Holdcraft and Mary French, reported that it was orderly accomplished.

Minutes of Evesham Monthly Meeting of Women Friends:

5" of 11 mo. 1761. Wm. Holdcraft and Mary French appeared and declared their intentions of taking each other in marriage.

10" of 12" mo. 1761. Wm. Holdcraft and Mary French appeared and signified the continuation of their intention of marriage. Nothing obstructing they are allowed to proceed.

7" of 1" mo. 1762. The overseers appointed to attend the marriage of Wm. Holdcraft & Mary French report that it was orderly accomplished.

129—THOMAS FRENCH (Thomas, 1; Thomas, 6; Robert, 35).

> b. 12th mo. 26th, 1745.
> d. 2nd mo. 2nd, 1785.
> m. April 22nd, 1769, Mercy Cox, daughter of
> Newberry and Elizabeth Cox.
> She b. 8th mo. 26th, 1746.
> d. 2nd mo. 1st, 1807.

312—ELIZABETH FRENCH   b. 2nd mo. 4th, 1770.
                         m. 11th mo. 15th, 1796, Joseph Jones.

313—JAMES FRENCH   b. 3rd mo. 13th, 1773.
                         m. 5th mo. 17th, 1801, Mary Rogers.

314—THOMAS FRENCH, JR.   b. 3rd mo. 13th, 1773.
                         d. 1st mo. 23rd, 1852.
                         m. sup., 1798, Esther Cattel, at Red Stone
                         Meeting, Fayette County, Penna.
                    She b. 3rd mo. 28th, 1780.
                         d. 7th mo. 27th, 1856 (no issue).

315—HANNAH FRENCH   b. 6th mo. 7th, 1775.
                         m. 5th mo., 1797, Anthony Morris, Jr.

316—JOSEPH FRENCH   b. 1st mo. 23rd, 1778.
                         d. 1st mo. 23rd, 1778.

317—ROBERT FRENCH   b. 4th mo. 24th, 1779.
                         m. 2nd mo. 25th, 1807, Ann Street.

318—BARZILLAI FRENCH   b. 7th mo. 23rd, 1781.
                         m. 11th mo. 1st, 1810, Mary Yates.

319—ELIJAH FRENCH   b. 5th mo. 4th, 1784.
                         m. 3rd mo. 4th, 1807, Susannah Curle.

MEETING RECORDS

Evesham Monthly Meeting Minutes:
At a Monthly Meeting held at Evesham ye 8th of ye 3rd mo. 1770.
Thos. French produced an acknowledgement for outgoing in marriage which
was read and referred for Consideration.

At a Monthly Meeting held at Evesham ^{ye} 5th of ^{ye} 4th Mo. 1770. Thomas Frenches acknowledgement is now accepted of & is in the following words—

The 8th of ^{ye} 3^d mo. 1770. To ^{ye} monthly meeting at Evesham,—Dear Friends, Whereas I ^{ye} Subscriber hereof have been Educated in ^{ye} principles of Truth, But for want of adhearing to ^{ye} true teacher, have so farr Diviated from ^{ye} good rules Established by Friends as to Consummate my marriage Contrary to ye good order, & by so Doing have Brought Sorrow on myself & friends For which misconduct I am heartily Sorry, hopeing this with my orderly walking for the Future may again Bring me under ^{ye} Care & notice of Friends is the hearty Desire of your friend.

Thomas French

[Women's Meeting]

9" of 7" mo. 1772   Mary French requests to be taken under the care of Friends. Ann Stokes and Esther and Rebecca Roberts are to visit her and enquire into the motive of her request.

6—8 mo. 1772. Friends having considered the request of Mary the wife of Thos. French and having nothing to object but that her request may be granted with desires for her further groath in the Truth.

5—3 mo. 1784. Friends from the Preparative Meeting at Chester report, that Thomas French and wife makes request for their daughter Elizabeth French to be joined in membership with Friends. Two Friends are appointed to visit her.

9th 4th Mo. 1784. The Friends appointed to visit Elizabeth French report that they have had an opportunity with her to some good degree of satisfaction; and having the concurrence of the Men's Meeting, this meeting concludes to grant the request.

[Men's Meeting]

9th 4th Mo. 1784. The Women inform that Tho's. French requests that his Daughter Eliz: (a minor) may be received under friends Care & they having visited her and expressing their satisfaction, She is accordingly received and they are desired to acquaint her therewith.

At a Monthly Meeting held at Evesham ye 9th of 7th Mo. 1784. A Certificate was desired for Thos. French Marcy his Wife & their Seven Children vizt. Eliz., James, Thomas, Hannah, Robert, Barzillai & Elijah to Mount Holly; therefore Jos. Hunt & Abrm. Warrington are appointed to make the necesſary enquiry and if nothing appears to obstruct prepare one and produce it to next meeting.

[Women's Meeting]

9" 7 Mo. 1784. Marcy French requests to be included with her husband and children (to wit) Eliz. James, Thos. Hannah, Robert, Barzillai and Elijah in a certificate to Friends of Mount Holly Monthly Meeting. Abigail Stokes and Elizabeth Cattle are appointed to make the necessary inquiry concerning her, and give their account to Friends appointed to draw it.

[Men's Meeting]

At a Monthly Meeting held at Evesham ^{ye} 6th of 8th Mo. 1784.— The Friends appointed reported some obstruction in preparing a Cert. for Thomas French and Family; which being considered they are desired to continue their care therein.

At a Monthly Meeting held at Evesham the 10th of the 9th M^{o}. 1784 The Friends appointed to prepare a Certificate for Thos. French and Family are continued to the service.

At a Monthly Meeting held at Evesham the 8th of 10th M^{o}. 1784. The Friends appointed to prepare a Certificate for Thos. French and Family are continued to the service.

At a Monthly Meeting held at Evesham ^{ye} 5th of 11th M^{o}. 1784. The Friends appointed to prepare a certificate for Thos. French & Family are continued to the service.

At a Monthly Meeting held at Evesham the 10th of 12th Mo. 1784. The Friends appointed to prepare a certificate for Thos. French and Family are continued to the service.

At a Monthly Meeting held at Evesham the 7th of 1st Mo. 1785. The Friends appointed to prepare Certificate for Thomas French and Family are continued to the service.

At a Monthly Meeting held at Evesham the 11th of 2^{d} Mo. 1785. The Friends appointed to prepare a Certificate for Thomas French and Family inform'd the Meeting that the obstruction heretofore reported, was removed, but that himself is deceased since last Meeting; and that his Widow and Children have a prospect of returning to reside within the limits of this Meeting; which being considered, it is apprehended that further care respecting a Certificate for them at present, maȳ be suspended.

[Women's Meeting]

11th of 2nd Mo. 1785. The men inform, that the request made in the 7 mo. last for a certificate on behalf of Thomas French and family having met with obstruction, which has since been removed: That himself is since deceased, and his family expecting still to continue members of this meeting: The request is therefore discontinued.

Record book of Sufferings of Friends of Evesham Monthly Meeting for non Compliance of Military duty.

12th Mo. 24th 1777. Taken from Thomas French, by Savory Toy Constable, by Virtue of a Law of New Jersey & warrent under ye hands & Seals of Peter Stretch and William Hough, one Calf & 25 Bushels of Indian Corn rated — — — £6: 0: 0   Fines Demanded £26: 5: 0—

Thomas French

SIGNATURE TO MARRIAGE BOND, 1769

COMB-BACK CHAIR, 1790

131—ROBERT FRENCH, JR. (Thomas, 1; Thomas, 6; Robert, 35).

          b. 3rd mo. 10th, 1749.

          d. 1811.

          m. First, 2nd mo. 15th, 1785, Hannah Warring-
ton, daughter of Thomas and Mary (Roberts)
Warrington.

    She b. 1760.

          d. 4th mo. 4th, 1786.

          m. Second, 5th mo. 1803, Elizabeth Stokes [170],
daughter of John and Hannah (Stockdell)
Stokes.

    She b. 5th mo. 31st, 1759.

          d. 1st mo. 26th, 1847.

320—MARY FRENCH   b. 1st mo. 6th, 1786.
                         m. 3rd mo. 24th, 1808, Josiah Roberts.

ROBERT FRENCH, JR.

Robert French, Jr., the third son of Robert French [35] was a life-long
resident of the vicinity of Moorestown, N. J., and a worthy and useful citizen.
Having learned the trade of mason, he pursued that calling in connection with
farming at the old homestead, inherited from his father.   In 1782 he became
a trustee of the property granted to Friends of Chester Preparative Meeting,
Moorestown, including care of the old meeting house ground and graveyard,
and also of that on which the present meeting house and school building
stand, on the south side of Main Street, and continued a trustee for nearly
thirty years.   He was master mason in the construction of the meeting house
built in 1802.   All his life he was active in the affairs of Chester Preparative Meeting and Evesham Monthly Meeting.   His wise counsel and faithful coöperation were sought concerning many matters of weight, such as
discipline, marriage, education, orderly living, attendance upon worship,
temperance, philanthropy, setting up of meetings, etc.   The meeting records
relating to him are remarkable.   He set a consistent example and exercised
wide influence.   He was overseer of highways of Chester Township in 1798.
His wife, Elizabeth (Stokes) French, survived him many years.   In her will,
dated 3rd mo. 21st, 1839, proved Feby. 16, 1847, she made the kindly request
that her wearing apparel be placed with her executors, in trust, " to be dis-

ROBERT FRENCH HOUSE, NEAR MOORESTOWN, N. J.

posed of as they may think best amongst the poorer class of women in the vicinity of Moorestown or elsewhere."

MEETING RECORDS

Evesham Monthly Meeting Minutes:

At a Monthly Meeting held at Evesham ye 6th of 12th mo. 1781— Robert French appointed as one of a Committee to consider & report their judgment respecting the time of admitting and passing of Marriages.

At a Monthly Meeting held at Evesham ye 8th of ye 8th Mo. 1782— Wm. Rogers on behalf of the committee appointed to collect an account of the sufferings of friends within the compass of this Meeting requested an additional number thereto there being two members Dec'd. since appointment & William Matlack one of the surviving members requested a release which was granted & Enoch Evans, Job Collins, John Roberts, Joshua Hunt & Robert French are added in the room of such as are dec'd or released from the service.

At a Monthly meeting held at Evesham the 7th of 1st Mo. 1785. Robert French Son of Robert French dec'd. and Hannah Warrington Daughter of Thomas Warrington appeared and declared their intentions of Marriage with each other his Mother being present consented, and the Meeting being inform'd that her Father was also consenting: Wm. Matlack and John Collins are appointed to inquire into his clearness and conversation and report to next Meeting.

At a Monthly Meeting held at Evesham the 11th of. 2^d Mo. 1785. Robert French and Hannah Warrington appeared and declared the continuation of their Intentions of Marriage with each other, the Friends appointed reporting nothing to obstruct their proceedings they are at liberty to consumate their marriage and John Collins and Joshua Hunt are appointed to be present, see that good order be kept, and report to next Meeting.

At a Monthly Meeting held at Evesham the 11th of 3rd Mo. 1785. The Friends appointed to attend the Marriage of Robert French and Hannah Warrington reported that is was orderly accomplished.

[Women's Meeting]

7th. 1st Mo. 1785. Robert French and Hannah Warrington appeared and declared their intentions of marriage with each other, his mother being present consented.

11th of 2nd Mo. 1785. Robert French and Hannah Warrington appeared and signified the continuation of their intentions of marriage with each other, and nothing appearing to obstruct they are at liberty to consumate the same.

11—3 mo. 1785. The Friends appointed to attend the marriage of Robert French and Hannah Warrington, reported that it was orderly accomplished.

[Men's Meeting]

At a Monthly Meeting held at Evesham the 9th of the 5th Mo. 1788— Robert French being sometime since appointed by this Meeting to inspect the Account of Friends Sufferings now requested to be released thereform, which was granted.

At a Monthly meeting held at Evesham the 10th of 2^d mo. 1792— It being divers times heretofore proposed, and now again revived the expediency of selecting several Minutes of Advices from our Book of Discipline which might be profitably communicated to Parents and heads of Families, in a meeting of conferrence for that purpose appointed; which after being solidly deliberated upon it appeared the united sense that John Collins, Wm Roberts, John Roberts, Rob't. French, Samuel Roberts senr., Wm. Rogers, Bethuel Moore, Enoch Evans, Joshua Lippincott, Job Haines, Job Collins, Jos^a Owen and Joshua Stokes be appointed to take the subject under their weighty consideration, & report their service to next Meeting.

At a Monthly Meeting held at Evesham 10th of 5th mo. 1793— A proposition relative to the division of this meeting being divers times heretofore suggested for consideration, and the subject at last meeting being revived and weightily deliberated upon, it appeared the prevailing sense that could the proposed division be effected with that uniting harmony the nature of the case required, it might be productive of real advantage to the members of this Meeting, and the benefit of Society; in consequence whereof divers friends were then verbally appointed to attend the several prepara- tive meetings constituting this, in order to obtain their unanimous sense and Judgment thereon: who now reported, that agreeable to the tenour of their appointment they have attended the several preparative meetings, who appear generally united that the proposed division might be beneficial should it be concluded with that unamity the subject requires; which report being weightily deliberated upon, it appeared the united sense that the following named friends be appointed to take the subject matter relative to the mode and manner of sd. proposed division into solid deliberation, proceed theirin as they may be enabled in the wisdom of Truth, and report thereon to this meeting when necessary, vizt. Jno. Collins, Abraham Warrington, Jno. Roberts, Robert French, Joseph Roberts, Joshua Matlack, Wm. Roberts, Reuben Matlack, Wm. Rogers, Theo. Hollinshead, Enoch Evans, Isiah Haines, Joshua Lippincott, Isaac Borton, Stacy Haines, Wm. Haines, Thos. Lippincott, Jno. Haines Junr., Wm. Allison, Jos. Owen, Jno. Haines, Job Collins, Sam'l. Shinn, Barzillai Braddock, Joshua Stokes, Lawrence Webster & Job Prickett: who agree to meet at this place next second day week at the eleventh Hour.

At a Monthly Meeting held at Evesham the 11th of 10th mo. 1793. Friends from the preparative meeting at Chester reported that Robert French requesting to be released from ye station of an Overseer, they were united in proposing for consideration the appointment of Abraham Warrington to succeed him therein; which on deliberation appears to be fully concurred with.

At a Monthly Meeting held at Evesham the 8th of 11th Mo. 1793— Friends from the preparative meeting at upper Evesham reported that divers members residing at a place called new hopewell within their limits, request liberty for holding meetings of worship every other first day, and the third 5th day in each month for five months next ensuing, at a house of Jonathan Jones beginning at the eleventh hour; which being attended to with a good degree of solid weight & sympathy wherein it appeares the prevailing sense that sd. meetings be held agreeable to request for three months, the first of which to be held next first day, & that Job Collins, Isaac Borton, Jos. Owen, Ephraim Stratton and Robert French be appointed to have the overst. thereof, & report their sense thereon in the second mo. next.

At a Monthly Meeting held at Evesham the 10th of 1st mo. 1794 The consideration of the Extracts being resumed by reading them again at this time, & after a time of mature deliberation, it appeared the prevailing sense, that Robert French, Jno. Hunt, Jno. Collins, Jno. Borton, Jno. Maxwell, Wm. Rogers, Stacy Haines and Henry Warrington be appointed to unite with the Overseers in giving further attention to the subject of the right Education of our Youth and Others in endeavouring to promote a consistency with our profession in their Dress & general deportment; and report their service herein to this Meeting in the ninth mo. next.

At a Monthly Meeting held at Evesham the 11th of 4th Mo. 1794 Joseph Engle on behalf of the Committee in negro-cases proposed for consideration, the appointment of a meeting for the benefit of that people, which is concurred with, to be held at this place next first day Week, beginning at the third Hour P. M: and Jno. Collins, Jacob Hollinshead, Robert French, Job Haines, Joseph Engle, and Wm. Rogers are appointed to have the oversight thereof, and report to next Meeting.

At a Monthly Meeting held at Evesham the 6th of 6th Mo. 1794. Report was now made that the select Meetings of Ministers & Elders held at this place are much smaller than heretofore, in consequence of the establishment of upper Evesham monthly meeting; and apprehending it consistent with Discipline, that the appointment of select members should be an act of the monthly meeting, Abraham Warrington, Jno. Collins, Robert French, Jno. Roberts, Wm. Snowdon, Wm. Rogers, Job Haines and Gabriel Davis are desired to take the subject under weighty deliberation, & as way may open propose to the Monthly meeting for approbation, such friends as they may apprehend qualified for that Station—who agree to meet at Chester meeting House, next third Day.

At a Monthly Meeting held at Evesham the 11th of 7th Mo. 1794
The Committee appointed to deliberate on the subject of nominating select members to this Meeting having attended thereto were united in proposing Rob't. French and Job Haines to that Station, which being severally considered, were, after weighty deliberation, concurred with; and the Clk. directed to notify the next Quarterly meeting of Ministers and Elders thereof, by transmitting a copy of this Minutes consents thereto.

At a Monthly Meeting held at Evesham the 5th of 12th mo. 1794.
The preparative meeting at Chester inform that divers of their Members, living somewhat remote from said meeting, have requested the liberty of holding three meetings in friends lower School House in Chester aforesaid to be held the first, first days following our monthly meetings in the first, second, & third months, beginning at the Eleventh hour A. M.: which being deliberated upon with a good degree of solid weight, there appeared a union in granting said request, & appointmt. of Robert French, Abraham Warrington and Saml. Lippincott to have the oversight thereof, & report theron to this meeting in the 4th mo. next.

11th of 9th Mo. 1795 The Book of Discipline was delivered to Rob't French for the present Month.

At a Monthly Meeting held at Evesham the 9th day of 10th month 1795
The Friends appointed to have the oversight of Meetings held in Chester lower School house, reported they had been held to general satisfaction And a request being now made for liberty to hold three meetings in the former manner with the addition of three to be held on the fifth day week succeeding each first day Meeting which being solidly weighed said request is granted and Robert French, Abraham Warrington and Henry Warrington are appointed to have the oversight thereof and report to this Meeting in the first month next.

At a Monthly Meeting held at Evesham the 6th of 11th Mo. 1795
The Committee appointed to take into consideration the altering this House to accommodate the Quarterly Meeting reported some attention thereto yet further deliberation thereon appearing necessary they are continued with the addition of Robert French, Bethuel Moore, Joseph Roberts, Lucas Gibbs, Wm. Roberts and Joshua Roberts and report to this Meeting as occasion may require.

At a Monthly Meeting held at Evesham the 8th of 1st month 1796
Agreeable to the conclusion of last Meeting the consideration of the weighty
subjects recommended in the Extracts being resumed and divers weighty
Observations being made thereon tending to excite more vigilance in guard-
ing against giving way to the inordinate pursuit of the grandeur of the
World too manifest amongst us in the extravagance of our dress and Household Furniture and the neglect of attending our Religious Meetings and
giving way to a sleepy disposition when assembled, also the Subject of Spirituous Liquors being revived the following named friends are desired to
take the latter subject under care and persue such further steps as may
appear necessary to discourage the unnecessary Use of this Article and
enable us to transmit a cleare account of our progress therein to the Quarterly Meeting in the 9th month next Vizt. Sam'l. Lippincott, Joseph Matlack,
Henry Warrington, Robert French, Ab^{r}m. Engle, Gabriel Davis, Job
Haines, Wm. Rogers & Stacy Haines.

At a Monthly Meeting held at Evesham the 5th of 2nd Mo. 1796
The deviations pointed out in the Extracts respecting the neglect of attending meetings giving way to Sleeping when aſsembled and the extravagance
observable in Dreſs, Addreſs, Household furniture &c coming weightily,
before this Meeting the following named friends are desired to unite with
the Overseers in endeavouring as ability may be afforded to promote a reformation in these respects (vizt.) John Collins, Job Haines, Robert French,
Wm. Haines, Joseph Matlack, Cox Haines, John Roberts, Henry Warrington, and William Rogers to report to this meeting as occasion may require.

At a Monthly Meeting held at Evesham the 7th of 10th mo. 1796.
The Committee appointed to the oversight of the Meetings last held in
Chester lower School House reported they had been held to a good degree
of satisfaction and a request being now made for liberty to continue three
Months longer in they were held last Winter with which the Meeting concurs
and appoint Joseph Warrington, Joseph Matlack, Saml. Lippincott and
Robert French to have the oversight thereof and report to this Meeting in
the first Month next.

At a Monthly Meeting held at Evesham the 9th of 12th Mo. 1796
The Clk. produced the Extracts from the Minutes of our last Yearly Meeting which were read and the several weighty subjects therein reccommended
being considered it appeared the united sense of the Meeting that the following named friends be appointed to take the subject of Spirituous Liquors
under their care and labour to promote a reformation therein as they may
be enabled and make report to this Meeting so as to enable us to send up
a clear account of the progress made therein to our next Yearly Meeting
(vizt.) Abrm. Brown, Joseph Matlack, Reuben Matlack, Robert French,
William Snowdon, Bethuel Moore, Stacy Haines and Gabriel Davis.

At a Monthly Meeting held at Evesham the 5th of 5th Mo. 1797
The subject matter of making Suitable provision at this place to accomo-
date the Quarterly Meeting as noted in the foregoing Minute being resumed
and deliberated upon with a good degree of condescension, the meeting
uniting in the appointment of the following Friends to take under consideration the digesting a plan and computing the expence of making the
necessary alterations in this House for the purpose above mentioned (viz.)
John Roberts, Wm. Rogers, Lucas Gibbs, Job Haines, Joshua Sharp, Levi
Ballinger, Robert French, Zebedee Wills, Isiah Haines, Wm. Wilkins, John
Borton, Gabriel Davis, Joseph Engle, Isaac Snowdon, Sam'l. Lippincott,
Sam'l Matlack, Jacob Hollingshead, Jeremiah Matlack, John Warrington,
& Samuel Roberts Senr. who are directed to proceed therein, and report
to this Meetg. as occasion may require.

At a Monthly Meeting held at Evesham the 5th of 1st Mo. 1798
The Preparative Meeting of Chester propose for consideration the discon-
tinuing of the practice of having what is called Groom's Men &c. at the
time of accomplishing marriages; which being considered and spoken to
the Meeting united in the appointment of Robert French, John Collins,
Abraham Brown, John Roberts, William Roberts, Joshua Roberts, Edward
Hilliar, Gabriel Davis, William Rogers, Levi Ballinger, William Haines,
Job Haines, John Borton and Zebedee Wills to unite with the Committee
of the Women's Meeting on the subject, proceed therein as way may open,
and report thereon to next or future Meeting.

At a Monthly Meeting held at Evesham the 11th of 10th mo. 1799.
Two meetings for the benefit of black people were appointed. Robert
French, John Roberts, Joseph Matlack, Job Haines, Gabriel Davis and
William Snowden are appointed to the oversight thereof and report to next
meeting.

At a Monthly Meeting held at Evesham the 6th of the 6th month 1800.
The Extracts from the Minutes of our last Yearly Meeting being produced;
on being read, the Subject of Distillation, dealing in and unnecessary use
of Spiritous Liquors coming under Solid deliberation, and most of the
Quarter's Committee thereon being present, and earnest care and solicitude
evidently prevailing in the minds of many friends for the advancement of
this weighty Concern; for which purpose the following friends are appointed
to have the subject under their care, proceed therein as way may open and
report to this meeting on or before the 3^d month next. Viz. Thomas Lippincott, Robert French, John Matlack, John Roberts, Isaac Snowden, Job
Haines, Jacob Borton & Zebedee Wills.

5th—of 12th mo. 1800.—The preparative meeting of Chester propose for
consideration the appointment of a solid committee to Join the Overseers

MOORESTOWN (CHESTER) MEETING HOUSE, 1802

MOORESTOWN (CHESTER) MEETING HOUSE, 1802

in taking into consideration the state of Society with respect to the support of our Discipline and attention to other advice of the Body conveyed in the Extracts, particularly the last: On deliberation the meeting united in the appointment of John Collins, William Rogers, Hinchman Haines, Job Haines, Joseph Matlack, Samuel Lippincott, Robert French, John Hunt, James Hemingway, Levi Ballinger, and William Roberts to that service; to proceed therein as Truth may open the way and report to next or future Meeting.

5th of 6th Mo. 1801. The Extracts from the minutes of our last Yearly Meeting being read, and the subject of distilling, dealing in, and unnecessary use of Spiritous liquors coming under consideration, the following friends are appointed to have the subject under their care, proceed therein as way may open, and report their service to this meeting so as to enable us to send up a clear account to our next Yearly Meeting,—Viz. Abraham Warrington, John Matlack, Caleb Atkinson, Robert French, John Maxell, Joseph Haines, and Samuel Matlack.

10th of 7th Mo. 1801. Pursuant to the conclusion of last meeting, some parts of the Extracts being again revived, and the subject of the boarding-school coming under consideration the following friends are appointed to attend the sitting of our several ensuing Preparative meetings; and as way may open endeavor to promote liberality in affording some further assistance in that important concern; also, attend to the direction of our last Yearly meeting in the revival of former advices therefrom; and report to next or future Meeting. Joseph Matlack, Abraham Warrington, John Collins, Robert French, Job Haines, Gabriel Davis and William Rogers.

At a monthly Meeting held at Evesham the 11th of 6th mo. 1802 The Extracts being read, and the subject of distilling, dealing in, and common use of spiritous Liquors, coming under weighty consideration; the Meeting united in the appointment of the following friends to have the subject under their care, proceed therein as way may open, and report thereon to this meeting in the 3^d mo. next, Vizt. John Mazell, Levi Ballinger, William Rogers, John Hunt Junr., Samuel Roberts, Robert French, Morgan Hollinshead, Joshua Roberts, Joseph Warrington Jr., William Evans, Henry Warrington and Samuel Lippincott.

8th of 7th month 1803. The minute of our last Quarterly meeting relative to the practice of distilling and vending spiritous Liquors, together with some paragraphs of our last and former Extracts on that subject, being read; and being favoured with the company of most of our Quarterly meetings committee under that appointment; a concern for the advancement of friends Testimony herein, was felt to prevail: and the following

24

friends were appointed to join in a labor to promote a reformation in these respects; and as way may open, endeavour to discourage the unnecessary use of those Liquors. Viz.—Jacob Borton, William Wilkins, Jos. Haines, Zebedee Wills, Robert French, Wm. Roberts, Morgan Hollinshead, John Hunt, Abraham Warrington, Henry Warrington Junr., Joshua Lippincott and Wm. Borough, who are directed to report thereon at, or previous to, our meeting in the 4th month next.

7th of 1st Mo. 1803.   Abraham Warrington Junr. produced an Acknowledgment for laying a wager on a horse race, thereby expressing sorrow therefor, which being read and considered with a good degree of weight, & John Collins and Robert French expressing a willingness to take an opportunity with him on the occasion, they are therefore appointed thereto; and report their sense of his disposition of mind to next meeting.

8th of the 4th month 1803.   Robert French and Elizabeth Stokes appeared and declared their intention of marriage with each other.

6th of 5th Month 1803.   Robert French and Elizabeth Stokes appeared and signified the continuation of their intention of marriage with each other; and the friends appointed reporting nothing to obstruct their proceeding, they are, therefore, at liberty to consumate their marriage agreeably to good order; for the preservation of which, John Matlack and Morgan Hollinshead are appointed to be present and report to next meeting.

10th of 6th Mo. 1803.   The friends appointed to attend the marriage of Robert French and Elizabeth Stokes report it orderly accomplished.

[Women's Meeting]
At the Monthly Meeting of Women Friends held at Evesham the 8th of 4th Month 1803, Robert French and Elizabeth Stokes appeared and expressed their intentions of marriage with each other, the meeting appoints Mary Gibbs and Rebecca Hollinshead to enquire respecting her clearness of other like engagements and report to next meeting.

6—5 mo. 1803.   Robert French and Elizabeth Stokes appeared and expressed the continuance of their intentions of marriage with each other and no obstruction appearing they are at liberty to accomplish their marriage agreeably to good order, Mary Gibbs and Rebecca Cowperthwaite are appointed to be present and report to next meeting.

At a Monthly Meeting held at Evesham the 10th of the 6th Month 1803. The friends appointed to attend the marriage of Robert French and Elizabeth Stokes report it orderly accomplished.

Record book of Sufferings of Friends of Evesham Monthly Meeting for non Compliance of Military duty. Being An Account of Friends Sufferings within the Compass of Evesham Monthly Meeting for refusing to pay a Tax for procuring Powder & other Military Stores & for refusing to be Active in Military Services. The Sums Demanded: Goods taken: the Value thereof; by whom taken, & by what Authority is as followeth.

Taken from Robert French by sd. Toy, one Mare rated £20:0:0. Fines Demanded £23:5:0—12th mo. 23ᵈ 1777

Taken from Robert French 11th mo. 24th 1780 by Peter Bankson a Saddle, rated at £1:10:0   Fine Demanded £30—

Taken from Robert French 10th mo. 27th 1780 by William Venhorn one Hog rated £1:10:0—Tax Demanded £51:4:6—

Was Taken from Robert French 5th Mo. 29th 1781—by Samuel Ivens Constable: one sheep, rated £0:7:6

10/31—1782 Taken from Robert French by Joseph Brackney a Heifer rated at £4:0:0—Taxes Demanded not Assertained

11th mo. 29—1782— Taken from Robert French by Samuel Ivens for Sundry Taxes a Cow & one Hog rated £6:5:0 Demands not assertained.

11th Mo. 25" 1783—Taken from Robert French by Jacob Cooper Constable (by virtue of a Warrant signed Darling Conrow) two hogs valued 5£, a Heifer 3£, two Sheep 7£, and 10 Bushels of Indian Corn 1£ 10 S. Demand £6:13ˢ·:6ᵈ

7th Mᵒ. 22ᵈ 1784 Taken from Robert French by said Wiley, by virtue of a Warrant signed as above, a Cart rated at 4£, two Sheep at 15/ and a Grindstone at 10/ Whole Amount 5£:5 S:0—Demand 3£:9 S:2d

2nd Mo. 4th 1790. Taken from Robert French by the Authority aforesaid (John Griffith Deputy Constable) 5 sheep rated 3£:15S:0—Sum demanded not ascertained.

2ud Mo. 1802 Taken from Robert French by Josiah Gibbs Deputy Constable 3 bu. of Corn valued at 4/6 Amt. £1 8s. 0d. for a Demand of £1 3s. 6d.—by an Execution signed Thomas Adams.

2nd Mo. 5th 1802 Taken from Robert French by Israel Hammell Dep. Constable 7—3/4 Bushˢ of Corn valued at 4/6 Amt. £4 6s. 5d. for a Demand of £3 3s. 6d. by an Execution signed Edward French.

WILL OF ROBERT FRENCH, JR., 1808

I, Robert French of the township of Chester, County of Burlington and State of New Jersey, being of sound mind and memory, do make and publish this for my last will and testament. First, I give and bequeath to my dear wife Elizabeth French the sum of four hundred dollars, and all the household goods she brought to me and one milch cow to be paid to her in sixty days after my decease. Second, I bequeath to my said dear wife half of the profits of my plantation during her natural life, to be paid to her yearly which annuity I give in lieu of dower out of my estate, and if not accepted as such in thirty days after my decease then my will is that the said annuity be void.

Third, all the residue of my estate after payment of debts both real and personal I give and devise to my daughter Mary Roberts in fee simple, to her, her heirs and assigns forever—I appoint my dear wife Elizabeth French and my son-in-law Josiah Roberts, executors of this my testament and last will. In witness whereof I have hereto set my hand and seal this second day of ninth month in the year of our Lord one thousand eight hundred and eight.

Signed, sealed, published and declared by the said Robert French to be his testament and last will in the presence of us: Andrew Hollinshead, Job Hollinshead, Morgan Hollinshead.

I, Robert French make this codicil to my testament and last will, besides what I have bequeathed to my beloved wife in my last will to which this is a codicil; if she should choose to reside on my plantation, I leave her the privilege of half the house to live in and fire wood brought to the door sufficient for her use, but if she should choose to live in her own house it is my will that my executors deliver to her seven cords of wood every year at her door as long as she remains my widow, besides which I give her one good bed, bedstead and bedding to be her own.

In witness whereof I have hereunto set my hand and seal this ninth day of second month in the year of our Lord one thousand eight hundred and eleven 1811

MOORESTOWN MEETING HOUSE (ORTHODOX), 1897

MOORESTOWN MEETINGS

About the year 1700 the meeting at Chester was established and was called the Adams' Meeting, from its being located upon their land. By a deed of James and Esther Adams, dated 9th of 4th mo. 1700, we learn that a meeting house already stood there, viz.: " To the Trustees of the Religious Society of Friends, for one acre of land lying and being on the west side of the King's highway, with all that house or building now erected, and being upon said acre of land, called the Quaker Meeting House." It was of logs and was destroyed by fire. In 1721 a house built of stone succeeded it, and was located in what is now the burial ground, on the north side of the street. In the ensuing years repairs and additions became necessary, costing upwards of $1,500. Amongst those who generously contributed, both money and labor, were Charles French [42], Jonathan French [31] and Mathew Allen, Jr. This place of worship was used by the Friends of the vicinity for over eighty years, when owing to increase in population, it became necessary to provide a new meeting house. In 1781 a lot of something over two acres, on the south side of the main street, was purchased " for the sum of ninety-six pounds, five shillings and seven pence, gold and silver." Twenty years later a large brick meeting house was built, and this has been used since 1802. The old building was torn down and much of the material used in the construction of a school house within the new enclosure. In 1829, Orthodox Friends built a frame meeting house on the same lot, which they used until a few years ago, when they erected a large modern brick building. After the removal of the meeting the ground on the north side of the street was used for burial purposes only. About 1740 a member of the meeting planted a strong young sycamore tree near the old meeting house. For more than a century it has been the pride of the community, and today, though fully one hundred and seventy years old, it is as vigorous as ever. Moorestown originally was called Chestertown at one end and Rodmantown at the other, and was also known as Adams, after pioneer families. Finally it took its permanent name from one Thomas Moore, an enterprising settler, who was one of the early inn keepers, though his first house only contained four rooms. During its entire history of over two centuries, Moorestown has been one of the most distinctive Quaker communities in the United States.

132—JAMES FRENCH (Thomas, 1; Thomas, 6; Robert, 35).

> b. 3rd. mo. 1st, 1751.
>
> m. First, July 24th, 1773, Mary Clark; Rev. Jacob Duche performing ceremony; Christ Church record, Philadelphia.
>
> m. Second, October 12th, 1779, Sarah Ferguson.

321—CHARLES FRENCH m. ——— ———.

322—JOSEPH FRENCH

> b. 11th mo. 3rd, 1781.
> m. September 2nd, 1804, Martha Newton.

323—JAMES FRENCH

324—ROBERT FRENCH

325—THOMAS FRENCH

> b. 1st mo. 3rd, 1795.
> m. First, Elizabeth Talbott.
> m. Second, 6th mo. 27th, 1827, Martha Bryan.

MARRIAGE BOND

Know all Men by these Prefents,———

That we James French and William Cox of the County of Burlington—are held and firmly bound unto His Excellency William Livingston Esq. Governor and Commander in Chief of New Jersey, &c. in the Sum of Five Hundred Pounds current lawful Money of New Jersey, to be paid to the faid William Livingston Esqʳ Governor, &c. his Succefsors and Afsigns; for which Payment well and truly to be made, we bind our felves, our Heirs, Executors and Adminiftrators, and every of them, jointly and feverally, firmly by thefe Prefents: Sealed with our Seals, dated the twelfth Day of October—Anno Domini One Thousand Seven Hundred and Seventy Nine.

The Condition of this Obligation is fuch, That whereas there is a Mutual Contract of Marriage between James French—of the one party, and Sarah Ferguson—of the other party, and the Parties have complied with the Terms prefcribed in an Act of the General Afsembly of New-Jersey, made in the Year of our Lord One Thoufand Seven Hundred and Nineteen, intitled, An Act to prevent clandeftine Marriages.

Now if it fhall hereafter appear that the Certificates produced, or either of them, have been fraudulent, or that either the aforefaid James French or the aforefaid Sarah Ferguson—had not the Confent of their Parents,

Guardians, or Persons under whofe Care they were, figning the faid Certificates; or that the faid James French—or the faid Sarah Ferguson—or either of them, had fome lawful Let or Impediment of Pre-contract, Affinity or Consanguinity, to hinder their being joined in the Holy Bands of Matrimony, and afterwards of living together as Man and Wife; then this Obligation to ftand and remain in full force and Virtue, otherwife to be void and of none Effect.—

James French

Sealed and Delivered
in the Prefence of   Willm Cox   [SEAL]
BowesReed

The New Jersey marriage license law of 1719 was a measure specially enacted to prevent clandestine marriages of minors, but it was not in practice thus regarded exclusively. The provisions of the act were exact and elaborate and evidently were held in great public respect for many years. But as time passed and colonial power weakened, "marriage by license" became less popular and marriage bonds, like that filed by James French, when he contracted a second marriage, rapidly fell into disuse about the time of the Revolution. There are about ten thousand of these bonds on file in Trenton. The act remained nominally in force or at least on the colonial statute books, until 1795. Its chief beneficiaries, financially, were the rural justices of the peace. The clergy were much opposed to it, and in Pennsylvania a similar law was strongly attacked by Bishop White.

FOOT WARMER, 1750

135—ANN FRENCH (Thomas, 1; Thomas, 6; Robert, 35).

> b. 10th mo. 26th, 1758.
> d. 4th mo. 9th, 1842.
> m. 12th mo. 1781, Samuel Carr, son of Caleb Carr.
> He b. 10th mo. 22nd, 1754.
> d. 6th mo. 29th, 1832.

326—HANNAH CARR

> b. 9th mo. 12th, 1782.
> m. 3rd mo. 12th, 1807, Thomas Middleton, son of John and Martha Middleton, of Evesham, N. J.

327—CALEB CARR

> b. 7th mo. 28th, 1784.
> d. 4th mo. 18th, 1842.
> m. 11th mo. 13th, 1834, Mary Stockton, daughter of Samuel and Abigail Stockton.
> She d. 10th mo. 29th, 1852.

328—JEREMIAH CARR

> b. 9th mo. 27th, 1786.
> d. 11th mo. 15th, 1786.

329—SAMUEL CARR, JR.

> b. 3rd mo. 24th, 1788.
> m. Patience ———.

330—MARY F. CARR

> b. 9th mo. 27th, 1791.
> m. 10th mo. 17th, 1816, Aaron Lippincott, son of Samuel and Theodocia Lippincott, of Evesham, N. J.

331—ISAAC CARR

> b. 11th mo. 4th, 1793.
> m. 1st mo. 11th, 1816, Ann Craft, daughter of George and Elizabeth Craft of Mansfield, N. J.

332—ROBERT CARR

> b. 12th mo. 9th, 1795.

333—THOMAS CARR

> b. 2nd mo. 4th, 1798.
> d. 2nd mo. 28th, 1798.

MEETING RECORDS

Evesham Monthly Meeting Minutes:

At a Monthly Meeting held at Evesham ^{ye} 8th of ^{ye} 11th mo. 1781. Sam'l Carr son of Caleb Carr & Ann French Daughter of Robert French dec'd, appeared & declared their Intentions of Marriage with each other, the young man residing within ^{ye} Compass of Mount Holly Monthly Meeting was Informed that a Certificate from there would be expected at their next appearance. The Young Woman's mother being present consented and the young man produced his father's in writing.

At a Monthly Meeting held at Evesham ^{ye} 6th of 12th mo. 1781— Sam'l Carr & Ann French appeared & signified the Continuation of their intentions of Marriage with each other, he produced a certificate from the Monthly Meeting at Mount Holly to the satisfaction of this. Therefore they are at Liberty to consumate their s'd Intentions & Enoch Evans & Joshua Lippincott are appointed to be present & see that good order be kept & report to next meeting.

At a Monthly Meeting held at Evesham ^{ye} 10th of ^{ye} 1st Mo. 1782. The friends appointed to attend the marriage of Samuel Carr & Ann French reported that it was orderly accomplished.

Minutes of Evesham Monthly Meeting of Women Friends:

8th 11th Mo. 1781. Samuel Carr and Ann French appeared and declared their intentions of marriage with each other, therefore two friends are appointed to make the needful enquiry into her clearnefs of marriage and report to next Meeting; the young woman's mother being present consented, and he produced his Father's consent in writing.

10th 1st Mo. 1782. The friends appointed to attend the marriage of Samuel Carr and Ann French reported that it was orderly accomplished.

138—ANN FRENCH (Thomas, 1; Charles, 8; Charles, 42).

b. September 24th, 1740.

d. 2nd mo. 4th, 1840, buried in Evesham Burying Ground.

m. 12th mo. 12th, 1757, Jacob Wilkins, son of Thomas Wilkins.

334—URIAH WILKINS.   b. 8th mo. 22nd, 1758.

m. October 18th, 1792, Elizabeth Eyre.

335—HANNAH WILKINS   b. 2nd mo. 20th, 1761.
         m. October 28th, 1783, Benjamin Burrough, son of Samuel and Mary Burrough.

336—SAMUEL WILKINS   b. 11th mo. 10th, 1763.
         d. 1st mo. 14th, 1766.

337—ANNA WILKINS   b. 7th mo. 25th, 1767.
         m. January 17th, 1797, Asa Eyre; Edward French [121], Justice of Peace, performing ceremony.

338—JACOB WILKINS   b. 3rd mo. 22nd, 1770.
         m. 1794, Theodosia Lippincott.

339—ISAAC WILKINS   b. 12th mo. 7th, 1772.
         m. April 4th, 1796, Ann Hollingshead [377].

340—THOMAS WILKINS   b. 10th mo. 12th, 1775.
         d. 4th mo. 26th, 1848.

341—CHARLES WILKINS   b. 2nd mo. 12th, 1779.
         m. First, Lydia Hazelton.
         m. Second, 1808, Sarah Striker.

MEETING RECORDS

Haddonfield Monthly Meeting Minutes:

14—11 mo. 1757 Jacob Wilkins son of Thos. Wilkins and Anne French daughter of Chas. French appeared and declared their intentions of marriage with each other. Parents being present consented, and James Cattle & Wm. Evens are appointed to make ye needful enquiry into ye young mans clearness and conversation.

12—12 mo. 1757. Jacob Wilkins & Ann French appeared and signified ye continuation of their intention of marriage with each other, ye friends appointed to make enquiry reported nothing to obstruct & they are at liberty to consumate their said intentions.

Haddonfield Minutes of ye Mo: Meeting of Women Friends:
Women friends of ^{ye} monthly meeting being met at Haddonfield ye 14th of 11^m 1757
Jacob Wilkins & Ann French signified their intentions of taking each other in marriage friends appointed to make ^{ye} usual inquirie are Jane Midleton & Rachel Coperthwait & report to next meeting.

Women fr^{ds} of ^{ye} m^{o}ly meeting being met at Had^{n}f^{ld} ^{ye} 12th of 12^m 1757 Jacob Wilkins & Ann French Signified ^{ye} Continuation of their intentions of marriage confent of Parents appearing & return of inquirers clear fr^{ds} consent to ye accomplishm^t theirof according to ^{ye} good order among fr^{ds} & app^{ts} Han^a French & Kizia Heritage to attend it, to see good order kept, & report to next m^{t}g.

Women friends of ^{ye} m^{o}ly Meeting being met at Had^{n}f^{ld} ^{ye} 9th of 1st m^o 1758 reported ^{ye} afores^d marriage was orderly accomplish$^{t.}$

Evesham Monthly Meeting Minutes:
At a Monthly Meeting held at Evesham ^{ye} 10th of ^{ye} 12th Mo. 1778. Jos^h Stokes, Jos^h Roberts, Jacob Wilkins & Sam'l. French are appointed to take in subscriptions for ^{ye} journal of our friend John Churchman, & report to next meeting.

At a Monthly Meeting held at Evesham ^{ye} 7th of 10th Mo. 1779. This meeting was Inform'd that ^{ye} Journals of our Dec'd friend John Churchman being almost compleated, therefore Jacob Wilkins, Samuel French, Joseph Roberts & Joseph Stokes are directed to call upon ^{ye} Subscribers, & Receive ^{ye} Money & pay ^{ye} same to John Lippincott as soon as they conveniently can.

Ann (French) Wilkins departed this life 2nd mo. 4th 1840 in the one hundreth year of her age; having attended Evesham Monthly Meeting until she was passed 96 years old, and retained all her faculties in a remarkable manner.
Appearing sensible that she was nearing her close she was heard to say, 'Come sweet Jesus, come quickly, not my will but Thine be done.' She was the mother of eight children, only three of whom survived her; she had forty-four grandchildren and seventy great grand children at the time of her death

139—ABIGAIL FRENCH (Thomas, 1; Charles, 8; Charles, 42).

b. January 18th, 1742.

d. 2nd mo. 20th, 1797, in Gloucester Co., N. J.

m. 9th mo., 1760, John Brick, 3rd, son of Judge John and Ann (Nicholson) Brick.

He b. 11th mo. 10th, 1733, in Salem County, N. J.

d. 1780, in Gloucester Co., N. J.

342—JOHN BRICK, 4TH	m. February 19th, 1783, Mercy Hartley; Rev. Robert Blackwell performing ceremony; Christ Church record, Philadelphia.
343—SAMUEL BRICK	
344—WILLIAM BRICK	m. Mary Inskeep.
345—ANN BRICK	m. 5th mo. 16th, 1799, William Roberts.
346—ABIGAIL BRICK	m. Captain Jacob Stokes.
347—SARAH BRICK	m. James Hale.

ANCESTRY OF JOHN BRICK, 3RD

John Brick, progenitor of the Brick family in West Jersey, came from England to Salem soon after the founding of the colony, in 1675. About 1690 he bought 1000 acres of land located along a stream which afterward became known as Stow creek and the dividing line between Salem and Cumberland counties. Ten years later he built a grist and saw mill and the village which grew up was called Jerico. For nearly half a century the pioneer John Brick was an active and influential man in the community. He died in 1753. His son, Joseph, succeeded to the ownership of the mills, and his son, John, was given 240 acres of land in Salem county. Many years later the mills became the property of the Wood family. John Brick, Jr., who in 1728 married Ann Nicholson, granddaughter of Samuel Nicholson, progenitor, an original Salem settler, became a prominent citizen. He represented Salem county in the Assembly, 1745–46, and was appointed a Common Pleas Judge for the new county of Cumberland, 1748, serving also as one of the managers in the building of the new court house. He died in 1758, leaving two sons and six daughters, amongst whom he divided a considerable estate. His son, John (3rd), born in 1733, who, in 1760, married Abigail French, was a prosperous farmer and business man. He left an estate located chiefly in Gloucester county, where he had bought of Charles Read, in 1766, three tracts of land, aggregating about 250 acres, for £1600.

MEETING RECORDS

Haddonfield Monthly Meeting Minutes:

11—8 mo. 1760. John Brick son of John deceased and Abigail French daughter of Chas. French appeared and declared their intentions of marriage with each other. Y$_e$ young man belonging to Salem Monthly Meeting was acquainted that a certificate from thence would be expected at their next appearance; he produced his mother's consent in writing, her parents being present gave theirs.

8—9 mo. John Brick and Abigail French appeared and signified the continuance of their intentions of marriage with each other and he produced a certificate from Salem Monthly Meeting to the satisfaction of this. They are left at liberty to consumate their said intentions.

10—11 mo. 1760. The Friends appointed to attend the marriage of John Brick and Abigail French report that it was orderly accomplished.

Haddonfield Minutes of ^{ye} Mo: Meeting of Women Friends:

Women friends of ^{ye} monthly meeting being met at Had^{n}f^{ld} ^{ye} 11th of 8th m^o 1760

Jno Brick & Abigail French, signify^d their intentions of taking each other in marraig, fr^{ds} appointed to make ye uſual inquiry are Jane Midleton & Rebecca Roberts, & to make their report to next m^{o}ly meeting. & ^{ye} young man belongin to Salem, a certificate expecte^d next m^{t}g.

Women friends of ^{ye} monthly meeting being met at Had^{n}f^{ld} ^{ye} 8th of 9^m 1760

Jno Brick & Abigail French, signified ^{ye} continuation of their intentions of taking each other in marraig, Couſent of Parents appearing, & return of inquierr^s clear, fr^{ds} consent to ^{ye} accomplishment thereof, according to ye good order among fr^{ds}, & appoints Rebecca Roberts & Caziah Heritage to attend s^d accomplishm^t, to see good orders kept, & make their report to next m^{o}ly meeting.

Women friends of ^{ye} m^{o}ly m^{t}g being met at Had^{n}f^{ld} ye 10th of 11^m 1760 Report^d ^{ye} marriag of Jno Brick & Abigail French, was orderly accomplish^d, being hindred by Sickneſs in its Proper Season.

SUMMARY OF WILL OF JOHN BRICK, 3RD, 1780

John Brick Gloucester Town & Co. New Jersey " being sick & weak "
Date—2 Mo—(Feby) 29—1780   Proved April 21—1780 at Timber Creek.
Wife—Abigail sole use & profits of my plantation until son John is 25.
Children—John Brick, that part of my plantation I purchased of Charles
Read Lyeing the Easterly side of the great Road Leading from Gloucester to Salem, Bounding by Little Timber Creek the Lands of Isaac Burroughs Late of John Mickle deceased Samuel Harrison and said Road to the Bridge, Leading over said Creek. If he die before he is 25 years of age, & without lawful issue this land to descend unto my son Samuel & lands devised to Samuel shall then descend to son W^m

Samuel   when 21 rest of my plantation & ⅓ of my cedar swamp, & rest of cedar swamp to son John

William £150 to be paid to him, by son John Brick out of the land above bequeathed to him, Money equal to a Spanish peace of Eight at seven Shillings and six pence, Son Samuel also to pay son William £150 of like money. Both payments to be made when William is 21.

Three Daughters   Ann ⎫
                  Abigail ⎬ all the remainder of my Personal Estate to be equally divided share and share alike and each one's share to be paid her when 18.   If either of my daughters marry before she arrives at 18 years of age, her share to be paid her then.
                  Sarah ⎭

Exrs— ⎰ Wife, Abigail Brick
       ⎱ Bro-in-law, Samuel French

John Brick

Witnesses   Hannah Bispham   John Bispham Junr.
            Martha Harrifon   Saml Clement

Abigail Brick

Samuel French   Signatures of Executors

Inventory of John Brick late of Town of Gloucester—
Date April 11—1780

Total £568—1—8

Sam¹ Harrison ⎱ Apprs.
Joſeph Clement ⎰
Affirmed to at Timber Creek
April 21—1780
  Before Joᵇ Hugg Surrogᵗ.

Upon her death, in 1797, the estate of Abigail Brick, who died intestate, was administered by her brother, Charles French [143], the inventory showing personal property
valued at, approximately, £700.

FAMILY PIECES, 1770

140—JACOB FRENCH (Thomas, 1; Charles, 8; Charles, 42).

b. April 28th, 1745.

d. 10th mo. 28th, 1827.

m. 12th mo. 3rd, 1772, Elizabeth Stokes, daughter
of Joshua and Amy (Hinchman) Stokes.

She d. 2d mo. 5th, 1837; buried in Friends' Burying
Ground, Moorestown, N. J.

348—RACHEL FRENCH	b. 8th mo. 13th, 1773.
	d. in Burlington, N. J., unmarried.
349—AMY FRENCH	b. 12th mo. 3rd, 1774.
	m. 11th mo. 20th, 1799, John Pope.
350—ABIGAIL FRENCH	b. 12th mo. 27th, 1777.
	m. 1801, Joseph Jones.
351—RICHARD FRENCH	b. 7th mo. 6th, 1781.
	m. Hannah Lippincott.
352—JOSHUA FRENCH	b. 10th mo. 30th, 1787.
	m. 10th mo. 3rd, 1817, Elizabeth H. Beck.

Elizabeth (Stokes) French was great-great-aunt of Edward C. Stokes, Governor of
New Jersey, 1905–1908.

Joshua Stokes, son of Thomas and Rachel (Wright) Stokes, married Amy Hinchman,
of Haddonfield Monthly Meeting, 1741; he died 1779.

MEETING RECORDS

Evesham Monthly Meeting Minutes:

At a Monthly Meeting held at Evesham ye 8th of ye 10th mo. 1772.
Jacob French by John Hunt requested a certificate to ye monthly meeting
at Haddonfield in order for marriage with a member thereof. Therefore
Enoch and Joseph Roberts are appointed to make ye needful Enquiery and
prepare one & produce it to next meeting.

At a Monthly Meeting held at Evesham ye 5th of ye 11th mo. 1772.
The Friends appointed produced a certificate on behalf of Jacob French
which was read approved and signed by ye Clerk.

Whereas Jacob French, son of Charles French, of the Township of ... in the County of Gloucester in the Province of New Jersey, Yeoman, and Elizabeth Stokes, daughter of Richard Stokes, of the same Township & County, Yeoman, Declared their Intentions of Marriage with each other, before several Monthly Meetings of the People called Quakers, at Haddonfield in the County aforesaid, according to the good order used amongst them, and having Consent of Parents and Parties concerned, their said proposals of Marriage were allowed of by the said Meetings.

— NOW These are to Certify whom it may concern, that for the full accomplishing of their said Intention, this thirtieth day of the ninth month, in the year of our Lord One thousand seven hundred and seventy five, they the said Jacob French and Elizabeth appeared in a Public meeting of the said People at Haddonfield aforesaid, and the said Jacob taking the said Elizabeth Stokes by the hand, did in a solemn manner openly Declare, that he took the said Elizabeth Stokes to be his Wife, promising through Divine assistance, to be unto her a loving and faithful Husband, until Death should separate them, and then and there in the same Assembly, the said Elizabeth Stokes did in like manner Declare, that she took the said Jacob French to be her Husband, promising through the like Divine assistance, to be unto him a loving and faithful Wife, until Death should separate them. And moreover they the said Jacob French and Elizabeth Stokes (she according to the custom of Marriage)

(and we whose names are here under written have subscribed) hereto doe ... the whole amongst ...
and subscriptions have as witnesses there ... Set our hands, the Day and Year ...

Haddonfield Minutes of ^{ye} Mo: Meeting of Women Friends:
At a Monthly Meeting of Women friends held at Haddonfield the 12th of the 10th M° 1772
Jacob French & Elizabeth Stokes (Daughter of Joshua Stokes) signified their Intentions of Marriage with each other. Mary Lippincott & Elizabeth Bates are appointed to make ^{ye} usual Enquery & report to next Meetg.

At a Monthly Meeting of Women friends held at Haddonfield the 9th of 11th M° 1772
Jacob French & Elizabeth Stokes Signified ^{ye} continuation of their intentions of Marr^{ge}, consent of Parties concerned app^{g} & return of Enquir^{s} clear concern^{g} ^{ye} young Woman, and ^{ye} young man producing a Certificate from Evesham signifying his clearneſs there, Fr^{ds} consent to ^{ye} accomplishm^{t} thereof according to good order established amongst Friends. Mary Lippincott & Elizabeth Bates to attend, see good order. kept & report to next Meeting.

At a Monthly Meeting of Women friends at Haddonfield the 14th of 12th M° 1772
Report ^{ye} afores^{d} marr^{g} orderly accomplished.

A RELIC OF THE NURSERY, 1749

141—SAMUEL FRENCH (Thomas, 1; Charles, 8; Charles, 42).

> b. September 17th, 1748, in Waterford township, Gloucester Co., N. J.
>
> d. 7th mo. 8th, 1814.
>
> m. 4th mo. 7th, 1769, Sarah Heulings, daughter of Jacob, Jr., and Agnes (Buckman) Heulings of Evesham township, Burlington Co., N. J.
>
> She b. 8th mo. 12th, 1753.
>
> d. 6th mo. 7th, 1806.

353—URIAH FRENCH
> b. 7th mo. 13th, 1770.
> m. 6th mo. 3rd, 1802, Mary Ivins.

354—JACOB FRENCH
> b. 4th mo. 30th, 1773.
> m. First, Sarah Ellis.
> m. Second, Hannah (Pancoast) Cooper.

355—AGNES FRENCH
> b. 2nd mo. 24th, 1775.
> m. 12th mo. 20th, 1792, Amasa Moore.

356—CHARLES FRENCH, JR.
> b. 4th mo. 22nd, 1777.
> m. First, 12th mo. 27th, 1798, Martha Hazelton.
> m. Second, 11th mo. 3rd, 1808, Esther (Davis) Lippincott.
> m. Third, 11th mo. 28th, 1810, Priscilla Moore.

357—SAMUEL FRENCH, JR.
> b. 4th mo. 10th, 1779.
> m. First, 3rd mo. 28th, 1811, Hannah Ivins.
> m. Second, 10th mo. 3rd, 1816, Rebecca Clark.

358—ANN FRENCH
> b. 5th mo. 12th, 1781.
> d. 2nd mo. 28th, 1782.

359—SARAH FRENCH
> b. 11th mo. 24th, 1783.
> m. 2nd mo. 8th, 1810, John V. Clark.

360—JOSEPH CLEMENT FRENCH
> b. 7th mo. 20th, 1786.
> m. First, Elizabeth P. Ellis.
> m. Second, 9th mo. 7th, 1848, Nancy Vanneman.

361—ANN HEULINGS FRENCH
> b. 9th mo. 29th, 1788.
> d. 12th mo. 18th, 1812.

1748 SAMUEL FRENCH 1814

1753 SARAH (HEULINGS) FRENCH 1806

SAMUEL FRENCH

Samuel French [141] spent the early years of his married life as a farmer in the upper part of Waterford township, then Gloucester, now Camden county, N. J. It is evident that about 1771 he took charge of an extensive tract of land, upwards of 1000 acres, located in Greenwich, now Harrison township, Gloucester county. This estate, the property of James Budd, was sold by Sheriff Joseph Hugg, in 1771, to Charles French [42] and by his will, 1785, descended to his son Samuel French. In 1784 the latter purchased 125 acres in the same neighborhood and in 1794 and 1810 added to his holdings, until he became possessed of over 1300 acres, being one of the largest land owners in that section. Upon his death, 1814, farms were assigned to his five sons, as detailed in his will, a lengthy document, revealing a careful administrative mind. The saw mill property, with 115 acres, given to Uriah, had been in his charge for some years. Charles was continued in possession of a desirable place; Jacob, also, in another nearby location, and with a goodly portion of land given to Joseph, the remainder of the great plantation was entrusted to Samuel, Jr., including the homestead.

An accompanying outline map, taken from an ancient time-worn parchment, shows the general location of four of these farms. The homesteads reproduced are in excellent condition. The chimneys were built with old-fashioned fire-places, the heavy timbers and rafters are of oak, now hard as stone, the weather-boarding of cedar. Only one house, that of Jacob French and built by him, is of brick. These venerable dwellings, with probably one exception, are considerably over one hundred years old and with care will last many years. In the pioneer homestead General Samuel G. French was born. Here he spent his boyhood days, attending school at Mullica Hill, three miles distant, until be entered the United States Military Academy at West Point in 1839. This property passed out of possession of the family upon the death of his father Samuel French, Jr., [357] in 1852.

Samuel French [141] was a prosperous and influential man in his community. He sat as a representative of Gloucester county in the Assembly at Trenton during the sessions of 1795–96–97–1800–01–02. He took an active part in the proceedings, upon several occasions giving striking manifestation of his devotion to the principles of Friends. He served on several important committees. A bill concerning the College of New Jersey, at Princeton, in

SAMUEL FRENCH

Samuel French [141] spent the early years of his married life as a farmer in the upper part of Waterford township, then Gloucester, now Camden county, N. J. It is evident that about 1771 he took charge of an extensive tract of land, upwards of 1000 acres, located in Greenwich, now Harrison township, Gloucester county. This estate, the property of James Budd, was sold by Sheriff Joseph Hugg, in 1771, to Charles French [42] and by his will, 1785, descended to his son Samuel French. In 1784 the latter purchased 125 acres in the same neighborhood and in 1794 and 1810 added to his holdings, until he became possessed of over 1300 acres, being one of the largest land owners in that section. Upon his death, 1814, farms were assigned to his five sons, as detailed in his will, a lengthy document, revealing a careful administrative mind. The saw mill property, with 115 acres, given to Uriah, had been in his charge for some years. Charles was continued in possession of a desirable place; Jacob, also, in another nearby location, and with a goodly portion of land given to Joseph, the remainder of the great plantation was entrusted to Samuel, Jr., including the homestead.

An accompanying outline map, taken from an ancient time-worn parchment, shows the general location of four of these farms. The homesteads reproduced are in excellent condition. The chimneys were built with old-fashioned fire-places, the heavy timbers and rafters are of oak, now hard as stone, the weather-boarding of cedar. Only one house, that of Jacob French and built by him, is of brick. These venerable dwellings, with probably one exception, are considerably over one hundred years old and with care will last many years. In the pioneer homestead General Samuel G. French was born. Here he spent his boyhood days, attending school at Mullica Hill, three miles distant, until he entered the United States Military Academy at West Point in 1839. This property passed out of possession of the family upon the death of his father Samuel French, Jr., [357] in 1852.

Samuel French [141] was a prosperous and influential man in his community. He sat as a representative of Gloucester county in the Assembly at Trenton during the sessions of 1795–96–97–1800–01–02. He took an active part in the proceedings, upon several occasions giving striking manifestation of his devotion to the principles of Friends. He served on several important committees. A bill concerning the College of New Jersey, at Princeton, in

SAMUEL FRENCH HOMESTEAD, NEAR MULLICA HILL, N. J.

From a photograph taken in 1906

the session of 1796, contained provisions he could not approve and he voted against it. The same day he voted against a bill concerning cavalry and artillery. Two days later, February 19, 1796, he voted against a bill for organizing and training the militia of the state. He was watchful of the interests of his constituents and supported a measure providing for rebuilding and keeping in repair the main highway bridge over Great Timber Creek. He voted against a motion to dismiss a pending bill to prevent the importation of slaves into New Jersey, looking to their release and protection from abuse. He served on a special committee to consider a petition of Indians for their removal to New York. November 10, 1800, Samuel French presented a bill, " An Act for relief of Josiah Hunt " who had lost a note issued to him by the state of New Jersey for the depreciation of his pay as a soldier of the United States. Josiah Hunt had presented a petition and Samuel French, as a member of the committee to whom his case was referred, wrote the report which he submitted.

Throughout a manhood life of nearly fifty years Samuel French manifested the qualities of a conscientious, vigorous, industrious and honorable ancestry. He took intelligent interest in all public affairs, and set a consistent example as a member of the religious society with which he was actively connected for half a century, leaving the memory of a well spent and successful life.

Sarah Heulings, wife of Samuel French, was the great-granddaughter of William Buckman who, in 1682, came to Pennsylvania from Billinghurst, Sussex county, England, with William Penn, in the ship " Welcome." Thomas Buckman, youngest son of William Buckman and his second wife, Elizabeth Wilson, was born 4th mo. 8th, 1707, died 1734, married 3rd mo. 26th, 1726, Agnes Penquite, born 1705, daughter of John and Agnes (Sharp) Penquite. Agnes Buckman, daughter of Thomas and Agnes (Penquite) Buckman, was born 2nd mo. 6th, 1732, married 9th mo. 27th, 1750, Jacob Heulings, Jr., and their daughter, Sarah Heulings, married 4th mo. 7th, 1769, Samuel French [141]. Jacob Heulings, Jr., was the son of Jacob and Dorothy (Eves) Heulings, and grandson of William and Dorothy (Eves) Heulings who were married in 1680. William Heulings served as justice of peace for Burlington County, 1703; died 1713. Jacob and Dorothy (Eves) Heulings both died in 1758.

MEETING RECORDS

Evesham Monthly Meeting Minutes:

At a Monthly Meeting held at Evesham ^{ye} 9th of ye 3rd Mo. 1769 Samuel French son of Charles French & Sarah Hulings Daughter of Jacob Hulings Jr. Dec'd. appeared & Declared their Intentions of marriage with Each other. Therefore John Roberts & John Cowperthwaite are appointed to make ^{ye} usual Enquiry Concerning him, & report to next meeting, parents being present Consented.

At a Monthly Meeting held at Evesham ^{ye} 6th of ^{ye} 4th Mo. 1769. Samuel French & Sarah Hulings appeared & signified ^{ye} Continuation of their Intentions of marriage with Each other the Friends appointed to make Enquiery reporting nothing to obstruct their proceeding Therefore they are at Liberty to Consumate their said Intentions according to good order & Joshua Lippincott & Isaac Evans are appointed to be present & see that good order be kept, & report to next meeting.

[Women's Meeting]

9" of 3^d mo. 1769. Samuel French and Sarah Heulings appeared and declared their intentions of marriage with each other, parents present consented.

6th of ^{ye} 4th Mo. 1769. Samuel French and Sarah Heulings appeared and signified ^{ye} continuation of their said intention of marriage with each other and return of enquirers clear they are at liberty to consumate their said intention according to good order.

4" 5 mo. 1769. Friends appointed to attend the marriage of Samuel French reported that it was orderly accomplished.

[Men's Meeting]

At a Monthly Meeting held at Evesham ^{ye} 4th of ^{ye} 2nd Mo. 1779. Solomon Haines, Samuel French, Jno. Haines, Enoch Evans & Bethual Moore produced acknowledgements for paying fines in Lieu of their personal service in ^{ye} Militia contrary to ^{ye} Rules Established in ^{ye} Society which were read and Received.

At a Monthly Meeting held at Evesham ^{ye} 9th of ^{ye} 3^d mo. 1780.— Samuel French by Edward Darnel requested a Certificate to reccommend himself, Wife & children to the Monthly Meeting at Haddonfield, therefore Enoch Evans & John Maxell Junr. are appointed to make ^{ye} usual Enquiry & prepare one & produce it to next meeting.

At a Monthly Meeting held at Evesham ^{ye} 6th of ^{ye} 4th Mo. 1780. The friends appointed produced a Certificate on behalf of Sam'l. French, wife and children, which was read approv'd & Sign'd by the Clk. & sent to the Women for their signing.

[Women's Meeting]

9"—3 mo. 1780 Sarah French requested our certificate to be inclosed with her husband and children to joyu Friends of Haddonfield Monthly Meeting, therefore two friends are appointed to enquire into her life and conversation and give their account to ^{ye} friends appointed to draw it.

Haddonfield Minutes of ^{ye} Mo: Meeting of Women Friends:

At a Monthly Meeting of Women friends held at Haddonfield the 8th of the 5th Month, 1780.

A certificate was produced from Evesham Monthly Meeting Recommending Samuel French & wife Sarah & their Daughter Agneſs to the care of this which was read and Received.

Samuel French spent his early life subject to Evesham Monthly Meeting, as will be noted. In 1780, some years after he removed to the lower part of Gloucester County, he became a member of Haddonfield Monthly Meeting. From various records, it is evident that the family attended worship at Mickleton, or Upper Greenwich, as it was then called, that being the nearest meeting to their residence. After Woodbury became a Monthly Meeting, 1785, Samuel French and family appear to have been united therewith, although the record of transfer it not attainable. Later the meeting at Mullica Hill was the home place of worship.

WILL OF SAMUEL FRENCH, 1803

In the name of God, Amen. I Samuel French of the township of Greenwich, County of Gloucester and State of New Jersey being at this time in a poor state of health but of sound mind and memory, not knowing but what my dissolution may be near, do make and publish this for my last will and Testament.

First, I give and bequeath to my dear wife Sarah French one hundred pounds, to be paid to her by my executors, hereafter named as soon as it can be collected after my decease. Or she may take the whole or any part of the above said one hundred pounds at the praisement as she may think proper, and also six silver table spoons and nine silver tea spoons and the priviledge of two rooms in the house where I now dwell of her choice, and priviledge of the Oven, Pump, Cellar and fruit of all kinds for her own use, all kinds of sauce of vegitable production sufficient for her own use, with her firewood delivered at the door, Hay and grain sufficient to keep a horse and Hay and pasture for a cow.

Second I bequeath to my son Uriah French my tract of land whereon the Saw Mill stands, bounded as follows Beginning at a stone for a corner

near said Mill and runs thence North thirty-seven and one half degrees
West twelve chains and sixty-five links to a White oak thence North eighty-
nine degrees West three chains and twelve links to an Elm thence North
seventy-nine West five chains and forty-five links to a Black Oak thence
North forty-two degrees West four chains and thirty links to a Black Oak
thence North four degrees and thirty minutes East twenty-one chains and
fifty links to a Hickory thence South fifty-six degrees West fifteen chains
thence North twenty-two degrees West six chains and thirty links thence
South fifty-three degrees West ten chains and forty links thence South
twenty degrees East thirty-four chains and fifty links thence South eighty-
eight degrees three chains thence South six degrees and thirty minutes East
twelve chains and sixty links thence North seventy-two degrees and thirty
minutes East twelve chains and thirty links thence North thirty-one degrees
East four chains and sixty links thence South eighty-five degrees East
thirty-four chains and fifty links thence North seventy-seven degrees and
thirty minutes East six chains and seventy-five links thence North eighteen
degrees West three chains and forty links thence North eighty-six degrees
West five chains and twenty-eight links thence South thirty-five degrees
West one chain and seventy-two links thence North eighty-four degrees
and thirty minutes West five chains thence North twelve degrees and thirty
minutes East nine chains and sixty links thence South seventy degrees and
thirty minutes East twelve chains to the place of beginning. Containing
one hundred and fifteen acres, more or less, together with all the appurtenances to the Mill belonging. And also I bequeath unto my son Uriah
my silver watch, and it is my will that my son Uriah do pay unto my wife
Sarah French, yearly and every year the sum of forty dollars during her
natural life

Thirdly—I bequeath to my son Jacob French the plantation whereon he
now lives with all the appurtenances except the part of said land which
lays over the Cohawkin Road between Iredell's and Allen's land—and it
is my will that my son Jacob do pay unto my wife Sarah French the sum
of forty dollars yearly and every year during her natural life.

Fourthly I give and bequeath to my son Charles French all that my
tract of land I purchased of Hewit, bounding as follows beginning at a
stake near a large Gum near Clems run and runs from thence North
twenty-six degrees and thirty minutes West fifty-five chains thence South
seventy-three degrees West seventeen chains and thirty links thence South
seventy degrees West twenty-six chains thence South twelve degrees and
thirty minutes West nine chains and sixty links thence South eighty-four
degrees and thirty minutes East five chains thence North thirty-five degrees
East one chain and seventy-two links thence South eighty-six degrees East
five chains and twenty-eight links thence South eighteen degrees East three
chains and forty links thence South twenty-six degrees and thirty minutes
East one chain and seventy-five links thence South eighty degrees East nine

said ▓▓ ▓▓ ▓▓ ▓▓ North thirty-seven and one-half degrees
West twelve ▓▓ and sixty-five links to a White oak thence North eighty-
one degrees West three chains and twelve links to an Elm thence North
twenty-nine West five chains and forty-five links to a Black Oak thence
North forty-two degrees West four chains and thirty links to a Black Oak
thence North four degrees and thirty minutes East twenty-one chains and
fifty links to a Hickory thence South fifty-six degrees West fifteen chains
thence North twenty-two degrees West six chains and thirty links thence
South fifty-three degrees West ten chains and forty links thence South
twenty degrees East thirty-four chains and fifty links thence South eighty-
eight degrees three chains thence South six degrees and thirty minutes East
twelve chains and sixty links thence North seventy-two degrees and thirty
minutes East twelve chains and thirty links thence North thirty-one degrees
East four chains and sixty links thence South eighty-five degrees East
thirty-four chains and fifty links thence North seventy-seven degrees and
thirty minutes East six chains and seventy-five links thence North eighteen
degrees West three chains and forty links thence North eighty-six degrees
West five chains and twenty-eight links thence South thirty-five degrees
West one chain and seventy-two links thence North eighty-four degrees
and thirty minutes West five chains thence North twelve degrees and thirty
minutes East nine chains and sixty links thence South seventy degrees and
thirty minutes East twelve chains to the place of beginning. Containing
one hundred and fifteen acres, more or less, together with all the appurtenances to the Mill belonging. And also I bequeath unto my son Uriah
my silver watch, and it is my will that my son Uriah do pay unto my wife
Sarah French, yearly and every year the sum of forty dollars during her
natural life

Thirdly—I bequeath to my son Jacob French the plantation whereon he
now lives with all the appurtenances except the part of said land which
lays over the Cohawkin Road between Iredell's and Allen's land—and it
is my will that my son Jacob do pay unto my wife Sarah French the sum
of forty dollars yearly and every year during her natural life.

Fourthly I give and bequeath to my son Charles French all that my
tract of land I purchased of Hewit, bounding as follows beginning at a
stake near a large Gum near Clems run and runs from thence North
twenty-six degrees and thirty minutes West fifty-five chains thence South
seventy-three degrees West seventeen chains and thirty links thence South
seventy degrees West twenty-six chains thence South twelve degrees and
thirty minutes West nine chains and sixty links thence South eighty-four
degrees and thirty minutes East five chains thence North thirty-five degrees
East one chain and seventy-two links thence South eighty-six degrees East
five chains and twenty-eight links thence South eighteen degrees East three
chains and forty links thence South twenty-six degrees and thirty minutes
East one chain and seventy-five links thence South eighty degrees East nine

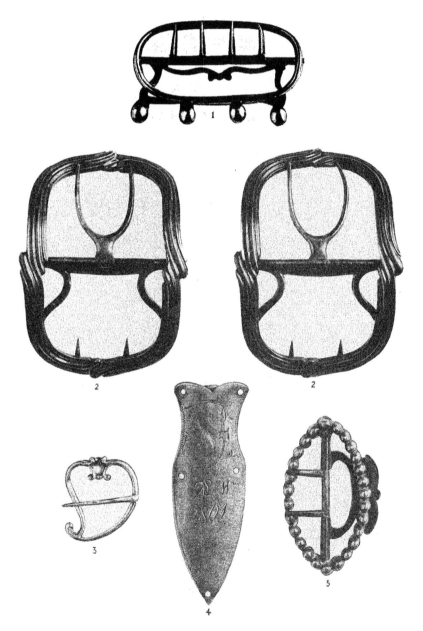

1. Silver Knee Buckle belonging to Charles French (42), marked "C. F."
2. Silver Shoe Buckles belonging to Samuel French (141)

chains and thirty links thence South thirty-five degrees East nine chains and fifty links thence South seventy-five degrees and thirty minutes East thirty-three chains thence North forty-one degrees East two chains thence South sixty-five degrees East ten chains to the place of beginning Containing one hundred and forty-two and one half acres, with all the appurtenances thereto belonging, and it is my will that my son Charles do pay unto my wife Sarah the sum of forty dollars yearly and every year during her natural life

Fifthly, I give and bequeath unto my son Samuel French the plantation whereon I now dwell bounding as follows beginning at a Maple bush corner to Iredell's land and runs from thence North sixty-nine and one half degrees East thirty chains and fifty links thence East ten chains thence North forty-one degrees East twenty-five chains thence North seventy five degrees and a half East thirty-three chains thence North thirty-five degrees West nine chains and fifty links thence North eighty degrees West nine chains and thirty links thence North twenty-six degrees and thirty minutes West one chain and seventy-five links thence South seventy-seven degrees and thirty minutes West six chains and seventy-five links thence North eighty-five degrees West thirty-four chains and fifty links thence South thirty-one degrees West two chains and thirty-nine links thence South seventy-four degrees East seven chains and forty links thence South twenty-two degrees and thirty minutes East four chains and ten links thence South forty-eight degrees and thirty minutes East four chains and ninety links thence South eighty-one degrees East four chains thence South thirty degrees and thirty minutes East six chains and thirty-five links thence South thirty-three degrees West nine chains and seventy-two links thence South fifty-one and one half degrees East eight chains and seventy-five links thence North seventy degrees East three chains and ninety links to Raccoon Creek thence up the several courses thereof to the place of Beginning, containing two hundred and twenty-two acres and twenty-five perches of land be the same more or less together with all the appurtenances thereunto belonging, and also I bequeath unto my son Samuel my sorrel mare together with my saddle and bridle.

Sixthly—I bequeath unto my daughter Agnes Moore the sum of fifty pounds to be paid by my Executors hereafter named in two years after my decease

Seventhly I bequeath to my son Joseph French the residue of my plantation whereon I now live bounded as follows beginning at a stone corner to Iredell's land and runs from thence North six and one half degrees West thirty-six chains and forty links thence North seventy-two degrees and thirty minutes East twelve chains and thirty links thence North thirty-one degrees East two chains and twenty-one links thence South seventy-four degrees East seven chains and forty links South twenty-two degrees and thirty minutes East four chains and ten links South forty-eight degrees and thirty minutes East four chains and ninety links thence eighty-one degrees East four chains thence South thirty degrees and thirty minutes East six chains and thirty-five links thence South thirty-three degrees West nine chains and seventy-two links thence South fifty-one degrees and thirty minutes East eight chains and seventy-five links thence South seventy degrees East twenty-eight chains and ninety links to the place of beginning containing ninety-two acres three roods and fifteen Perches of land be the same more or less, and also I bequeath unto my son Joseph all the land over the Cohawken road that I purchased of Joseph Gardiner lying between Allen's and Iredell's land, and also I bequeath unto my son Joseph twenty-five acres of land off the Egypt Tract adjoining the Cohawken Road and Joseph Allen's land and also I bequeath unto my son Joseph a certain Road that lies along Joseph Allen's line.

Eighthly I bequeath to my daughter Sarah French two hundred pounds to be paid by my Executors hereafter named in one year after my decease.

Ninthly I bequeath unto my daughter Ann French two hundred pounds to be paid by my executors as abovesaid when my daughter Ann shall arrive at the age of eighteen.

Tenthly all the unappropriated Rights that I am possessed of at my decease I equally bequeath unto my five sons namely Uriah, Jacob, Charles, Samuel and Joseph.

Eleventhly I order and empower my executors hereafter named to sell all the residue of my lands that has not been heretofore bequeathed and that after paying all my just debts and legacies as aforesaid the remainder of monies if any more be, to be equally divided between my beloved wife and three daughters namely Agnes Moore, Sarah and Ann French, and lastly I order my executors to sell all my moveable estate except what is taken by widow at the Praisement and the monies to be divided between my beloved wife and daughters as abovesaid after paying as abovesaid and lastly I appoint my two eldest sons namely Uriah and Jacob French Executors of this my last Will. In Witness whereof I have hereto set my hand and seal this twenty-third day of the seventh month in the year of our Lord one thousand eight hundred and three

Samuel French

Sealed, signed published and declared by
the said Samuel French to be his testament and last will in the presence of us
    Rebecca Zane
    Isaac Eacrit
    Joshua Haines
Will proved August 11, 1814.

SUMMARY OF INV. OF ESTATE OF SAMUEL FRENCH, 1814

An Inventory of the Goods and Effects of Samuel French late of the township of Greenwich County of Gloucester and State of New Jersey, deceased, as shown to us the subscribers and appraised this 4th. day of August 1814

Wearing apparel and Desk..................................... 20
Table & chairs, crockreware & sund.......................... 11.75
Books, Looking glass, Cubboard and furn...................... 13.25
two Beds and beding... 35.50
Seven Chairs and beding..................................... 28.50
Hogshead, tubs & pail & sund................................ 2.50
Meal Chest, Tea Cettle & sund............................... 2.25
Book accounts 152.64

                          $266.39

        Josiah Moore Joseph Allen

IN MEMORIAM

When sorrowing o'er some stone I bend,
Which covers all that was a friend,
And from her hand, her voice, her smile,
Divides me—for a little while,
Then Saviour seest the tears I shed—
For Thou didst weep o'er Lazarus dead.

Died on Thursday the 17th inst, Miss Ann French, youngest daughter of Samuel French, Esq., of Gloucester County, New Jersey. The sudden and premature death of this amiable young Lady has caused an universal gloom to pervade the minds of her relations and friends. With a mind highly cultivated, a taste refined, a judgment sound, a heart filled with benevolence and charity, and manners the most bland and insinuating, she could not fail to attract the attention and gain the esteem of those with whom she associated. To love and revere Miss French, it was only necessary to be acquainted with her. As a child she was affectionate and obedient, as a friend, frank and sincere. Although in the midst of youth and lovliness, with prospects flattering, she did not shrink at the approach of the King of terrors, but with a firm and unshaken confidence in the promise of her Saviour, she looked for immortality and bliss beyond the grave. The chasm occasioned in society by her death will not soon be filled— Lamented Maid thou art gone!—Our longing eyes will n'er behold thy lovely form again!—Thy spotless soul has urged its way to Heaven—Bright cherubims welcome thy arrival on the shores of deliverance and felicity. Thy friends will long cherish the remembrance of thy many virtues and strive to make them their own.

CHATELAINE
BELONGING
ANN H. FREN

A tribute to the memory of Ann Heulings French [361]; from a newspaper of 1812.

MULLICA HILL MEETING AND SCHOOL

In the latter part of the seventeenth century one Eric Molica, an adventurous Swede, belonging to one of the early colonies on the Delaware, ascended the winding stream which has become historic as Raccoon creek. He took up a large tract of land and founded a prosperous settlement, afterward known as Mullica Hill. He had eight children and lived to round out almost a century. Indians were numerous and their name for the creek was Naraticon, or Raccoon, on account of great numbers of that lively animal in the dense forests which lined its banks. The soil was wonderfully fertile, as it is today after two hundred years' cultivation. Many curious Swedish traditions have long prevailed. Greenwich was the first township organized by the Gloucester County Court, in 1694. Friends early came to the vicinity and prospered greatly. They were separated from regular meeting places and asked permission to assemble otherwise. The first society in Mullica Hill appears to have been organized in 1797, meetings being held in the school house. This was continued until 1804 when the present large and substantial brick meeting house was built, at a most desirable location, on a high piece of ground, on the south side of the creek.

As education was always in the minds of Friends, this community was no exception. The history of Mullica Hill School may be traced back through a period of one hundred and eighty-seven years, embracing five different buildings. The first of these was built of cedar logs, with oiled paper for window lights. It served from about 1720 until 1756, when a frame house was built. In 1790 a larger and more comfortable building was erected, the result of awakened public interest. Samuel French [141] was one of the principal subscribers to the building fund, his younger children and some of his grandchildren attending the school for many years. This building was heated by an immense stove, the first luxury of the kind known in that part of the country. In 1824 building number four was erected, largely out of the materials of the old school house. In 1855 a two-story school house was built, and this, with all needful conveniences, has been used ever since. Charles French, son of Samuel French, was one of the trustees in charge of this property, including the meeting house and graveyard, from 1801 until 1833.

d eight children and lived to round out

MULLICA HILL MEETING HOUSE, 1804

We whose Names are underwritten animated by motives of public Spirit do agree & promise to pay towards building and erecting a Schoolhouse on the Lot of Ground generously given by Jacob Spicer to Friends ~~for that Purpose~~ To be paid to the Managers on demand witness our Hands the 5th Day of the 5th Mo. 1789. ————

	£	S		
Rebekah Lippincott	10	7	6 Paid in full	£ p.
Joseph Gibson Junr	15	0	0 Paid in part	14 2 7
Samuel French	12	10	0 Paid in full	£ S
Aaron Pancoast	10	0	0 Paid in part	8 2 0
Benjamin Moore	7	10	0 Paid in full —
Joseph Allen	6	1	5 Paid in full
Hannah Elles	2	16	0 Paid in full
Abraham Iredell	1	14	0 Paid in full
Ephraim Gardnier	7	10	0 Paid in full
Agnes Robert	5	00	0 Paid in full
Benjamin Hootten	5	0	0 Paid in full

SUBSCRIPTIONS TO FRIENDS' SCHOOL, MULLICA HILL, 1789

MICKLETON (UPPER GREENWICH) MEETING

Friends living between Mullica Hill and Woodbury, about 1740, built a small frame meeting house on a lot of ground granted for that purpose by Solomon Lippincott. The meeting was a branch of Haddonfield Monthly Meeting until 1785, when it was united with Woodbury meeting. In 1798 a large and commodious brick meeting house was built, which has been in use ever since. This is located one and a half miles east of the former one, the old lot being held for a burying ground. In 1808 a large brick school house was erected, the school being under the special care of the meeting and becoming a noted educational institution. The meeting at Mickleton was first known as Lippincott's and later as Upper Greenwich. This meeting was the place of worship of Samuel French and family for many years, prior to the setting up of a meeting in Mullica Hill, in 1797.

DESK BELONGING TO SAMUEL FRENCH [141]

PLAN OF
FRENCH'S ESTATE
GRENWICH TOWNSHIP
GLOUCESTER COUNTY
N. J.

URIAH FRENCH

115 ACRES.

CHARLES FRENCH
142 ½ ACRES

☐ HOUSE.

JOSEPH FRENCH

92 A. 3 R. 15 P.

☐ HOMESTEAD

SAMUEL FRENCH

222 A. 25 P

FRENCH FARMS IN GLOUCESTER COUNTY, N. J.

From an old map prepared by Samuel French [141] about 1790. The farm allotted to Jacob French was located near that of his brother Joseph.

WILL OF JACOB HEULINGS, JR., 1758

In the Name of God Amen, I Jacob Heulings of Evesham in the County of Burlington and Provience of West New Jersey Being Sick and Weak of Body but of Sound and perfect Disposing mind and memory bleſsed be almighty God for the Same and Calling to mind the Mortality of my Body and that it is appointed for all men Once to Dye DO make and Ordain this my Last will and Testament in manner and fform ffollowing VIZ My mind and will is that all my Just Debts and ffuneral Charges be Duly paid and Discharged by my Executors hereafter named as Soon as Conveniently Can be after my Decease; IMPRIMIS I Give my Son Jacob Heulings all that my Land and Plantation Whereon I now Dwell to Hold to him my said Son Jacob Heulings and to his heirs and Aſsigns fforever He paying thereout to his three Sisters Theodosia, Sarah, and Agnes Heulings the Sum of Six Hundred Pounds in manner ffollowing That is to Say to my Daughter Theodosia Heulings the sum of Two hundred pounds in One year after my said Son arrives at the Age of Twenty One Years To my Daughter Sarah Heulings the Like sum of Two hundred pounds in two years after my Said Son arrives at the age aforesaid AND to My Daughter Agnes Heulings the Like Sum of Two Hundred pounds in three years after my said Son arrives at the Age af^d AND my mind and Will is that if Either of my Said Daughters Should Dye before she arrives at the age and Time ffixed for their Receiving their respective Legacies to be paid in manner aforesaid that then her Legacy So Dying Shall be Equally Divided between the other two Surviving Daughters, I ALSO Give to my said Son Jacob Heulings my part and Share of a Certain Cedar Swamp Lying on ae Brook called Kettle Runn To Hold to him his Heirs and Assigns fforever Item I Give and Devise to my Loving wife Agnes Heulings all the use of my Land and Plantation So Given and Bequeathed as aforesaid until my Said Son Jacob Heulings arrives at the Age of Twenty Years PROVIDED that She Continue my widdow So Long and Commit no Wast thereon To Enable her to bring up my Children and to Give them Good Education BUT if it Should So happen that my said wife Should Marry Again before my Said Son arrives at The Age aforesaid THEN my will is that my Other Executors Shall Have the Care of Leasing my Place Educating and Bringing up my Children and Other Affairs of my Estate AND that they Let my wife have the Liberty of Living on the said Plantation after her Marriage on Such Terms as my Other Executors Shall See most Convenient for the benefit of My Children ITEM I do Give to my aforesaid wife all the remainder of my Estate be it what it will or where it will AND Do Nominate Constitute and Appoint my said Wife Agnes Heulings and my Brother-in-Law Micajah Wills and my Own Brother William Heulings Executors of this my Last will-Testament and Do ffrustrate and Make void all fformer Wills by me

WILL OF JACOB HEULINGS, JR., 1758

In the Name of God Amen, I Jacob Heulings of Evesham in the County of Burlington and Provience of West New Jersey Being Sick and Weak of Body but of Sound and perfect Disposing mind and memory blefsed be almighty God for the Same and Calling to mind the Mortality of my Body and that it is appointed for all men Once to Dye DO make and Ordain this my Last will and Testament in manner and fform ffollowing VIZ My mind and will is that all my Just Debts and ffuneral Charges be Duly paid and Discharged by my Executors hereafter named as Soon as Conveniently Can be after my Decease; IMPRIMIS I Give my Son Jacob Heulings all that my Land and Plantation Whereon I now Dwell to Hold to him my said Son Jacob Heulings and to his heirs and Afsigns fforever He paying thereout to his three Sisters Theodosia, Sarah, and Agnes Heulings the Sum of Six Hundred Pounds in manner ffollowing That is to Say to my Daughter Theodosia Heulings the sum of Two hundred pounds in One year after my said Son arrives at the Age of Twenty One Years To my Daughter Sarah Heulings the Like sum of Two hundred pounds in two years after my Said Son arrives at the age aforesaid AND to My Daughter Agnes Heulings the Like Sum of Two Hundred pounds in three years after my said Son arrives at the Age af^d AND my mind and Will is that if Either of my Said Daughters Should Dye before she arrives at the age and Time ffixed for their Receiving their respective Legacies to be paid in manner aforesaid that then her Legacy So Dying Shall be Equally Divided between the other two Surviving Daughters, I ALSO Give to my said Son Jacob Heulings my part and Share of a Certain Cedar Swamp Lying on ae Brook called Kettle Runn To Hold to him his Heirs and Assigns fforever Item I Give and Devise to my Loving wife Agnes Heulings all the use of my Land and Plantation So Given and Bequeathed as aforesaid until my Said Son Jacob Heulings arrives at the Age of Twenty Years PROVIDED that She Continue my widdow So Long and Commit no Wast thereon To Enable her to bring up my Children and to Give them Good Education BUT if it Should So happen that my said wife Should Marry Again before my Said Son arrives at The Age aforesaid THEN my will is that my Other Executors Shall Have the Care of Leasing my Place Educating and Bringing up my Children and Other Affairs of my Estate AND that they Let my wife have the Liberty of Living on the said Plantation after her Marriage on Such Terms as my Other Executors Shall See most Convenient for the benefit of My Children ITEM I do Give to my aforesaid wife all the remainder of my Estate be it what it will or where it will AND Do Nominate Constitute and Appoint my said Wife Agnes Heulings and my Brother-in-Law Micajah Wills and my Own Brother William Heulings Executors of this my Last will-Testament and Do ffrustrate and Make void all fformer Wills by me

MICKLETON (UPPER GREENWICH) MEETING HOUSE, BUILT 1798

made and Declare this and no Other to be my Last Will and Testament
IN TESTIMONY whereof I the said Jacob Heulings have hereunto Set
my Hand and Affixed my Seal this thirty ffirst day of March ANNO
DOM; One thousand Seven hundred and Fifty Eight 1758

Signed Sealed published pronounced and Declared by the within named
Jacob Heulings as and for his Last will and Testament in the Presence of
us with the words / then / ae Brook Called / ffirst interlined

    Hannah Z. Thorn
    Her ✕ mark
    Abraham Heulings
    Elizabeth Buckman

By the Honble. John Reading Esq., President of His Majesty's Council
and Commander in Chief in and over his Majefty's Province of New Jerfey
and Territories thereon depending in America, &c.

To all to whom thefe Presents fhall come or may concern, Greeting.

Know ye, That at Burlington on the Day of the Date hereof, before
Samuel Peart Surrogate, being thereunto delegated and appointed, the laft
Will and Teftament of Jacob Heulings late of the County of Burlington,
Deceafed (a Copy whereof is hereunto annexed) was proved; and is
approved and allowed of by me. The faid Deceafed having while he lived,
and at the Time of his Death, Goods, Chattels and Credits within this
Province, by Means whereof the Proving the faid Will, and the granting
Adminiftration, of all and fingular the faid Goods, Chattels and Credits,
and alfo the auditing, allowing, and finally difcharging the Account thereof,
doth belong unto me. And the Adminiftration of all and fingular the
Goods, Chattels and Credits of the faid Deceafed, and any Way concerning his Will, was granted unto Agnefs Heulings, Micajah Wills and
William Heulings Executors in the faid Will named, being firft duly
affirmed well and faithfully to Adminifter the fame, and to make and
exhibit a true and perfect Inventory of all and fingular the faid Goods,
Chattels and Credits, and alfo to render a juft and true Account of their
Adminiftration, when thereunto lawfully required.

IN TESTIMONY whereof, I have caufed the Prerogative Seal of the
Province of New-Jerfey to be hereunto affixed, this Thirtieth Day of May
in the Year of Our Lord One Thoufand Seven Hundred and fifty eight.

                              Charles Read Reg.

INVENTORY OF THE ESTATE OF JACOB HEULINGS, JR., 1758

A true and perfect Inventory of the Goods and Chattles, rights and Credits of Jacob Heulings Late of Evesham in the County of Burlington and provence of New Jerfey yeoman Deceafed as was appraifed this 24th. of april Annoi Dom, 1758

	£	s.	d.	£	s.	d.
to his Purfe and apparrel	18	2	9			
to Silver Watch	8			26	2	9

	£	s.	d.	£	s.	d.
to horfe Bridle and Saddle	16	0	0			
to two pare of three year old Steers	11	10	0			
to a 2 year old Colt	11	0	0			
to 7 Milch Cows	21	0	0			
to 4 young cattle	6	10	0			
to 3 Calves	1	15	0			
to a Bay mare	15	0	0			
to 2 Draugted Crosbars, 2 Plows and 2 Pair Gears	15	18	0	98	13	0

	£	s.	d.	£	s.	d.
to an Ax	0	5	0			
to Bay Mare Bigg with fold	6	0	0			
to Green Corn Rye in Lower field } to " " " in upper " }	7	0	0			
to 6 acres of wheat	2	0	0			
to 11 Sheep and 8 Lambs	6	0	0			
to 21 Hoggs in the wood Pafter	10	0	0	31	5	0

	£	s.	d.	£	s.	d.
to Rye and flax in the Barn and Mill	3	0	0			
Goods in the Room						
to set of high Draws and Glafs	4	0	0			
to Bed and furniture	7	10	0			
to walnut table	1	5	0			
to a tea Table	1	0	0			
to a pine Cheft	0	5	0			
to Striped Druget 4 yds	0	12	0			
to 15 yrds. of worped ———	3	0	0			
to table Linnen	1	5	0	18	17	0
				174	17	0

thee Room continued	£	s.	d.	£	s.	d.
to and Irons	0	5	0			
to warming pan	0	15	0			
to Saddle Baggs	0	3	0			
to Corner Cupboard and Sundrys therein	2	10	0			
to 2 Spinning wheels and Reel	0	15	0			
to Great Wheel	0	10	0			
to ½ Doz. Chares and Arm Chare	1	0	0			
to ½ Doz. tea Spoons and tongs	1	12	0			
to Sundrys on the mantle-Shelf	0	7	6			
to Conductor Generalis	0	5	0			
to old Books	0	5	0			
to Sundrys as Lancets knives and other things	0	5	0	6	12	6

to Goods in the houſse						
to Pewter and knives and forks	3	0	0			
to Bed and furniture	9	0	0			
to Sundrys pots kettle and sundry Small artecles.	3	5	0	15	5	0

In the Chamber						
to a Box Iron and 2 heaters	0 2	5 16 1	0 0			
to 6 Dear Skinns						
to flock Bed						
to Negro man Named Tip and Bed	40					
to tubs and flower	0					
to 8 lb. yern	0	12	0			
to an old Sadle	0	5	0	46	2	0

In the Aft Chamber						
to a feather Bed, 2 pillows Sheet and Blanket	1	15	0			
to a Bagg of feathers	2	0	0			
to Wool Baskets Cards and feathers and Sundrys	0	10	0			
to 4 Bush. wheat	0	10	0	4	15	0

In the Cellar						
to 3 hogsheds and 2——	0	15	0			
to ½ barrel of——	0	10	0			
to one Barrel of Cyder	0	5	0			
to Sundrys of tubs and Pails &c	1	0	0			
to a tub of Lard 60 lbs	1	0	0	3	10	0
				75	4	0

out of Doors	£	s.	d.	£	s.	d.
to Horse Gears	0	5	0			
to Sundrys of tubbs	0	10	0			
to powdering tubb	0	5	0			
to Bacon in the Smoak houfe	8	0	0			
to a waggon	6	0	0			
to 3 Shoats	0	15	0			
to Indian Corn in the Cribb	2	0	0			
to 4 yokes and Chains and Sundry Utensils of husbandry	3	10	0	21	5	0
to a hive of Bees	0	5	0			
to Two Deer and Bells	1	0	0	1	5	0
				14	10	0
				75	4	0
				193	17	0
				£283	11	0
to a Boar	0	10	0			

Jofhua Ballinger } Appraisers
James Cattell   }

E & O Excepted

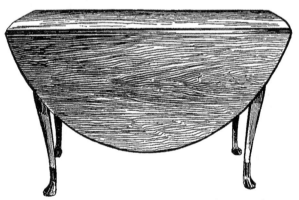

wALNUT tABLE wItH fALlINg LEAVES, sArAh (HEULINGS) fRENCH

AGNES SHARP PENQUITE

John Penquite, who came from Parish Kayne, Cornwall, England, in 1683, was the third white settler in what is now Wrightstown township, Bucks Co., Pa. He was an enterprising and prosperous farmer and active and zealous Friend. Meetings were held at his house for over twenty years, until the building of the first meeting house, in 1721. The present meeting house, a picture of which is herewith given, was built in 1787. In 1690 John Penquite married, at Shrewsbury, N. J., Agnes Sharp, who came from England in 1686, and who became a highly respected minister among Friends, devoting over 70 years to useful work in the religious field. She died in 1758. John Penquite died 1719.

"A Teſtomony from Wrights Town Monthly-Meeting in Bucks county Pennſylvania, concerning our ancient friend and Siſter Agnes Penquite, who departed this life, the 20th day of the eleventh month 1758, being upwards of one hundred years old.

" She brought a certificate with her from Europe, dated the 6th day of the Second month 1686. She was of an innocent pious life and converſation, a good example in attending meetings both on firſt and week-days, until a few years before her death. She was a miniſter above Seventy years; her teſtimony, tho' generally Short, was moſtly to Satsifaction and edification; and in her declining age, when nature Seemed almoſt Spent, She appeared more divinely favoured than common, to the admiration of Some. When She could no longer attend meetings, She would often, at meal times, appear in prayer, with praiſes to the Lord, to the comfort and Satisfaction of thoſe preſent; and frequently Signified, 'She had the evidence of divine peace.' Not long before her departure She Said, 'That her Sweet Lord had not forſaken her, but was Still with her to comfort and refreſh her in her old age.' Thus She was removed from time to eternity, like a Shock of corn fully ripe."

WRIGHTSTOWN MEETING HOUSE, 1787

142—ELIZABETH FRENCH (Thomas, 1; Charles, 8; Charles, 42).

> b. February 18th, 1750, in Waterford Township, Gloucester Co., N. J.
> d. 5th mo. 25th, 1812.
> m. First, 10th mo., 1768, James Wills, son of Micajah and Rebecca (Heulings) Wills.
> m. Second, 4th mo. 11th, 1787, Moses Wills, son of Daniel and Elizabeth (Woolston) Wills.
> He b. 11th mo. 15th, 1737.
> d. 1st mo. 30th, 1807.

362—LETTICE WILLS

> b. 11th mo. 5th, 1771.
> m. 8th mo. 25th, 1795, William Rowand.

363—ANN WILLS

> b. March, 1775.
> m. First, 4th mo. 8th, 1795, Evan Clement, M.D.
> m. Second, 1799, John Blackwood, M.D.

364—REBECCA WILLS

> b. 1780.
> m. 5th mo. 15th, 1799, Samuel Woolman.

365—ELIZABETH WILLS

> m. October 23rd, 1800, Thomas Wood.

366—CHARLES WILLS

> b. 1787.
> d. 9th mo. 9th, 1806.

367—MOSES WILLS, JR.

> b. 12th mo. 17th, 1792.
> m. 12th mo. 17th, 1818, Rebecca Wright Black.

MOSES WILLS married, first, March 31st, 1764, Margaret Wills; she died 3rd mo. 7th, 1782. They had the following children:

ELIZABETH WILLS

> b. 12th mo. 29th, 1764.
> d. 8th mo. 28th, 1790.
> m. 5th mo. 4th, 1785, Joseph Burr, son of Robert Burr, of Ruland, Pa.

MARY WILLS

> b. 3rd mo. 17th, 1766.
> m. 3rd mo. 11th, 1789, John Haines, son of Ephraim Haines, of Chester Township, Burlington Co., N. J.

HOPE WILLS	b. 7th mo. 15th, 1768.
HANNAH WILLS	b. 6th mo. 20th, 1770. m. 12th mo. 14th, 1809, John Lancaster.
ABEL WILLS	b. 8th mo. 15th, 1772. d. 11th mo. 13th, 1774.
RUTH WILLS	b. 3rd mo. 4th, 1775. d. 3rd mo. 1st, 1781.
RACHEL WILLS	b. 6th mo. 24th, 1777. m.. 4th mo. 7th, 1803, David Mickle, son of William Mickle, of Greenwich, N. J.
AARON WILLS	b. 11th mo. 29th, 1779. d. 2nd mo. 20th, 1781.

By will dated December 13, 1779, proved December 21, 1780, Elizabeth Wills made the following bequests to her great-grandchildren, daughters of her granddaughter Margaret Wills, wife of Moses Wills: Elizabeth £5 and six silver tea-spoons; Mary £5, two pewter dishes, six plates and two porringers; Hope, £5 and chest of drawers; Hannah £5 and pair of sheets; Ruth £5, six napkins and a table-cloth; Rachel £5, a pair of silver buttons and warming pan. The money was to be paid to their father, Moses Wills, and kept at interest until children became of age.

MEETING RECORDS

Evesham Monthly Meeting Minutes:

At a Monthly Meeting held at Evesham ye 8th of ye 9th mo. 1768. James Wills son of Micajah Wills & Elizabeth French daughter of Charles French appeared & Declared their Intentions of marriage with each other. Therefore Joshua Lippincott and Jacob Evans are appointed to make ye needful Enquiery Concerning & report to next meeting, parents being present consented.

At a Monthly Meeting held at Evesham ye 6th of ye 10th Mo. 1768. James Wills & Elizabeth French appeared & signified ye continuation of their Intentions of marriage with Each other ye friends appointed to make Enquiery reporting nothing to obstruct their proceeding, therefore they are at Liberty to Consumate their said Intentions according to good order, & Joshua, & Enoch Roberts are appointed to be present & see that good order be kept & report to next meeting.

At a monthly meeting held at Evesham ye 10th of ye 11th Mo. 1768. The Friends appointed to attend ye marriage of James Wills & Elizabeth French reported that it was orderly accomplished.

Minutes of Evesham Monthly Meeting of Women Friends:

8—9 mo. 1768. Jas. Wills and Elizabeth French appeared and declared their intentions of marriage with each other. Esther and Rebecca Roberts to make needful enquiry concerning her.

6" of 10" mo. 1768. Jas. Wills and Elizabeth French appeared and signified the continuation of their intention of marriage with each other, and inquiry having been made they are left at liberty to proceed in marriage.

SUMMARY OF WILL OF ELIZABETH (FRENCH) WILLS, 1812

Elizabeth Wills of Northamton Burlington Co., N. J., widow

Proved June, 27—1812.

Children Lettice Rowand, wife of Wm Rowand interest of $120 her life and at her death to her female children in equal shares

Ann, wife of Doc^r John Blackwood use of $120. her life and at her death divided equally among all her children

Rebecca, wife of Samuel Woolman use of $120. her life, then divided equally among all her children

Elizabeth, wife of Thomas Wood, interest of $120. her life, then to be equally divided among her 3 children, viz Richard, Charles and Ann Wood

Marcy Burr daughter of Joseph Burr $20.

Moses Mickle son of David Mickle $30. when 21

Sarah   "   sister of Moses, to have above^{sd} $30 when 18, if her brother dies before day of payment.

Granddaughters Martha Woolman ⎱ a Bed, Bolster and pillows
            Ann Wood   ⎰ with one coverlid to each

Son Moses Wills the remainder of my money wether in Cash Bonds Bills or otherwise, also all sheets, pillow cases, best Bed Bed-stead 6 of my best blankets, 2 Coverleds, best bed-quilt Table Cloths Napkins &c marked with the letters M & W, my Walnut Dining Table, Mahogany Breakfast Table, Cherry tree ſtand, my brase and Irons all my Books, &c.

Rest of household goods between my 4 Daughters; Lettice to have my six silver Table Spoons in her share for life, then to her Daughter Elizabeth Rowand

Executor—Son Moses Wills
Witnesses—Saml Black
            Nathan W. Black
            Wm Black

A true and perfect Inventory of all and Singular the Goods chattels monies and effects Elizabeth Wills of the Township of Mansfield in the County of Burlington New Jersey, dec^d taken at her late dwelling the 5th day of June 1812.

Cash and Wearing Apparrel.................................. 67.17½
Obligations to the amount of................................. 1717.92
Household Goods Kitchen furniture &c........................ 339.42½
                                                            ─────────
                                                            $2124.52

Appraised the day and year above written by   Joseph Wills
                                                 George Haines

Affirmed to 7th day of July, 1812 ⎱ Joseph Wills one of the apprs.
    before Abrm. Brown Surrg ⎰ Moses Wills Executor.

PARLOR CHAIR, 1760

143—CHARLES FRENCH 3RD (Thomas, 1; Charles, 8; Charles, 42).

   b. October 25th, 1753, in Waterford Township, Gloucester Co., N. J.

   d: April 6th, 1834 (Sunday morning), buried in Trinity P. E. Churchyard, Moorestown, N. J.

   m. May 29th, 1783, Sabilla Stokes, daughter of Joseph and Atlantic ˙ (Bispham) Stokes; Rev. Robert Blackwell performing ceremony; Christ Church record, Philadelphia.

  She b. December 6th, 1757.

   d. November 4th, 1845, buried in Trinity P. E. Churchyard, Moorestown, N. J.

368—ANN FRENCH
  b. August 14th, 1784.
  m. 6th mo. 20th, 1811, Joshua M. Hollingshead, M.D.

369—JOSEPH FRENCH
  b. September 2nd, 1786.
  m. December 9th, 1813, Mary Stokes.

370—HOPE FRENCH
  b. February 22nd, 1789.
  d. August 29th, 1805.

371—ATLANTIC FRENCH
  b. September 21st, 1791.
  m. March 19th, 1812, Gilbert Page.

372—ELIZABETH FRENCH
  b. April 15th, 1794.
  d. April 20th, 1854.
  m. October 21st, 1841, John Gill, son of John and Annie (Smith) Gill; Rev. A. B. Patterson of Trinity P. E. Church, Moorestown, N. J., performing ceremony.
  He b. 7th mo. 9th, 1795.
  d. 4th mo. 12th, 1884.

373—SABILLA FRENCH
  b. June 21st, 1796.
  d. September 10th, 1880.

374—SARAH FRENCH
  . December 4th, 1799.
  b. October 2nd, 1854.

375—CHARLES FRENCH
  b. October 26th, 1801.
  d. August 29th, 1802.

CHARLES FRENCH FARMHOUSE, NEAR FELLOWSHIP, N. J. (WEST FRONT), 17—AND 1785

THE

Atlantic Bispham, born March 22nd, 1737, was the daughter of Joshua and Mary (Lawrence) Bispham, who were married in Bickerstaff, England, 1729, and sailed from London for America, December 13th, 1736, in the ship " Mary and Hannah," Henry Lavage, Captain. Owing to the fact of her being born on this voyage, she was named Atlantic by the captain of the vessel, who, tradition states, gave her a silk dress, in further honor of the event. The ship arrived at Philadelphia April 26th, 1737, after a trip of five months. Atlantic Bispham married, in 1757, Joseph Stokes, for many years an honored and useful citizen of Moorestown, N. J.

· CHARLES FRENCH, 3RD

Upon coming into possession of the homestead, near Fellowship, in 1784, Charles French, 3rd, son of Charles French, Jr. [42], continued in operation the old colonial grist mill on the home plantation, the site of which can still be traced, on the bank of the Pensaukin Creek, and in 1816 purchased another property of the same kind, with a saw mill and 37 acres of land, in the same neighborhood, for $10,000. In 1800 he purchased three acres, a valuable site, near the center of Moorestown, and in 1818 bought 33 acres additional. Hither he removed, about 1820, having built one of the finest brick mansions of the time, in which he resided until his death. His widow, under a life tenancy, occupied the place until her death, and, in 1845, it was sold, later becoming the property of the Society of Friends, under whose direction it is used as a delightful retreat and boarding-home for aged Friends.

While living in Moorestown, Charles French became a partner with William Roberts in a large woolen mill industry, at Mt. Holly. He acted as executor and adviser in the settlement of many estates and also performed several responsible trusts as assignee. His business activities continued until the close of a long and honored life. Old-time residents of Moorestown and vicinity remember him as one of the most useful citizens of that community. The work of his executors revealed the fact that he had quadrupled, in value, the estate with which he began, half a century before, being possessed of over 1,000 acres of land in Burlington and Gloucester Counties, with farm houses, two grist mills and the mansion house in Moorestown and a large amount of personal property. The mansion was sold for $10,000; the farm homestead for $13,700 and other properties at advanced prices.

The old French farm home, near Fellowship, has a most interesting history. As elsewhere stated, it was bought by Charles, Jr., in 1747, who soon after went there to live. In 1785 Charles, 3rd, shortly after his marriage, built a large brick addition to the old house, the initials of his own name and those of his wife appearing on the end, as shown in one of the accompanying illustrations. This house is a splendid old-time exhibit, solid and enduring, with brick-paved and enclosed apartments in the great cellar for ample storage purposes. The masonry is a marvel of expert work. The long slanting roof of the older part, running to within a few feet of the ground, is moss-covered, while the great oaken doors and immense fire-place, with brick-enclosed boiler annex for pig-killing time uses, tell the story of farm life one hundred and fifty years ago. The original dwelling was probably built about 1730. Here some of the children of Charles French, Jr., were born and reared and all the children of Charles, 3rd. Here were the joyous scenes of marriage festivities and family reunions and other events covering a period of nearly seventy-five years.

Five sisters of Charles, 3rd, went forth, with glad anticipation, to their new homes. Two of his brothers brought brides, to receive the parental benediction, and he, likewise, came from Christ Church, Philadelphia, with Sabilla (Stokes) to spend nearly forty years together in the old homestead. In the old chimney corners sat Charles and Ann, at eventide, as the years came on apace. Here their life stories ended, happily not far apart, joining the one child who left them at the dawn of womanhood. A little later, the years passing swiftly, three of the second generation that grew up under the family roof-tree, went forth, with chosen partners, each followed by the prayers and blessings of Charles and Sabilla. Three daughters tarried to comfort and care for them when the shadows lengthened. Hither, at various times of special interest, came troops of cousins and other relatives, young and old, from neighboring and, for those days, distant communities. In the great "living room" there were feasts and merry-makings, while fascinating stories of colonial and revolutionary times were told after candle light. The last survivor of those happy occasions is Mary (French) Burrough [725], great granddaughter of Charles and Ann, who recently observed her 82nd birthday. The touching memories of this old homestead would fill many pages in themselves.

CHARLES FRENCH FARMHOUSE, NEAR FELLOWSHIP, N. J. 17— AND 1785

MEETING RECORDS

Charles [143] and Sabilla (Stokes) French

Evesham Monthly Meeting Minutes:
At a Monthly Meeting held at Evesham ye 4th of ye 1st Mo. 1781. Friends from ye Preparative Meeting of Chester reported that Charles French Junr. hath been treated with for paying Military Fines in lieu of Personal Service.—and the Neglect of attending Meetings, therefore John Hunt and William Matlack are appointed to treat further with him and report to next meeting.

At a Monthly Meeting held at Evesham ye 8th of ye 3^d mo. 1781. The Friends appointed reported that they have had an opportunity with Charles French Junr. who did not appear convinced of the Inconsistency of his Conduct in paying his Military Fine and the Neglect of attending Meetings: Therefore this Meeting disowns him according to our Discipline and John Hunt & John Roberts are appointed to give him a copy of the Minute & acquaint him of his Priviledge of an Appeal & report to next Meeting.

At a Monthly Meeting held at Evesham ye 5th of ye 4th mo. 1781. The Friends appointed to give Charles French Jr. a Copy of this Meeting's Minute against him, having not Comply'd therewith they are continued to the service.

At a Monthly Meeting held at Evesham ye 10th of 5th Mo. 1781— The Friends Appointed reported that they have given Charles French Junr. a copy of the Disownment against him according to appointment.

[Women's Meeting]
6"—2 Mo. 1783. Friends from the Preparative Meeting at Chester report that Sabillah French (formerly Stokes) has been visited for going out in her marriage; after a time of deliberation thereon, this meeting appoints Hannah French, Elizabeth Grinsdale and Martha Dudley to visit her, and report their sense respecting her to next meeting.

5"—3d mo. 1784. The Friends appointed to visit Sabillah French report that they have had an opportunity with her, and that she appeared in some degree of tendernefs, but did not desire Friends forebearance; after a time of deliberate consideration the meeting to refer her case to the care of the Mens-meeting.

[Men's Meeting]

At a Monthly Meeting held at Evesham y° ... of ... Mo. 1784.
The Women friends inform that they have treated with Sabilla French
(formerly Stokes) for outgoing in marriage and communicating the
before an hireling Minister that she appeared tender but did not incline to
make the necessary satisfaction therefor; which being considered John
Cattell and Jno. Roberts are appointed to inform her that the Meeting has
come to a Judgement to disown her, prepare a Minute accordingly & produce it to next Meeting.

9ᵗʰ 4ᵗʰ mo. 1784 The Friends appointed reported that they have delivered the Meetings Message to Sabilla French (late Stokes) and now produced an Essay of a Minute disowning her which being read is approved
and the Cl'k signed the same; John Hunt and Sam'l Allinson are appointed
to visit, give her a Copy and acquaint her with her right of appeal.

At a Monthly Meeting held at Evesham y° 7ᵗʰ of yᵉ 5ᵗʰ Mo. 1784.
One of the Friends appointed to give Sabilla French a copy of the disownment against her reported that they have not comply'd therewith for the
above reason, (occasioned by reason of the other friends being indisposed).
They are also continued to the service.

At a Monthly-meeting held at Evesham the 11ᵗʰ of the 6ᵗʰ M°. 1784
The friends appointed reported that they have given Sabilla French a Copy
of the Disownment against her according to appointment and she said she
should not appeal.

WILL OF CHARLES FRENCH [143], 1833

Let this be recorded, that I Charles French of Moorestown in the Township of Chester, County of Burlington & State of New Jersey; being of
sound mind & disposing memory; Blessed be the Most High for all his
mercies extended to me; but knowing the uncertainty of time here: Do
make & ordain this my last Will & Testament, in manner & form following, viz.

Imprimis. I direct my herein after named executors, to pay all my just
debts & funeral expences out of my personal estate as early after my decease
as convenient.

Item. I give & devise unto my dear & well beloved wife Sabilla French,
all that part of the plantation & tract of land whereon I dwell situate
in Moorestown aforesaid now in my occupancy, together with all & singular, the buildings & improvements of what kind or nature soever, thereon ·

CHARLES FRENCH HOUSE, MOORESTOWN, N. J., BUILT ABOUT 1820

erected & made, for & during her natural life. I do further give & bequeath
to my beloved wife aforesaid all my household goods & kitchen furniture,
together with so much of the farming utensils, & stock as she may choose,
including the Carriage, two of the best horses & harnefs:—Also the sum
of four hundred dollars, payable quarterly out of the interests & rents of
my estate.—Provided she accept the above in lieu of her full right of
Dower.

Item. It is my will that my four daughters, namely Ann Hollinshead,
Elizabeth French, Sabilla French & Sarah French should have homes &
live with their mother as they heretofore have done in my life time; also
after her death, during the space of one year, to enjoy all the privileges
of said premises, household goods stock &c, thereon, including the Carriage, horses & harnefs, by allowing a reasonable compensation therefor.
And provided they or any of them agree to take the premises, as a part of
their share of my estate; they & my executors shall nominate men to value
it accordingly—in which case I give & devise the same, with all & singular
of its appurtenances, to such of them my said daughters so agreeing, &
their heirs & afsigns, forever.

Item. It is my Will & I hereby authorize and impower my executors
to make sales, at such times & in such manner as may appear to them best,
of all my real estate whatsoever & wheresoever situated in the State of
New-Jersey, with all & singular of their appurtenances, for the best prices
they can obtain for the same, & that they make & execute good & sufficient
titles therefor;—excepting neverthelefs, a limit of the time on the premises
whereon I now dwell;—the sales of which if not taken at valuation by my
daughters as aforesaid, to be suspended till the expiration of the privileges
herein before reserved.

Item. I give & devise to my daughter Atlantic Page, my house & lot,
in second street between Tammany & Green St. Philadelphia (3ᵈ door
below Green) to her my said daughter & to her heirs;—which premises
& their appurtenances, I value at six thousand dollars & to be considered
as so much of her dividend of my estate.

Item. I give & devise to my two Grand-children Sabilla & Mary Ann
French, my house & lot in Seventh Street, between Green & Coats St. Philadelphia, equally, share & share alike, to them & their heirs—which premises & their appurtenances, I value at two thousand five hundred dollars,
to be considered as part of their share of my estate

Item. I give & bequeath to each of my daughters, Elizabeth French,
Sabilla French, & Sarah French as much of my personal effects, as each of
their sisters Ann Hollinshead & Atlantic Page received at her outfit.

Item. I give & bequeath to my daughter Ann Hollinshead;—to the children & the legal representatives of the deceased (if any) of my son Joseph
French, (viz.) Sabilla, Mary Ann, Deborah, Elizabeth & Sarah French;—to
my daughters Atlantic Page, Elizabeth French, Sabilla French & Sarah

French, all the residue & remainder of the proceeds & valuations of my estate, in equal division, share & share alike (my herein named Grand children to take one share) which bequest I do give to my said children &c. their heirs & assigns for their benefit & advantage forever.—Excepting out of the share to my aforementioned grand-children the sum of two thousand five hundred dollars, and on the account of Sabilla & Mary Ann French,—and out of the share to my daughter Atlantic Page the sum of six thousand dollars as aforesaid, & all the above recited shares subject to the annuity of my wife.

Item. I appoint my daughter Elizabeth French & my nephew Joseph Stokes, to have the charge of that share of my estate which may fall to my son Joseph French's children; to be kept at interest in Bank Stock or otherwise;—the income of which so far as necessary, to be expended in their education, & as they respectively attain the age of twenty one years, the full share to be paid over to them; but in case of intermarriage, previous thereto, one half to be paid & no more & the remaining half at the age aforesaid; allowing the valuation of my house & lot in Seventh St. taken out of the share of my estate set off, for the children of my son Joseph dec[d] from & out of the shares of Sabilla and Mary Ann French, to whom it is given.

Lastly.—I nominate, constitute & appoint my daughter Elizabeth French executrix, my Brother-in-law Joseph Matlack & my nephew Hugh F. Hollinshead, Executors of this my Testament & last Will.—

In witness whereof, I have hereunto set my hand & seal this ninth—day of the fourth month (April) in the year of our Lord eighteen hundred & thirty three. 1833.

Charles French (seal)

sign'd, seal'd, publish'd & declar'd by the said Charles French to be his testament & last will, in the presence of us—

Henry Warrington
Joseph Hooton
William Hooton

REAR LAWN, CHARLES FRENCH HOUSE, MOORESTOWN, N. J.

State of New Jersey

Burlington County ſs; William Hooton one of the Witneſses to the fore-going Will alledging himself to be conscientiously scrupulous of taking an oath and being duly Affirmed according to Law on his solemn Affirma-tion did declare and say that he saw Charles French the Testator therein named sign and seal the same, and heard him publish pronounce and declare the foregoing Writing to be his last Will and Testament and that at the doing thereof the said Testator was of sound and disposing mind and memory, as far as this Affirmant knows and as he verily believes;—and that Henry Warrington and Joseph Hooton the other subscribing Evidences were present at the same time, and signed their names as Witneſses to the said Will, together with this Affirmant, in the presence of the said Testator.—

Affirmed at Mount Holly the 23ᵈ
day of May A D—1834—before me—
   Charles Kinsey
     Surrogate.

           William Hooton

State of New Jersey

Burlington County ſs; Elizabeth French Executrix and Joseph Matlack and Hugh F. Hollinshead Executors in the within Testament named sever-ally alledging themselves to be conscientiously scrupulous of taking an oath and being duly Affirmed according to Law on their solemn Affirmations sev-erally did declare and say that the Within Instrument contains the true last Will and Testament of Charles French the Testator therein named so far as they know and as they verily believe, that they will well and truly perform the same by paying first the debts of the said deceased and then the Legacies in the said Testament Specified, so far as the goods chattels and credits of the said deceased can thereunto extend; and that they will make and exhibit into the prerogative office at Trenton a true and perfect Inventory of all and Singular the goods, chattels and credits of the said deceased; that have or shall come to their knowledge or poſseſsion, or to the poſseſsion of any other person or persons for their use, and render a just and true account, when thereunto lawfully required.—

Affirmed at Mount Holly the 23ᵈ
day of May A D—1834 before me
Charles Kinsey
   Surrogate

   Elizabeth French
   Joseph Matlack
   Hugh F. Hollingshead.

INVENTORY OF ESTATE OF CHARLES FRENCH, 1834

A true and perfect Inventory of all and Singular the goods and chattles rights and credits moneys and effects of Charles French late of the Township of Chester County of Burlington Deceased made by us whose names are hereunto Subscribed this twenty second day of the fifth Month Anno Domini 1834—

Silver watch & wearing apparel............................	60.00
Cash on hand silver................................... 186.56	
gold 50	1843.56
Bank notes 1607	
household goods & kitchen furniture.........................	1010.50
Ceder bords plank Joice &c................................	94.00
waggons plows and other farming utinseals...................	297.50
horses horned cattle hogs &c..............................	342.25
light waggons gig and Sundry harnefs.......................	135.00
rye oats and corn..	185.50
old iron & chains &c.......................................	6.50
Sundrys on the farm at Charles Becks.......................	41.50
bonds and notes drawing interest together with bank Stock &c....	12623.67
Stock on the farm on the ferry road........................	27.00
	$16666.98

Appraised by us whose names are hereunto
Subscribed the day and year above written
            Jo⁸ Hugg
            William Hooton.

    State of New Jersey,
    Burlington County SS. William Hooton one of the Appraisers of the above Inventory alledging himself to be conscientiously scrupulous of taking an oath and being duly affirmed, according to Law, did declare and say, that the goods, chattels and credits in the above Inventory set down and specified, were by him appraised according to their just and true respective rates and values after the best of his judgment and understanding and that Jo⁸ Hugg, the other appraiser, whose name is thereto subscribed was present at the same time, and consented in all things to the doing thereof, and that they appraised all things that were brought to their view for appraisement

    Affirmed the 23ᵈ day of May }
    A D. 1834, before me   }   William Hooton
        Charles Kinsey
            Surrogate.

1794   ELIZABETH (FRENCH) GILL   1854

1795   JOHN GILL   1884

State of New Jersey

Burlington County, SS. Elizabeth French Executrix and Joseph Matlack and Hugh F. Hollinshead Executors of the last Will and Testament of Charles French in the within Inventory named, deceased, severally alledging themselves to be conscientiously scrupulous of taking an oath, and being severally duly affirmed according to law, did severally declare and say, that the within writing contains a true and perfect Inventory of all and singular the goods, chattels and credits of the said deceased, as far as have come to their knowledge or poſseſsion, or to the poſseſsion of any other person or persons for their use.—

Elizabeth French

Joseph Matlack

Hugh F. Hollingshead

Affirmed, the 23ᵈ day of May A D. 1834 before me

Charles Kinsey

Surrogate

JOHN GILL

John Gill, the fourth of the name in this country, was the great grandson of the pioneer who came to Haddonfield, N. J., or the wilderness site thereof, in 1706, as the business agent of Elizabeth Haddon, afterwards Elizabeth Estaugh. He was born on the homestead plantation, still remaining in the family and now known as " Gillford." He followed farming, being also a devotee of healthful rural sports, until the death of his father, in 1839, when he removed to Haddonfield. Shortly after, having married Elizabeth French, of Moorestown, he built the present mansion, the third on the same site, on the old King's Highway, or Main Street. The shrubbery of this notable place is more than one hundred years old and the twenty acres of beautiful lawn adjoining have not been ploughed for fully one hundred and twenty-five years. This ground was part of the historic Indian field, or cleared space occupied by the natives when the white man first came to that section.

During his lifetime John Gill took an active interest in public affairs, serving as an efficient legislator. In 1842 he was elected president of the State Bank, Camden, reëlected when it became a national bank, in 1865, and held this responsible post for over forty years, or until his death, in 1884. Under his wise, yet liberal, management this bank became one of the leading financial institutions of the state. He was always the sympathetic friend of the small borrower, especially the farmer of limited means, who needed assistance until his crops could be made available. Mr. Gill also took an active interest in public affairs. During the session of 1832 he represented Gloucester County in the lower house of the legislature, and in 1848 was chosen Senator from Camden County. He had lively personal recollections of the last Indians in New Jersey, in his boyhood days, and while a legislator cheerfully voted for the generous appropriation in behalf of the remnant of former tribes, whose ancient fishing and hunting rights in that state were thus redeemed, at their earnest request.

SUMMARY OF WILL OF ELIZABETH (FRENCH) GILL, 1853

Dated Haddonfield Dec 8, 1853   Proved Camden May 27, 1854

One fifth of Estate to Sister, Sabilla French
"   "   "   "   "   "   Sarah French
"   "   "   "   " be divided between four nieces, daughters of brother Joseph, namely, Sabilla S. Mary Anne, Deborah H and Elizabeth French.

Income of one fifth part of Estate to Sister Atlantic Page, wife of Gilbert Page, during his and her life. Should she survive her husband, she then to receive said full share of estate.

One fifth part of estate to be divided between nephews Charles F. Hollingshead and H. H. Hollingshead.

Wearing apparel to sisters, silverware to nieces and grand nieces, stating, as feme covert (i. e., not having absolute right of disposal) "nothing doubting that my said husband (John Gill) will gladly and faithfully carry into effect my wishes thereunto."

"My beloved husband John Gill to have and take all my furniture as it now stands; also fifteen silver desert spoons and six large spoons and the income of my stock in the Commercial Bank and the residue of my maiden property not herein before devised. But in case of my said husband's marriage, I give the above named silver to my three nieces, Sabilla S., Mary Ann and Deborah H. French; also my Commercial Bank Stock. And in case of (his) marriage or death, my husbands two daughters,

During his lifetime John Gill took an active interest in public affairs, serving as an efficient legislator. In 1842 he was elected president of the State Bank, Camden, reëlected when it became a national bank, in 1865, and held this responsible post for over forty years, or until his death, in 1884. Under his wise, yet liberal, management this bank became one of the leading financial institutions of the state. He was always the sympathetic friend of the small borrower, especially the farmer of limited means, who needed assistance until his crops could be made available. Mr. Gill also took an active interest in public affairs. During the session of 1832 he represented Gloucester County in the lower house of the legislature, and in 1848 was chosen Senator from Camden County. He had lively personal recollections of the last Indians in New Jersey, in his boyhood days, and while a legislator cheerfully voted for the generous appropriation in behalf of the remnant of former tribes, whose ancient fishing and hunting rights in that state were thus redeemed, at their earnest request.

SUMMARY OF WILL OF ELIZABETH (FRENCH) GILL, 1853

Dated Haddonfield Dec 8, 1853   Proved Camden May 27, 1854

One fifth of Estate to Sister, Sabilla French
"   "   "   "   "   "   Sarah French
"   "   "   "   " be divided between four nieces, daughters of brother Joseph, namely, Sabilla S. Mary Anne, Deborah H and Elizabeth French.

Income of one fifth part of Estate to Sister Atlantic Page, wife of Gilbert Page, during his and her life. Should she survive her husband, she then to receive said full share of estate.

One fifth part of estate to be divided between nephews. Charles F. Hollingshead and H. H. Hollingshead.

Wearing apparel to sisters, silverware to nieces and grand nieces, stating, as feme covert (i. e., not having absolute right of disposal) "nothing doubting that my said husband (John Gill) will gladly and faithfully carry into effect my wishes thereunto."

" My beloved husband John Gill to have and take all my furniture as it now stands; also fifteen silver desert spoons and six large spoons and the income of my stock in the Commercial Bank and the residue of my maiden property not herein before devised. But in case of my said husband's marriage, I give the above named silver to my three nieces, Sabilla S., Mary Ann and Deborah H. French; also my Commercial Bank Stock. And in case of (his) marriage or death, my husbands two daughters,

JOHN GILL HOUSE, KING'S HIGHWAY, HADDONFIELD, N. J., BUILT 1841

Rebecca M. Willits and Anna S. Gill, to have and take my dinner and tea sets, Anna to have her choice. And after the decease of my husband, I give all the residue of my furniture, and all other of my maiden property which I wish my said husband to have during his natural life, at his decease, to my above named legatees, with bank stock, bonds & notes."

John Gill, Executor.

INVENTORY OF ESTATE OF ELIZABETH F. GILL, 1854

A true and perfect inventory of and singular the goods and chattels rights and credits of Elizabeth F. Gill, late of Haddonfield in the county of Camden and State of New Jersey, deceased, made by John Gill, Executor, and Samuel Nicholson and John K. Roberts, two disinterested freeholders, this twenty fourth day of May, A. D. 1854.

Purse and Apparel	$ 493.00
Household Goods	1,295.87
34 shares stock in Western Bank	2,312.00
24 shares stock in Farmers & Mechanics Bank	1,680.00
18 shares stock in Commercial Bank	1,080.00
Bonds and Notes esteemed good	7,199.85
	$14,060.72

Samuel Nicholson ⎱ appraisers
John K. Roberts ⎰

John Gill, Executor.

Affirmed May 27, 1854   Mark Ware, Surrogate.

SOFA BELONGING TO CHARLES FRENCH, 3RD, [143]

NEW JERSEY IN THE WAR OF 1812

For many years prior to the second conflict with England the people of the United States suffered vastly more from injustice, insolent disregard of their rights and downright persecution, than ever the colonies endured. American commerce had almost been destroyed. Nearly a thousand vessels had been unlawfully seized and a multitude of seamen impressed into the British service. The situation was exasperating; still, recognizing its apparent helplessness, especially on the sea, the nation was averse to war. It was earnestly hoped that the wrongs committed would cease. Sectional and commercial agitation resulted in serious division of public sentiment. When, June 18th, 1812, the lower house of Congress declared war, this was most impressively shown.

Out of 128 members present and voting, 79 supported the resolution and 49 opposed it. A change of 16 votes would have defeated the war measures, since almost universally regarded by statesmen and historians as a grave and lamentable mistake, full of peril. The votes of Massachusetts, Connecticut, New York, New Jersey, Pennsylvania and Delaware, showed 27 for war and 34 against; 4 out of 6 from New Jersey being recorded for peace. The Philadelphia " Gazette," the leading Federalist paper of the country, printed a fourteen column article signed by many influential citizens, bitterly denouncing the war, while its news columns were filled with reports of public indignation meetings held in almost every state. In New England town bells were tolled, shops closed and business suspended. Three governors refused to heed the call of the Federal government for militia. Volunteer enlistments were slow, only about one tenth the number asked for promptly responding. Two widely different elements comprised a large and influential peace party, one actuated by humanitarian principles, in which Friends were conspicuous; the other manufacturers, merchants and shipping men, apprehensive of disastrous losses.

On the 4th of July, 1812, a convention of the friends of peace in New Jersey, composed of leading and influential citizens from every part of the state, assembled at Trenton. Charles French, 3rd [143], headed the delegation from Gloucester county and Edward French [121] was a representative from Burlington county, and, later, he was a member of the district Congressional Convention at Salem. The Trenton convention issued a patriotic, wise and most impressive address, declaring for the maintenance of honorable peace and urging negotiation to that end. It was suggested that delegates should be elected to a convention to meet at the same place August 11th, to nominate Presidential Electors and candidates for Congress; it was also urged that peace party candidates for the legislature and county offices should be selected in the counties. The nominating convention met at Trenton, August 11th, and adjourned until September 15th. Thirteen counties were represented by twenty-five delegates, nominations were made for Electors and Congressmen, and another stirring address issued and widely circulated.

On the opposite page is given in facsimile, copy of a hand bill of those exciting days advertising the movement in Gloucester county, in which Franklin Davenport, Charles French, 3rd, Samuel Clement, Isaac Kay, John Gill and many other prominent citizens were actively interested. The influence of Friends in this worthy effort to promote peace and the public welfare was everywhere recognized.

No person will pull this down but an Enemy to PEACE.

WOODBURY,
NEW-JERSEY.

PURSUANT to Public Notice given, a *numerous* meeting of the PEOPLE of the County of Gloucester, Friends of Peace and the blessings to be derived from a Government administered on the principles and according to the example of the illustrious WASHINGTON. met at the Court-House, the 1st of August, 1812, for the purpose of selecting suitable persons, who, at this truly alarming situation of our common country, will make use of all constitutional means to obtain a *repeal* of the act of Congress declaring *war*, promote a settlement of all differences with Great-Britain, upon *honorable* terms, and by these means shield us from all the horrors of national distresses, and the more dreaded miseries of civil dissension and sacrifices—*Franklin Davenport*, acted as Chairman, and *Wm. Watson*, Secretary.

After some impressive observations, made on the occasion by J. B. Caldwell, James Sloan, R. L. Armstrong. Dr, Hopkins, and others, the Meeting proceeded to the appointment of a Committee from the several Townships of the County, to report a TICKET for the above important service, and for Sheriff and Coroners, to be voted for at the ensuing Election—when the following persons were agreed upon:

Waterford, Charles French, Levi Ellis, Joseph C. Swett.
Newton, James Hurly, Joseph Roberts, William E. Hopkins.
Gloucester Township, Samuel Clement, Job Eldridge, Samuel B. Lippincott.
Gloucester Town, Isaac Kay, Isaac Dowden, Isaac Browning.
Deptford, Edmund Brewer, J. L. Howell, J. B. Caldwell.
Greenwich, Jacob Lippincott, Samuel P. Paul, Edmund Wetherby.
Woolwich, John Gill, Joseph Chatham, John Benson.
Weymouth,
G. Eggharbour, } Peter Steelman, Benjamin Scull, Daniel Carrell, Wm, Watson.
Galloway,

The Committee, after a short space of time, reported the following Ticket for the consideration of the meeting:

> *Council*—JAMES HOPKINS.
> *Assembly*—ISAAC PINE, JOS. C. SWETT, DANIEL CARRELL.
> *Sheriff*—JOSEPH V. CLARK.
> *Coroners*—JOS. M. BISPHAM, JOS. JAMES, JOHN ESTELL.

Whereupon it was unanimously resolved, That this meeting do fully approve of the above Ticket, that they will support the same by every constitutional mean in their power, and they do recommend to those people of the county of Gloucester disposed to think and act with them at this trying crisis of our public calamities, to appoint committees in their several townships, to aid in the great and good work.

The Committee also report, that should any thing occur, by which the above persons, or either of them, cannot be voted for at the ensuing election, the following persons be put on nomination to supply any deficiency: Council, M. C. Fisher—Assembly, Charles French, J. B. Caldwell, Wm. Watson—Sheriff, John Baxter—Coroners, Daniel Baker, Wm. Cooper, James Bacon.

The meeting proceeded to the appointment of "two delegates, to meet other delegates, on Tuesday the 11th of August, inst. at 2 o'clock, P. M. at Trenton, for the purpose of agreeing on fit persons to be nominated as *Electors* of President and Vice-President of the United States, and as *Members of Congress* for this state—whereupon Franklin Davenport and James B. Caldwell were chosen—and in case of their absence, Joshua L. Howell, Joseph V. Clark or Matthew Gill, jun. be requested to supply their or either of their places.

Ordered that 300 copies of the foregoing proceedings be printed in handbills, for the use of the county, and that the same be published in the newspapers of this and our neighbouring states, favourable to the peace, happiness and protection of the American people.

FRANKLIN DAVENPORT, Chairman.

WM. WATSON, *Secretary*.

144—ELEANOR FRENCH (Thomas, 1; Charles, 8; Charles, 42).

> b. March 19th, 1756, in Waterford Township, Gloucester Co., N. J.
>
> d. 7th mo., 1850.
>
> m. First, 11th mo. 23rd, 1775, Hugh Hollingshead, son of Hugh Hollingshead.

He d. 1786.

> m. Second, Joseph Matlack.

376—AGNES HOLLINGSHEAD b. 8th mo. 6th, 1776.
> m. William Page, M.D.

377—ANN HOLLINGSHEAD   b. 2nd mo. 2nd, 1779.
> m. April 4th, 1796, Isaac Wilkins [339].

378—ABIGAIL HOLLINGSHEAD
> b. 6th mo. 28th, 1781.
> m. November 31st, 1802, William Stockton, son of William and Mary Stockton.

379—HOPE HOLLINGSHEAD   b. 11th mo. 29th, 1783.
> m. 4th mo. 23rd, 1807, D. Bassett.

380—HUGH FRENCH HOLLINGSHEAD
> b. 6th mo. 18th, 1786.
> m. Martha Mickle.

381—CHARLES FRENCH MATLACK, M.D.
> m. Sarah Ann Maule.

MEETING RECORDS

Evesham Monthly Meeting Minutes:
At a monthly meeting held at Evesham y[e] 5th of y[e] 10th mo. 1775. Hugh Hollingshead son of Hugh Hollingshead Dec'd & Ellioner French daughter of Charles French appeared & Declared their intentions of marriage with Each other Therefore Joshua Roberts and John Lippincott are appointed to make y[e] usual Enquiery & report to next meeting, parents being present consented.

At a monthly meeting held at Evesham ye 9th of ye 11th mo. 1775. Hugh Hollinshead & Ellioner French appeared & signified the continuation of their intentions of marriage with Each other the Friends appointed to made Enquiery reporting nothing to obstruct their proceeding Therefore they are. at Liberty to Consumate their said Intentions according to good order & Joshua & Enoch Roberts are appointed to be present & see that good order be kept & report to next meeting.

At a monthly meeting held at Evesham ye 7th of ye 12th mo. 1775. The Friends appointed to attend ye marriage of Hugh Hollingshead & Elioner French reported that it was orderly accomplished.

Minutes of Evesham Monthly Meeting of Women Friends:

5—10 mo. 1775. Hugh Hollingshead and Elloner French appeared and declared their intentions of marriage with each other. Therefore Rebeckah Roberts and Esther Hunt are appointed to make ye necessary enquiry concerning her.

9—11 mo. 1775. Hugh Hollingshead and Ellioner French appeared and signified ye continuation of their intentions of marriage with each other, and having ye return of enquirers clear therefore they are at liberty to consumate their said intentions according to good order.

7—12 mo. 1775. The friends appointed to attend ye marriage of Hugh Hollingshead and Elioner French reported that it was orderly accomplished.

Hugh Hollingshead died intestate in 1786, and his estate was administered by his wife and Jacob Hollingshead. Inventory of personal estate taken April 6, 1786, showed a valuation of £623 4s. 7d. The following interesting list of articles is quoted from the inventory:

A Silver Watch & Buckles
A " Ferry " Flat
A Dusk, a case of Drawers
A Cloc in the Parler
Sundry articles in Parler Bowfat (buffet)
1 dozen Silver Spoons
Chaney in Bowfat
time of bound boy Jeremiah Durell
time of ditto John Wills

      Tho Hollinshead ⎫
      Mofes Wills   ⎬ Apprs.

Eleanor Hollinshead

SIGNATURE OF ADMINISTRATRIX

145—HOPE FRENCH (Thomas, 1; Charles, 8; Charles, 42).

>> b. November 5th, 1763, in Waterford Township, Gloucester Co., N. J.
>> d. 8th mo. 19th, 1834.
>> m. 1st mo., 1780, William Black, 3rd, son of William and Mary (Gibbs) Black.
> He b. 2nd mo. 20th, 1759.
>> d. 10th mo. 7th, 1839.

382—ANN BLACK

> b. 8th mo. 12th, 1780.
> m. 6th mo. 12th, 1816, John Bishop.

383—CHARLES FRENCH BLACK

> b. 1st mo. 20th, 1783.
> d. 4th mo. 9th, 1787.

384—SAMUEL BLACK

> b. 10th mo. 22nd, 1786.
> m. 10th mo. 17th, 1816, Charlotte Biddle.

385—NATHAN WRIGHT BLACK

> b. 10th mo. 21st, 1790.
> m. 1st mo. 31st, 1828, Sarah Ellis.

386—REBECCA WRIGHT BLACK

> b. 8th mo. 23rd, 1792.
> m. 12th mo. 17th, 1818, Moses Wills, Jr.

387—WILLIAM BLACK, 4TH

> b. 4th mo. 12th, 1795.
> m. First, 4th mo. 12th, 1820, Ann Taylor Newbold.
> m. Second, Mary (Newbold) Adams.

388—CHARLES BLACK

> b. 3rd mo. 8th, 1799.
> m. Mary Vail.

389—GEORGE BLACK

> b. 1st mo. 15th, 1802.
> m. 9th mo. 22nd, 1838, Hannah M. Atkinson.

390—MARY BLACK

> b. 8th mo. 18th, 1805.
> d. 7th mo. 26th, 1812.

ANCESTRY OF WILLIAM BLACK, 3RD

Prominent among the early settlers of West Jersey were William Black and wife Alice (Taylor), who came from England in the Flie-boat " Martha," which sailed from Hull late in the summer of 1677. He had signed the "Concessions and Agreements" in 1676, and upon settling at Burlington, took up a large quantity of land in Mansfield, Springfield and Chesterfield townships, much of which still remains in possession of members of the family. He was a zealous Friend, highly esteemed and respected, and held several offices of trust under colonial government. He died in 1702, leaving wife, Alice, four sons, Thomas, William, John, Samuel, and daughter, Mary. Alice (Taylor) Black died 1709.

John Black, son of William and Alice (Taylor) Black, m. 10th mo. 4th, 1706, Sarah Rockhill: Chesterfield Mo. Meeting records. He died in Springfield township in 1744; intestate, leaving a considerable amount of property, and his estate was administered by Thomas Black of same place.

William Black, son of John and Sarah (Rockhill) Black, m. 1740, Christine Page, and had children, Ezra, b. 1740; Achsah, b. 1742; Ann, b. 1743; John, b. 1745; Edward, b. 1746; Joseph, b. 1748. In August, 1754, William m. second, Mary Gibbs, daughter of Isaac and Mary (Shreve) Gibbs. Their children were Ann, b. 1755; Mary, b. 1757; William, b. 1759. William Black died Jany., 1760; and by will dated Dec. 31, 1759, proved Jany. 30, 1760, bequeathed to his son Edward 100 acres of land in Chesterfield, Burlington Co.; to Ezra, the home plantation in Chesterfield, with instructions to care for his grandmother; to John and William, lands and plantation in Mansfield, Burlington Co., to be equally divided between them when they arrived at the age of 21; to daughter Achsah, £200, one-half when 18, other half when 21; to daughter Ann, £100, to be paid by son Ezra, one-half when she was 18, other half when 21; to wife Mary, £200, etc., to bring up younger children. Mary (Gibbs) Black married, second, Samuel Burroughs, and died in 1807, at the age of 81.

The descendants of William Black the pioneer have been men of strong character, who have made deep impressions upon the annals of their time. In the " Pennsylvania Chronicle " Jan., 1768, an interesting article appeared from a correspondent in Mansfield, Burlington Co., from which we quote:

> An early settler in this neighbourhood, acquired a large estate—he had
> five farms or plantations, and as many sons; and for each son, he intended
> one of the places, and his mind in that respect was well known in his

family; he however neglected to get his will reduced into writing, and died without one, so that as the English laws, in regard to descents, take place in this province, the whole landed estate, became the property of the eldest son. This he knew, but tho' he had then a family of children of his own, he, without hesitation or delay, ordered deeds to be drawn, and cheerfully executed them; to convey to each brother the plantation designed for him by their common father. The name of this just man was William Black, and as he has been deceased several years, its hoped that the mentioning of it, can give no offence to any body, nay, rather may it not be called a tribute due to such virtue, and the more necessary as his private way of living prevented him from being much known, and his religious profession from directing any marble monument to be erected to his memory.

MEETING RECORDS

Evesham Monthly Meeting Minutes:

At a Monthly Meeting held at Evesham ye 9th of ye 12th Mo. 1779— William Black son of William Black Dec'd. & Hope French Daughter of Charles French appeared & Declared their Intentions of Marriage with Each other y^e Young Man residing within y^e Compass of Haddonfield Monthly Meeting was acquainted that a Certificate from thence would be expected at their next appearance. Parents being present consented.

At a Monthly Meeting held at Evesham the 6th of y^e 1st M$^{o.}$ 1780 William Black & Hope French appeared and signified the continuation of their Intentions of Marriage with each other & he produced a Certificate from the Monthly Meeting at Haddonfield to the satisfaction of this, therefore they are at liberty to consumate their said Intentions according to good order & John Hunt & John Roberts are appointed to be present & see that good order be kept & report to next Meeting

At a Monthly Meeting held at Evesham the 10th of the 2^d Mo. 1780. The friends appointed to attend the Marriage of William Black & Hope French reported that it was orderly accomplished as usual.

Minutes of Evesham Monthly Meeting of Women Friends:

9"—12 mo. 1779. William Black and Hope French appeared and declared their intentions of marriage with each other. Parents present consenting.

6"—1 mo. 1780. Wm. Black and Hope French appeared ye second time and signified their intentions of marriage, and he produced a certificate from Haddonfield monthly meeting to ye satisfaction of this and having return of inquirers clear they are left at liberty to consumate their said intentions.

10"—2 mo. 1780. The Friends appointed to attend ye marriage of Wm. Black and Hope French report it was orderly accomplished.

SUMMARY OF WILL OF WILLIAM BLACK, 3RD, 1834

William Black—Mansfield Township, Burlington Co. N. J.

"being favoured with sound mind and memory"

Date 11 Mo. (Nov) 18th 1834.   Proved Oct 7—1839.

Children Sam¹ Black 3 Lots of Meadow Land—as follows.

    N° 1 purchased of Sam¹ Vaughn & wife by deed dated 7 Mo. 2ᵈ 1803 recorded in Book N. 501 &c at Mᵗ Holly.

    N° 2 purchased of John L. Hancock & wife July 18—1818 recorded in Book H² 338 &c in Clerks office Mt. Holly.

    3ᵈ bought of Exʳˢ of Jacob Keelor dec'd recorded in Clerk's Office in Mt. Holly. All described in deeds.—

Nathan Wright Black $5000, in addition to what I have advanced him heretofore

William Black Jr. $3000, above what he has had heretofore.

Charles Black—3 lots purchased of Mary Stevens deed dated Sept 27—1834 recorded Book B³ 423 at Mt. Holly, also 4 other lots which I purchased—

    Lot 1. of Joshua S. Earl Esqʳ at Sheriff's Sale he being then Sheriff of Burlington Co. by deed dated March 30—1825

    Lot 2. purchased of Jonathan Scattergood & wife—July 5, 1833—Book H³ 216 at Mt. Holly.

    Lot 3—purchased of Benj Shreve & wife April 11—1791

    Lot 4 (wood lot) purchased of Sam¹ Fenimore

George Black—House & lot I purchased of Dr. John Brognard, in the village of Columbus, & buildings thereon, also $1500.

Ann Bishop wife of John Bishop $2000.

Rebecca Wills $3000. & my eight day clock.

Housekeeper—Mary Craft $40.

Grand-daughters Mary Black ⎫
    Charlotte Black ⎪
    Abigail Ann Black ⎬ Children of son Samuel Black
    Emeline   " ⎪ $100 each when 18
    Rebecca   " ⎪
    Elizabeth   " ⎭

    Mary Bishop ⎫
    Rebecca   " ⎬ daughters of John Bishop $100 each

    Mary T. Black dau. of son Wᵐ Black Jr $100

Grandson Wᵐ Black, son of Nathan W. Black $100.

William Black

Executors
            Saml Black
Sons   *George Black*

Son-in-law   *Moses Wills*

Witnesses   Israel Nixon
            Aaron B. Rainier
            Chas. Mickle

INVENTORY OF ESTATE OF WILLIAM BLACK, 1839

A true and perfect Inventory of all and Singular the goods, chattels, rights and credits of William Black, late of the township of Mansfield in the county of Burlington and State of New Jersey, deceased made the 16th day of October, 1839.

Purse ....Dolls.   4.80
Wills & Black's Note of hand & Interest..........................484.
Thomas Starkey's   do   "   do 68.85
John Emley's   do   "   do 57.90
Dearbon waggon & harnís .... 30.
House hold good's & kitchen furniture ....181.

      Amount Dolls.826.55
Appraised by us   { Thomas Starkey
                { William E. Boulton
    Affirmed to Oct 17—1839

ANCIENT FAMILY PIECE

147—CHARLES FRENCH (Thomas, 1; Charles, 8; Uriah, 43).

m. 4th mo. 7th, 1773, Rebecca Taylor, daughter of Jacob and Abigail Taylor, of Chesterfield Township, Burlington Co., N. J.

d. 4th mo. 8th, 1809, in Philadelphia.

391—ELIZABETH FRENCH   b. 2ud mo. 15th, 1780.
d. 9th mo. 15th, 1793.

392—ANN FRENCH   b. 1st mo. 15th, 1782.
d. 10th mo. 15th, 1793.

393—CHARLES CREIGHTON FRENCH
b. 9th mo. 20th, 1784.
m. 12th mo. 5th, 1809, Mercy (Gilpin) Chapman.

394—JAMES FRENCH   b. 5th mo., 1787.
d. 10th mo. 15th, 1793.

CHARLES FRENCH

Charles French [147] and Samuel Crawford were old-style Philadelphia grocery merchants, their place of business being at 43 North Water Street, on the south side of " Old Ferry Alley," which was the first alleyway below Arch Street, and adjoining the store of Elliston & Perot. They also occupied the wharf, which was the second from Arch Street, next to the ferry slip. Their business was quite extensive, including large imports from the East Indies. For a time they had a branch store on Race Street, near Front. Charles French was thus engaged for over twenty-five years and having acquired a competency he retired, living near Third and Arch Streets. During the yellow fever epidemic of 1793 he lost three of his four children, two dying the same day. When the only surviving child and son, Charles Creighton French, attained his majority, in 1805, he engaged in the same line of business in which his father had been successful, locating his store at 48 North Front Street.

Charles French took into his employ, and into his home, a bright boy named Joseph Harrison, who later married the daughter of Mr. Crawford. Their son, Joseph Harrison, Jr., made a large fortune by building railroads in Russia. His widow, who died in 1906, left a choice collection of valuable paintings to the Philadelphia Academy of Fine Arts.

MEETING RECORDS

Philadelphia Monthly Meeting Minutes:

At a Monthly Meeting of Friends of Philadelphia held in our Meeting house in Fourth Street the 26th day of the Second Month 1773.

The Meeting was informed that Charles French who ſerved his apprenticeship with John Parish in this city, and has been an attender of our Meetings for worship, and is of a sober conduct, but not having brought a Certificate on his coming among us, has been in doubt respecting his right of membership on that account, and being about to enter into an Engagement of marriage with a young woman who is a member of Chesterfield Monthly Meeting, is desirous his case may be taken under consideration, and if the Meeting thinks proper, that he may have a Certificate to enable him to accomplish his intentions agreeably to the good order of our Discipline: John Pemberton and William Wilson are desired to take an opportunity of further conversing with him and to make such further Enquiry concerning him, as may appear necefsary and if no objection appears to prepare a Certificate suitable to the occasion, for the consideration of the Meeting next Month.

At a Monthly Meeting of Friends of Philadelphia held in our Meeting house on Fourth Street the 26th of Third Month 1773.

Certificate prepared for Charles French to Chesterfield Monthly Meeting.

Minutes of Chesterfield Monthly Meeting of Women Friends:

4th of 3^d mo. 1773. Charles French and Rebecca Taylor laid their proposal of marriage the first time before this meeting, two friends are appointed to make enquiry of the young womans clearness of others & report.

1" of 4" mo. 1773 Charles French and Rebecca Taylor appeared the second time, he declared they containued their intentions of marriage, and he producing a certificate from Philadelphia Monthly Meeting two friends are appointed to attend the marriage & make report.

6" of 6" mo. 1773 The Friends appointed to attend the marriage of Chas. French and Rebecca Taylor report they saw nothing but what was orderly.

MARRIAGE CERTIFICATE

Whereas Charles French of ye City of Philadelphia Son of Uriah French Late of Haddonfield in the County of Gloſter Dec'd, And Rebeckah Taylor Daughter of Jacob Taylor of Chesterfield in ye County of Burlington Weſtern devision of ye Province of New Jersey Haveing declared their Intentions of Marriage with Each other before Severial Monthly Meetings of ye People call'd Quakers at Chesterfield aforesaid According to ye Good order used Amongst them Whose Proceedings there in—After a deliberate Consideration thereof and haveing Consent of parents and Relations conceru^d nothing appearing to obstruct were approved of By said Meeting.

Now these are to Certify all whome it May Concern that for ye full accomplishing their said Intentions, this Seventh day of ye fourth Month One Thouſand Seven hundred and Seventy Three The said Charles French and Rebeckah Taylor appeared in a Publick Meeting of the s^d People and others, at there publick Meeting house in Bordentown, in the County of Burlington, afores^d And the said Charles French takeing the s^d Rebeckah Taylor by the Hand, did in a Solemn Manner Openly Declare that he took her to be his Wife promising by Divine Aſsistance to be unto her a faithfull and Loveing Husband, untill death Seperates them. And then and there in the said Aſsembly the Said Rebeckah Taylor did in Like Manner declare that She took the Said Charles French to be her Husband promising by Divine Aſsistance to be unto him a faithfull and Loveing Wife Untill Death Should Seperate them, And moreover the Said Charles French & Rebeckah Taylor she according to ye Custom of Marriage Aſsumeing the name of her Husband, as a further Confirmation Thereof, did then and there to these Presents set there hands And we whose names are heare Under Subscribed being preſent at the Solomnisation of ye s^d Marriage & Subscription in Manner beforeſ^d as Witneſses thereunto have also to these preſents Set our hands the day and year above written

Charles French
Rebeckah French

Joanna Brooks	Achsah Quicksall	
Bershaba Smith	Ann Curtis	Jacob Taylor
Isaac Wright	Mary Brown	Abigail Taylor
Hope Kay	Elisabeth Watson	Mary Crighton
Joseph Borden Junr	Ann Brooks	Samuel French
Wm Ivins	Elisabeth Taylor	Lewis Taylor
Thos Watson	Jonathan Wright	Mary Thay
Jo^s Duer	Ann Allison	Mary French
Mary Wright	Mary Crighton	Charles Taylor
Fretwell Wright	Amos Taylor	Mary Watson
Lydia Taylor	Ruth Alliſon	Rebeckah Potts
Henry Budd	Ann Ivins	Amy Watson
James Laurie	Margret Corman	

28

Philadelphia Monthly Meeting Minutes:

At a Monthly Meeting of Friends of Philadelphia held in our Meeting house on Fourth Street the 26ᵗʰ day of Seventh Month 1776.

It is agreed to acquaint our next Monthly Meeting that Charles French has been treated with ſeveral Months since for aſsociating to learn warlike exercises, and tho' he declined the practice for a Considerable time, and gave expectation that he would not again engage therein, yet it appears he has not kept his resolution,—William Savery and David Bacon are appointed to administer such further admonition & advice as his deviation requires.

At a Monthly Meeting of Friends of Philadelphia held the 27ᵗʰ day of the 9ᵗʰ Month—1776.

Charles French of this city, Bricklayer, who was educated and made profeſsion with us, hath in this time of outward Commotion so far deviated from our Christⁿ peaceable principles as to engage with others in learning the art of Wars, for ᵂᶜʰ he had been treated with in brotherly love, but as he doth not appear convinced of our religious principles herein, we testify he hath disunited himself from fellowship wᵗʰ us, until he becomes convinced of his deviation & makes such acknowledgment as the nature of his case require, wᶜʰ we desire he may be enabled to do through the aſsistance of Divine Grace.

SUMMARY OF WILL OF CHARLES FRENCH, 1804

Charles French city of Philᵃ (Merchant) sick & weak in Body.

Date—11 Mo 3ᵈ 1804   Proved—April 12—1809.

Wife—Rebekah in lieu of her Dower one full equal ½ part of my monies, Goods, chattels, outstanding Debts Rights Credits & effects whatsoever & wheresoever generally 1 full equall ½ part of all & singular my Estate Real & personal & mixed whatsoever & wheresoever as her absolute property & for the proper use of her & her heirs & Assigns forever—

Son—Charles C. French One full equal half part of my monies Goods Chattels outstanding debts, Rights Credits and Effects whatsover and wheresoever generally. One like full equal half part of all my Estate Real, personal & mixed whatsoever & wheresoever to him his heirs & Assigns forever. If he die under age without issue my wife Rebekah French to enjoy that portion intended for Son Charles during her natural life.

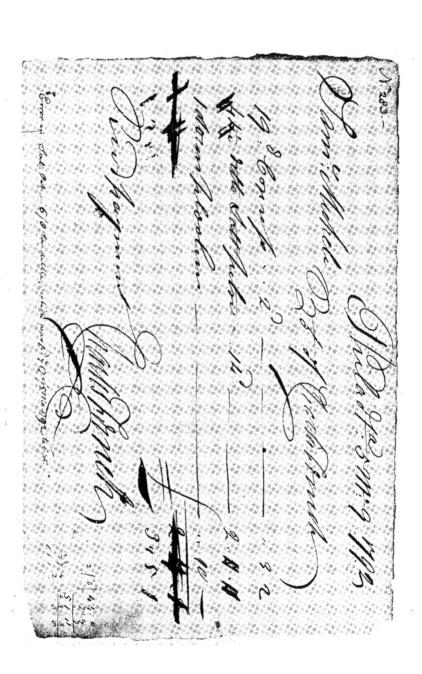

BILL FOR MERCHANDISE BOUGHT OF CHARLES FRENCH, 1792

Nieces—Mary French ⎫
        Hope French ⎬ (daughters of my Bro: Samuel French) at death of
        my wife to receive ⅔ of what was to have been my Son Charles
        C. French's, to be equally divided, but if either die under age
        without issue, her share to go to survivor.

Legatees John Taylor   ⎫
        Charles French Taylor ⎬ Children of my wife's Bro: Enoch
        Taylor dec'd—⅓ of what was intended for my Son Charles C.
        French to be equally divided, & if either of them die under age
        & without issue, his share to go to survivor.

Exrs—Wife—Rebekah French
      Son—Charles C. French
Witnesses—
      Sam: Smith
      William Ashby
      P. Thomson

INVENTORY OF ESTATE OF CHARLES FRENCH, 1809

Inventory of an Appraisement of the Effects of the Estate of Charles
French late of the City of Phil[a] Deceased—

Cash in Bank of Penna	3928.04
Cash lent Dunn & French	1600.
Cash lent Jacob Clements	600.
Interest due from Jacob Clements	98.39
" due from Hannah Clements	50.
Cash lent John Porter	20.
Schuylkill Bridge Shares	37.
Rachel Miller's Note of Hand	90.
Mathias Baili's " Do	37.56
Bond & Judgment against Nathaniel Donald	451.18
4000 p[r] nankeens	3760.
1 Case India Sewing Silk	610.
Dunn & French's Note of hand	1000.
Plate	200.
Furniture	611.
	$13093.17

148—SAMUEL FRENCH (Thomas, 1; Charles, 8; Uriah, 43).

> m. First, November 11th, 1775, Mary Wayne.
> m. Second, Elizabeth ————.
> He d. 1812.
> She d. 1813.

395—MARY FRENCH

396—HOPE FRENCH   m. ———— Webster.

Samuel French, son of Uriah French [43], and later stepson of Hugh Creighton, was deeply imbued with the patriotic spirit of Revolutionary days. As a young man he enlisted in the Gloucester County militia, and it is evident that he saw active service. New Jersey State records show that on May 1st, 1784, he was awarded certificate No. 517 for the depreciation of his pay as a Continental soldier during the war, amounting to £3. 3s. 9d. In "Votes and Proceedings of the General Assembly of the State of New Jersey, 1776–1780," is the note, "July 16, 1776, Cash paid Samuel French for a coffin for a Prifoner £1 10 0." Samuel French was a long time resident of Newton township, Gloucester county, N. J. Dying intestate, in 1812, his estate was administered by his second wife, Elizabeth, the inventory of the personal estate showing a total of $285.00. Elizabeth French died about a year later, leaving an estate which amounted to $296.00.

INVENTORY OF ESTATE OF SAMUEL FRENCH, 1812

Inventory of goods and chattels rights and credits of Samuel French late of township of Newton. Made February 28, 1812

Wearing Apparel	20
Bed & Bedding in East Room up stairs	18
Case of Drawers	10
Bed Clothing	30
Up Stairs and Trunk	2
Bed & Bedding in Front Room up stairs	25
One pine Chest do	2
One Bed in West Room up stairs	10
An unfinished desk	6
Two small pieces of Worsted & Wool	6
Carpenter Tools	5
Lot of lumber	5
One Mahogany Table in Parlor	12
Walnut Breakfast Table	3

½ Dozen Chairs	6
Looking glass	6
Andirons, shovel & tongs	5
Tea tackling, queensware & pewter	12
One ten plate stove in kitchen	16
Kitchen furniture	16
Spinning wheel	2
Tubs & sundry articles in cellar	8
Axes, hoes, forks and sundries	6
Two Cows	36
Four sheep	12
Wood saw	1
Cash	5.90
	$285.90

Jacob Glover ⎱
James Hurley ⎰ Apprs.

Elizabeth French Administratrix of Samuel French dec^d. being duly affirmed saith that the within writing contains a true and perfect Inventory of all and singular the goods Chattles and Credits of the said deceased as far as have come to her knowledge or poſseſsion or to the poſseſsion of any other person or persons for her use

Aff^d. 9th day of March
1812 Before me
Jas. Matlach Surr.

149—ELEAZER FENTON (Thomas, 1; John, 9; Rachel, 47).

b. 1723.

d. November 10th, 1789.

m. November 7th, 1753, Elizabeth Atkinson, daughter of John and Hannah (Shinn) Atkinson; ceremony performed by Rev. Colin Campbell, Rector of St. Mary's P. E. Church, Burlington, N. J.

She b. 2nd mo. 1st, 1731.

397—SAMUEL FENTON   b. 1755.
                        d. February 27th, 1814.

398—HANNAH FENTON b. March 30th, 1761.
          d. March 6th, 1805.
          m. November 6th, 1777, Jacob Shinn, Jr.

399—ELEAZER FENTON, JR. b. June 8th, 1762.
          d. March 28th, 1816.
          m. November 11th, 1788, Elizabeth Clark,
           daughter of Thomas and Deborah (Denny)
           Clark.
      She b. August 13th, 1769.
          d. February 23rd, 1824.

153—THOMAS BUZBY, JR. (Thomas, 1; Mary, 11; Thomas Buzby, 50).

       b. 2nd mo. 4th, 1739.
       m. 1765, Tabitha Hugg.
     She b. 1st mo. 18th, 1745.
       d. 1st mo. 16th, 1784.

400—JOHN BUZBY   b. 8th mo. 24th, 1766.

401—THOMAS BUZBY, 3RD b. 12th mo. 25th, 1768.
          d. 9th mo., 1816.
          m. 11th mo. 16th, 1788, Hannah Haines,
           widow of Ephraim Haines.
      She d. 1815.

402—WILLIAM BUZBY b. 11th mo. 25th, 1773.
          d. 3rd mo. 8th, 1798.

403—ISAAC BUZBY   b. 4th mo. 24th, 1775.

404—BENJAMIN BUZBY b. 8th mo. 17th, 1778.

405—HANNAH BUZBY b. 4th mo. 10th, 1781.

DESCENDANTS OF THOMAS BUZBY, 3RD

Thomas and Hannah (Haines) Buzby [401] had sons, Thomas, Benjamin and Isaac, and daughter Hannah. Hannah Buzby, daughter of Thomas and Hannah (Haines) Buzby, married June 6th, 1799, Miles Foster; Edward French [121] Justice of the Peace, performing ceremony. Concerning this marriage, Burlington Monthly Meeting Minutes, 4th mo. 7th, 1800, state " Hannah Foster, late Buzby, had her birthright amongst us, the People called Quakers, for want of attending to the dictates of Truth in her own mind, has deviated from the good order amongst us by accomplishing her marriage contrary thereto with one not in membership . . . for which conduct she has been treated with, but not being disposed to condemn the same, we disown the said Hannah Foster from being a member of our Religious Society until she manifests a desire by a suitable acknowledgment to be reconciled to Friends."

Hannah Foster, daughter of Miles and Hannah (Buzby) Foster, married Joseph Banes. He died in Santa Lucia, Cuba, 1842. Josephine Banes, daughter of Joseph and Hannah (Foster) Banes, was born in Matanzas, Cuba; died July 31st, 1862, in Philadelphia; married September 23rd, 1851, James Harwood Closson; Rev. Charles Brown, Logan Square Presbyterian Church, Philadelphia, performing ceremony. James Harwood Closson, born September 23rd, 1826, son of John Closson [b. Oct. 14th, 1797] and wife Mary Libhart Loucks [b. Sept. 15th, 1799; d. Mar. 16th, 1879, in Phila.], was Captain in the 91st Regiment of Penna. Vol. during the Civil War, and was killed in action at Hatchers Run, Va., November 22nd, 1864. James Harwood Closson, Jr., M.D., son of Capt. James Harwood and Josephine (Banes) Closson, born November 27th, 1861, married October 22, 1891, in Second Presbyterian Church, Germantown, Mary Eldredge Bell, daughter of Samuel Wilson Bell, president of the Farmers' & Mechanics' Bank of Philadelphia, and wife Mary E. Bancroft; Rev. C. H. P. Nason performing ceremony. The children of James Harwood Closson, Jr., M.D., and wife Mary Eldredge Bell, are: Josephine Banes Closson, born September 12th, 1893; James Harwood Closson, 3rd, born June 18th, 1896; Mary Bancroft Closson, born December 24th, 1898.

James Harwood Closson, Jr., M.D., was educated in private and public schools of Philadelphia, Lafayette College, Easton, Pa., and Hahnemann Medical College, Philadelphia, from which he graduated in 1886. He served for a year as resident physician at the Childrens Homeopathic Hospital, Philadelphia, and in 1887 entered into partnership with Dr. John Malin, a leading homeopathic physician of Germantown, Philadelphia, who died two years later and to whose extensive practice Dr. Closson succeeded, at 53 West Chelton Ave., and where he has continued, becoming prominent in his profession. He is a member and former president of the Philadelphia Homeopathic Society, Secretary of the Pennsylvania Homeopathic Society, member of the American Institute of Homeopathy, the Pennsylvania Historical Society, the Netherlands Society, Pennsylvania Genealogical Society, Colonial Society of Pennsylvania, Sons of the Revolution, New Jersey Society of Pennsylvania, the Union League and other organizations. He is visiting physician at St. Luke's Hospital and much interested in the religious work of the Brotherhood of Andrew and Philip. On the paternal side Dr. Closson is a descendant of the first burgess and one of the original settlers of Germantown, the author of the earliest protest against slavery, Abraham Op den Graeff.

154—AMOS BUZBY (Thomas, 1; Mary, 11; Thomas Buzby, 50).

b. 7th mo. 20th, 1742.

d. 6th mo. 10th, 1815.

m. First, Patience Springer.

She d. 2nd mo. 18th, 1790.

m. Second, Rebecca Matlack.

406—MARY BUZBY   b. 7th mo. 24th, 1769.
m. 5th mo. 19th, 1792, at Ancocas, N. J., Robert Middleton, son of Amos and Elizabeth Middleton, of Upper Freehold Township, Monmouth Co., N. J.

407—JOSEPH BUZBY   b. 1st mo. 14th, 1771.
m. 4th mo. 16th, 1794, Beulah Woolman.

408—NICHOLAS BUZBY   b. 11th mo. 16th, 1773.
m. 1798, Hannah Heaton.

409—MARGARET BUZBY   b. 10th mo. 26th, 1774.
m. 11th mo. 5th, 1800, Samuel Hilliard, Jr.

410—HUDSON BUZBY   b. 2ud mo. 1st, 1777.
m. 11th mo. 12th, 1800, Rachel Woolman.

411—HANNAH BUZBY   b. 1st mo. 5th, 1779.
m. 11th mo. 13th, 1799, at Ancocas, N. J., Richard Heaton, son of John and Rachel Heaton of Willingborough Township, Burlington Co., N. J.

412—AMOS BUZBY, JR.   b. 3rd mo. 14th, 1781.
d. 9th mo. 6th, 1851.

413—DANIEL BUZBY   b. 2ud mo. 10th, 1783.
d. 10th mo. 26th, 1785.

Children of Amos and Rebecca (Matlack) Buzby.

414—JOHN BUZBY   b. 11th mo. 5th, 1794.
d. 8th mo. 12th, 1826.

415—WILLIAM BUZBY   b. 9th mo. 22nd, 1796.
d. 7th mo. 5th, 1822.

416—GEORGE BUZBY   b. 12th mo. 3rd, 1798.
m. Esther ———.

417—JOSEPH BUZBY

418—ROBERT C. BUZBY   b. 12th mo. 14th, 1800.
m. Elizabeth ———.

156—WILLIAM BUZBY, JR. (Thomas, 1; Mary, 11; William Buzby, 53).

b. 10th mo. 23rd, 1751.
d. 12th mo. 28th, 1814.
m. 6th mo. 9th, 1773, Susannah Deacon.
She b. 4th mo. 17th, 1749.
d. 5th mo. 22nd, 1835.

419—BEULAH BUZBY   b. 1st mo. 16th, 1774.

420—PHINEAS BUZBY   b. 10th mo. 3rd, 1775.
d. 11th mo. 5th, 1776.

421—WILLIAM BUZBY, 3RD   b. 10th mo. 8th, 1777.
m. 1st mo., 1804, Ann Lippincott.

422—JONATHAN BUZBY   b. 11th mo. 16th, 1779.

423—MARY W. BUZBY   b. 10th mo. 28th, 1783.
m. 5th mo. 13th, 1824, Jeremiah Bunting, son
of William and Margaret Bunting, of
Middletown Township, Bucks County, Pa.

424—JOSEPH BUZBY   b. 8th mo. 8th, 1787.
m. 1813, Mary Haines.

425—ELIZABETH BUZBY   b. 10th mo. 30th, 1789.
m. 11th mo. 17th, 1808, John Gummere.

426—MARTHA BUZBY   b. 11th mo. 25th, 1792.
m. Dubre Knight.

427—ABEL BUZBY   b. 7th mo. 19th, 1795.
m. 5th mo. 14th, 1834, Rachel W. Buzby
[868], daughter of Nicholas and Hannah
(Heaton) Buzby.

157—ELIZABETH BUZBY (Thomas, 1; Mary, 11; William Buzby, 53).

m. 5th mo. 13th, 1767, Samuel Haines, Jr., son of Samuel and Lydia (Stokes) Haines, of Northampton Township, Burlington Co., N. J.

428—WILLIAM HAINES   b. 4th mo. 17th, 1768.
                          m. Mary Eayre.

429—MARY HAINES   b. 11th mo. 15th, 1770.
                          m. 7th mo. 15th, 1789, Jacob Hollingshead.

430—AARON HAINES   b. 3rd mo. 25th, 1773.
                          m. October 29th, 1795, Martha Stokes [452],
                             daughter of Jarves and Elizabeth (Rogers)
                             Stokes.

431—ABEL HAINES   b. 9th mo. 30th, 1775.
                          m. October 30th, 1800, Elizabeth Stokes [457],
                             daughter of Jarves and Elizabeth (Rogers)
                             Stokes.

432—JOSEPH HAINES   b. 4th mo. 1st, 1778.
                          d. 1793.

433—ELIZABETH HAINES   b. 7th mo. 15th, 1780.
                          d. unmarried.

434—SAMUEL HAINES, 3RD   b. 12th mo. 13th, 1783.
                          m. Susannah Chapman.

SAMUEL HAINES, JR., married second, 10th mo. 15th, 1788, Mary Stevenson, daughter of Cornell Stevenson. Their children were:

LYDIA HAINES   b. 7th mo. 31st, 1789.

ROBERT HAINES   b. 1st mo. 2nd, 1791.
                          m. Edith Rogers.

SARAH HAINES   b. 11th mo. 31st, 1792.
                          d. 7th mo. 17th, 1795.

EZRA HAINES   b. 9th mo. 26th, 1795.
                          m. First, Lucy Bishop.
                          m. Second, Phoebe Pierce.

HANNAH HAINES   b. 1798.
                          m. Joseph R. Bishop.

165—MARY STOKES (Thomas, 1; Rachel, 4; Mary Allen, 18; Hannah Stockdell, 72).

> b. 8th mo. 15th, 1745.
> d. 10th mo. 13th, 1829.
> m. Isaac Newton.

435—JOHN NEWTON	m. Rachel Sharp.
436—SAMUEL NEWTON	d. unmarried.
437—MARY NEWTON	m. Samuel Garwood, son of Israel Garwood.
438—HANNAH NEWTON	d. unmarried.

166—JOHN STOKES, 3RD (Thomas, 1; Rachel, 4; Mary Allen, 18; Hannah Stockdell, 72).

> b. 6th mo. 22nd, 1747.
> m. Susannah Newton.

439—WILLIAM STOKES	m. Eleanor Long.
440—MARY STOKES	m. Thomas Lester.
441—HANNAH STOKES	m. Joshua Paul.
442—ELIZABETH STOKES	m. David Roberts.
443—RACHEL STOKES	m. Timothy Smith.
444—JOHN STOKES	d. unmarried.
445—SUSAN STOKES	m. James Bryan.
446—SAMUEL STOKES, M.D.	m. Susan Meyers.
447—STOCKDELL STOKES	m. Eliza Eastburn.

167—DAVID STOKES (Thomas, 1; Rachel, 4; Mary Allen, 18; Hannah
           Stockdell, 72).

        b. 11th mo. 12th, 1751.
        d. 9th mo. 27th, 1830.
        m. 4th mo. 15th, 1784, Ann Lancaster, daughter
           of John and Elizabeth (Barlow) Lancaster, of
           Richland, Pa.
     She b. 1759.
        d. 9th mo. 25th, 1835.

448—ISRAEL STOKES   b. 11th mo. 7th, 1785.
                              m. Sarah Borton, daughter of Joshua and
                                Elizabeth N. (Woolman) Borton.

449—JOHN L. STOKES   b. 2ud mo. 24th, 1788.
                              d. 9th mo., 1822.
                              m. Rachel Burr, daughter of Caleb and
                                Martha Burr.

450—CHARLES STOKES   b. 8th mo. 12th, 1791.
                              d. 2ud mo. 27th, 1882.
                              m. Tacy Jarrett, daughter of William and
                                Ann (Lukens) Jarrett.

451—DAVID STOKES   b. 2ud mo. 25th, 1794.
                              d. 1st mo. 22nd, 1817, unmarried.

CHARLES STOKES [450]

For more than half a century Charles Stokes, of Rancocas, was one of
the best known and most useful citizens of Burlington county. A great-great-
grandson of Thomas Stokes, the progenitor of the family in West Jersey, he
inherited in marked degree the qualities of a vigorous ancestry. Farm life
and school teaching occupied his early years, after which he pursued survey-
ing, conveyancing and management of real estate as his calling, with the
performance of responsible public duties. He was a member of the General
Assembly in 1831 and of the Legislative Council in 1836-37. In 1836 he
was appointed by Governor Vroom Master in Chancery, "as a token of long

and appreciative friendship, which shall be as long as life." In 1844 he served efficiently as a member of the convention to revise the state constitution. He surveyed the Camden & Amboy railroad from the Rancocas River to Burlington. He also laid out Beverly, Delanco, Edgewater and other towns. He was long time surveyor of Willingborough township, making, from books of original surveys, the map of that section, showing pioneer locations, herewith reproduced. He was long noted for his zealous and consistent advocacy of the temperance cause. He was also firm in his devotion to peace principles and signed vigorous protests against the wars of 1812, 1848 and 1860. As an earnest minded Friend he was known throughout the country, having sat in Philadelphia Yearly Meeting as a representative from Burlington Quarterly, for sixty-five years, a record unequaled in the Society. He enjoyed remarkable health until within a short time of his death, in 1882, at the advanced age of 90 years. As the genealogical record shows, David Stokes [167], father of Charles Stokes [450], was a son of Hannah Stockdell, great granddaughter of Thomas ffrench, progenitor.

168—JARVES STOKES (Thomas, 1; Rachel, 4; Mary Allen, 18; Hannah Stockdell, 72).

> b. 11th mo. 10th, 1753.
> d. 12th mo. 14th, 1804.
> m. November 27th, 1773, Elizabeth Rogers, daughter of William and Martha (Esturgans) Rogers.

452—MARTHA STOKES
b. 6th mo. 26th, 1774.
m. October 29th, 1795, Aaron Haines [430], son of Samuel and Elizabeth (Buzby) Haines.

453—HANNAH STOKES
b. 8th mo. 11th, 1775.
m. 2ud mo. 11th, 1795, at Ancocas, N. J., Granville Woolman, son of Asher and Rachel (Norcross) Woolman, of Northampton Township, Burlington Co., N. J.
He b. 1st mo. 1st, 1774.

454—JOHN STOKES
b. 4th mo. 11th, 1777.
m. 1798, Elizabeth Woolman, daughter of Asher and Rachel (Engle) Woolman.

455—WILLIAM STOKES
b. 1st mo. 14th, 1779.
d. 8th mo. 17th, 1838.
m. 4th mo. 8th, 1798, Hannah Hatcher, of Burlington County, N. J.
She b. 8th mo. 11th, 1775.
d. 4th mo. 18th, 1858.

456—JARVES STOKES, JR.
b. 11th mo. 5th, 1780.
m. Abigail Woolman, daughter of Asher and Rachel (Engle) Woolman.

457—ELIZABETH STOKES
b. 5th mo. 29th, 1782.
m. October 30th, 1800, Abel Haines [431], son of Samuel and Elizabeth (Buzby) Haines.

458—EDITH STOKES
b. 2nd mo. 22nd, 1784.
d. in infancy.

459—JOSEPH STOKES
b. 2ud mo. 26th, 1787.
d. 8th mo. 23rd, 1851.
m. 1812, Harriet Stockton, daughter of Richard and Sarah Stockton.
She d. 2nd mo. 17th, 1874.

460—MARY STOKES
b. 11th mo. 18th, 1788.
d. 1875, unmarried.

461—ESTHER STOKES.
b. 1st mo. 22nd, 1791.
m. Joseph Butterworth, son of John M. and Rachel (Eayre) Butterworth.

462—STOCKDELL STOKES
b. 10th mo. 12th, 1792.
m. Wilhelmina Metzgar.

463—SAMUEL STOKES
b. 8th mo. 13th, 1794.
d. 10th mo. 11th, 1860.
m. Amy Middleton.
She d. 10th mo. 13th, 1874.

464—MORDECAI STOKES
b. 3rd mo. 6th, 1796.
d. in infancy.

465—SARAH STOKES   b. 2nd mo. 24th, 1798.
       d. 6th mo. 23rd, 1851.
       m. 8th mo. 4th, 1825, Uriah Haines, son of George and Edith (Woolman) Haines.
       He b. 2nd mo. 10th, 1800.
       d. 3rd mo. 13th, 1874.

466—MORDECAI STOKES, 2ND   b. 3rd mo. 22nd, 1800.
       d. 8th mo. 29th, 1835.
       m. Sarah Thompson.

169—HANNAH STOKES (Thomas, 1; Rachel, 4; Mary Allen, 18; Hannah Stockdell, 72).

       b. 10th mo. 12th, 1756.
       d. 6th mo. 16th, 1790.
       m. First, 4th mo. 9th, 1794, at Ancocas, N. J., Jacob Haines, son of Samuel and Lydia (Stokes) Haines, of Chester Township, Burlington Co., N. J.
       m. Second, George Browning.

467—HANNAH HAINES   m. Benjamin R. Morgan [472], son of Isaac and Sarah (Ridgway) Morgan.

468—STOKES HAINES   m. 12th mo. 17th, 1818, Lockey Ann French [555], daughter of Joseph and Elizabeth (Zane) French.

171—RACHEL STOKES (Thomas, 1; Rachel, 4; Mary Allen, 18; Hannah Stockdell, 72).

       b. 2nd mo. 2nd, 1765.
       m. 10th mo. 12th, 1785, Joseph Hackney, Jr., son of Joseph Hackney, of Chester Township, Burlington Co., N. J..

469—JOSEPH HACKNEY, 3RD.

470—JOHN HACKNEY

181—SARAH RIDGWAY (Thomas, 1; Rachel, 4; Rebecca Sharp, 21;
Mary Coate, 89).

b. 6th mo. 17th, 1764.

m. 12th mo. 21st, 1785, Isaac Morgan, son of
Joseph and Mary (Stokes) Morgan.

471—MARY MORGAN   m. Joel Middleton.

472—BENJAMIN R. MORGAN   m. Hannah Haines [467], daughter of Jacob
                         and Hannah (Stokes) Haines.

473—HANNAH MORGAN   m. Eli Stokes.

474—ISAAC MORGAN

475—GRIFFITH MORGAN   m. Elizabeth Roberts.

476—JOSEPH MORGAN   m. Mary Burrough.

477—JUDITH MORGAN   m. First, Arthur Roberts.
                         m. Second, Thomas Stiles.

RICHARD RIDGWAY AND DESCENDANTS

None of the early settlers of Pennsylvania and New Jersey was more successful and
influential than Richard Ridgway. Descended from notable English ancestry, he arrived
at Burlington in September, 1679. With a number of his fellow homeseekers he crossed
the Delaware, purchased land and founded a settlement known for many years thereafter
as Crewcorne, and which was the site of the present town of Morrisville, Bucks Co.,
Pa. As elsewhere noted, these pioneers in the wilderness were early beset with a special
annoyance and peril, in consequence of the sale of liquor to the Indians. A petition
addressed to Governor Andros, of New York, April ye 12th, 1680, by the inhabitants of
Crewcorne, quaintly describes existing conditions:

"To ye Worthy Governor of New Yorke.
"Whereas, wee ye Inhabitants of ye new Seated Towne near ye falls of
Dellaware (called Crewcorne) findeing ourselves aggrieved by ye Indians
when drunk, informeth, that wee be and have been in great danger of our
Lives, of our houses burning, of our goods stealing and of our Wives and
Children affrighting, Insomuch that wee are afeard to go about our Lawful
affairs, least when we come home we finde ym and our concerns damnified.
These things considered, wee doe humbly & jointly desire that ye selling
of brandy and strong liquors to ye Indians may be wholly suppressed, when
if done wee hope wee shall live peaceably. Willi. Biles, Rich. Ridgway,
Samuel ffeild, John Akarman, Robt. Lucas, Robt. Scholey, Tho. Scholey,
Darius brinson, William Cooper, George Browne."

Richard Ridgway prospered at Crewcorne, but he was a man of large views and purposes. He bought additional tracts of desirable land in Pennsylvania, and in the fall of 1690 bought, of ~~Gov.~~ Daniel Coxe, of West Jersey, 600 acres in the upper part of Burlington County, near Stony Brook, along the East Jersey line, locating there with his family for a time. Later he sold this property, and in the spring of 1697 purchased of John Hollinshead 600 acres at Mattacopeny, Burlington Co. A few months later he bought of Jane Ogburn 90 acres in the same section, transferring this property, with 100 acres additional, to his son Thomas, two years thereafter. Still other land purchases and sales by Richard Ridgway are recorded about 1700. He also became a land owner in East Jersey and for a time resided at the ancient settlement of Piscataway, now in the upper part of Middlesex County, one of his grantee's being the original Richard Stockton, father of his second wife, Abigail Stockton, and founder of the Stockton family in New Jersey. He returned to Burlington County and settled finally in Springfield township, where he became active in public affairs, serving as one of the county judges at different periods between 1700 and 1720. He died in 1722, leaving an estate of considerable size. His will, dated September 21, 1722, proved April 5, 1723, appointed wife Abigail executrix, with sons Thomas and Job and son-in-law Henry Clothier as assistants. Inventory showed personal property to the value of £207 11s. His widow survived him about three years. Her will was proved December 19, 1726; inventory of personal estate amounted to £141 15s.

Richard Ridgway was twice married, first to Elizabeth Chamberlayne, of Wiltshire, England, with whom he came to America. She died at Crewcorne, March 31, 1692. He married second, February 1, 1693/4, Abigail Stockton. By his first marriage he had seven children, viz., Thomas, Richard, Elizabeth, William, Sarah, Josiah and Joseph. There were seven children also by the second marriage, namely, Job, Mary, Jane, Abigail, John, Joseph and Sarah. Four children died in infancy—William, both Sarahs, and the first Joseph. The eldest son, Thomas, born in England in 1677, died 1724/5, in early life located in the Egg Harbor section and became the progenitor of a large branch of the family. Richard Ridgway, Jr., born at Crewcorne 1680, died 1718/9, located in Springfield township, Burlington County, and his descendants, likewise those of his brothers and sisters, have been numerous and prosperous.

Sarah (Ridgway) Morgan [181], daughter of Joseph Ridgway of Springfield township, was a great, great granddaughter of Thomas ffrench and Richard Ridgway, progenitors.

WALNUT DRESSING TABLE, 1700

29

.

INDEX

INDEX OF NAMES OF PERSONS.

452

INDEX OF NAMES OF PLACES.

HISTORICAL INDEX.

WASHINGTON'S LETTERS TO COL. SHREVE.

(Associated Press Cablegram.)
London, March 1, 1909.—Four letters or
documents signed by Washington were sold
at auction at Sotheby's today for $210 to a
London dealer. The letters are addressed
chiefly to Colonel Israel Shreeve, commanding in New Jersey and are dated between
February, 1777, and January, 1781.

NOTE. The foregoing refers to Col. Israel Shreve [107], pages 307 to 325 of
this volume.

END OF VOLUME I.

CPSIA information can be obtained
at www.ICGtesting.com
Printed in the USA
BVOW11s2241200917
495397BV00013B/121/P